THE LEGAL
RESEARCH
AND WRITING
HANDBOOK

NINTH EDITION

THE LEGAL RESEARCH AND WRITING HANDBOOK

A BASIC APPROACH FOR PARALEGALS

ANDREA B. YELIN

HOPE VINER SAMBORN

Wolters Kluwer

Printed in Canada.

1 2 3 4 5 6 7 8 9 0

ISBN 978-1-5438-2618-0

Library of Congress Cataloging-in-Publication Data
Names: Yelin, Andrea B., author. I Samborn, Hope Viner, author.
Title: The legal research and writing handbook : a basic approach for
    paralegals / Andrea B. Yelin, DePaul University; Hope Viner Samborn.
Description: Ninth edition. I New York : Wolters Kluwer, [2022] I Series:
    Paralegal series I Includes bibliographical references and index. I
    Summary: "Introductory textbook on legal writing and research for
    paralegal students"—Provided by publisher.
Identifiers: LCCN 2021052734 (print) I LCCN 2021052735 (ebook) I ISBN
    9781543826180 (paperback) I ISBN 9781543826197 (ebook)
Subjects: LCSH: Legal research—United States. I Legal composition. I Legal
    assistants—United States—Handbooks, manuals, etc.
Classification: LCC KF240 .Y45 2022 (print) I LCC KF240 (ebook) I DDC
    340.072/073—dc23/eng/20211109
LC record available at https://lccn.loc.gov/2021052734
LC ebook record available at https://lccn.loc.gov/2021052735

About Wolters Kluwer Legal & Regulatory U.S.

Wolters Kluwer Legal & Regulatory U.S. delivers expert content and solutions in the areas of law, corporate compliance, health compliance, reimbursement, and legal education. Its practical solutions help customers successfully navigate the demands of a changing environment to drive their daily activities, enhance decision quality and inspire confident outcomes.

Serving customers worldwide, its legal and regulatory portfolio includes products under the Aspen Publishers, CCH Incorporated, Kluwer Law International, ftwilliam.com and MediRegs names. They are regarded as exceptional and trusted resources for general legal and practice-specific knowledge, compliance and risk management, dynamic workflow solutions, and expert commentary.

To David, Rachel, and Henry with all my love.
You are the greatest joy!
—ABY

To my dear children Eve, Sarah,
and Benjamin for being amazing teachers, students,
and human beings, and to my husband,
Randy for being my favorite teacher, friend, and
partner. You all have all my love and thanks.
—HVS

SUMMARY OF CONTENTS

CONTENTS

CHAPTER 2   LEGAL AUTHORITIES AND HOW TO USE THEM   21

PART 2   LEGAL WRITING

CHAPTER 15   GETTING READY TO WRITE

CHAPTER 16   CLEAR WRITING AND EDITING

CHAPTER 20   QUESTIONS PRESENTED AND CONCLUSIONS OR BRIEF ANSWERS

CHAPTER 21   FACTS

LIST OF
ILLUSTRATIONS

PREFACE

As paralegals, you can be invaluable to attorneys and clients when you have adequately mastered legal research and writing skills. This book is a step-by-step guide that explores the twists and turns of legal research and writing, teaching you how to avoid the dead ends and conquer obstacles along the way. Examples, exercises, and checklists help make it a smooth and enjoyable road.

Part 1 features an introduction to the legal system and legal authorities: the state and federal legislatures, the courts, and administrative agencies. It explains the relationship between state and federal governments and between other governing bodies.

The research component of Part 1 begins with print resources. Proficiency in hard-copy research will bring you greater success when performing research using a computer. You will also learn how to use online resources. All significant resources will be explored, and you will learn how they are interrelated and how to find the best sources for your particular project. Legal writing pointers are integrated throughout the research chapters where relevant.

Part 2 focuses on basic legal writing, with an emphasis on legal memoranda and letters—the most common documents that paralegals draft. Objective memos inform the attorney of all of the relevant law, both for and against the client's position. Having paralegals brief cases expedites the research process. Delegating research and writing tasks to the paralegal is cost-effective for the client and saves the client money.

Part 2 also guides you step-by-step through the legal writing process. You will be introduced to the case brief, the legal memorandum, the questions presented statement, the brief answer, and the facts statement. You will learn how to identify the legal issues and relevant facts of a case and how to organize and present them in a written brief or memorandum. As the culmination of your legal writing skills, you will learn to synthesize—to distill a general legal concept that applies to a case and then state it in writing (citing more than one case or statute). Synthesis is essential to writing most case-related documents. A clear methodology—IRAC—will introduce you to the important components of synthesis: Issue, Rule, Application, and Conclusion. Using IRAC, you will learn to synthesize effectively and consistently.

A valuable reference tool, *The Legal Research and Writing Handbook* reviews letter writing, grammar, and editing—all essential skills you will use every day as a paralegal. Also, the examples and citation appendix will help you draft documents.

The book includes hands-on exercises that reinforce the concepts presented in the book and provide you with practical applications for future work experiences. Practice pointers and ethics alerts included in this text are designed to guide you in your day-to-day work as a paralegal. This edition provides Net Notes to help you navigate the Internet to review points raised in the text. Computer resources, both paid and free, are integrated throughout the book.

You should view *The Legal Research and Writing Handbook* as a launching point from which to begin developing your research and writing skills. You will want to refer to the guidelines and concepts in this book throughout your career as you continue to expand in knowledge and experience.

November 2021

Andrea B. Yelin
Hope Viner Samborn

ACKNOWLEDGMENTS

We would like to acknowledge all of the people who have helped us create this text and who have shaped its contents.

Thank you to Betsy Kenny for helping us to hone our continuing revisions of the text and the teacher's manual and for countless hours spent guiding us. Thanks to Lisa Wehrle for her great job copyediting the first and second editions of this text. Thanks to Dana Wilson and Nicholas Lasoff for editing the eighth edition, and thanks to Tom Daughhetee of The Froebe Group for editing the seventh edition. Thank you to Lisa Connery for your help with the copyediting for the ninth edition. Huge thanks to Stacie Goosman, of Wolters Kluwer, for the editorial direction and support.

Thanks to Sylvia Rebert at Progressive Publishing Alternatives for her work on the sixth edition, to Julie Grady and Rebecca Logan for their assistance with the fifth edition, to Candice Adams for her assistance with the fourth edition, and to Peggy Rehberger, Melody Davies, Ellen Greenblatt, Curt Berkowitz, Suzanne Rapcavage, and Barbara Roth for their editing and additional help with the text. Thank you to Dave Herzig, Steve Silverstein, and Lou McGuire for their terrific marketing of the text.

Thanks to Loyola University Law School Library in Chicago, Thomson Reuters, LexisNexis, Shepard's, and the Arlington Heights Memorial Public Library for assistance in obtaining illustrations for this book.

Thanks also to Patricia Scott, Joe Mitzenmacher, Julie Grant, Nan Norton, and Fred LeBaron of Loyola University Chicago Law School for all of your assistance past and present. A special debt of gratitude goes to Fred LeBaron, once again, for his invaluable wise counsel and professional guidance.

Thanks to Allen Moye, Anne Hudson, and Michael Schiffer as well as to the staff at the DePaul University College of Law Rinn Law Library.

Thanks to Jean Hellman Ryan, Alice Perlin, Jennifer Brendel, and Pete Vandenberg for the opportunity to teach in your wonderful programs.

Thank you to Eve Samborn, Sarah Samborn, Ben Samborn, and Lauren Grodsky for their research contributions.

Thanks to our families and friends, whose continued support has helped us to revise this text. A very special thank you to the WONDERFUL Barbara and Leon!

We continue to be indebted to the people whose assistance, direction, and support led to the first edition of this text and ultimately this revised text as well as individuals who helped with our text *Basic Legal Writing for Paralegals*, a project that led to some of the revisions in this text.

To that end, we thank Jean Hellman Ryan, former director of the Loyola University Chicago, Institute for Paralegal Studies, who encouraged us to write our first book and who introduced us to Carolyn O'Sullivan of Little, Brown and Company—the company that first published our book. Thanks to Carolyn O'Sullivan, Betsy Kenny, Lisa Wehrle, Joan Horan, John Lyman, Katie Byrne Butcher, and Kaesmene Banks for their assistance with our books. We also thank our students who have helped us to hone the text and the exercises. Their writing and use of the exercises helped form the skeleton for the book and then mold its contents. Their continued use of the book assisted us in revising the text. Our students have taught us more than we ever could teach them, and we appreciate all that they have done. Some of our students who deserve special thanks for their critiques, suggestions, and encouragement include Kelly Barry, Amy Berezinski, Nanette Boryc, Mara Castello, Patricia Cochran, Jessie Cohen, Nan Crotty, Beverly Dombroski, Susanne Grant, Stephen Gromala, Chris Harrigan, Marion Kahle, Michael Luckey, Mitchell McClure, Brenda Mondul, Cheryl Morgan, Patricia Naqvi, Melissa Pederson, Shay Robertson, Louise Tessitore, and Amy Widmer.

The students in DePaul University's Writing, Rhetoric & Discourse class, Topics in Professional Writing: Legal Writing, provided invaluable insights. The students in Advanced Legal Research at Loyola University Chicago School of Law were immensely helpful for walking through many of the hypotheticals and illustrations.

Thanks to Terri Rudd, David Harris, Marc Steer, the late Debbie Freudenheim, and Linda Kahn for their insightful ideas and assistance with earlier editions.

Finally, we would like to thank the following publishers for allowing us to reprint the illustrations listed below.

Illustration 3-3. Reprinted with permission of Thomson Reuters.

Illustration 3-4. Reprinted with the permission of LexisNexis.

Illustrations 3-5, 3-6, 3-9, and 3-10. Reprinted with permission of Thomson Reuters.

Illustrations 4-1, 4-3, 4-5, 4-6, 4-7, 4-8, 4-9, 4-10. Reprinted with permission of Thomson Reuters.

llustrations 5-1, 5-2, 5-3, and 5-4. Reprinted with the permission of LexisNexis. For Illustrations, and, see online document for complete report.

Illustration 5-5. Reprinted with permission of Thomson Reuters.

Illustrations 6-1, 6-2, 6-3, 6-4, 6-5, 6-6, 6-7, 6-8, and 6-9. Reprinted with permission of Thomson Reuters.

Illustration 6-10. Copyright © 1981 by the American Law Institute. Reprinted with permission. All rights reserved.

Illustration 6-11. Uniform Law Commission showing the Uniform Controlled Substances Act. © 2021 by the Uniform Law Commission. Reprinted with permission. All rights reserved.

Illustration 7-5. Reprinted with permission of Thomson Reuters.

Illustration **7-6** Reprinted with the permission of LexisNexis.

Illustration 7-9, 7-11 and 7-12 Reprinted with permission of Thomson Reuters.

Illustration 7-13. Vermont Statutes Online –Vermont State Statutes database

Illustrations 8-1 and 8-2. Reprinted with permission of Thomson Reuters.

Illustration 18-1. Reprinted with permission of Thomson Reuters.

Illustration 18-4. Reprinted with the permission of LexisNexis.

Illustration 18-6. Reprinted with the permission of LexisNexis. (Abridged decision- see online document for complete decision.)

LEGAL
RESEARCH

INTRODUCTION TO LEGAL RESEARCH AND WRITING

CHAPTER OVERVIEW

Before you begin to research and to write about a legal problem, you must understand your role as a paralegal. You are an important member of a team. To function effectively, you must know which legal system governs and how that system operates. This chapter first considers your role in researching a legal problem and communicating it to your supervising attorney. Next, it discusses the legal system. It focuses on the organization of the U.S. federal government, which is divided into three separate branches: the legislative, the executive, and the judicial. It also provides a general explanation of how state governments are structured. Finally, the role of major governmental bodies is explored.

A. INTRODUCTION TO LEGAL RESEARCH AND WRITING

1. The Role of the Paralegal in Legal Research and Writing

Legal research and legal writing are among the tasks paralegals can perform efficiently and cost-effectively for law firms and their clients. But to do so effectively, you must understand the legal system and a variety of legal concepts. You must be able to use all the research tools available to lawyers and their staffs. Paralegals retrieve information regarding the law as well as nonlegal information, such as financial information and test results.

▼ Why Do Paralegals Perform Research?

Often research is done to determine whether a client has a case. We write an office memo to predict an outcome for the client. This requires that we evaluate all relevant law for and against the client's position. Other times, paralegals must research a particular issue raised after a case has been filed. Some research is done to support motions to be filed with courts. Research also may be done when a client is involved in a transaction and the attorney must determine the law and the steps to take in the transaction.

▼ What Tasks Do Paralegals Handle in the Research and Writing Process?

In practice, paralegals act as an arm of an attorney. The amount of research and the type of assignments paralegals perform vary throughout the country.

In some law offices, paralegals undertake all of the research in preparation for the filing of motions but attorneys draft the motions. In others, paralegals research and prepare rough drafts of motions. Once a research project is completed, you must communicate your research results effectively. To do this, you must understand the fundamentals of legal writing and be able to write detailed, clear, and thoughtful memoranda. Paralegals often are asked to prepare memoranda that summarize their research results. Some paralegals who work with judges prepare rough drafts of court decisions. This book is designed to help you complete each of these tasks.

When you are assigned a research problem, you are expected to work as a professional. You should complete the assignment in a timely fashion. More important, however, the written research results must be accurate, complete, and current. To make sure that your research skills are current and your search results are accurate, we will include references to online resources and search strategies throughout the text. This book will introduce you to query formation when you use commercial databases. After using this book, you will be able to form a research strategy and know the methods of using particular resources so you can analyze, organize, and communicate the results of your research in professional documents.

ETHICS ALERT

Paralegals work under the supervision of attorneys, except in very limited, statutorily sanctioned situations. As a result, all research results and client memoranda should be submitted to an attorney before they are provided to a client. Work submitted to clients containing legal opinions should never be signed by a paralegal.

B. INTRODUCTION TO THE U.S. LEGAL SYSTEM

1. The Organization of the Legal System

The United States consists of a multitiered system of government. The **federal government** and the **state governments** are the top two tiers. See Illustration 1-1.

Several lower-tier governmental bodies, including **city, village, township**, and **county governments**, exercise authority over the citizens of the United States. For the most part, your research will concern either federal or state law. It is important to know about the federal and state systems and how to find the law they generate. The knowledge of these systems, the types of laws they adopt, and how to find legal standards for these systems later can be applied to any research you undertake

ILLUSTRATION 1-1. U.S. and State Government Systems

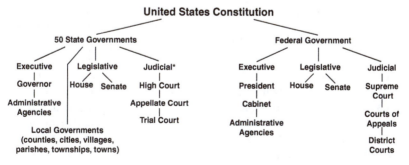

*Most, but not all, state courts consist of three tiers.

concerning other government bodies and their laws. You will use the information you find as authorities in a writing project.

▼ How Did the Federal and State Systems Originate?

Representatives of the states adopted a **constitution** for the United States that is the framework for the operation of this federal/state system of government. To that end, the U.S. Constitution creates three branches of government and defines their powers. You can think of the Constitution as an umbrella over all of the United States' governing bodies as it covers questions of not only federal government powers, but some state powers as well. The Constitution reserves for the states all the remaining powers not specifically designated to the federal government bodies. In addition, the Constitution establishes the rules for the relationship between the federal and state governments. The U.S. Constitution is the supreme law of the United States. For example, Congress, the legislative body of the federal government, cannot enact a law that is contrary to the U.S. Constitution. The state legislatures similarly are prevented from adopting laws that violate provisions of the U.S. Constitution.

2. Components of the Federal System and Governing Law

The federal government consists of three branches of government: the legislative, the executive, and the judicial. The U.S. Constitution created each branch and defines the relationship between them. The Constitution establishes a system in which each branch of government can monitor the activities of the other branches to prevent abuses. Each branch has the ability to alter actions of another branch. In this way, the Constitution provides **checks** and **balances** concerning the actions of each branch of government.

In general, the legislative branch creates the laws, the executive branch enforces the laws, and the judicial branch interprets the laws.

a. The Legislative Branch

The **legislative branch** of the federal government is called the **Congress**. It is comprised of two houses or chambers called the **Senate** and the **House of Representatives**. Both houses are comprised of individuals who are elected. The Congress creates laws called **statutes**. Some statutes are new rules of law. Other statutes either supersede or amend existing statutes or adopt court-made law. Court-made law is referred to as **case law** or the **common law**. One pervasive example of this is patent law. Many laws were adopted based on court decisions concerning this area of the law. The statutes and the U.S. Constitution comprise one body of law called **enacted law**. The laws enacted by the federal government apply to all U.S. citizens and residents.

NET NOTE

Congress.gov provides access to federal legislative information including House and Senate bills.

▼ How Is Legislation Enacted?

Anyone can propose that Congress adopt a new law, and either chamber can introduce a law for consideration. When a proposed law is introduced, it is called a **bill**. Before the bill can become a law, both chambers must approve it. If both houses approve the same version of the bill, it is sent to the chief of the executive branch, our **President**. The President can sign or veto the bill or withhold action on it. If the President signs the bill, it becomes law. If the President does not act within ten days and the legislative session is still in progress, the bill becomes law. If the President vetoes the bill, Congress may override the veto by a two-thirds majority vote of each house.

If the President fails to act on the bill within the ten days and the legislature is out of session, the bill does not become law. This action is called a **pocket veto**.

Once a piece of legislation becomes law, its first form is a slip law. The slip law on the federal level is called a Public Law. At the end of the legislative session, all the laws passed in the session are published in a set called the Statutes at Large. The Statutes at Large are the federal session laws. The process of codification is when the individual laws are inserted, according to subject, into the United States Code. The official United States Code is updated every six years. In the interim, we rely on the unofficial codes—the United States Code Annotated (Thomson Reuters West) and the United States Code Service (LexisNexis). The United States Code has 54 titles, with each title covering a separate subject.

b. The Executive Branch

The **executive branch** of the government, headed by the President, is the primary enforcer of the law. The President appoints the cabinet and oversees many federal agencies. The executive branch is responsible for the day-to-day management of the federal government. With the assistance of the Vice President, the cabinet members, and the heads of federal agencies, the President helps to guide the day-to-day operations of the government. The President can issue executive orders to direct the operations of various agencies and the actions of the citizens of the United States. In addition, the President is the commander-in-chief of the armed forces and with the advice and consent of the Senate, he can enter into treaties. Most federal administrative agencies are under direct control of the executive branch. See Illustration 1-2.

ILLUSTRATION 1-2.   **The Government of the United States**

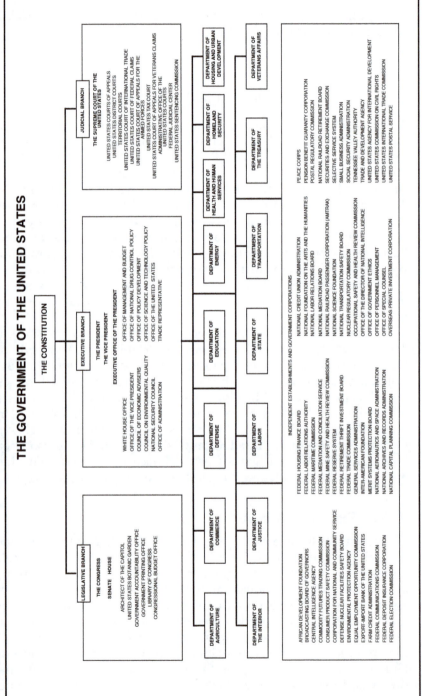

As the country's top executive, the President has the authority to control many administrative agencies. However, some administrative agencies are independent. For example, the Department of Justice, which includes the Office of the Attorney General, is part of the executive branch. However, the Federal Trade Commission is an independent agency.

Administrative agencies enforce many of the laws of the United States. These agencies are responsible for the daily regulation of activities controlled by federal law. For a listing of some of the many administrative agencies, see Illustration 1-2.

NET NOTE

Check govinfo.gov for the Code of Federal Regulations (C.F.R.), where you will find the final federal regulations. Proposed regulations and final regulations before they are published in the C.F.R. are located in the Federal Register—federalregister.gov. You can also find executive orders in the Federal Register at federalregister.gov.

Congress creates the agencies and delegates some of its own power to them because it alone is unable to handle the day-to-day enforcement of the overwhelming number of federal laws. Agencies, however, have the staff and often the technical expertise to deal with the daily enforcement of Congress's enacted laws. To do this, agencies often make rules that explain in detail how individuals should act to comply with congressional mandates. In some cases, agencies hold hearings to enforce the law. These agencies, therefore, function in quasi-judicial and quasi-legislative roles.

PRACTICE POINTER

Check the table of contents in the daily Federal Register to see agency activity. You can bookmark federalregister.gov and click "Current Issue."

For example, Congress enacted the Consumer Product Safety Act and delegated its enforcement power to the U.S. Consumer Product Safety Commission. Congress charged the commission with the responsibility for the daily enforcement of that act. As part of the commission's duties, it adopts rules or regulations. It also has administrative hearings, which often result in decisions.

In some cases, agencies use their **police powers** to enforce the law. For example, the U.S. Environmental Protection Agency will assist in prosecuting individuals or corporations that violate the Clean Air Act or other laws designed to protect the environment.

NET NOTE

Search for federal agencies and information about a particular agency at search.usa.gov. Details about cabinet members, proclamations, executive orders, and issues facing the executive branch can be found at www.white house.gov. Another government source of information is www.usa.gov. You can find a complete list of all government agencies at www.usa.gov.

c. The Judicial Branch

The third branch of government is the **judicial branch**. The federal judicial system includes three levels of courts that resolve disputes. See Illustration 1-3.

The entry-level court, in the federal judicial system, is the **trial court**. In that court, disputes are heard and decided by either a judge or a jury. The second level or intermediate level of courts is called

ILLUSTRATION 1-3.   Federal Judicial System

appellate courts. These courts consider appeals of decisions of the trial court. The final level is the **U.S. Supreme Court**. Its decisions cannot be appealed to any court.

NET NOTE

The website www.uscourts.gov provides links to all the U.S. appellate and district courts and U.S. bankruptcy courts, as well as the U.S. Supreme Court. Information is provided about judges, court personnel, locations, and court rules.

▼ Who Can Bring an Action in Federal Court?

A court can only consider a case if it has **jurisdiction** to hear it, that is, if the court is authorized to consider such cases. The federal court can consider all cases involving issues of federal law. In addition, it may hear cases involving disputes between parties of different states. Such cases are called **diversity cases**. Cases in which both the plaintiff, who is the party bringing the lawsuit, and the defendant are citizens of different states are examples of diversity cases. Diversity cases often involve issues of state law.

ETHICS ALERT

If you are assisting an attorney in preparing a claim, check with the supervising attorney to be certain that the claim is made in a court that has jurisdiction over such a claim.

PRACTICE POINTER

Ask the supervising attorney if the issue is controlled by federal or by state law.

---

i. The Trial Courts

The **trial court** is the court that hears the facts concerning a dispute. It is generally the first place in which a party can seek a remedy in federal court. In that way, it is considered a court of **original jurisdiction**. However, this court also hears appeals from some administrative agencies and the federal bankruptcy courts. Some administrative agency decisions, however, are appealed directly to the appellate courts.

In the federal system, the trial courts are known as the **district courts**. These courts decide disputes when a party (which can be a person, corporation, or other entity) brings an action against another party. In such cases, the trial courts often are asked to interpret congressional enactments such as statutes, ordinances, charters, or executive branch–created laws, including agency rules or decisions. When a court interprets a statute or regulation, it is overseeing the actions of other government branches. Courts often consult a body of law called the common law before rendering any decisions. Common law is court-created law found in the judicial opinions or cases; it is not found in the statutes.

ii. The Appellate Courts

The federal trial courts' decisions can be appealed to one of the 13 **federal appellate courts** known as the **U.S. Courts of Appeals**. See Illustration 1-3. This second tier of federal courts is broken into numbered and named **circuits**. Eleven circuits are known as the First through Eleventh. The remaining circuits are the Federal Circuit and the District of Columbia Circuit. The circuits are geographic, except for the Federal Circuit. See Illustration 1-4. An online map is available at www.uscourts.gov. These courts decide issues of law posed in appeals of trial court decisions located within its circuit. These courts do not consider new factual evidence. Witnesses are not brought before these courts. The Court of Appeals for the Federal Circuit has nationwide jurisdiction to hear appeals in specialized cases such as those arising from decisions of the Court of Federal Claims or the Court of International Trade. Decisions of the federal appellate courts can be appealed to the U.S. Supreme Court.

iii. The Supreme Court

The U.S. Supreme Court is the highest court in the United States. See Illustration 1-3. The U.S. Constitution establishes this court. Today nine justices, appointed by the President and confirmed by the U.S. Senate, sit on this tribunal. The U.S. Supreme Court has discretion to consider many issues. This discretion to consider an issue or to review a lower court's holding is called **certiorari**. If the court decides not to hear an issue, it denies certiorari. The effect is that the decision of the appellate court is final. If the U.S. Supreme Court decides to hear an issue, it grants certiorari. It then will consider whether the appellate court's decision should stand. By law, the U.S. Supreme Court alone has the authority to hear appeals of a state court of last resort decision when a substantial federal constitutional issue is presented. The U.S. Supreme Court also may hear a dispute between two states. The

Supreme Court also has original jurisdiction—that is the right—to directly take actions and proceedings in which ambassadors, other public ministers, consuls, or vice consuls of foreign states are parties. It also has original jurisdiction in all controversies between the United States and a state. The U.S. Supreme Court site, www.supremecourt.gov, is an excellent resource for recent decisions, and to monitor the status of pending decisions. Many opinions are posted the same day that they are decided. Additionally, the site allows access to the briefs for the U.S. Supreme Court cases. The Supreme Court briefs are terrific resources for the researcher. An example of a U.S. Supreme Court opinion, *Shelby County v. Holder*, 570 U.S. 529 (2013), is available at https://www.supremecourt.gov/opinions/12pdf/12-96_6k47.pdf.

NET NOTE

The Federal Judicial Center provides information about the federal judiciary and its history. See www.fjc.gov.

---

3. Relationship Between Federal and State Governments

▼ Can a Federal Court Decide an Issue of State Law?

Yes. A federal court can decide an issue of state law if the state issue is presented with a related federal issue or if the state question is raised in a dispute between parties of different states in a case called a diversity action.

▼ What Effect Does a Federal Decision Have on State Law?

A federal court decision generally cannot change state law. It may persuade the state courts to review state law, but its decision usually does not force any change in the law. These decisions, therefore, are advisory for future litigants but must be followed by the parties directly involved in the case in which the decision was rendered. Because states are separate sovereigns, in almost all cases only the state governing bodies can change state law. One exception to this rule does exist. The U.S. Supreme Court can determine whether state law violates the U.S. Constitution. If such a violation is found, the decision of the U.S. Supreme Court could invalidate state law.

▼ Are Federal and State Agencies Part of One Governing Body?

No. The federal government is one sovereign or governing body and the state is a separate governing body or sovereign. That means that the state cannot control the federal government agencies or change

ILLUSTRATION 14.   Circuit Map of the U.S. Courts of Appeals

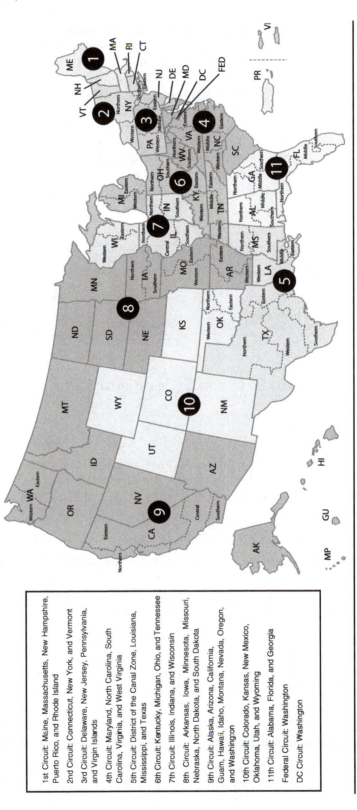

1st Circuit: Maine, Massachusetts, New Hampshire, Puerto Rico, and Rhode Island

2nd Circuit: Connecticut, New York, and Vermont

3rd Circuit: Delaware, New Jersey, Pennsylvania, and Virgin Islands

4th Circuit: Maryland, North Carolina, South Carolina, Virginia, and West Virginia

5th Circuit: District of the Canal Zone, Louisiana, Mississippi, and Texas

6th Circuit: Kentucky, Michigan, Ohio, and Tennessee

7th Circuit: Illinois, Indiana, and Wisconsin

8th Circuit: Arkansas, Iowa, Minnesota, Missouri, Nebraska, North Dakota, and South Dakota

9th Circuit: Alaska, Arizona, California, Guam, Hawaii, Idaho, Montana, Nevada, Oregon, and Washington

10th Circuit: Colorado, Kansas, New Mexico, Oklahoma, Utah, and Wyoming

11th Circuit: Alabama, Florida, and Georgia

Federal Circuit: Washington

DC Circuit: Washington

Found at the U.S. Courts website, www.uscourts.gov.

federal law. In general, the federal government branches cannot control the state government or change state law.

Also, state legislation may not conflict with federal law. States do hold broad autonomy to form their governments and to pursue legislative goals that are not in conflict with federal laws. The Tenth Amendment reserves to the states all powers not specifically granted to the federal government. For instance, the laws concerning the sale of alcohol are delegated to the states. The laws concerning U.S. citizenship are delegated to the federal government.

PRACTICE POINTER

Often attorneys choose to bring a case in a federal rather than state court or the other way around for tactical reasons. Sometimes an attorney wants to bring an action in federal court because the case will be heard more quickly than in state court where the docket is crowded. More often the reason for bringing an action in a particular court is based solely on the law that serves as the basis for the claim.

---

4. Organization of State Governments

Most state governments are organized in a manner similar to that of the federal government. State governments are governed by constitutions. That constitution defines the organization of the state's government and the relationship between the branches of government. The states have legislative, executive, and judicial branches.

The legislative branches operate in a manner similar to that of Congress and often feature two chambers. Some legislatures enact enabling laws that create administrative agencies and provide such agencies with the responsibility for the daily enforcement of state laws. The chief executive in each state is a governor.

Each state has a judicial system. However, not all state systems mirror the federal government's three-tier court system. Each state establishes which courts can hear different disputes. Some states have a three-tier system similar to that of the federal judicial branch. In some states, the intermediate appellate court is eliminated. The following systems do not include an intermediate appellate court: Delaware, Maine, Montana, New Hampshire, Rhode Island, South Dakota, Vermont, West Virginia, and Wyoming.

PRACTICE POINTER

The Supreme Court may not be the highest court in a state. This is the case in New York. Check the *Bluebook*, Table 1, for state court information.

NET NOTE

For more information about the state trial courts, see the National Center for State Courts website, www.ncsc.org. Information about court structures and links to the courts are provided.

▼ What Are the Duties of the State Courts?

In most state court systems, trial courts determine the facts and legal issues of a case. A trial court might include a family, a municipal, or a small claims court. The jurisdiction of these courts is generally limited, sometimes according to the amount of money in dispute.

The next level generally is an appellate level court. However, as noted above, some states do not have this level. As in the federal court system, this court usually does not hear new facts or evidence. Instead, it decides whether the lower court erred in deciding substantive law or procedural issues. Finally, most states have another appellate level court, similar to the U.S. Supreme Court, which is the final arbiter of disputes. In some states, there are two such courts—one for criminal cases and the other for civil cases. Texas and Oklahoma are two states that have such courts.

PRACTICE POINTER

An appellate court may hear facts and evidence if it is the court of original jurisdiction.

▼ Can State Courts Decide Issues of Federal Law?

Yes, state courts can decide issues of federal law. Although a state court decision concerning federal law does not change the federal law, it may persuade federal governing bodies to change federal law. The state court decision's impact is limited to the case in which the federal issue was presented, and therefore only parties involved in that case are bound or required to follow that ruling.

The federal government controls all issues of federal law. The state governments exercise authority over all issues of state law. These areas are not always well defined. In some areas, both the state and federal governments exercise authority. For example, both the state and federal governments control how industries dispose of their wastes. Do not be discouraged if you have difficulty separating state and federal issues in some cases. Many times courts struggle with these issues.

CHAPTER SUMMARY

In this chapter, you learned about the branches of the U.S. government and their functions, as well as the general structure of the state governments. The United States has three branches of government: the legislative, the executive, and the judicial. All of these branches were created by the U.S. Constitution, which guides their activities. In addition, administrative agencies enforce the laws created by the legislature.

The legislature, which consists of the House of Representatives and the Senate, creates laws called statutes.

The executive branch enforces the laws of the United States. The administrative agencies issue proposed and final regulations. The judicial branch resolves disputes and interprets the laws and writes opinions that form the common law. You will find the common law in cases.

The judicial branch is comprised of a three-tier court system. The highest court is the U.S. Supreme Court; the middle courts are the U.S. Courts of Appeals; and the trial or lowest courts are the U.S. District Courts. All three branches of government create law.

KEY TERMS

administrative agencies
appellate courts
balances
bill
case law
certiorari
checks
circuits
city government
codification
common law
Congress
constitution
county government
district courts
diversity cases
enacted law
executive branch

federal appellate court
federal government
House of Representatives
judicial branch
jurisdiction
legislative branch
original jurisdiction
pocket veto
police powers
President
Senate
state governments
statutes
township government
trial court
U.S. Courts of Appeals
U.S. Supreme Court

EXERCISES

SELF-ASSESSMENT

1. What is the role of the President, the courts, and the Congress?
2. Can the Rhode Island legislature adopt a law that violates the U.S. Constitution? Why or why not?
3. What type of law do legislatures create?
4. Briefly, how does Congress create a law?

5. What branch of the government handles day-to-day regulatory issues?
6. How are administrative agencies empowered?
7. What are the trial courts of the United States called?
8. What U.S. court is the highest court?
9. Is a decision of the U.S. Supreme Court enacted law or common law?
10. Do appellate courts generally decide issues of fact?
11. How is the legal system organized in the United States?
12. Why does the Constitution establish multiple U.S. government branches?
13. What government bodies are parts of the legislative branch?
14. List at least two entities within the executive branch.
15. What is the federal court system, and what are its duties?
16. What do trial courts do?
17. What is the U.S. Supreme Court, and what does it do?

APPLICATION OF BASIC RESEARCH CONCEPTS

18. Explain the relationships among the state courts in your state.
19. What is the name of the intermediate court in your state, if any?
20. Diagram how a case would go through your state court system.
21. Draw a flowchart of how a case would travel through the federal court system.
22. What is the name (not title) of the top state executive in your state?
23. What are the names of two executive agencies within your state government?
24. Go to the White House website. Note two of the links provided on the site.
25. Go to your state's website. Does it provide links to the legislature? Does it provide links to the courts? If it provides a link to the courts, click on the link for the highest court in your state. Can you obtain opinions?

REVIEW QUESTIONS

26. Draw a diagram of your state government.
27. How many houses does your legislature have? What are the names of each chamber?
28. Diagram your state court system. Is there an intermediate court?
29. Draw a flowchart of the federal bill process.
30. Draw a flowchart of the state bill process for your state.
31. Who is the chief executive?
32. Go to the National Center for State Courts website and review the structure of your state court.
33. What are the monetary requirements for filing an action in the trial court in your state?
34. Go to www.usa.gov and click around the site to find links to the Congressional Budget Office and the Domestic Policy Council.
35. What are the branches of the U.S. government and what are the responsibilities of each branch?
36. What are the laws created by Congress called?
37. What is the body of law created by the courts called?
38. Name the judges on your high court. Where did you find this information?
39. Find your state's website. Note it.

40. Find a website for your state courts. Note it.
41. Find a website for your state legislature. Note it.

DISCUSSION TOPIC

42. List areas of legal authority that are delegated to the states and to the federal government. One area that is delegated to the states is the sale of alcohol. Can you think of other areas that are only controlled by the states and areas that are controlled by the federal government?

LEGAL AUTHORITIES AND HOW TO USE THEM

CHAPTER OVERVIEW

In researching legal issues, you must have goals and understand the value of the legal authorities you find. This chapter explains the concept of legal authority and the determination of governing law. It discusses the value of various authorities and how authorities interrelate with each other. You will learn which authorities should determine the outcome of a case and which authorities merely provide persuasive support for a case. You will learn how to determine which authorities to use in documents you write.

A. DETERMINATION OF GOVERNING LAW

To determine what law controls your case, you must first determine the jurisdiction. Next, you must identify the current law that applies to your case. To do this, you must examine the hierarchy of authorities. You then consider relevant precedent and dicta.

1. Jurisdiction

Jurisdiction is a complex concept that has several different definitions. In the broadest sense, jurisdiction is the right of a state or of the federal government to apply its laws to a dispute and to exercise control over a conflict. Jurisdiction also is defined as a geographic area such as a state that has the right to interpret and apply its law to a particular case. When a court or a governing body has jurisdiction over a case or situation, it has the authority to adjudicate the case or outcome of the situation.

▼ What Factors Determine Which Jurisdiction Governs Your Case?

A variety of factors affect which jurisdiction governs a claim in a particular case, including where the dispute arose, the parties involved in the case, and the nature of the dispute. Sometimes making this determination is a complex task. Ask the assigning attorney to assist you in making this determination. Various statutes, procedural rules, and cases also can assist you in understanding which court has jurisdiction. For example, federal court jurisdiction is specified by federal law. One type of federal jurisdiction is diversity jurisdiction. It establishes jurisdiction for disputes involving citizens of different states. However, in some cases, citizenship can be difficult to determine. For example, the determination of a corporation's citizenship may require you to investigate where decisions are made about the corporation's operations.

2. Precedent

You already have learned that the courts generate decisions of cases that become law. The basic statement of the rule of law decided by the court is the **holding**. If the court is presented with more than one issue, the decision includes more than one holding. The holding also is called the **precedent**. Other courts use past **precedents** to decide cases.

Theoretically, the lower courts must follow decisions or precedents of the higher courts in their jurisdiction. This theory is called **stare decisis**. The idea behind it is that parties should be able to rely on what the courts have done in the past. Doing so allows parties to predict how a court is likely to rule in their cases.

The doctrine of stare decisis makes your job as a researcher important. You must determine what the courts have decided in the past to assist the attorneys in predicting what the court is likely to do, or likely to be persuaded to do, in your case. Sometimes a court will not follow precedent. Even though stare decisis and precedent are the controlling doctrines, courts often decide cases based on the facts before them and the changes in society. This allows the law, through the holdings, to evolve and to meet contemporary needs. Holdings are what you must consider after reviewing the theories of hierarchy of authorities.

3. Hierarchy of Authorities

Once you have determined the jurisdiction, you then must identify the current law that applies to the case. To determine what law applies to your case, you must determine the **hierarchy of authorities**. This is a system in which legal authorities such as court decisions, statutes, administrative rules and decisions, and constitutions are ranked according to the effect they have in controlling the law of a governing body. You can think of this in part as a chain of command. For example, U.S. Supreme Court cases outrank federal appeals and trial courts concerning issues of federal law. Determining the hierarchy of authorities can be simple or complex depending in large part on the system of government and structure of the courts, the law applicable to the dispute, and the underlying claim. The currency of an authority and competing laws within a jurisdiction are other factors that help researchers determine whether one authority outranks another.

a. Currency

You must first determine which authority is most current. Suppose you find that the law governing your case is a federal law and the case involves a question of federal constitutional law. At first glance the highest legal authority would appear to be the U.S. Constitution because it is the supreme law of the United States and because the legal issue in question is constitutional in nature. However, if the U.S. Supreme Court has interpreted the Constitution on the issue presented in your case, then its decision is more current, and the Court would therefore be the highest legal authority.

In another case that does not involve a constitutional issue, a federal statute might be the highest authority. This would depend on whether a court had interpreted the statute. If a federal court had interpreted the statute's language and that language affected the issue involved in your case, you would need to determine the hierarchy of authority by researching whether the court decision or a statute and any amendment is more recent. The most current authority is the highest authority.

EXAMPLE OF THE HIERARCHY QUESTION BETWEEN A STATUTE AND A CASE

Your case involves a legal issue that was addressed in a statute that was enacted on December 1, 2020. The court cases you have found that may have a bearing on this legal issue involved in this case were decided before December 1, 2020. Therefore, the statute—the most current authority—is the highest authority concerning this issue. For another example, see Illustration 2-1.

b. Levels of Court

Next, you must consider the level of each authority, that is, where the court or government body ranks in order of its authority. The trial courts, appellate courts, and U.S. Supreme Court do not carry the same weight. For example, a decision of the highest court, the U.S. Supreme Court, would be at the top of the hierarchy of authorities of federal court decisions. Its decisions would control those of other federal courts.

Except for the U.S. Supreme Court, all the federal courts are within defined groups called **circuits**. Within each circuit are a group of district courts and one circuit court of appeals. The key to the relationship between the federal courts is that the district courts, which are the entry-level courts or trial courts, must follow decisions of the U.S. Circuit Court of Appeals within its circuit. A district court does not have to follow decisions of appellate courts that are outside of its circuit. A Texas district court is within the Fifth Circuit. Appeals of its decisions generally are made to the U.S. Court of Appeals for the Fifth Circuit. Therefore, the Texas district court must follow the precedents established in the decisions of the U.S. Court of Appeals for the Fifth Circuit. It does not have to follow the precedents set in the decisions of the U.S. Court of Appeals for the Sixth Circuit. For a review of the circuit divisions, review Chapter 1. Decisions of appellate courts outside of a circuit, however, often are used to persuade an appellate court to make a certain decision if it has not addressed that issue earlier. Such a decision is **persuasive authority** discussed later in this chapter.

ILLUSTRATION 2-1.   Example of Ranking Authorities

The problem presented is whether the Fourth Amendment of the U.S. Constitution was violated when the Federal Bureau of Investigation agents obtained GPS tracking data from a phone app provider.

Applicable law:

U.S. Constitution

The USA Freedom Act (2015)—a statute that ended bulk surveillance of Americans.

ILLUSTRATION 2-1. *Continued*

A Supreme Court case (2018) in which the Court determined that the Fourth Amendment of the U.S. Constitution protected individuals against the state's "unrestricted access to a wireless carrier's database of physical location information."

Rank of authorities and reason for the ranking:

1. Supreme Court case 2018 interpreting the Constitution would be first. It is the most current authority.
2. The next authority is likely to be the USA Freedom Act if it directly addresses this point. It is the second most current authority.

PRACTICE POINTER

Create a chart that lists the primary and secondary authorities to consider for each jurisdiction in which you often undertake research.

---

c. Conflicting Decisions Between Circuits

Each circuit is independent of the other circuits. Therefore, decisions from two or more different circuits may conflict. Each appellate court can make its decision independent of any decisions concerning the same issue rendered by other appellate courts. If two appellate courts have conflicting decisions concerning the same issue, how can you, as a researcher, decide what law governs? You must determine what circuit court authority is **mandatory authority** for your case. Mandatory authority is a court decision that a lower court in the same jurisdiction must follow. If the question is a particularly significant federal issue, check if the U.S. Supreme Court has decided the issue or is about to render a decision concerning such an issue. If so, a decision of the Supreme Court—the highest level of court—will be at the top of the hierarchy of authority.

Often, however, one appellate court may be guided in its decision by the decision of another appellate court. Review the example below.

EXAMPLES OF HIERARCHY BETWEEN COURTS

The U.S. District Court for the Northern District of Illinois, which is in Chicago, falls in the Seventh Circuit. See Illustration 1-4. If the federal district court in Illinois was asked to determine whether federal law permitted a union to charge a fee to nonmembers for activities that benefit nonmembers, it would be bound to follow the U.S. Court of Appeals for the Seventh Circuit concerning this issue. This is because this appellate court is a higher court than the district court within the Seventh Circuit. Appeals from the Illinois district court generally are taken to the Seventh Circuit Court of Appeals. If the U.S. Sixth Circuit Court of Appeals in Cincinnati handed down a decision on this issue that conflicted with the Seventh Circuit Court of Appeals, the District Court for the Northern District of Illinois, a trial court, would be bound to follow the decision of the Seventh Circuit Court of Appeals, as it is within the Seventh Circuit and the Seventh Circuit Court of Appeals is above the Illinois district court in rank and status. The Illinois court is not within the Sixth Circuit. Therefore, the Sixth Circuit Court of Appeals is not above the Illinois district court in rank and status. The Illinois court would not be bound to follow the decision of the U.S. Court of Appeals for the Sixth Circuit in Cincinnati. However, the Seventh Circuit decision would be considered **mandatory binding authority** for the Illinois court. The Sixth Circuit opinion would be **primary persuasive authority**. The Sixth Circuit decision would be a very persuasive authority if the Seventh Circuit appellate court had not already ruled on the same issue of law. The Illinois district court facing a decision in a union fee case or even the Seventh Circuit Court of Appeals may be guided by the Sixth Circuit opinion, a persuasive authority rather than mandatory or binding authority.

The U.S. District Court for the Northern District of Ohio, based in Cleveland, falls within the Sixth Circuit. See Illustrations 1-4 and 2-2. That district court must follow decisions of the Sixth Circuit appellate court, not those of the Seventh Circuit Court of Appeals in Chicago, because decisions of the Sixth Circuit Court would be mandatory binding authority for the Ohio court. Decisions of the Seventh Circuit would be primary persuasive authorities for the Ohio court.

ILLUSTRATION 2-2.   Hierarchy Chart for Above Example

U.S. Supreme Court	
Sixth Circuit	*Seventh Circuit*
U.S. Court of Appeals for the Sixth Circuit	U.S. Court of Appeals for the Seventh Circuit
U.S. District Courts in Kentucky, Michigan, Ohio, and Tennessee	U.S. District Courts in Illinois, Indiana, and Wisconsin

d. State and Federal Decisions Concerning an Issue

What happens if the issue in your case involves both state and federal decisions? How do you make sense of the hierarchy of authorities in such cases? The key is to determine which court has jurisdiction or the right to hear the case. The court systems of the state and federal governments operate in tandem. As explained above, the federal courts may decide issues of both federal or state law. For example, a federal diversity case may involve a negligence issue—a state law issue.

Next, you must determine whether federal or state law applies. If you find this difficult, ask the assigning attorney. The federal courts should look to decisions of the highest court of the state to make a determination of state law. The federal court decision, however, does not bind later state court decisions.

State courts also may decide issues of either federal or state law. The state court decisions concerning federal law are merely persuasive authority, however, because federal courts are not required to follow these decisions. State courts will look to federal courts for guidance in deciding issues of federal law. However, they are not bound to follow those decisions. Similarly, a state court may decide a federal age discrimination issue, but the federal courts can disregard that decision when facing the same question.

e. Conflicts in Federal and State Authority

Although the federal and state governments are independent governments, they sometimes regulate some of the same areas, such as environmental pollution. In some cases, the federal government by congressional action will control an area extensively, and a state will attempt to monitor the same area. Who controls varies. Often, a determination of which of the **conflicting authorities** governs is decided by reviewing the Constitution. Other times, federal or state law might specify which law governs.

The federal courts sometimes are asked to decide who controls. The courts may look to the Constitution for guidance or may consider who has pervasively regulated an area. For example, if a case involves a section of the U.S. Constitution, the U.S. Supreme Court is the final authority. In other cases, it depends on the area being regulated. Areas such as trade secrets or environmental law often are regulated by the state and federal government, so conflicts often arise.

f. State Court Decisions

Each group of state courts is a separate court system. State courts of one state are not required to follow decisions that courts of other states render. Often, however, state courts consider other states' court decisions for guidance concerning how to decide a case. Decisions of one state's courts are merely advisory or persuasive decisions for another state's courts, not decisions that control the law of the first state.

4. Dicta

Courts may address an issue that is not directly presented by the parties. In such cases, a court states what it would do if it was presented directly with the issue. When the court makes such statements, they are called **dicta.** Dicta are not holdings. Dicta do not have the same force and effect as holdings. They are not authoritative, and lower courts are not bound to follow such statements.

You might use dicta when no court has ever been asked directly to decide the issue in question. Dicta may explain how a court would decide an issue if it was directly presented to the court. Because of this, the dicta might help you to predict how a court might decide an issue. Dicta from one case may be used to persuade a court in another case to decide an issue in a certain manner. Although dicta may be helpful, finding dicta is not the goal of your research.

B. TYPES OF LEGAL RESOURCES

Your task is to find primary authority "on point" or "on all fours" with your case. In other words, you are seeking cases that are similar in fact and in legal issue to your case and whose holdings address an issue presented in your case — "on all fours."

1. Primary Authority

Primary authority is law generated by a government body. Cases decided by any court are primary authority. Legislative enactments such as constitutions, statutes, rules, ordinances, or charters are primary authorities. See Illustration 2-3. Administrative agency rules and decisions also are primary authorities.

These authorities often are published chronologically. However, statutes are arranged by subject. Some sources of primary authorities will be more appropriate for your research than others. In some cases, primary authority is mandatory or binding authority, because a government body, most often a court, must follow that authority when it makes future decisions. Courts are required to follow decisions of higher courts in the same state or the same federal circuit. The words *mandatory* and *binding* are interchangeable.

ILLUSTRATION 2-3.   Types of Authorities and Finding Tools

Primary Authorities	*Secondary Authorities*	*Finding Tools*
Court decisions	Encyclopedias	Digests
Statutes	*American Law Reports*	Citators
Agency rules and regulations	Periodicals	Updaters
	Law reviews	Case and Statute Annotations
Constitutions	Dictionaries	
Charters	Thesauri	
Ordinances	Model codes	
Adopted pattern jury instructions	Unadopted uniform laws	
Court rules	Treatises	
State-adopted model code provisions	Restatements of the Law	
State-adopted uniform laws		

▼ How Do You Determine Whether a Case Is Mandatory or Binding?

To determine whether a case is mandatory or binding, you must consider the rank of the authorities. Follow the steps below.

1. Determine the jurisdiction that applies to your case. Then, look to the hierarchy of the courts within that jurisdiction.
2. Note what court decided the case you are reviewing.
3. Determine whether this is a court within the jurisdiction that applies to your case.
4. If the court is within the appropriate jurisdiction, you must determine the level of that court within the court system. Is it a trial court or an appellate court? Is it the highest court of the system? States often have rules that specify the effect of a court decision on other courts within the same system. In general, the lower courts in a system must follow the decisions of the highest court in the system. The rules concerning which courts must follow the decisions of the intermediate-tier courts vary by jurisdiction. Consult the rules for that jurisdiction.

An authority is mandatory only if it controls or shapes the law of a particular jurisdiction. Examples of such authorities include state appellate court opinions or state statutes.

▼ When Is a Case or Statute Persuasive Authority?

An authority is persuasive when it is made by a court outside of a particular jurisdiction. Decisions of one state court are not binding on courts of other states. Such a decision, however, may be a persuasive authority. Decisions of the Arizona Supreme Court are mandatory or binding on the lower courts in Arizona, but these decisions are merely persuasive primary authority in Michigan.

A decision is also persuasive rather than mandatory if it is made by a court whose decisions according to the law do not bind other courts. For example, decisions of the federal trial courts do not have to be followed by other federal courts. Therefore, these decisions are only persuasive primary authority.

Persuasive authority can be invaluable in persuading a court. This is especially true in decisions concerning statutory interpretation that involve statutes that are identical. For example, Kansas and Ohio adopted the same comparative negligence statute at different times. Kansas courts faced challenges concerning the statutory language. The decisions were highly persuasive authority when Ohio courts faced similar challenges years later, particularly since it was likely that the Ohio legislators were aware of the Kansas interpretations when they adopted the Ohio statute.

▼ What Process Should You Undertake to Decide When to Use Persuasive Authority?

Consider whether the highest court in your jurisdiction has decided a case on point. If it has not made such a decision, then persuasive authority is valuable. Determine how current the highest court's decision is on the legal issue. If it is outdated and a persuasive decision is far more recent, consider presenting it to the court along with the court's own decision. Review facts of the case. If the highest court in your jurisdiction has decided the issue of law in your case, but the facts are not on point, consider a persuasive authority. If the facts in your case are on point with the facts at issue in the persuasive authority and those facts differ significantly from the facts that were at issue in the case the highest court in your jurisdiction already decided, persuasive authority can be presented to the court. Review Illustrations 2-4 through 2-6 for more information about court decisions and persuasive authority.

ILLUSTRATION 2-4.   When to Use Persuasive Authority

Your Jurisdiction	*Persuasive Authority*
No decision on point	Decision or decisions on point
Decisions on point very old	Recent decision on point
Facts differ substantially	Facts are very similar
No decision based on a new statute or public policy	Decision based on similar statute or public policy

ILLUSTRATION 2-5.   Court Decisions and State Courts

Type of Decision		*Type of Authority*
Decisions of highest court of state (usually the state Supreme Court, but in New York the state Supreme Court is a mid-level appellate court)	=	Mandatory/binding primary authority for mid-level and trial courts in the same state.
Decisions of mid-level appellate courts	=	Mandatory/binding primary authority for trial courts in most states. Primary authority, but not binding on higher state courts.
Decisions of trial courts	=	Primary authority, but not binding on higher courts. These may be binding on administrative agencies and administrative courts depending upon state statutes.
Decisions of U.S. Supreme Court regarding issues of federal constitutional law	=	Mandatory/binding primary authority for all state courts.
Decisions of U.S. Supreme Court regarding issues of federal or state law	=	Primary persuasive authority.
Decisions of federal appellate courts and federal trial courts	=	Primary persuasive authority for all state courts.

ILLUSTRATION 2-6. Court Decisions and Federal Courts

Decisions of U.S. Supreme Court	=	Mandatory/binding primary authority for all federal courts.
Decisions of federal appellate courts	=	Mandatory/binding primary authority for U.S. District Court (federal trial courts) within the circuit of the Federal Appellate Court. Primary persuasive authority for all trial courts outside of the circuit.

For example:

Decisions of Tenth Circuit Court of Appeals ≠ mandatory binding for Ohio federal trial court in Ohio that is in the Sixth Circuit.

Decisions of the Sixth Circuit = mandatory/ binding primary authority for Ohio federal trial courts within the circuit.

Decisions of trial courts	=	Primary authority, but not binding on higher courts. These may be binding on administrative agencies and administrative courts depending upon statutes.
Decisions of all state courts	=	Primary persuasive authority for all federal courts.

PRACTICE POINTER

Use persuasive authority if you do not have a mandatory binding or controlling primary authority on point. For statutory disputes, determine whether legislators would have been aware of the persuasive authority when the statute was adopted. If so, you can argue that the authority should be considered as very persuasive.

2. Secondary Authority

Another type of authority is **secondary authority.** Such authority is not generated by government bodies. Instead, secondary authority includes commentary written by attorneys or other experts. It is not law. Secondary authority is a tool for finding and understanding primary authority. Secondary authority is persuasive only, and it is never binding or mandatory. In general, an attorney would not base an argument to a court on a secondary authority.

Secondary authorities or sources are helpful in understanding an issue of law, in discovering other issues, and in finding primary authorities that are often mentioned within the secondary authorities. Sometimes secondary authorities help to interpret a primary authority for you and the court. Secondary sources include treatises, Restatements of the Law, dictionaries, encyclopedias, legal periodicals,

American Law Reports, books, and thesauri. See Illustration 2-3. Often these sources direct you to cases, statutes, and other primary authorities.

Some secondary authorities are more persuasive than others. Many courts consider Restatements and some treatises as authoritative and these sources can be noted in court documents and legal reports called motions and memoranda addressed to the courts and attorneys. However, most secondary authorities should not be noted in these court documents.

Uniform codes are a type of secondary authority often mistaken for a primary authority. Many uniform codes exist throughout the country. These are suggested laws, often devised by experts. If a state adopts the uniform code in total or in part, the adopted statute, not the underlying uniform code, is primary authority. The recommended or uniform code, however, remains as a very persuasive secondary authority.

PRACTICE POINTER

If you have a primary authority on point, do not cite a secondary authority to make the same point.

PRACTICE POINTER

Secondary authorities are rarely cited in court documents. However, some secondary authorities carry significant persuasive weight, for example, commentaries to uniform laws.

3. Finding Tools

To find primary and secondary authorities, often you need to consult **finding tools**, such as digests and citators. See Illustration 2-3. These finding tools are neither primary nor secondary authority. They should never be noted or cited in memoranda or court documents. Among the finding tools are **digests**, which are books containing case abstracts arranged according to publisher-assigned topics rather than in chronological order. **Annotated statutes** also include case abstracts written by the publishers. **Citators**, such as *Shepard's*®, provide you with listings of cases and some secondary authorities.

> ## PRACTICE POINTER
>
> Attorneys do not look favorably on paralegals who cite finding tools as authority.

4. Hybrid Sources of Authority

Hybrid sources of authority contain primary authorities, secondary authorities, regulations, cases, and finding tools. Hybrid sources of authority include looseleaf services and formbooks. These resources can be useful in finding multiple authorities. However, be certain that you distinguish the primary and secondary authorities and finding tools and that in most cases, you cite only the primary authorities.

5. Nonlegal Sources

You often must consult nonlegal sources, such as newspapers or corporate information statements. These sources are not authoritative. Never use nonlegal sources to determine the law that governs a case. However, nonlegal sources can assist you in your work. Sometimes it is necessary to cite these sources as relevant **factual authority** in a motion or a brief. For example, a state certified document that indicates whether a corporation is incorporated in a particular state may be presented to a court when the court is considering the corporate citizenship. Nonlegal sources often provide insight into the purpose behind a court decision or the enactment of a law.

C. USE OF AUTHORITIES OR SOURCES IN YOUR LEGAL WRITING

1. Essential Sources to Cite

Primary authority is the key type of authority you should use in any form of legal writing such as a legal memorandum (discussed in detail later in this book). As explained earlier, primary authority is the highest authority in the chain of command. In particular, you should use primary, binding authority for the jurisdiction in which your action will be filed or is pending. Primary, binding authority that is tailored to your case — that is, one that is similar in fact and legal issues to your case — is best. However, do not ignore primary, binding authority that does not support your client's case. Attorneys have an ethical obligation to consider such authority in deciding whether to pursue a case and often must cite such authority to a court. If you have not found any primary, binding authority that matches your case facts or legal issues, then consider primary, persuasive authority that matches your case facts or legal issues. For example, if you are working on a case in the federal district court in Florida and you cannot find a U.S. Supreme Court or an Eleventh Circuit appellate court decision on point, you can use a case from the federal Second Circuit Court of Appeals if it has considered a similar case. If, however, you are writing a legal memorandum for an attorney, you should mention all primary, persuasive authorities, both for and against a particular case if you cannot find any primary, binding authorities. An attorney needs to know the cases that support his or her client's position as well as those that oppose it.

2. Valuable Sources to Cite

Primary, persuasive authorities are valuable sources to cite if you do not have primary, binding authority that is similar in fact and law to your case. However, some secondary authorities such as Restatements of Law or treatises are very persuasive and can be cited when you lack primary authority on point. When you cite these secondary authorities, you need to be careful to note, however, that you did not have any primary authority on point.

3. Sources Never to Cite

Do not cite digests, the annotations in secondary authorities, or the case abstracts listed in the annotated statutes. Citing these nonauthorities can result in serious consequences, including ethics law violations. Nonlegal sources such as newspapers should not be cited to support a legal issue. Only cite these sources to support factual statements.

ETHICS ALERT

Attorneys must cite applicable primary, mandatory authority to a court in a motion or memorandum even if the authority does not support your client's position. Do not cite a secondary authority favorable to your side in place of the primary, mandatory authority.

CHECKLIST

1. Review all of your sources of authority.
2. Divide the sources into primary and secondary authorities and finding tools.

3. Make a list of all of the primary authorities.
4. Separate primary authorities that are applicable to the jurisdiction that applies in the case you are handling.
5. Make a ranking of those primary authorities—determine which are binding and which are merely persuasive. To rank these authorities, determine which authority is highest in the chain of command as explained in the hierarchy of authority section of this chapter. Consider which authority is most current and which authority is precedential in value rather than merely dicta.
6. Determine whether these binding authorities match your facts or legal issues.
7. Determine whether the primary persuasive authorities match your facts or legal issues.
8. Make a ranking of the secondary authorities and determine whether these match your facts or legal issues.
9. Start your analysis and written summary with the primary, binding authorities that match your facts and legal issues.
10. Next incorporate primary, persuasive authorities that match your facts and legal issues. However, you should use these authorities only if the primary, binding authority does not match your facts or legal issues in total.
11. Finally, consider incorporating secondary authorities into your writing if none of the primary authorities address your facts or legal issues.
12. Never cite a secondary authority when you have a primary binding authority on point.
13. Never cite a newspaper article or a finding tool to support a legal issue. Nonlegal sources such as newspapers should be cited only to support a factual issue.

IN-CLASS EXERCISE

FACTS

You are a paralegal in the state in which you live. You have been assigned to research whether an individual can bring an action in state court against a car dealer and the car manufacturer of a car that has been trouble-ridden since the individual purchased it eight months ago.

RESEARCH RESULTS

You have found a statute that explains lemon law actions in your state; two cases in your state that interpret the statute; a federal case that explains the lemon law's application in your state; a case from another state that explains the lemon law; an encyclopedia explanation of the statute; a periodical article in a bar journal about lemon law actions in your state; and a newspaper article that explains how to bring a lemon law action and what actions are barred.

DISCUSSION QUESTIONS FOR THE CLASS

1. What type of authority is the lemon law statute in your state?
2. What type of authority are the two cases from your state?
3. What type of authority is the case from another state?
4. What type of authority is the federal case?
5. What type of authority is the encyclopedia reference to the statute?
6. What type of authority is the periodical article?
7. What type of authority is the newspaper article?
8. Which, if any, authorities might be binding or mandatory authorities?
9. Which authorities might be noted in a memorandum to a court?

Determine whether the authorities are primary mandatory, primary persuasive, or secondary authorities, and rank authorities according to which authorities to use first, second, third, and so on, if at all.

CHAPTER SUMMARY

In this chapter, you learned that determining governing law involves examining jurisdiction and the hierarchy of authorities. You also learned how precedent and dicta influence governing law. As a researcher, your goal is to find cases that are similar to yours in fact and legal issue and whose holdings address an issue presented in your case. In reaching this goal, you first seek primary authorities because these authorities carry more weight with the courts than secondary authorities. Primary authorities include court decisions, statutes, court rules, constitutions, and administrative rules and regulations.

Some primary authorities are binding. If an authority is binding, a court must follow that authority. Other authorities are merely persuasive. Such authorities provide guidance to the courts and often are followed by the decision-making tribunal.

As you are researching, you often will refer to secondary authorities. Secondary authorities provide you with information to understand primary authorities. Generally, secondary authorities are commentaries prepared by experts in a particular field. These authorities often include citations to primary authorities. Secondary authorities are persuasive only. Therefore, you would rely on a primary authority rather than a secondary authority. Secondary authorities include encyclopedias, treatises, and legal periodicals.

Finding tools are designed to assist you in your research, but they are not considered authorities. These tools provide you with citations to primary and secondary authorities. Finding tools include annotated statutes, digests, and citators. The statutes and the cases are primary authorities, but the annotations are the finding tools. Cite these primary authorities in documents addressed to courts and attorneys, not the annotations.

Finally, you learned how to incorporate these authorities into your legal writing. You learned that primary, binding authority is the best authority to use to support a legal proposition. Primary, persuasive, and some secondary authority also may be cited. Finding tools and nonlegal sources should not be used to support a legal theory.

KEY TERMS

annotated statutes

binding authority

circuits

citators

conflicting authorities

dicta

digests

factual authority

finding tools

hierarchy of authorities

holding

hybrid sources of authority

jurisdiction

mandatory authority

persuasive authority

precedent

primary authority

secondary authority

stare decisis

EXERCISES

COURT SYSTEMS

Self-Assessment

1. What is the highest court of your state? Where can you find this information on the Internet? Give a website.
2. Within your state's court system, what type of authority are decisions made by the highest court named in Question 1?
   a. primary binding
   b. primary persuasive
   c. secondary binding
   d. secondary persuasive
3. What is the name of the trial court of your state?
4. Are the trial court's decisions binding on the highest court of the state?
5. What is the highest court of the federal system of government?
6. Within the federal system of government, what type of authority are decisions made by the highest court named in Question 5?
   a. primary binding
   b. primary persuasive
   c. secondary binding
   d. secondary persuasive
7. What is the name of the trial court of the federal government?
8. Are decisions of any federal trial court binding on any federal appellate court?
9. Are all federal appellate court decisions binding on every federal trial court? Why or why not?
10. Can state courts decide issues of federal law?

11. Can federal courts decide issues of state law?
12. What is primary authority?
13. What is binding or mandatory authority?
14. When would you use primary authority?

PRACTICE SKILLS

15. Can the Arizona Legislature adopt a law that contradicts the U.S. Constitution?
16. Must the U.S. Circuit Court of Appeals for the Ninth Circuit follow a decision of the U.S. Supreme Court concerning a federal issue?
17. Must an Arkansas trial court follow a decision of the U.S. Supreme Court concerning an issue of federal law?
18. You are a paralegal assigned to research the components necessary to create a valid will in your state. List in order the types of authorities you would consult and why. Next, rank the authorities according to whether they are primary mandatory, primary persuasive, or secondary.
19. You are a paralegal who has just researched what constitutes a breach of contract in a case involving the delivery of dairy products in Wisconsin. Rank the following authorities and list whether each is a primary binding, primary persuasive, or secondary authority.
    a. A Wisconsin Supreme Court case involving a breach of contract dispute
    b. A Wisconsin statute that defines breach of contract
    c. A Wisconsin statute that defines the term *delivery* in a contract
    d. A Wisconsin trial court case involving a breach of contract dispute
    e. An Illinois Supreme Court case involving a breach of contract dispute
    f. A Uniform Commercial Code section concerning breach of contract. (The Wisconsin statute is derived in part from this section but does not adopt it in total.)
20. You are researching the question of whether a company that employs 50 individuals is an employer under the federal law regulating age discrimination in employment. Your case is pending in the federal district court in Toledo, Ohio. You learn that the definitions in the age discrimination statute were derived from those already in the sex discrimination statute. Rank the following authorities and list whether each is a primary binding, primary persuasive, or secondary authority.
    a. The federal age discrimination in employment statute that defines the term *employer*
    b. The federal sex discrimination in employment statute that defines the term *employer*
    c. A U.S. Supreme Court case that interprets the definition of *employer* contained in the federal age discrimination in employment statute
    d. A U.S. Supreme Court case that interprets the definition of *employer* contained in the federal sex discrimination in employment statute
    e. A decision of the Northern District Court of Ohio, Western Division, concerning the definition of *employer* under the federal age discrimination in employment statute
    f. A law review article in the *University of Toledo Law Review* concerning the definition of *employer* contained in the federal age discrimination in employment statute

g. A section of an employment law treatise that explains the definition of *employer* under the federal age discrimination in employment statute

h. An Ohio Supreme Court case that explains the definition of *employer* under the federal age discrimination in employment statute

Which authorities would you use in a legal memorandum you are writing for an attorney and why?

21. You are asked to research the validity of a New York statute that bars high school students from wearing t-shirts bearing antigovernment slogans. Your case is pending in the state court of New York. Rank the following authorities and list whether each is a primary binding, primary persuasive, or secondary authority.

a. The New York statute in question

b. The U.S. Constitution's First Amendment regarding free speech

c. A U.S. Supreme Court case that prohibits states from banning the wearing of symbols by high school students because such a ban violates the U.S. Constitution

d. A case decided by the highest court in New York that holds that the statute is invalid

e. A California case involving an identical statute adopted in California that holds that the statute is valid

f. An encyclopedia entry that states that such bans are invalid

g. A newspaper article in *The National Law Journal* that predicts that the U.S. Supreme Court will invalidate the New York statute

Which authorities would you use in a legal memorandum you are writing for an attorney and why?

22. A local school expelled a student for writing profane words to describe her school and cheerleading squad on her Instagram page. You are asked to research the validity of an Indiana statute that allows schools to expel students who violate codes of conduct for extracurricular activities. The case is pending in the state court of Indiana. Rank the following authorities and list whether each is a primary binding, primary persuasive, or secondary authority.

a. The Indiana statute in question

b. The U.S. Constitution's First Amendment regarding free speech

c. A U.S. Supreme Court decision that found that a Snapchat post was off-campus speech and that regulation of such speech violated the First Amendment to the U.S. Constitution. *Mahanoy Area School District v. B.L.* Slip Opinion No. 20-255 (June 23, 2021).

d. A case decided by the highest court in Indiana that holds that the statute is invalid

e. A California case involving an identical statute adopted in California that holds that the statute is valid

f. An encyclopedia entry that states that such bans are invalid

g. A newspaper article in *The National Law Journal* that predicts that the U.S. Supreme Court will invalidate the Indiana statute

Which authorities would you use in a legal memorandum you are writing for an attorney and why?

COURT DECISIONS

CHAPTER OVERVIEW

In Chapters 1 and 2, you learned about our system of government and were introduced to the concept of legal authorities. This chapter focuses on one of those legal authorities—case law, which is a primary authority. The chapter describes where to find U.S. Supreme Court cases and other federal court decisions as well as the location of many state court opinions. It also explains where you can find the most recent court decisions. You are then introduced to a topical system for locating cases and are shown how to use this system.

A. REPORTERS

Court decisions are often referred to as **case law.** Case law is one of the primary sources of our law, on both the state and the federal levels.

Finding and reading past court decisions is therefore vital to any lawyer or paralegal working on a client's case.

Several publishers publish court decisions in various forms. Some publishers have devised **reporting systems** for organizing these court decisions. The major reporting system is called **West's® National Reporter System** created by West Publishing, now a Thomson Reuters product. It includes books called **reporters** that contain many federal and state decisions in chronological order. Several other companies and government agencies also publish court decisions in chronologically arranged reporters. In all cases, the decisions are selectively reported. Many decisions never appear in print or online. Libraries are discontinuing the use of print reporters in favor of computer databases and court websites.

In the past, most states either published their own print reporters or designated a commercial reporter as the official state report of a case. Today, some states designate their online case reports as official reports decisions rather than the print materials.

1. Bench Opinions

The U.S. Supreme Court provides the text of **bench opinions** immediately after the Court announces an opinion from the bench. It is a pamphlet that has the opinion of the majority, the plurality, and any concurring or dissenting opinions written by the justices. These opinions are available from the Court's Public Information Office, electronically through the Court's website, and through Project Hermes. Project Hermes is a subscription service and most subscribers are universities, news media outlets, and publishing houses.

2. Slip Opinions

The next *printed* version of a U.S. Supreme Court decision, and often the first printed version of other court decisions, is called a **slip opinion.** See Illustration 3-1. Sometimes, the slip opinion is the only report of a court's action because the case is never published in a reporter or other service. This is usually what happens with trial court decisions, especially state court decisions. However, many court slip opinions, including those of the U.S. Supreme Court, are readily available to the public online at a court website, usually within minutes after a decision is announced. The U.S. Supreme Court continues to have a slip opinion on its website until the decision is published in bound volumes. In some instances, you need to know the name of the case to find a case on a court website. However, many court websites allow you to search by keyword. Most are available free or for a minimal charge. In addition, computerized legal research services such as Thomson Reuters' Westlaw® and Westlaw Edge®, both commonly called **Westlaw®**, and RELX Inc.'s Lexis+ and Lexis® formerly called Lexis Advance®,

(Lexis) include many slip opinions online. ***United States Law Week***, a service of Bloomberg Law, allows subscribers to access the full text of U.S. Supreme Court opinions quickly. Bloomberg's Supreme Court Today tracker provides the status of final decisions and it is updated within an hour of orders or decisions.

An official U.S. Supreme Court slip opinion contains a syllabus. See Illustration 3-1. It is written by the Reporter of Decisions. It is not part of the decision.

ETHICS ALERT

Newspaper reports of slip opinions of court cases also are quickly available, usually within a few days of the court's decision; however, these should never be quoted in a memorandum for an attorney or in a motion or memorandum to the court because such reports have no force within the law. In addition, they may be incorrect. Only quote or cite information that comes directly from the official court opinion.

---

a. Supreme Court Slip Opinions

For the U.S. Supreme Court, you can retrieve U.S. Supreme Court slip opinions from its website. Cases and the docket files can be searched by keywords.

b. Other Slip Opinions

Slip opinions for other federal courts and state courts can be secured from the court, the Internet, and through services such as Westlaw and Lexis. In some states, the website version of the high court's opinions have become the official report of the court's decision.

▼ How Are Pending or Unreported Opinions Such as Slip Opinions Cited in Memorandums to the Court or to Attorneys?

Most court rules and many attorneys require sources be cited based on *The Bluebook: A Uniform System of Citation* (21st ed. 2021) (the *Bluebook*) or the *ALWD Guide to Legal Citation* (7th ed. 2021) (*ALWD*). Review the local court rules and ask the attorneys at your firm or office about the preferred citation format. Slip opinions are cited according to **Rule 10.8.1** of the *Bluebook* or **Rule 12.15** of *ALWD*. Updates for the *Bluebook* can be found at www.legalbluebook.com. In addition, the *Bluebook* offers online citation subscriptions. Users must register to receive any updates. Both citation manuals yield the same citation in this case. In

ILLUSTRATION 3-1. A Portion of a Supreme Court Slip Opinion

OCTOBER TERM, 2020   1

Syllabus

NOTE: Where it is feasible, a syllabus (headnote) will be released, as is being done in connection with this case, at the time the opinion is issued. The syllabus constitutes no part of the opinion of the Court but has been prepared by the Reporter of Decisions for the convenience of the reader. See *United States* v. *Detroit Timber & Lumber Co.,* 200 U. S. 321, 337.

SUPREME COURT OF THE UNITED STATES

Syllabus

(B) MAHANOY AREA SCHOOL DISTRICT *v.* B. L., A MINOR, BY AND THROUGH HER FATHER, LEVY, ET AL.

CERTIORARI TO THE UNITED STATES COURT OF APPEALS FOR THE THIRD CIRCUIT

(C) No. 20–255. (D) Argued April 28, 2021—(E) Decided June 23, 2021

Mahanoy Area High School student B. L. failed to make the school's varsity cheerleading squad. While visiting a local convenience store over the weekend, B. L. posted two images on Snapchat, a social media application for smartphones that allows users to share temporary images with selected friends. B. L.'s posts expressed frustration with the school and the school's cheerleading squad, and one contained vulgar language and gestures. When school officials learned of the posts, they suspended B. L. from the junior varsity cheerleading squad for the upcoming year. After unsuccessfully seeking to reverse that punishment, B. L. and her parents sought relief in federal court, arguing *inter alia* that punishing B. L. for her speech violated the First Amendment. The District Court granted an injunction ordering the school to reinstate B. L. to the cheerleading team. Relying on *Tinker* v. *Des Moines Independent Community School* [District] subsequent motion for summary [judgment] that B. L.'s punishment violated [the First Amendment because her Snap]chat posts had not caused [substantial disruption at the school]. The Third Circuit affirmed the j[udgment] reasoned that *Tinker* did not a[pply] to regulate student speech occurring off campus.

> A Syllabus
> B Case name
> C Docket number
> D Date argued
> E Date decided

Held: While public schools may have a special interest in regulating some off-campus student speech, the special interests offered by the school are not sufficient to overcome B. L.'s interest in free expression in this case. Pp. 4–11.

    (a) In *Tinker*, we indicated that schools have a special interest in regulating on-campus student speech that "materially disrupts class-

ILLUSTRATION 3-1. *Continued*

2   MAHANOY AREA SCHOOL DIST. *v.* B. L.

Syllabus

Ⓐ work or involves substantial disorder or invasion of the rights of others." 393 U. S., at 513. The special characteristics that give schools additional license to regulate student speech do not always disappear when that speech takes place off campus. Circumstances that may implicate a school's regulatory interests include serious or severe bullying or harassment targeting particular individuals; threats aimed at teachers or other students; the failure to follow rules concerning lessons, the writing of papers, the use of computers, or participation in other online school activities; and breaches of school security devices. Pp. 4–6.

Cite as: 594 U. S. ____ (2021)   3

Syllabus

Ⓐ stances where the school did not stand *in loco parentis*. And the vulgarity in B. L.'s posts encompassed a message of criticism. In addition, the school has presented no evidence of any general effort to prevent students from using vulgarity outside the classroom. Pp. 9–10.

(4) The school's interest in preventing disruption is not supported by the record, which shows that discussion of the matter took, at most, 5 to 10 minutes of an Algebra class "for just a couple of days" and that some members of the cheerleading team were "upset" about the content of B. L.'s Snapchats. App. 82–83. This alone does not satisfy *Tinker's* demanding standards. Pp.

(5) Likewise, there is little to s **A Syllabus**
in, or disruption of, the school's eff **F Summary of how the**
school cheerleading squad. P. 11. **judges voted concerning the decision**

964 F. 3d 170, affirmed.

Ⓕ BREYER, J., delivered the opinion of the Court, in which ROBERTS, C. J., and ALITO, SOTOMAYOR, KAGAN, GORSUCH, KAVANAUGH and BARRETT, JJ., joined. ALITO, J., filed a concurring opinion, in which GORSUCH, J., joined. THOMAS, J., filed a dissenting opinion.

ILLUSTRATION 3-1. *Continued*

Cite as: 594 U. S. ____ (2021)   1

Opinion of the Court

NOTICE: This opinion is subject to formal revision before publication in the preliminary print of the United States Reports. Readers are requested to notify the Reporter of Decisions, Supreme Court of the United States, Washington, D. C. 20543, of any typographical or other formal errors, in order that corrections may be made before the preliminary print goes to press.

SUPREME COURT OF THE UNITED STATES

_____

No. 20–255

_____

MAHANOY AREA SCHOOL DISTRICT, PETITIONER *v.* B. L., A MINOR, BY AND THROUGH HER FATHER, LAWRENCE LEVY AND HER MOTHER, BETTY LOU LEVY

ON WRIT OF CERTIORARI TO THE UNITED STATES COURT OF APPEALS FOR THE THIRD CIRCUIT

[June 23, 2021]

JUSTICE BREYER delivered the opinion of the Court.

A public high school student used, and transmitted to her Snapchat friends, vulgar language and gestures criticizing both the school and the school's cheerleading team. The student's speech took place outside of school hours and away from the school's campus. In response, the school suspended the student for a year from the cheerleading team. We must decide whether the Court of Appeals for the Third Circuit correctly held that the school's decision violated the First Amendment. Although we do not agree with the reasoning of the Third Circuit panel's majority, we do agree with its conclusion that the school's disciplinary action violated the First Amendment.

I
A

B. L. (who, together with her parents, is a respondent in this case) was a student at Mahanoy Area High School, a public school in Mahanoy City, Pennsylvania. At the end of her freshman year, B. L. tried out for a position on the

Ⓖ

G Body of the decision

either case, you should provide the docket number, the court, and the full (but abbreviated) date of the most recent disposition of the case.

slip opinion cite: *Gillespie v. Willard City Bd. of Educ.*, No. C87-7043 (N.D. Ohio Sept. 28, 1987)

with page cite: *Gillespie v. Willard City Bd. of Educ.*, No. C87-7043, slip op. at 3 (N.D. Ohio Sept. 28, 1987)

ETHICS ALERT

Always check the local court rules and orders to see if unpublished cases may be cited.

---

3. Preliminary Prints

After a U.S. Supreme Court slip opinion is released, it is published in **preliminary print.** These include the opinions, announcements, tables, and indexes. Commercial publishers also distribute **advance sheets** that contain the full text of federal and state decisions and often are paginated using the same page numbers that will be used when the decision is published in the bound reporter. Many advance sheets contain publisher's notes called **headnotes** that are designed to assist readers. These notes summarize points of law in a case and have a topic and number assigned to them. These topics and numbers assist you in finding additional cases. The timing of the publication of advance sheets varies by publisher. After decisions appear in advance sheets, they are published in the bound reporters. Many print advance sheet publications and bound volumes are being phased out as many courts and fee-based online services now send users slip opinions via e-mail or make them available on their court website.

4. Bound Reporters

a. U.S. Supreme Court Decisions

A U.S. Supreme Court case is first presented as a bench opinion, published as a slip opinion, then as a preliminary print, and finally as a report in a bound volume. For U.S. Supreme Court cases, the official, government-printed reporter is *United States Reports.* See Illustration 3-2. Illustration 3-2 includes a syllabus or summary of the case. For this court, the syllabus is not part of the court's decision and should not be quoted in any documents submitted to the court. It has no force of law. In some courts, however, a syllabus is part of the opinion. Check local court rules and orders. This illustration also indicates the docket number, the decision date, the date argued, and the case name. The attorneys representing the parties are noted. On page 4 of the illustration, the author of the opinion, Ruth Bader Ginsburg, is noted. It also indicates whether any justices concurred or dissented. Then the decision begins. In this case, justices both concurred and dissented. Those decisions also are included in the slip opinion. See Illustration 3-2 pages 7 and 8. This reporter, however, is not published quickly, nor does it contain any research aids. Because of this delay, commercial publishers have created reporter systems that contain the same decisions as those published in ***U.S. Reports.*** Full-text electronic versions of *U.S. Reports* are available on the supremecourt.gov website from 1991 to the present.

Electronic versions of the *U.S. Reports* are available at the U.S. Supreme Court website. If there is a discrepancy between the print and PDF versions of *U.S. Reports*, the print version controls.

Commercial publishers offer these decisions as well. All U.S. Supreme Court decisions are available from Thomson Reuters, a commercial publisher, in a print reporter called the ***Supreme Court Reporter.*** See Illustration 3-3. Lexis distributes the same full text of U.S. Supreme Court decisions in a print reporter called *United States Supreme Court Reports, Lawyers' Edition.* Most people simply call it the ***Lawyers' Edition.*** Both publishers provide these resources in a similar format online through their respective databases, Westlaw and Lexis.

Within both unofficial reporters, the case opinions should be identical to the decisions that appear in the official *U.S. Reports.* The reports in these commercially published reporters, however, also contain references prepared by the publishers to assist you in your research. These references direct you to other sources that may help you understand a point of law. For example, a publisher may direct you to a treatise that contains commentary about a point of law raised in the case reported. In addition, these references may assist you in locating other cases on point.

▼ What Happens if the Language of a Decision in the Commercial Reporters Varies from the Language in *U.S. Reports?*

If the decision text contained in either the *Supreme Court Reporter* or the *Lawyers' Edition* varies from the official, government-printed report, the language in *U.S. Reports* governs.

▼ Is U.S. Supreme Court Docket Information Available without Charge on the Internet?

Yes. For U.S. Supreme Court docket, schedules, general information, and links to decisions, see www.supremecourt.gov. This site also provides oral argument transcripts and argument audio in recent cases.

ILLUSTRATION 3-2. **Pages from** *U.S. Reports*

OCTOBER TERM, 1995   515

Syllabus

⑤ UNITED STATES *v.* VIRGINIA ET AL.

CERTIORARI TO THE UNITED STATES COURT OF APPEALS FOR
THE FOURTH CIRCUIT

① No. 94–1941.   Argued ④ January 17, 1996—Decided June 26, 1996* ②

Virginia Military Institute (VMI) is the sole single-sex school among Virginia's public institutions of higher learning.   VMI's distinctive mission
is to produce "citizen-soldiers," men prepared for leadership in civilian
life and in military service.   Using an "adversative method" of training
not available elsewhere in Virginia, VMI endeavors to instill physical
and mental discipline in its cadets and impart to them a strong moral
code.   Reflecting the high value alumni place on their VMI training,
VMI has the largest per-student endowment of all public undergraduate
institutions in the Nation.   The United States sued Virginia and VMI,
alleging that VMI's exclusively male admission policy violated the Fourteenth Amendment's Equal Protection Clause.   The District Court
ruled in VMI's favor.   The Fourth Circuit reversed and ordered Virginia to remedy the constitutional violation.   In response, Virginia proposed a parallel program for women: Virginia Women's Institute for
Leadership (VWIL), located at Mary Baldwin College, a private liberal
③ arts school for women.   The District Court found that Virginia's proposal satisfied the Constitution's equal protection requirement, and the
Fourth Circuit affirmed.   The appeals court deferentially reviewed Virginia's plan and determined that provision of single-gender educational
options was a legitimate objective.   Maintenance of single-sex programs, the court concluded, was essential to that objective.   The court
recognized, however, that its analysis risked bypassing equal protection
scrutiny, so it fashioned an additional test, asking whether VMI and
VWIL students would receive "substantively comparable" benefits.
Although the Court of Appeals acknowledged that the VWIL degree
lacked the historical benefit and prestige of a VMI degree, the court
nevertheless found the educational opportunities at the two schools sufficiently comparable.

Held:
   1. Parties who seek to defend gender-based government action must
demonstrate an "exceedingly persuasive justification" for that action.
E. g., Mississippi Univ. for Women v. *Hogan,* 458 U. S. 718, 724.   Nei-

---

*Together with No. 94–2107, *Virginia et al.* v. *United States,* also on
certiorari to the same court.

---

1 Docket number	**4 Date argued**
2 Decision Date	**5 Case name**
3 Syllabus written by reporter	

ILLUSTRATION 3-2. *Continued*

516 UNITED STATES *v.* VIRGINIA

Syllabus

ther federal nor state government acts compatibly with equal protection when a law or official policy denies to women, simply because they are women, full citizenship stature—equal opportunity to aspire, achieve, participate in and contribute to society based on their individual talents and capacities. To meet the burden of justification, a State must show "at least that the [challenged] classification serves 'important governmental objectives and that the discriminatory means employed' are 'substantially related to the achievement of those objectives.'" *Ibid.*, quoting *Wengler* v. *Druggists Mut. Ins. Co.*, 446 U. S. 142, 150. The justification must be genuine, not hypothesized or invented *post hoc* in response to litigation. And it must not rely on overbroad generalizations about the different talents, capacities, or preferences of males and females. See, *e. g.*, *Weinberger* v. *Wiesenfeld*, 420 U. S. 636, 643, 648. The heightened review standard applicable to sex-based classifications does not make sex a proscribed classification, but it does mean that categorization by sex may not be used to create or perpetuate the legal, social, and economic inferiority of women. Pp. 531–534.

2. Virginia's categorical exclusion of women from the educational opportunities VMI provides denies equal protection to women. Pp. 534–546.

(③) (a) Virginia contends that single-sex education yields important educational benefits and that provision of an option for such education fosters diversity in educational approaches. Benign justifications proffered in defense of categorical exclusions, however, must describe actual state purposes, not rationalizations for actions in fact differently grounded. Virginia has not shown that VMI was established, or has been maintained, with a view to diversifying, by its categorical exclusion of women, educational opportunities within the Commonwealth. A purpose genuinely to advance an array of educational options is not served by VMI's historic and constant plan to afford a unique educational benefit only to males. However well this plan serves Virginia's sons, it makes no provision whatever for her daughters. Pp. 535–540.

(b) Virginia also argues that VMI's adversative method of training provides educational benefits that cannot be made available, unmodified, to women, and that alterations to accommodate women would necessarily be so drastic as to destroy VMI's program. It is uncontested that women's admission to VMI would require accommodations, primarily in arranging housing assignments and physical training programs for female cadets. It is also undisputed, however, that neither the goal of producing citizen-soldiers, VMI's *raison d'être*, nor VMI's implementing methodology is inherently unsuitable to women. The District Court made "findings" on "gender-based developmental differences" that restate the opinions of Virginia's expert witnesses about typically male or typically female "tendencies." Courts, however, must take "a hard

ILLUSTRATION 3-2. *Continued*

Syllabus

look" at generalizations or tendencies of the kind Virginia pressed, for state actors controlling gates to opportunity have no warrant to exclude qualified individuals based on "fixed notions concerning the roles and abilities of males and females." *Mississippi Univ. for Women,* 458 U. S., at 725. The notion that admission of women would downgrade VMI's stature, destroy the adversative system and, with it, even the school, is a judgment hardly proved, a prediction hardly different from other "self-fulfilling prophec[ies], see *id.,* at 730, once routinely used to deny rights or opportunities. Women's successful entry into the federal military academies, and their participation in the Nation's military forces, indicate that Virginia's fears for VMI's future may not be solidly grounded. The Commonwealth's justification for excluding all women from "citizen-soldier" training for which some are qualified, in any event, does not rank as "exceedingly persuasive." Pp. 540–546.

3. The remedy proffered by Virginia—maintain VMI as a male-only college and create VWIL as a separate program for women—does not cure the constitutional violation. Pp. 546–558.

(a) A remedial decree must closely fit the constitutional violation; it must be shaped to place persons unconstitutionally denied an opportunity or advantage in the position they would have occupied in the absence of discrimination. See *Milliken* v. *Bradley,* 433 U. S. 267, 280. The constitutional violation in this case is the categorical exclusion of women, in disregard of their individual merit, from an extraordinary educational opportunity afforded men. Virginia chose to leave untouched VMI's exclusionary policy, and proposed for women only a separate program, different in kind from VMI and unequal in tangible and intangible facilities. VWIL affords women no opportunity to experience the rigorous military training for which VMI is famed. Kept away from the pressures, hazards, and psychological bonding characteristic of VMI's adversative training, VWIL students will not know the feeling of tremendous accomplishment commonly experienced by VMI's successful cadets. Virginia maintains that methodological differences are justified by the important differences between men and women in learning and developmental needs, but generalizations about "the way women are," estimates of what is appropriate for *most women,* no longer justify denying opportunity to women whose talent and capacity place them outside the average description. In myriad respects other than military training, VWIL does not qualify as VMI's equal. The VWIL program is a pale shadow of VMI in terms of the range of curricular choices and faculty stature, funding, prestige, alumni support and influence. Virginia has not shown substantial equality in the separate educational opportunities the Commonwealth supports at VWIL and VMI. Cf. *Sweatt* v. *Painter,* 339 U. S. 629. Pp. 547–554.

ILLUSTRATION 3-2.   *Continued*

518   UNITED STATES *v.* VIRGINIA

Syllabus

③   (b) The Fourth Circuit failed to inquire whether the proposed remedy placed women denied the VMI advantage in the position they would have occupied in the absence of discrimination, *Milliken,* 433 U. S., at 280, and considered instead whether the Commonwealth could provide, with fidelity to equal protection, separate and unequal educational programs for men and women. In declaring the substantially different and significantly unequal VWIL program satisfactory, the appeals court displaced the exacting standard developed by this Court with a deferential standard, and added an inquiry of its own invention, the "substantive comparability" test. The Fourth Circuit plainly erred in exposing Virginia's VWIL plan to such a deferential analysis, for "all gender-based classifications today" warrant "heightened scrutiny." See *J. E. B.* v. *Alabama ex rel. T. B.,* 511 U. S. 127, 136. Women seeking and fit for a VMI-quality education cannot be offered anything less, under the Commonwealth's obligation to afford them genuinely equal protection. Pp. 554–558.

⑦ No. 94–2107, 976 F. 2d 890, affirmed; No. 94–1941, 44 F. 3d 1229, reversed and remanded.

⑥ GINSBURG, J., delivered the opinion of the Court, in which STEVENS, O'CONNOR, KENNEDY, SOUTER, and BREYER, JJ., joined. REHNQUIST, C. J., filed an opinion concurring in the judgment, *post,* p. 558. SCALIA, J., filed a dissenting opinion, *post,* p. 566. THOMAS, J., took no part in the consideration or decision of the case.

⑧   *Paul Bender* argued the cause for the United States in both cases. With him on the briefs were *Solicitor General Days, Assistant Attorney General Patrick, Cornelia T. L. Pillard, Jessica Dunsay Silver,* and *Thomas E. Chandler.*
   Theodore B. Olson argued the cause and filed briefs for respondents in No. 94–1941 and petitioners in No. 94–2107. With him on the briefs were *James S. Gilmore III,* Attorney General of Virginia, *William H. Hurd,* Deputy Attorney General, *Thomas G. Hungar, D. Jarrett Arp, Robert H. Patterson, Jr., Anne Marie Whittemore, William G. Broaddus, J. William Boland, Griffin B. Bell,* and *William A. Clineburg, Jr.*†

   †Briefs of *amici curiae* urging reversal in No. 94–1941 were filed for the State of Maryland et al. by *J. Joseph Curran, Jr.,* Attorney General of Maryland, and *Andrew H. Baida,* Assistant Attorney General, and by the Attorneys General for their respective jurisdictions as follows: *Margery*

---

6 Summary of how judges voted concerning the decision
7 Citations to lower court cases
8 Attorneys who argued and briefed case

ILLUSTRATION 3-2.   *Continued*

Opinion of the Court

⑩ JUSTICE GINSBURG delivered the opinion of the Court.

⑨ Virginia's public institutions of higher learning include an incomparable military college, Virginia Military Institute (VMI).   The United States maintains that the Constitution's equal protection guarantee precludes Virginia from reserving exclusively to men the unique educational opportunities VMI affords.   We agree.

S. Bronster of Hawaii, *Scott Harshbarger* of Massachusetts, *Frankie Sue Del Papa* of Nevada, *C. Sebastian Aloot* of the Northern Mariana Islands, and *Theodore R. Kulongoski* of Oregon; for the Employment Law Center et al. by *Patricia A. Shiu* and *Judith Kurtz;* and for the National Women's Law Center et al. by *Robert N. Weiner, Marcia D. Greenberger, Sara L. Mandelbaum, Janet Gallagher, Mary Wyckoff, Steven R. Shapiro,* and *Susan Deller Ross.*

Briefs of *amici curiae* urging affirmance in No. 94–1941 were filed for the State of South Carolina et al. by *Charles Molony Condon,* Attorney General, *Treva Ashworth,* Deputy Attorney General, *Kenneth P. Woodington,* Senior Assistant Attorney General, *Reginald I. Lloyd,* Assistant Attorney General, and *M. Dawes Cooke, Jr.;* and for Kenneth E. Clark et al. by *James C. Roberts* and *George A. Somerville.*

Briefs of *amici curiae* were filed in both cases for the State of Wyoming et al. by *William U. Hill,* Attorney General of Wyoming, *Thomas W. Corbett, Jr.,* Attorney General of Pennsylvania, and *Bradley B. Cavedo;* for Bennett College et al. by *Wendy S. White;* for the Center for Military Readiness et al. by *Mellissa Wells-Petry* and *Jordan W. Lorence;* for the Employment Law Center et al. by *Patricia A. Shiu* and *Judith Kurtz;* for the Independent Women's Forum et al. by *Anita K. Blair* and *C. Douglas Welty;* for Mary Baldwin College by *Craig T. Merritt* and *Richard K. Willard;* for the South Carolina Institute of Leadership for Women by *Julianne Farnsworth;* for Wells College et al. by *David M. Lascell;* for Women's Schools Together, Inc., et al. by *John C. Danforth* and *Thomas C. Walsh;* and for Nancy Mellette by *Valorie K. Vojdik, Henry Weisburg, Suzanne E. Coe,* and *Robert R. Black.*

Briefs of *amici curiae* were filed in No. 94–1941 for the American Association of University Professors et al. by *Joan E. Bertin* and *Ann H. Franke;* and for Rhonda Cornum et al. by *Allan L. Gropper.*

Da[...] 9 Text of decision *[...]man Redlich,*

Barb[...] 10 Justice who wrote the majority's opinion *Seymour* filed

a brief for the Lawyers Committee for Civil Rights Under Law as *amicus curiae* in No. 94–2107.

ILLUSTRATION 3-2. *Continued*

520   UNITED STATES *v.* VIRGINIA

Opinion of the Court

I

Founded in 1839, VMI is today the sole single-sex school among Virginia's 15 public institutions of higher learning. VMI's distinctive mission is to produce "citizen-soldiers," men prepared for leadership in civilian life and in military service. VMI pursues this mission through pervasive training of a kind not available anywhere else in Virginia. Assigning prime place to character development, VMI uses an "adversative method" modeled on English public schools and once characteristic of military instruction. VMI constantly endeavors to instill physical and mental discipline in its cadets and impart to them a strong moral code. The school's graduates leave VMI with heightened comprehension of their capacity to deal with duress and stress, and a large sense of accomplishment for completing the hazardous course.

VMI has notably succeeded in its mission to produce leaders; among its alumni are military generals, Members of Congress, and business executives. The school's alumni overwhelmingly perceive that their VMI training helped them to realize their personal goals. VMI's endowment reflects the loyalty of its graduates; VMI has the largest per-student endowment of all public undergraduate institutions in the Nation.

Neither the goal of producing citizen-soldiers nor VMI's implementing methodology is inherently unsuitable to women. And the school's impressive record in producing leaders has made admission desirable to some women. Nevertheless, Virginia has elected to preserve exclusively for men the advantages and opportunities a VMI education affords.

II

A

From its establishment in 1839 as one of the Nation's first state military colleges, see 1839 Va. [9 Text of opinion] has remained financially supported by Virginia and "subject to

ILLUSTRATION 3-2. *Continued*

---

558   UNITED STATES *v.* VIRGINIA

REHNQUIST, C. J., concurring in judgment

There is no reason to believe that the admission of women capable of all the activities required of VMI cadets would destroy the Institute rather than enhance its capacity to serve the "more perfect Union."

*   *   *

For the reasons stated, the initial judgment of the Court of Appeals, 976 F. 2d 890 (CA4 1992), is affirmed, the final judgment of the Court of Appeals, 44 F. 3d 1229 (CA4 1995), is reversed, and the case is remanded for further proceedings consistent with this opinion.

It is so ordered.

JUSTICE THOMAS took no part in the consideration or decision of these cases.

CHIEF JUSTICE REHNQUIST, concurring in the judgment.

The Court holds first that Virginia violates the Equal Protection Clause by maintaining the Virginia Military Institute's (VMI's) all-male admissions policy, and second that establishing the Virginia Women's Institute for Leadership (VWIL) program does not remedy that violation. While I agree with these conclusions, I disagree with the Court's analysis and so I write separately.

I

(11)   Two decades ago in *Craig* v. *Boren*, 429 U. S. 190, 197 (1976), we announced that "[t]o withstand constitutional challenge, . . . classifications by gender must serve important governmental objectives and must be substantially related to achievement of those objectives." We have adhered to that standard of scrutiny ever since. See *Califano* v. *Goldfarb*, 430 U. S. 199, 210–211 (1977); *Califano* v. *Webster*, 430 U. S. 313, 316–317 (1977); *Orr* v. *Orr*, 440 U. S. 268, 279 (1979); *Caban* v. *Mohammed*, 441 U. S. [11 Concurrence] *avis* v. *Passman*, 442 U. S. 228, 234–235, 235, n. 9 (1979); *Personnel Administrator of Mass.* v. *Feeney*, 442 U. S. 256, 273 (1979);

ILLUSTRATION 3-2.   *Continued*

566   UNITED STATES *v.* VIRGINIA

Scalia, J., dissenting

no interest in a women's school of civil engineering, or in a men's school of nursing.

In the end, the women's institution Virginia proposes, VWIL, fails as a remedy, because it is distinctly inferior to the existing men's institution and will continue to be for the foreseeable future. VWIL simply is not, in any sense, the institution that VMI is. In particular, VWIL is a program appended to a private college, not a self-standing institution; and VWIL is substantially underfunded as compared to VMI. I therefore ultimately agree with the Court that Virginia has not provided an adequate remedy.

Justice Scalia, dissenting.

Today the Court shuts down an institution that has served the people of the Commonwealth of Virginia with pride and distinction for over a century and a half. To achieve that desired result, it rejects (contrary to our established practice) the factual findings of two courts below, sweeps aside the precedents of this Court, and ignores the history of our people. As to facts: It explicitly rejects the finding that there exist "gender-based developmental differences" supporting Virginia's restriction of the "adversative" method to only a men's institution, and the finding that the all-male composition of the Virginia Military Institute (VMI) is essential to that institution's character. As to precedent: It drastically revises our established standards for reviewing sex-based classifications. And as to history: It counts for nothing the long tradition, enduring down to the present, of men's military colleges supported by both States and the Federal Government.

Much of the Court's opinion is devoted to deprecating the closed-mindedness of our forebears with regard to women's education, and even with regard to the treatment of women in areas that have nothing to do [**12 Dissenting opinion**]d-minded they were—as every age is, including our own, with regard to matters it cannot guess, because it simply does not

⑫

Federal courts offer docket information online. Many state appellate trial court websites are limited and will provide you with docket information only.

▼ Why Use the Commercial Reporters Rather Than the Official Reports?

You should review U.S. Supreme Court cases in either the *Supreme Court Reporter* or in the *U.S. Supreme Court Reports, Lawyers' Edition*. They contain a variety of publisher's headnotes or case abstracts that assist you in your research. Often, they include additional references, such as encyclopedia cites. These headnotes summarize points of law found in a case. They also include a publisher's topic designation and number. These topics and numbers tie into the commercial publisher's indexes of legal issues called **digests.** These digests are organized by topic and numbers. Digests will be discussed in detail in Chapter 4.

Cases published in the *Supreme Court Reporter* also contain headnotes similar to what is shown in the Westlaw version of this case. See Illustration 3-3. The *Supreme Court Reporter* cases include topics and numbers, called **Key Numbers.** In Illustration 3-3, the first headnote includes the topic Constitutional Law along with a description of the Key Number. In the print versions the Key Numbers are included. Online a hyperlink is provided to the Key Number and the cases that cite this headnote. Also included in the text is the publisher's case abstract of a point of law. West Publishing Company has devised a system of organizing federal and state cases according to topics coupled with Key Numbers. See Chapter 4 for a more detailed explanation of this system. Across the top of the page in Illustration 3-3 is the citation to the *Supreme Court Reporter.* Above the name of the case are the official citation to the *U.S. Reports* and a citation to the *Lawyers' Edition* report of this case is included along with a *United States Law Week* citation. In addition to the official **syllabus** of the court, Thomson Reuters (formerly West) provides a summary of each case called a **synopsis.** This synopsis should not be cited because it is not authoritative.

Note the small numbers with the single * in front of them in the text of the decision shown in Illustration 3-3. Those numbers indicate the page number in which that text would appear in the official reports. The numbers with the two * indicate the page number for the West unofficial print report of the decision.

The *Lawyers' Edition* also includes headnotes, or the publisher's summaries of points of law presented in each case. See Illustration 3-4. This illustration is a Lexis screen shot showing headnotes that are included in the printed version of this case that appears in the *U.S. Supreme Court Reports, Lawyers' Edition*. These headnotes are arranged by publisher-designated topics and numbers in a series of volumes called *United States Supreme Court Digest, Lawyers' Edition*. Headnotes and

ILLUSTRATION 3-3.   Pages from Westlaw Computerized Version of *Supreme Court Reporter* Report of the *United States v. Virginia*, 518 U.S. 515 (1996)

(7) U.S. v. Virginia, 518 U.S. 515 (1996)

(8) 116 S.Ct. 2264, 135 L.Ed.2d 735, 64 USLW 4638, 96 Cal. Daily Op. Serv. 4694...

KeyCite Yellow Flag - Negative Treatment
Declined to Extend by Veasey v. Abbott, 5th Cir.(Tex.), April 27, 2018

116 S.Ct. 2264 (6)
Supreme Court of the United States

UNITED STATES, Petitioner,

(1)   v.

VIRGINIA et al.

VIRGINIA, et al., Petitioners,

v.

UNITED STATES.

(2) Nos. 94–1941, 94–2107.

(3)   Argued Jan. 17, 1996.

(4)   Decided June 26, 1996.

(5) **Synopsis**
United States sued Commonwealth of Virginia alleging equal protection violation in

maintaining military college exclusively for males. The United States District Court for the Western District of Virginia, 766 F.Supp. 1407, entered judgment for Commonwealth. Appeal was taken. The Fourth Circuit Court of Appeals, 976 F.2d 890, vacated and remanded. On remand, the Commonwealth moved for approval of a proposed remedial plan, and the District Court, Jackson L. Kiser, Chief Judge, 852 F.Supp. 471, approved proposal. Appeal was taken. The Court of Appeals, Niemeyer, Circuit Judge, 44 F.3d 1229, affirmed. United States sought certiorari. After granting certiorari, the Supreme Court, Justice **Ginsburg**, held that: (1) Commonwealth failed to show exceedingly persuasive justification for excluding women from citizen-soldier program offered at Virginia military college in violation of equal protection; (2) remedial plan offered by Commonwealth to create separate program for women at another college did not afford both genders benefits comparable in substance to survive equal protection evaluation; and (3) use of substantive comparability inquiry to review remedial plan was plain error.

Initial judgment of Court of Appeals affirmed; final judgment of Court of Appeals reversed and remanded.

Chief Justice Rehnquist filed opinion concurring in judgment.

Justice Scalia filed dissenting opinion.

Justice Thomas took no part in consideration or decision of case.

West Headnotes (15)

(9) [1]   (10) **Constitutional Law** ⟜ Sex or gender

(11) Under equal protection analysis, parties who seek to defend gender-based government action must demonstrate exceedingly persuasive justification for that action. U.S.C.A. Const.Amend. 14.

83 Cases that cite this headnote

(9) [2]   **Constitutional Law** ⟜ Sex or gender

Focusing on differential treatment or denial of opportunity for which relief is sought, court reviewing official classification based on gender under equal protection analysis must determine whether proffered justification is exceedingly persuasive. U.S.C.A. Const.Amend. 14.

(12) 92 Cases that cite this headnote

(9) [3]   **Constitutional Law** ⟜ Sex or Gender

Burden of justification for official classification based on gender under equal protection analysis is demanding and it rests entirely on the state. U.S.C.A. Const.Amend. 14.

32 Cases that cite this headnote

(9) [4]   **Constitutional Law** ⟜ Sex or gender

In justifying official classification based on gender under equal protection analysis, state must show at least that challenged classification serves important governmental objectives and that discriminatory means employed are substantially related to achievement of those objectives. U.S.C.A. Const.Amend. 14.

1 Case name	4 Date decided	7 Official citation	10 Topics
2 Docket number	5 Synopsis	8 Parallel citations	11 Headnote text
3 Date argued	6 Supreme court reporter citation	9 Headnote	12 Number of cases that cite to the headnote

ILLUSTRATION 3-3. *Continued*

U.S. v. Virginia, 518 U.S. 515 (1996)
116 S.Ct. 2264, 135 L.Ed.2d 735, 64 USLW 4638, 96 Cal. Daily Op. Serv. 4694...

[12] **Federal Civil Procedure** ⇐ Nature and extent of relief in general

Remedial decree must closely fit constitutional violation; it must be shaped to place persons unconstitutionally denied opportunity or advantage in position they would have occupied in absence of discrimination.

9 Cases that cite this headnote

[13] **Constitutional Law** ⇐ Discrimination and Classification

Proper remedy for an unconstitutional exclusion from opportunity or advantage based on discrimination aims to eliminate, so far as possible, discriminatory effects of the past and to bar like discrimination in the future.

4 Cases that cite this headnote

[14] **Education** ⇐ Curriculum, Degrees, Grades, and Credits

Constitutional Law ⇐ Single-sex institutions

Remedial plan offered by Commonwealth of Virginia for equal protection violations related to exclusion of women from citizen-soldier program offered at Virginia military college to create separate program for women at another college did not afford both genders benefits comparable in substance so as to survive equal protection evaluation; separate college afforded women no opportunity to experience the rigorous military training for which male school was famed, female school's student body, faculty, course offerings, finances and facilities hardly matched male school and graduates from female school could not anticipate benefits associated with male school's 157–year history, prestige, and its influential alumni network. U.S.C.A. Const.Amend. 14.

25 Cases that cite this headnote

[15] **Constitutional Law** ⇐ Single-sex institutions

Use of "substantive comparability" inquiry to review remedial plan offered by Commonwealth of Virginia for equal protection violations related

to exclusion of women from citizen-soldier program offered at Virginia military college was plain error; rather than deferential analysis, all gender based classifications warranted heightened scrutiny. U.S.C.A. Const.Amend. 14.

44 Cases that cite this headnote

2267   *515 *Syllabus

Virginia Military Institute (**VMI**) is the sole single-sex school among Virginia's public institutions of higher learning. **VMI's** distinctive mission is to produce "citizen-soldiers," men prepared for leadership in civilian life and in military service. Using an "adversative method" of training not available elsewhere in Virginia, **VMI** endeavors to instill physical and mental discipline in its cadets and impart to them a strong moral code. Reflecting the high value alumni place on their **VMI** training, **VMI** has the largest per-student endowment of all public undergraduate institutions in the Nation. The United States sued Virginia and **VMI**, alleging that **VMI's** exclusively male admission policy violated the Fourteenth Amendment's Equal Protection Clause. The District Court ruled in **VMI's** favor. The Fourth Circuit reversed and ordered Virginia to remedy the constitutional violation. In response, Virginia proposed a parallel program for women: Virginia Women's Institute for Leadership (VWIL), located at Mary Baldwin College, a private liberal arts school for women. The District Court found that Virginia's proposal satisfied the Constitution's equal protection requirement, and the Fourth Circuit affirmed. The appeals court deferentially reviewed Virginia's plan and determined that provision of single-gender educational options was a legitimate objective. Maintenance of single-sex programs, the court concluded, was essential to that objective. The court recognized, however, that its analysis risked bypassing equal protection scrutiny, so it fashioned an additional test, asking whether **VMI** and VWIL students would receive "substantively comparable" benefits. Although the Court of Appeals acknowledged that the VWIL degree lacked the historical benefit and prestige of a **VMI** degree, the court nevertheless found the educational opportunities at the two schools sufficiently comparable.

Held:

1. Parties who seek to defend gender-based government action must demonstrate an "exceedingly persuasive

13 Court syllabus

ILLUSTRATION 3-3. *Continued*

U.S. v. Virginia, 518 U.S. 515 (1996)

116 S.Ct. 2264, 135 L.Ed.2d 735, 64 USLW 4638, 96 Cal. Daily Op. Serv. 4694...

justification" for that action. *E.g., Mississippi Univ. for Women v. Hogan,* 458 U.S. 718, 724, 102 S.Ct. 3331, 3336, 73 L.Ed.2d 1090. Neither ***516** federal nor state government acts compatibly with equal protection when a law or official policy denies to women, simply because they are women, full citizenship stature—equal opportunity to aspire, achieve, participate in and contribute to society based on their individual talents and capacities. To meet the burden of justification, a State must show "at least that the [challenged] classification serves 'important governmental objectives and that the discriminatory means employed' are 'substantially related to the achievement of those objectives.' " *Ibid.,* quoting *Wengler v. Druggists Mut. Ins. Co.,* 446 U.S. 142, 150, 100 S.Ct. 1540, 1545, 64 L.Ed.2d 107. The justification must be genuine, not hypothesized or invented *post hoc* in response to litigation. And it must not rely on overbroad generalizations about the different talents, capacities, or preferences of males and females. See, *e.g., Weinberger v. Wiesenfeld,* 420 U.S. 636, 643, 648, 95 S.Ct. 1225, 1230–1231, 1233, 43 L.Ed.2d 514. The heightened review standard applicable to sex-based classifications does not make sex a proscribed classification, but it does mean that categorization by sex may not be used to create or perpetuate the legal, social, and economic inferiority of women. Pp. 2274–2276.

2. Virginia's categorical exclusion of women from the educational opportunities VMI provides denies equal protection to women. Pp. 2276–2282.

(a) Virginia contends that single-sex education yields important educational benefits and that provision of an option for such education fosters diversity in educational approaches. Benign justifications proffered in defense of categorical exclusions, however, must describe actual state purposes, not rationalizations for actions in fact differently grounded. Virginia has not shown that VMI was established, or has been maintained, with a view to diversifying, by its categorical exclusion of women, educational opportunities ****2268** within the Commonwealth. A purpose genuinely to advance an array of educational options is not served by VMI's historic and constant plan to afford a unique educational benefit only to males. However well this plan serves Virginia's sons, it makes no provision whatever for her daughters. Pp. 2276–2279.

(b) Virginia also argues that VMI's adversative method of training provides educational benefits that cannot be made available, unmodified, to women, and that alterations to accommodate women would necessarily be so drastic as

to destroy VMI's program. It is uncontested that women's admission to VMI would require accommodations, primarily in arranging housing assignments and physical training programs for female cadets. It is also undisputed, however, that neither the goal of producing citizen-soldiers, VMI's *raison d'être,* nor VMI's implementing methodology is inherently unsuitable to women. The District Court made "findings" on "gender-based developmental differences" that restate the opinions of Virginia's expert witnesses about typically male or typically female "tendencies." Courts, however, must take "a hard ***517** look" at generalizations or tendencies of the kind Virginia pressed, for state actors controlling gates to opportunity have no warrant to exclude qualified individuals based on "fixed notions concerning the roles and abilities of males and females." *Mississippi Univ. for Women,* 458 U.S., at 725, 102 S.Ct., at 3336–3337. The notion that admission of women would downgrade VMI's stature, destroy the adversative system and, with it, even the school, is a judgment hardly proved, a prediction hardly different from other "self-fulfilling prophec[ies]", see *id.,* at 730, 102 S.Ct., at 3339, once routinely used to deny rights or opportunities. Women's successful entry into the federal military academies, and their participation in the Nation's military forces, indicate that Virginia's fears for VMI's future may not be solidly grounded. The Commonwealth's justification for excluding all women from "citizen-soldier" training for which some are qualified, in any event, does not rank as "exceedingly persuasive." Pp. 2279–2282.

3. The remedy proffered by Virginia—maintain VMI as a male-only college and create VWIL as a separate program for women—does not cure the constitutional violation. Pp. 2282–2287.

(a) A remedial decree must closely fit the constitutional violation; it must be shaped to place persons unconstitutionally denied an opportunity or advantage in the position they would have occupied in the absence of discrimination. See *Milliken v. Bradley,* 433 U.S. 267, 280, 97 S.Ct. 2749, 2757, 53 L.Ed.2d 745. The constitutional violation in this case is the categorical exclusion of women, in disregard of their individual merit, from an extraordinary educational opportunity afforded men. Virginia chose to leave untouched VMI's exclusionary policy, and proposed for women only a separate program, different in kind from VMI and unequal in tangible and intangible facilities. VWIL affords women no opportunity to experience the rigorous military training for which VMI is famed. Kept away from the pressures, hazards, and psychological bonding

ILLUSTRATION 3-3. *Continued*

U.S. v. Virginia, 518 U.S. 515 (1996)
116 S.Ct. 2264, 135 L.Ed.2d 735, 64 USLW 4638, 96 Cal. Daily Op. Serv. 4694...

characteristic of **VMI's** adversative training, VWIL students will not know the feeling of tremendous accomplishment commonly experienced by **VMI's** successful cadets. Virginia maintains that methodological differences are justified by the important differences between men and women in learning and developmental needs, but generalizations about "the way women are," estimates of what is appropriate for *most women,* no longer justify denying opportunity to women whose talent and capacity place them outside the average description. In myriad respects other than military training, VWIL does not qualify as **VMI's** equal. The VWIL program is a pale shadow of **VMI** in terms of the range of curricular choices and faculty stature, funding, prestige, alumni support and influence. Virginia has not shown substantial equality in the separate educational opportunities the Commonwealth supports at VWIL and **VMI.** Cf. *Sweatt v. Painter,* 339 U.S. 629, 70 S.Ct. 848, 94 L.Ed. 1114. Pp. 2282–2286.

*518 b) The Fourth Circuit failed to inquire whether the proposed remedy placed women denied the **VMI** advantage in the position they would have occupied in the ****2269** absence of discrimination, *Milliken,* 433 U.S., at 280, 97 S.Ct., at 2757, and considered instead whether the Commonwealth could provide, with fidelity to equal protection, separate and unequal educational programs for men and women. In declaring the substantially different and significantly unequal VWIL program satisfactory, the appeals court displaced the exacting standard developed by this Court with a deferential standard, and added an inquiry of its own invention, the "substantive comparability" test. The Fourth Circuit plainly erred in exposing Virginia's VWIL plan to such a deferential analysis, for "all gender-based classifications today" warrant "heightened scrutiny." See *J.E.B. v. Alabama ex rel. T.B.,* 511 U.S. 127, 136, 114 S.Ct. 1419, 1425, 128 L.Ed.2d 89. Women seeking and fit for a **VMI**-quality education cannot be offered anything less, under the Commonwealth's obligation to afford them genuinely equal protection. Pp. 2286–2287.

976 F.2d 890 (C.A.4 1992), affirmed; 44 F.3d 1229 (C.A.4 1995), reversed and remanded.

 GINSBURG, J., delivered the opinion of the Court, in which STEVENS, O'CONNOR, KENNEDY, SOUTER, and BREYER, JJ., joined. REHNQUIST, C.J., filed an opinion concurring in the judgment, *post,* p. 2287. SCALIA, J., filed a dissenting opinion, *post,* p. 2291. THOMAS, J., took no part in the consideration or decision of the case.

14 Summary of judicial opinions	17 Majority opinion
15 Attorneys	author
16 Court opinion	

Attorneys and Law Firms (15)

Paul Bender, Washington, DC, for U.S.

Theodore B. Olson, Washington, DC, for Virginia, et al.

1995 WL 745011 (Resp.Brief)

Opinion

(17)

*519 Justice GINSBURG delivered the opinion of the Court.

Virginia's public institutions of higher learning include an incomparable military college, Virginia Military Institute (**VMI**). The United States maintains that the Constitution's equal protection guarantee precludes Virginia from reserving exclusively to men the unique educational opportunities **VMI** affords. We agree.

*520 I

Founded in 1839, **VMI** is today the sole single-sex school among Virginia's 15 public institutions of higher learning. **VMI's** distinctive mission is to produce "citizen-soldiers," men prepared for leadership in civilian life and in military service. **VMI** pursues this mission through pervasive training of a kind not available anywhere else in Virginia. Assigning prime place to character development, **VMI** uses an "adversative method" modeled on English public schools and once characteristic of military instruction. **VMI** constantly endeavors to instill physical and mental discipline in its cadets and impart to them a strong moral code. The school's graduates leave **VMI** with heightened comprehension of their capacity to deal with duress and stress, and a large sense of accomplishment for completing the hazardous course. (16)

VMI has notably succeeded in its mission to produce leaders; among its alumni are military generals, Members of Congress, and business executives. The school's alumni overwhelmingly perceive that their **VMI** training helped them to realize their personal goals. **VMI's** endowment reflects the loyalty of its graduates; **VMI** has the largest per-student endowment of all public undergraduate institutions in the Nation.

Neither the goal of producing citizen-soldiers nor **VMI's** implementing methodology is inherently unsuitable to women. And the school's impressive record in producing

Reprinted with permission of Thomson Reuters.

digests are explained in detail later in Chapter 4. You should not quote from these headnotes because they are not authoritative. Compare the headnotes in Illustration 3-3 to those in Illustration 3-4. They are different because one is prepared by Lexis and the other is written by the Thomson Reuters staff. Their headnote systems are based on different topics and classifications.

▼ How Do You Locate a Reported Case?

Cases have citations that are similar to addresses. For example, "116 S.Ct. 2264" is a citation. The number "116" is the volume of the reporter that contains the case. "S.Ct." is the abbreviation for the *Supreme Court Reporter* that contains the case, and finally, "2264" is the first page the case appears on within the reporter. See Illustration 3-3. Another example of a citation is "581 N.E.2d 885." The number "581" indicates the volume that contains the case. "N.E.2d" is the abbreviation for the reporter, the *North Eastern Reporter Second Series.* The last number, "885," is the first page of the case. This citation identifies the case, *Thompson v. Economy Super Marts.* See Illustration 3-5.

At the top of Illustration 3-5, next to the circled 1 is this same West's *North Eastern Reporter* citation. Above the name of the case, you can find the official (that is, state government–printed) citation and a citation to *West's Illinois Decisions* reporter. Review Illustration 3-6. It is a PDF of the Westlaw report of this case. It is similar to the one in the printed *North Eastern Reporter.* Citations also appear in this report. However, the official citation to the Ill.App.3d appears at the top of the page.

▼ How Are U.S. Supreme Court Cases Cited?

Cite U.S. Supreme Court cases according to *Bluebook* Rule 10. Once a U.S. Supreme Court case is published in an advance sheet of the *U.S. Reports,* the *U.S. Reports* citation, and only the *U.S. Reports* citation, is the proper citation. Do not include parallel citations with the official *U.S. Reports* cite.

Correct: *Erie R.R. v. Tompkins,* 304 U.S. 64 (1938)

Incorrect: *Erie R.R. v. Tompkins,* 304 U.S. 64, 58 S. Ct. 817, 82 L. Ed. 1188 (1938)

The citation would be the same based on *ALWD* **Rule 12.4(b)(3)**.

However, if a Supreme Court opinion has been published in West's *Supreme Court Reporter* but not yet in *U.S. Reports,* the *Supreme Court Reporter* citation should be used. *See Bluebook* and *ALWD* Rule 12.4(b)(3). See the Citation Appendix for more detailed information.

ILLUSTRATION 3-4. Pages from Lexis screen shot of *United States v. Virginia*, 135 L.Ed 2d 735

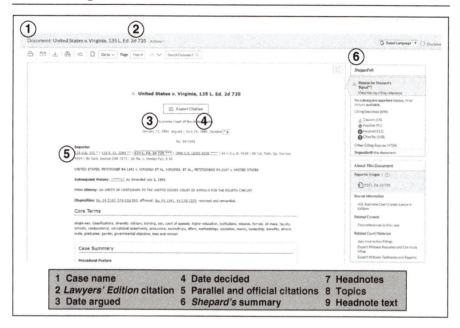

1 Case name	4 Date decided	7 Headnotes
2 *Lawyers' Edition* citation	5 Parallel and official citations	8 Topics
3 Date argued	6 *Shepard's* summary	9 Headnote text

ILLUSTRATION 3-4.   *Continued*

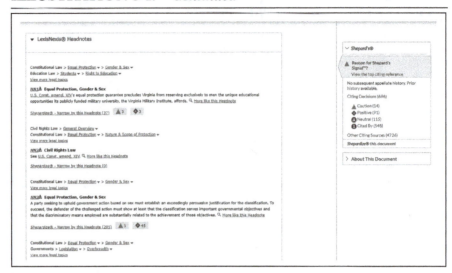

b. Other Federal Case Reports

▼ Where Do You Find Decisions of Other Federal Courts?

Many opinions of the U.S. Courts of Appeals can be found in Thomson West's *Federal Reporter*, now in the third series. In addition to printing the decisions of the U.S. Courts of Appeals, the current series contains some decisions of the Temporary Emergency Court of Appeals. See Illustration 3-7 for court coverage during specific years.

Thomson West's *Federal Supplement*, now in the third series, is a publication started in 1932 to connect with the *Federal Reporter*. It includes decisions of the U.S. District Courts, the U.S. Court of Claims from 1932 to 1960, the U.S. Court of International Trade (formerly known as the U.S. Customs Court), and the Judicial Panel on Multidistrict Litigation. See Illustration 3-7.

Thomson West's *Federal Appendix* is an offshoot of the *Federal Reporter*. It contains U.S. Court of Appeals decisions from 2001 to date that are not designated by the court for publication. Similar to the other Thomson West reporters, this publication contains headnotes and other enhancements.

Not all federal appellate court or district court decisions are published. In some instances, the judges of these courts determine whether to submit their decisions to the publishers. In other cases, the publishers selectively print decisions. Unpublished opinions are available from the courts.

ILLUSTRATION 3-5. West's *North Eastern Reporter, Thompson v. Economy Super Marts, Inc.*, 581 N.E.2d 885 (Ill. App. Ct. 1991) PDF Report from West

---

THOMPSON v. ECONOMY SUPER MARTS, INC.   Ill. **885**
Cite as 581 N.E.2d 885 (Ill.App. 3 Dist. 1991)

provided for both of them on the instrument. Therefore, the defendant argues, since the intention of the Bank was to obtain a mortgage of the premises from both joint tenants and only one joint tenant signed the mortgage, the instrument should be found to be unenforceable as was the contract in *Dineff.*

Dineff is clearly distinguishable from the instant case. In *Dineff*, the plaintiff was attempting to enforce an agreement to convey the entire interest in the jointly held property without the signatures of both cotenants. The court pointed out that there was no prayer for partial performance against the cotenant who had signed the agreement. (*Dineff*, 27 Ill.2d at 482, 190 N.E.2d at 311.) It is well established that one cotenant cannot convey the interest of another cotenant without proper authority.

Here, however, the plaintiff is not attempting to foreclose on the entire interest in the property. The foreclosure complaint is against only the undivided one-half interest of the joint tenant who signed the mortgage.

[4] We disagree with the defendant's argument that the clear intention of the parties required the defendant's signature

1 Citation to *West's North Eastern Reporter*
2 Citation to official reporter
3 Citation to unofficial reporter
4 Case name
5 Docket number
6 Syllabus by reporter editor
7 West Key Numbers and headnotes

that the names of both husband and wife appear in the body of the instrument and in the acknowledgment. The rule seems to be general that a deed naming two or more parties as grantors, executed by only a portion of them, is valid as to

those executing it." *Heckmann*, 283 Ill. at 513, 119 N.E. at 642.

It is clear that Mr. Stauffenberg intended to mortgage the real estate. There is nothing in the mortgage to indicate that it was not to be binding unless the defendant signed it also. We see no reason to deviate from the established rule that when a property owner attempts to convey a greater interest in the property than he actually has, that the conveyance is valid to the extent of his interest and void only as to the excess.

For the reasons stated above, the order of the trial court dismissing the complaint is reversed. This cause is remanded for further proceedings.

Reversed and remanded.

GORMAN and McCUSKEY, JJ., concur.

221 Ill.App.3d 263
163 Ill.Dec. 731

Cherryl E. THOMPSON,
Plaintiff–Appellant,

v.

ECONOMY SUPER MARTS, INC., a Division of Weems & Bruns Corp., a Corporation, and Weems & Bruns Corp., a Corporation, Defendants–Appellees.

No. 3–90–0662.

Appellate Court of Illinois,
Third District.

Nov. 8, 1991.

Customer allegedly injured when she slipped on lettuce leaf in produce section of grocery store brought negligence action against store owners. The Circuit Court, 12th Judicial Circuit, Will County, Michael H. Lyons, J., granted defendants' posttrial motion for judgment notwithstanding verdict after jury found customer to be 55% contributorily negligent and awarded her

ILLUSTRATION 3-5. *Continued*

damages. the Appellate Court, Haase, J., held that: (1) where foreign substance causing slip of business invitee is on premises due to negligence of proprietor or his servants, it is not necessary to establish their actual or constructive knowledge of the substance, but if substance is on premises through acts of third persons, time element during which substance was present is material factor to establish **(6)** knowledge of, or notice to, proprietor; (2) even where there is proof that foreign substance causing slip of business invitee was related to defendant's business, where no further evidence is offered other than presence of substance and occurrence of injury, defendant is entitled to directed verdict, as such evidence is insufficient to support necessary inference of negligence; and (3) evidence of negligence of grocery store was not sufficient to permit customer to recover from store owners.

Affirmed.

(7) **1. Negligence** ⟐32(2.8)

Defendant owes business invitee on defendant's premises duty to exercise ordinary care in maintaining premises in reasonably safe condition.

2. Negligence ⟐44, 48

Where business invitee is injured by slipping on premises, liability may be imposed if substance causing slip was placed by negligence of proprietor or his servants; or if substance was on premises through acts of third persons or there is no showing how it got there, liability may be imposed if it appears that proprietor or his servant knew of presence of substance, or that substance was there sufficient length of time so that in exercise of ordinary care its presence should have been discovered.

3. Negligence ⟐48

Where foreign substance causing slip of business invitee is on premises due to negligence of proprietor or his servants, it is not necessary to establish their actual or constructive knowledge of the substance, but if substance is on premises through acts of third persons, time element during which substance was present is material

factor to establish knowledge of, or notice to, proprietor.

4. Negligence ⟐136(22)

Where there is proof that foreign substance causing slip of business invitee was product sold or related to defendant's operations and invitee offered some further evidence, direct or circumstantial, however slight, such as location of substance or business practices of defendant from which it could be inferred that it was more likely that defendant or his servants, rather than a customer, dropped the substance on the premises, trial court should allow negligence issue to go to jury.

5. Negligence ⟐121.1(8)

Even where there is proof that foreign substance causing slip of business invitee was related to defendant's business, where no further evidence is offered other than presence of substance and occurrence of injury, defendant is entitled to directed verdict, such evidence being insufficient to support necessary inference of negligence.

6. Negligence ⟐134(5)

Evidence of negligence of grocery store was not sufficient to permit customer allegedly injured when she slipped on lettuce leaf in produce section of store to recover from store, even though leaf was described as wilted and was found near unsupervised produce section where vegetables were packed on ice; no direct or circumstantial evidence made it more likely that store's servants, rather than customer, dropped the leaf, and customer presented no evidence that ice which packed produce was directly above water spot or any evidence regarding how ice was packed or how easy it might have been to jar ice loose and spill it to the floor.

James J. Morici, Jr., argued, Anesi, Ozmon & Rodin, Ltd., Chicago, for Cherryl E. Thompson.

Kenneth T. Garvey, Robert Spitkovsky, Jr. and Kevin P. O'Connell, argued, Bresnahan & Garvey, Chicago, for Economy Super Marts, Inc.

ILLUSTRATION 3-5. *Continued*

Justice HAASE delivered the opinion of the Court.

The plaintiff, Cherryl E. Thompson, brought this negligence action against the defendants, Economy Super Marts, Inc. and Weems & Bruns Corp., to recover damages for personal injuries she sustained when she slipped on a lettuce leaf in the produce section of the defendants' grocery store. A jury awarded the plaintiff $12,974.96 in recoverable damages after finding that she was 55% contributorily negligent. Thereafter, the trial court granted the defendants' post-trial motion for a judgment notwithstanding the verdict. The plaintiff appeals from that decision.

The plaintiff testified at trial that on July 3, 1986, she picked up a watermelon in the produce section of the defendants' store and began to walk through the produce aisle. At that point, she slipped and fell on a lettuce leaf and water. She had not seen the leaf or the water before her fall and did not know how long they were there. She noted that the lettuce leaf was green and brown, had dirt on it, and appeared beat up. According to the plaintiff, her fall occurred about two or three feet to the left of the produce aisle. She also stated that the fruits and vegetables in the produce aisle were kept on ice.

Terida Thompson, the plaintiff's daughter, substantially corroborated the plaintiff's testimony. Additionally, she stated that the lettuce leaf looked old and like it had been there awhile. She further stated that she had walked through the produce aisle once before the accident occurred and did not see any water or a lettuce leaf on the floor prior to the plaintiff's fall.

Gene Pesavento, the assistant store manager, testified that it was his duty to make sure that all areas in the grocery store were clear and free of debris. He agreed that the produce department requires constant surveillance to ensure that debris is not left on the floor. He also agreed that debris poses a tripping hazard.

Pesavento further testified that no one was specifically charged with the responsibility of constantly monitoring the floor of the produce department. He explained

that the defendants' employees knew that they were supposed to keep an eye on the entire store, and not specifically one area.

Phil Woock, the store's general manager, testified that he was not working at the time of the plaintiff's accident. He stated that the store's floor was dry mopped and swept every night in July, 1986. In addition, the floors were swept during the day as needed, and spills were cleaned as needed. The floors were professionally mopped and waxed every Wednesday night, and the plaintiff's accident occurred on a Thursday. Woock further testified that a part-time employee was on duty in the produce department at the time of the accident, but he could have been working in the back room when it occurred. Woock also testified that all store workers have the responsibility of keeping the floor clean if no one is working in the produce department at a particular time.

Donald Schreiner and Rubin Amazan each testified that they were working at the store at the time of the plaintiff's accident, but did not witness the fall. They both stated that they did not observe a lettuce leaf on the floor after inspecting the floor following the accident.

Based on the foregoing evidence, the jury found that the plaintiff suffered $28,833.24 in damages, but it awarded her only $12,974.96 because it found that she was 55% contributorily negligent. Thereafter, the defendants filed a post-trial motion requesting that the trial court enter a judgment notwithstanding the verdict. The trial court subsequently granted the defendants' motion, finding that: (1) no evidence was presented that the defendants had actual or constructive notice of the lettuce leaf and water for a sufficient length of time that its presence should have been discovered; and (2) the jury's award of damages was a compromise verdict and could not be sustained.

On appeal, the plaintiff initially argues that the trial court erred in granting a judgment notwithstanding the verdict. She contends that the court mistakenly found that she did not present any evidence that

ILLUSTRATION 3-5. *Continued*

the defendants had actual or constructive notice of the lettuce leaf.

[1–3] It is well-settled that a defendant owes a business invitee on the defendant's premises a duty to exercise ordinary care in maintaining the premises in a reasonably safe condition. (*Ward v. K Mart Corp.* (1990), 136 Ill.2d 132, 143 Ill.Dec. 288, 554 N.E.2d 223; *Perminas v. Montgomery Ward & Co.* (1975), 60 Ill.2d 469, 328 N.E.2d 290.) Where a business invitee is injured by slipping on the premises, liability may be imposed if the substance was placed there by the negligence of the proprietor or his servants, or, if the substance was on the premises through acts of third persons or there is no showing how it got there, liability may be imposed if it appears that the proprietor or his servant knew of its presence, or that the substance was there a sufficient length of time so that in the exercise of ordinary care its presence should have been discovered. (*Olinger v. Great Atlantic & Pacific Tea Co.* (1961), 21 Ill.2d 469, 173 N.E.2d 443; *Wroblewski v. Hillman's, Inc.* (1963), 43 Ill.App.2d 246, 193 N.E.2d 470.) Thus, where the foreign substance is on the premises due to the negligence of the proprietor or his servants, it is not necessary to establish their knowledge, actual or constructive; whereas, if the substance is on the premises through acts of third persons, the time element to establish knowledge or notice to the proprietor is a material factor. *Blake v. Dickinson* (1975), 31 Ill.App.3d 379, 332 N.E.2d 575.

[4, 5] Where there is proof that the foreign substance was a product sold or related to the defendant's operations, and the plaintiff offers some further evidence direct or circumstantial, however slight, such as the location of the substance or the business practices of the defendant, from which it could be inferred that it was more likely that the defendant or his servants, rather than a customer, dropped the substance on the premises, the trial court should allow the negligence issue to go to the jury. (*Donoho v. O'Connell's, Inc.* (1958), 13 Ill.2d 113, 148 N.E.2d 434.) However, even where there is proof that the foreign substance was related to the defendant's business, but no further evi-

dence is offered other than the presence of the substance and the occurrence of the injury, the defendant is entitled to a directed verdict, such evidence being insufficient to support the necessary inference. *Olinger v. Great Atlantic & Pacific Tea Co.* (1961), 21 Ill.2d 469, 173 N.E.2d 443; *Wroblewski v. Hillman's, Inc.* (1963), 43 Ill. App.2d 246, 193 N.E.2d 470.

[6] The plaintiff argues that she satisfied the requirements set forth in *Donoho* of introducing "further evidence, however slight, such as the location of the substance or the business practice of the defendant, from which it could be inferred that it was more likely that the defendant or his servants, rather than a customer, dropped the substance on the premises." She contends that evidence of the wilted lettuce leaf and the fact that it was found near the unsupervised produce section where vegetables were packed on ice was sufficient to allow the case to go to the jury under *Donoho*.

We disagree. The Illinois Supreme Court in *Donoho* undertook an extensive analysis of the circumstances under which negligence could be inferred from the conduct of the defendant when it was uncertain who was responsible for the foreign substance dropped on the premises. In *Donoho*, the plaintiff slipped and fell on an onion ring at the defendant's restaurant. It was unknown who dropped the onion ring. Yet, the court found that from the circumstantial evidence, it could be reasonably inferred that it was more likely that the onion ring was on the floor through the acts of the defendant's servants rather than a customer. The court based its decision on the additional circumstantial evidence that the onion ring on which the plaintiff slipped was located by a table cleared by a bus boy, under the bus boy's practice of clearing tables food particles could drop to the floor, and testimony that after the bus boy cleared the table in question no one else ate there before the plaintiff fell.

In the present case, however, there was no direct or circumstantial evidence indicating that it was more likely that the defendants' servants dropped the item than a customer. Furthermore, the plaintiff did not present any evidence that the ice, which

ILLUSTRATION 3-5. *Continued*

PEOPLE v. SOLANO
Cite as 581 N.E.2d 889 (Ill.App. 3 Dist. 1991)

Ill. **889**

packed the produce, was directly above the water spot. Nor did she present any evidence regarding how the ice was packed or how easy it might have been to jar it loose spilling it to the floor. Moreover, there was no specific evidence that the plaintiff's business practice was unusual or created any special hazard.

The plaintiff also relies on *Perminas v. Montgomery Ward & Company* (1975), 60 Ill.2d 469, 328 N.E.2d 290, in support of her position. In *Perminas*, the plaintiff slipped on a skateboard-like object in an aisle of the defendant's store. There, one of the defendant's employees actually had knowledge that the object was creating a dangerous condition. The court imposed liability on the defendant because the defendant, after receiving notice through its employee that its product was creating a dangerous situation, failed to return its premises to a safe condition or warn its customers.

We find that the plaintiff's reliance on *Perminas* is misplaced. In the present case, unlike *Perminas*, the defendants did not have actual or constructive knowledge of the situation. Furthermore, the record in the instant case does not contain any evidence regarding the length of time the substance was on the floor from which it could be inferred that the defendants had constructive notice.

After reviewing the evidence in the aspect most favorable to the plaintiff, we conclude that the evidence so overwhelmingly favored the defendants that no contrary verdict could ever stand. Accordingly, we find that the trial court properly granted the defendants' motion for a judgment notwithstanding the verdict. Our resolution of the foregoing issue renders the parties' remaining issues moot.

The judgment of the circuit court of Will County is affirmed.

Affirmed.

McCUSKEY, J., and STOUDER, P.J., concur.

221 Ill.App.3d 272

163 Ill.Dec. 735

The PEOPLE of the State of Illinois, Plaintiff–Appellee,

v.

Juan SOLANO, Defendant–Appellant.

No. 3–91–0067.

Appellate Court of Illinois, Third District.

Nov. 8, 1991.

Sixteen-year-old defendant was convicted of reckless homicide and driving under the influence of alcohol by the 13th Judicial Circuit Court, LaSalle County, James Lanuti, J., and he appealed. The Appellate Court, McCuskey, J., held that: (1) degree of harm to passenger in defendant's car was aggravating factor that trial judge could consider in imposing sentence, and (2) trial judge could likewise consider defendant's prior underage drinking and level of alcohol in defendant's blood.

Affirmed.

1. Criminal Law ⬩1147, 1208.2

Sentencing is matter of judicial discretion and, absent abuse of discretion by trial court, sentence may not be altered on review.

2. Criminal Law ⬩986.2(1)

Defendant's history, character and rehabilitative potential, along with the seriousness of defendant's offense, need to protect society, and need for deterrence and punishment, must be equally weighed at sentencing.

3. Criminal Law ⬩986(3), 1144.17

Sentencing judge is presumed to have considered mitigating circumstances before court, and there is no requirement that judge recite and assign value to each circumstance presented.

4. Automobiles ⬩359

Trial judge sufficiently considered motorist's rehabilitative potential, young age,

ILLUSTRATION 3-6.   West's *North Eastern Reporter, Thompson v. Economy Super Marts, Inc.*, 581 N.E.2d 885 (Ill. App. Ct. 1991), PDF Report from Westlaw

Thompson v. Economy Super Marts, Inc., 221 Ill.App.3d 263 (1991)   **(3)**

(4) 581 N.E.2d 885, 163 Ill.Dec. 731   **(5)**

(11)   KeyCite Yellow Flag - Negative Treatment

Distinguished by Wiegman v. Hitch-Inn Post of Libertyville, Inc., Ill.App. 2 Dist., October 13, 1999

221 Ill.App.3d 263
Appellate Court of Illinois,
Third District.

(1)   Cheryl E. **THOMPSON**,
Plaintiff-Appellant,

v.

ECONOMY SUPER MARTS, INC., a
Division of Weems & Bruns Corp., a
Corporation, and Weems & Bruns Corp.,
a Corporation, Defendants-Appellees.   **(7)**

(2)   No. 3-90-0662.
|
Nov. 8, 1991.

(6) **Synopsis**
Customer allegedly injured when she slipped on lettuce leaf in produce section of grocery store brought negligence action against store owners. The Circuit Court, 12th Judicial Circuit, Will County, Michael H. Lyons, J., granted defendants' posttrial motion for judgment notwithstanding verdict after jury found customer to be 55% contributorily negligent and awarded her damages. the Appellate Court, Haase, J., held that: (1) where foreign substance causing slip of business **(7)** invitee is on premises due to negligence of proprietor or his servants, it is not necessary to establish their actual or constructive knowledge of the substance, but if substance is on premises through acts of third persons, time element during which substance was present is material factor to establish knowledge of, or notice to, proprietor; (2) even where there is proof that foreign substance causing slip of business invitee was related to defendant's business, where no further evidence is offered other than presence of substance and occurrence of injury, defendant is entitled to directed verdict, as such evidence is insufficient to support necessary inference of **(7)** negligence; and (3) evidence of negligence of grocery store was not sufficient to permit customer to recover from store owners.

Affirmed.

West Headnotes (6)

(8)   **(9)**

[1]   Negligence ⟳ Care Required of Store and
Business Proprietors

Defendant owes business invitee on defendant's premises duty to exercise ordinary care in maintaining premises in reasonably safe condition.

12 Cases that cite this headnote

[2]   Negligence ⟳ Water and Other Substances

Where business invitee is injured by slipping on premises, liability may be imposed if substance causing slip was placed by negligence of proprietor or his servants; or if substance was on premises through acts of third persons or there is no showing how it got there, liability may be imposed if it appears that proprietor or his servant knew of presence of substance, or that substance was there sufficient length of time so that in exercise of ordinary care its presence should have been discovered.

(10)   17 Cases that cite this headnote

[3]   Negligence ⟳ Water and Other Substances

Where foreign substance causing slip of business invitee is on premises due to negligence of proprietor or his servants, it is not necessary to establish their actual or constructive knowledge of the substance, but if substance is on premises through acts of third persons, time element during which substance was present is material factor to establish knowledge of, or notice to, proprietor.

12 Cases that cite this headnote

[4]   Negligence   Buildings and Other Structures

Where there is proof that foreign substance causing slip of business invitee was product sold or related to defendant's operations and invitee offered some further evidence, direct or circumstantial, however slight, such as location of substance or business practices of defendant

1 Case name	**7 Headnote**	
2 Docket number	**8 Topic**	
3 Official citation	**9 Subtopic**	
4 Unofficial *N.E. Reporter* citation	**10 Number of cases citing**	
5 Unofficial Illinois Decisions citation	**to headnote**	
6 Synopsis	**11 KeyCite summary**	

ILLUSTRATION 3-6. *Continued*

Thompson v. Economy Super Marts, Inc., 221 Ill.App.3d 263 (1991)

581 N.E.2d 885, 163 Ill.Dec. 731

from which it could be inferred that it was more likely that defendant or his servants, rather than a customer, dropped the substance on the premises, trial court should allow negligence issue to go to jury.

14 Cases that cite this headnote

[5] **Negligence** — Slips and Falls in General

7 Even where there is proof that foreign substance causing slip of business invitee was related to defendant's business, where no further evidence is offered other than presence of substance and occurrence of injury, defendant is entitled to directed verdict, such evidence being insufficient to support necessary inference of negligence.

6 Cases that cite this headnote

[6] **Negligence** — Buildings and Other Structures

7 Evidence of negligence of grocery store was not sufficient to permit customer allegedly injured when she slipped on lettuce leaf in produce section of store to recover from store, even though leaf was described as wilted and was found near unsupervised produce section where vegetables were packed on ice; no direct or circumstantial evidence made it more likely that store's servants, rather than customer, dropped the leaf, and customer presented no evidence that ice which packed produce was directly above water spot or any evidence regarding how ice was packed or how easy it might have been to jar ice loose and spill it to the floor.

3 Cases that cite this headnote

Attorneys and Law Firms

886 *263 ***732 James J. Morici, Jr., argued, Anesi, Ozmon & Rodin, Ltd., Chicago, for Cherryl E. **Thompson.

(13) Kenneth T. Garvey, Robert Spitkovsky, Jr. and Kevin P. O'Connell, argued, Bresnahan & Garvey, Chicago, for **Economy** Super Marts, Inc.

> **12 Opinion**
> **13 Attorneys**

Opinion

**887 ***733 Justice HAASE delivered the opinion of the Court.

(12) The plaintiff, Cherryl E. **Thompson**, brought this negligence action against the defendants, **Economy** Super Marts, Inc. and Weems & Bruns Corp., to recover damages for personal injuries she sustained when she slipped on a lettuce leaf in the produce section of the defendants' grocery store. A jury awarded the plaintiff $12,974.96 in recoverable damages after finding that she was 55% contributorily negligent. Thereafter, the trial court granted the defendants' post-trial motion for a judgment notwithstanding the verdict. The plaintiff appeals from that decision.

The plaintiff testified at trial that on July 3, 1986, she picked up a watermelon in the produce section of the defendants' store and began ***264** to walk through the produce aisle. At that point, she slipped and fell on a lettuce leaf and water. She had not seen the leaf or the water before her fall and did not know how long they were there. She noted that the lettuce leaf was green and brown, had dirt on it, and appeared beat up. According to the plaintiff, her fall occurred about two or three feet to the left of the produce aisle. She also stated that the fruits and vegetables in the produce aisle were kept on ice.

Terida **Thompson**, the plaintiff's daughter, substantially corroborated the plaintiff's testimony. Additionally, she stated that the lettuce leaf looked old and like it had been there awhile. She further stated that she had walked through the produce aisle once before the accident occurred and did not see any water or a lettuce leaf on the floor prior to the plaintiff's fall.

Gene Pesavento, the assistant store manager, testified that it was his duty to make sure that all areas in the grocery store were clear and free of debris. He agreed that the produce department requires constant surveillance to ensure that debris is not left on the floor. He also agreed that debris poses a tripping hazard.

Pesavento further testified that no one was specifically charged with the responsibility of constantly monitoring the floor of the produce department. He explained that the defendants' employees knew that they were supposed to keep an eye on the entire store, and not specifically one area.

ILLUSTRATION 3-6.   *Continued*

Thompson v. Economy Super Marts, Inc., 221 Ill.App.3d 263 (1991)

581 N.E.2d 885, 163 Ill.Dec. 731

Phil Woock, the store's general manager, testified that he was not working at the time of the plaintiff's accident. He stated that the store's floor was dry mopped and swept every night in July, 1986. In addition, the floors were swept during the day as needed, and spills were cleaned as needed. The floors were professionally mopped and waxed every Wednesday night, and the plaintiff's accident occurred on a Thursday. Woock further testified that a part-time employee was on duty in the produce department at the time of the accident, but he could have been working in the back room when it occurred. Woock also testified that all store workers have the responsibility of keeping the floor clean if no one is working in the produce department at a particular time.

Donald Schreiner and Rubin Amazan each testified that they were working at the store at the time of the plaintiff's accident, but did not witness the fall. They both stated that they did not observe a lettuce leaf on the floor after inspecting the floor following the accident.

Based on the foregoing evidence, the jury found that the plaintiff suffered $28,833.24 in damages, but it awarded her only $12,974.96 because it found that she was 55% contributorily negligent. Thereafter, ***265** the defendants filed a post-trial motion requesting that the trial court enter a judgment notwithstanding the verdict. The trial court subsequently granted the defendants' motion, finding that: (1) no evidence was presented that the defendants had actual or constructive notice of the lettuce leaf and water for a sufficient length of time that its presence should have been discovered; and (2) the jury's award of damages was a compromise verdict and could not be sustained.

On appeal, the plaintiff initially argues that the trial court erred in granting a judgment notwithstanding the verdict. She contends that the court mistakenly found that she did not present any evidence that ****888 ***734** the defendants had actual or constructive notice of the lettuce leaf.

(14) **[1]   [2]   [3]**   It is well-settled that a defendant owes a business invitee on the defendant's premises a duty to exercise ordinary care in maintaining the premises in a reasonably safe condition. (*Ward v. K Mart Corp.* (1990), 136 Ill.2d 132, 143 Ill.Dec. 288, 554 N.E.2d 223; *Perminas v. Montgomery Ward & Co.* (1975), 60 Ill.2d 469, 328 N.E.2d 290.) Where a business invitee is injured by slipping on the premises, liability may be imposed if the substance was placed there by the negligence of the proprietor or his servants, or, if the substance was on the premises through acts of third persons or

there is no showing how it got there, liability may be imposed if it appears that the proprietor or his servant knew of its presence, or that the substance was there a sufficient length of time so that in the exercise of ordinary care its presence should have been discovered. (*Olinger v. Great Atlantic & Pacific Tea Co.* (1961), 21 Ill.2d 469, 173 N.E.2d 443; *Wroblewski v. Hillman's, Inc.* (1963), 43 Ill.App.2d 246, 193 N.E.2d 470.) Thus, where the foreign substance is on the premises due to the negligence of the proprietor or his servants, it is not necessary to establish their knowledge, actual or constructive; whereas, if the substance is on the premises through acts of third persons, the time element to establish knowledge or notice to the proprietor is a material factor. *Blake v. Dickinson* (1975), 31 Ill.App.3d 379, 332 N.E.2d 575.

[4]   [5]   Where there is proof that the foreign substance was a product sold or related to the defendant's operations, and the plaintiff offers some further evidence direct or circumstantial, however slight, such as the location of the substance or the business practices of the defendant, from which it could be inferred that it was more likely that the defendant or his servants, rather than a customer, dropped the substance on the premises, the trial court should allow the negligence issue to go to the jury. (*Donoho v. O'Connell's, Inc.* (1958), 13 Ill.2d 113, 148 N.E.2d 434.) However, even where there is proof that the ***266** foreign substance was related to the defendant's business, but no further evidence is offered other than the presence of the substance and the occurrence of the injury, the defendant is entitled to a directed verdict, such evidence being insufficient to support the necessary inference. *Olinger v. Great Atlantic & Pacific Tea Co.* (1961), 21 Ill.2d 469, 173 N.E.2d 443; *Wroblewski v. Hillman's, Inc.* (1963), 43 Ill.App.2d 246, 193 N.E.2d 470.

[6]   The plaintiff argues that she satisfied the requirements set forth in *Donoho* of introducing "further evidence, however slight, such as the location of the substance or the business practice of the defendant, from which it could be inferred that it was more likely that the defendant or his servants, rather than a customer, dropped the substance on the premises." She contends that evidence of the wilted lettuce leaf and the fact that it was found near the unsupervised produce section where vegetables were packed on ice was sufficient to allow the case to go to the jury under *Donoho.*

We disagree. The Illinois Supreme Court in *Donoho* undertook an extensive analysis of the circumstances under which negligence could be inferred from the conduct of the defendant when it was uncertain who was responsible for the

14 Text that corresponds with headnotes

ILLUSTRATION 3-6. *Continued*

Thompson v. Economy Super Marts, Inc., 221 Ill.App.3d 263 (1991)

581 N.E.2d 885, 163 Ill.Dec. 731

foreign substance dropped on the premises. In *Donoho,* the plaintiff slipped and fell on an onion ring at the defendant's restaurant. It was unknown who dropped the onion ring. Yet, the court found that from the circumstantial evidence, it could be reasonably inferred that it was more likely that the onion ring was on the floor through the acts of the defendant's servants rather than a customer. The court based its decision on the additional circumstantial evidence that the onion ring on which the plaintiff slipped was located by a table cleared by a bus boy, under the bus boy's practice of clearing tables food particles could drop to the floor, and testimony that after the bus boy cleared the table in question no one else ate there before the plaintiff fell.

In the present case, however, there was no direct or circumstantial evidence indicating that it was more likely that the defendants' servants dropped the item than a customer. Furthermore, the plaintiff did not present any evidence that the ice, which ****889 ***735** packed the produce, was directly above the water spot. Nor did she present any evidence regarding how the ice was packed or how easy it might have been to jar it loose spilling it to the floor. Moreover, there was no specific evidence that the plaintiff's business practice was unusual or created any special hazard.

The plaintiff also relies on *Perminas v. Montgomery Ward & Company* (1975), 60 Ill.2d 469, 328 N.E.2d 290, in support of her position. In ***267** *Perminas,* the plaintiff slipped on a skateboard-like object in an aisle of the defendant's store. There, one of the defendant's employees actually had knowledge that the object was creating a dangerous condition.

The court imposed liability on the defendant because the defendant, after receiving notice through its employee that its product was creating a dangerous situation, failed to return its premises to a safe condition or warn its customers.

We find that the plaintiff's reliance on *Perminas* is misplaced. In the present case, unlike *Perminas,* the defendants did not have actual or constructive knowledge of the situation. Furthermore, the record in the instant case does not contain any evidence regarding the length of time the substance was on the floor from which it could be inferred that the defendants had constructive notice.

After reviewing the evidence in the aspect most favorable to the plaintiff, we conclude that the evidence so overwhelmingly favored the defendants that no contrary verdict could ever stand. Accordingly, we find that the trial court properly granted the defendants' motion for a judgment notwithstanding the verdict. Our resolution of the foregoing issue renders the parties' remaining issues moot.

The judgment of the circuit court of Will County is affirmed.

Affirmed.

McCUSKEY, J., and STOUDER, P.J., concur.

All Citations

221 Ill.App.3d 263, 581 N.E.2d 885, 163 Ill.Dec. 731

End of Document

Reprinted with permission of Thomson Reuters.

ILLUSTRATION 3-7.   West's *Federal Reporter* and *Federal Supplement Coverage*

Federal Reporter Coverage (F., F.2d, F.3d)	
U.S. Circuit Courts	1880 to 1912
Commerce Court of the United States	1911 to 1913
U.S. District Courts	1880 to 1932
U.S. Court of Claims (1960 to 1982)	1929 to 1932
U.S. Court of Appeals (formerly United States Circuit Court of Appeals)	1891 to date
U.S. Court of Customs and Patent Appeals	1929 to 1982
U.S. Emergency Court of Appeals	1943 to 1961
Temporary Emergency Court of Appeals	1972 to 1993
Federal Supplement Coverage (F. Supp., F. Supp. 2d)	
U.S. District Courts	1932 to date
U.S. Court of Claims	1932 to 1960
U.S. Court of International Trade (formerly U.S. Customs Court)	1956 to date
Judicial Panel on Multidistrict Litigation	1968 to date

PRACTICE POINTER

Check all applicable rules whenever you plan to use an unpublished case as an authority for a point of law.

▼ How Are *Federal Reporter* and *Federal Supplement* Decisions Cited?

Cite *Federal Reporter* and *Federal Supplement* decisions according to *Bluebook* **Rules 10.1** through **10.6** or *ALWD* **Rule 12**. The case name is placed first and underlined. Next, place the volume number. The reporter abbreviation is next. Note that for the *Federal Reporter*, the abbreviation is "F." If the *Federal Reporter* cited belongs to the second or third series, "2d" or "3d" should be placed next to the "F." For the *Federal Supplement*, the reporter is abbreviated "F. Supp.," "F. Supp. 2d," or "F. Supp. 3d." The page number follows the abbreviation for the reporter. Next, in parentheses you should place an abbreviation that denotes the appropriate court and then the date of the decision. Be certain to include a geographic designation for the district courts.

***Federal Reporter* case**	*Zimmerman v. N. Am. Signal Co.*, 704 F.2d 347 (7th Cir. 1983) — *Bluebook* format
***Federal Supplement* case**	*Musser v. Mountain View Broad.*, 578 F. Supp. 229 (E.D. Tenn. 1984) — *Bluebook* format

▼ Are Decisions Published in Any Other Reporters?

Several publishers of topical resources and specialized reporters also publish some federal decisions. Sometimes they duplicate opinions found in the West series. West also publishes some specialized reporters, such as the ***Federal Rules Decisions*** (F.R.D.). This reporter contains decisions in which a federal rule of civil or criminal procedure is at issue. *Federal Rules Decisions* includes not only cases but speeches, articles, and other resources to assist in understanding the federal rules. Another specialized reporter is *West's Education Law Reporter.* It is a compilation of selected state and federal education–related decisions from 1982 to date. It also includes information about grants, awards, and regulations of the U.S. Department of Education and articles written by education experts.

5. State Reporters

▼ Where Can You Find State Court Decisions?

Some states continue to publish state decisions in their own reporters. In those states, the state publication is the official reporter. Some states authorize private publishers to publish the official reports for them. For example, West's regional reporters have been adopted as official state reporters in various states. However, some states are now designating the online report as the official state report and discontinuing the publication of print reporters.

▼ Are There Any Unofficial Reports of State Cases?

Yes. In addition to its publication of some states' official reporters, Thomson West, part of Thomson Reuters, publishes seven **regional reporters** that contain state cases. See Illustrations 3-8 and 3-9. The regional reporters are not based on actual geographic regions. For example, Illinois is in the American Midwest region, but the regional reporter that contains Illinois decisions is the *North Eastern Reporter.* However, publication frequency varies. Most reporters are updated irregularly with advance sheets.

The regional reporters contain decisions from several different states. Some states have designated the West regional reporter as the official reporter of their state decisions.

ILLUSTRATION 3-8   West's Regional Reporters Coverage

Regional Reporter	*States Covered*
Atlantic Reporter (A., A.2d, or A.3d)	Connecticut, Delaware, Maine, Maryland, New Hampshire, New Jersey, Pennsylvania, Rhode Island, Vermont, and the District of Columbia
North Eastern Reporter (N.E., N.E.2d, or N.E.3d)	Illinois, Indiana, Massachusetts, New York, and Ohio
North Western Reporter (N.W. or N.W.2d)	Iowa, Michigan, Minnesota, Nebraska, North Dakota, South Dakota, and Wisconsin
Pacific Reporter (P., P.2d, or P.3d)	Alaska, Arizona, California, Colorado, Hawaii, Idaho, Kansas, Montana, Nevada, New Mexico, Oklahoma, Oregon, Utah, Washington, and Wyoming
South Eastern Reporter (S.E. or S.E.2d)	Georgia, North Carolina, South Carolina, Virginia, and West Virginia
South Western Reporter (S.W., S.W.2d, or S.W.3d)	Arkansas, Kentucky, Missouri, Tennessee, and Texas
Southern Reporter (So., So. 2d, or So. 3d)	Alabama, Florida, Louisiana, and Mississippi

PRACTICE POINTER

In theory, the text of a case published in the state reporter should be identical to that in the regional reporter. If the two differ, then the language of the official version governs.

▼ Why Would You Use the Regional Reporter Rather Than the Official State Reporter?

The regional reporter contains the publisher's headnotes designed to assist you. See Illustrations 3-5 and 3-6. These notes guide you to the publisher's topical index of cases called a digest. You also might use the regional reporter because it is published sooner than the official reporter. Review Illustration 3-5. Review the headnotes and the format. Next review Illustration 3-6. This is a Westlaw PDF of the *Thompson* case. The format is similar to the printed *North Eastern Reporter* report of the case. In this case, the official and parallel citations are provided. Headnotes are listed with the specific topic, but the Key Numbers do not appear. Hyperlinks provided in the PDF will take researchers with

ILLUSTRATION 3-9.   National Reporter System

Reprinted with permission of Thomson Reuters.

a Westlaw subscription to the online Key Number. Online researchers can use hyperlinks to search Key Numbers by jurisdiction. This report also notes the number of cases that cite that Key Number. The synopsis and the headnote case abstracts in the PDF are identical to the print report.

▼ How Are State Cases Cited?

Cite a state case according to *Bluebook* **Rule 10.3.1.(b)** and *ALWD* **Rule 12.6(c)(4) and Rule 12.6(c)(5)**. If you are citing a state case in a document submitted to a court in the same state, you should provide the citations required by local rule. However, the *Bluebook* generally directs you to cite to the regional reporter. In states where the official reporter citation is required, you will likely be required to provide the regional citation as well. The official citation should be listed first. Some states now require a public domain citation rather than a citation to an official print reporter.

Bluebook **Rule 10.3.3** requires that you cite public domain citations as follows: case name, followed by the year of the decision, the deciding court, and the sequential number of the decision. In some jurisdictions, the sequential number of the decision is the docket number. If available, a parallel cite must be listed. To cite to a specific portion of the decision, you may add a reference to the paragraph.

public domain citation   *State v. Kienast,* 1996 S.D. 111 ¶2, 553 N.W.2d 254

Cite to what *ALWD* refers to as neutral citations rather than public domain citations, according to **Rule 12.11** of the *ALWD* guide. First, use the format specified by the court or include the case name, the year of the decision, the state's two-letter postal code abbreviation, the court abbreviation if decided by a court other than the state's high court, the opinion number, and then a pinpoint citation reference. The above case would be cited as follows:

State v. Kienast, 1996 SD 111, 553 NW2d 254.

6. Computerized Reporting

▼ Can You Find Decisions on the Internet and through Fee-Based Computer Services?

Yes. Published and unpublished federal and state decisions are available online through the court websites for free or for a nominal fee. Although online cases found at court websites can be accessed at a low cost 24 hours a day, these cases often lack research aids. To access Web-based cases through the Internet, go directly to a court's website. All federal courts are required to offer websites and to include on those websites access to all written opinions, even if the opinions are not published. The United States courts also provide the public with electronic access to case and docket information of the federal appellate, district, and bankruptcy cases. Online, federal and state court websites are great resources to find a specific decision or for targeted research. Many allow you to search the full text of a decision. However, not all court websites provide full-text searching or decisions online. Many trial court websites are limited and will provide you with docket information only.

Commercial sources such as Westlaw, Lexis, Bloomberg Law, and Fastcase also provide decisions online. On Westlaw and Lexis, cases are organized into databases or files and can be accessed through keyword and other searches. Unlike most cases that may be found on the Internet, cases that appear within these databases contain publishers' research aids such as headnotes. Like many other commercial services, Westlaw, Lexis, and Fastcase now use a search query bar similar to

Google that allows users to conduct broad searches without terms and connectors. Connectors are special words or symbols devised to link your search terms together to indicate your search term's placement in the text of the document and the proximity of the search terms in relation to one another. The use of terms and connectors called Boolean search might make your search more targeted. For example, you enter terms and require the terms to be within the same sentence, the same paragraph, or within three words. You can filter your request by jurisdiction, topic, or type of format such as cases, statutes, or news articles.

PRACTICE POINTER

Finding a case through free resources can often be a cost-effective way merely to read a specific case. Before using any cost-based, online services, ask the attorney assigning the research project if it is within the budget.

If you know the case citation or a case name, you can easily find the case on Westlaw, Lexis, or Fastcase. On Westlaw, begin at the search page. Westlaw search pages may vary in display depending on the subscription. The main search bar is next to the words Thomson Reuters Westlaw. On the right side of the bar, it shows the jurisdiction to be searched. A pull-down menu within the box that says "All Federal" allows you to set your search to other jurisdictions that are separate databases within the Westlaw platform. See Illustration 3-10.Westlaw allows users to enter a citation or keywords in a search box similar to that found on a Google search page. Users can search multiple databases at once in a search that is similar in feel to a Google search. On the left side of the search bar, a drop-down menu allows researchers to limit the content or databases to be searched. An advanced search allows users to insert terms to be searched and Boolean connectors.

On a Lexis search page, you can search by citation or by party name. To search by citation, enter the citation in the search box. You do not need to be in a database to retrieve cases using these search tools. Fastcase also has a search function. Your query can be entered into the search bar and can be filtered by jurisdiction. For example, you can limit your search to only Pennsylvania state cases. It allows for search by keyword with or without Boolean connectors, natural language, and citation. You also can add an alert so that you can receive an e-mail concerning cases that meet your search criteria.

ILLUSTRATION 3-10.   Finding a Case in Westlaw

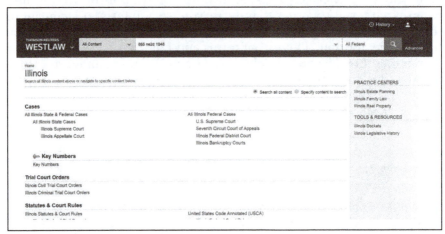

Reprinted with permission of Thomson Reuters.

PRACTICE POINTER

Check court rules for citing and relying on opinions available on the Internet. Many courts may prohibit researchers from citing a Web case if it is available in a reporter, an online database, or a printed source, such as a looseleaf.

▼ What Free Resources Allow Researchers to Search for Federal and State Cases?

Fastcase is free with some bar memberships. Many state bar associations offer this service. In addition, you can find many legal resources at no cost at https://www.law.cornell.edu/. Google Scholar also allows you to search for federal and state cases. A Google Scholar search can be limited to a particular jurisdiction such as the Court of Appeals for the Eighth Circuit or the state of Arizona. It is not as comprehensive as Westlaw and Lexis and does not include any editorial enhancements.

Justia offers free full-text keyword searches of all U.S. Supreme Court decisions at https://www.justia.com/. It also allows you to subscribe free to receive daily U.S. Supreme Court opinion summaries. Here is a link to Justia's opinion and summary of the *Mahanoy Area School District* case mentioned above: https://supreme.justia.com/cases/fede ral/us/594/20-255/. Links also are provided to briefs and filings as well as links to Oyez, where a recording of the argument can be found. Oyez is a free service from Cornell's Legal Information Institute, Justia, and Chicago-Kent College of Law. It archives U.S. Supreme Court multimedia files and calls itself "the most complete and authoritative source for all of the Court's audio" since 1955.

The Caselaw Access Project publishes U.S. case law for free at https://case.law/. It includes "all official, book-published United States case law—every volume designated as an official report of decisions by a court within the United States," according to its website. Full case text can be viewed or downloaded free if you register for an account. You can conduct a full-text search and filter your search by date, case name, docket number, reporter, jurisdiction, citation, or court.

PACER (Public Access to Court Electronic Records) is a service offered by the federal government that provides access to federal cases and case information. Despite its keyword and other search capabilities, PACER is cumbersome to use and does not include the editorial enhancements offered by commercial publishers. In addition, PACER users are charged for printing or downloading documents.

PRACTICE POINTER

Most free resources do not include any of the types of editorial enhancements found on Westlaw or Lexis. They can be a good starting point, but they have very limited value unless you know exactly what you are seeking.

▼ How Do You Know Whether a Case Is Published or Available Online Only?

Westlaw and Lexis provide the citations for all cases that are published in print. If this information is absent or the publisher indicates that it is not published, it is not. Instead, Westlaw provides its own citation for this case. Lexis also indicates its own citation for cases it publishes only online.

▼ How Are Decisions Reported Only on Westlaw or Lexis Cited?

Bluebook **Rule 10.8.1** and *ALWD* **Rule 12.14(b)** explain how you should cite an unpublished decision found only on either Westlaw or Lexis. (If a decision is published in a hard-copy reporter, you should not use the Westlaw or Lexis citation.)

For both Westlaw and Lexis, the *Bluebook* citation would first state the case name. After the case name is the docket number. In the example that follows, that number is "No. 82-C-4585." Next is the year of the decision. For Westlaw cases, the next item would be "WL" for Westlaw. The Westlaw number assigned to the case follows that. If a spot cite is provided, precede the screen or page number with an asterisk. Finally, in the parentheses, place the court and the full date.

Westlaw cite   *Clark Equip. Co. v. Lift Parts Mfg. Co.*, No. 82-C-4585,
(***Bluebook***)   1985 WL 2917, at *1 (N.D. Ill. Oct. 1, 1985)

The *ALWD* citation based on **Rule 12**, especially **Rule 12.14(b)**, would be as follows (the docket number and the abbreviation for company is dropped because it is the second business designation).

Westlaw cite   *Clark Equip. Co. v. Lift Parts Mfg.*, 1985 WL 2917, at *1
(***AWLD***)   (N.D. Ill. Oct. 1, 1985)

For Lexis citations, the *Bluebook* requires that you state the name of the case, the docket number, the year of the decision, the name of the Lexis file that contains the case, the name "LEXIS" to indicate that the case is found on Lexis, and the document number. Last, place the court and the full date in parentheses.

Lexis cite   *Barrett Indus. Trucks v. Old Republic Ins. Co.*,
(***Bluebook*** and   No. 87-C-9429, 1990 U.S. Dist. LEXIS 142, at *1
ALWD)   (N.D. Ill. Jan. 9, 1990)

CHAPTER SUMMARY

In this chapter, you learned about case law and about the reporters that contain Supreme Court, federal, and state decisions. Case law consists of court-adopted decisions. These decisions are primary authorities. These authorities generally are organized chronologically. Several publishers have established case reporters that are books, usually in series format, which contain court decisions.

Decisions are first published in slip opinions, generally a typed set of pages. Next, advance sheets are published. These decisions usually look similar to the final case reporter version of a decision.

Next, bound reporters that carry the case decision reports are published. For the Supreme Court decisions, three reporters are available. The *United States Reports* is published by the government. The *United States Supreme Court Reports, Lawyers' Edition* is published by Lexis. The *Supreme Court Reporter* is published by Thomson West. The commercial publishers' reports include publishers' notes and annotations, such as headnotes designed to assist you in your research.

Many other federal court decisions are published in the *Federal Supplement, Federal Reporter,* and *Federal Appendix*. State court decisions often are found in a state-published case reporter and in regional reporters. These commercial reporters have headnotes that assist you in your research. These headnotes contain case abstracts concerning a point of law raised in a case and a topic and number that refer you to a topical system for finding additional similar cases discussed in the next chapter.

Today, slip and other opinions often are available free of charge or for a nominal fee on the Internet from official court sites.

KEY TERMS

advance sheets

bench opinion

case law

digests

Federal Appendix

Federal Reporter

Federal Rules Decision

Federal Supplement

headnotes

Key Numbers

Lawyers' Edition

Lexis

National Reporter System

preliminary print

regional reporter

reporters

reporting systems

slip opinion

Supreme Court Reporter

syllabus

United States Law Week

U.S. Reports

Westlaw

EXERCISES

SELF-ASSESSMENT

1. List the three reporters that contain the decision in Illustration 3-5.
2. What reporter or reporters would you look in to find a published Illinois Supreme Court decision?
3. What reporter or reporters would you look in to find a published U.S. Court of Appeals decision decided in 2021?
4. What reporter or reporters would you look in to find a U.S. District Court decision from 1930?
5. What is contained in the *Federal Rules Decisions*?
6. What sources would you look in to find a U.S. Supreme Court decision one to two weeks after the case was decided by the Court? (List at least four sources.)
7. What is the advantage of using the *Lawyers' Edition* to review a Supreme Court case?
8. What is the advantage of using a West's regional reporter in researching rather than the *Illinois Reports*?
9. When you are beginning a research assignment, what is the first thing that you should determine? How is this determined?
10. Are headnotes cited? Why, or why not?

PRACTICE SKILLS

11. Find 507 F. Supp. 1091. What is the Key Number and topic for the second headnote?
12. Find 825 F.2d 257. What court decided this case?

13. Find 819 F.2d 630. What is the docket number for this case? List the names of the attorneys who argued this case.
14. Find 373 N.E.2d 1371. List the presiding judge and the date the case was decided.
15. Find 432 N.E.2d 1123. List the official citation for this case, the name of the plaintiff, and the name of the defendant.
16. Find 222 N.E.2d 561. List the name of the judge who wrote the opinion.
17. Find the Government Printing Office's U.S. Supreme Court decisions on the Internet. What is the website address?
18. Go to the U.S. Courts website. What links to other courts are available? Please provide the websites for at least three links.
19. Go to the U.S. Fifth Circuit Court of Appeals website. Find the court's local rules. What is the Web address for these rules?

4

DIGESTS AND TOPICAL CLASSIFICATION SYSTEMS

CHAPTER OVERVIEW

This chapter focuses on the use of **digests**, topically organized indexes, and online topical classification systems. You will be taught how to use both the online topical systems and the Thomson Reuters digests developed by the former West Publishing Company (West). These digests and other Thomson Reuters products first published by West

Publishing Company often are referred to as West products. The West digest system is the largest and most diverse topical organization of the law. The skills you learn will help you to use other publishers' digests and online topical classification systems. Topical searching, as well as research, using headnotes and Key Numbers will be explored.

A. CONTENT OF DIGESTS AND ONLINE TOPICAL CLASSIFICATION SYSTEMS ORGANIZATION

▼ What Are Digests and Online Topical Classification Systems, and What Do They Contain?

Publishers have developed systems called digests that index the law by topics or legal issues. For example, the West digests contain at least 450 topics. A list of some of the West topics is shown in Illustration 4-1. West migrated its digest system to an easily searchable online platform on Westlaw. Other publishers have similarly taken their print digests online and some are creating only online systems. Online resources are making print resources obsolete and many libraries and law firms have discontinued their print digests subscriptions in favor of online resources. However, understanding the organization and use of print digests is still useful when you try to learn online topical research strategies. If available, print resources can be browsed for brainstorming relevant topics. Therefore, this chapter will detail how to do topical research online and in print.

1. Headnotes and Key Numbers

Publishers continually revise their topical systems. Both online and in print digests, you find **headnotes** or case abstracts in which the publishers assign a topic and number to a point of law. The headnotes assist you in finding other cases that are relevant to the issues presented in your case. Cases are read by publishers' editors, and these editors put each issue into a topic category. The specific legal issue is then assigned a number to accompany the topic. This enables you to match cases discussing the same issues of law. Digests also contain references to the publisher's other resources such as law review articles.

The Thomson Reuters' West American Digest System, commonly called the West digest system, features the **West Key Number System**®. This system is divided into digest topics, such as bankruptcy, civil rights, criminal law, negligence, double jeopardy, and damages. LexisNexis's Michie publishes a digest for U.S. Supreme Court cases called *U.S. Supreme Court Digest, Lawyers' Edition*. Other publishers also prepare state digests. West's state digests contain references to decisions of

ILLUSTRATION 4-1. Partial List of West's Digest Topics

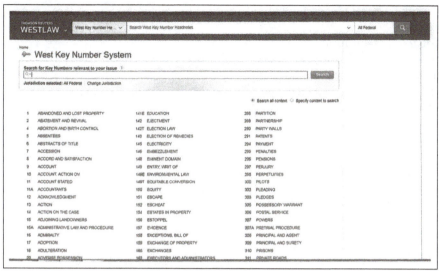

Reprinted with permission of Thomson Reuters.

federal courts sitting within that state that pertain to the state's legal issues. West's regional digests contain abstracts of state cases. In addition to these digests, West and other publishers print topical digests, such as the *West's Education Law Digest.*

2. Types of Digests

The ***West American Digest System*** is a comprehensive set of all of West's reported federal and state cases. See Illustration 4-2. This system includes the *Century Digest,* which contains cases decided between 1658 and 1897. It does not contain Key Numbers. However, a West index allows you to cross-reference cases in the first and second *Decennial Digest* to convert them to the equivalent Key Number.

ILLUSTRATION 4-2. Assorted Digests

American Digest System
West's General Digests
Century Digest
Decennial Digests
General Digests

Digests That Abstract All U.S. Supreme Court Cases
U.S. Supreme Court Digest (West)
U.S. Supreme Court Digest, Lawyers' Edition

ILLUSTRATION 4-2. *Continued*

Other Federal Court Digests
Federal Digest
Modern Federal Practice Digest
West's Federal Practice Digest 2d
West's Federal Practice Digest 3d
West's Federal Practice Digest 4th
West's Federal Practice Digest 5th contains all of the federal court cases reported by West, including U.S. Supreme Court cases

State Cases
West Regional Digests: indexes cases reported in the reporter bearing the same name
    North Western Digest
    South Eastern Digest
    Pacific Digest
    Atlantic Digest

West does not publish a digest for the *North Eastern Reporter*, the *Southern Reporter*, or the *South Western Reporter.*
Individual State Digests: West publishes digests for most of the 50 states and the District of Columbia; however, it publishes a combined digest for South Dakota and North Dakota and a combined digest for West Virginia and Virginia. It does not publish separate digests for Utah, Delaware, and Nevada. Digest summaries for those cases appear in their respective regional digest products.

Specialized Digests
West's Bankruptcy Digest
West's Military Justice Digest
West's Education Law Digest

The *Decennial Digests* is a multiple-volume digest that includes state and federal court cases from all U.S. jurisdictions from 1997 to date. Presented in ten-year increments, it contains points of law that are summarized in headnotes and classified using the West Key Number System®. Older *Decennial Digests* contain all of the abstracts from West's regional, state, and federal digests. *General Digests* also are included in this system. These also include all West cases and are presented in one-year increments. These older print digests, however, are falling out of favor; instead, researchers are turning to Westlaw and Lexis to search for older cases.

United States Supreme Court opinions are indexed in a digest called the *United States Supreme Court Digest*, in *West's Supreme Court Digest*, and in *West's Federal Practice Digest* series.

3. Organization of Digests and Online Topical Classification Systems

▼ How Are Digests and Online Topical Classification
Systems Organized?

Most systems are organized first by topic. Case abstracts of points of law or headnotes are prepared by the publisher, and these points of law are then assigned topics. Within each topic, points of law are assigned numbers. In the West system, this match of a topic and a number is called a Key Number. Lexis has a similar classification system in print and online. Once a researcher masters one system, the other system is easy to navigate.

Key Numbers are the cornerstones of the West system. Key Numbers correspond to specific points of law presented in a case. See the illustrations in Chapter 3, specifically Illustrations 3-5 and 3-6. The case abstracts are not authoritative and should never be cited. These case abstracts contain a publisher's summary of a point of law, the case name, and a citation.

Illustration 4-3 shows pages from *West's Illinois Digest*. On the second page of the illustration, the *Thompson* case is noted in the second column by the circled 3. Note that the case abstract contained on this digest page is identical to the first headnote contained in Illustrations 3-5 and 3-6. However, the Key Number is different than the one shown in Illustration 3-5, a copy of the print report of the *Thompson* case. This is because publishers constantly update topical classification systems such as West's Key Number System®. At the top of Illustration 4-3 is the word *Negligence*. This indicates the topic. Next to it is a key and the number 1076. This is the Key Number. The deciding court and the year of the decision are noted at the beginning of the abstract. See the court next to the circled 4 in Illustration 4-3.

The theory of the Key Number system is that if you have a good case on point and you want to find similar cases on point, you look under the topic and the Key Number assigned to the point in your case. The case abstracts listed under that topic and Key Number should be similar to your case. To find cases similar to the point of law noted in the first headnote of the *Thompson* case, you would review Negligence Key Number 1076 in the hardcopy digest and any updates. Review the language of a case that corresponds to the headnote or headnotes of interest to you as a researcher. Then, compare it with case language that corresponds with the headnote or headnotes you want to review. The two cases will address similar issues, but the headnotes will not be identical. Now review the case text itself to ensure that the text actually says what the headnote or headnotes indicate. A case generally has multiple key numbers because a case abstract and a corresponding topic and Key Number are prepared for each point of law raised in a case.

ILLUSTRATION 4-3. Sample Pages from *West's Illinois Digest*

---

①   ②

🗝1076 **NEGLIGENCE**   38A Ill D 2d—128

For later cases, see same Topic and Key Number in Pocket Part

Storekeeper is not insurer of his customer's safety.

> Mick v. Kroger Co., 224 N.E.2d 859, 37 Ill.2d 148, 21 A.L.R.3d 926.

Ill. 1961. Store owner owed business invitee duty of exercising ordinary care to maintain premises in a reasonably safe condition.

> Olinger v. Great Atlantic & Pacific Tea Co., 173 N.E.2d 443, 21 Ill.2d 469.

A proprietor of a store is not an insurer against all accidents and injuries to customers coming to his place of business.

> Olinger v. Great Atlantic & Pacific Tea Co., 173 N.E.2d 443, 21 Ill.2d 469.

Ill. 1958. Restaurant proprietor owes a business invitee duty of exercising ordinary care in maintaining premises in reasonably safe condition.

> Donoho v. O'Connell's, Inc., 148 N.E.2d 434, 13 Ill.2d 113.

Ill. 1955. Where operator of bowling alley maintained adjacent to the bowling alley an automobile parking lot for use of its patrons, and a patron was injured in the parking lot, relation of injured patron to operator of bowling alley was that of a "business invitee" to whom operator of bowling alley owed duty to exercise reasonable care for safety of patron while he was on the parking lot.

> Geraghty v. Burr Oak Lanes, 125 N.E.2d 47, 5 Ill.2d 153.

Where operator of bowling alley maintained an automobile parking lot adjacent to the bowling alley for the use of its patrons, operator of bowling alley owed pa[ ] automobile in the pa[1 Key Number] exercise ordinary ca[2 Topic]g lot in a reasonable [ ] use in a manner consistent with purpose of the invitation, or at least not to lead patron into a dangerous trap, or expose him to unreasonable risk, and to give him adequate and timely notice and warning of any latent or concealed perils, which were known to operator of bowling alley but not to patron.

> Geraghty v. Burr Oak Lanes, 125 N.E.2d 47, 5 Ill.2d 153.

Ill. 1948. The general rule is that the owner is not liable for negligence where the invitee is using a portion of the premises to which invitation has not been extended and which the owner would not reasonably expect the invitee to use in connection with the conduct of business on the premises.

> Briney v. Illinois Cent. R. Co., 81 N.E.2d 866, 401 Ill. 181.

Ill.App. 1 Dist. 2003. Duty of reasonable care of store owner, based on distraction exception to open and obvious rule, encompassed risk that customer, while exiting store, would be distracted by unattended shopping cart and trip and fall over irregular pavement.

> Green v. Jewel Food Stores, Inc., 278 Ill.Dec. 875, 799 N.E.2d 740, 343 Ill.App.3d 830, rehearing denied.

A business operator generally owes his customers a duty to exercise reasonable care to maintain his premises in a reasonably safe condition.

> Green v. Jewel Food Stores, Inc., 278 Ill.Dec. 875, 799 N.E.2d 740, 343 Ill.App.3d 830, rehearing denied.

Ill.App. 1 Dist. 2003. A tavern operator is not an insurer of its patrons.

> Sameer v. Butt, 277 Ill.Dec. 697, 796 N.E.2d 1063, 343 Ill.App.3d 78, rehearing denied.

Ill.App. 1 Dist. 2002. In an action based upon negligence, general rule regarding duty of a business occupier of any premises is that it must provide a reasonably safe means of ingress to and egress from premises, but ordinarily it will not be held liable for any injuries incurred on a public sidewalk under control of municipality, even though sidewalk may also be used for ingress or egress to premises.

> Friedman v. City of Chicago, 267 Ill. Dec. 627, 777 N.E.2d 430, 333 Ill. App.3d 1070.

Ill.App. 1 Dist. 2002. Store, tavern, or restaurant owners owe a duty of ordinary care to their business invitees.

> Salazar v. Crown Enterprises, Inc., 262 Ill.Dec. 906, 767 N.E.2d 366, 328 Ill.App.3d 735, appeal denied 266 Ill.Dec. 447, 775 N.E.2d 9, 199 Ill.2d 579.

Ill.App. 1 Dist. 1999. Person is a "business invitee" on the land of another if (1) the person enters by express or implied invitation, (2) the entry is connected with

† This Case was not selected for publication in the National Reporter System
For legislative history of cited statutes, see West's Smith-Hurd Illinois Compiled Statutes Annotated

ILLUSTRATION 4-3. *Continued*

①☞1076 NEGLIGENCE ②   38 Ill D 2d—420

For later cases, see same Topic and Key Number in Pocket Part

to such licensee is to not wilfully or wantonly injure him.

> Wesbrock v. Colby, Inc., 43 N.E.2d 405, 315 Ill.App. 494.

Where plaintiff, after making some purchases in defendant's store, was injured when she fell down basement steps as she attempted to make use of telephone located in stairway of store which was not intended for public use, and there was no evidence that clerk who showed plaintiff where telephone was had authority to give plaintiff permission to use it, plaintiff at time she received her injuries was a "licensee", and not an "invitee", and hence could not recover for her injuries, in absence of any willful or wanton misconduct by defendant.

> Wesbrock v. Colby, Inc., 43 N.E.2d 405, 315 Ill.App. 494.

Ill.App. 2 Dist. 1942. Although one operating a business to which the public is invited is not an "insurer" of safety of patrons, he has the duty to use reasonable care to keep premises in a reasonably safe condition so that patrons will not be injured by reason of any unsafe condition of the premises, and a failure to do so is actionable negligence in case an injury results therefrom.

> Crump v. Montgomery Ward & Co., 39 N.E.2d 411, 313 Ill.App. 151.

An owner of store in propping open the doors at entrance of store owed the same duty to its invitees to use reasonable care for their safety as it did to provide safe equipment.

> Crump v. Montgomery Ward & Co., 39 N.E.2d 411, 313 Ill.App. 151.

Ill.App. 2 Dist. 1939. The law raises on the part of a proprietor of a store an implied invitation to the public to come into his building or upon his premises should they seek to do business with him, and he is under a legal obligation to exercise ordinary and reasonable care to make his premises safe for the protection of his customers.

> Todd v. S. S. Kresge Co., 24 N.E.2d 899, 303 Ill.App. 89.

A proprietor of a store is not an insurer against all accidents and injuries to customers coming to his place of business.

> Todd v. S. S. Kresge Co., 24 N.E.2d 899, 303 Ill.App. 89.

Ill.App. 3 Dist. 1993. Person is "business invitee" on land of another if that person enters land by express or implied invitation, if entry is connected with owner's business or with activity conducted by owner on land, and if owner receives benefit.

> Leonardi v. Bradley University, 192 Ill.Dec. 471, 625 N.E.2d 431, 253 Ill.App.3d 685, appeal denied 198 Ill.Dec. 544, 633 N.E.2d 6, 155 Ill.2d 565.

Ill.App. 3 Dist. 1993. Store owner did not assume duty to remove all tracked-in water from its store when it placed two mats near its outside entrance; owner's duty extended only to maintaining with reasonable care the mats it installed.

> Roberson v. J.C. Penney Co., 191 Ill.Dec. 119, 623 N.E.2d 364, 251 Ill.App.3d 523.

④Ill.App. 3 Dist. 1991. Defendant owes business invitee on defendant's premises duty to exercise ordinary care in maintaining premises in reasonably safe condition.

> Thompson v. Economy Super Marts, Inc., **③** 163 Ill.Dec. 731, 581 N.E.2d 885, 221 Ill.App.3d 263.

Ill.App. 3 Dist. 1987. A "business invitee" is one who enters upon the premises of another in response to an express or implied invitation for the purpose of transacting business in which the parties are mutually interested.

> Simmons v. Aldi-Brenner Co., 113 Ill.Dec. 594, 515 N.E.2d 403, 162 Ill.App.3d 238, appeal denied 119 Ill.Dec. 398, 522 N.E.2d 1257, 119 Ill.2d 575.

The owner or occupier of land owes to persons present on the premises as business invi[...]nd reas[...]are reas[...]es.

> **1 Key Number**
> **2 Topic**
> **3 *Thompson* case**
> **4 Deciding court**

[...]ec. [...]38, [...]22

[...]ers

must be founded on fault.

> Simmons v. Aldi-Brenner Co., 113 Ill.Dec. 594, 515 N.E.2d 403, 162 Ill.App.3d 238, appeal denied 119 Ill.Dec. 398, 522 N.E.2d 1257, 119 Ill.2d 575.

Ill.App. 3 Dist. 1985. Storekeeper is not insurer of customer's safety.

> Nicholson v. St. Anne Lanes, Inc., 91 Ill. Dec. 9, 483 N.E.2d 291, 136 Ill.App.3d 664, appeal denied.

Ill.App. 3 Dist. 1982. Duty of owner of commercial enterprise to provide reasonably safe means of ingress and egress from place of business for use of his patrons is not abrogated by presence of accumulation of ice or snow which is natural.

> Kittle v. Liss, 64 Ill.Dec. 307, 439 N.E.2d 972, 108 Ill.App.3d 922.

Ill.App. 3 Dist. 1980. Duty owed to business invitee is to exercise ordinary care in maintaining premises in a reasonably safe condition.

> Hayes v. Bailey, 36 Ill.Dec. 124, 400 N.E.2d 544, 80 Ill.App.3d 1027.

For legislative history of cited statutes

Reprinted with permission of Thomson Reuters.

> ### PRACTICE POINTER
>
> The same West digest system is used for all states. Therefore, you can find a good case in one state and look up the relevant Key Number in another state's digest. That will lead you to cases that are similarly decided in the second state.

B. GUIDE TO THE PRINT DIGEST SYSTEMS

▼ How Do You Use a Digest System?

You might use one of several methods for finding cases within a digest: the descriptive word index method, the topic outline method, and the one good case method.

1. Descriptive Word Index Method

▼ What Is the Descriptive Word Index Method?

One method you might use is the **descriptive word index method.** This index is included in each West digest. Other digest series have similar indexes. Before you review the digest, brainstorm for words that might be indexed. You must separate the facts into various categories. These categories will assist you in brainstorming.

To categorize the materials, first review the facts. Select only the important or relevant facts. How do you determine which facts are relevant? Facts are relevant if they might have a bearing on the outcome of a case. These are facts that the courts will look at to make their determinations of the law.

Suppose that you are asked to research the claims a client might have against a supermarket for a slip-and-fall accident in a grocery store. In this case, your client slipped on a banana peel in the produce section of the supermarket while she was speaking on a cell phone.

First, determine what facts are legally relevant. How do you as a researcher make this determination? You must first determine the legal issues presented. Negligence is one theory. The question posed is: Was the store owner negligent? The second question to consider is: Was the woman also negligent? Negligence is a broad area of the law.

Next, you should brainstorm to develop a list of possible words to review in the digest. Brainstorming is important because a publisher might index a subject differently than you would index it. For example, slip-and-fall accidents at hotels or motels are not indexed under hotel or motel in the West digest. Instead, they are found under the topic Innkeepers.

Consider the people, the places, and the things involved in your case, as well as the basis for any action and any defenses. These are manageable categories. Consider also the relationships between people. In this case, we have a grocer and a patron. Next, think about the location of the incident. Where did the accident occur? It occurred in the produce section of a grocery store. Finally, determine what happened. A woman slipped on a banana peel while talking on a cell phone.

Next, develop a relationship between the facts to one another. For example, does the grocer owe a duty to his patron to prevent the patron from slipping and falling inside his store? Does the patron owe a duty to herself to ensure that she does not fall?

Once you have determined these relationships, you should find synonyms for the words you plan to research. Use a thesaurus or an encyclopedia to find synonyms and other additional search words. For example, *grocer* might be indexed, but other words might be used in its place. Try *store owner, market owner,* or *shopping center owner.* For *patron,* an index might contain the words *customer, shopper,* or *invitee,* a legal term of art. Cases may have dealt with a shop owner's liability for a slip-and-fall accident, but banana peels may not have been involved. Research slip-and-fall accidents that occurred on surfaces covered with food or other slippery items such as snow or water as well as those that occurred on dry surfaces.

Now frame the legal issues: Did the owner clean the floor? If so, did he do it in a timely fashion? Did the owner ensure his patrons' safety? Was the woman negligent because she walked while talking on her cell phone?

The results of your brainstorming session for the grocery slip and fall might be recorded as indicated in Illustration 4-4.

Once you have brainstormed, review the descriptive word index. Look under the most obvious topics first, such as negligence, slip and fall, customer, or grocery store. Once you have reviewed these words, the digest will lead you to topics and Key Numbers. See Illustration 4-5.

ILLUSTRATION 4-4. Results of Brainstorming Session

People or Parties	*Place*	*Things*
Customer	Grocery store	Banana peel
Patron	Shopping center	
Buyer	Supermarket	
Purchaser	Shop	
Shopper	Store	
Grocer		
Supermarket		
Grocery store		
Store		
Shop		
Shopping center		

Activity	*Action*	*Defense*
Slip	Negligence	Contributory negligence
Fall	Negligence	Comparative negligence

Illustration 4-5 is a sample page from *West's Illinois Digest 2d* Descriptive Word Index. Under the entries for *premises liability* and *stores and business proprietors,* you see a variety of subtopics such as Standard of Care and Insurer of Safety. Many of these subtopics refer you to the Negligence topic with the designation "Neglig." The number next to the topic designation is the Key Number. Under the subtopics Standard of Care and Insurer of Safety, the notation is "Neglig 1076." This topic and Key Number should have cases that are relevant. After reviewing this page, if you have access to current print materials you would retrieve the volume with the Negligence topic and Key Number and review a page similar to Illustration 4-3. Under Key Number 1076 in Illustration 4-3, you can find a case abstract that refers to headnote 1 of the *Thompson v. Economy Super Marts* case.

2. Topic Outline Method

▼ What Is the Topic Outline Method?

Another method you can use to locate cases in print is the **topic outline method.** If you were asked to research a slip-and-fall problem similar to the one noted above, you might already suspect that negligence is the designated topic. You then would find the negligence topic in the appropriate volume of the digest series. At the beginning of the topic, you would review a topic outline, which is similar to a table of contents. Review the outline and note the Key Numbers that might be relevant to your case. Note any related topics.

3. One Good Case Method

▼ What Is the One Good Case Method?

You also can use the **one good case method** to find cases when you already have found a case on point. If you have a West report of the case, the report will contain headnotes or abstracts with topic and Key Number designations. See Illustrations 3-5 and 3-6. Note the topic and Key Number designations for the points contained in the case that are relevant to your research; next, go to the relevant digest. For example, if you were researching an issue of federal law, you would review first the *Federal Practice Digest, 5th.* However, if you are researching a question of Massachusetts law, you should review *West's Massachusetts Digest.* Review the cases under the Negligence Key Number 1076. Case abstracts found in the *West's Massachusetts Digest* will be similar to those found in the *Illinois Digest* for the same Negligence Key Number. Review the case abstracts. The case abstracts contained in the digests will be identical to the headnotes. Compare Illustrations 3-5 and 4-3; note headnote 1 of the *Thompson* case and the case abstract on the digest page. They are identical.

ILLUSTRATION 4-5. Sample Page from *West's Illinois Digest 2d* Descriptive Word Index

---

66A Ill D 2d–45   **PREMISES**

References are to Digest Topics and Key Numbers

PREMISES LIABILITY—Cont'd
STATUS of entrant—Cont'd

Exceeding invitation or license, **Neglig** ⇔ 1052
Invitee. See subheading INVITEE, under this heading.
Licensee. See subheading LICENSEE, under this heading.
Rejection of status distinctions, **Neglig** ⇔ 1053
Relative degrees of care, **Neglig** ⇔ 1051
Standard of care dependent on status, **Neglig** ⇔ 1036
Trespasser. See subheading TRESPASSERS, under this heading.

STATUTES, **Neglig** ⇔ 1002

STATUTORY requirements,
Duty of care, **Neglig** ⇔ 1025
Safe workplace laws. See subheading SAFE workplace laws, under this heading.
Standard of care, **Neglig** ⇔ 1079
Violation of requirements in general,
Building and structures in general, **Neglig** ⇔ 1101
Firefighters, **Neglig** ⇔ 1210
Plaintiff's conduct or fault, **Neglig** ⇔ 1295
Police, **Neglig** ⇔ 1210
Stairs and ramps, hand and guard rails, **Neglig** ⇔ 1110(3)
Swimming pools, **Neglig** ⇔ 1129

STORE and business proprietors,
Breach of duty,
Criminal acts of third persons, **Neglig** ⇔ 1162
Displays and shelves, **Neglig** ⇔ 1119
Falling merchandise, **Neglig** ⇔ 1119
Third persons, acts of, **Neglig** ⇔ 1162
Business invitee. See subheading BUSINESS invitee, under this heading.
Duty of care,
Generally, **Neglig** ⇔ 1022-1024
Criminal acts of third persons, **Neglig** ⇔ 1024
Discovery, **Neglig** ⇔ 1023
Foreseeability, **Neglig** ⇔ 1022
Ice and snow, **Neglig** ⇔ 1022
Inspection, **Neglig** ⇔ 1023
Third persons, acts of, **Neglig** ⇔ 1024
Warning, **Neglig** ⇔ 1022
→ Standard of care,
Generally, **Neglig** ⇔ 1076-1078
Criminal acts of third persons, **Neglig** ⇔ 1078
Discovery, **Neglig** ⇔ 1077
Inspection, **Neglig** ⇔ 1077

PREMISES LIABILITY—Cont'd
STORE and business proprietors—Cont'd
Standard of care—Cont'd
Insurer of safety, **Neglig** ⇔ 1076   ←
Third persons, acts of, **Neglig** ⇔ 1078

STRICT liability,
Buildings and structures in general, **Neglig** ⇔ 1101
Floors, cleaning or waxing, **Neglig** ⇔ 1104(8)

STRUCTURAL work laws,
Safe workplace laws, **Neglig** ⇔ 1204(7)

SUBCONTRACTORS,
Construction, demolition and repairs, **Neglig** ⇔ 1205(9)
Injury or loss, **Neglig** ⇔ 1251

SUPPLIERS,
Construction, demolition and repairs, **Neglig** ⇔ 1205(10)

SWIMMING pools,
Attractive nuisance doctrine, **Neglig** ⇔ 1177
Breach of duty, **Neglig** ⇔ 1129
Complaint, **Neglig** ⇔ 1524(4)
Evidence,
Burden of proof, **Neglig** ⇔ 1565
Presumptions and inferences, **Neglig** ⇔ 1596
Weight and sufficiency, **Neglig** ⇔ 1671
Hotels and motels, **Inn** ⇔ 10
Jury instructions, **Neglig** ⇔ 1737
Jury questions and directing verdict, **Neglig** ⇔ 1709
Plaintiff's conduct or fault, **Neglig** ⇔ 1290
Proximate cause, **Neglig** ⇔ 1234
Violation of statutory requirements, **Neglig** ⇔ 1129

THEATERS. See heading **THEATERS AND SHOWS**, generally.

THIRD persons, acts of,
Breach of duty,
Generally, **Neglig** ⇔ 1161-1162
Store and business proprietors, **Neglig** ⇔ 1162
Duty of care,
Generally, **Neglig** ⇔ 1019
Store and business proprietors, **Neglig** ⇔ 1024
Plaintiff's conduct or fault, **Neglig** ⇔ 1292
Standard of care,
Generally, **Neglig** ⇔ 1070
Store and business proprietors, **Neglig** ⇔ 1078

Reprinted with permission of Thomson Reuters.

▼ Once You Have a Relevant Topic or Key Number,
What Comes Next?

Once you find a relevant topic and Key Number using any of these methods, then you can check that topic and Key Number in any update pamphlets called **pocket parts.** These are infrequently updated. The best next step is to review the Key Number or topic in an online database. For Key Numbers, that would be Westlaw. Lexis also allows you to search its topical classification system online.

PRACTICE POINTER

Never quote from headnotes in legal memoranda to an attorney or the court. These statements are not law.

PRACTICE POINTER

Because editors have different perspectives and each publisher highlights its own legal resources, headnotes for one case will differ between publishers.

C. ONLINE TOPICAL CLASSIFICATION SYSTEM RESEARCH

▼ Can Topical Classification Systems Be Searched Online?

You can search online for topics and Key Numbers on Westlaw only. However, topics and Lexis headnotes may be searched on Lexis through its topical classification system. Because Westlaw is a Thomson Reuters product, it has exclusive access to the Key Number system. Westlaw's online search tools allow researchers to use this Key Number system to access a broad range of cases. Researchers can use several different online search methods including some that are similar to the descriptive word index method, the topic outline method, and the one good case method.

1. Browse Topical Classifications

▼ How Do You Browse Topical Classifications Online?

The best way to search topical classification systems online is to draw from techniques used in both the descriptive word index and topic outline methods. First, you should brainstorm for words that might be used within the classification system. Use the strategy suggested in the descriptive word index method above. The next step is more akin to the topic outline method as it involves browsing the topics online.

To browse online for Key Numbers, you can access the West Key Number Digest on Westlaw. Westlaw provides an extensive listing of topics. See Illustrations 4-1 and 4-6. Topics such as Negligence have subtopics. You can easily expand the Negligence topic on the screen to view the subtopics with a simple mouse click. See an example of these expanded topics in Illustration 4-6. You can see the subtopic is Premises Liability and additional subtopics below that include Standard of Care with a Key Number range of k1030-k1079. Those Key Numbers deal with that topic. In a negligence case involving a slip and fall on a business premises or at a store, these would be relevant. Standard of care is the issue raised in the negligence case involving a slip and fall. You might search the Key Number 1076. Illustration 4-7 shows a PDF printout of the results of a search on Westlaw of the Key Number 1076 in Illinois. The jurisdiction is shown on the side of the illustration. Researchers can limit their searches to a particular jurisdiction.

Note that the headnote abstracts shown in Illustration 4-7 are similar to one another.

The West Key Number System® is altered frequently. When the headnote topics are revised, numbers change. For older cases, online cases will indicate the former Key Number. See Illustration 4-8. This illustration shows some of the *Thompson* case headnotes as shown on Westlaw. Note the headnote number 5. In the print case shown in

ILLUSTRATION 4-6.   Listing of Topics

ILLUSTRATION 4-7.   Westlaw: Results of Search

WESTLAW

NARROW:

Select Multiple Filters

Search within results

Key Number   Select

Jurisdiction
☐ Illinois   225

Date
All

Select Multiple Filters

Search other sources:
News
Dockets
Intellectual Property
Public Records
Company Investigator

Back to k1076 —In general

1076 —In general (225)
Jurisdiction: Illinois   Change

1 - 20   Sort by: Topic then Date ▼

☐ Select all items   No items selected

272 NEGLIGENCE (Up to 10,000)
  272XVII Premises Liability 5,330
    272XVII(C) Standard of Care 1,325
      272k1075 Care Required of Store and Business Proprietors 267
        272k1076 In general 225

☐   **1. Bulduk v. Walgreen Co.**
Appellate Court of Illinois, First District, First Division.   August 29, 2016   2015 IL App (1st) 150166-B

Headnote: Generally, a business operator owes its invitees a duty to exercise reasonable care in maintaining the premises in a reasonably safe condition for use by its invitees.

   Document Preview: TORTS - Premises Liability. Material fact issues as to whether cleaning machine in store was open and obvious precluded summary judgment.

☐   **2. Bulduk v. Walgreen Co.**
Appellate Court of Illinois, First District, First Division.   October 5, 2015   2015 IL App (1st) 150166

Headnote: Generally, a business operator owes its invitees a duty to exercise reasonable care in maintaining the premises in a reasonably safe condition for use by its invitees.
1 Case that cites this legal issue

   Document Preview: TORTS - Premises Liability. Issue of material fact as to whether cleaning machine in aisle of drug store was open and obvious danger precluded summary judgment.

☐   **3. Garest v. Booth**
Appellate Court of Illinois, First District, First Division.   May 19, 2014   2014 IL App (1st) 121045

Headnote: A person may be a business invitee of a landowner if: (1) the person enters by express or implied invitation; (2) the entry is connected with the owner's business or with an activity conducted by the owner of the land; and (3) the owner receives a benefit.

   Document Preview: TORTS - Premises Liability. Contractor owed duty of care to pedestrian only in the construction of building, not as a premises owner.

☐   **4. Hougan v. Ulta Salon, Cosmetics and Fragrance, Inc.**
Appellate Court of Illinois, Second District.   November 18, 2013   2013 IL App (2d) 130270

Headnote: A business owner generally has a duty to provide a reasonably safe means of ingress to and egress from the business.
3 Cases that cite this legal issue

   Document Preview: TORTS - Premises Liability. Store that leased property did not owe duty of care to patron standing on common area under exclusive control of lessor.

☐   **5. Marshall v. Burger King Corp.**
Supreme Court of Illinois.   June 22, 2006   222 Ill.2d 422

Headnote: Special relationship between a business invitor and invitee gives rise to an affirmative duty on the part of invitors to aid or protect invitees against unreasonable risk of physical harm; overruling Stutz v. Kamm, 204 Ill.App.3d 898, 149 Ill.Dec. 935, 562 N.E.2d 399. Restatement (Second) of Torts §§ 314A, 344.
10 Cases that cite this legal issue

   Document Preview: TORTS - Negligence. Restaurant owed duty to protect customers from unreasonable risk of physical harm posed by out-of-control cars.

ILLUSTRATION 4-7.   *Continued*

Westlaw

6. Marshall v. Burger King Corp.
Supreme Court of Illinois.   June 22, 2006   222 Ill.2d 422

Headnote: Fast food restaurant, an establishment open to the general public for business purposes, was in a special invitor-invitee relationship with its customers, giving rise to duty to aid or protect customers against unreasonable risk of physical harm.   Restatement (Second) of Torts §§ 314A, 344.

11 Cases that cite this legal issue

Document Preview: TORTS - Negligence. Restaurant owed duty to protect customers from unreasonable risk of physical harm posed by out-of-control cars.

7. Pageloff v. Gaumer
Appellate Court of Illinois, Third District.   April 19, 2006   365 Ill.App.3d 481

Headnote: The operator of a business owes his invitees a duty to exercise reasonable care to maintain his premises in a reasonably safe condition for use by the invitees.

1 Case that cites this legal issue

Document Preview: TORTS - Premises Liability. Campground owner owed no duty to customer who tripped on a walnut to keep ground clear of fallen walnuts.

8. Pageloff v. Gaumer
Appellate Court of Illinois, Third District.   April 19, 2006   365 Ill.App.3d 481

Headnote: Campground and its owner did not have a duty to keep the ground clear of fallen walnuts and, thus, could not be liable to camper who tripped on a walnut that fell from a tree near her campsite for breach of such a duty; camper was aware of the existence of the walnuts and of the tripping danger posed by them, burden of guarding against injury caused by fallen walnuts would be extremely onerous, and imposing such a burden on campground owner would, as a practical matter, result in an inability to have walnut trees near campgrounds.

1 Case that cites this legal issue

Document Preview: TORTS - Premises Liability. Campground owner owed no duty to customer who tripped on a walnut to keep ground clear of fallen walnuts.

9. Pageloff v. Gaumer
Appellate Court of Illinois, Third District.   April 19, 2006   365 Ill.App.3d 481

Headnote: Campground and its owner had no duty to warn camper who tripped on a walnut that fell from a tree near her campsite of the danger posed by walnuts and other items on the ground in wooded campgrounds; campground customers were already well aware of the potential for a trip or fall caused by stepping on such items.

Document Preview: TORTS - Premises Liability. Campground owner owed no duty to customer who tripped on a walnut to keep ground clear of fallen walnuts.

10. Green v. Jewel Food Stores, Inc.
Appellate Court of Illinois, First District, Second Division.   September 9, 2003   343 Ill.App.3d 830

Headnote: Duty of reasonable care of store owner, based on distraction exception to open and obvious rule, encompassed risk that customer, while exiting store, would be distracted by unattended shopping cart and trip and fall over irregular pavement.

4 Cases that cite this legal issue

Document Preview: TORTS - Negligence. Duty of reasonable care of store owner encompassed risk that customer would be distracted and fall.

11. Green v. Jewel Food Stores, Inc.
Appellate Court of Illinois, First District, Second Division.   September 9, 2003   343 Ill.App.3d 830

Headnote: A business operator generally owes his customers a duty to exercise reasonable care to maintain his premises in a reasonably safe condition.

2 Cases that cite this legal issue

Document Preview: TORTS - Negligence. Duty of reasonable care of store owner encompassed risk that customer would be distracted and fall.

12. Sameer v. Butt
Appellate Court of Illinois, First District, Fifth Division.   June 27, 2003   343 Ill.App.3d 78

Headnote: A tavern operator is not an insurer of its patrons.

Document Preview: REAL PROPERTY - Premises Liability. Stabbing of concert goer was not foreseeable despite similar stabbing minutes earlier.

ILLUSTRATION 4-7. *Continued*

Westlaw

☐ **13. Cobb v. Martin IGA & Frozen Food Center, Inc.**
Appellate Court of Illinois, Fifth District.   February 10, 2003   337 Ill.App.3d 306

Headnote: The general duty of reasonable care of possessor of land has toward its business invitees does not extend to all risks of harm encountered by invitees while on defendant's premises.   Restatement (Second) of Torts §§ 318, 344, 390.
1 Case that cites this legal issue

Document Preview: REAL PROPERTY - Premises Liability. Grocery store company had no duty to protect customer who was injured when child ran into her with cart.

☐ **14. Cobb v. Martin IGA & Frozen Food Center, Inc.**
Appellate Court of Illinois, Fifth District.   February 10, 2003   337 Ill.App.3d 306

Headnote: The duty owed by a possessor of land to a business invitee is not absolute.   Restatement (Second) of Torts §§ 318, 344, 390.
1 Case that cites this legal issue

Document Preview: REAL PROPERTY - Premises Liability. Grocery store company had no duty to protect customer who was injured when child ran into her with cart.

☐ **15. Friedman v. City of Chicago**
Appellate Court of Illinois, First District, Sixth Division.   September 6, 2002   333 Ill.App.3d 1070

Headnote: In an action based upon negligence, general rule regarding duty of a business occupier of any premises is that it must provide a reasonably safe means of ingress to and egress from premises, but ordinarily it will not be held liable for any injuries incurred on a public sidewalk under control of municipality, even though sidewalk may also be used for ingress or egress to premises.
5 Cases that cite this legal issue

Document Preview: TORTS - Negligence. Genuine issue of material fact precluded summary judgment in negligence action.

☐ **16. Salazar v. Crown Enterprises, Inc.**
Appellate Court of Illinois, First District, Second Division.   March 12, 2002   328 Ill.App.3d 735

Headnote: Store, tavern, or restaurant owners owe a duty of ordinary care to their business invitees.

Document Preview: REAL PROPERTY - Premises Liability. Owners of vacant building were not liable for homeless person's beating death.

☐ **17. Elizondo v. Ramirez**
Appellate Court of Illinois, Second District.   July 17, 2001   324 Ill.App.3d 67

Headnote: The relationship of business invitor and invitee did not exist between property owners and guest at party killed by another guest, although money was charged for attendance and 50 to 70 people attended, where party was not a business open to the public.

Document Preview: TORTS - Negligence. Party host and owners of apartment were not business invitors of guest killed at party.

☐ **18. Elizondo v. Ramirez**
Appellate Court of Illinois, Second District.   July 17, 2001   324 Ill.App.3d 67

Headnote: The relationship of business invitor and invitee, which imposes a duty of care, may arise where the owner or occupier of land holds the land open to the public for business purposes.

Document Preview: TORTS - Negligence. Party host and owners of apartment were not business invitors of guest killed at party.

☐ **19. Elizondo v. Ramirez**
Appellate Court of Illinois, Second District.   July 17, 2001   324 Ill.App.3d 67

Headnote: The collection of a small fee, by someone who, absent the fee, would otherwise clearly not be a business invitor, is insufficient to establish the special relationship of business invitor and invitee that would allow the imposition of negligence liability for the criminal acts of third parties.

Document Preview: TORTS - Negligence. Party host and owners of apartment were not business invitors of guest killed at party.

☐ **20. Elizondo v. Ramirez**
Appellate Court of Illinois, Second District.   July 17, 2001   324 Ill.App.3d 67

Westlaw

Headnote: To establish the relationship of business invitor-invitee sufficient to impose a duty to guard against the criminal acts of third parties, the premises involved must be a business open to the general public.

Document Preview: TORTS - Negligence. Party host and owners of apartment were not business invitors of guest killed at party.

ILLUSTRATION 4-8. West Key Number System: Revised and Former Key Number

Reprinted with permission of Thomson Reuters.

Illustration 3-5, the topic and Key Number are Negligence 121.1 (8). The online case shows the current topic and Key Number Negligence, but the Key Number is now 1594. If you searched that Key Number online in Illinois, Westlaw would show the *Thompson* case.

2. Words or Terms Search of Topical Classification Systems Online

Another way to search is to enter search terms in a publisher's search box as shown in Illustration 4-9. In this case, the search of the words "store owner duty of care to invitee" yields the negligence Key Numbers shown in the illustration, including Key Numbers 1076 and 1078. The results will show a list of cases similar to those found in Illustration 4-7. You can click on the cases to review them online. You can narrow your court decision search to one state, multiple states, all states, a federal circuit, multiple federal circuits, tax courts, military courts, federal district courts, bankruptcy courts, federal courts of appeals, the United States Supreme Court, or all federal courts.

Lexis also offers the ability to search by topics. One way to search is to use the Lexis search page. You can enter specific terms or you can select the natural language method. Using that method, a researcher can enter terms without using Lexis search connectors. The natural language search in Lexis will yield results similar in part to those found on Westlaw using the Key Numbers discussed above. Try this search on both Westlaw and Lexis and compare the results.

ILLUSTRATION 4-9.   Searching Terms in the Search Box

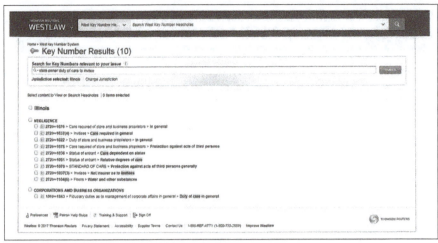

Reprinted with permission of Thomson Reuters.

3. One Good Case Method Online

▼ What Is the One Good Case Method Online?

Another method of locating a Key Number is similar to the one good case method used for the print digest. This type of search is particularly invaluable when you are undertaking research for a state case and you do not have access to that state's digest. Suppose you are presented with a slip-and-fall issue similar to the one discussed in the headnote of the *Thompson* case. You need to find Michigan cases, but you have only the *Thompson* case on point. You can use the Key Number you found in the *Thompson* case to search for the relevant Michigan case on the computer. In this case, it would be negligence Key Number 1708. If you search that Key Number and specify Michigan as the jurisdiction, you will see the results shown in Illustration 4-10. This illustration is a printout of the Michigan search results for Key Number 1708. Review the abstracts. You will see that they are similar to the legal issues presented in the *Thompson* case headnote 4.

Lexis also allows you to search by headnotes online. But the search is limited to Lexis-created headnotes and does not correspond to the West system.

ETHICS ALERT

Never cite to digests or portions of the digest abstracts. It is not a primary or secondary authority. Digests are merely finding tools to assist you as a researcher.

ILLUSTRATION 4-10.   Westlaw: Michigan Search Results for Key Number 1708

WESTLAW

NARROW:

Select Multiple Filters

Search within results

Key Number   Select

Jurisdiction
☐ Michigan   52

Date
All

Select Multiple Filters

Search other sources:
News
Dockets
Intellectual Property
Public Records
Company Investigator

Back to k1708 —Buildings and other structures

1708 —Buildings and other structures (52)
Jurisdiction: Michigan   Change

1 - 20   Sort by: Topic then Date ▼

☐ Select all items   No items selected

272 NEGLIGENCE **5.331**
  272XVIII Actions **1,696**
    272XVIII(D) Questions for Jury and Directed Verdicts **770**
      272⟞1708 Premises Liability **132**
        272⟞1708 Buildings and other structures. **52**

☐   **1. Clark v. Kmart Corp.**
Supreme Court of Michigan.   October 23, 2001   465 Mich. 416

Headnote: Evidence that check-out lane had been closed for about an hour before customer fell was sufficient to create jury question as to whether dangerous condition caused by grapes that were scattered on floor of lane, which condition led to customer's injury, existed for a sufficient period of time to put store on constructive notice of the condition.
122 Cases that cite this legal issue

   Document Preview: REAL PROPERTY - Premises Liability. Evidence showing time grapes had been on floor prior to customer's fall created jury question as to store's liability.

☐   **2. Abke v. Vandenberg**
Court of Appeals of Michigan.   January 11, 2000   239 Mich.App. 359

Headnote: Whether allegedly dangerous condition presented by loading dock and truck bay in dark area of retail produce outlet's supply barn was open and obvious, and, even if condition was open and obvious, whether condition was unreasonably dangerous, so that business operator had duty to warn invitee of condition, were questions for jury in action brought by customer for injuries sustained when he fell off dock into truck bay while being led through supply barn.
23 Cases that cite this legal issue

   Document Preview: REAL PROPERTY - Premises Liability. Whether danger posed by loading dock in merchant's storage barn was open and obvious was jury issue.

☐   **3. Knight v. Gulf & Western Properties, Inc.**
Court of Appeals of Michigan.   September 21, 1992   196 Mich.App. 119

Headnote: Whether warehouse owner breached duty owed to real estate agent was question for jury in real estate agent's premises liability action against owner arising from real estate agent's fall off interior loading dock after showing vacant warehouse on behalf of potential buyers; real estate agent presented sufficient evidence to establish that owner had duty to warn real estate agent of dangers inside warehouse or to take other precautions to protect him against harm from those dangers and, in light of real estate agent's awareness of inadequate interior lighting and interior loading dock, it was for jury to decide whether owner should have reasonably anticipated that real estate agent would choose to proceed even when confronted by the obvious danger.
7 Cases that cite this legal issue

   Document Preview: PREMISES LIABILITY - Open and Obvious Danger. Evidence could not support finding that real estate agent encountered known or obvious danger and, thus, premises owner was not entitled to special open and obvious danger instructions.

☐   **4. Constantineau v. DCI Food Equipment, Inc.**
Court of Appeals of Michigan.   August 17, 1992   195 Mich.App. 511

Headnote: Evidence in premises liability case raised fact issue for jury as to whether business invitee who was injured when he slipped on dangerous staircase moved inside owner's building with permission and while accompanied by owner, or whether he ventured into parts of building without permission or invitation and became trespasser.
3 Cases that cite this legal issue

   Document Preview: PREMISES LIABILITY - Invitees. Business invitee could become trespasser by venturing into area without permission.

ILLUSTRATION 4-10. *Continued*

5. Berryman v. K Mart Corp.
Court of Appeals of Michigan.   February 18, 1992   193 Mich.App. 88

Headnote: Whether store owner owed customer duty, whether owner breached that duty by creating condition that was dangerous, whether condition caused customer's injury, and whether she suffered damages presented questions for jury in customer's negligence action against owner for injuries sustained in slip-and-fall, given customer's testimony that she had fallen on wet spot on floor in store, that she observed after she fell that floor was streaky, as if it had been mopped, and that there were no signs or warnings that floor was wet, and that she later saw store employee with mop and bucket, and owner admitted that his premises were maintained solely by its employees.
24 Cases that cite this legal issue

Document Preview: Customer and spouse brought action against store owner to recover for injuries sustained by customer in slip-and-fall accident and to recover for loss of consortium.   The Wayne Circuit Court, Samuel A. Turner, J., directed verdict for store owner, and customer and spouse appealed.   The Court of Appeals, Connor, J., held that: (1) negligence and loss of consortium claims presented questions for jury; (2) spouse did not have to testify in support of loss of consortium claims; and (3) refusal to permit expert to testify was abuse of discretion. Reversed and remanded.

6. Evans v. Johnson
Court of Appeals of Michigan.   February 6, 1984   131 Mich.App. 776

Headnote: In a slip and fall case brought against executor of estate of deceased lessee and operator of bar, question of whether at time of plaintiff's injury executor had been operating the bar long enough to have become aware of alleged defect on the premises allegedly giving rise to the injury, and was thus legally chargeable, instead of the estate, with failure to exercise due care, was a question for jury.

Document Preview: In a slip and fall case, plaintiff brought action against executor of estate of deceased lessee and operator of bar, alleging that her injuries resulted from defects on the premises. The Detroit Common Pleas Court, Arthur Bowman, J., entered judgment for the executor on a jury verdict of no cause of action, and plaintiff appealed. The Wayne Circuit Court, Henry J. Szymanski, J., affirmed the judgment, and plaintiff appealed by leave granted. The Court of Appeals, Allen, J., held that: (1) executor, who was in control and possession of the premises at the time the injury occurred, was personally liable if he had been in control and possession of the premises long enough to have become aware, or long enough for a reasonable person to become aware, of the alleged defect, and (2) whether executor had been operating the bar long enough to have become aware of the defect, and thus to be chargeable, in place of the estate, with failure to exercise due care, was a question...

7. Ritter v. Meijer, Inc.
Court of Appeals of Michigan.   September 19, 1983   128 Mich.App. 783

Headnote: In personal injury action arising from slip and fall on grape in grocery store, fact that plaintiff described grape as being white and wet did not preclude presumption that it was dirty or partially discolored or withered, and trial court's denial of directed verdict at close of plaintiff's evidence could be sustained on basis of such presumption.
4 Cases that cite this legal issue

Document Preview: In personal injury action arising from slip and fall on grape in grocery store, the Oakland Circuit Court, Hilda R. Gage, J., denied grocery store's motion for directed verdict at close of plaintiffs' evidence, and subsequently entered judgment on jury verdict for plaintiff, and store appealed. The Court of Appeals held that: (1) finding that plaintiff had made a prima facie case could be sustained, and (2) evidence that grape had previously been slapped on sufficiently established that it had been there long enough to give store actual or constructive notice. Affirmed.

8. Gage v. Ford Motor Co.
Court of Appeals of Michigan.   December 3, 1980   102 Mich.App. 310

Headnote: Whether defendant owned and maintained faulty scale and whether defendant exercised its duty as an invitor to exercise reasonable care not to injure plaintiff's decedent and to warn decedent of latent dangers of which it knew or reasonably should have known was question of fact for jury in action for fatal injuries sustained by decedent while standing on scale.

Document Preview: Suit was instituted for fatal injuries sustained by plaintiff's decedent while standing on a scale at defendant's steel plant. The Circuit Court, Wayne County, Joseph B. Sullivan, J., entered judgment on verdict in favor of plaintiff, and defendant appealed. The Court of Appeals held that: (1) contract whereby employer of plaintiff's decedent was permitted to remove steel wastes or slag from a steel plant owned by defendant was a license or permit, rather than a lease, and did not absolve defendant from liability for injury sustained by plaintiff's decedent, where it was evident that use of property by decedent's employer was dependent on continuance of slag operation and that employer could use property only for that purpose, consideration was measured on a per-pound basis, rather than a monthly or annual lease, and defendant was permitted to enter land and to give decedent's employer instruction on how to keep it safe; and (2) whether defendant...

9. Florence v. Wm. Moors Concrete Products, Inc.
Court of Appeals of Michigan, Division No. 1.   August 30, 1971   35 Mich.App. 613

Headnote: Evidence of negligence of building owner and engineer was sufficient to present jury issue in death action arising from collapse of floor composed of preformed concrete planks.

ILLUSTRATION 4-10. *Continued*

Document Preview: Wrongful death action. The Circuit Court, Wayne County, Thomas J. Foley, J., entered judgment for defendants and plaintiffs appealed. The Court of Appeals, Holbrook, J., held, inter alia, that plaintiffs were entitled to be present during rereading of charge to jury. Reversed and remanded.

10. Hall v. Wood
Court of Appeals of Michigan, Division No. 3. August 25, 1970 26 Mich.App. 135

Headnote: In suit by repairman and his wife against tavern proprietors and others to recover for the injuries repairman sustained when, while at tavern to pick up a cash register in need of repair, he fell through open trap door in backroom of tavern, the record raised several questions of fact (including whether repairman made careful observations while in the backroom, the amount of illumination in the room, and whether the open trap door should have been obvious to a person using ordinary care) requiring determination by a jury of both the alleged negligence of defendants and contributory negligence of the repairman.

Document Preview: Suit by repairman and his wife against tavern proprietors and others to recover for the injuries repairman sustained when, while at the tavern to pick up a cash register in need of repair, he fell through an open trap door in a backroom of the tavern. The Calhoun County Circuit Court, Ronald M. Ryan, J., entered judgment in favor of defendants, and plaintiffs appealed. The Court of Appeals, Byrns, J., held that the record raised several questions of fact (including whether repairman made careful observations while in the backroom, the amount of illumination in the room, and whether the open trap door should have been obvious to a person using ordinary care) requiring determination by a jury of both the alleged negligence of defendants and contributory negligence of the repairman. Judgment affirmed.

11. Preston v. Sleziak
Court of Appeals of Michigan, Division No. 3. February 24, 1969 16 Mich.App. 18

Headnote: Evidence in action by social guests for injuries sustained when homemade elevator broke presented jury question as to whether defendants had failed properly to inspect or test elevator.

Document Preview: Action by social guests against host for injuries sustained when homemade elevator broke. The Circuit Court, Kent County, Stuart Hoffius, J., rendered judgment on verdict for defendants, and plaintiffs appealed. The Court of Appeals, R. B. Burns, P.J., held that plaintiffs were invitees, and that instruction that guests were licensees whom defendant had only duty not to injure by active or affirmative negligence and to warn of any dangers which guests were not likely to discover was erroneous. Reversed and remanded.

12. Serinto v. Borman Food Stores
Supreme Court of Michigan. May 6, 1968 380 Mich. 637

Headnote: Testimony of grocery store customer that she had been in store 45 or 50 minutes without hearing any sound resembling a jar breaking prior to the time she slipped and fell on broken jar of mayonnaise in aisle was insufficient to justify submitting to jury the question of whether store owner had constructive notice of existence of broken jar on aisle floor.
13 Cases that cite this legal issue

Document Preview: Action by store customer for damages sustained in fall on store floor and by her husband for medical expenses, and for loss of services and consortium. The Circuit Court, Wayne County, Halford I. Streeter, J., entered a judgment for the customer and her husband and the store owner appealed. The Court of Appeals, 3 Mich.App. 163, 142 N.W.2d 32, reversed and leave was granted to appeal. The Supreme Court, Kelly, J., held that proprietor of store is liable for injury to customer resulting from unsafe condition in store, though not caused by his employees' negligence, if condition is known or has existed long enough that it should have been known to proprietor, but evidence of owner's constructive notice of broken jar was insufficient to warrant submitting the question to jury. Affirmed. Adams, O'Hara, and Kavanagh, JJ., dissented.

13. Fries v. Merkley
Court of Appeals of Michigan, Division No. 2. November 21, 1967 8 Mich.App. 177

Headnote: Under evidence that owners of dairy receiving plant failed to remove butter fat-soap solution from plant floor, that owners failed to provide adequate lighting and that they failed to provide safety device or services as was common throughout dairy industry, question of owners' negligence was for jury in action by motor truck hauler of raw milk for injuries sustained in fall on owners' premises.

Document Preview: Action by motor truck hauler of bulk raw milk against owners of dairy receiving plant for injuries sustained when hauler slipped and fell on butter fat-soap solution on plant floor. The Circuit Court of Genesee County, Stewart A. Newblatt, J., rendered judgment in favor of the hauler and the plant owners appealed. The Court of Appeals, McGregor, J., held that under evidence that owners of dairy receiving plant failed to remove butter fat-soap solution from plant floor, that owners failed to provide adequate lighting and that they failed to provide safety device or services as was common throughout dairy industry, question of owners' negligence was for jury. Affirmed.

14. Pollack v. Oak Office Bldg.
Court of Appeals of Michigan, Division No. 1. June 27, 1967 7 Mich.App. 173

Headnote: Although evidence of slipperiness of floor alone is insufficient to establish liability for injury sustained in fall on floor, evidence of excessive oil or wax, skid marks, or soiled clothes will constitute sufficient evidence to give rise to factual question proper for jury determination.
4 Cases that cite this legal issue

ILLUSTRATION 4-10. *Continued*

Document Preview: Negligence action for injuries resulting from slipping and falling on allegedly excessively waxed hallway floor in defendant's building. The Circuit Court, Wayne County, George E. Bowles, J., after jury verdict for plaintiff, denied defendant's motion for judgment non obstante veredicto or for new trial, and defendant appealed. The Court of Appeals, Holbrook, J., held that evidence sustained jury verdict finding defendant building owner guilty of negligence concerning excessively waxed hallway floor resulting in fall and injury to plaintiff office worker. Affirmed.

15. McCord v. U.S. Gypsum Co.
Court of Appeals of Michigan, Division No. 1.   November 9, 1966   5 Mich.App. 126

Headnote: Conflicting testimony as to visibility of skylight on roof through which invitee fell presented fact question for jury.
1 Case that cites this legal issue

Document Preview: Action for resultant injuries when independent contractor's employee stepped on skylight on roof and fell 30 or 40 feet to floor below. The Circuit Court, Wayne County, Charles Kaufman, J., entered judgment upon verdict for plaintiff, and defendant appealed. The Court of Appeals, Gillis, J., held, inter alia, that conflicting testimony as to visibility of skylight on roof through which invitee fell presented question of fact for jury. Judgment affirmed.

16. Serinto v. Borman Food Stores
Court of Appeals of Michigan, Division No. 1.   May 11, 1966   3 Mich.App. 183

Headnote: Evidence in case involving fall on a broken jar of mayonnaise by customer in store was insufficient to raise a question of fact as to store's notice of the dangerous condition, so that court erred in submitting the question to the jury.
6 Cases that cite this legal issue

Document Preview: Action by customer and her husband against store for injuries sustained in a fall. The Circuit Court, Wayne County, Halford I. Streeter, J., found for customer, and appeal was taken. The Court of Appeals, Watts, J., held that evidence in case involving fall on a broken jar of mayonnaise by customer in store was insufficient to raise a question of fact as to store's notice of the dangerous condition, so that court erred in submitting the question to the jury. Reversed. Lesinski, C.J., dissented.

17. Miller v. Miller
Supreme Court of Michigan.   September 2, 1964   373 Mich. 519

Headnote: Evidence, in action by social guest for injuries sustained when she fell down a stairway after defendant husband advised her to kick open a stuck door in his home, presented questions for the jury as to whether plaintiff was a gratuitous invitee, as to whether the sticking door was a dangerous defect likely to be undiscovered by plaintiff, as to whether defendants were negligent in failing to disclose such defect if any, and as to whether defendant husband was negligent in advising plaintiff to kick the door.
6 Cases that cite this legal issue

Document Preview: Action for personal injuries sustained by social guest when she fell down a stairway after defendant husband advised her to kick open a stuck door in his home. The Circuit Court, Bay County, Richard G. Smith, J., entered judgment for defendants and plaintiff appealed. The Supreme Court, Souris, J., held that evidence presented questions for the jury as to whether plaintiff was a gratuitous invitee, as to whether the sticking door was a dangerous defect, likely to be undiscovered by plaintiff, as to whether defendants were negligent in failing to disclose such defect if any, and as to whether defendant husband was negligent in advising plaintiff to kick the door. Reversed and remanded. Kelly, Dethmers and O'Hara, JJ., dissented.

18. Sparks v. Luplow
Supreme Court of Michigan.   December 27, 1963   372 Mich. 198

Headnote: Evidence raised jury question as to whether storekeeper was negligent in not seeing and removing banana from floor prior to plaintiff's fall.
7 Cases that cite this legal issue

Document Preview: Action for injuries sustained by the plaintiff as the result of a fall in a store. The Circuit Court, Saginaw County, Eugene Snow Huff, J., rendered judgment on a verdict for the plaintiffAnd the defendant appealed. The Supreme Court, Kavanagh, J., held that evidence raised jury questions as to whether storekeeper was negligent in not seeing and removing banana from the floor prior to plaintiff's fall and as to whether plaintiff was contributorily negligent in not observing the banana before stepping on it. Affirmed.

19. DeSmit v. J.C. Penney Co.
Supreme Court of Michigan.   March 8, 1963   369 Mich. 527

Headnote: Whether slope of terrazzo entryway to defendant's department store became insecure in the windy, snowy and cold weather on morning that pedestrian fell while leaving store, whether defendant was knowledgeably forewarned of condition, whether pedestrian of ordinary prudence might not have known that sloping terrazzo surface when wet or icy becomes inordinately slippery, whether defendant took all indicated measures necessary and whether defendant was negligent and plaintiff was contributorily negligent were jury questions.
2 Cases that cite this legal issue

ILLUSTRATION 4-10. *Continued*

> **Document Preview:** Action for injuries sustained by plaintiff when leaving defendant's store. The Circuit Court, Kalamazoo County, Lucien F. Sweet, J., entered judgment for plaintiff and defendant appealed. The Supreme Court held that whether slope of terrazzo entryway to defendant's department store became insecure in windy, snowy and cold weather on morning that pedestrian fell while leaving store, whether defendant was knowledgeably forewarned of condition, whether pedestrian of ordinary prudence might not have known that sloping terrazzo surface when wet or icy becomes inordinately slippery, whether defendant took all indicated measures necessary, and whether defendant was negligent and plaintiff was contributorily negligent were jury questions. Affirmed.
>
> **20. Ackerberg v. Muskegon Osteopathic Hospital**
> Supreme Court of Michigan.   May 18, 1962   366 Mich. 596
>
> **Headnote:** Evidence presented question for jury as to whether hospital had a duty to construct a guard or protection around rear platform used by general public entering and leaving emergency entrance of hospital in excited state, with respect to father who took his small daughter into emergency room and then walked out on emergency platform when he became dizzy and thereafter fell from the platform.
>
> 6 Cases that cite this legal issue
>
> **Document Preview:** Action against hospital for injuries sustained by father as result of a fall from platform located in front of emergency entrance. The Circuit Court, Muskegon County, Morris K. Davis, J., directed a verdict against the father, and the father appealed. The Supreme Court, Kavanagh, J., held that the evidence presented a question for the jury as to whether the hospital had a duty to construct a guard or a protection around the rear platform used by the general public entering and leaving emergency entrance of hospital in excited state, with respect to father who took his small daughter into emergency room and then walked out on emergency platform when he became dizzy and thereafter fell from the platform. Order reversed and case remanded.

Reprinted with permission of Thomson Reuters.

CHAPTER SUMMARY

In this chapter, you learned about digests that can assist you in locating similar cases on point. The digests are tied to the commercial reporters' headnotes that contain case abstracts concerning a point of law raised in a case. Each headnote contains a topic and a number that refer you to a topical system for finding additional similar cases. West's National Reporter System® is linked to its digest system both in print and online. This system enables researchers to find applicable topics in one state and review the same topics in a different state digest to find similar cases. The online databases also allow researchers to research multiple states.

When you research a legal issue in a digest, you can review its index to find a relevant topic and number that directs you to cases on point. In the West system, the numbers are called Key Numbers. Another method for using the digest is to review the outline presented before each topic. You also might find a good case on point and locate other similar cases by using the digest topic and numbers listed in the publisher's headnotes that appear at the beginning of a case reporter.

In the next chapter, you will learn how to ensure that the cases you found are good law.

KEY TERMS

descriptive word index method
digests
headnotes
one good case method

pocket parts
topic outline method
West American Digest System
West Key Number System®

EXERCISES

SELF-ASSESSMENT
COMPUTER EXERCISES FOR DIGEST TOPICS

1. Search for Negligence Key Number 1076, cases in all 50 states. Print the search and the first page of the citation list of the cases.
2. Prepare and list a headnote search of topic Bankruptcy 3079 in Minnesota. Print your search and the first page of the list of cases you find.
3. Find 713 N. E2d 1285. What are the topic number and Key Number for headnote 2?
4. Find 984 F.2d 214 on Westlaw.
   a. What is the name of the case?
   b. Who are the plaintiffs?
   c. Who are the defendants?
   d. What are the topic number and Key Number for headnote number 4?
   e. What is the former Key Number for that headnote?
   f. Is the appellee's brief for this case available on Westlaw? If so, how would you find it?
5. Find 2013 WL 6452336.
   a. What is the name of the case?
   b. Who are the plaintiffs?
   c. Who are the defendants?
   d. Who is the deciding judge?
   e. What headnote involves the topic 272k1076?

PRACTICE SKILLS

6. Research the following issue in the appropriate print digest if possible, online on Westlaw, and on Lexis. Your firm's client was fired from her job because she was 69 years old. She had worked for 40 years in this position. When she was fired, she was replaced with a 25-year-old woman. Your firm's client has a master's degree; the 25-year-old has a bachelor's degree. You only need to consider what federal law claims she might have against her former employer. Her case would be brought in the U.S. District Court for the Northern District of Ohio. *Brainstorm:* What words would you review? What topics and Key Numbers did you find? List them. List two relevant cases.

7. You must determine whether a former employee can assert the attorney-client privilege in your state when a third party, not the former employee, brings an action against the former employer. *Brainstorm:* What words would you review? What topics and Key Numbers did you find? List them and the source. List two relevant cases.

8. Read the following fact situation. Answer the questions following the situation.

FACTS

Nate Late, a business owner, has two partners in the operation of Loose Cannon Manufacturing in Gurnee, Illinois. He owns 33 percent of a $3 million company. Late is ill, but not dying. He is grooming a 26-year-old, Ivan T. All, to run the business. He tells his family he likes All and wants to teach him the business. Nate Late dies.

The most current will leaves Late's estate to his wife of 24 years, Shirley Late, and his only son, Lou Sier. Mr. All tells Mrs. Late that her husband told All he intended to give the 26-year-old his one-third interest in Loose Cannon. This conversation took place in front of a bank president. No written record exists concerning Late's intention to give his stock to All. However, family members knew that Late intended for All to run the business and for All to get something if the business was sold. None of the family believed that Late intended to give the business to newcomer Ivan T. All. Late's shares of stock were never given to All. The shares were in the safety deposit box shared by Late and his wife.

Mrs. Late said that Mr. Late planned to give her the shares. He told her this when he opened the joint safety deposit box and gave her the key.

You work for a firm that has been retained by Mrs. Late. She would like to know if All can prove that Mr. Late gave All Mr. Late's interest in the company.

DIGEST QUESTIONS

a. What digest is appropriate for this problem?
b. How would you find the appropriate digest topics? Note in detail two methods for finding the appropriate digest topics. Next, review two topics.
c. What topics did you review?
d. Did you find additional topics that should be reviewed? If so, review those now.
e. What topics and Key Numbers are relevant to this problem?
f. Find these topics and Key Numbers online on Westlaw. List them.
g. Review the case abstracts listed under one of the topics and Key Numbers for your jurisdiction. Which cases are relevant? Review two cases.
h. What relevant topics did you find in the Lexis topical classification system? How did you find them?
i. Using Lexis, find one relevant case in your jurisdiction.

VALIDATING

CHAPTER OVERVIEW

This chapter teaches you how to ensure that a case that you find is good law and how to find additional cases using citators. To ensure that a case is current or is still good law, you must validate or update your research findings. A case is good law if its ruling has not been reversed or overruled by another court's decision. Validating or Shepardizing, as it is commonly called, is one of the most important tasks you must do as a researcher. It is also referred to as cite checking. To do this, you must review citators.

A. *SHEPARD'S*®

▼ What Is a Citator?

Citators are services that note when a court has mentioned or relied on a case. They also note when a law or statute is mentioned. The citator may be found on the computer or in print, however, print citators are not used very often. Most law firms and libraries no longer subscribe to these print resources. In addition, some states require that online resources be used to supplement any print citator research. To ensure that an authority is current, online citators must be reviewed. The *Shepard's* **citator system** has long been one of the most pervasive. It can be accessed through Lexis. KeyCite is a well-regarded and widely used citator offered by Westlaw. Fastcase has a citator called Authority Check. Attorneys, practitioners, and paralegals often use one or more of these citators. However, some may use one of the other available citators. Check with attorneys in your firm to determine which citators to use. Once you learn how to use one service, you will be able to master another easily.

Citators are used to validate an authority such as a case. In addition, you can use them to locate relevant primary authorities, including cases and statutes, and secondary authorities, such as law review articles that may assist you in finding additional primary authorities or in understanding the legal issues presented in your research. You also can review citators to determine the direct history of a case. This history describes the progress of a specific case and all the decisions made by different courts pertaining to it.

▼ Why Use *Shepard's*?

Shepard's can be used to research almost every federal and state case reported in print in the past 200 years. It includes some cases considered unreported because they only appear online. Among the authorities that can be Shepardized are cases, statutes, constitutions, codes, jury instructions, administrative decisions, copyrights, trademarks, patents, and regulations, as well as secondary authorities including Restatements. More information about Shepardizing statutes can be found in Chapter 7 and updating regulations is covered in Chapter 9.

▼ What Information Does *Shepard's* Provide for Researchers and How Do You Use *Shepard's* Online?

Shepard's provides a list of parallel citations and the history of the case you are reviewing. The **case history** explains whether the case has been appealed and the results of that appeal. If it is a trial court case, *Shepard's* indicates whether it was appealed and lists the appellate citation.

The biggest benefit of *Shepard's* is that it provides a detailed report of all Lexis cases that mention or cite the case you are Shepardizing or reviewing.

You can access *Shepard's* online at Lexis during any point in your research. Various methods are available to access *Shepard's* with the click of a button. You also can enter shep: and the citation in the search bar. It cannot be accessed through Westlaw. When you are reviewing a case, a *Shepard's* preview box is shown on the side of the screen. This preview box provides a summary of the treatments of decisions that cite the decision you are viewing. See Illustration 5-1. These treatments are represented by graphics called *Shepard's* signals. For Shepard's case reports, the following signals are used.

ILLUSTRATION 5-1.   Lexis: Screen Shot of the Top of the *Thompson* Case

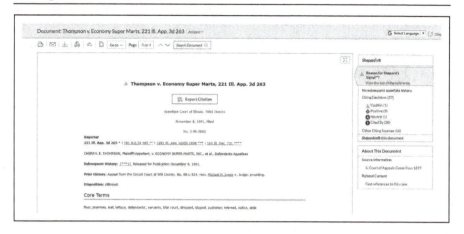

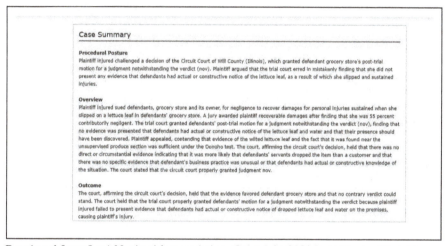

- A red stop sign warns researchers that a case may be overruled in whole or in part. This also indicates that the case may have been superseded, or departs from the case you are Shepardizing without explicitly overruling the case.
- An orange "Q" indicates that a portion of the case has been questioned by a court—meaning that the validity or precedential value of the case is in question.
- A yellow triangle cautions the researcher about a case's negative history. This means that a case may have been criticized by a court, limited, modified, corrected, or clarified.
- A green diamond with a plus sign indicates that the case has received positive treatment from a citing court. This type of treatment could be that the court affirmed the case or followed it.

- An "A" in a blue octagon indicates that the citing case reference is a neutral treatment but it interprets or clarifies the case being Shepardized.
- An "I" in a blue octagon indicates that the case was cited, but that the case did not merit analysis.

Within this preview box, you can see how many cases have been designated as negative, positive, or neutral types of treatments. *Shepard's* also will designate what its editors consider to be top citing references. *Shepard's* is designed to allow you to easily access the cases selected as top citing references. *Shepard's* reports feature the Reason for the Shepard's Signal.™ It provides researchers with the citing reference that had the most influence on the Shepard's Signal designation. Illustration 5-2 is an example of such a report. A recent *Shepard's* enhancement, Shepard's® At Risk indicator identifies when a specific point of law in a case is at risk of being overruled. Such cases are marked with "At Risk."

Although these signals can guide you in your legal research, you must determine for yourself whether a case is still good law. A case may not be good law concerning one point of law; however, you still need to determine whether that point concerns the issue you are researching. To thoroughly do your job as a researcher, you need to read the case yourself.

When you are reviewing the *Shepard's* report itself—see Illustration 5-3, the *Shepard's* report for the *Thompson* case shown in Illustrations 3-5 and 3-6—*Shepard's* indicates all of the cases that mention the case you are Shepardizing. You also can filter results by headnote, court, court's analysis, type of motion, or timeframe. The *Shepard's* screen shows tabs

ILLUSTRATION 5-2.   Reason for Shepard's Signal

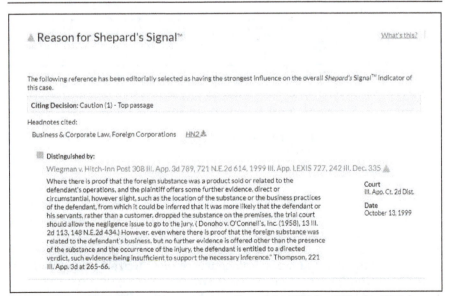

ILLUSTRATION 5-3. *Shepard's* Report of the *Thompson* Case

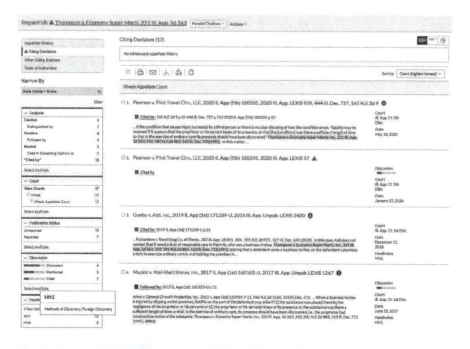

ILLUSTRATION 5-3.   *Continued*

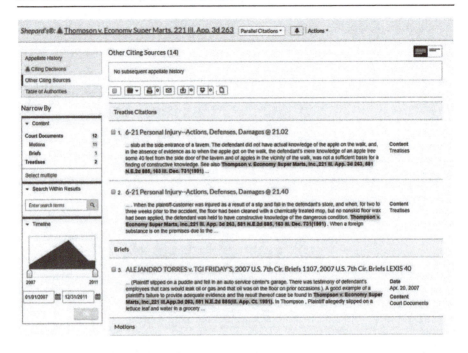

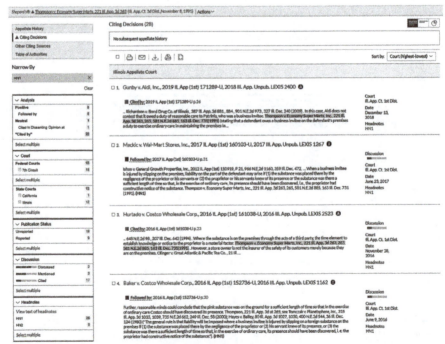

similar to those found when using Internet search engines. In addition to the tab of citing cases, there is a tab for Other Citing Sources that includes secondary sources such as treatises and Restatements that can be easily accessed through the link provided and a tab for the Table of Authorities—a list of cases cited in the case you are Shepardizing.

At the top of the *Shepard's* result for the *Thompson* case is a yellow triangle. That triangle indicates that a researcher should use caution before relying on the *Thompson* case. That is because of the possible negative treatment of this case. In addition to the preview box, a flag is placed next to the name of the *Thompson* case in Illustration 5-1. That flag is yellow and indicates researchers should be cautious when citing the *Thompson* case.

After you retrieve the *Shepard's* report of citing cases, you will be able to perform searches to narrow your results or use the set filters *Shepard's* provides. Review the left side of each of the pages in Illustration 5-3. You can see the set filters *Shepard's* provides. You can filter the *Shepard's* report so that you retrieve only the cases that have a negative impact on your case. You also can retrieve cases that contain only a particular headnote or those decided by a specific court. You also may filter your search results to include a particular jurisdiction, published or unpublished status, headnote, vital points of law, or fact patterns, dates, or other *Shepard's* treatments such as *followed by* or *overruled*. The first screen shot of Illustration 5-3 shows a partial report called citing decisions. The report is a list of decisions that cite the *Thompson* case. The second page of Illustration 5-3 also shows citing decisions but limits the results to cases decided by the Illinois appellate court. The third screen shot of Illustration 5-3 shows a partial report of other citing sources. Those sources may include treatises or court documents such as motions and briefs. The fourth page of Illustration 5-3 is a partial report of citing decisions limited to cases that apply to headnote 1 of the *Thompson* case. Another type of search you can perform is to seek opinions by a particular judge. You also can narrow the result to search for briefs, pleadings, or motions.

Shepard's also will provide a graphic of trends in courts' treatment of a case that may indicate that a case may not be good law. This view can be accessed by clicking on the Grid View. See Illustration 5-4. You can get an overview of the analysis by court or by date. Again, with a simple click, you can access cases with a specific treatment.

Shepard's also provides links to other citing references such as treatises. *Shepard's* also allows you to immediately access the citing cases and other references online by clicking the hyperlinked number.

PRACTICE POINTER

Note that the *Shepard's* citations are not *Bluebook* abbreviations for the reporters and that the number for each series is placed on top of the reporter abbreviations.

ILLUSTRATION 5-4.   Example of the Grid View for the
Thompson **Case**

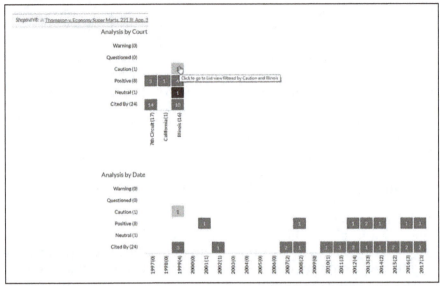

ETHICS ALERT

Some courts may sanction attorneys if they provide cases that are no longer good law to support their claims. Disciplinary action may be taken against an attorney who fails to use online resources to validate an authority.

Shepard's Alerts provide information about changes to a *Shepard's* report of a particular case. These alerts are e-mailed to researchers at whatever interval the user specifies. These alerts can be tailored to provide specific information only, such as the negative treatment of a case or changes to the citation. To receive this, you set up a *Shepard's* alert online. It can be done by clicking "*Shepard's* Alert" found within the *Shepard's* report.

B. KEYCITE

Westlaw provides a service called **KeyCite** that competes with *Shepard's*. KeyCite, however, is not offered in print. KeyCite provides the direct history of a case as well as any case that affects the precedential value of a case. This information is listed under the "History" tab. KeyCite retrieves all citing references that are contained within Westlaw, including thousands of unpublished decisions as well as published cases, secondary sources, appellate briefs, trial motions, memoranda, and affidavits. Review the screen shots of the KeyCite report of the *Thompson* case in Illustration 5-5. There is a flag on the top far left. Online you would see that the color is yellow. Now review the Westlaw PDF report of the *Thompson* case in Illustration 3-6. At the top of the case in the left-hand corner is a yellow flag and the words "negative treatment." This summarizes why the case has a yellow flag and quickly alerts researchers that citing this case may be a problem.

On the top left side of the first screen shot of Illustration 5-5 it states that this KeyCite report shows a list of citing references. In this case, it says 29 cases cite the *Thompson* case. Citing sources are listed on the left side with a number next to these sources that include secondary sources, appellate court documents, and trial court orders and documents. On the left side of the screen shot shown in Illustration 5-5, you can see the options for narrowing this KeyCite search. On the side of the report as shown in the second screen shot of Illustration 5-5, you can select one or more of those items to review. On that page, the box for reported cases is selected so the results show only reported cases that cite to the *Thompson* case. In the third screen shot of the same illustration, the search of the KeyCite report for *Thompson* is limited to secondary sources that cite to the case. You also can filter your request by court, by date, by headnote, by type of documents, or by treatments. Similar to *Shepard's*, KeyCite displays different tabs to allow you to select the materials you would like to see. The KeyCite report contains the following tabs:

- History indicating the case history for the case that is the subject of the KeyCite.
- Citing references indicating all cases, trial court orders, administrative decisions, secondary sources, appellate court documents, and others that have cited the case that is the subject of the KeyCite.
- Negative Treatment shows all of the cases that have provided a negative treatment of the case.
- Filings.
- Table of Authorities.

For example, the fourth screen shot of Illustration 5-5 shows the Negative Treatment tab for the *Thompson* case. When a report shows citing decisions such as the first two screen shots of Illustration 5-5, the KeyCite report indicates the treatment KeyCite's editors thought was merited based on the citing case's comments about the *Thompson* case. For example, the notation next to the first two cases indicates the case received negative treatments. You also can see that those two cases were distinguished from the *Thompson* case. It provides a citation for the citing case and a link to the full case. In addition, the KeyCite report shows the date of the case and indicates the West headnotes in the *Thompson* case that are referenced in the citing case. The fifth screen shot of Illustration 5-5 shows that eight cases cite to headnote 1 of the *Thompson* case.

KeyCite uses a system of colored flags to alert you to the history:

- A red case flag warns that the case is no longer good law for at least one of the points of law.
- A yellow flag warns that there is some negative treatment, but that the case has not been explicitly overruled or reversed.
- If a case has been appealed to the U.S. Court of Appeals or the U.S. Supreme Court, it will have a blue striped flag.

Note the flag at the top of the first page of Illustration 5-5. It is a yellow flag, which indicates that the case has some negative history. That negative treatment is shown in the listing of citing cases discussed above.

In addition, Westlaw has developed a more in-depth treatment indicator that involves green bars that note the depth of the treatment a court provides to a case. This treatment is noted in the column in Illustration 5-5 under Depth of Treatment. Four bars means that the case was examined. Three bars mean it was discussed, and two bars

ILLUSTRATION 5-5. KeyCite Report of *Thompson* Case

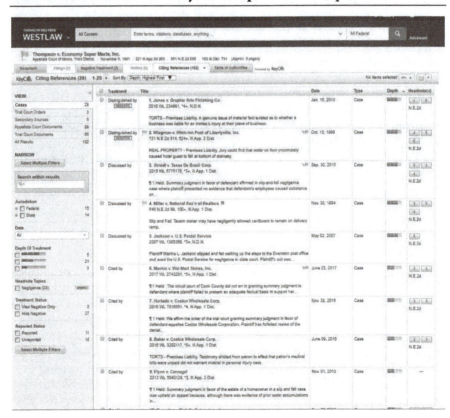

ILLUSTRATION 5-5. *Continued*

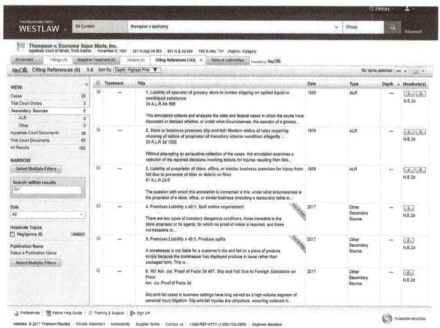

ILLUSTRATION 5-5. *Continued*

Reprinted with permission of Thomson Reuters.

indicate it was cited. One bar means that the case was mentioned. Westlaw's headnotes and topics and key numbers also are incorporated into the KeyCite display under the column "Headnotes."

KeyCite allows you to receive automatic status updates concerning cases. You can indicate how often you would like to be updated and results can be sent to you via e-mail. Also similar to *Shepard's,* you can save or e-mail research results.

▼ What Is the Difference Between *Shepard's* and KeyCite?

Researchers have noted recently that the services are very similar in nature. However, some citing references, such as some secondary authorities or treatises, may be unique to one system or the other.

▼ Why Would You Use Both KeyCite and *Shepard's*?

Using both services provides an extra check on the accuracy of the citation. In addition, different research databases and publishers may result in dissimilar results. Each publisher also provides references to secondary sources that might assist you in your research. For more information about secondary sources, consult Chapter 6.

▼ How Do I Access KeyCite?

From any Westlaw screen, you can access KeyCite for a particular case. If you are already viewing a case, you can access KeyCite with a click of the mouse. You also can enter a KeyCite request in the Westlaw search box — keycite: and the citation or kc: and the citation.

C. OTHER CITATORS

Various services such as Fastcase and Bloomberg offer citators. These services have fewer features, however, and may not provide the same level of analysis provided by the big two in the marketplace. Authority Check, the Fastcase citator, shares the negative treatment of a case with a red flag. A gray or clear flag indicates no negative treatment. It also provides citing references for cases and other authorities. You can click on the Authority Check flag while viewing a case and it will provide you with the precedential value of the case. You also can filter the Authority Check results by jurisdiction. As of July 2021, Fastcase was revising its Authority Check. It will combine its artificial intelligence capabilities with a review of cases by individuals. The goal is to provide more nuanced case analysis. To do this it will be providing different shades of red for cases that might not be good law. Instead of solely a red flag, it will provide flags for review granted, disavowed, superseded by statute, superseded by regulation, superseded by constitutional amendment, abrogated by other case, disapproved, overruled, reversed, or vacated.

Westlaw Edge, Thomson Reuter's newest online subscription, offers artificial intelligence searches in addition to its traditional KeyCite to caution researchers that a point of law in a case is at risk of being overruled based on its "reliance on an overruled or otherwise invalid prior decision," according to Thomson Reuters. Artificial intelligence is used to make this determination. For example, a court may directly overrule a case, but fail to mention another case that relied on the overruled case. The case that was not mentioned by the court overruling the first case would be assigned the overruling risk symbol, an orange symbol with an exclamation point.

CASE CITE-CHECKING CHECKLIST

1. Make a list of the cases you need to cite check.
2. To be thorough, search cases in both of the following sources or services: *Shepard's* and KeyCite.

SHEPARD'S CHECKLIST

1. Click on the *Shepard's* citation button and type in the citation.
2. Check for red, orange, or yellow signals and review citing references.
3. Click on the hyperlink to review any citing authority that may challenge the validity of the case.

KEYCITE CHECKLIST

1. Type the citation in the search box.
2. Check for red or yellow signals and review citing references.
3. Click on the hyperlink to review any citing authority that may challenge the validity of the case.

CHAPTER SUMMARY

In this chapter, you learned that you must ensure that the law or authority you are citing is still current or valid. To determine this, you must validate or update your research findings. This process often is called Shepardizing. Citators not only assist you in validating the law, but also provide you with citations to other authorities. You can validate an authority both in print and online.

The next chapter discusses resources called secondary authorities that help you understand legal issues and find primary authorities.

KEY TERMS

case history

citators

KeyCite

negative history

Shepardizing

Shepard's citator system treatment

EXERCISES

SELF-ASSESSMENT

Lexis

1. Shepardize the following citations:
   a. 64 N.W.2d 38
   b. 150 Ill. App. 3d 21
   c. 326 U.S. 310
2. For 326 U.S. 310, limit your treatment to negative treatment only. What are the results?

Westlaw

3. Perform a KeyCite search for the following citations:
   a. 64 N.W.2d 38
   b. 150 Ill. App. 3d 21
   c. 326 U.S. 310

PRACTICE SKILLS

4. Shepardize and KeyCite all of the following cases on the computer. Print out the first page of each result.
   a. *Consolidation Coal Co. v. Bucyrus-Erie Co.*, 89 Ill. 2d 103, 432 N.E.2d 250 (1982)
   b. *United States v. Upjohn*, 449 U.S. 383 (1981)
   c. *People v. Adam*, 51 Ill. 2d 46, 280 N.E.2d 205 (1972)
   d. *Cox v. Yellow Cab Co.*, 61 Ill. 2d 416, 337 N.E.2d 15 (1975)
   e. *Archer Daniels Midland Co. v. Koppers Co.*, 138 Ill. App. 3d 276, 485 N.E.2d 1301 (1985)
5. Shepardize 713 N.E.2d 1285. Note that it is cited by 754 N.E.2d 448. Now, go to that case. What is the name of that case?
6. Perform a KeyCite search for 507 F. Supp. 1091 on Westlaw. List some of the cases that have yellow flags.
7. Perform a KeyCite for 2002 WL1592517 (CA 7. Ill.). Can you perform a KeyCite for this case on Westlaw? Can you Shepardize this case on *Shepard's*?
8. Perform a KeyCite for 106 S. Ct 1415.
   a. What is the name of the case?
   b. Is there any signal indicating the validity of the case? If so, what is it?

9. Shepardize the following cases online.
   a. 816 F.2d 630
   b. 373 N.E.2d 1371
   c. 432 N.E.2d 1123
   d. 222 N.E.2d 561
10. Find 984 F.2d 218 online on Thomson Reuters Westlaw.
    a. Is there a signal that indicates whether the case is good law?
    b. If so, what is the signal and what does it indicate?
    c. Does it apply to the entire case? If no, what part of the case does it apply to?
11. Shepardize the citations listed below online.
    a. 361 N.E.2d 325
    b. 80 Ill. App. 3d 315
    c. 571 F. Supp. 1012
12. Shepardize the following citations online.
    a. 129 F.R.D. 515
    b. 432 N.E.2d 250
    c. 449 U.S. 383
    d. 423 F.2d 487
13. Shepardize 581 N.E. 2d 19.
    a. What color flag, if any, appears at the top? If so, why does it appear?
    b. What is the topic of the third headnote?
    c. What year was this case decided?
    d. Who were the attorneys involved in the case?
    e. What is the name of the judge who wrote the opinion?
    f. How many cases cite headnote 6?
    g. Under headnote 7, what case does the court say plaintiff relied upon?
    h. What does the court say about that case?

CHAPTER **6**

SECONDARY AUTHORITY

CHAPTER OVERVIEW

Secondary authorities are used to understand, analyze, and tie together primary authorities, or the law. Secondary authorities explain the law and the legal rules, and they provide insight into primary authorities. Cases, statutes, and administrative regulations—all primary authorities—are frequently cited in secondary sources. Secondary authorities are useful tools for finding citations to law supporting a legal issue.

This chapter details the many sources of secondary authority, how to use the sources, and how to update them. Citation information is given for each source.

A. SECONDARY AUTHORITY: WHAT IT IS AND WHERE TO FIND IT

▼ What Is Secondary Authority?

Secondary authority describes, analyzes, and comments on primary authority. Secondary authority provides commentary on the law. Any analytical or critical discussion of the law is considered secondary authority. Generally, individuals, institutions, and publishers create secondary sources.

Secondary authority compares and contrasts judicial opinions and indicates how the law is evolving. Sometimes a secondary source presents aspirational law—that is, how the law should be, but has not necessarily been adopted by a jurisdiction. The American Law Institute (the Restatements) does this, and this can be seen in the Restatements and Uniform Laws (the Uniform Laws National Conference of Commissioners on Uniform State). Also, a secondary source will often tell the researcher which cases are most important and which have little merit. If you do not understand a legal rule or are concerned about how to apply a legal rule, consult a secondary source for guidance. Secondary sources are easier to read than primary authority because they are written in a narrative format. Secondary sources discuss statutes and administrative materials, expounding on the policy motivations for enacting legislation and the accompanying regulations.

▼ Why and When Do You Use a Secondary Source?

Secondary sources are used to explain the law or a particular legal concept. Secondary sources discuss the legal rules directly without requiring the reader to unearth the issues and the holdings from the texts of judicial decisions. Secondary authority provides insight into a legal topic by discussing the most important relevant cases and statutes and by explaining how that law is applied to the facts. Because secondary sources comment on, describe, and analyze primary sources, a researcher obtains citations to primary authority. By providing access to citations, secondary sources are great finding tools. A researcher uses secondary authority to gain insight into a legal topic as well as to obtain citations to primary sources.

Paralegals use secondary sources when they are unfamiliar with a legal issue or topic and need a broad overview of the concepts written in a text format that is easily understandable. Use secondary authority to learn the vocabulary used before searching on commercial databases. (See Chapter 10.) Using secondary authority provides access to primary sources because of the great number of footnotes and citations found in the secondary source so that you can access the relevant general rules.

▼ What Are the Sources of Secondary Authority?

Generally, any source that comments on, analyzes, criticizes, describes, or projects the status of the law is a secondary source. Any source that states what the law should be is a secondary source. Some secondary sources are considered more prestigious and carry more persuasive authority than others. For instance, the Restatements of Law are very well respected, as are scholarly law review articles. The major sources of secondary authority are dictionaries, thesauri, encyclopedias, *American Law Reports* (A.L.R.), hornbooks, treatises, Restatements, Uniform Laws, legal periodicals, and newspapers. We will discuss each source separately, give examples, and illustrate which research situation would mandate their respective use.

PRACTICE POINTER

Secondary sources are great finding tools for primary authority, particularly case law. Use the secondary source to understand how case law fits together and to obtain citations. Always read the primary source that you find cited in the secondary authority—that is, the case, the statute, or the regulation—yourself to see if it is applicable to your research. Also, be sure to Shepardize or KeyCite any primary source before you rely on it as a source of authority. Update all statutes and regulations, too.

B. DICTIONARIES

▼ What Is a Legal Dictionary?

The **legal dictionary** provides the legal definition of a word or term. Sometimes a case is mentioned that contains the judicial definition of that word. The two most common legal dictionaries are *Black's Law Dictionary* and *Ballentine's Law Dictionary*.

▼ When Would a Legal Dictionary Be Used?

Researchers use a legal dictionary when they do not understand the **legal meaning** of a word or term. The emphasis is on the legal meaning because the legal definition of a word often differs from its lay meaning. Sometimes you will be assigned a research project where you cannot answer or resolve the issue without first figuring out what the terms mean.

EXAMPLE

Ms. Associate asks you if Mr. Blackacre can obtain an easement by necessity to access his farm from the road by crossing his neighbor's property. You do not know what an easement is, nor do you know what an easement by necessity is. To research the issue effectively, you would use a legal dictionary to look up easement and easement by necessity.

Examples of dictionary entries of the word *easement* are provided in Illustration 6-1. The entries in the legal dictionary are in alphabetical order. Under the word *easement* are the various types of easements.

▼ How Would You Cite to a Legal Dictionary?

The information for the citation format for dictionaries is found in **Rule 15.8** of the *Bluebook* with an excellent example at B15.1, and in **Rule 22.1** of *ALWD*.

> *Easement,* <u>Black's Law Dictionary</u> (11th ed. 2019) — *Bluebook* format; note that the title is either underlined or italicized in *Bluebook* format.

> *Easement, Black's Law Dictionary* (11th ed. 2019) — *ALWD* format

ALWD states that the pinpoint page is not included because the term is the reference. No editor is included in a citation to *Black's Law Dictionary.*

▼ Are Legal Dictionaries Available Online?

Black's Law Dictionary is available on Westlaw. The directory screen, which changes constantly, indicates exactly where the dictionary is located within the Westlaw database. The contents of *Black's* online are identical to the hardcopy version. To search for a definition online, enter the word that you want to be defined. In our example, you would enter the word *easement.* A free online legal dictionary is available at http://dictionary.law.com. A plain English legal dictionary is found at http://www.nolo.com/dictionary.

ILLUSTRATION 6-1. Definition of *Easement* in *Black's Law Dictionary*

EASEMENT, Black's Law Dictionary (11th ed. 2019)

Black's Law Dictionary (11th ed. 2019), easement

EASEMENT

Bryan A. Garner, Editor in Chief

Preface | Guide | Legal Maxims | Bibliography

easement (eez-mənt) (14c) *Property.* **1.** An interest in land owned by another person, consisting in the right to use or control the land, or an area above or below it, for a specific limited purpose (such as to cross it for access to a public road). • The land benefiting from an easement is called the *dominant estate*; the land burdened by an easement is called the *servient estate.* Unlike a lease or license, an easement may last forever, but it does not give the holder the right to possess, take from, improve, or sell the land. The primary recognized easements are (1) a right-of-way, (2) a right of entry for any purpose relating to the dominant estate, (3) a right to the support of land and buildings, (4) a right of light and air, (5) a right to water, (6) a right to do some act that would otherwise amount to a nuisance, and (7) a right to place or keep something on the servient estate. **2.** A document granting such an interest; specif., an easement deed or easement agreement. **3.** EASEMENT AREA. — Also termed *private right-of-way*; *easement agreement.* See SERVITUDE (1). Cf. PROFIT À PRENDRE.

- **access easement.** (1933) An easement allowing one or more persons to travel across another's land to get to a nearby location, such as a road. • The access easement is a common type of easement by necessity. — Also termed *easement of access*; *easement of way*; *easement of passage.*

- **adverse easement.** See *prescriptive easement.*

- **affirmative easement.** (1881) An easement that forces the servient-estate owner to permit certain actions by the easement holder, such as discharging water onto the servient estate. — Also termed *positive easement.* Cf. *negative easement.*

> "Positive easements give rights of entry upon the land of another, not amounting to profits, to enable something to be done on that land. Some are commonplace, examples being rights of way across the land of another and rights to discharge water on to the land of another. Others are more rare, such as the right to occupy a pew in a church, the right to use a kitchen situated on the land of another for the purpose of washing and drying clothes, and the right to use a toilet situated on the land of another." Peter Butt, *Land Law* 305 (2d ed. 1988).

- **agricultural-preservation easement.** See *land-conservation easement.*

- **ancillary easement.** See *secondary easement.*

- **apparent easement.** (1851) A visually evident easement, such as a paved trail or a sidewalk.

- **appendant easement.** See *easement appurtenant.*

- **appurtenant easement.** See *easement appurtenant.*

- **avigational easement.** (1962) An easement permitting unimpeded aircraft flights over the servient estate. — Also termed *avigation easement*; *aviation easement*; *flight easement*; *navigation easement.*

- **blanket easement.** (1917) See *floating easement.*

- **common easement.** (18c) An easement allowing the servient landowner to share in the benefit of the easement. — Also termed *nonexclusive easement.*

- **conservation easement.** (1965) *Property.* A real-estate covenant binding a parcel of land in a way that preserves a native plant or animal, a natural or physical feature of the land, or some aspect of the land that has some historical, cultural, or scientific significance. • The easement is a recorded, perpetual, individually tailored agreement creating a nonpossessory interest in real property, the interest being held by a government entity or by a qualified nonprofit. It permanently restricts or imposes

Reprinted with permission of Thomson Reuters.

C. ENCYCLOPEDIAS

1. Generally

▼ What Is a Legal Encyclopedia?

Just as the *Encyclopedia Britannica* divides the realm of knowledge into subjects and discusses each subject broadly (for example, the subject Insects), a **legal encyclopedia** divides the law into topics and offers broad coverage of the legal rules pertaining to each topic. The discussion is thorough but not too detailed and is oriented to the reader with legal knowledge, although not necessarily of the particular subject in question. Legal encyclopedias synthesize the relevant sources so that they are easy to understand, as you do not have to locate the rule in the case or the statute. Encyclopedias provide generalized commentary on the law.

There are topical legal encyclopedias such as the *Encyclopedia of the American Constitution* that cover specialized subject areas. There are encyclopedias such as ***American Jurisprudence*** and ***Corpus Juris Secundum*** that are national in scope. Finally, there are state law encyclopedias such as *Illinois Law and Practice* and *Florida Jurisprudence Second*. There are legal encyclopedias for most states.

NET NOTE

A terrific video on using legal encyclopedias is found at https://guides.ll.georgetown.edu/c.php?g=362053&p=2445621.

▼ Why Would You Use an Encyclopedia?

An encyclopedia is very helpful when beginning research in an area of the law in which you have no basic knowledge of the subject or the issues. Encyclopedias divide the law into topics and subtopics and provide a generalized, clearly written discussion of the issues and the general rules. A working vocabulary and a knowledge of the general rules are obtained when using an encyclopedia. In addition, encyclopedias give credit to every tenet mentioned, so they are a marvelous source for citations.

After reading the encyclopedia entry, you must always read the cases and statutes, the primary authority, cited in the references to determine if they are relevant to your problem.

▼ When Do You Cite an Encyclopedia as Authority?

As a general rule, encyclopedias should never be cited as authority. Encyclopedias are not scholarly sources, and authorship is institutional rather than individual. This does not detract from their helpfulness in providing a broad overview of the legal topic and in providing citations to primary source materials.

A researcher should use primary source references, even from other jurisdictions, obtained from the encyclopedia rather than cite to the encyclopedia's text. Always read the case or statute that the encyclopedia cites and rely on the primary source for authority. Even if you cannot locate primary authority from the jurisdiction needed, it is still better to use the law from another jurisdiction, as persuasive but not binding authority, than to use an encyclopedia as authority.

The two predominant encyclopedias that are national in scope are *American Jurisprudence*, commonly referred to as Am. Jur. and Am. Jur. 2d (second series), and *Corpus Juris Secundum*, known as C.J.S. However, many law libraries are no longer updating C.J.S. Both Am. Jur. 2d and C.J.S. are published by Thomson Reuters and are organized by topic in a similar fashion.

Both encyclopedias cover the individual legal disciplines in a generalized manner. Discussion is thorough but not overly detailed. The encyclopedias provide many more references to case law than to statutes and regulations. The footnotes and citations included in the sections provide citations to primary authorities. You must always read the primary source that you rely on, not only the encyclopedia's interpretation of it.

State encyclopedias also exist. In Illinois, *Illinois Law and Practice* is the encyclopedia that deals with issues of state law. *Illinois Law and Practice* is published by West and contains references to many other West publications, particularly the digests with the topics and Key Numbers. Check with your librarian for the encyclopedia in your state.

2. *American Jurisprudence*

▼ What Is Contained in *American Jurisprudence*?

American Jurisprudence, commonly called Am. Jur., is published by West and references other publications such as the *American Law Reports* (A.L.R.). The encyclopedia is in the second edition. The entire set is divided into topics, and the topics are arranged alphabetically.

Illustration 6-2 shows the topic outline for Easements and Licenses in Am. Jur. 2d. Notice that under the topics of Easements are various subtopics. The initial discussion of the subtopic Easements in gross begins with a category entitled "Transfer of Easement."

The editors attempt to divide the entire body of American law into labeled topics. This gives the reader a subject approach to the law and lets you, the researcher, find general legal rules from the cases and statutes that are cited. The text explores each legal topic by providing the most important law that is relevant or the controlling legal doctrine on that particular topic, then discusses the exceptions to the general rules. The encyclopedia is considered to be a secondary source because

ILLUSTRATION 6-2. Topic Outline for Easements and Licenses at 25 Am. Jur. 2d 668 (2014)

it offers discussion and commentary on the law and synthesizes, or puts together, many cases. The encyclopedia does not create law. Of course, there is extensive footnoting to give proper credit or attribution to the authority discussed. This makes the encyclopedia a great finding tool, although not a substitute for reading the primary source material. The encyclopedia is a good place to begin research when you do not understand the topic and need a broad overview of the discipline. The encyclopedia provides the general rules, the broadest rules, for each topic. Reading an encyclopedia section will help you form effective online searches because you will learn the vocabulary used for the issue. From reading about the topic, you will acquire case and statute citations to relevant materials.

Am. Jur. is organized by topic, and the volumes are updated with pocket parts. The pocket parts are called **Cumulative Supplements** and are generally published annually. Each volume of Am. Jur. is numbered, and the topics and sections contained within the volume are listed on the spine; for example, Volume 25 of Am. Jur. contains Domestic Abuse and Violence to Elections, §§ 1-198. At the beginning of each topic is an outline listing every related subtopic. Each section within a topic refers to a subtopic; for example, under the topic of Easements and Licenses, captions indicate categories within the topics such as VI. Transfer of Easement. Under Transfer of Easement, § 79 is entitled "Easements in Gross." The text of Am. Jur. 2d repeats the topic and subtopic heading. See Illustration 6-3.

Notice that the topic or subtopic is first discussed generally, then the subissues are explored. To update the information found in the main volume, refer to the pocket part, or supplement, under the topic and then under the section. See Illustration 6-4. In our example, the supplement has no additional material updating § 79, but there is material updating other sections. Always check the pocket part, regardless of how recent the main volume publication date is, to see if there are any new cases. A sample page of the pocket part is provided although § 79 is not listed.

Narrative text generally is omitted in the pocket part, but new and updating citation references are included. This means that citations to new cases published that support the legal premises discussed in the main text are listed so that you can find the most recent authority for the legal premise. This is the same format as the pocket part in C.J.S.

Am. Jur. updates its topics with a volume entitled *New Topic Service* in which current topics, complete with text and footnotes, are contained. Am. Jur. also publishes the *Desk Book*, which contains facts, charts, tables, statistics, and court rules of interest to attorneys. The *Desk Book* is published annually.

ILLUSTRATION 6-3.   Portion of Easement Entry at 25 Am. Jur. 2d § 79 (2014)

EASEMENTS AND LICENSES   § 79

§ 78   Right to remove obstructions

Research References

West's Key Number Digest, Easements ⬅60
Fence as nuisance, 80 A.L.R.3d 962
Remedy of tenant against stranger wrongfully interfering with his posses-
    sion. 12 A.L.R.2d 1192
Servient Estate Owner's Wrongful Obstruction of Right of way Easement,
    100 Am. Jur. Trials 337
Am. Jur. Legal Forms 2d § 203:37 (Disposition of brush and timber)

An easement owner has a right to remove obstructions unreasonably interfering with use of the easement[1] so long as there is no breach
of the peace.[2] However, the easement holder will be liable for the removal of an obstruction that is outside the scope of the easement
holder's grant.[3]

VI.   TRANSFER OF EASEMENT

Research References

West's Key Number Digest
Easements ⬅22, 24

A.L.R. Library
A.L.R. Index, Easements; Right of Way; Servient Owners
West's A.L.R. Digest, Easements ⬅22, 24

§ 79   Easements in gross

Research References

West's Key Number Digest, Easements ⬅24
Am. Jur. Legal Forms 2d § 203:47 (Assignment permitted—Exception of
    right to construct additional pipelines); § 203:48 (Assignment prohibited—
    Exception of certain subsidiaries)

Generally, an easement in gross is a purely personal right that is
not assignable,[1] absent evidence of the parties' intent to the contrary,
and it terminates upon the death of the person for whom it was

---

[Section 78]

[1]Pioneer Irr. Dist. v. City of
Caldwell, 153 Idaho 593, 288 P.3d 810
(2012); DeHaven v. Hall, 2008 SD 57, 753
N.W.2d 429 (S.D. 2008) (the dominant
estate owner may remove trees and earth
that obstruct an easement roadway).

[2]Pioneer Irr. Dist. v. City of
Caldwell, 153 Idaho 593, 288 P.3d 810
(2012).

[3]Conley v. Whittlesey, 133 Idaho
265, 985 P.2d 1127 (1999) (a grantee
removed a cedar tree located 35 feet from
the existing road where the easement
enjoyed by the grantee was only 12 feet
in width).

[Section 79]

[1]Beckstead v. Price, 146 Idaho 57,
190 P.3d 876 (2008); Meade v. Ginn, 159
S.W.3d 314 (Ky. 2004); Tarason v. Wesson

751

ILLUSTRATION 6-3. *Continued*

§ 79   AMERICAN JURISPRUDENCE 2D

created.[2] However, there is some authority for the view that easements in gross that are taken for commercial purposes, especially those for public utility purposes, such as railroads, telephone lines, and pipelines, are freely transferable.[3]

When the evidence demonstrates that the parties clearly intended that an easement in gross be assignable, it is.[4] If acquired by contract, an easement in gross may be made assignable by the terms of the instrument creating the right.[5]

§ 80   Easements appurtenant

Research References

West's Key Number Digest, Easements ☞24
Am. Jur. Legal Forms 2d § 94:88 (Consent required for assignment or sublicense)

An easement appurtenant runs with the land and may be transferred.[1] An appurtenant easement is tied to the dominant estate, is conveyed with a conveyance of that estate, and cannot be conveyed independently thereof.[2]

A transfer of real property passes all easements attached to the property,[3] in accordance with the fundamental rule that all easements appurtenant to real property and created expressly by deed will pass

Realty, LLC, 2012 ME 47, 40 A.3d 1005 (Me. 2012); Newman v. Michel, 224 W. Va. 735, 688 S.E.2d 610 (2009).

[2]Tarason v. Wesson Realty, LLC, 2012 ME 47, 40 A.3d 1005 (Me. 2012).

An agreement created an easement in gross which was not transferred to the grantee's successor in interest where the easement provided a right of access to a river, which was granted to the grantees and their immediate families; identified no dominant or servient estate; and gave a right of access to people who might have no interest in the land itself, such as immediate family members, while in contrast, another easement in the agreement clearly identified a dominant estate and servient estate, identified the location of the easement, and was granted to the grantees and their "heirs and assigns" rather than specifically to the grantees. King v. Lang, 136 Idaho 905, 42 P.3d 698 (2002).

As to what constitutes an easement in gross, see § 10.

[3]Canova v. Shell Pipeline Co., 290

F.3d 753 (5th Cir. 2002).
[4]Wentworth v. Sebra, 2003 ME 97, 829 A.2d 520 (Me. 2003).
[5]Meade v. Ginn, 159 S.W.3d 314 (Ky. 2004).

[Section 80]
[1]Kankakee County Bd. of Review v. Property Tax Appeal Bd., 226 Ill. 2d 36, 312 Ill. Dec. 638, 871 N.E.2d 38 (2007); U.S. v. Blackman, 270 Va. 68, 613 S.E.2d 442 (2005).

An easement appurtenant which runs with the land is not a mere privilege to be enjoyed by the person to whom it is granted or by whom it is reserved; it passes by a deed of such person to the grantee. Heg v. Alldredge, 157 Wash. 2d 154, 137 P.3d 9 (2006).
[2]Box L Corp. v. Teton County ex rel Board of County Commissioners of Teton County, 2004 WY 75, 92 P.3d 811 (Wyo. 2004).
[3]Leichtfuss v. Dabney, 2005 MT 271, 329 Mont. 129, 122 P.3d 1220 (2005); Mansur v. Muskopf, 159 N.H. 216, 977

752

Reprinted with permission of Thomson Reuters.

ILLUSTRATION 6-4. Sample Page: Westlaw Volume 25 Am. Jur. 2d § 79 Showing All Updates through May 2021

---

§ 79. Easements in gross, 25 Am. Jur. 2d Easements and Licenses § 79

---

25 Am. Jur. 2d Easements and Licenses § 79

American Jurisprudence, Second Edition | May 2021 Update

Easements and Licenses in Real Property
Jill Gustafson, J.D.

VI. Transfer of Easement

§ 79. Easements in gross

Topic Summary   Correlation Table   References

West's Key Number Digest

- West's Key Number Digest, Easements ⬤⟳24

Forms

- Am. Jur. Legal Forms 2d § 203:47 (Assignment permitted—Exception of right to construct additional pipelines)
- Am. Jur. Legal Forms 2d § 203:48 (Assignment prohibited—Exception of certain subsidiaries)

Generally, an easement in gross is a purely personal right that is not assignable,[1] absent evidence of the parties' intent to the contrary, and it terminates upon the death of the person for whom it was created.[2] However, there is some authority for the view that easements in gross that are taken for commercial purposes, especially those for public utility purposes, such as railroads, telephone lines, and pipelines, are freely transferable.[3]

When the evidence demonstrates that the parties clearly intended that an easement in gross be assignable, it is.[4] If acquired by contract, an easement in gross may be made assignable by the terms of the instrument creating the right.[5]

ILLUSTRATION 6-4. *Continued*

Footnotes

1   Beckstead v. Price, 146 Idaho 57, 190 P.3d 876 (2008); Meade v. Ginn, 159 S.W.3d 314 (Ky. 2004);

Tarason v. Wesson Realty, LLC, 2012 ME 47, 40 A.3d 1005 (Me. 2012); Newman v. Michel, 224 W. Va. 735, 688 S.E.2d 610 (2009).

2   Tarason v. Wesson Realty, LLC, 2012 ME 47, 40 A.3d 1005 (Me. 2012).

An agreement created an easement in gross which was not transferred to the grantee's successor in interest where the easement provided a right of access to a river, which was granted to the grantees and their immediate families; identified no dominant or servient estate; and gave a right of access to people who might have no interest in the land itself, such as immediate family members, while in contrast, another easement in the agreement clearly identified a dominant estate and servient estate, identified the location of the easement, and was granted to the grantees and their "heirs and assigns" rather than specifically to the grantees. King v. Lang, 136 Idaho 905, 42 P.3d 698 (2002).

As to what constitutes an easement in gross, see § 10.

3   Canova v. Shell Pipeline Co., 290 F.3d 753 (5th Cir. 2002).

4   Wentworth v. Sebra, 2003 ME 97, 829 A.2d 520 (Me. 2003).

5   Meade v. Ginn, 159 S.W.3d 314 (Ky. 2004).

Reprinted with permission of Thomson Reuters.

▼ How Do You Use Am. Jur.?

There are four basic methods of using Am. Jur. 2d.

1. **Access Am. Jur. on Lexis or Westlaw.** Although costly, you can search by word or term. This is particularly helpful when you have an unusual term. All updates are integrated into the page or section retrieved so that you do not have to consult pocket part supplements. Searching Am. Jur on Lexis or Westlaw is the most efficient way to use the encyclopedia.
2. **The index method.** This is the most efficient approach when using the hardcopy version. At the end of the set is a multivolume index that is printed annually. Entries are organized by descriptive word and topic and include subtopics as cross-references. An example of the index from Am. Jur. 2d is shown in Illustration 6-5.
3. **The table method.** If you have a statutory cite, use the separate Am. Jur. 2d volume entitled *Table of Statutes, Rules and Regulations Cited.* If you have a relevant *United States Code* (U.S.C.) or U.S.C.S., *Code of Federal Regulations,* or Uniform Law citation, the tables will indicate the precise topic and section where it is discussed.
4. **The topic outline.** This is the least efficient method. In this method you review the topics outlined at the beginning of each topic section.

▼ What Is the Citation Format for Am. Jur.?

Bluebook **Rule 15.8** and *ALWD* **Rule 22.3** cover print legal encyclopedias. Note the section is the pinpoint cite, so there is no need for page numbers. The cite format is as follows:

> 25 Am. Jur. 2d *Easements and Licenses* § 79 (2004 & Supp. 2021) — *Bluebook* and *ALWD* formats

If the encyclopedia is available in print and on a commercial database, you may cite to the database. For example:

> 25 Am. Jur. 2d *Easements and Licenses* § 79, Westlaw (database updated May 2021) — *Bluebook* **Rule 15.9** and *ALWD* **Rule 22.3(f)**

3. State Law Encyclopedias

▼ Are There Any Legal Encyclopedias for State Law?

Yes, almost every jurisdiction has a legal encyclopedia. Illinois, for example, has *Illinois Law and Practice,* commonly known as I.L.P. I.L.P. is published by West and refers the reader to the other West resources such as the Key Numbers and the digests. West publishes many state encyclopedias such as *Florida Jurisprudence Second* and *Texas Jurisprudence Third.*

4. Online Encyclopedia Services

▼ Are Legal Encyclopedias Available on Lexis or Westlaw?

Legal encyclopedias are available online. Am. Jur. is on Lexis and Westlaw. Selected portions of C.J.S. are on Westlaw. C.J.S. is not available on Lexis. The Cornell University Legal Information Institute has a free legal encyclopedia called Wex that can be accessed at http://topics.law.cornell.edu/wex.

D. *AMERICAN LAW REPORTS*

▼ What Are *American Law Reports?*

The *American Law Reports* (A.L.R.), published by West, contain annotations on narrow, well-defined legal topics. Each volume contains at least a half-dozen annotations, or in-depth articles, about a legal issue as well as the pivotal case that prompted the examination of the issue inspiring the editors to write the annotation. Subjects common to A.L.R. are torts, property, contracts, sales, and criminal law. Federal and state law are combined in A.L.R. until 1969. A.L.R. Federal (A.L.R. Fed.) began to be published in 1969. A.L.R. is in its sixth series. In print and updated with pocket part supplements are A.L.R., A.L.R.2d, A.L.R.3d, A.L.R.4th, A.L.R.5th, A.L.R.6th, and A.L.R.7th. A.L.R. is published sequentially, just like case reporters, so that when a number of annotations are written, although they may bear no subject relationship to one another (just as with opinions), a volume of A.L.R. is published. A new volume is published about every six weeks.

Each volume of A.L.R. contains cases and annotations. The first section in each volume is a list entitled Subjects Annotated in this Volume. This provides a cross-reference for the annotations in the volume. The next section is Table of Cases Reported, which lists the full-text decisions in the volume. Because every annotation is developed from a pivotal legal decision, A.L.R. reprints the full text of that decision before the annotation. Beginning with A.L.R.5th, the decisions are now found in the back of each volume.

As an example, let's look at the annotation entitled *Locating Easement of Way Created by Necessity.* The first page containing library references leads you to many other relevant practice aids. See Illustration 6-6. The next entry is a detailed outline of the annotation so that if you are interested in only a portion of the discussion, you can focus your research efforts. There is also an index, just for each annotation, so that you can see which subjects are discussed by section. See Illustration 6-7. Following the annotation's index is the Table

ILLUSTRATION 6-5. Sample Page: Westlaw Am. Jur. 2d General Index, Easements, Sample Pages Updated July 2021

AMJUR Index

American Jurisprudence, Second Edition
Index updated July 2021

American Jurisprudence 2d General Index

EASEMENTS

EASEMENTS

See also Licenses in Real Property (this index)
Generally, Easements § 1 to 111
Abandonment, Easements § 85
Access to make repairs or improvements, Easements § 73
Actions and remedies
    generally, Easements § 96 to 104
    burden of proof, Easements § 100
    damages, below
    defenses, Easements § 99
    evidence, Easements § 100
    extent of relief, Easements § 104
    injunctions, Easements § 101
    landlord and tenant, Easements § 96
    limitation of actions, Easements § 99
    nature of relief, Easements § 104
    parties, Easements § 96, 97
    pleadings, Easements § 98
    punitive damages, Easements § 103
    standing, Easements § 96, 97
    title and ownership, Easements § 96
    weight and sufficiency of evidence, Easements § 100
Adjoining Landowners (this index)
Adverse or hostile use. Prescription, below
Adverse possession
    prescription, Easements § 39
    termination or extinguishment, Easements § 89
Affirmative easements, Easements § 7
Agreement, creation by, Easements § 16
Airspace, avigation easements as defense to trespass, Aviation § 8
Alterations
    generally, Easements § 74
    access to make repairs or improvements, Easements § 73
    building or structure, alteration of, Easements § 90
Apparent easements
    generally, Easements § 8
    preexisting uses, Easements § 25

Reprinted with permission of Thomson Reuters.

ILLUSTRATION 6-6. Total Client-Service Library References at 36 A.L.R.4th 769 (1985)

ANNOTATION

LOCATING EASEMENT OF WAY CREATED BY NECESSITY

by

William B. Johnson, J.D.

TOTAL CLIENT-SERVICE LIBRARY® REFERENCES

25 Am Jur 2d, Easements and Licenses §§ 64–69

Annotations: See the related matters listed in the annotation, infra.

9 Am Jur Pl & Pr Forms (Rev), Easements and Licenses, Forms 41–48

3 Am Jur Proof of Facts 2d 647, Abandonment of Easement; 5 Am Jur Proof of Facts 2d 621, Intent to Create Negative Easement; 33 Am Jur Proof of Facts 2d 669, Extent of Easement Over Servient Estate

22 Am Jur Trials 743, Condemnation of Easements

L Ed Index to Annos, Real Property; Trespass

ALR Quick Index, Access; Adjoining or Abutting Landowners; Easements; Ingress and Egress; Place or Location; Right of Way; Trespass; Way by Necessity

Federal Quick Index, Adjoining Landowners and Property; Easements and Right of Way; Ingress; Place and Location; Trespass

Auto-Cite®: Any case citation herein can be checked for form, parallel references, later history, and annotation references through the Auto-Cite computer research system.

Reprinted with permission of Thomson Reuters.

of Jurisdictions Represented. Then Illustration 6-8 shows the Table of Cases, Laws, and Rules accessed on Westlaw. The Table of Cases, Laws, and Rules makes A.L.R. a unique resource because each annotation includes every relevant statute or case from all of the appropriate jurisdictions. Think of an annotation as a survey of law on a particular issue. This is a windfall for the researcher. If possible, obtain this table on either Lexis or Westlaw because new cases are added weekly.

▼ How Do You Use A.L.R.?

There are three basic methods of using A.L.R.

1. **The computerized method.** This is the best method of accessing A.L.R. annotations when available. Lexis has the full text of A.L.R. online, and so does Westlaw. Using online access permits you to search for relevant annotations using the words that you think would appear in an annotation on point. All of the updated cases,

ILLUSTRATION 6-7.   Outline of Annotation at 36 A.L.R.4th 770 (1985)

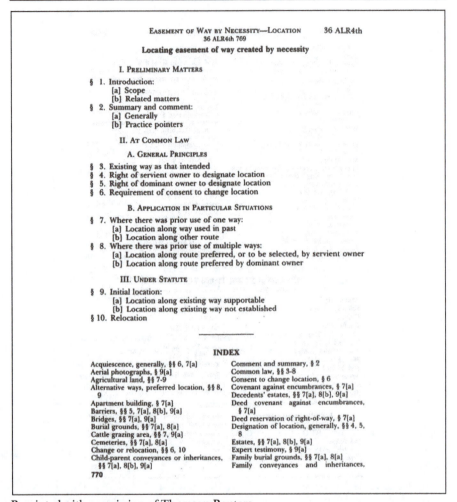

Reprinted with permission of Thomson Reuters.

statutes, and regulations are included online. The A.L.R. online is updated weekly but the hardcopy supplement is printed annually.

2. **The index method.** A.L.R. has a subject index for A.L.R.2d through A.L.R.5th, A.L.R.6th, A.L.R. 7th, A.L.R. Fed., A.L.R. Fed. 2d, A.L.R. Fed. 3rd, and *U.S. Supreme Court Reports, Lawyers' Edition.* See Illustration 6-9. It also contains a *Table of Statutes, Rules, and Regulations.* A.L.R. (first series) has a separate index. The index method requires that you find descriptive words for the issue or topic you are researching in one of A.L.R.'s indexes. The index is very detailed and has a pocket part supplement to update it. This is a very efficient method.

A.L.R. also has a separate index entitled the *Quick Index*, which covers the broadest topics and index entries for A.L.R.3rd through A.L.R.7th. The A.L.R. Index is available on Westlaw. Limit your source to A.L.R. and enter your terms in the search bar. If you have a specific phrase or group of words, then you may consider entering the terms in quotes. For the example in Illustration 6-9, the search terms were: "easement of way created by necessity." The phrase is in quotation marks because the exact phrase is searched. The online index is easy to use, you can use phrases that may appear in an annotation or any relevant term, it is updated frequently, and you can link to the annotation with a click. See Illustration 6-9.

3. *Shepard's.* This is also an excellent way to find A.L.R. annotations. *Shepard's* lists any A.L.R. citations where the case you are Shepardizing is cited. When you Shepardize a case, check to see if there are any A.L.R. references; they would appear at the end of the citation list.

▼ Why Would You Use A.L.R.?

A.L.R. is best consulted when you are researching a narrow, well-defined issue, similar to how you might use a law review article. The major difference between A.L.R. and a law review article is that A.L.R. provides you with indexed terms, an outline, a table of law from other jurisdictions, and library references to encyclopedias, form books, and digest topics. A.L.R., however, is not considered nearly as scholarly as a law review article. An A.L.R. annotation will provide you with a good understanding of a narrow, well-defined legal issue if an annotation is available on point. A.L.R. annotations are great finding tools because you are led to relevant primary authority, which you then must read.

ILLUSTRATION 6-8. Westlaw Table of Cases, Laws, and Rules in William B. Johnson, Annotation, *Locating Easement of Way Created by Necessity*, 36 A.L.R.4th 769 (1985 & Supp. 2021) — (Westlaw through July 8, 2021)

Table of Cases, Laws, and Rules

Arkansas
Nation v. Ayres, 340 Ark. 270, 9 S.W.3d 512 (2000) — 9[a]
White v. Grimmett, 223 Ark. 237, 265 S.W.2d 1 (1954) — 10

California
Kripp v. Curtis, 71 Cal. 62, 11 P. 879 (1886) — 4, 5, 7[a]

Colorado
De Reus v. Peck, 114 Colo. 107, 162 P.2d 404 (1945) — 2[b]

Georgia
Wyatt v. Hendrix, 146 Ga. 143, 90 S.E. 957 (1916) — 9[b]

ILLUSTRATION 6-8. *Continued*

Indiana
Kaiser v. Somers, 80 Ind. App. 89, 138 N.E. 20 (1923) — 7[a]
Ritchey v. Welsh, 149 Ind. 214, 48 N.E. 1031 (1898) — 4, 5, 6, 8[b]
Thomas v. McCoy, 30 Ind. App. 555, 66 N.E. 700 (1903) — 4, 5

Kentucky
Bentley v. Hampton, 28 Ky. L. Rptr. 1083, 91 S.W. 266 (Ky. 1906) — 6, 7[a]
Roland v. O'Neal, 122 S.W. 827 (Ky. 1909) — 4, 6, 8[b]

Louisiana
Bandelin v. Clark, 7 La. App. 64, 1927 WL 3637 (1st Cir. 1927) — 9[a]
Breeden v. Lee, 2 La. App. 126, 1925 WL 3669 (1st Cir. 1925) — 2[b], 9[b]
Broussard v. Etie, 11 La. 394, 1837 WL 818 (1837) — 9[b]
Bulliard v. Delahoussaye, 481 So. 2d 747 (La. Ct. App. 3d Cir. 1985) — 9[b]
Collins v. Reed, 316 So. 2d 134 (La. Ct. App. 3d Cir. 1975) — 9[a]
Corley v. C & J Frye Properties, LLC, 176 So. 3d 439 (La. Ct. App. 2d Cir. 2015) — 10
Dalton v. Graham, 295 So. 3d 437 (La. Ct. App. 2d Cir. 2020) — 9[a], 9[b]
Dickerson v. Coon, 71 So. 3d 1135 (La. Ct. App. 2d Cir. 2011) — 6.5
Howes v. Howes, 499 So. 2d 314 (La. Ct. App. 1st Cir. 1986) — 9[a]
Inabnet v. Pipes, 241 So. 2d 595 (La. Ct. App. 2d Cir. 1970) — 10
Littlejohn v. Cox, 15 La. Ann. 67, 1860 WL 5503 (1860) — 9[b]
Martini v. Cowart, 23 So. 2d 655 (La. Ct. App. 2d Cir. 1945) — 9[a]
Mercer v. Daws, 186 So. 877 (La. Ct. App. 2d Cir. 1939) — 9[a], 10
Morgan v. Culpepper, 324 So. 2d 598 (La. Ct. App. 2d Cir. 1975) — 9[b]
Phillips Energy Partners, LLC v. Milton Crow Ltd. Partnership, 166 So. 3d 428 (La. Ct. App. 2d Cir. 2015) — 9[a]
Rieger v. Norwood, 401 So. 2d 1272 (La. Ct. App. 1st Cir. 1981) — 9[a]
Roberson v. Reese, 376 So. 2d 1287 (La. Ct. App. 2d Cir. 1979) — 9[b]
Watson v. Scott, 349 So. 2d 982 (La. Ct. App. 2d Cir. 1977) — 9[a], 9[b]

Maine
Rumill v. Robbins, 77 Me. 193, 1885 WL 3147 (1885) — 4, 5, 8[a]

Maryland
Hancock v. Henderson, 236 Md. 98, 202 A.2d 599, 9 A.L.R.3d 592 (1964) — 2[b], 7[b]
Michael v. Needham, 39 Md. App. 271, 384 A.2d 473 (1978) — 2[b], 7[a], 7[b]
Stair v. Miller, 52 Md. App. 108, 447 A.2d 109, 36 A.L.R.4th 764 (1982) — 3, 7[b]
Stansbury v. MDR Development, L.L.C., 390 Md. 476, 889 A.2d 403 (2006) — 7[a]
Stansbury v. MDR Development, L.L.C., 161 Md. App. 594, 871 A.2d 612 (2005) — 3
USA Cartage Leasing, LLC v. Baer, 429 Md. 199, 55 A.3d 510 (2012) — 6.5
USA Cartage Leasing, LLC v. Baer, 202 Md. App. 138, 32 A.3d 88 (2011) — 6.5
Zimmerman v. Cockey, 118 Md. 491, 84 A. 743 (1912) — 2[b], 7[a]

Massachusetts
Bass v. Edwards, 126 Mass. 445, 1879 WL 9206 (1879) — 7[b]
Davis v. Sikes, 254 Mass. 540, 151 N.E. 291 (1926) — 4, 5, 6, 7[a]

Michigan
Douglas v. Jordan, 232 Mich. 283, 205 N.W. 52, 41 A.L.R. 1437 (1925) — 4, 6, 7[a]

ILLUSTRATION 6-8. *Continued*

Moore v. White, 159 Mich. 460, 124 N.W. 62 (1909) — 4, 8[a], 8[b]
Powers v. Harlow, 53 Mich. 507, 19 N.W. 257 (1884) — 4, 5

Minnesota
Bode v. Bode, 494 N.W.2d 301 (Minn. Ct. App. 1992) — 4, 5

Mississippi
Broadhead v. Terpening, 611 So. 2d 949 (Miss. 1992) — 6.5
Ganier v. Mansour, 766 So. 2d 3 (Miss. Ct. App. 2000) — 10
Quin v. Sabine, 183 Miss. 375, 183 So. 701 (1938) — 3, 6, 8[b]
Vinoski v. Plummer, 893 So. 2d 239 (Miss. Ct. App. 2004) — 3

Missouri
Chase v. Hall, 41 Mo. App. 15, 1890 WL 1638 (1890) — 5
Daniels v. Richardson, 762 S.W.2d 55 (Mo. Ct. App. W.D. 1988) — 5
Merrick v. Lensing, 622 S.W.2d 260 (Mo. Ct. App. E.D. 1981) — 9[a]
Welch v. Shipman, 357 Mo. 838, 210 S.W.2d 1008 (1948) — 9[b]

Montana
Herrin v. Sieben, 46 Mont. 226, 127 P. 323 (1912) — 4, 5, 8[a], 8[b]

New Jersey
Manning v. Port Reading R. Co., 54 N.J. Eq. 46, 33 A. 802 (Ch. 1896) — 7[a]

New York
Fritz v. Tompkins, 18 Misc. 514, 41 N.Y.S. 985 (Sup 1896) — 4, 5, 7[a]
Hines v. Hamburger, 14 A.D. 577, 43 N.Y.S. 977 (2d Dep't 1897) — 4, 5, 6, 7[a]
Palmer v. Palmer, 150 N.Y. 139, 44 N.E. 966 (1896) — 4, 5, 7[a]

North Carolina
Harris v. Greco, 69 N.C. App. 739, 318 S.E.2d 335 (1984) — 7[a]
Oliver v. Ernul, 277 N.C. 591, 178 S.E.2d 393 (1971) — 3, 4, 7[a]

Oklahoma
Jones v. Weiss, 1977 OK 188, 570 P.2d 948 (Okla. 1977) — 4, 7[a], 7[b]

South Carolina
Brasington v. Williams, 143 S.C. 223, 141 S.E. 375 (1927) — 4, 5, 8[b]
Graham v. Causey, 284 S.C. 339, 326 S.E.2d 412 (Ct. App. 1985) — 7[b]

Tennessee
McMillan v. McKee, 129 Tenn. 39, 164 S.W. 1197 (1914) — 4, 5, 8[a]
Pearne v. Coal Creek Min. & Mfg. Co., 90 Tenn. 619, 18 S.W. 402 (1891) — 7[a], 7[b]

Texas
Grobe v. Ottmers, 224 S.W.2d 487 (Tex. Civ. App. San Antonio 1949) — 4, 5, 6, 7[a]
Missouri-Kansas-Texas Ry. Co. of Texas v. Cunningham, 273 S.W. 697 (Tex. Civ. App. Amarillo 1925) — 4, 5, 6
Parker v. Bains, 194 S.W.2d 569 (Tex. Civ. App. Galveston 1946) — 6, 8[b]
Samuelson v. Alvarado, 847 S.W.2d 319 (Tex. App. El Paso 1993) — 4, 6

Vermont
Jenne v. Piper, 69 Vt. 497, 38 A. 147 (1897) — 4, 7[a]

West Virginia
Bosley v. Cabot Oil & Gas Corp. of West Virginia, 624 F. Supp. 1174 (S.D. W. Va. 1986) (applying West Virginia law) — 9[a]
Johnson v. Lunsford, 113 W. Va. 270, 168 S.E. 382 (1933) — 8[a]

Wisconsin
McCormick v. Schubring, 2003 WI 149, 672 N.W.2d 63 (Wis. 2003) — 7[a]

Reprinted with permission of Thomson Reuters.

ILLUSTRATION 6-9. Sample Page of A.L.R. Index— Easements Accessed on Westlaw

---

EASEMENTS, A.L.R. Index

A.L.R. Index

American Law Reports
Index updated July 2021

Index to Annotations

EASEMENTS

EASEMENTS

Abandonment of property
> loss of private easement by nonuse, 25 ALR2d 1265, 62 ALR5th 219
> private easement in way vacated, abandoned, or closed by public, 150 ALR 644

Access
> loss or impairment of landowner's access to existing controlled-access road or highway as compensable taking absent government condemnation or occupation of landowner's realty, 93 ALR6th 363
> misuse of easement, what constitutes, and remedies for, misuse of easement, 111 ALR5th 313
> roads. Access roads, in this topic
> scope of prescriptive easement for access (easement of way), 79 ALR4th 604

Access roads
> grant which does not specify location, 24 ALR4th 1053, § 5, 8, 13(b)
> inadequate access, way of necessity where a means of access does exist, but is claimed to be inadequate, inconvenient, difficult, or costly, 10 ALR4th 447
> locating easement of way created by necessity, 36 ALR4th 769
> part of land is inaccessible, 10 ALR4th 500

Adjoining landowners and property
> forced sale, power of court to order land owner to sell land to another if other's structures encroach on the land, 29 ALR7th Art. 11, § 4, 9, 10
> may an easement or right of way be appurtenant where the servient tenement is not adjacent to the dominant, 15 ALR7th Art. 1

Adoption as period of prescription for easement the period prescribed by statute of limitations with reference to adverse possession as including condition of color of title or right or other conditions imposed by that statute, 112 ALR 545

Adverse possession
> boundaries, easement by prescription for use of land near boundary line, 58 ALR 1037
> building, adverse possession based on encroachment of building or other structure, 2 ALR3d 1005, § 3(a, b), 8 to 11
> loss of private easement by nonuser or adverse possession, 25 ALR2d 1265, 62 ALR5th 219
> prescriptive easements
>> adoption as period of prescription for easement the period prescribed by statute of limitations with reference to adverse possession as including condition of color of title or right or other conditions imposed by that statute, 112 ALR 545
>> neighborly accommodation as defense against adverse possession or prescriptive easement, 56 ALR7th Art. 8
> prescriptive easements, in this topic
> presumptions and evidence respecting identification of land on which property taxes were paid to establish adverse possession, 36 ALR4th 843, § 6(a)
> private easement, loss by adverse possession or nonuse, 25 ALR2d 1265, 62 ALR5th 219

Reprinted with permission of Thomson Reuters.

It is best not to cite A.L.R. annotations and not to rely on them as authority unless absolutely necessary. Cite to the primary source materials that A.L.R. annotations provide after reading the primary authority to determine its relevance.

▼ How Do You Cite to an A.L.R. Annotation?

Citation style for the hardcopy A.L.R. is found in *Bluebook* **Rule 16.7.6** and *ALWD* **Rule 22.5**, as follows:

> William B. Johnson, Annotation, *Locating Easement of Way Created by Necessity*, 36 A.L.R.4th 769 (1985 & Supp. 2021).

You can cite to a commercial database if you retrieved the A.L.R. annotation on Lexis or Westlaw. According to *Bluebook* **Rule 15.9**, if a source is available in both print and on a commercial database, you may cite to the database. You must include the complete citation described in **Rule 16.7.6** as well as a cite to the database. *Bluebook* **Rule 16.8**. The underlying goal here is for the reader to be able to access the source with the citation you provide.

> William B. Johnson, Annotation, *Locating Easement of Way Created by Necessity*, 36 A.L.R.4th 769, Westlaw (1985 & database updated April 19, 2021) *Bluebook* format

> William B. Johnson, Annotation, *Locating Easement of Way Created by Necessity*, 36 A.L.R.4th 769 (Westlaw through April 19, 2021) *ALWD* format

▼ How Do You Update an A.L.R. Annotation?

A.L.R. (first series) Volumes 1 to 175 are updated in the *Blue Book of Supplemental Decisions*. This is a separate set of books that comes out every two years that updates the annotations in Volumes 1 to 175. It also indicates where annotations have been superseded or supplemented in later editions or series of the A.L.R. Entries are organized by volume and page numbers.

A.L.R.2d is updated by using the separate set entitled the *A.L.R.2d Later Case Service*. All entries are found by volume and page numbers.

To update A.L.R.3d, 4th, 5th, 6th, 7th or Fed., Fed. 2nd, and Fed. 3rd Annotations, consult the pocket part supplement to the volume to see if additional annotations and new statute and case law references are mentioned. Pocket parts are issued at least annually.

For any annotation, if using hardcopy resources, consult the Annotation History Table in the Tables volume to see if the annotation is superseded.

The best and easiest way to update an A.L.R. annotation is to access the annotation on either Westlaw or Lexis. This may be costly in practice, so it is still important to know how to use the books. The books will also show you all the features that the A.L.R. offers. Try to read the annotation in hardcopy format, as this is the most economical method. When you retrieve the annotation on a commercial database, weekly additions of new cases integrate the updates into the annotations. You will also be told if the annotation is superseded.

▼ Can A.L.R. Annotations Be Shepardized?

A.L.R. annotations can be Shepardized to see where they are cited in reported opinions and to see if a case reprinted in the A.L.R. has a parallel cite in a reporter. Most researchers do not Shepardize annotations because they are not primary authority but rather lead you to primary sources on point.

E. TREATISES AND HORNBOOKS

▼ What Are Treatises and Hornbooks?

Both hornbooks and treatises are secondary sources because they provide commentary, analysis, and criticism of the law and are written by private parties. Treatises and hornbooks help the researcher to understand the topic and, through cited references, provide citations to cases and statutes. **Treatises** are scholarly works, generally multivolume sets, that examine one legal topic, such as contracts, in great detail and with very broad coverage. **Hornbooks**, also scholarly but designed for the student of law, are generally one-volume works providing an overview of a single legal topic. The authors of hornbooks and treatises are legal scholars.

▼ How Do You Find a Thorough Treatise or Hornbook?

The best place to look for a hornbook or treatise is in the law library. The librarian will be able to refer you to the treatises that are best for the legal topic you are researching. You can also check the online catalog for treatise titles. There is a treatise for almost every legal subject. Many hornbooks are published by West Publishing Co. At the beginning of a West hornbook is a list entitled *Hornbook Series and Basic Legal Texts*, which provides all of the hornbooks categorized by legal subject.

▼ Which Treatises Are Most Noteworthy?

The following example treatises are well known and respected.

Corbin, *Contracts*
Herzog, *Bankruptcy Forms and Practice*
LaFave, *Principles of Criminal Law*
McCormick, *Evidence*
Rotunda and Nowak, *Constitutional Law*

▼ Why Do You Use a Treatise?

There are a few approaches to using a treatise. Because the treatise covers a single legal topic and is written like a text, rather than like a case opinion, it is easy to find relevant information. The amount of relevant information may present the only problem when using a treatise: So much detail is provided that you may lose sight of the focus of your research. A treatise is used to find a very detailed analysis of a point of law or a legal rule. A hornbook is used to find an overview of a point of law or a legal rule. Both sources provide the general rules of law, its exceptions, and information on how the law is evolving. Often, a treatise or hornbook offers discussion of how the legal rules are applied in specific situations or in specific factual scenarios. You should use a treatise or a hornbook to educate yourself in a legal discipline or when an encyclopedia does not offer adequate detail in the discussion of a topic.

PRACTICE POINTER

You can use Google Scholar, at http://scholar.google.com, to find books, too.

▼ How Do You Use a Treatise or Hornbook?

There are three methods of using a treatise or a hornbook, generally.

1. **The table of contents method.** Treatises and hornbooks have detailed tables of contents that serve as outlines of the legal topics covered. A chapter or a subchapter often discusses the area you are researching.
2. **The table method.** Hornbooks and treatises contain tables of cases and tables of statutes. Use the relevant table when you have an excellent case or statute on point and want to understand the

significance of the primary source in the context of the subject as a whole.

3. **The index method.** A subject index is found at the end of every treatise and hornbook. The index is a good place to start if you have found a word like *easement* and want to find out its relevance in property law.

▼ Are Treatises Ever Relied on as Authority?

Treatises are occasionally relied on as authority in a document when no primary authority is available on point and when it is necessary to show the progression or evolution of the law. Because scholars write treatises, they are considered to be very prestigious sources of secondary authority. Hornbooks should not be relied on for authority because they are designed for the student and are one-volume versions of treatises that support the study of the particular legal discipline.

▼ How Do You Cite to a Hornbook and a Treatise?

Bluebook **Rule 15.1** covers citation style for treatises and hornbooks. *ALWD* **Rule 20.1** uses the same format:

Wayne LaFave, *Search and Seizure: A Treatise on the Fourth Amendment* § 1.1 (6th ed. 2020).

▼ Are Treatises Available Online?

More and more treatise titles are appearing online. Westlaw, because it is part of West, makes an increasing number of treatise titles available online, and its list is growing. For instance, *Search and Seizure* is available on Westlaw in the database, "searchszr." Often updates are available online so that you can access the newest case references. Lexis also has an expanding number of treatises available. The benefit of using a treatise online is that you can perform full-text searching whereby you construct a query and retrieve relevant information with your own selection of terms rather than relying on any of the traditional research methods and the publisher's index entries. Some treatises are now available on the Internet.

▼ How Are Treatises and Hornbooks Updated?

Treatises are updated in two ways: pocket parts or supplements, which are published at least annually, and new editions. This updating format is most commonly used in hardcopy treatises. Always check to see that you are working with the most recent edition available and to see if there is a pocket part or updating supplement.

F. RESTATEMENTS OF THE LAW

▼ What Are Restatements?

Restatements of the Law, published by the American Law Institute, are the most prestigious source of secondary authority. The subjects covered are agency, conflict of laws, contracts, foreign relations, judgments, property, restitution, security, torts, and trusts. There is a Restatement on Security, but this set is only in the first edition. Each of the legal disciplines mentioned comprises a separate set of the Restatements. The authors of the Restatements write every rule of law from these legal disciplines in a form that resembles a code and not a judicial opinion. The drafters of the Restatements are "restating" the law. The purposes are to codify the common law holdings so that a researcher does not have to unearth the legal rule from the text of an opinion and to make common law principles straightforward and succinct, like statutes. The Comments and the Illustrations are most helpful in understanding the application of the rule. The Reporter's Note, following the Illustrations, contains case references in which the Restatement section has been cited. See Illustration 6-10.

NET NOTE

Washburn University has an excellent research guide for the Restatements at http://washburnlaw.edu/library/research/guides/restatements.html.

▼ How Are the Restatements Updated?

Most of the Restatements are in their second series. A few, such as Trusts, are in the third series. The rules, the codified-type versions of the legal principles, are updated in the appendix. Additional case references are also included in the appendix. The appendix is organized by section in the same order as the main text. The appendix is updated annually by pocket part supplements that are organized in the same manner as the main volume, by section. Also, the *Cumulative Annual Supplement* lists newer cases citing to the particular Restatement provision.

▼ How Do You Use the Restatements?

1. **The online method.** The Restatements are available on Lexis and Westlaw. This is an efficient method to use when you know the significant vocabulary words that describe the subject. If you are unfamiliar with the terminology or the words used to describe

ILLUSTRATION 6-10.   Sample Pages from Restatement (Second) of Contracts

on Illustration 6 to former § 267. Beach v. First Fed. Sav. & Loan Ass'n, 140 Ga. App. 882, 232 S.E.2d 158 (1977). Illustration 5 is adapted from Illustration 7 to former § 267.

Comment c. See former § 272. Illustration 6 is based on Illustration 1 to former § 268 and on Kane v. Hood, 30 Mass. (13 Pick.) 281 (1832). Illustration 7 is based on Illustration 2 to former § 268.

Comment d. This Comment replaces former § 273. See 3A Corbin, Contracts § 689 (1951); 6 Williston, Contracts § 887C (3d ed. 1962). Illustration 8 is based on Illustration 2 to former § 273 and on Beecher v. Conradt, 13 N.Y. (3 Kern.) 108 (1855); see also Kennelly v. Shapiro, 22? A.D. 488, 226 N.Y.S. 692 (1928).

Comment e. On the origin of the principle, see 6 Williston, Contracts §

830 (3d ed. 1962); Murray, Contracts § 162 (2d rev. ed. 1974). That a substantial failure to make timely progress payments is a material breach when the payments are required by a construction contract, see United States ex rel. Micro-King Co. v. Community Science Technology, Inc., 574 F.2d 1292, 1295 n.3 (5th Cir. 1978).

Comment f. Illustration 9 is based on Stewart v. Newbury, 220 N.Y. 379, 115 N.E. 984 (1917). See also Illustration 1 to former § 270. Illustration 10 is based on Clark v. Gulesian, 197 Mass. 492, 84 N.E. 94 (1908). The facts in Illustration 11 are taken from New Era Homes v. Forster, 299 N.Y. 303, 86 N.E.2d 757 (1949). Illustration 12 is based on Comment a to former § 270 and Illustration 1 to former § 268.

TOPIC 2. EFFECT OF PERFORMANCE AND NON-PERFORMANCE

§ 235.   Effect of Performance as Discharge and of Non-Performance as Breach

(1) **Full performance of a duty under a contract discharges the duty.**

(2) **When performance of a duty under a contract is due any non-performance is a breach.**

Comment:

a. *Discharge by performance.* Under the rule stated in Subsection (1), a duty is discharged when it is fully performed. Nothing less than full performance, however, has this effect and any defect in performance, even an insubstantial one, prevents discharge on this ground. The defect need not be wilful or even negligent. Although a court may ignore trifling departures, performance that is merely substantial does not result in discharge under Subsection (1). See Comment d to § 237. A duty may, of course, be discharged on some other ground. See Chapter 12. For example, a duty that has not been fully

ILLUSTRATION 6-10. *Continued*

> performed may be discharged on the ground of impracticability of performance. See Chapter 11.
>
> **Illustration:**
>
> 1. A contracts to build a house for B for $50,000 according to specifications furnished by B. A builds the house according to the specifications. A's duty to build the house is discharged.
>
> b. *Effect of non-performance.* Non-performance is not a breach unless performance is due. Performance may not be due because a required period of time has not passed, or because a condition has not occurred (§ 225), or because the duty has already been discharged (Chapter 12) as, for example, by impracticability of performance (Chapter 11). In such a case non-performance is justified. When performance is due, however, anything short of full performance is a breach, even if the party who does not fully perform was not at fault and even if the defect in his performance was not substantial. Non-performance of a duty when performance is due is a breach whether the duty is imposed by a promise stated in the agreement or by a term supplied by the court (§ 204), as in the case of the duty of good faith and fair dealing (§ 205). Non-performance includes defective performance as well as an absence of performance.
>
> **Illustrations:**
>
> 2. The facts being otherwise as stated in Illustration 1, A builds the house according to the specifications except for an inadvertent variation in kitchen fixtures which can easily be remedied for $100. A's non-performance is a breach.
>
> 3. A contracts with B to manufacture and deliver 100,000 plastic containers for a price of $100,000. The colors of the containers are to be selected by B from among those specified in the contract. B delays in making his selection for an unreasonable time, holding up their manufacture and causing A loss. B's delay is a breach. His duty of good faith and fair dealing (§ 205) includes a duty to make his selection within a reasonable time.
>
> 4. A contracts with B to repair B's building for $20,000, payment to be made "on the satisfaction of C, B's architect, and the issuance of his certificate." A makes the repairs but does not ask C for his certificate. B does not pay A. B's non-performance is not a breach. It is justified on the ground that performance is not due because of the non-occurrence of a condition. See Illustration 5 to § 227.

the legal principles, then the online method is very costly and not very efficient. Lexis and Westlaw provide current case citations for Restatement sections. The Restatement is easy to use online.

2. **The index method.** Use the index at the end of the set by looking up various descriptive words pertaining to your issue.
3. **The table of cases method.** When you have an excellent case on point, use the table of cases, organized in alphabetical order by plaintiff, to find references in the Restatements. This is the most efficient method when you have a specific case on point. Be sure to check the pocket part to locate references to newer cases.

▼ Can the Restatements Be Shepardized?

Yes, the Restatements can be Shepardized in the *Shepard's Restatement of Law Citations*. The *Shepard's* for the Restatements does not in any way validate the authority because the Restatements are secondary sources. *Shepard's*, in this instance, is a citator telling the researcher which cases contain citations to the particular Restatement section. Finding a case that cites your Restatement section may be helpful because a court may adopt the language from the Restatement section. On Lexis, you can Shepardize the Restatement provision when the section is on the screen.

▼ Are the Restatements Available Online?

Yes, as mentioned earlier, the Restatements are available online on both Lexis and Westlaw. The advantage of searching the Restatements online is that you do not have to rely on indexing terms. However, using the Restatements online can be very expensive if you are unfamiliar with the legal terms used.

▼ How Are the Restatements Cited?

Bluebook **Rule 12.9.4** indicates that the Restatements are cited as follows:

> RESTATEMENT (SECOND) OF CONTRACTS § 235 (AM. L. INST. 1981) — *Bluebook*. Note the use of large and small capitals may be used for stylistic purposes in court documents but is not required. See *Bluebook* **Rule B2.**

> Restatement (Second) of Contracts § 235 (Am. L. Inst. 1981) — *ALWD* **Rule 23.1**

Note that for both the *Bluebook* and *ALWD* format, the year is the date that the Restatement was published. You can find the year of publication on the title page of the Restatement volume.

When you are citing to a comment that follows the Restatement section, **Rule 3.4** of the *Bluebook* and *ALWD* **Rule 23.1** applies. For example:

> RESTATEMENT (SECOND) OF CONTRACTS § 235 cmt. a (AM. L. INST. 1981) — *Bluebook* format

> Restatement (Second) of Contracts § 235 cmt. a (Am. L. Inst. 1981) — *ALWD* format **Rule 23.1**

ALWD considers a comment a form of a pinpoint reference like a page number or an illustration. Note that in Restatement cites, *ALWD* only requires the use of small and large capitals in the citation when used in academic footnotes.

G. UNIFORM LAWS

Uniform Laws are secondary authority until they are adopted by a state legislature. The goal of the Uniform Laws is to provide consistency and reliability for state statutory authority to facilitate commerce, transactions, and relationships. The uniformity of statutory authority in many, many areas works to create a comprehensive set of statutory authority that provides consistency among the states. The Uniform Commercial Code is an example of a Uniform Law that has been adopted by many states. However, each state legislature must adopt the particular Uniform Law for the law to be binding authority in the jurisdiction. If a state legislature fails to adopt the Uniform Law or has yet to adopt the Uniform Law, the particular provision is a secondary source. Uniform Laws are very prestigious secondary sources. The legislative fact sheets provide insight into the provision's intent.

▼ Where Do You Find Uniform Laws?

Uniform Laws are available at the Uniform Law Commission site, http://uniformlaws.org. This free site is the most economical way to find, to update, and to read Uniform Laws. It provides all the Uniform Laws, in alphabetical order by title. You can obtain the text of the individual Uniform Law. On the site, when you click on the individual acts, you will be linked to the legislative fact sheet, act summary, and why the state should adopt the Uniform Law. This information is very helpful when you are trying to unearth the intent of a state statute that was originally a Uniform Law. You can use this information when you do not have a case that interprets and applies a statute. Additionally, this information is pertinent when your state has not adopted the statute, but you want to use the Uniform Law to show that your state should adopt the provision. Also, you will see a map of the United States showing the states that adopted the particular Uniform Law as a state statute and the state legislatures where the Uniform Law is currently introduced.

The site http://uniformlaws.org does have limitations, as it does not provide case references where the Uniform Law is cited. http://uniformlaws.org also does not include citations to the state codes where you can find the adopted Uniform Law.

The best way to find citations to cases that cite to a particular Uniform Law is to use *The Uniform Laws Annotated*, published by Thomson Reuters. The set also includes the precise code sections where the adopted Uniform Law is located in the particular state statute. *The Uniform Laws Annotated* is a multivolume set, organized by general topics. You can use *The Uniform Laws Annotated* on Westlaw and in print. All the updates are included in the Westlaw format whereas you need to consult the pocket part of each volume in the hardcopy version.

ILLUSTRATION 6-11. Uniform Law Commission Site — Sample Screen Shots

UNIFORM CONTROLLED SUBSTANCES ACT (1994) *
(Last Revised or Amended in 1995)

Drafted by the

NATIONAL CONFERENCE OF COMMISSIONERS
ON UNIFORM STATE LAWS

and by it

APPROVED AND RECOMMENDED FOR ENACTMENT
IN ALL THE STATES

at its

ANNUAL CONFERENCE
MEETING IN ITS ONE-HUNDRED-AND-THIRD YEAR
IN CHICAGO, ILLINOIS
JULY 29 - AUGUST 5, 1994

WITH PREFATORY NOTE AND COMMENTS

COPYRIGHT 1994
By
NATIONAL CONFERENCE OF COMMISSIONERS
ON UNIFORM STATE LAWS

December 28, 1995

* The Conference changed the designation of the Controlled Substances Act (1990)(1994) from Uniform to Model as approved by the Executive Committee on July 11, 2006.

ILLUSTRATION 6-11. *Continued*

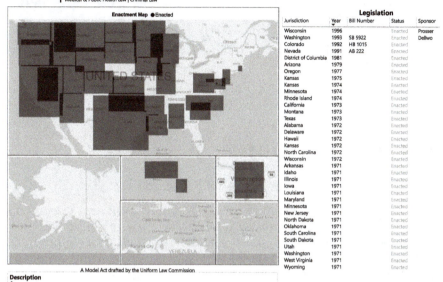

1990 | Controlled Substances Act

| Medical & Public Health Law | Criminal Law

Jurisdiction	Year	Bill Number	Status	Sponsor
Wisconsin	1996		Enacted	Prosser
Washington	1993	SB 5922	Enacted	Dellwo
Colorado	1992	HB 1015	Enacted	
Nevada	1991	AB 222	Enacted	
District of Columbia	1981		Enacted	
Arizona	1979		Enacted	
Oregon	1977		Enacted	
Kansas	1975		Enacted	
Kansas	1974		Enacted	
Minnesota	1974		Enacted	
Rhode Island	1974		Enacted	
California	1973		Enacted	
Montana	1973		Enacted	
Texas	1973		Enacted	
Alabama	1972		Enacted	
Delaware	1972		Enacted	
Hawaii	1972		Enacted	
Kansas	1972		Enacted	
North Carolina	1972		Enacted	
Wisconsin	1972		Enacted	
Arkansas	1971		Enacted	
Idaho	1971		Enacted	
Illinois	1971		Enacted	
Iowa	1971		Enacted	
Louisiana	1971		Enacted	
Maryland	1971		Enacted	
Minnesota	1971		Enacted	
New Jersey	1971		Enacted	
North Dakota	1971		Enacted	
Oklahoma	1971		Enacted	
South Carolina	1971		Enacted	
South Dakota	1971		Enacted	
Utah	1971		Enacted	
Washington	1971		Enacted	
West Virginia	1971		Enacted	
Wyoming	1971		Enacted	

A Model Act drafted by the Uniform Law Commission

Description

The Model Controlled Substances Act (MCSA) provides fundamental law in the fight against narcotic and dangerous drugs and promotes uniformity between state and federal drug laws.

Cornell's Legal Information Institute provides access to select Uniform Laws in the areas of commercial code, probate code, evidence, as well as under the topics of matrimonial, family and health law, and business and finance. The site provides the precise code cite for the state statute where the particular Uniform Law was adopted. This site is free and is an easy way to access state statutes that are the adoption of a Uniform Law. See www.law.cornell.edu/uniform.

▼ How Do You Update a Uniform Law?

The easiest way to update a Uniform Law is to check http://uniform laws.org for amendments or changes to the Uniform Law at issue.

▼ How Do You Validate a Uniform Law?

Because a Uniform Law is a secondary source until it is adopted by a jurisdiction, validation is not performed. You can search to see where a Uniform Law is cited in case law. You can perform this search on Westlaw or Lexis. It is best to check if the Uniform Law was adopted by a particular state. Once the Uniform Law is adopted by the state, it is then primary authority and you can validate the particular state statute cite with Shepard's or KeyCite.

▼ How Do You Cite a Uniform Law?

Uniform Laws are called "Uniform Acts" in the *Bluebook*. You can also cite to the *Uniform Laws Annotated* if your material is from that source. Use these formats:

> Certificate of Title Act § 2 (Unif. Law Comm'n 2005) — *Bluebook* **Rule 12.9.4**
>
> Unif. Certificate of Title Act § 2 (2005) — *ALWD* **Rule 23.6**

H. LEGAL PERIODICALS

▼ What Are Legal Periodicals?

Legal periodicals are secondary sources ranging from very prestigious to very practical forms of authority. Scholarly law review articles are considered the most prestigious, and bar journals and commercial publications are considered the most pragmatic. The major categories of legal periodicals are:

1. academic law reviews
2. bar journals and practitioner's periodicals
3. commercial journals and newsletters
4. legal newspapers
5. blogs

Every conceivable subject is covered in a legal periodical. Some legal periodicals focus on a particular practice area, like estate planning. The different forms of legal periodicals have different attributes. Although not scholarly, legal blogs are a source of very current commentary on legal events and legislation.

▼ Why Would You Use a Legal Periodical?

Legal periodicals are published quickly and keep abreast of new legal issues and laws. They are a terrific place to obtain articles discussing the impact of a Supreme Court decision or the enactment of new legislation because such information is published very quickly, far faster than any text could be printed. Also, certain legal periodicals (for example, the practitioner's journals, the journals that pertain to specific bar association sections, the commercial journals, and newsletters) cover discrete legal subject areas and enable paralegals, practitioners, and researchers to keep up with all of the new developments in their respective practice areas. The website for a particular legal periodical or journal is also a terrific resource. You can also use Google to search for blogs and publications on a particular topic. When using a search engine such as Google, you may receive an abundance of hits that might not all be relevant.

The legal newspapers provide up-to-date information about the legal profession, the courts and significant opinions, the federal and state legislatures and significant laws, and information about law firms and the business of law. Legal newspapers also write about major and interesting cases and clients. Legal newspapers provide great insight into the realities of legal practice. Additionally, national newspapers such as *The New York Times, The Washington Post,* and *The Wall Street Journal* offer up-to-the-minute coverage of legal events with timely articles on seminal cases, U.S. Supreme Court activity, and pending legislation. National newspapers are a terrific resource to follow activity in the U.S. Congress. The papers' websites are updated very frequently and often provide links to the legislation or court decision under discussion.

Academic law review articles are very scholarly and are excellent finding tools because of the voluminous number of cited references in each article. Academic law review articles are often theoretical and discuss the application of a particular legal doctrine or a trend in the law. Sometimes authors of law review articles suggest how the law should hold on certain issues. Because the academic law reviews are a very prestigious source of secondary authority, sometimes these resources are relied on for persuasive purposes when no primary authority is available on point.

▼ How Do You Obtain Relevant Legal Periodical Articles?

First, the researcher must decide the type of information needed. For example, is scholarly material required, or is practical information on drafting a will needed? After deciding on the type of information required for the project, the source should be selected accordingly. If scholarly material is required, then an academic law review would be appropriate. If practical information is needed, then a practitioner's journal, bar association section newsletter, or commercial publication dealing with the legal discipline is appropriate. If the researcher needs information about a law firm, a client, or a very recent (two-week-old) Supreme Court decision, then a legal newspaper is the ideal source.

Almost all legal periodicals, regardless of format, are indexed. The major indexes are:

Current Law Index (1980 to present): The most comprehensive hardcopy index. Published monthly, by Gale.
Current Index to Legal Periodicals.
HeinOnline: An easy-to-use subscription database.
Index to Foreign Legal Periodicals (1960 to present).
LegalTrac: Online subscription version of hardcopy *Current Law Index.*

There are many ways to access legal periodicals for free. Google Scholar, found at http://scholar.google.com, is a free search engine for citations to legal articles and law journals. It provides abstracts of articles. Also, many law reviews have their own websites. Start with the law school website.

▼ Are Legal Periodicals Available on Lexis and Westlaw?

Yes, legal periodicals are available online on both Lexis and Westlaw. Both databases have full-text articles, cover to cover, of an increasing number of law reviews. Also, the NEWS library on Lexis contains the full-text copies of legal newspapers. Westlaw has the full-text articles from an increasing number of law reviews. Most law reviews have websites, so you may be able to access the journal directly. It is a costly way to obtain a citation to a law review article when you search on Lexis or Westlaw.

▼ How Do You Cite to a Law Review or Law Journal?

Bluebook **Rule 16**, with **Table 13** for periodical title abbreviations, and *ALWD* **Rule 21**, with **Appendix 5 online** for abbreviations, cover the citation form:

> Mitchell N. Berman, *Justification and Excuse, Law and Morality*, 53 Duke L.J. 1 (2003).

A legal newspaper is cited according to *Bluebook* **Rule 16.6** and *ALWD* **Rule 21.3(f)**. For example:

> Wayne Smith, *Remote Access: Striking a Balance*, Law Tech. News, Jan. 2005, at 11.

▼ What Is a Blog?

Blogs are a very current source of information. The material may or may not be verified or edited. You will often not have links to primary authority. However, blogs cannot be overlooked for their up-to-the-minute commentary and policy coverage.

To cite to a blog, consult **Rule 18.1** in the *Bluebook*, referred to as dynamic webpages, for an example of the basic citation form. Sometimes blogs are called Direct Internet Resources because they do not have any print equivalent. The citation formats for blogs are in *Bluebook* **Rule 18.2.2** and *ALWD* **Rule 31.2**.

CHAPTER SUMMARY

Secondary authorities describe, analyze, and criticize primary sources. You use secondary authorities to educate yourself about a legal topic and to find citations to primary sources.

The major sources of secondary authority are dictionaries, thesauri, encyclopedias, *American Law Reports* (A.L.R.), hornbooks, treatises, Restatements of the Law, Uniform Laws, and legal periodicals.

The dictionary and the thesaurus are used to find definitions and synonyms. Encyclopedias are used to educate yourself about a legal topic. *American Law Reports* contain articles called annotations that explore a legal issue in depth. Hornbooks are written for the student of law and cover a single legal subject. Treatises cover a single legal subject but go into great detail. Restatements of the Law, produced by the American Law Institute, attempt to organize common law holdings from cases into a format resembling statutes. Legal periodicals include academic law reviews, bar association and legal specialty publications, and legal newspapers. Law reviews are the most scholarly form of legal periodicals. Law review articles contain many citations to primary authority and are known for research accuracy.

Updating and correctly citing secondary authorities are important in your research process. Generally, it is best to rely on primary authority when writing a memo or a brief. Rely on secondary authority when there is no primary authority on point.

KEY TERMS

American Jurisprudence
American Law Reports
Corpus Juris Secundum
Cumulative Supplements
hornbooks
legal dictionary
legal encyclopedia

legal meaning
legal periodicals
Restatements of the Law
secondary authority
thesaurus
treatises
Uniform Laws

EXERCISES

SELF-ASSESSMENT

1. What are the *American Law Reports*? What is found in the *American Law Reports*? List two research features that the *American Law Reports* provides in an annotation. What is the common abbreviation for the *American Law Reports*?
2. What are hornbooks?
3. What is a legal encyclopedia? What do you use a legal encyclopedia for when researching?
4. What are the Restatements of Law?
5. What is a secondary authority? Provide three examples of secondary authority.
6. What is a treatise?

COMPARING SECONDARY AUTHORITIES

7. Look up the word *easement* in a legal dictionary. Now look up the same word in Am. Jur. 2d and then in your state legal encyclopedia. How is the term treated in each encyclopedia? How is this different from a dictionary?

ENCYCLOPEDIA RESEARCH

8. Locate the section in Am. Jur. 2d discussing *easements by necessity*. First, try to locate the section by using the index method, then by the topic outline method. Go to the encyclopedia volume for the sections that you found. Examine the treatment of *easements by necessity*. Do you see any cases from your state? Now update the section in the pocket part. Are there any new case references?

9. Look up *Pawnbroker* in the index of Am. Jur. 2d. Are there any encyclopedia sections discussing pawnbrokers? Now look up *Pawnbroker* in your state legal encyclopedia. Are there any relevant cases or statutes from your state?

10. Use Am. Jur. 2d. Is there a topic called *gaming*? What similar topic covers the subject of gaming in Am. Jur. 2d? Go to the index in Am. Jur. 2d and look up *gaming*. Where are you led? Compare the text in the main volume of Am. Jur. 2d that covers a topic similar to the *gaming* topic in C.J.S. How are the topics similar and how are they different? Does Am. Jur. 2d have a pocket part to the main volume that updates the topics? Using the index to Am. Jur. 2d, look up *casinos*. What do you find?

11. Look up *negligence* in a law dictionary. Look up *negligence* in Am. Jur. 2d. What did you find in each source? How do the sources differ in their treatment of *negligence*?

12. How are Am. Jur. 2d and C.J.S. similar? How are they different? What research benefits do you obtain when consulting a legal encyclopedia? Does a legal encyclopedia lead you to other library resources or research tools? List two of the additional research tools.

PRACTICE SKILLS

13. Read the following fact situation, which you first encountered in Chapter 4. Answer the questions following the situation.

FACTS

Nate Late, a business owner, has two partners in the operation of Loose Cannon Manufacturing in Gurnee, Illinois. He owns 33 percent of a $3 million company. Late is ill, but not dying. He is grooming a 26-year-old, Ivan T. All, to run the business. He tells his family he likes All and wants to teach him the business. Nate Late dies.

The most current will leaves Late's estate to his wife of 24 years, Shirley Late, and his only son, Lou Sier. Mr. All tells Mrs. Late that her husband told All he intended to give the 26-year-old his one-third interest in Loose Cannon. This conversation took place in front of a bank president. No written record exists concerning Late's intention to give his stock to All. However, family members knew that Late intended for All to run the business and for All to get something if the business was sold. None of the family believed that Late intended to give the business to newcomer Ivan T. All. Late's shares of stock were never given to All. The shares were in the safe deposit box shared by Late and his wife.

Mrs. Late said that Mr. Late planned to give her the shares. He told her this when he opened the joint safety deposit box and gave her the key.

You work for a firm that has been retained by Mrs. Late. She would like to know if All can prove that Mr. Late gave All Mr. Late's interest in the company.

    a. What topics might be relevant to this question?

    b. How would you determine where to find those topics?

    c. List the steps that you would take.

    d. Take those steps. Note what you find.

    e. Select two topics for review. Review those topics. Which topics were most relevant?

    f. What additional information did you find to determine the answer to Mrs. Late's question?

    g. Where did you find that information?

14. Use Google Scholar to find a citation to an article about using Facebook as evidence for a divorce.

15. Consult Google Scholar. Is there a citation to an article on the topic of easements to make repairs?

16. On Westlaw, search Pennsylvania legal encyclopedia or *Pennsylvania Jurisprudence* for an entry on easements concerning "Private Ways and Alleys."

17. Consult *Florida Jurisprudence Second* on Westlaw. List citations to sections concerning easements, alleys, and rights-of-way.

CHAPTER 7

CONSTITUTIONS AND STATUTES

CHAPTER OVERVIEW

Constitutions and statutes occupy the top rung in the hierarchy of authority. Constitutions are the highest form of legal authority, followed by statutes. In ordinary legal dilemmas, statutes are often the controlling law. In our society statutes govern relationships like marriage and adoption, transactions like banking, and behavior like criminal acts. Learning how to find relevant statutes and constitutional provisions is very important for effective legal research.

This chapter details the research methods used to find, update, cite, and validate constitutions and statutes. The legislative process that charts the path that a statute takes from initial sponsorship through codification is outlined. This chapter gives you the skills you need to perform constitutional and statutory research.

A. CONSTITUTIONS

▼ What Is a Constitution?

A **constitution** is a document that establishes the legal structure of a state or nation and the basic legal principles that control the operation of the government and the conduct of its citizens.

▼ What Is the Relationship Between the Federal Constitution and the State Constitutions?

The U.S. Constitution is, in essence, the supreme law of the land. The state constitutions are the supreme law of each particular state. The federal constitution takes precedence over any state constitution.

▼ Who Determines Whether a Statute Violates the U.S. Constitution?

Federal courts determine whether a statute violates the U.S. Constitution, and state courts determine if their respective state constitutions are being violated. Although courts determine if a statute violates the constitution, courts cannot rewrite or repeal statutes; only legislatures can. Under the separation of powers of the branches of the government only the U.S. Congress can repeal or redraft legislation or amend the U.S. Constitution. If a federal court determines that a state constitutional provision violates the U.S. Constitution, then the court must deem that section of the state constitution unconstitutional. However, the appropriate legislature can only amend or repeal the provision.

▼ Can Federal and State Constitutions Be Validated?

Yes, federal and state constitutions can be validated. KeyCite on Westlaw and *Shepard's®* on Lexis indicate if a court of law has interpreted or applied a section of the U.S. Constitution in question. KeyCite and *Shepard's* serve to validate the authority and are finding tools to obtain relevant case law decisions applying the constitutional section or amendment at issue in your research. For a full discussion of how to validate authority, see Chapter 5.

Illustration 7-1 shows the *Go-Bart* decision and where the Fourth Amendment is discussed in the case. State constitutions can also be validated with *Shepard's* or KeyCite. See Chapter 5, on validating authorities.

ILLUSTRATION 7-1.   Page from Decision in *U.S. Reports* That Discusses the Fourth Amendment

---

344   OCTOBER TERM, 1930.

Syllabus.   282 U. S.

to do business within a state.   In those cases the judgment of this Court in no way restricts the further exercise of the legislative power of the state in any constitutional manner.   Here the Commission is ousted from the exercise of power which Congress has given it, and an order is sanctioned authorizing an issue of securities which it cannot be said the Commission has approved, and which this Court does not purport to say is appropriate under the statute.

Mr. Justice Holmes and Mr. Justice Brandeis concur in this opinion.

GO-BART IMPORTING COMPANY et al. *v.* UNITED STATES.

CERTIORARI TO THE CIRCUIT COURT OF APPEALS FOR THE SECOND CIRCUIT.

No. 111. Argued November 25, 1930.—Decided January 5, 1931.

1. A warrant issued by a United States Commissioner, addressed only to the Marshal and his deputies, and based upon, and reciting the substance of, a complaint that was verified merely on information and belief and that did not state an offense,—*held* invalid on its face, and no authority to prohibition officers to make an arrest. P. 355.

2. Acting under color of an invalid warrant of arrest, and falsely claiming to have a search warrant, prohibition agents entered the office of a company, placed under arrest two of its officers, and made a general search of the premises. They compelled by threats of force the opening of a desk and safe, and seized therefrom and from other parts of the office, papers and records belonging to the company and its officers. The officers of the company were arraigned before a United States Commissioner, and by him held on bail further to answer the complaint (U. S. C., Title 18, § 591), while the seized papers were held under the control of the United States Attorney in the care and custody of the prohibition agent in charge. The company, and its two officers individually, before

ILLUSTRATION 7-1.   *Continued*

GO-BART CO. *v.* UNITED STATES.   345

344   Syllabus.

an information or indictment had been returned against them,
applied to the District Court for an order to enjoin the use of the
seized papers as evidence and directing their return. On a rule
against the United States to show cause, the United States Attorney
appeared and opposed the motion and an affidavit of the agent in
charge was also filed in opposition. The applications were denied.
Held:

(1) In the proceedings before him, the Commissioner acted
merely as an officer of the District Court in a matter of which it
had authority to take control at any time. P. 353.

(2) Notwithstanding the order to show cause was addressed to
the United States alone, the proceeding was in substance and effect
against the United States Attorney and the prohibition agent in
charge, the latter being required by the Prohibition Act to report
violations of it to the former and being authorized by the statute,
subject to the former's control, to conduct such prosecutions; and
both these officers were subject to the proper exertion of the disciplinary powers of the court. P. 354.

(3) The District Court had jurisdiction summarily to determine
whether the evidence should be suppressed and the papers returned
to the petitioners. P. 355.

(4) The company being a stranger to the proceedings before
the Commissioner, the order of the District Court as to it was
final and appealable. P. 356.

(5) There being no information or indictment against the officers
of the company when the application was made, and nothing to
show that any criminal proceeding would ever be instituted in that
court against them, it follows that the order was not made in or
dependent upon any case or proceeding pending before the court,
and therefore the order as to them was appealable. *Id.*

→ (6) The Fourth Amendment forbids every search that is unreasonable, and is to be liberally construed. P. 356.

(7) Assuming that the facts of which the arresting officers had
been previously informed were sufficient to justify the arrests
without a warrant, nevertheless the uncontradicted evidence requires a finding that the search of the premises was unreasonable.
Marron v. *United States*, 275 U. S. 192, distinguished. P. 356.

(8) The District Court is directed to enjoin the United States
Attorney and the agent in charge from using the papers as evidence
and to order the same returned to petitioners. P. 358.

40 F. (2d) 593, reversed.

▼ Where Are Federal and State Constitutions Found?

The full text of the current version of the U.S. Constitution as well
as all the amendments are contained in the first volume of the annotated versions of the *United States Code* (U.S.C.), the *United States Code*

Service (U.S.C.S.), and the *United States Code Annotated* (U.S.C.A.). Encyclopedias are also sources of unannotated versions of the U.S. Constitution. Additionally, the full text of the U.S. Constitution is available at www.congress.gov/constitution-annotated/.

State constitutions are located in the first volume of the respective state code. Both the unannotated and the annotated state codes contain the state constitutions.

▼ How Do You Cite Federal or State Constitutions?

Bluebook **Rule 11** and *ALWD* **Rule 13** outline the format. The U.S. Constitution cite includes the particular article, section, and clause.

U.S. Const. art. II, § 2, cl. 1

This cite is used when you are referring to the body of the Constitution. A special citation format is required when you are referring to an amendment.

U.S. Const. amend. II

State constitutions are indicated by the name of the state in the *Bluebook* abbreviated format. *Bluebook* **Table 1** and *ALWD* **Appendix 1** indicate the accepted state name abbreviation. The postal abbreviation is not always used. The state of Washington's postal abbreviation is WA, but the citation abbreviation is Wash. A section of the Washington state constitution would be cited as follows:

Wash. Const. art. I, § 2

Years or dates are not included in citations to federal or state constitutions that are current. Parenthetical notations after the citation indicate the year only if a constitutional provision was repealed or amended. An example is the Eighteenth Amendment to the U.S. Constitution prohibiting the sale of liquor. This amendment was later repealed by the Twenty-First Amendment. *Bluebook* **Rule 11** and *ALWD* **Rule 13.3(b)** use this example for the Prohibition amendment:

U.S. Const. amend. XVIII (repealed 1933).—*Bluebook* and *ALWD* format

If more information is available, you can use this format:

U.S. Const. amend. XVIII, *repealed by* U.S. Const. amend. XXI.— *Bluebook* and *ALWD* format

▼ Are Constitutions Available on Lexis and Westlaw?

The full text of the U.S. Constitution, in its current format, is available on Lexis. Westlaw has the full text of the current U.S. Constitution as well. The individual state constitutions are available on both Lexis and Westlaw.

▼ Are There Any Hardcopy Digests or Other Finding Tools
That Assist with Researching Federal Constitutional Issues?

Yes, the *United States Supreme Court Digest* (for a detailed explanation of how to use digests, see Chapter 4). Also, *Shepard's* and KeyCite are terrific finding tools in that they provide cases and secondary sources citing to the particular part of the constitution you are researching. There are annotations discussing constitutional issues in the *American Law Reports Federal.*

Do not overlook hornbooks and treatises. An excellent treatise on constitutional law is:

American Constitutional Law by Fisher

A treatise is the best place to start researching a constitutional law issue. Treatises explain the legal issues and indicate which cases are the most important. Treatises are particularly helpful in the area of constitutional law because the issues are very complex and require a high level of analysis. For more information on secondary sources, see Chapter 6.

B. STATUTES

▼ What Are Statutes?

Statutes are the laws enacted by either a federal or a state legislature. The business of the legislature is to enact laws. Statutes, both state and federal, as well as municipal and county ordinances and charters, are primary authority.

PRACTICE POINTER

Read the daily *New York Times, Washington Post,* or *The Wall Street Journal* to stay current with the activity in Congress.

---

1. The Legislative Process

▼ How Is a Statute Created Through the Federal Legislative Process?

Anyone can propose **legislation.** Very often special interest groups and law firms propose legislation. Once the legislation is proposed, a **sponsor** in the ranks of Congress must be found to introduce the legislation.

Legislation is generally introduced in the U.S. House of Representatives, but it can be introduced in the U.S. Senate. For purposes of our discussion, assume the legislation is introduced in the House. Once introduced, it is called a **slip bill.** The slip bill is given a numerical designation and is referred to the appropriate **House committee** and then often referred to a **subcommittee.** A committee print of the bill is created. Hearings are conducted on the bill to determine its impact and effectiveness. Various experts may testify at the hearings to give input as to the possible effects of the legislation or to offer insight as to the purpose the legislation will serve. The tangible result of the hearings is the transcript of the testimony. This records the testimony of experts and lobbyists and their exhibits.

The next stage is the presentation of the committee's report. The **committee report** is a very informative resource because it generally includes the purpose of the bill and the public policies that the bill addresses. The bill is then debated on the floor of the House. The *Congressional Record,* which prints all activity occurring on the floor of both the House and the Senate, prints the transcripts of the debates. More policy information can be gathered from the debates. Flaws in the legislation can also be discerned from the text of the debates. The bill must pass by vote in the chamber of Congress in which it was initiated. In our example, the bill began in the House, so it would have to pass in the House before going to the Senate for approval.

When a bill is passed by the House and sent to the Senate, it must be referred to the appropriate committee and follow the identical route as it did in the first chamber. When the Senate passes its version of the bill, it may differ from the original House bill. Before the bill can become law, both chambers must pass the same version of the bill. If the House and the Senate pass different versions of the bill, the bill is referred to a **conference committee**, which issues a conference committee report and the conference committee version of the bill. The conference committee version is then submitted for votes in both chambers.

If both congressional chambers approve the same version, the bill is sent to the President for signing. If the President signs the bill, it becomes a slip law. If the President **vetoes** the bill, that is, refuses to approve it, the bill goes back to the Congress, and Congress may override the veto by a two-thirds majority vote in both the House and the Senate. If the President does not sign or veto the bill within ten days and the legislature is still in session, the bill automatically becomes law. Occasionally, the President uses a pocket veto. A **pocket veto** occurs when there are fewer than ten days left in the legislative session and the President neither signs nor vetoes the bill, but merely waits for the session to expire. If the session expires before the President acts on the bill, the bill dies because it did not survive the legislative session. If the sponsors are still interested in passing this legislation, it must be reintroduced, in either chamber, at the beginning of the next legislative session. If both chambers pass the bill in the same exact version, then it is sent again to the President for signing. The President has the same choices: sign or veto. If the President signs the bill, it becomes a slip law.

NET NOTE

Consult www.congress.gov. This site is a terrific resource for legislative information that extends back to the 93rd Congress for many resources. This site is updated the morning after each session's adjournment, so it is a valuable source for current legislative activity and for bill tracking.

▼ What Are Slip Laws?

Slip laws are the first written presentation of enacted laws from a legislative body. Slip laws are identified by numbers, for example, Pub. L. No. 96-242. This cite is for a federal session law, or **public law**, for the amendments (to include the definition of "recycled wool") to the statute with the popular name: the Wool Products Labeling Act of 1939. The 96 indicates the congressional or legislative session, in this case the 96th Congress. The 242 indicates that it is the 242nd law passed by the 96th Congress. Slip laws are published in the order in which they are enacted.

Slip laws can be obtained at federal government depository libraries (many university and large city libraries are government depository libraries), http://congress.gov, or www.gpo.gov/fdsys. Slip laws can also be obtained from the law's sponsor in Congress. The *United States Code Annotated,* the *United States Code Service,* and the *United States Code Congressional and Administrative News* have advance services that publish the slip laws. You can get the slip laws on Lexis and on Westlaw, too. Advance services are paperbound volumes that contain updated information published in advance of the bound volume or supplement.

▼ What Are Session Laws?

At the end of a congressional session, all of the laws created during the course of the session are numbered and given the designation of **session laws.** Session laws on the federal level, also known as public laws, are added to the *Statutes at Large* and receive a *Statutes at Large* citation.

See Illustration 7-2 for the amendment to the Wool Products Labeling Act in the *Statutes at Large* at 94 Stat. 344. The text for the amendment to the Act, to include "recycled wool" in the *Statutes at Large*, is identical to what is found in the earlier slip law. You can find the *Statutes at Large*, from 1951 to date, at govinfo.gov.

▼ What Are the *Statutes at Large*?

The **Statutes at Large** are the compilation of the slip laws from the session of Congress that just ended. After each congressional session ends, the slip laws from that session are bound into at least one volume to form the *Statutes at Large*. The laws are published in chronological order rather than codified like the statutes because they document all legislation enacted during the congressional session. Unfortunately, the *Statutes at Large* volumes are not produced immediately after a congressional session. The *Statutes at Large* contain the public laws, or slip laws, as well as presidential proclamations and private laws. The wording of the session laws in the *Statutes at Large* is identical to the public law. The federal codes have tables indicating the *Statutes at Large* citation for a public law. See Illustration 7-2 for a reprint of the *Statutes at Large*. The *Statutes at Large*, beginning with the 82nd Congress, is available at govinfo.gov. See Illustration 7-8 for an example of the *Statutes at Large* and Public Law Numbers Table.

▼ What Is Codification?

Finally, the session laws are codified. **Codification** means that the session laws are grouped by subject and placed in the statutes according to their titles, which contain particular subject areas of the law. Sometimes the process of organizing and placing the laws, as passed, according to their respective subject, is called classification. Unlike cases, which are published as the opinions are written, federal statutes are arranged by a defined group of 54 subject categories called titles. See Illustration 7-3 for the list of titles. Statutes are updated during the course of a legislative session if the legislature proposes amendments or revisions. For instance, The Wool Products Labeling Act of 1939 was amended.

The most comprehensive finding tool for the appropriate statute, after it is codified, is an annotated statute set because we rely on unofficial codes for up-to-date information, editorial enhancements, and detailed indices. A new version of the official *United States Code* appears approximately every six years. An official *United States Code* was published in 2012 and in 2018. In the interim, the code is updated by slip laws and session laws because Congress works continually to create and enact legislation. The *United States Code Annotated* on Westlaw and the *United States Code Service* on Lexis are updated weekly to include all new congressional activity affecting the statute section you are researching. When accessing the relevant code section on either Lexis or Westlaw, there is no need to consult a pocket part supplement as all of the updates are integrated into the material retrieved. (See Illustration 7-6, for example.)

ILLUSTRATION 7-2.   Sample Session Law Published in
Statutes at Large

---

94 STAT. 344 PUBLIC LAW 96–242—MAY 5, 1980

Public Law 96–242
96th Congress

An Act

May 5, 1980
[H.R. 4197]

Wool Products
Labeling Act,
amendment.
15 USC 68.

To amend the Wool Products Labeling Act of 1939 with respect to recycled wool.

Be it enacted by the Senate and House of Representatives of the United States of America in Congress assembled, That (a) section 2(c) of the Wool Products Labeling Act of 1939 (54 Stat. 1128) is amended to read as follows:

"(c) The term 'recycled wool' means (1) the resulting fiber when wool has been woven or felted into a wool product which, without ever having been utilized in any way by the ultimate consumer, subsequently has been made into a fibrous state, or (2) the resulting fiber when wool or reprocessed wool has been spun, woven, knitted, or felted into a wool product which, after having been used in any way by the ultimate consumer, subsequently has been made into a fibrous state.".

Repeal.

(b) Subsection (d) of section 2 of the Wool Products Labeling Act of 1939 is repealed.

(c) Subsections (e), (f), (g), (h), and (i) of section 2 of the Wool Products Labeling Act of 1939 and all references thereto are redesignated as subsections (d), (e), (f), (g), and (h), respectively.

(d) Section 2(d) of such Act, as redesignated by subsection (c) of this section, is amended by striking out ", reprocessed wool, or reused wool" and inserting in lieu thereof "or recycled wool".

15 USC 68b.

SEC. 2. Section 4(a)(2)(A) of the Wool Products Labeling Act of 1939 is amended—

(1) by striking out "(2) reprocessed wool; (3) reused wool" and inserting in lieu thereof "(2) recycled wool";

(2) by striking out "(4)" and inserting in lieu thereof "(3)"; and

(3) by striking out "(5)" and by inserting in lieu thereof "(4)".

Effective date.
15 USC 68 note.

SEC. 3. The amendments made by this Act shall take effect with respect to wool products manufactured on or after the date sixty days after the date of enactment of this Act.

Approved May 5, 1980.

LEGISLATIVE HISTORY:

HOUSE REPORT No. 96–795 (Comm. on Interstate and Foreign Commerce).
SENATE REPORT No. 96–655 (Comm. on Commerce, Science, and Transportation).
CONGRESSIONAL RECORD, Vol. 126 (1980):
    Mar. 11, considered and passed House.
    Apr. 23, considered and passed Senate.

ILLUSTRATION 7-3. Table of U.S.C. Titles from uscode.house.gov

```
Front Matter
*Title 1—General Provisions
Title 2—The Congress
*Title 3—The President
*Title 4—Flag And Seal, Seat Of Government, And The States
*Title 5—Government Organization And Employees; and Appendix
Title 6—Domestic Security
Title 7—Agriculture
Title 8—Aliens And Nationality
*Title 9—Arbitration
*Title 10—Armed Forces
*Title 11—Bankruptcy; and Appendix
Title 12—Banks And Banking
*Title 13—Census
*Title 14—Coast Guard
Title 15—Commerce And Trade
Title 16—Conservation
*Title 17—Copyrights
*Title 18—Crimes And Criminal Procedure; and Appendix
Title 19—Customs Duties
Title 20—Education
Title 21—Food And Drugs
Title 22—Foreign Relations And Intercourse
*Title 23—Highways
Title 24—Hospitals And Asylums
Title 25—Indians
Title 26—Internal Revenue Code
Title 27—Intoxicating Liquors
*Title 28—Judiciary And Judicial Procedure; and Appendix
Title 29—Labor
Title 30—Mineral Lands And Mining
*Title 31—Money And Finance
*Title 32—National Guard
Title 33—Navigation And Navigable Waters
*Title 35—Patents
*Title 36—Patriotic And National Observances, Ceremonies, And Organizations
*Title 37—Pay And Allowances Of The Uniformed Services
*Title 38—Veterans' Benefits
*Title 39—Postal Service
*Title 40—Public Buildings, Property, And Works
*Title 41—Public Contracts
Title 42—The Public Health And Welfare
Title 43—Public Lands
*Title 44—Public Printing And Documents
Title 45—Railroads
*Title 46—Shipping
Title 47—Telecommunications
Title 48—Territories And Insular Possessions
*Title 49—Transportation
Title 50—War And National Defense; and Appendix
*Title 51—National And Commercial Space Programs
Title 52—Voting And Elections
Title 53—[Reserved]
*Title 54—National Park Service And Related Programs
Popular Names and Tables
```

Constant updating is an essential component of statutory research. For instance, Pub. L. No. 96-242 (1996) updated the Wool Products Labeling Act of 1939 by amending the language of the statute to include recycled wool. Look carefully at Illustrations 7-4, 7-5, and 7-6 for amendments following the statute. These illustrations show how different publications provide information. Illustration 7-4 shows the text of the statute in the official *United States Code* for 2018. The official code does not show research enhancements or citing references. Looking at the unofficial codes in Illustrations 7-5 and 7-6, you will see legislative history references, relevant *Code of Federal Regulations* citations, research aids including practice materials and secondary sources, as well as cases citing the code section.

Staying current is essential when using statutory authority, because Congress passes new legislation continually during its sessions. When you retrieve statutes on uscode.house.gov, govinfo.gov, Lexis, and Westlaw, the code sections will indicate that the statute reflects updates current through a recent date. If you use hardcopy sources, always check the year of the code volume and the year of the supplement, or pocket part, when researching statutory authority. The best way to make sure that the statute is in its most current form is to use the most recent compilation of an annotated statute and to update it with the pocket part supplements and the advance sheets for the code section. When you pull up the statute section on Westlaw or Lexis, all the updates are included. You can also view the code section at http://uscode.house.gov. When you retrieve a section at uscode.house.gov, a date will appear at the top of the screen indicating that the statute is current through a specific date. For instance, 15 U.S.C. § 68 viewed on uscode.house.gov on July 26, 2021 had the following note at the top of the screen: "Text contains those laws in effect on July 25, 2021." The currency should be noted wherever you retrieve a statute.

Now look at Illustration 7-12, which is a sample page from the pocket part showing the updates for 15 U.S.C.A. § 77a. The entry shows new amendments or legislative activity since the publication of the statute section in the main volume that would affect the text of the section. The pocket part provides important updating information for the statute section including annotations that reference cases that cited the statute section. The pocket parts are important to check when updating your research, as they provide additional research sources as well.

Alternatively, if cost is not an issue, access the code section on either Lexis or Westlaw, and the updates will be integrated into the statute cite retrieved. This is shown in Illustration 7-6, 15 U.S.C.S. § 68 accessed on Lexis. When accessing either the U.S.C.A. on Westlaw or the U.S.C.S. on Lexis, there is no need to use pocket parts or advance sheets, because all of the amendments, legislative updates, annotations, and citing references are updated weekly.

ILLUSTRATION 7-4. Sample Page Showing 15 U.S.C. § 68 Obtained from uscode.house.gov

15 USC 68: Definitions
Text contains those laws in effect on July 25, 2021

From Title 15-COMMERCE AND TRADE
    CHAPTER 2-FEDERAL TRADE COMMISSION; PROMOTION OF EXPORT TRADE AND PREVENTION OF UNFAIR METHODS OF COMPETITION
    SUBCHAPTER III-LABELING OF WOOL PRODUCTS
Jump To:
    Source Credit
    References In Text
    Amendments
    Effective Date
    Short Title
    Miscellaneous

§68. Definitions

As used in this subchapter-

(a) The term "person" means an individual, partnership, corporation, association, or any other form of business enterprise, plural or singular, as the case demands.

(b) The term "wool" means the fiber from the fleece of the sheep or lamb or hair of the Angora or Cashmere goat (and may include the so-called specialty fibers from the hair of the camel, alpaca, llama, and vicuna) which has never been reclaimed from any woven or felted wool product.

(c) The term "recycled wool" means (1) the resulting fiber when wool has been woven or felted into a wool product which, without ever having been utilized in any way by the ultimate consumer, subsequently has been made into a fibrous state, or (2) the resulting fiber when wool or reprocessed wool has been spun, woven, knitted, or felted into a wool product which, after having been used in any way by the ultimate consumer, subsequently has been made into a fibrous state.

(d) The term "wool product" means any product, or any portion of a product, which contains, purports to contain, or in any way is represented as containing wool or recycled wool.

(e) The term "Commission" means the Federal Trade Commission.

(f) The term "Federal Trade Commission Act" means the Act of Congress entitled "An Act to create a Federal Trade Commission, to define its powers and duties, and for other purposes", approved September 26, 1914, as amended, and the Federal Trade Commission Act approved March 21, 1938.

(g) The term "commerce" means commerce among the several States or with foreign nations, or in any Territory of the United States or in the District of Columbia, or between any such Territory and another, or between any such Territory and any State or foreign nation, or between the District of Columbia and any State or Territory or foreign nation.

(h) The term "Territory" includes the insular possessions of the United States and also any Territory of the United States.

(Oct. 14, 1940, ch. 871, §2, 54 Stat. 1128 ; Pub. L. 96–242, §1, May 5, 1980, 94 Stat. 344 .)

REFERENCES IN TEXT

The Act of September 26, 1914, referred to in subsec. (f), is act Sept. 26, 1914, ch. 311, 38 Stat. 717 , as amended, which is classified generally to subchapter I (§41 et seq.) of this chapter. For complete classification of this Act to the Code, see section 58 of this title and Tables.

The Federal Trade Commission Act approved March 21, 1938, referred to in subsec. (f), is act Mar. 21, 1938, ch. 49, 52 Stat. 111 , as amended. For complete classification of this Act to the Code, see Tables.

AMENDMENTS

1980-Subsec. (c). Pub. L. 96–242, §1(a), substituted "recycled wool" for "reprocessed wool" as term defined, designated existing definition as cl. (1), and added cl. (2).

Subsecs. (d) to (i). Pub. L. 96–242, §1(b)–(d), redesignated subsecs. (e) to (i) as (d) to (h), respectively, and, in subsec. (d) as so redesignated, substituted "containing wool or recycled wool" for "containing wool, reprocessed wool, or reused wool". Former subsec. (d), which defined term "reused wool", was struck out.

EFFECTIVE DATE OF 1980 AMENDMENT

Pub. L. 96–242, §3, May 5, 1980, 94 Stat. 344 , provided that: "The amendments made by this Act [amending this section and section 68b of this title] shall take effect with respect to wool products

ILLUSTRATION 7-4.   *Continued*

manufactured on or after the date sixty days after the date of enactment of this Act [May 5, 1980]."

EFFECTIVE DATE

Act Oct. 14, 1940, ch. 871, §12, 54 Stat. 1133 , provided that: "This Act [this subchapter] shall take effect nine months after the date of its passage."

SHORT TITLE OF 2006 AMENDMENT

Pub. L. 109–428, §1, Dec. 20, 2006, 120 Stat. 2913 , provided that: "This Act [amending section 68b of this title and enacting provisions set out as a note under section 68b of this title] may be cited as the 'Wool Suit Fabric Labeling Fairness and International Standards Conforming Act'."

SHORT TITLE

Act Oct. 14, 1940, ch. 871, §1, 54 Stat. 1128 , provided that: "This Act [this subchapter] may be cited as the 'Wool Products Labeling Act of 1939'."

SEPARABILITY

Act Oct. 14, 1940, ch. 871, §13, 54 Stat. 1133 , provided that: "If any provision of this Act [this subchapter], or the application thereof to any person, partnership, corporation, or circumstance is held invalid, the remainder of the Act and the application of such provision to any other person, partnership, corporation, or circumstance shall not be affected thereby."

TRANSFER OF FUNCTIONS

For transfer of functions of Federal Trade Commission, with certain exceptions, to Chairman of such Commission, see Reorg. Plan No. 8 of 1950, §1, eff. May 24, 1950, 15 F.R. 3175, 64 Stat. 1264, set out under section 41 of this title.

2. Reading and Understanding Statutes

▼ How Do You Read a Statute?

Each word of a statute is read for its plain meaning. Statutes are drafted using as few words as possible to state the law. The courts resolve any ambiguities that arise when applying a statute. Often litigation involves the application or interpretation or violation of a statute. When a statute has not been applied in a case previously, it is a case of first impression. Remember that the text of the statute does not discuss policy issues but policy and political climate influence how a statute will be applied. Think of the goals that the government seeks to further and this will provide insight into relevant policy arguments concerning the application of a particular statutory provision.

The focus of statutory analysis is that legislation is adopted to apply to situations that will arise after the legislation goes into effect. An activity that existed prior to the passage of the particular legislation is **grandfathered** if the legislation includes language that does not prohibit this existing activity from continuing. For instance, suppose a city passes an ordinance forbidding the operation of commercial businesses in residentially zoned neighborhoods. Under a grandfather clause, an existing business would be permitted to continue its operation; the legislation would apply only to businesses opened after the legislation took effect.

ILLUSTRATION 7-5. Sample Pages Showing 15 U.S.C.A. § 68 (West 2020)

Ch. 2 FEDERAL TRADE COMMISSION 15 § 68

ters charged in complaints was vested in first instance in Commission under §§ 61 to 65 of this title, would, in Supreme Court's discretion, be reviewed by writ of certiorari in view of hardship imposed on defendants by long postponed appellate review, coupled with attendant infringe-ment of asserted congressional policy of conferring primary jurisdiction on the Commission. United States Alkali Export Ass'n v. United States, U.S.N.Y.1945, 65 S.Ct. 1120, 325 U.S. 196, 89 L.Ed. 1554. Federal Courts ⬯ 3126

§ 66. Short title

This subchapter may be cited as the "Webb-Pomerene Act".

(Apr. 10, 1918, c. 50, § 6, as added Pub.L. 94–435, Title III, § 305(c), Sept. 30, 1976, 90 Stat. 1397.)

HISTORICAL NOTES

Revision Notes and Legislative Reports
1976 Acts. House Report Nos. 94–499, 94–1343, and 94–1373, see 1976 U.S. Code Cong. and Adm. News, p. 2572.

LAW REVIEW AND JOURNAL COMMENTARIES

Joint ventures and the Export Trading Company Act. Dennis Unkovic. 5 J.L. & Com. 373 (1985).

Research References

Treatises and Practice Aids
8 Callmann on Unfair Competition, Trademarks, and Monopolies Appendix 2 § 2:5 (4th Ed.), Webb-Pomerene Act.
4 E-Commerce and Internet Law 31.03[1], Credit Cards.
23 Federal Procedure, Lawyers Edition § 54:45, Generally.
32 Federal Procedure, Lawyers Edition § 75:3, Laws Administered by FTC.
6 Newberg on Class Actions § 20:16 (5th ed.), Parties Exempted from Antitrust Liability.
3 West's Federal Administrative Practice § 3304, Federal Laws Enforced by the FTC—Competition.

SUBCHAPTER III—LABELING OF WOOL PRODUCTS

CROSS REFERENCES

"Textile fiber product" defined as not including product required to be labeled under this subchapter for purposes of textile fiber products identification, see 15 USCA § 70.

§ 68. Definitions

As used in this subchapter—

(a) The term "person" means an individual, partnership, corporation, association, or any other form of business enterprise, plural or singular, as the case demands.

(b) The term "wool" means the fiber from the fleece of the sheep or lamb or hair of the Angora or Cashmere goat (and may

ILLUSTRATION 7-5. *Continued*

15 § 68   **COMMERCE AND TRADE** **Ch. 2**

include the so-called specialty fibers from the hair of the camel, alpaca, llama, and vicuna) which has never been reclaimed from any woven or felted wool product.

(c) The term "recycled wool" means (1) the resulting fiber when wool has been woven or felted into a wool product which, without ever having been utilized in any way by the ultimate consumer, subsequently has been made into a fibrous state, or (2) the resulting fiber when wool or reprocessed wool has been spun, woven, knitted, or felted into a wool product which, after having been used in any way by the ultimate consumer, subsequently has been made into a fibrous state.

(d) The term "wool product" means any product, or any portion of a product, which contains, purports to contain, or in any way is represented as containing wool or recycled wool.

(e) The term "Commission" means the Federal Trade Commission.

(f) The term "Federal Trade Commission Act" means the Act of Congress entitled "An Act to create a Federal Trade Commission, to define its powers and duties, and for other purposes", approved September 26, 1914, as amended, and the Federal Trade Commission Act approved March 21, 1938.

(g) The term "commerce" means commerce among the several States or with foreign nations, or in any Territory of the United States or in the District of Columbia, or between any such Territory and another, or between any such Territory and any State or foreign nation, or between the District of Columbia and any State or Territory or foreign nation.

(h) The term "Territory" includes the insular possessions of the United States and also any Territory of the United States.

(Oct. 14, 1940, c. 871, § 2, 54 Stat. 1128; Pub.L. 96–242, § 1, May 5, 1980, 94 Stat. 344.)

HISTORICAL NOTES

Revision Notes and Legislative Reports
   1980 Acts. Senate Report No. 96–655, see 1980 U.S. Code Cong. and Adm. News, p. 782.

References in Text
   The Act of September 26, 1914, referred to in subsec. (f), is Act Sept. 26, 1914, c. 311, 38 Stat. 717, as amended, which is classified generally to subchapter I (§ 41 et seq.) of this chapter. For complete classification, see 15 U.S.C.A. § 58 and Tables.
   The Federal Trade Commission Act approved March 21, 1938, referred to in

subsec. (f), is Act Mar. 21, 1938, c. 49, 52 Stat. 111, as amended. For complete classification, see Tables.

Amendments
   1980 Amendments. Subsec. (c). Pub.L. 96–242, § 1(a), substituted "recycled wool" for "reprocessed wool" as the term defined, designated the existing definition as cl. (1), and added cl. (2).
   Subsec. (d). Pub.L. 96–242, § 1(b) to (d), redesignated subsecs. (e) to (i) as (d) to (h), respectively, and, in subsec. (d) as so redesignated, substituted "containing wool or recycled wool" for "containing

ILLUSTRATION 7-5. *Continued*

wool, reprocessed wool, or reused wool". Former subsec. (d), which defined the term "reused wool", was struck out.

Effective and Applicability Provisions

1980 Acts. Section 3 of Pub.L. 96–242 provided that: "The amendments made by this Act [amending this section and section 68b of this title] shall take effect with respect to wool products manufactured on or after the date sixty days after the date of enactment of this Act [May 5, 1980]."

1940 Acts. Section 12 of Act Oct. 14, 1940, provided that: "This Act [this subchapter] shall take effect nine months after the date of its passage."

Transfer of Functions

All executive and administrative functions of the Federal Trade Commission were, with certain reservations, transferred to the Chairman of such Commission by 1950 Reorg. Plan No. 8, § 1, eff. May 24, 1950, 15 F.R. 3175, 64 Stat.

1264, set out as a note under section 41 of this title.

Separability of Provisions

Section 13 of Act Oct. 14, 1940, provided that: "If any provision of this Act [this subchapter], or the application thereof to any person, partnership, corporation, or circumstance is held invalid, the remainder of the Act and the application of such provision to any other person, partnership, corporation, or circumstance shall not be affected thereby."

Short Title

2006 Amendments. Pub.L. 109–428, § 1, Dec. 20, 2006, 120 Stat. 2913, provided that: "This Act [amending 15 U.S.C.A. § 68b and enacting provisions set out as a note under 15 U.S.C.A. § 68b] may be cited as the 'Wool Suit Fabric Labeling Fairness and International Standards Conforming Act'."

1940 Acts. Section 1 of Act Oct. 14, 1940, provided that: "This Act [this subchapter] may be cited as the 'Wool Products Labeling Act of 1939'."

CODE OF FEDERAL REGULATIONS

Regulations under specific acts of Congress,
Textile Fiber Products Identification Act, see 16 CFR § 303.1 et seq.
Wool Products Labeling Act, see 16 CFR § 300.1 et seq.

LAW REVIEW AND JOURNAL COMMENTARIES

Drop dead stylish: Mitigating environmental impact of fur production through consumer protection in the Truth in Fur Labeling Act of 2010. Comment, 19 Penn St. Envtl. L. Rev. 267 (Spring 2011).

Research References

ALR Library
16 American Law Reports, Federal 361, Jurisdiction of Federal District Court to Entertain Attacks on Federal Trade Commission's Actions.
65 American Law Reports 2nd 225, What Constitutes False, Misleading, or Deceptive Advertising or Promotional Practices Subject to Action by Federal Trade Commission.
79 American Law Reports 1200, Validity and Construction of Statute Creating Federal Trade Commission.
149 American Law Reports 349, Justiciable Controversy Within Declaratory Judgment Act as Predicable Upon Advice, Opinion, or Ruling of Public Administrative Officer.

Encyclopedias
61 Am. Jur. Proof of Facts 3d 501, Proof of Identity of Fiber, Fabric, or Textile.
24 Am. Jur. Trials 1, Defending Antitrust Lawsuits.
54A Am. Jur. 2d Monopolies, Restraints of Trade, and Unfair Trade Practices § 1237, Generally.
54A Am. Jur. 2d Monopolies, Restraints of Trade, and Unfair Trade Practices § 1239, Enforcement.

Forms
16 Federal Procedural Forms § 65:225, Introduction.

ILLUSTRATION 7-5. *Continued*

15 § 68   **COMMERCE AND TRADE   Ch. 2**

16 Federal Procedural Forms § 65:228, Labeling Requirements—Wool Products.

16 Federal Procedural Forms § 65:260, FTC Complaint—Wool Products Not Labeled, or Deceptively Labeled [15 U.S.C.A. §§ 45(A)(1), 68, 68a, 68b(A)(1), (2); 16 C.F.R. §§ 3.11, 300.1 et seq.].

16 Federal Procedural Forms § 65:262, Provisions in FTC Order—Respondent Ordered to Cease and Desist from Failing to Label or Falsely and Deceptively Labeling Wool Products, from Importing Wool Products Without Posting Bond, and from Furnishing a False Guaranty [15 U.S.C.A. §§ 45, 68, 68a, 68b; 16 C.F.R. §§ 3.54, 300.1 et seq.].

16 Federal Procedural Forms § 65:263, Petition for Review—Judicial Review of FTC Order to Cease and Desist from Acts and Practices in Violation of Wool Products Labeling Act [15 U.S.C.A. §§ 45(C), 68a, 68b(A)(2), 68g(B); Fed. R. App. P. 15].

Treatises and Practice Aids

7 Callmann on Unfair Competition, Trademarks, and Monopolies § 25:10 (4th Ed.), Jurisdiction of the Commission Under the Wool and Fur Products Labeling Acts and Textile Fiber Products Identification Act.

8 Callmann on Unfair Competition, Trademarks, and Monopolies Appendix 4 § 4:1 (4th Ed.), Wool Products Labeling Act of 1939.

8 Callmann on Unfair Competition, Trademarks, and Monopolies Appendix 4 § 4:4 (4th Ed.), Textile Fiber Products Identification Act.

4 Eckstrom's Licensing in Foreign and Domestic Operations Appendix 19B, Agreement Between United States and Commission of the European Communities Regarding Competition Laws.

32 Federal Procedure, Lawyers Edition § 75:3, Laws Administered by FTC.

5 McCarthy on Trademarks and Unfair Competition § 27:56 (5th ed.), False Representations as to the Nature or Qualities of Goods and Services—Methods of Proof—Proving Falsity.

5 McCarthy on Trademarks and Unfair Competition § 29:54 (5th ed.), Country of Origin Marking Requirements.

6 McCarthy on Trademarks and Unfair Competition Appendix A2 B, B Other Statutes Having a Relation to Trademarks.

3 West's Federal Administrative Practice § 3305, Federal Laws Enforced by the FTC—Consumer Protection.

Notes of Decisions

Purpose   1
Reprocessed wool   2
Wool product   3

────────

1. Purpose

Sections 68 to 68j of this title were intended to protect consumers against concealment of substitutes for wool in products claimed to be made wholly or partially of wool. Marcus v. F. T. C., C.A.2, 1965, 354 F.2d 85. Antitrust And Trade Regulation ☞ 164

2. Reprocessed wool

To the extent that woven or felted wool waste entered into garnetter's operation,

his garnett was "reprocessed wool" and not a product of reprocessed wool within §§ 68 to 68j of this title. Carr v. F. T. C., C.A.1, 1962, 302 F.2d 688. Antitrust And Trade Regulation ☞ 164

3. Wool product

Garnett, composed exclusively of ordinary wool waste which had never been processed was not a "wool product" within §§ 68 to 68j of this title and producer of garnett was not covered. Carr v. F. T. C., C.A.1, 1962, 302 F.2d 688. Antitrust And Trade Regulation ☞ 164

§ 68a.   Misbranding declared unlawful

The introduction, or manufacture for introduction, into commerce, or the sale, transportation, or distribution, in commerce, of any wool

614

Reprinted with the permission of Thomson Reuters.

ILLUSTRATION 7-6.   Sample Pages Showing 15 U.S.C.S. § 68 Accessed on Lexis

15 USCS § 68

Current through Public Law 117-27, approved July 22, 2021, excepting Part V of Subtitle A of Title 10, as added by Public Law 116-283 (effective 1/1/2022).

United States Code Service > TITLE 15. COMMERCE AND TRADE (Chs. 1 — 119) > CHAPTER 2. FEDERAL TRADE COMMISSION; PROMOTION OF EXPORT TRADE AND PREVENTION OF UNFAIR METHODS OF COMPETITION (§§ 41 — 77) > LABELING OF WOO...

Congress continually enacts new Public Laws. This retrieval of the statute is current through Public Law 117-27. 117 is the 117th Congress and 27 is the 27th law passed by the 117th Congress.

§ 68. Definitions

As used in this Act

(a) The term "person" means an individual, partnership, corporation, ... enterprise, plural or singular, as the case demands.

(b) The term "wool" means the fiber from the fleece of the sheep or la... (and may include the so-called specialty fibers from the hair of the ca... never been reclaimed from any woven or felted wool product.

(c) The term "recycled wool" means (1) the resulting fiber when wool has been woven or felted into a wool product which, without ever having been utilized in any way by the ultimate consumer, subsequently has been made into a fibrous state, or (2) the resulting fiber when wool or reprocessed wool has been spun, woven, knitted, or felted into a wool product which, after having been used in any way by the ultimate consumer, subsequently has been made into a fibrous state.

(d) The term "wool product" means any product, or any portion of a product, which contains, purports to contain, or in any way is represented as containing wool or recycled wool.

(e) The term "Commission" means the Federal Trade Commission.

(f) The term "Federal Trade Commission Act" means the Act of Congress entitled "An Act to create a Federal Trade Commission, to define its powers and duties, and for other purposes," approved September 26, 1914, as amended, and the Federal Trade Commission Act approved March 21, 1938.

(g) The term "commerce" means commerce among the several States or with foreign nations, or in any Territory of the United States or in the District of Columbia, or between any such Territory and another, or between any such Territory and any State or foreign nation, or between the District of Columbia and any State or Territory or foreign nation.

(h) The term "Territory" includes the insular possessions of the United States and also any Territory of the United States.

History

HISTORY:

Act Oct. 14, 1940, ch 871, § 2, *54 Stat. 1128*; May 5, 1980, *P. L. 96-242*, § 1, *94 Stat. 344*.

ILLUSTRATION 7-6.   *Continued*

NOTES TO DECISIONS

1.Generally

2.Purpose

3.Wool

4.Recycled wool

5.Wool product

> **Case annotations for cases citing to the statute.**

1. Generally

Wool Products Labeling Act is applicable only to wool products, and not to wool itself or reprocessed wool itself. *Carr v. Federal Trade Com., 302 F.2d 688, 1962 Trade Cas. (CCH) ¶ 70216, 1962 U.S. App. LEXIS 6045 (1st Cir. 1962).*

2. Purpose

In passing Wool Products Labeling Act (*15 USCS §§ 68–68j*), Congress intended to protect consumers against concealment of substitutes for wool in products claimed to be made wholly or partially of wool. *Marcus v. Federal Trade Com., 354 F.2d 85, 1965 Trade Cas. (CCH) ¶ 71633, 1965 U.S. App. LEXIS 3617 (2d Cir. 1965).*

3. Wool

Page 4 of 6

15 USCS § 68

Garnett composed exclusively of ordinary wool waste which has never been processed constitutes wool and not wool product. *Carr v. Federal Trade Com., 302 F.2d 688, 1962 Trade Cas. (CCH) ¶ 70216, 1962 U.S. App. LEXIS 6045 (1st Cir. 1962).*

4. Recycled wool

Garnett of wool which has been processed is no more than reprocessed wool. *Carr v. Federal Trade Com., 302 F.2d 688, 1962 Trade Cas. (CCH) ¶ 70216, 1962 U.S. App. LEXIS 6045 (1st Cir. 1962).*

Because the Wool Products Labeling Act, *15 USCS §§ 68* et seq., requires recycled garments and fabrics, including cashmere, to be labeled as such, whenever a label represents that a garment contains the unqualified term "cashmere," the law requires that the garment contain only virgin cashmere; thus Act, is essentially telling consumers that garments labeled "cashmere" can be presumed to be virgin cashmere as if it had been explicitly stated. *Cashmere & Camel Hair Mfrs. Inst. v. Saks Fifth Ave., 284 F.3d 302, 2002-1 Trade Cas. (CCH) ¶ 73628, 2002 U.S. App. LEXIS 5361 (1st Cir.)*, cert. denied, *537 U.S. 1001, 123 S. Ct. 485, 154 L. Ed. 2d 396, 2002 U.S. LEXIS 8095 (2002).*

ILLUSTRATION 7-6. *Continued*

> The U.S.C.S. includes references to administrative regulations.

Research References & Practice Aids

Code of Federal Regulations:

Federal Trade Commission—Rules and regulations under the Wool Products Labeling Act of 1939, *16 CFR 300.1* et seq.

Federal Trade Commission—Rules and regulations under the Textile Fiber Products Identification Act, *16 CFR 303.1* et seq.

Am Jur:

54A Am Jur 2d, Monopolies, Restraints of Trade, and Unfair Trade Practices §§ 1237, 1239.

Am Jur Proof of Facts:

61 Am Jur Proof of Facts 3d, Proof of Identity of Fiber, Fabric, or Textile, p. 501.

13 Am Jur Proof of Facts, Textile Identification and Clothing Hazards, p. 649.

Corporate and Business Law:

5 *Antitrust Laws and Trade Regulation, 2nd Edition (Matthew Bender), ch 76*, Enforcement by the Federal Trade Commission: An Overview § 76.02.

5 *Antitrust Laws and Trade Regulation, 2nd Edition (Matthew Bender), ch 81*, Remedial Powers of the Federal Trade Commission § 81.03.

> Citations to secondary authority.

Reprinted from LexisNexis with permission. Copyright 2021 LexisNexis. All rights reserved.

▼ What Type of Legal Authority Are Statutes?

Statutes are primary authority because codes and statutes are the laws created by the legislature. Statutes are the authority to rely on when researching. When researching, first determine the relevant jurisdiction and then check the appropriate code to see if there is a statute on point. If there is a relevant statute on point, the statute takes precedence over case law holdings that were decided prior to the statute's enactment. Statutes are enacted to control conduct like criminal acts, relationships like marriage and adoption, and transactions like banking that occur frequently in our society. Court decisions applying and interpreting statutes already enacted must be consulted to assess how a statute has been applied and analyzed.

▼ What Is the Relationship Between Statutes and Case Law?

Most cases today revolve around the application or the interpretation of a statute. Courts determine whether an individual or an institution — public, private, or government — violated a statute or whether the statute itself is unconstitutional. People, institutions, municipalities, and even state governments go to court to determine if a statute is unconstitutional. Often at issue in a case is whether a party complied with a statute's requirements.

3. How to Find Federal Statutes

▼ Where Are Federal Statutes Found?

The official, government-issued compilation of the federal statutes is the *United States Code,* or U.S.C. See Illustration 7-4, the current version, 2019, of 15 U.S.C. § 68. The last completely updated official version of the United States Code was published in 2018 and the next official publication is in 2024, but the Office of the Law Revision Counsel will post the updated code when available. The most cost-effective way to access the *United States Code* is at www.gpo.gov/fdsys or at uscode.house.gov. The official code is published only every six years, so you would have to search the section at http://uscode.house.gov to obtain information about subsequent legislative activity.

Of course, on the government sites you would not obtain any of the research enhancements or annotations, but the ease of use is remarkable, especially if you know the code section or a keyword in the provision. Here you can search "wool labeling and recycled wool." The U.S.C. contains most of the laws created by the U.S. Congress. The U.S. Government Printing Office publishes the U.S.C. Another terrific Internet resource for federal and state codes is Cornell's Legal Information Institute at www.law.cornell.edu.

The U.S.C. is organized by title. The titles are numbered 1–54 with Title 53 reserved for future needs. Each title covers a specific subject area over which the U.S. Congress has the authority to draft legislation. For example, Title 15 contains all statutes dealing with commerce and trade. When a new piece of legislation is enacted that pertains to commerce and trade, which includes labeling provisions, it is placed in Title 15. Changes to a statute are called amendments. In our example, the original statute was amended in Pub. L. No. 96-242 to include language regarding recycled wool. When new statutes are enacted that replace existing statute sections, the older sections are then superseded. This differs from case law because new decisions overrule prior decisions' holdings; they do not supersede them. Sometimes only a portion of an existing statute changes when a new public law is enacted, as in our example with the addition of new language to change "reprocessed wool" to "recycled wool." A statute is repealed when it is revoked and is no longer in force.

▼ How Often Is the U.S.C. Updated?

An official version of the U.S.C. is published every six years. Supplements updating the existing code are published annually. During the course of the six years, new legislation is passed all of the time. It is not included in the official code until the annual supplement is published. There might be a great time lag between the law's enactment and the production of the annual supplement. New legislation retains the slip format until it becomes a session law and gets a *Statutes at Large* citation. It is important to check to see if the legislation has been repealed or superseded by a slip law or a session law in the intervening years between publications of the official code and during the time between publications of the annual supplements. You will notice that Congress updates statutes with the same steps (slip law, session law, public law) as it employs to enact new legislation, as discussed earlier in this chapter.

▼ Is the U.S.C. the Only Codified Version of the Federal Statutes?

No. There are two unofficial versions of the U.S.C., the **United States Code Annotated** (U.S.C.A.) published by West and the **United States Code Service** (U.S.C.S.) published by LexisNexis. Both the U.S.C.A. and the U.S.C.S. contain the text of the laws found in the U.S.C. and also include case law annotations and excellent updating services. Unlike case law where the official and the unofficial reporters have different volume numbers and different pagination for the same case, the citations for the unofficial codes have the same title and section designations as the U.S.C. cite. For example, the following are citations to the identical statute:

26 U.S.C. § 61 (2018)

26 U.S.C.A. § 61 (West) (Note that the date is optional if the statute is currently in force.)

26 U.S.C.S. § 61 (LexisNexis 2021)

▼ What Do the Unofficial Codes Contain?

The unofficial codes contain references to cases that construe and apply the code section. See Illustrations 7-5 and 7-6. They are called annotated codes because they contain the case law annotations. The unofficial codes contain references to law review articles dealing with the particular code section as well as ties to the respective publisher's resources. The U.S.C.A. and U.S.C.S. are excellent research tools. See Illustrations 7-4, 7-5, and 7-6 for a comparison of the official and the unofficial codes.

The U.S.C.A., because it is published by Thomson Reuters, the publisher of West and Westlaw products, links the researcher to all of the other West publications. See Illustration 7-5. References are given to topic and Key Numbers, if they are available, so that the subject covered by the code section can be examined in the *West Digests* to find pertinent case law. (See Chapter 4 for a detailed discussion of digests.) References to West secondary sources and law journals are given as well. (See Chapter 6.) References to the *United States Code Congressional and Administrative News* (U.S.C.C.A.N.), published by West and containing compilations of legislative histories for major public laws since the 1950s, are contained in the U.S.C.A. (The U.S.C.C.A.N. is discussed fully in Chapter 8.) Also, references to administrative laws, the *Code of Federal Regulations*, are provided for certain statutes. (Administrative materials are discussed in Chapter 9.)

The U.S.C.S., published by LexisNexis, provides references to other publications that are relevant to the particular code section. See Illustration 7-6. This illustration was downloaded from Lexis. Note how the updating is integrated into the material retrieved. Westlaw has a similar feature in the U.S.C.A. database. The U.S.C.S. includes related statute citations and pertinent secondary source references as well as case annotations. U.S.C.S. has consistent references to the *Code of Federal Regulations*. (See Chapter 9.)

Aside from providing excellent updates, case law annotations, and law review citations, the annotated or unofficial federal codes provide the researcher with an entry into the entire research network created by the respective publisher.

▼ Is There Any Difference Between the U.S.C.S. and the U.S.C.A.?

The U.S.C.S. provides consistent references to relevant *Code of Federal Regulations* (C.F.R.) citations; the U.S.C.A. does not consistently include administrative law citations. Overall, then, the U.S.C.S. is better for researching administrative issues. The U.S.C.A. provides Key Numbers and topics relating to the West Digest System as well as electronic searching tips for Westlaw query formulation.

▼ Why Would You Use an Annotated Set of the U.S.C.?

As mentioned earlier, the annotated codes, available in hard copy and on Lexis and Westlaw, offer a host of references to secondary source publications produced by the respective code's publisher as well as case law annotations. You would use an annotated, or unofficial code, because the updating either integrated into the site on the commercial database, or through pocket parts, bound supplements, and advance session law pamphlets is very timely. Between publication of the official statutes every six years, consult an unofficial version of the U.S.C. to determine if a statute has been updated, modified, amended, or superseded. The unofficial versions contain references to any new legislation that relates to the code section, even if it is a session law. If using a hardcopy code, always check the volume's pocket part for updates as well as the advance pamphlets.

▼ How Useful Are Annotated Statutes as Finding Tools?

Annotated codes are excellent finding tools for retrieving cases that interpret the statute section in question. You do not cite to the research points and abstracts following the code section, although they are very helpful in your research. When using an annotated code section on point, you are also linked to many other resources produced by the particular code's publisher. For example, within the U.S.C.A. you would find citations to encyclopedia sections. In addition, because of the excellent updating services, the annotated codes allow you to find subsequent legislation that relates to the statute section.

▼ What Are the Research Methods Used to Find Relevant Statutes?

The research methods are the same for the U.S.C., the U.S.C.A., and the U.S.C.S. Generally, you can start your search with Google or Wikipedia when looking for a statute. Use the popular name of the statute in your search, such as "The Wool Products Labeling Act." You will then have to obtain the most current version of the statute. It is best to use uscode.house.gov if you have the title and section for a federal statute because the statute is updated. This is the least expensive way to read a statute and to update it. However, the Google, Wikipedia, and the government sites do not provide validation and do not provide citing references. The following methods to find statutory authority are listed in order of efficiency.

1. **Starting with Google.** Often you will learn about a statute when you read the news. In the news, the statute is often referred to by its popular name. You can then Google the popular name to see the text of the statute. You may read a section in Wikipedia that provides some background on the statute. You will likely obtain a citation. You can also read the statute on a government website such as govinfo.gov or uscode.house.gov.
2. **Popular name table.** The popular name table is found online and in a separate set of volumes, generally paperbound, in the unofficial codes. Almost every statute passed in Congress has a popular name; it is either a last name of the sponsor or a description of the Act's intent. If you have a popular name but not a title and section number, you can use the popular name table. The popular name table will tell you where to find the Act in the *United States Code.*

On the govinfo.gov site, under the United States Code, the table is called Popular Name Tool. Illustration 7-7 shows a screen from the Popular Name Tool and indicates that the Wool Products Labeling Act is codified at 15 U.S.C. §§ 68 et seq. All of the popular names for all of the code sections are listed in alphabetical order with the corresponding title and section numbers of the Act, the public law numbers, and the *Statutes at Large* citations. The popular name table, or popular name tool, is an excellent research tool for finding public law numbers quickly. Notes or short titles in the popular name table generally describe how a particular public law is inserted into the code. Because the code is organized by subject and the public laws are passed sequentially, the public laws must sometimes be broken down into parts by specific subject and classified in the code in various sections. The notes or short titles often explain the organization of the particular public law within the code. The popular name table is a good source for updated information.

3. **Conversion table.** The conversion table is online at uscode.house. gov, Table III, and in hardcopy form at the end of the U.S.C. set, in the tables volume, as well as in the tables volume in the U.S.C.A. and in the U.S.C.S. This table lets you find the U.S.C. citation if you have a *Statutes at Large* citation. Illustration 7-8 shows, using Table III on uscode.house.gov, how to convert the public law number into a *Statutes at Large* citation to ultimately locate the code section. For example, you would obtain the citation of 94 Stat. 344 from Pub. L. No. 96-242. The table also converts the public law number into a U.S.C. citation. (The public law number helps you find the legislative history of the Act in the U.S.C.C.A.N. also. See Chapter 8 for more information on the U.S.C.C.A.N.)

4. **The search term and index method.** You can find a relevant statute by using some of the significant terms from the Act in the search bar. Use the terms that you read about or that are used in the Act to search in either the government databases or on Lexis or Westlaw. You can also find the relevant code section by using the index in an annotated code set. Very often a word from the popular name of the statute is cited in the index. The index is in alphabetical order. In Illustration 7-9, from the U.S.C.A., our example focuses on the subject heading, "Wool." Note that the index entry contains many terms describing the subject matter of the statute. You will often find related statutory provisions when you scan an index.

5. **The title outline.** If you know the particular title where the statute section is located but don't know the section number, you can look at the title outline to see if any entry in the particular title is appropriate. Illustration 7-10 shows the outline of Subchapter III—Labeling of Wool Products—in Title 15. You must have a very clear idea of what you are looking for and knowledge about the statute's language to use the title outline method effectively. Use this method only if you cannot find a statute section by any other means.

ILLUSTRATION 7-7.   Popular Name Table, from Popular Name Tool from the Government Printing Office, uscode.house.gov

Page 373   ACTS CITED BY POPULAR NAME

Women's Educational Equity Act of 1978
Pub. L. 89–10, Apr. 11, 1965, title IX, part C (§ 931 et seq.), as added Pub. L. 95–561, title VIII, § 802, Nov. 1, 1978, 92 Stat. 2298 (20 U.S.C. 3341 et seq.)

Women's Educational Equity Act of 1994
Pub. L. 89–10, title V, part B (§ 5201 et seq.), as added Pub. L. 103–382, title I, § 101, Oct. 20, 1994, 108 Stat. 3695

Women's Educational Equity Act of 2001
Pub. L. 89–10, title V, part D, subpart 21 (§ 5611 et seq.), as added Pub. L. 107–110, title V, § 501, Jan. 8, 2002, 115 Stat. 1867

Women's Educational Equity Amendments of 1984
Pub. L. 98–511, title IV, Oct. 19, 1984, 98 Stat. 2389
Short title, see 20 U.S.C. 6301 note

Women's Entrepreneurship and Economic Empowerment Act of 2018
Pub. L. 115–428, Jan. 9, 2019, 132 Stat. 5509
Short title, see 22 U.S.C. 2151 note

Women's Health and Cancer Rights Act of 1998
Pub. L. 105–277, div. A, § 101(f) [title IX], Oct. 21, 1998, 112 Stat. 2681–337, 2681–436
Short title, see 42 U.S.C. 201 note

Women's Health Research and Prevention Amendments of 1998
Pub. L. 105–340, Oct. 31, 1998, 112 Stat. 3191
Short title, see 42 U.S.C. 201 note

Women's Naval Reserve Act
July 30, 1942, ch. 538, 56 Stat. 730

Women's Progress Commemoration Act
Pub. L. 105–341, Oct. 31, 1998, 112 Stat. 3196 (16 U.S.C. 470a note)

Women's Suffrage Centennial Commemorative Coin Act
Pub. L. 116–71, Nov. 25, 2019, 133 Stat. 1147 (31 U.S.C. 5112 note)

Women's Suffrage Centennial Commission Act
Pub. L. 115–31, div. G, title IV, § 431(a)(3) [S. 847, § 1], May 5, 2017, 131 Stat. 502 (36 U.S.C. note prec. 101)

Women Veterans Health Programs Act of 1992
Pub. L. 102–585, title I, Nov. 4, 1992, 106 Stat. 4944
Short title, see 38 U.S.C. 101 note

Wood Residue Utilization Act of 1980
Pub. L. 96–554, Dec. 19, 1980, 94 Stat. 3257 (16 U.S.C. 1681 et seq.)
Short title, see 16 U.S.C. 1600 note

Woodrow Wilson Memorial Act of 1968
Pub. L. 90–637, Oct. 24, 1968, 82 Stat. 1356 (20 U.S.C. 80e et seq.)
Short title, see 20 U.S.C. 80e note

Woodrow Wilson Memorial Bridge Authority Act of 1995
Pub. L. 104–59, title IV, Nov. 28, 1995, 109 Stat. 627

Wool and Woolens Act (Tariff)
Mar. 2, 1867, ch. 197, 14 Stat. 559; R.S. §§ 2504, 2912, 2916

Wool Manufacturer Payment Clarification and Technical Corrections Act
Pub. L. 107–210, div. E, title L, subtitle A, § 5101, Aug. 6, 2002, 116 Stat. 1041

Wool Products Labeling Act of 1939
Oct. 14, 1940, ch. 871, 54 Stat. 1128 (15 U.S.C. 68 et seq.)
Short title, see 15 U.S.C. 68 note

Wool Suit and Textile Trade Extension Act of 2004
Pub. L. 108–429, title IV, Dec. 3, 2004, 118 Stat. 2600
Short title, see 7 U.S.C. 7101 note

Wool Suit Fabric Labeling Fairness and International Standards Conforming Act
Pub. L. 109–428, Dec. 20, 2006, 120 Stat. 2913
Short title, see 15 U.S.C. 68 note

Work Hours and Safety Act of 1962
Pub. L. 87–581, Aug. 13, 1962, 76 Stat. 357

Work Made For Hire and Copyright Corrections Act of 2000
Pub. L. 106–379, Oct. 27, 2000, 114 Stat. 1444
Short title, see 17 U.S.C. 101 note

Work Relief and Public Works Appropriation Act of 1938
June 21, 1938, ch. 554, 52 Stat. 809

Worker Adjustment and Retraining Notification Act
Pub. L. 100–379, Aug. 4, 1988, 102 Stat. 890 (29 U.S.C. 2101 et seq.)
Short title, see 29 U.S.C. 2101 note

Worker Economic Opportunity Act
Pub. L. 106–202, May 18, 2000, 114 Stat. 308
Short title, see 29 U.S.C. 201 note

Worker, Homeownership, and Business Assistance Act of 2009
Pub. L. 111–92, Nov. 6, 2009, 123 Stat. 2984
Short title, see 26 U.S.C. 1 note

Worker, Retiree, and Employer Recovery Act of 2008
Pub. L. 110–458, Dec. 23, 2008, 122 Stat. 5092
Short title, see 29 U.S.C. 1001 note

Workers' Family Protection Act
Pub. L. 102–522, title II, § 209, Oct. 26, 1992, 106 Stat. 3420 (29 U.S.C. 671a)
Short title, see 29 U.S.C. 671a(a)

Workers Technology Skill Development Act
Pub. L. 103–382, title V, part D (§ 541 et seq.), Oct. 20, 1994, 108 Stat. 4051 (29 U.S.C. 2701 et seq.)
Short title, see 29 U.S.C. 2701 note

Workforce Innovation and Opportunity Act
Pub. L. 113–128, July 22, 2014, 128 Stat. 1425 (29 U.S.C. 3101 et seq.)
Short title, see 29 U.S.C. 3101 note

Workforce Investment Act of 1998
Pub. L. 105–220, Aug. 7, 1998, 112 Stat. 936 (29 U.S.C. 2801 et seq.)

ILLUSTRATION 7-8. *Statutes at Large* and Public Law Numbers Table

96th Cong. 94 Stat.	Pub. L.	Section	Page	U.S.C. Title	U.S.C. Section	Status
				TABLE III—STATUTES AT LARGE		Page 1204
1980—Apr. 3	96-225	...	310	50	4564	
	96-226	1	311	31	1 nt	Rev. T.
		101	311	31	67	Rev. T.
		102	312	31	54	Rev. T.
		103	314	31	53	Rev. T.
		104(a), (b)(1)	314, 315	31	42, 43	Rev. T.
		104(b)(2)	315	31	43 nt	Rev. T.
		201, 202	315	42	3523, 7138	Rep.
	96-227	1	317	25	761 nt	Elim.
		2	317	25	761	Elim.
		3	317	25	762	Elim.
		4	318	25	763	Elim.
		5	319	25	764	Elim.
		6	319	25	765	Elim.
		7	320	25	766	Elim.
		8	322	25	767	Elim.
		9	322	25	768	Elim.
7	96-229	2(d)	327	42	4963a	
		2(e)	327	42	4963	
		4	328	42	4969a	
		5	328	42	4970	
8	96-230		329	5	905	
11	96-234	1, 2	333	7	1445e	
		3	333	15	714b	
22	96-236	1	336	7	3601	
		2	336	7	3602	
		3	336	7	3603	
		4	337	7	3604	
		5, 6	337	7	3605, 3606	Rep.
30	96-239		341	29	1461	
May 3	96-241	1	343	5	5312 nt	Elim.
		2	343	22	2651 nt	
5	96-242	1	344	15	68	
		2	344	15	68b	
		3	344	15	68 nt	
16	96-243		345	7	2014 nt	Elim.
19	96-244	1	346	16	470h-1	Rev. T. 54
		2	346	16	470t	Rev. T. 54
21	96-245		347	29	161	
23	96-246		348	16	1535	
	96-247	1	349	42	1997 nt	
		2	349	42	1997	
		3	350	42	1997a	
		3A		42	1997a-1	
		4	350	42	1997b	
		5	351	42	1997c	
		6	352	42	1997d	
		7	352	42	1997e	
		8	353	42	1997f	
		9	354	42	1997g	
		10	354	42	1997h	
		11	354	42	1997i	
		12	354	42	1997j	
	96-248	1	355	16	1132 nt	
26	96-249	1	357	7	2011 nt	
		101(a)	357	7	2012	
		101(b)	357	7	2019	
		102, 103	357, 358	7	2014	
		104-106	358	7	2014	Rep.
		104-106	358	7	2014 nt	
		107, 108	358, 359	7	2014	
		109, 110	359	7	2015	
		111	360	7	2012	
		112	361	7	2014	
		113	361	7	2020	
		114, 115	361	7	2015	
		116-120	361, 362	7	2020	
		121	363	7	2025	
		122, 123	363	7	2020	
		124	363	7	2024	
		125, 126	364	7	2025	
		127(a)(1)	365	26	6103	
		127(a)(2)(A)-(C)	366	26	6103	
		127(a)(2)(D)	366	26	7213	
		127(a)(3)	366	26	6103 nt	
		127(b)(1)	366	42	503	
		127(b)(2)	367	42	504	
		127(b)(3)	367	42	503 nt	
		128, 129	367	7	2025	
		130-132(a)	367, 368	7	2026	
		132(b)	368	7	2026 nt	
		133	368	7	2026	
		134	368	7	2027	
		135	369	7	2012	
		136-138	369, 370	7	2014	
		139, 140	370	7	2015	
		201	370	7	2027	

ILLUSTRATION 7-9.   U.S.C.A General Index Showing the entry "Wool," Accessed on Westlaw

Wool

Generally: 15 USCA § 68 et seq.
Adjustments, Loans: 7 USCA § 9040
Advertisements, Fraud: 15 USCA § 68b
Agriculture Wool Apparel Manufacturers Trust Fund: 7 USCA § 7101 NT
Analyses: 15 USCA § 68d
Antitrust Laws. Monopolies and Combinations,
    Fraud: 15 USCA § 68g , 15 USCA § 68f
    Misbranding: 15 USCA § 68a
    Stamps, Removal: 15 USCA § 68c
    Tags, Removal: 15 USCA § 68c
Apparel Manufacturers Trust Fund: 7 USCA § 7101 NT
Appeal and Review, Loans: 7 USCA § 7996
Base Acres, Payment: 7 USCA § 7901 et seq.
Boards and Commissions. Commission: 15 USCA § 68 et seq.
    Condemnation: 15 USCA § 68e
    Definitions: 15 USCA § 68
    Injunctions: 15 USCA § 68e
    Labeling Act: 15 USCA § 68d
    Misdemeanors: 15 USCA § 68h
Bonds (Officers and Fiduciaries)
Brands, Marks and Labels. Labels: 15 USCA § 68a et seq.
    Affixing Labels: 15 USCA § 68c
    Cashmere: 15 USCA § 68b
    Guarantees: 15 USCA § 68g
    Imported Products: 15 USCA § 68f
    Misbranding: 15 USCA § 68a et seq.
    Mutilation: 15 USCA § 68c
    Removal: 15 USCA § 68c
Carbonizing: 19 USCA § 1562
Cashmere: 15 USCA § 68b
Charges. Rates and Charges,
    Loans,
        Deficiencies, Payment: 7 USCA § 9035
        Markets and Marketing: 7 USCA § 9032
    Markets and Marketing, Loans: 7 USCA § 7932
    Payment: 7 USCA § 7914 , 7 USCA § 7913
Clothing, Agriculture Wool Apparel Manufacturers Trust Fund: 7 USCA § 7101 NT
Combinations. Monopolies and Combinations,
    Fraud: 15 USCA § 68g , 15 USCA § 68f
    Misbranding: 15 USCA § 68a
    Stamps, Removal: 15 USCA § 68c

ILLUSTRATION 7-10.   Outline of Sections in Title 15 U.S.C., Commerce and Trade, §§ 68–68j, Labeling of Wool Products

---

SUBCHAPTER III—LABELING OF WOOL PRODUCTS

68.	Definitions.
68a.	Misbranding declared unlawful.
68b.	Misbranded wool products.
68c.	Stamp, tag, label, or other identification.
68d.	Enforcement of subchapter.
68e.	Condemnation and injunction proceedings.
68f.	Exclusion of misbranded wool products.
68g.	Guaranty.
68h.	Criminal penalty.
68i.	Application of other laws.
68j.	Exceptions from subchapter.

PRACTICE POINTER

When you obtain a statute on the government websites it is very cost effective. After reading the statute on the government site, look at the statute in an unofficial code, either in hard copy or online, to obtain research enhancements, links to administrative code references, case annotations, and research enhancements. Last, validate the statute cite on Lexis with *Shepard's* or on Westlaw with KeyCite.

▼ How Do You Cite Federal Statutes?

Always cite to the official statutory compilation, if it is the most current version. The first entry in the citation is the title number, then the abbreviation for the statutory compilation, and then the section or paragraph number. *Bluebook* **Rule 12** and *ALWD* **Rule 14** detail the various rules on citing statutes and codes, state or federal. For example, Title 12, § 211 of the U.S.C. would be cited as:

12 U.S.C. § 21.

Note that if the statute is obtained from a current code volume and the statute is currently in force, there is no need to include a date, as including the date is optional. Also, you need to include the publisher of the code in parentheses unless the code was published by or published under the direction of a federal or state government.

You always cite to the official code, the U.S.C., unless you are relying on an unofficial code for updating purposes. Because the government sites provide highly reliable, authenticated versions of the United States Code, there is no need to provide a URL when citing to the United States Code if accessed via govinfo.gov or uscode.house.gov.

The year included in the citation is the year that the code volume was published, not the year that the statute was enacted. The publication date is printed either on the title page of the bound volume or on the back of the title page. If a pocket part supplement is used, include that date as well.

15 U.S.C.A. § 68 (West Supp. 2020) — citation to only the pocket part.

You can also cite the statute as: 15 U.S.C.A. § 68 (West 2020 and Supp. 2020).

In this example, the first year mentioned, 2020, is the year that the particular volume of the code was published. The second date, 2020, is the year of the pocket part supplement that updates the code volume.

If a code section is well known by a popular name, then include the name in the citation:

Wool Products Labeling Act of 1939, 15 U.S.C. §§ 68 - 68j.

4. Validating and Updating Statutes

▼ How and Why Would You Validate Federal Statutes?

Remember, it is important to validate and update statutes. You cannot rely on a particular statute until you have both updated and validated it. We discussed updating earlier in this chapter; it concerns finding any new legislative activity that affects the statute section. Validating tells you how a court interpreted or applied a statute. *Shepard's* and KeyCite provide citations to cases and secondary sources that cite the statute section. The cases provide insight into how a statute is used in a specific situation with a specific set of facts. After all, statutes generally do not include facts. *Shepard's* and KeyCite also provide the analytical treatment indicating how a court of law interprets or applies a statute section. *Shepard's* contains analysis that tells you whether the statute is constitutional, unconstitutional, valid, or invalid. See Illustration 7-11 for a portion of a case applying a statute. See Chapter 5 for a thorough discussion of *Shepard's* and KeyCite. Validating indicates whether a court deems the statute constitutional or unconstitutional, valid or invalid. A court cannot repeal, supersede, or amend legislation as this activity is under the purview of the legislature. The court's discussion and application of a statute is very helpful in providing insight into how a statute is used in a certain factual scenario.

Shepardizing and KeyCiting statutes also includes information indicating whether the statute has been repealed or amended. You

ILLUSTRATION 7-11. Pages from *Decision in the Federal Reporter* That Cites to 15 U.S.C. § 68

---

302   284 FEDERAL REPORTER, 3d SERIES

IV.

The plaintiff also challenges on appeal the district court's analysis of his claim for damages arising out of the alleged malpractice. The district court, in an effort to provide a "complete record of factual findings," analyzed the case backwards, starting with an assessment of damages, then proceeding to causation, negligence, and duty, in that order. Although we understand why the court engaged in this method of analysis, rather than simply concluding its ruling after finding there was no duty to disclose, such analysis resulted in extraneous factual findings. Therefore, because the district court did not need to reach the issue of damages, any findings regarding damages are dicta; the district court did not actually award any damages. As a result, plaintiff's claims of error in computing the damages are premature. *See United States v. Ottati & Goss, Inc.,* 900 F.2d 429, 443 (1st Cir.1990) (refusing

CASHMERE & CAMEL HAIR MANU-FACTURERS INSTITUTE, f/k/a Camel Hair & Cashmere Institute of America, Inc., and L.W. Packard & Co., Inc., Plaintiffs, Appellants,

v.

SAKS FIFTH AVENUE, Harve Benard, Ltd. and Filenes Basement, Defendants, Appellees.

No. 00–2341.

United States Court of Appeals, First Circuit.

Heard Dec. 6, 2001.

Decided April 1, 2002.

Fabric wholesaler and trade association brought action against garment manu-

---

in cases where there is a "trade-off" between the health of the mother and the child, "pregnant women routinely choose" and "should" choose a cesarean section "for the benefit of their fetuses," even though the risk to the woman is higher than from a vaginal delivery).

8. We emphasize that a duty to disclose, if it exists, does *not* necessarily indicate any duty to offer or to perform a C-section if the doctor

does not consider one to be warranted in his medical judgment. *See Canterbury,* 464 F.2d at 781 (separating physician's duty "to treat [and diagnose] his patient skillfully" from his "obligation to communicate specific information to the patient"). The duty to disclose is intended to be limited, so as not to unduly burden the practice of medicine. *See Harnish,* 439 N.E.2d at 243.

ILLUSTRATION 7-11. *Continued*

CASHMERE & CAMEL HAIR MFRS. v. SAKS FIFTH AVE. 315
Cite as 284 F.3d 302 (1st Cir. 2002)

Because defendants do not dispute that overstating cashmere content is a literal falsity claim, we apply a presumption of consumer deception in plaintiffs' favor on this claim. Based on this presumption, and defendants' failure to present evidence to rebut it, Packard has satisfied its burden of demonstrating consumer deception on its cashmere content claim.

[15, 16] Whether literal falsity is involved in plaintiffs' claim that defendants improperly labeled their goods as cashmere rather than recycled cashmere, however, is a contentious issue. Defendants argue that this claim is, by definition, one of implied falsity—that is, a representation that is literally true but in context becomes likely to mislead. *See Clorox,* 228 F.3d at 33 (defining an implied falsity claim as one in which the "advertisement, though explicitly true, nonetheless conveys a misleading message to the viewing public"). As further support for their argument, defendants offer a simple syllogism: all suits based on implied messages are im-

falsity claim. *See id.* However, we disagree with defendants' assertion that all claims that rely on implied messages are necessarily implied falsity claims. In *Clorox,* this Court noted that "[a]lthough factfinders usually base literal falsity claims upon the explicit claims made by an advertisement, they may also consider any claims the advertisement conveys by 'necessary implication.'" *Id.* at 34–35. We explained that "[a] claim is conveyed by necessary implication when, considering the advertisement in its entirety, the audience would recognize the claim as readily as if it had been explicitly stated." *Id.* at 35.

After drawing all reasonable inferences in favor of the nonmoving party, a rational factfinder could conclude that plaintiffs' recycled cashmere claim is one of literal falsity. The Wool Products Labeling Act, 15 U.S.C. § 68 *et seq.,* requires recycled garments and fabrics, including cashmere, to be labeled as such. As a result, whenever a label represents that a garment

---

13. Defendants also argue that before the presumption of consumer deception can apply to a literal falsity claim for damages, the plaintiff must demonstrate that the defendant intentionally deceived the consuming public. None of the five circuit cases cited *supra,* however, speaks of the intent to deceive as a prerequisite to applying a presumption of consumer deception on a literal falsity claim. As discussed in more detail below, the intent

to deceive is an independent basis for triggering a presumption of consumer deception. *See William H. Morris Co. v. Group W, Inc.,* 66 F.3d 255, 258 (9th Cir.1995) (ruling, on an implied falsity claim, that "[i]f [defendant] intentionally misled consumers, we would presume consumers were in fact deceived and [defendant] would have the burden of demonstrating otherwise").

Reprinted with permission of Thomson Reuters.

must update statutory authority by using the code's pocket part supplement and advance sheets. Most important, validating a code section indicates the judicial treatment or interpretation of a statute, meaning how courts of law have looked at a statute's application and at whether its application was discriminatory or affected too broad or too narrow a group of people. Judges then determine if the statute has been complied with or if the statute is unconstitutional or constitutional in whole or in part. See Illustration 7-11, where 15 U.S.C. § 68 is cited in a case to see how a court applies a statute with a set of facts.

▼ How Do You Update Statutes?

To update statutes to ensure that you have the most recent version, you must take the following steps.

1. Check the statute cite on uscode.house.gov, as it will tell you that it is updated to a certain date. This website provides updates in a very timely manner. The legislation amending the statute is available.

    Updating statutory authority on Lexis or Westlaw is achieved through the point-and-click method. Once you have the relevant statutory provision on the screen, there will be a caption indicating that the statute is current through a particular date or session law. Citations to any slip laws or session laws updating the statute will be provided. Merely point and click the identifying citation, and you will link to the updating document. Before you perform this on either Lexis or Westlaw, call customer service for guidance.

    You can also use an unofficial code, the U.S.C.A. or the U.S.C.S. After finding the appropriate code section, consult the pocket part supplement at the end of the volume or the separately published pamphlet that updates the particular volume. You would turn to the back of the volume containing the initial entry and open the pocket part supplement to see if the section is mentioned. The entries in the supplement are in numerical order just as they are in the main volume. If a section is not affected, it is just skipped over and the next affected section, in sequential order, is mentioned. Note that sometimes the material updating the code volume contains too many pages to be included in a pocket part so that a supplementary pamphlet, a separate paperback-bound pamphlet, is published.

2. If you are using hardcopy statutes, to further update a federal code section, scan the *United States Code Service Advance Service,* the U.S.C.C.A.N. advance sheets (the paperbound pamphlets that are issued monthly containing the session laws from the Congress), or the U.S.C.A. statutory supplement to find relevant slip laws from recent congressional sessions. Look for entries that are similar in name to the code section you are updating. This can also be done for state statutes by using the state session law reporter.

3. If a state statute is being updated, it is best to consult the state legislative information website. You can obtain state legislative information at www.llsdc.org/state-legislation, which has an updated list of all 50 states' legislative telephone numbers and state legislature's websites, with separate access information for each chamber when available.
4. You can track pending legislation for the 50 states on Lexis and on Westlaw in the respective state bill tracking files.
5. Review the U.S.C.A. statutory supplement and advance sheets for federal statutes. These resources indicate whether a section of the U.S.C. has been amended, repealed, or created.
6. KeyCite or Shepardize the statute to get updates and to check validity (how a court applied and construed the statute).

5. How to Find State Statutes

▼ How Does State Statutory Research Compare with Federal Statutory Research?

State statutory research closely parallels federal statutory research. To perform state statutory research, you would likely start with Google and then consult the state's statutes online. Alternatively, in hard copy you would use the index method, the title outline method, the popular name table, or the conversion table approach, just as you would with the federal materials. You should use the annotated statute set, online or in print, for the state to be sure to obtain research enhancements and updates. Even the precise, succinct language of the state statutes is similar to the federal statutes and similar to the language used by other states, because of the canons of construction and models of statutory parallelism that are adopted by drafters of legislation.

State statutes are enacted by the state legislatures in the same manner as federal statutes and appear in the slip law format first, then become session laws, and finally are codified and incorporated into the state statutory codes. Current state legislation also can be found in state bar bulletins, legal newspapers, and on the Internet, or at the particular state's legislative website found at http://congress.gov. At the bottom of the screen locate the heading "Resources" and select "State Legislature Websites" from the list. This is the most cost-effective way to find and read a state statute. However, you can also search state legislation on Lexis or Westlaw, which are the only places where you can validate the statute and find annotations. An overlooked resource for state legislative information is the newspaper of a large city in the state or the newspaper of the state capital.

ILLUSTRATION 7-12. Sample Page Showing 2020 Pocket Part Entry for Volume 15 U.S.C.A.

COMMERCE AND TRADE

CHAPTER 2A—SECURITIES AND TRUST INDENTURES

SUBCHAPTER I—DOMESTIC SECURITIES

LAW REVIEW AND JOURNAL COMMENTARIES

White collar crime's gray area: The anomaly of criminalizing conduct not civilly actionable. Wendy Gerwick Couture, 72 Alb. L. Rev. 1 (2009).

§ 77a. Short title

HISTORICAL NOTES

Short Title

2012 Amendments. Pub.L. 112–142, § 1, July 9, 2012, 126 Stat. 989, provided that: "This Act [amending 15 U.S.C.A. § 77c] may be cited as the 'Church Plan Investment Clarification Act'."

Pub.L. 112–106, Title III, § 301, Apr. 5, 2012, 126 Stat. 315, provided that: "This title [Title III of Pub.L. 112–106, § 301 et seq., Apr. 5, 2012, 126 Stat. 315, enacting 15 U.S.C.A. § 77d–1, amending 15 U.S.C.A. §§ 77d, 77r, 78c, 78*l*, and 78*o*, and enacting provisions set out as notes under 15 U.S.C.A. §§ 77d, 77r, 78c, and 78*l*] may be cited as the 'Capital Raising Online While Deterring Fraud and Unethical Non-Disclosure Act of 2012' or the 'CROWDFUND Act'."

Notes of Decisions

4. Construction with other laws

Common law fraud and Securities Act claims alleged by investors in removed action against underwriters, sponsors, depositors, and originators of residential mortgage-backed securities (RMBS) concerned transactions involving territorial or foreign banking, and thus arose under laws of United States for purposes of jurisdiction-granting provision of Edge Act, even if complaint did not mention any loans originating in United States dependencies or any foreign banking transaction, since resolution of claims would turn, in part, on whether underlying mortgage loans complied with underwriting standards described in defendants' offering materials, and lending on property in territorial jurisdiction constituted "banking" within that jurisdiction. American Intern. Group, Inc. v. Bank of America Corp., S.D.N.Y.2011, 820 F.Supp.2d 555, motion to certify appeal granted, reconsideration denied 2011 WL 6778473, vacated and remanded 712 F.3d 775. Removal of Cases ☜ 20

14. Validity and enforcement of contracts

Federal law provides for the creation of mortgage-related securities; the pooling of mortgages into investment trusts is not some sort of illicit scheme that taints the underlying debt. Thompson v. Bank of America, N.A., C.A.6 (Tenn.) 2014, 773 F.3d 741, rehearing denied. Mortgages And Deeds Of Trust ☜ 1481; Securities Regulation ☜ 5.13

§ 77b. Definitions; promotion of efficiency, competition, and capital formation

(a) Definitions

When used in this subchapter, unless the context otherwise requires—

(1) The term "security" means any note, stock, treasury stock, security future, security-based swap, bond, debenture, evidence of indebtedness, certificate of interest or participation in any profit-sharing agreement, collateral-trust certificate, preorganization certificate or subscription, transferable share, investment contract, voting-trust certificate, certificate of deposit for a security, fractional undivided interest in oil, gas, or other mineral rights, any put, call, straddle, option, or

178

ILLUSTRATION 7-13. Sample Page Showing Vermont Statutes Online 9 V.S.A. § 2698 *available at* http://legislature .vermont.gov/statutes/

VERMONT **GENERAL ASSEMBLY**

The Vermont Statutes Online

Title 9 : Commerce And Trade

Chapter 073 : Weights And Measures

Subchapter 004 : Specific Weights And Measures

(Cite as: 9 V.S.A. § 2698)

§ 2698. Textile products

A person shall not keep for the purpose of sale, offer or expose for sale, or sell, any textile yard goods put up or packaged in advance of sale in a bolt or roll, or any other textile product put up or packaged in advance of sale in any other unit, for either wholesale or retail sale, unless that bolt or roll, or such other unit, is definitely, plainly, and conspicuously marked to show its net measure in terms of yards or its net weight in terms of avoirdupois pounds or ounces, subject, however, to the following limitations and requirements:

(1) Any unit of twine or cordage may be marked to show its net measure in terms of feet. Ready-wound bobbins that are not sold separately shall not be required to be individually marked, but the package containing those bobbins shall be marked to show the number of bobbins contained therein and the net weight or measure of the thread on each bobbin. Any unit of sewing, basting, mending, darning, crocheting, tatting, handknitting, or embroidery thread or yarn, except nylon handknitting yarn, that is not composed in whole or in part of wool, the net weight of which is less than two ounces avoirdupois, shall be marked to show its net measure in terms of yards as unwound from the ball or from the spool or other holder. Any retail unit of a textile product, sold only for household use, consisting of a package containing two or more similar individual units that are not sold separately, shall be marked to show the number of individual units in the package and the net weight or net measure of the product in each individual unit, but this proviso shall not apply where the individual units are separately marked. Any unit of yarn, composed in whole or in part of wool, sold to consumers for handiwork, shall be marked to show the net weight of such yarn, except that any such unit of tapestry, mending, or embroidery yarn, the net measure of which does not exceed 50 yards, may be marked to show its linear measures only.

(2) The marking required by this section shall in all cases be in combination with the name and place of business of the manufacturer, packer, or distributor of the product, or a trademark, symbol, brand, or other mark that positively identifies such manufacturer, packer, or distributor. Any such trademark, symbol, brand, or other mark that is employed to identify the manufacturer, packer, or distributor shall be filed with the Secretary.

(3) Reasonable tolerances may be permitted, and these may be included in regulations for the enforcement of this section that shall be issued by the Secretary.

(4) This section shall not apply to the following textile products when sold at wholesale in bulk by net weight: cordage, agricultural bag sewing threads, twines, yarns that are to be processed, and yarns that are to be industrially converted into end use products. (Added 1967, No. 102, § 32, eff. April 14, 1967; amended 1991, No. 227 (Adj. Sess.), § 7.)

PRACTICE POINTER

Always read a statute according to its plain meaning; that is, interpret the language just as it is written. After reading a statute, summarize the language in a few sentences, in your own words. This will help when you then want to use the statute in a written document. When you write a document, then your language and the statutory language won't contrast so sharply. Remember to cite to all statutory authority that you rely on, even if it is written in your own language. Be sure that any statute that you rely on is updated and validated.

▼ How Can You Tell Whether a State Code Is the Official
or the Unofficial Statutory Compilation?

Bluebook **Table T.1** and *ALWD* **Appendix 1 (B)** answer this question. Under each state in **Table T.1** is the boldface heading **Statutory compilations**, with information indicating the official format of the state code. *ALWD* indicates the official code with a red star and the preferred source with an asterisk. For example, in the *Bluebook*, under Wisconsin you find:

Statutory compilations: Cite to Wis. Stat. if therein.

This indicates that Wis. Stat., the *Bluebook* abbreviation for the *Wisconsin Statutes*, is the official statutory compilation for Wisconsin. Under the Statutory compilations heading, the names of the state code, in the official and the unofficial format, are listed along with the *Bluebook* abbreviation. Also, check the *Bluebook* and *ALWD* for guidance on citing to state statutes retrieved from a state website. See **Rule 18** of the *Bluebook* and *ALWD* **Rule 14.4** and **Appendix 1 (B)**.

Sometimes a state has more than one statutory compilation, or there is not an official compilation. When this occurs, follow the *Bluebook* or *ALWD* for guidance when citing.

6. Researching Statutes Online

▼ What Are the Features of Online Statutes?

a. United States Code

Yes, the complete texts of the U.S.C. and the U.S.C.A. (published by West) are available on Westlaw. The U.S.C.S. and the unannotated United States Code are available in full text on Lexis. See Illustration 7-6 for an example. Both Lexis and Westlaw have added the browse enhancement to the statutes databases, enabling you to view the code sections preceding and following the code section that you retrieved. The browse feature emulates flipping through code sections in a hardbound format because you often look at related code sections when you find the section of the statutes with information on point.

Now the government sites, uscode.house.gov, govinfo.gov, and congress.gov, provide access to highly reliable and authenticated copies of the federal statutes. In fact, you no longer have to indicate in the citation that you obtained the statute section from the government website if it is current.

Accessing statutes on government websites is very cost effective, as the sites are free. You can read the statutes on the government sites such as www.govinfo.gov, uscode.house.gov, or on the Cornell Legal Information Institute's site at www.law.cornell.edu. Govinfo.gov and uscode.house.gov are highly reliable, updated, and authenticated sources for the United States Code. However, you cannot validate, obtain citations to cases that interpret and apply the statute section, or obtain research enhancements on www.govinfo.gov, uscode.house.gov, congress.gov, or www.law.cornell.edu.

b. State Statutes

The full text of all 50 state statutory compilations is available on both Westlaw and Lexis. On Lexis, you can search all 50 state codes simultaneously. Slip laws are available for all 50 states on Lexis and Westlaw.

NET NOTE

Cornell's Legal Information Institute permits you to access and to search each state statutory compilation from all 50 states at no charge. The site is www.law.cornell.edu/states.

PRACTICE POINTER

Validation is available for all jurisdictions' statutes, state and federal.

When you access the United States Code on the Internet at uscode. house.gov, govinfo.gov, or www.law.cornell.edu, remember to validate any statutory provision, with *Shepard's* or KeyCite, to see how a court rules and how the statute was applied. Also, double check to see if the provision is current by consulting the last date updated on the site.

CHAPTER SUMMARY

This chapter led you through the legislative process, where you learned the steps a bill goes through to become law. Also, this chapter detailed constitutional and statutory research on the state and federal levels. You learned how to find, to cite, and to validate pertinent constitutional provisions. You learned about the different ways to perform statutory research—federal and state—and how to update, validate, and cite statutes.

KEY TERMS

codification	constitution
committee report	grandfathered
conference committee	House committee

legislation
pocket veto
public laws
session laws
slip bill
slip law
sponsor
statutes

Statutes at Large
statutory compilations
subcommittee
United States Code
United States Code Annotated
United States Code Service
Veto

EXERCISES

SELF-ASSESSMENT

1. Use the popular name table to find the Emmett Till Unsolved Civil Rights Crime Act of 2007. Please list all the information pertaining to the Act that you find in the popular name table.
2. List three ways to find a statute online. Name the sites consulted.

PRACTICE SKILLS

To answer Questions 3–11, look up the Americans with Disabilities Act of 1990.

3. What date was the Act enacted originally? Where is the information? List at least two places.
4. List the names of the four substantive titles of the Act. What are they called in the codified version?
5. Provide the public law number for the Act. List at least two places where this information is found.
6. Explain what the numbers included in the public law number mean.
7. Provide the U.S.C. citation for the Act. List the steps you followed to find this information.
8. Provide the *Statutes at Large* citation for the Act. List at least two places where this information is found.
9. What is the definition of *employer* under the Act?
10. Does the definition of *employer* under Title I of the Act differ in the U.S.C.A. from the definition found in the *Statutes at Large* when the law was originally enacted? If so, how?
11. Find the *United States Code* section for the Americans with Disabilities Act on the Internet at govingo.gov.

For Questions 12–18, look up the Energy Conservation and Production Act in the U.S.C.'s Popular Name Tool.

12. Write the U.S.C. citation in *Bluebook* format. (Remember to look at the most recent amendments.)
13. After you find the U.S.C. cite, look up the U.S.C.A. entry for the code section. Compare the entries and the annotations. Note the research enhancements that a West publication provides. Write down any Key Numbers and any U.S.C.C.A.N. references.
14. Look up the U.S.C.S. entry for the code section. Note the research aids that U.S.C.S. provides. Note that you see administrative regulation references in the U.S.C.S.

15. What C.F.R. citation is referred to in the code section? (Remember to use the supplements and the pocket parts to ensure that you are looking at the most current version of the statute.)
16. Are there any cases that discuss or interpret the statute? If so, look up two cases and see how the statute is treated in the opinions.
17. Shepardize the statute citation.
18. Find the statute on the Internet at uscode.house.gov or govinfo.gov.

For Questions 19–20, use your state statutes to find the sections that pertain to pawnbrokers and moneylenders.

19. Write the official state code cite in correct *Bluebook* format. Next, write the annotated cite if available. Compare the entries.
20. Are there any cases that discuss or interpret the statute? If so, look them up and see how the statute is treated in the opinion. Finally, Shepardize or KeyCite the statute citation.
21. Use uscode.house.gov or govinfo.gov to find the *United States Code* section containing the provisions concerning the definition of personal income for tax purposes.
22. Search either http://congress.gov or govinfo.gov for any federal bills or resolutions in the current Congress concerning the registration of sexual offenders.

LEGISLATIVE HISTORY

CHAPTER OVERVIEW

Paralegals are called on to monitor the status of bills and proposed legislation currently being considered on the federal and state levels and to compile legislative histories of laws already passed and codified to ascertain the policy or intended effect of the legislation. The process of compiling all of the components of the legislative process leading to the enactment of a statute, called **legislative history**, is growing in importance as the need for the interpretation of statutes in litigation increases.

A. LEGISLATIVE INFORMATION

Researching a legislative history requires that you retrace the law-making process of enacted law from the initial bill through the committee reports through the various versions of the bill to the final version and the enacted law. You will see that not all bills involve the proposal to create brand new laws. Some bills propose to amend existing laws, or statutes, as shown later in this chapter in Illustration 8-3.

Legislative histories are very informative because the information gathered from the committee reports and the speeches or legislative debates given on the floor of the legislative body provides insight into the purpose and intent of the legislation. Sometimes you may want to see an earlier version of a statute, even if that version is no longer in effect, because the statute is cited in an older case.

NET NOTE

A useful source of information on legislative history, including many links, is at www.llsdc.org/sourcebook. Look at the various links—all are helpful!

---

1. Finding the Text of Pending Legislation

Bills currently going through the process of being enacted into law are classified as **pending legislation.** Paralegals are called on to monitor pending legislation and to make sure that the information is as current as possible.

Lexis and Westlaw have current federal and state bills online. Lexis has the text of current pending federal bills as well as the full text of federal committee and conference reports dating back to the 101st Congress. The text of pending state bills from all 50 states is also available.

Westlaw has bills starting in 1995. Bill Tracking on Westlaw allows you to access pending legislation and the text of bills for states and the U.S. Congress online.

Use Congress.gov to access pending legislation and to monitor legislation. This site is free and updated continually when Congress is in session. The information extends back to the 93rd Congress for many legislative resources. The site is especially comprehensive beginning with the 104th Congress. You will find bills and actions relating to those bills. You can also obtain the committee reports that are essential resources when performing a legislative history, as they provide tremendous insight into the intent and scope of the legislation. The site is generally updated the morning after a congressional session on a particular bill adjourns. Congress.gov replaces Thomas.gov. Use Congress.gov to search for the components of a legislative history for laws passed beginning with the 93rd Congress and to monitor pending legislation.

On the state level, each state has a legislative library from which you can request the copy of the particular bill in question. If the librarian cannot provide a copy of the bill, he or she will generally direct you to the member of the state House or Senate who sponsored the bill or to the appropriate committee. Pending legislation for all 50 states can be tracked on Lexis and Westlaw. You can also contact the particular state legislature's library or the state representative directly.

NET NOTE

The website for the U.S. House of Representatives is www.house.gov. This site contains committee reports. Committee activities from the past three days are posted here. This is a good site to bookmark when you are tracking legislation, for it links you to bills in full-text format. It has a directory of House members complete with addresses, both postal and e-mail, and telephone numbers. This site posts activity currently on the House floor.

---

2. Tracking Pending Legislation

Congress.gov provides the capability to monitor pending federal legislation at no cost. Congress.gov goes back to 1973. On Congress.gov you can get the full text of bills soon after they are proposed. You can obtain committee reports from 104th Congress to the present day on Congress.gov.

You can also use govinfo.gov, 1993 to present, to monitor bills and the passage of legislation. To find Government Printing Office documents and links to the *Congressional Record, Congressional Bills*, and congressional publications, go to **govinfo.gov.**

On the state level, almost every state has either a state legislative website, a state bar association, or a state legislative library that provides information as to the status of bills that are currently being created and considered.

NET NOTE

The Law Librarians' Society of Washington, D.C., has a handy website that links you to all 50 state legislatures, state databases, and their respective telephone numbers. This site, at www.llsdc.org/state-legislation, includes state legislative history information.

Indiana University, Bloomington, Maurer School of Law Library has a state legislative history research guide for all 50 states at https://law.indiana.libguides.com/state-legislative-history-guides.

B. LEGISLATIVE HISTORIES

▼ Where Do You Find Copies of Public Laws?

Public laws, which are the federally enacted laws, can be obtained by contacting the law's sponsor in the House or the Senate. You can access the Public Laws at Congress.gov and at the Government Publishing Office, govinfo.gov, starting with the 93rd Congress. In addition to U.S.C.C.A.N., these can be obtained at a government depository library. (Many university libraries and large city libraries are government depository libraries.) The *United States Code Service* (U.S.C.S.) publishes paperback advance sheets with the public laws enacted during the prior month. The *United States Code Annotated* (U.S.C.A.) also prints paperback advance sheets each month that contain all of the public laws enacted during the prior month.

NET NOTE

The steps for tracing federal legislation can be found at guides.ll.georgetown .edu/legislative history.

▼ How Do You Research Legislative Histories of Laws That Are Already Enacted?

Commercial publishers compile the most accessible sources of legislative histories for laws that are already enacted. The most user-friendly, hardcopy source of commercially compiled federal legislative histories is the **United States Code Congressional and Administrative News** (U.S.C.C.A.N.). U.S.C.C.A.N., which began publication in the 1950s, was published originally by West, and is now published by Thomson Reuters. References to U.S.C.C.A.N. are provided in the U.S.C.A, which is also published by Thomson Reuters. Often a statute printed in the U.S.C.A. that was enacted since U.S.C.C.A.N.'s publication will contain a reference to the U.S.C.C.A.N. citation. U.S.C.C.A.N. includes select documents that were created during the legislative process that the statute underwent prior to enactment. However, U.S.C.C.A.N. only provides the legislative history for selected public laws and abridges the documents in the legislative history. U.S.C.C.A.N. generally includes the committee report for the legislation, which is the most insightful component of the legislative history.

U.S.C.C.A.N. is organized by congressional session; the congressional session is indicated on the spine of each volume. Each session's public laws, also indicated on the spine of each volume, and the legislative history of the public laws are arranged in numerical order according to public law number. See Illustrations 8-1 and 8-2.

U.S.C.C.A.N. is a good place to find legislative history and a copy of a public law, provided it is not too recent. It is quick to consult. For copies of recent public laws (one month old), consult the pamphlets at the end of the U.S.C.A., U.S.C.S., and U.S.C.C.A.N. sets.

Legislative histories are also available on Westlaw. The coverage begins in 1948. U.S.C.C.A.N. is also available on Westlaw, as it is a Thomson Reuters product.

Lexis has compiled legislative histories online for select, significant acts.

Congress.gov provides free access to legislative information, including public laws, beginning in the 93rd Congress. It also contains the *Congressional Record* beginning with the 101st Congress and committee reports starting with the 104th Congress, as well as links to federal government websites. However, the full text of bills from before 1993, the 103rd Congress, is not currently available on Congress.gov. Use this site to find legislative information from the current Congress that may impact a particular federal statute. You can search by bill number, by popular name, or by word. You can view the actual bill in PDF format.

▼ How Do You Use U.S.C.C.A.N. in Conjunction with the U.S.C.A.?

In Illustration 7-5, look at the reprint of 15 U.S.C.A. § 68 from the main code volume of the U.S.C.A. Notice the heading that follows the text of the statute: Historical Notes. It is in this part of the U.S.C.A. that you obtain references to the public laws that created the statute and to the appropriate U.S.C.C.A.N. cite that contains the legislative history for the public law for the amendments to § 68. We are interested in the amendments to the Wool Products Labeling Act of 1939 that concern the definition of recycled wool.

PRACTICE POINTER

When retrieving a document from a government website, use your software's "Find" feature to locate relevant text within the document.

ILLUSTRATION 8-1. Sample Pages from U.S.C.C.A.N. Showing Pub. L. No. 96-242

PUBLIC LAW 96–242 [H.R. 4197]; May 5, 1980

WOOL PRODUCTS LABELING ACT OF 1939— RECYCLED WOOL

For Legislative History of this and other Laws, see Table 1, Public Laws and Legislative History, at end of final volume

An Act to amend the Wool Products Labeling Act of 1939 with respect to recycled wool.

Wool Products Labeling Act, amendment. 15 USC 68.

Be it enacted by the Senate and House of Representatives of the United States of America in Congress assembled, That (a) section 2(c) of the Wool Products Labeling Act of 1939 (54 Stat. 1128) is amended to read as follows:

"(c) The term 'recycled wool' means (1) the resulting fiber when wool has been woven or felted into a wool product which, without ever having been utilized in any way by the ultimate consumer, subsequently has been made into a fibrous state, or (2) the resulting fiber when wool or reprocessed wool has been spun, woven, knitted, or felted into a wool product which, after having been used in any way by the ultimate consumer, subsequently has been made into a fibrous state.".

Repeal.

(b) Subsection (d) of section 2 of the Wool Products Labeling Act of 1939 is repealed.

(c) Subsections (e), (f), (g), (h), and (i) of section 2 of the Wool Products Labeling Act of 1939 and all references thereto are redesignated as subsections (d), (e), (f), (g), and (h), respectively.

(d) Section 2(d) of such Act, as redesignated by subsection (c) of this section, is amended by striking out ", reprocessed wool, or reused wool" and inserting in lieu thereof "or recycled wool".

15 USC 68b.

SEC. 2. Section 4(a)(2)(A) of the Wool Products Labeling Act of 1939 is amended—

(1) by striking out "(2) reprocessed wool; (3) reused wool" and inserting in lieu thereof "(2) recycled wool";

(2) by striking out "(4)" and inserting in lieu thereof "(3)"; and

(3) by striking out "(5)" and by inserting in lieu thereof "(4)".

Effective date. 15 USC 68 note.

SEC. 3. The amendments made by this Act shall take effect with respect to wool products manufactured on or after the date sixty days after the date of enactment of this Act.

Approved May 5, 1980.

LEGISLATIVE HISTORY:

HOUSE REPORT No. 96–795 (Comm. on Interstate and Foreign Commerce).
SENATE REPORT No. 96–655 (Comm. on Commerce, Science, and Transportation).
CONGRESSIONAL RECORD, Vol. 126 (1980):
    Mar. 11, considered and passed House.
    Apr. 23, considered and passed Senate.

94 STAT. 344

ILLUSTRATION 8-2. Sample Pages from U.S.C.C.A.N. Showing the Legislative History of Pub. L. No. 96-242

LEGISLATIVE HISTORY
P.L. 96–242

WOOL PRODUCTS LABELING ACT OF 1939— RECYCLED WOOL

P.L. 96–242, see page 94 Stat. 344

House Report (Interstate and Foreign Commerce Committee) No. 96–795, Mar. 4, 1980 [To accompany H.R. 4197]

Senate Report (Commerce, Science, and Transportation Committee) No. 96–655, Apr. 18, 1980 [To accompany H.R. 4197]

Cong. Record Vol. 126 (1980)

DATES OF CONSIDERATION AND PASSAGE

House March 11, 1980

Senate April 23, 1980

The Senate Report is set out.

SENATE REPORT NO. 96–655

[page 1]

The Committee on Commerce, Science, and Transportation, to which was referred the bill (H.R. 4197) to amend the Wool Products Labeling Act of 1939 with respect to recycled wool, having considered the same, reports favorably thereon without amendment and recommends that the bill do pass.

PURPOSE

H.R. 4197 would amend the Wool Products Labeling Act of 1939 by substituting the term "recycled wool" for the terms "reprocessed wool" and "reused wool" where these terms appear in the act. H.R. 4197 would also combine the definitions of "reprocessed wool" and "reused wool" into one definition for the term "recycled wool," and appropriately renumber subsections of the act accordingly. The amendments made by H.R. 4197 would beome effective 60 days after the date of enactment.

BACKGROUND AND NEED

The Wool Products Labeling Act of 1939, enacted October 14, 1940, provides for a system of labeling wool products introduced, manufactured for introduction, sale, transportation, or distribution in commerce. The failure to label wool products in accordance with the terms of the act is unlawful and is an unfair method of competition and an unfair and deceptive act or practice under the Federal Trade Commission Act.

[page 2]

The labeling terms required in the act are "wool," "reprocessed wool" and "reused wool." The term "wool" as used in the act means the fiber from the fleece of the sheep or lamb, or hair of angora or

782

ILLUSTRATION 8-2. *Continued*

WOOL PRODUCTS LABELING ACT
P.L. 96–242

cashmere goat (and may include the so-called specialty fiber from the hair of the camel, alpaca, llama, and vicuna) which has never been reclaimed from woven or felted wool products. The term "reprocessed wool" as used in the act means the resulting fiber when wool has been woven or felted into a wool product and which, without ever having been utilized in any way by the ultimate consumer, has subsequently been made into a fiber state. The term "reused wool" means the fiber which results when wool or reprocessed wool has been spun woven, knitted or felted into a wool product and which, after having been used in any way by the ultimate consumer, has subsequently been made into a fiber state again.

Since the fiber used in the production of "reprocessed wool" or "reused wool" goes through similar mechanical processes in order to be used in the remanufacture of wool products, the term "recycled" would be substituted for the terms "reprocessed" and "reused" since it more accurately describes the process involved.

The raw material for reprocessed wool comes from wool clippings and other wool products left over from manufacturing processes which is then recycled to its fibrous state. The raw material for reused wool stock comes from wool used in a wool product which has been used by the consumer and is then recycled to its fibrous state. The resulting fibers in each case are fibers of wool which are then made again into cloth, felt or some other wool product. As with wool or other fibers, that recycled wool fiber is frequently blended or combined with other fibers to produce the final product.

The steps in the recycling of wool are as follows:

Wool clippings and wool clothing or other wool products are sorted into more than 200 classifications before they are made into new cloth, felt, or other products. To prepare fibers for recycled wool, discarded wool products are first divided into those in good condition and those in poor condition. Products which are not suitable for fabrics are used for industrial purposes for roofing material.

The processed or used wool products are further graded. Knitted materials are separated from woven goods, woolens from worsteds. Pockets or linings of cotton or other materials are removed. The material is then sorted by color to permit its use where feasible without removing dyes. The material is usually carbonized which removes fibers and is thoroughly scoured to remove all soil and dirt. This makes the material sanitized.

After sorting has been completed, the products are placed in a machine that picks out the fibers used to produce wool stock. Clippings from cutting tables in garment plants are likewise sorted and graded in preparation for recycling.

Wool cloth, whether of 100-percent wool or recycled wool, is woven or otherwise fabricated in the same way. Wool stocks, both new wool and recycled wool, are blended to produce yarn which is then woven, knitted or blended for felt or other products. Fabrics are washed repeatedly to remove oil that is used to lubricate the fibers and all dirt that may be in the fabrics. The fabric is then dried in an oven at 240°F and sheared, finished, pressed, and ready for the manufacturer or home user.

[page 3]

After this processing, the wool fibers have been recycled, that is, entirely rebuilt into yarn, fabrics, and felt and subsequently into

ILLUSTRATION 8-2. *Continued*

> **LEGISLATIVE HISTORY**
> **P.L. 96-242**
>
> products for apparel or industrial use. Recycled wools are used primarily in heavy winter clothing, gloves, caps, felts and blankets.
> The Committee finds that the terms "reused wool" and "reprocessed wool" are unnecessary and often misleading to the consumer. Further, the terms also give a competitive advantage to foreign textile manufacturers who frequently do not comply with the rigid labeling requirements of the Wool Act.

Reprinted with permission of Thomson Reuters.

▼ What Are Other Ways to Find Relevant Legislative History in U.S.C.C.A.N.?

The popular name tables in the U.S.C., U.S.C.A., and U.S.C.S. provide references to the public law numbers for the statutes. If you have the public law number of a statute, then you can find the legislative history in U.S.C.C.A.N. because U.S.C.C.A.N. is organized by public law number.

▼ Is Legislative History Primary Authority?

Legislative history is not primary authority but is considered to be secondary authority because it provides material to interpret the statutes. In the legislative branch of our government, primary authority is limited to constitutions, statutes, codes, charters, and ordinances.

▼ How Do You Cite Legislative History Found in U.S.C.C.A.N.?

Legislative history materials found in U.S.C.C.A.N. follow *Bluebook* **Rule 13.4** and *ALWD* **Rule 15.7(f)**. The correct cite for a U.S. Senate Report reprinted in U.S.C.C.A.N. is:

S. Rep. No. 102-13, at 1 (1991), *as reprinted in* 1991 U.S.C.C.A.N. 12, 13.— *Bluebook* format in **Rule 13.4**

S. Rep. No. 102-13, at 1 (1991), *reprinted in* 1991 U.S.C.C.A.N. 12, 13.—*ALWD* format in **Rule 15.7(f)**

▼ How Do You Cite to a Legislative History of a Statute?

Bluebook **Rule 13** and *ALWD* **Rule 15** detail the format for the components of the legislative process: the bill, the committee report, the debates, and the transcripts of the hearings.

▼ What Are Some Other Sources of Legislative Information?

The *Congressional Record* contains the text of all of the proceedings from the floor of the U.S. Congress. It is published every day that Congress is in session. The *Congressional Record* has been in print since the 1870s. It is currently available on Lexis and Westlaw. You can view today's *Congressional Record* at Congress.gov. The *Congressional Record* is available at the Government Publishing Office, www.govinfo.gov, going back to 1994.

Proquest Congressional is a subscription database with coverage from 1969 to date. Proquest Congressional is thorough and provides exhaustive legislative information and resources. The database includes legislative histories for public laws—extending back for many years to 1970—along with congressional publications and hearings, and documents. The site also allows for Bill Tracking. You can view some materials, in digital format, dating back to 1789.

Sometimes it is necessary to consult a privately published legislative history. You should see your law librarian for this or contact the sponsor of the public law to find out more detailed information.

NET NOTE

The Library of Congress has a series of research resources in the blog, In Custodia Legis. The "Beginner's Guides" in the blog are especially helpful. "How to Locate a United States Congressional Committee Report: A Beginner's Guide" can be found at https://blogs.loc.gov/law/2015/10/how-to-locate-a-united-states-congressional-committee-report-a-beginners-guide/.

▼ How Do You Research State Legislative Histories?

Each state compiles legislative resources in a different manner, which complicates the task of research. Most states do not have commercially compiled legislative histories in hardcopy format. Some states have printed indexes, but the actual documents are on microfiche or on the particular state's legislative website. Each state has a legislative library that you can call for more information. Large public libraries and university libraries, particularly law school libraries, are good places to obtain state legislative history information. Session law services are available for every state at the state legislature's website. Consult www .congress.gov/state-legislature-websites to obtain the state's legislative website.

PRACTICE POINTER

Researching legislative histories can be time consuming. Ask the attorney who you are working for about a time budget for the project before performing a legislative history. Also, contact a librarian at a large academic law library for assistance when performing legislative histories.

▼ What Additional Sources for Legislative Information Are Available?

The following sources provide additional assistance in researching legislative information:

www.house.gov: To find bill information, representatives, and House of Representatives personnel. The House website provides biographical and contact information about every representative as well as their committees.

www.senate.gov: To find legislative information, senators, and Senate staff. The U.S. Senate website also offers information about every Senate committee as well as a biographical directory of Senate members.

The United States Government Manual: Searchable online at govinfo. gov/help/govman. Provides information about all agencies within all the branches of the federal government, including addresses and telephone numbers. Updated annually.

ILLUSTRATION 8-3. Congress.gov: Sample Page from 117th Congress Showing a Senate Bill to Amend the Internal Revenue Code

II

117TH CONGRESS
1ST SESSION **S. 2176**

To amend the Internal Revenue Code of 1986 to provide that floor plan
financing includes the financing of certain trailers and campers.

IN THE SENATE OF THE UNITED STATES

JUNE 22, 2021

Ms. ERNST (for herself and Mr. KING) introduced the following bill; which was
read twice and referred to the Committee on Finance

A BILL

To amend the Internal Revenue Code of 1986 to provide
that floor plan financing includes the financing of certain
trailers and campers.

1   *Be it enacted by the Senate and House of Representa-*

2   *tives of the United States of America in Congress assembled,*

3   **SECTION 1. SHORT TITLE.**

4   This Act may be cited as the "Travel Trailer and

5   Camper Tax Parity Act".

6   **SEC. 2. FLOOR PLAN FINANCING APPLICABLE TO CERTAIN**

7   **TRAILERS AND CAMPERS.**

8   (a) IN GENERAL.—Section 163(j)(9)(C) of the Inter-

9   nal Revenue Code of 1986 is amended by adding at the

10 end the following new flush sentence:

ILLUSTRATION 8-3. *Continued*

2

1 "Such term shall also include any trailer or camper which

2 is designed to provide temporary living quarters for rec-

3 reational, camping, or seasonal use and is designed to be

4 towed by, or affixed to, a motor vehicle.".

5   (b) EFFECTIVE DATE.—The amendment made by

6 this section shall apply to taxable years beginning after

7 December 31, 2020.

○

•S 2176 IS

CHAPTER SUMMARY

This chapter defined pending legislation and provided the tools to monitor pending legislation. U.S.C.C.A.N. is highlighted as the best and most efficient tool for compiling a legislative history of a federal statute. Both Congress.gov and the Government Publishing Office, govinfo.gov, offer easy access to legislative information and are very cost effective to use. You were also introduced to other resources to perform more detailed legislative histories, both federal and state.

KEY TERMS

Congress.gov

Congressional Record

Government Publishing Office, govinfo.gov

legislative history

pending legislation

public laws

United States Code Congressional and Administrative News

EXERCISES

SELF-ASSESSMENT

1. Name two components of a typical legislative history.
2. Why would you perform a legislative history of an act?
3. What information would you gather when performing a legislative history?

PRACTICE SKILLS

4. Find the legislative history of the Brady Handgun Violence Prevention Act. This is a federal act. Cite the legislative history of the Act in *Bluebook* format.
5. Find the legislative history of the Depository Library Act of 1964. This is a federal act. Cite the legislative history of the Act in *Bluebook* format.
6. Search Congress.gov to see if there are any bills from the current Congress that update or address the Brady Handgun Violence Prevention Act.
7. Search Congress.gov to find bills for the Rural America Energy Act of 2007.
8. Obtain any House or Senate bill numbers and the public law number for the Virginia Graeme Baker Pool and Spa Safety Act.

9

ADMINISTRATIVE MATERIALS AND LOOSELEAF SERVICES

CHAPTER OVERVIEW

In Chapter 7 you learned about the enactment of statutes and how to research them. Some statutes create administrative agencies and provide these agencies with a variety of powers. In this chapter, you learn about the creation of administrative agencies, the powers of these agencies, and the authority that they generate. You are shown how to locate these authorities as well as how to update and validate them. By the chapter's end, you will know how to use administrative materials and will understand their importance and relationship to other primary and secondary sources.

A. INTRODUCTION

▼ What Is Administrative Law?

Administrative rules and regulations are essential to the practice of law in a variety of areas, such as taxation, environmental law, education, and health care law. Federal and state administrative agencies regulate many aspects of our lives ranging from the safety of the products we purchase to the amount of hazardous wastes that can be placed in our landfills.

▼ How Can Administrative Agencies Create Law When This Is the Job of Congress?

Congress delegates its power to create law to **administrative agencies** by enacting **enabling statutes.** With these statutes, Congress charges these agencies with the daily enforcement of detailed regulations. This is both more efficient for Congress and also allows the development of these regulations by individuals with more expertise in an area than individual congressional representatives. The agencies create these detailed regulations through a process that involves solicitation of public opinions.

▼ How Do Administrative Agencies Operate?

On the federal level, administrative agencies often fall under the control of the executive branch of the government. To determine which executives control a particular agency, several sources should be consulted. The *United States Government Manual* provides information about all federal government agencies as well as an organization chart. Here is a link to the manual: www.usgovernmentmanual.gov. The organizational chart is one of the resources available on the manual's website.

This information includes a brief description of the agency's functions, how it was created, and how it is controlled. Although every cabinet post has an agency beneath it, some agencies are not associated with cabinet posts, such as the National Aeronautics and Space Administration (NASA). Often, agency staff members, other than those who hold cabinet posts, are hired because of their expertise and qualifications in an area of law. These experts do not leave their posts at the end of a legislative term.

Agencies often are called bureaus, boards, commissions, corporations, or administrations. All agencies create law in the form of **rules** or **regulations.** Agencies may function in an **adjudicatory** or **quasi-judicial** manner when they hear cases involving the application of a particular regulation and then issue written opinions of their findings.

Agencies create rules or regulations regularly, conduct hearings concerning particular issues, make decisions, and enforce Congress's mandates. The agency regulations adopted, or promulgated, are similar to statutes except that they are far more detailed. The administrative regulations explain how to apply the laws briefly outlined by Congress in the enabling legislation.

For example, Congress delegates to the U.S. Food and Drug Administration (FDA) authority to deal with the daily concerns regarding food products. The FDA regulates the labeling of all consumer food products based on a Congress-adopted law that created that FDA. The regulations are very specific. Among the details specified is the definition of principal display panel and the fact that it should be "large enough to accommodate all the mandatory label information required to be placed thereon." See the regulation shown in Illustration 9-1.

B. REGULATIONS

▼ How Are Regulations Adopted?

The process for adoption of regulations varies. The agency or the legislature determines what procedures must be followed before a regulation is adopted. In general, the agency requests comments from the public, conducts one or more hearings, and then decides whether to adopt a regulation. The agency concerns itself with the details. Agency regulations are revised, repealed, and created daily.

▼ What Type of Authority Is an Administrative Regulation or Rule?

The regulations and other documents adopted by federal agencies and published in the *Federal Register* and the *Code of Federal Regulations* (see next section) are primary authority because they are issued by a government body acting in its official law-making capacity.

C. FINDING ADMINISTRATIVE LAW

1. Generally

▼ Where Do You Find Federal Administrative Law?

Federal regulations are found in two official sources: the ***Code of Federal Regulations*** and the ***Federal Register.*** The *Code of Federal Regulations,* or the C.F.R. as it is known, contains all of the final administrative regulations. The C.F.R. is published annually, and different titles are published during different quarters of the year. The *Federal Register* is the daily newspaper for our administrative agencies and for our executive branch of the government. The *Federal Register* contains all of the proposed and final administrative regulations as well as executive orders and proclamations often issued by the president. Before any regulation or rule can become valid, it must be published in the *Federal Register.* This publication is available in print and online.

ILLUSTRATION 9-1.   C.F.R. Title 21, Part 101 Concerning Food Labeling

Pt. 101

of a food described in this section shall be exempt from declaration of the statements which paragraphs (a) and (b) of this section require immediately following the name of the food. Such exemption shall not apply to the outer container or wrapper of a multiunit retail package.

(e) All salt, table salt, iodized salt, or iodized table salt in packages intended for retail sale shipped in interstate commerce 18 months after the date of publication of this statement of policy in the FEDERAL REGISTER, shall be labeled as prescribed by this section; and if not so labeled, the Food and Drug Administration will regard them as misbranded within the meaning of sections 403 (a) and (f) of the Federal Food, Drug, and Cosmetic Act.

[42 FR 14306, Mar. 15, 1977, as amended at 48 FR 10811, Mar. 15, 1983; 49 FR 24119, June 12, 1984; 81 FR 59131, Aug. 29, 2016]

PART 101—FOOD LABELING

Subpart A—General Provisions

Sec.
101.1 Principal display panel of package form food.
101.2 Information panel of package form food.
101.3 Identity labeling of food in packaged form.
101.4 Food; designation of ingredients.
101.5 Food; name and place of business of manufacturer, packer, or distributor.
101.7 Declaration of net quantity of contents.
101.8 Vending machines.
101.9 Nutrition labeling of food.
101.10 Nutrition labeling of restaurant foods whose labels or labeling bear nutrient content claims or health claims.
101.11 Nutrition labeling of standard menu items in covered establishments.
101.12 Reference amounts customarily consumed per eating occasion.
101.13 Nutrient content claims—general principles.
101.14 Health claims: general requirements.
101.15 Food; prominence of required statements.
101.17 Food labeling warning, notice, and safe handling statements.
101.18 Misbranding of food.

Subpart B—Specific Food Labeling Requirements

101.22 Foods; labeling of spices, flavorings, colorings and chemical preservatives.

21 CFR Ch. I (4–1–20 Edition)

101.30 Percentage juice declaration for foods purporting to be beverages that contain fruit or vegetable juice.

Subpart C—Specific Nutrition Labeling Requirements and Guidelines

101.36 Nutrition labeling of dietary supplements.
101.42 Nutrition labeling of raw fruit, vegetables, and fish.
101.43 Substantial compliance of food retailers with the guidelines for the voluntary nutrition labeling of raw fruit, vegetables, and fish.
101.44 Identification of the 20 most frequently consumed raw fruit, vegetables, and fish in the United States.
101.45 Guidelines for the voluntary nutrition labeling of raw fruit, vegetables, and fish.

Subpart D—Specific Requirements for Nutrient Content Claims

101.54 Nutrient content claims for "good source," "high," "more," and "high potency."
101.56 Nutrient content claims for "light" or "lite."
101.60 Nutrient content claims for the calorie content of foods.
101.61 Nutrient content claims for the sodium content of foods.
101.62 Nutrient content claims for fat, fatty acid, and cholesterol content of foods.
101.65 Implied nutrient content claims and related label statements.
101.67 Use of nutrient content claims for butter.
101.69 Petitions for nutrient content claims.

Subpart E—Specific Requirements for Health Claims

101.70 Petitions for health claims.
101.71 Health claims: claims not authorized.
101.72 Health claims: calcium, vitamin D, and osteoporosis.
101.73 Health claims: dietary lipids and cancer.
101.74 Health claims: sodium and hypertension.
101.75 Health claims: dietary saturated fat and cholesterol and risk of coronary heart disease.
101.76 Health claims: fiber-containing grain products, fruits, and vegetables and cancer.
101.77 Health claims: fruits, vegetables, and grain products that contain fiber, particularly soluble fiber, and risk of coronary heart disease.
101.78 Health claims: fruits and vegetables and cancer.
101.79 Health claims: Folate and neural tube defects.

ILLUSTRATION 9-1. *Continued*

Food and Drug Administration, HHS §101.2

1 Title
2 Sections
3 Authority
4 *Federal Register* citation
5 Text

esters and risk of coronary heart disease (CHD).

Subpart F—Specific Requirements for Descriptive Claims That Are Neither Nutrient Content Claims nor Health Claims

101.91 Gluten-free labeling of food.
101.93 Certain types of statements for dietary supplements.
101.95 "Fresh," "freshly frozen," "fresh frozen," "frozen fresh."

Subpart G—Exemptions From Food Labeling Requirements

101.100 Food; exemptions from labeling.
101.108 Temporary exemptions for purposes of conducting authorized food labeling experiments.

APPENDIX A TO PART 101—MONIER-WILLIAMS PROCEDURE (WITH MODIFICATIONS) FOR SULFITES IN FOOD, CENTER FOR FOOD SAFETY AND APPLIED NUTRITION, FOOD AND DRUG ADMINISTRATION (NOVEMBER 1985)
APPENDIX B TO PART 101—GRAPHIC ENHANCEMENTS USED BY THE FDA
APPENDIX C TO PART 101—NUTRITION FACTS FOR RAW FRUITS AND VEGETABLES
APPENDIX D TO PART 101—NUTRITION FACTS FOR COOKED FISH

③ AUTHORITY: 15 U.S.C. 1453, 1454, 1455; 21 U.S.C. 321, 331, 342, 343, 348, 371; 42 U.S.C. 243, 264, 271.

④ SOURCE: 42 FR 14308, Mar. 15, 1977, unless otherwise noted.

EDITORIAL NOTE: Nomenclature changes to part 101 appear at 63 FR 14035, Mar. 24, 1998, 66 FR 17358, Mar. 30, 2001, 66 FR 56035, Nov. 6, 2001, and 81 FR 49895, July 29, 2016.

Subpart A—General Provisions

§101.1 Principal display panel of package form food.

⑤ The term *principal display panel* as it applies to food in package form and as used in this part, means the part of a label that is most likely to be displayed, presented, shown, or examined under customary conditions of display for retail sale. The principal display panel shall be large enough to accom-

modate all the mandatory label information required to be placed thereon by this part with clarity and conspicuousness and without obscuring design, vignettes, or crowding. Where packages bear alternate principal display panels, information required to be placed on the principal display panel shall be duplicated on each principal display panel. For the purpose of obtaining uniform type size in declaring the quantity of contents for all packages of substantially the same size, the term *area of the principal display panel* means the area of the side or surface that bears the principal display panel, which area shall be:

(a) In the case of a rectangular package where one entire side properly can be considered to be the principal display panel side, the product of the height times the width of that side;

(b) In the case of a cylindrical or nearly cylindrical container, 40 percent of the product of the height of the container times the circumference;

(c) In the case of any otherwise shaped container, 40 percent of the total surface of the container: *Provided, however,* That where such container presents an obvious "principal display panel" such as the top of a triangular or circular package of cheese, the area shall consist of the entire top surface. In determining the area of the principal display panel, exclude tops, bottoms, flanges at tops and bottoms of cans, and shoulders and necks of bottles or jars. In the case of cylindrical or nearly cylindrical containers, information required by this part to appear on the principal display panel shall appear within that 40 percent of the circumference which is most likely to be displayed, presented, shown, or examined under customary conditions of display for retail sale.

§101.2 Information panel of package form food.

(a) The term *information panel* as it applies to packaged food means that part of the label immediately contiguous and to the right of the principal display panel as observed by an individual facing the principal display panel with the following exceptions:

(1) If the part of the label immediately contiguous and to the right of

11

▼ Where Do You Find State Administrative Law?

States have agencies similar to those of the federal government. Most states have administrative materials that are organized and published in the same manner as those of the federal government.

The amount of administrative materials states publish sometimes is quite voluminous. Some states have an administrative register but do not publish an administrative compilation. Other states have an administrative compilation but do not publish an administrative register. Many states provide their administrative codes only at a website. A simple Google or other Internet search will show you whether the state publishes its administrative rules and regulations online or its administrative register. Most are easy to search by keyword. For example, the Pennsylvania Code can be found with an easy Google search at https://www.pacodeandbulletin.gov/. It is the official codification of the rules and regulation of the state's agencies.

Some of the state administrative codes overlap subjects covered in the federal code. For example, both the federal government and the state of Michigan regulate food labeling.

The coverage of state administrative regulations on Lexis and Westlaw is constantly changing. Therefore, check the directories. Using codes online, especially codes from the states, can be easier than trying to access print copies of the codes.

2. Specific Sources

a. *Federal Register*

The *Federal Register* is the official U.S. government publication of all regulations, proposed regulations, and notices of the federal administrative agencies. It also contains executive orders and other presidential documents. It is published Monday through Friday except on federal holidays. It often includes agency policy statements and discussions of comments received concerning agency actions. Documents are published in chronological order and are not codified. The *Federal Register* is available in print and on Westlaw and Lexis as well as on the Internet. The U.S. Government Publishing Office (U.S. GPO) provides the official *Federal Register* on the government's official website of government information, https://www.govinfo.gov/, formerly www.gpo.gov/fdsys/. A nonofficial version of the *Federal Register* is provided on its www .federalregister.gov website. The *Federal Register* is published in print and PDF files of the publication are found at the govinfo site, https://www.govinfo.gov/app/collection/fr./. This website is constantly evolving. In addition to the *Federal Register,* the GPO site provides access to official government documents such as the *Code of Federal Regulations,* federal statutes, congressional committee materials, congressional rules and procedures, judicial publications, and federal bills.

The *Federal Register* begins a new volume each year. The issues are consecutively paginated from the first day that the government offices are open during the year through the last day that the government offices are open during the year. For example, a March 1 *Federal Register* might contain pages 2600–4200. The March 2 *Federal Register* would begin on page 4201. It is not uncommon for the page number in the last issue to be 60,000.

▼ How Do You Search the *Federal Register?*

At either www.govinfo.gov, (the official website) or www.federalregister .gov, researchers can perform free, simple keyword or citation searches, search by agency name, or browse the publication. If you would like to browse a publication, select the browse function on either website. A list of publications including the *Federal Register* will appear in the alphabetical list of documents on the website. If you select the *Federal Register*, you will be asked to pick a year. After that you can select a month and date. Volumes of the *Federal Register* from 1936 to the present can be searched. You also can browse the *Federal Register*'s table of contents and index. You can simply click on the current index online and review a PDF version of the entire index. You will then see rules, proposed rules, and notices. See Illustration 9-2. The agency name, Food and Drug Administration, is shown in bold. Under the agency, rules, proposed rules, and notices are shown. Next to the number 5 in the illustration are the words "Uniform Compliance Date for Food Labeling Regulations — 462 (Jan 6)." This states the title of the rule. The number 462 indicates the *Federal Register* page number for 2021. The *Federal Register* publication date January 6 is listed next to the page number.

If you were to search for "food labeling" in the search bar of this website, the results would list rules, proposed rules, and notices. You can click hyperlinks on the left side of the page to browse a listing of rules, proposed rules, or notices. You can limit your search by publication date. You can retrieve the *Federal Register* pages as PDF files of the actual print publication. See Illustration 9-3. It is a sample of a *Federal Register* page from January 6, 2021. In the right corner of the page is the page number, 462. The date of the *Federal Register* is listed at the top of the page — Wednesday, January 6, 2021. The volume, 86, is listed at the top. Now review the new final rule that establishes January 1, 2024 as the date for uniform compliance for food labeling regulations. The agency is listed first — the Department of Health and Human Services, Food and Drug Administration. Next the C.F.R. citations, 21 C.F.R. part 101, is listed. It summarizes the regulation. When the action involves a final rule, a rule change, or correction, the *Federal Register* page will provide a brief summary and a more detailed summary of the agency's action. Next to the word "Action," you are told that this is a final rule. The effective date of the rule is provided. In addition, you are provided with methods and requirements for submitting comments. A contact person is listed as well as supplementary information. The *Federal Register* notation sometimes shows the congressional authority for a rule or amendment.

ILLUSTRATION 9-2. Page from *Federal Register* Index

Fish and Wildlife Service

Proposed Habitat Conservation Plan for the Sand Skink, Lake County, FL;
Categorical Exclusion – 16629 *(Mar 30)*
Sand Skink and Blue-Tailed Mole Skink; Osceola County, FL; Categorical
Exclusion – 16385 *(Mar 29)*
Sand Skink and Blue-Tailed Mole Skink; Polk County, FL; Categorical
Exclusion – 16384 *(Mar 29)*
Sand Skink, Orange County, FL; Categorical Exclusion – 16383, 16389
(Mar 29)
Incidental Take Permit Application:
Habitat Conservation Plan and Categorical Exclusion for the Threatened
Grizzly Bear; Flathead, Glacier, Lincoln, and Toole Counties,
Montana – 2445 *(Jan 12)*
Proposed Habitat Conservation Plan for the Sand Skink, Lake County, FL;
Categorical Exclusion – 24658 *(May 7)*
Intent to Grant Exclusive License:
World Wildlife Fund – 33343 *(Jun 24)*
Issuance of Permits:
Endangered Species; Marine Mammals – 16753 *(Mar 31)*
List of Bird Species to Which the Migratory Bird Treaty Act Does Not Apply;
Correction – 23422 *(May 3)*
Marianas Trench Marine National Monument; Monument Management
Plan; Extension of Public Comment Period – 27834 *(May 24)*
Marine Mammal Protection Act:
Stock Assessment Report for the Southern Sea Otter in California – 33334
(Jun 24)
Marine Mammal Protection:
Stock Assessment Reports for Two Stocks of Polar Bears – 33337 *(Jun 24)*
Marine Mammals and Endangered Species:
Incidental Take During Specified Activities; Proposed Incidental
Harassment Authorization for Southeast Alaska Stock of Northern Sea
Otters in the Queen Charlotte Fault Region, AK – 30613 *(Jun 9)*
Marine Mammals:
Incidental Take During Specified Activities; Proposed Incidental
Harassment Authorization for Northern Sea Otters in the Northeast
Pacific Ocean – 12019 *(Mar 1)*
Meetings:
Aquatic Nuisance Species Task Force – 30979 *(Jun 10)*
Convention on International Trade in Endangered Species of Wild Fauna
and Flora – 12199 *(Mar 2)*
Migratory Bird Hunting; Service Regulations Committee and Flyway
Council – 15957 *(Mar 25)*
Monument Management Plan:
Marianas Trench Marine National Monument – 11238 *(Feb 24)*
Permit Application:
Endangered and Threatened Species – 27645 *(May 21)*
Endangered and Threatened Species; Recovery – 16755 *(Mar 31)*
Endangered Species; Recovery – 16751 *(Mar 31)*
Foreign Endangered Species; Marine Mammals – 16754 *(Mar 31)*
Incidental Take and Proposed Habitat Conservation Plan for the Sand
Skink and Blue-Tailed Mole Skink; Osceola County, FL; Categorical
Exclusion – 16233 *(Mar 26)*
Permit Applications:
Endangered and Threatened Species – 28138 *(May 25)*
Record of Decision:
Highway Right-of-Way, Amended Habitat Conservation Plan and Issuance
of an Incidental Take Permit for the Mojave Desert Tortoise, and
Approved Resource Management Plan Amendments, Washington
County, UT – 4115 *(Jan 15)*
Requests for Nominations:
Sport Fishing and Boating Partnership Council – 28140 *(May 25)*
Updated Collision Risk Model Priors for Estimating Eagle Fatalities at Wind
Energy Facilities – 23978 *(May 5)*

(1) Food and Drug Administration

(2) RULES
Electronic Import Entries; Technical Amendments – 17059 *(Apr 1)*
Final Rule to Revoke the Standards for Lowfat Yogurt and Nonfat Yogurt
and to Amend the Standard for Yogurt:
Milk and Cream Products and Yogurt Products – 31117 *(Jun 11)*
Medical Devices:
Medical Device Classification Regulations to Conform to Medical Software
Provisions in the 21st Century Cures Act – 20278 *(Apr 19)*
Technical Amendments – 17065 *(Apr 1)*
New Animal Drug Applications:

Beta-Aminopropionitrile Fumarate; n-Butyl Chloride; Cupric Glycinate
Injection; Dichlorophene and Toluene; Orgotein For Injection;
Tetracycline Tablets – 10818 *(Feb 23)*
New Animal Drugs:
Approval of New Animal Drug Applications – 17061 *(Apr 1)*
Approval of New Animal Drug Applications; Change of Sponsor – 13181
(Mar 8)
Approval of New Animal Drug Applications; Changes of Sponsorship;
Change of Sponsor's Name and Address – 14815 *(Mar 19)*
Withdrawal of Approval of New Animal Drug Applications – 10819 *(Feb 23)*
Requirements for Foreign and Domestic Establishment Registration and
Listing for Human Drugs, Including Drugs That Are Regulated Under a
Biologics License Application, and Animal Drugs; Corrections – 17061
(Apr 1)
Securing Updated and Necessary Statutory Evaluations Timely – 5694
(Jan 19)
Securing Updated and Necessary Statutory Evaluations Timely;
Administrative Delay of Effective Date; Correction – 15404 *(Mar 23)*
Tobacco Products; Required Warnings for Cigarette Packages and
Advertisements; Delayed Effective Date – 3793 *(Jan 15)*
Uniform Compliance Date for Food Labeling Regulations – **(3)** 462 *(Jan 6)* **(5)**
PROPOSED RULES
Filing of Color Additive Petition:
Gardenia Blue Interest Group – 34664 *(Jun 30)*
Filing of Food Additive Petition:
Ag Chem Resources, LLC; Correction – 21984 *(Apr 26)*
General Mills, Inc. – 21675 *(Apr 23)*
Food Additive Petition:
Canadian Oilseed Processors Association; Withdrawal – 24564 *(May 7)*
(4) NOTICES
Agency Information Collection Activities; Proposals, Submissions, and
Approvals – 2674 *(Jan 13)*; 10107 *(Feb 18)*; 24628 *(May 7)*; 24867
(May 10); 27092 *(May 19)*; 30952 *(Jun 10)*
Agency Information Collection Activities; Proposals, Submissions, and
Approvals:
Accelerated Approval Disclosures on Direct-to-Consumer Prescription
Drug Websites – 31323 *(Jun 11)*
Adverse Experience Reporting for Licensed Biological Products; General
Records – 10975 *(Feb 23)*
Animal Food Labeling; Declaration of Certified and Non-Certified Color
Additives – 12690 *(Mar 4)*
Certification to Accompany Drug, Biological Product, and Device
Applications or Submissions – 10104 *(Feb 18)*
Class II Special Controls for Human Immunodeficiency Virus Serological
Diagnostic and Supplemental Tests and Human Immunodeficiency
Virus Nucleic Acid Diagnostic and Supplemental Tests – 33708 *(Jun 25)*
Class II Special Controls Guidance Document; Labeling Natural Rubber
Latex Condoms – 109 *(Jan 4)*; 24633 *(May 7)*
Class II Special Controls Guidance Document; Automated Blood Cell
Separator Device Operating by Centrifugal or Filtration
Principle – 10108 *(Feb 18)*
Current Good Manufacturing Practice for Finished Pharmaceuticals,
Including Medical Gases, and Active Pharmaceutical
Ingredients – 30960 *(Jun 10)*
Current Good Manufacturing Practice for Manufacturing, Processing,
Packing, and Holding of Finished Pharmaceuticals, Including Medical
Gases, and Active Pharmaceutical Ingredients – 12466 *(Mar 3)*
Current Good Manufacturing Practice, Hazard Analysis, and Risk-Based
Preventive Controls for Human and Animal Food – 14436 *(Mar 16)*
Current Good Manufacturing Practices and Related Regulations for Blood
and Blood Components; and Requirements for Donation Testing,
Donor Notification, and "Lookback" – 33713 *(Jun 25)*
Current Good Manufacturing Practices and Related Regulations for Blood
and Blood Components; Requirements for Donation Testing, Donor
Notification, and "Lookback" – 10582 *(Feb 22)*
Data to Support Drug Product Communications – 22970 *(Apr 30)*
Data to Support Drug Product Communications as Used by the Food and
Drug Administration – 5219 *(Jan 19)*
Dispute Resolution Procedures for Science-Based Decisions on Products
by the Center for Veterinary Medicine – 10581 *(Feb 22)*
Early Food Safety Evaluation of New Non-Pesticidal Proteins Produced by
New Plant Varieties Intended for Food Use – 12688 *(Mar 4)*
Electronic User Fee Payment Request Forms – 22669 *(Apr 29)*

1 Agency 2 Rules 3 Proposed rules
4 Notices 5 *Federal Register* page and date

ILLUSTRATION 9-3.   *Federal Register* Page from January 6, 2021

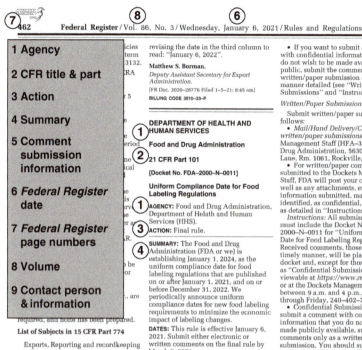

The left-hand annotation key reads:

1 Agency
2 CFR title & part
3 Action
4 Summary
5 Comment submission information
6 *Federal Register* date
7 *Federal Register* page numbers
8 Volume
9 Contact person & information

(7) 462   Federal Register / Vol. 86, No. 3 / Wednesday, January 6, 2021 / Rules and Regulations   (8)   (6)

...icies...term...3132....CRA...r 5

revising the date in the third column to read: "January 6, 2022".

Matthew S. Borman,
Deputy Assistant Secretary for Export Administration.
[FR Doc. 2020–28776 Filed 1–5–21; 8:45 am]
BILLING CODE 3510–33–P

DEPARTMENT OF HEALTH AND HUMAN SERVICES

Food and Drug Administration

21 CFR Part 101

[Docket No. FDA–2000–N–0011]

Uniform Compliance Date for Food Labeling Regulations

AGENCY: Food and Drug Administration, Department of Helath and Human Services (HHS).

ACTION: Final rule.

SUMMARY: The Food and Drug Administration (FDA or we) is establishing January 1, 2024, as the uniform compliance date for food labeling regulations that are published on or after January 1, 2021, and on or before December 31, 2022. We periodically announce uniform compliance dates for new food labeling requirements to minimize the economic impact of labeling changes.

DATES: This rule is effective January 6, 2021. Submit either electronic or written comments on the final rule by March 8, 2021.

ADDRESSES: You may submit comments as follows:

Electronic Submissions

Submit electronic comments in the following way:
• *Federal eRulemaking Portal:* https://www.regulations.gov. Follow the instructions for submitting comments. Comments submitted electronically, including attachments, to https://www.regulations.gov will be posted to the docket unchanged. Because your comment will be made public, you are solely responsible for ensuring that your comment does not include any confidential information that you or a third party may not wish to be posted, such as medical information, your or anyone else's Social Security number, or confidential business information, such as a manufacturing process. Please note that if you include your name, contact information, or other information that identifies you in the body of your comments, that information will be posted on https://www.regulations.gov.

• If you want to submit a comment with confidential information that you do not wish to be made available to the public, submit the comment as a written/paper submission and in the manner detailed (see "Written/Paper Submissions" and "Instructions").

Written/Paper Submissions

Submit written/paper submissions as follows:
• *Mail/Hand Delivery/Courier (for written/paper submissions):* Dockets Management Staff (HFA–305), Food and Drug Administration, 5630 Fishers Lane, Rm. 1061, Rockville, MD 20852.
• For written/paper comments submitted to the Dockets Management Staff, FDA will post your comment, as well as any attachments, except for information submitted, marked and identified, as confidential, if submitted as detailed in "Instructions."

Instructions: All submissions received must include the Docket No. FDA–2000–N–0011 for "Uniform Compliance Date for Food Labeling Regulations." Received comments, those filed in a timely manner, will be placed in the docket and, except for those submitted as "Confidential Submissions," publicly viewable at https://www.regulations.gov or at the Dockets Management Staff between 9 a.m. and 4 p.m., Monday through Friday, 240–402–7500.

• Confidential Submissions—To submit a comment with confidential information that you do not wish to be made publicly available, submit your comments only as a written/paper submission. You should submit two copies total. One copy will include the information you claim to be confidential with a heading or cover note that states "THIS DOCUMENT CONTAINS CONFIDENTIAL INFORMATION." We will review this copy, including the claimed confidential information, in our consideration of comments. The second copy, which will have the claimed confidential information redacted/blacked out, will be available for public viewing and posted on https://www.regulations.gov. Submit both copies to the Dockets Management Staff. If you do not wish your name and contact information to be made publicly available, you can provide this information on the cover sheet and not in the body of your comments, and you must identify this information as "confidential." Any information marked as "confidential" will not be disclosed except in accordance with 21 CFR 10.20 and other applicable disclosure law. For more information about FDA's posting of comments to public dockets, see 80 FR 56469, September 18, 2015, or access the information at: https://

required, and none has been prepared.

List of Subjects in 15 CFR Part 774

Exports, Reporting and recordkeeping requirements.

Accordingly, part 774 of the Export Administration Regulations (15 CFR parts 730 through 774) is amended as follows:

PART 774—THE COMMERCE CONTROL LIST

■ 1. The authority citation for part 774 continues to read as follows:

Authority: 50 U.S.C. 4801–4852; 50 U.S.C. 4601 *et seq.*; 50 U.S.C. 1701 *et seq.*; 10 U.S.C. 8720; 10 U.S.C. 8730(e); 22 U.S.C. 287c, 22 U.S.C. 3201 *et seq.*; 22 U.S.C. 6004; 42 U.S.C. 2139a; 15 U.S.C. 1824; 50 U.S.C. 4305; 22 U.S.C. 7201 *et seq.*; 22 U.S.C. 7210; E.O. 13026, 61 FR 58767, 3 CFR, 1996 Comp., p. 228; E.O. 13222, 66 FR 44025, 3 CFR, 2001 Comp., p. 783.

Supplement No. 5 to Part 774   [Amended]

■ 2. In Supplement No. 5 to part 774, amend the table, under the heading "0D521. Software" entry No 1, by

ILLUSTRATION 9-3. *Continued*

Federal Register / Vol. 86, No. 3 / Wednesday, January 6, 2021 / Rules and Regulations   463

www.govinfo.gov/content/pkg/FR-2015-09-18/pdf/2015-23389.pdf.

Docket: For access to the docket to read background documents or the electronic and written/paper comments received, go to *https://www.regulations.gov* and insert the docket number, found in brackets in the heading of this document, into the "Search" box and follow the prompts and/or go to the Dockets Management Staff, 5630 Fishers Lane, Rm. 1061, Rockville, MD 20852, 240–402–7500.

FOR FURTHER INFORMATION CONTACT: Carrol Bascus, Center for Food Safety and Applied Nutrition (HFS–24), Food and Drug Administration, 5001 Campus Dr., College Park, MD 20740, 240–402–3835.

SUPPLEMENTARY INFORMATION: We periodically issue regulations requiring changes in the labeling of food. If the compliance dates of these labeling changes were not coordinated, the cumulative economic impact on the food industry of having to respond separately to each change would be substantial. Therefore, we periodically have announced uniform compliance dates for new food labeling requirements (see *e.g.,* the **Federal Register** of October 19, 1984 (49 FR 41019); December 24, 1996 (61 FR 67710); December 27, 1996 (61 FR 68145); December 23, 1998 (63 FR 71015); November 20, 2000 (65 FR 69666); December 31, 2002 (67 FR 79851); December 21, 2006 (71 FR 76599); December 8, 2008 (73 FR 74349); December 15, 2010 (75 FR 78155); November 28, 2012 (77 FR 70885); December 10, 2014 (79 FR 73201); November 25, 2016 (81 FR 85156); and December 20, 2018 (83 FR 65294)). Use of a uniform compliance date provides for an orderly and economical industry adjustment to new labeling requirements by allowing sufficient lead time to plan for the use of existing label inventories and the development of new labeling materials.

We have determined under 21 CFR 25.30(k) that this action is of a type that does not individually or cumulatively have a significant effect on the human environment. Therefore, neither an environmental assessment nor an environmental impact statement is required.

This final rule contains no collections of information. Therefore, clearance by the Office of Management and Budget under the Paperwork Reduction Act of 1995 is not required.

We have examined the impacts of the final rule under Executive Order 12866, Executive Order 13563, Executive Order 13771, the Regulatory Flexibility Act (5

U.S.C. 601–612), and the Unfunded Mandates Reform Act of 1995 (Pub. L. 104–4). Executive Orders 12866 and 13563 direct us to assess all costs and benefits of available regulatory alternatives and, when regulation is necessary, to select regulatory approaches that maximize net benefits (including potential economic, environmental, public health and safety, and other advantages; distributive impacts; and equity). Executive Order 13771 requires that the costs associated with significant new regulations "shall, to the extent permitted by law, be offset by the elimination of existing costs associated with at least two prior regulations." We believe that this final rule is not a significant regulatory action as defined by Executive Order 12866.

The establishment of a uniform compliance date does not in itself lead to costs or benefits. We will assess the costs and benefits of the uniform compliance date in the regulatory impact analyses of the labeling rules that take effect at that date.

The Regulatory Flexibility Act requires us to analyze regulatory options that would minimize any significant impact of a rule on small entities. Because the final rule does not impose compliance costs on small entities, we certify that the final rule will not have a significant economic impact on a substantial number of small entities.

The Unfunded Mandates Reform Act of 1995 (section 202(a)) requires us to prepare a written statement, which includes an assessment of anticipated costs and benefits, before issuing "any rule that includes any Federal mandate that may result in the expenditure by State, local, and tribal governments, in the aggregate, or by the private sector, of $100,000,000 or more (adjusted annually for inflation) in any one year." The current threshold after adjustment for inflation is $156 million, using the most current (2019) Implicit Price Deflator for the Gross Domestic Product. This final rule would not result in an expenditure in any year that meets or exceeds this amount.

We have analyzed this final rule in accordance with the principles set forth in Executive Order 13132. We have determined that the rule does not contain policies that have substantial direct effects on the States, on the relationship between the National Government and the States, or on the distribution of power and responsibilities among the various levels of government. Accordingly, we have concluded that the rule does not contain policies that have federalism implications as defined in the Executive Order and, consequently, a federalism

summary impact statement is not required.

This action is not intended to change existing requirements for compliance dates contained in final rules published before January 1, 2021. Therefore, all final rules published by FDA in the **Federal Register** before January 1, 2021, will still go into effect on the date stated in the respective final rule. We generally encourage industry to comply with new labeling regulations as quickly as feasible, however. Thus, when industry members voluntarily change their labels, it is appropriate that they incorporate any new requirements that have been published as final regulations up to that time.

In rulemaking that began with publication of a proposed rule on April 15, 1996 (61 FR 16422), and ended with a final rule on December 24, 1996 (61 FR 67710) (together "the 1996 rulemaking"), we provided notice and an opportunity for comment on the practice of establishing uniform compliance dates by issuance of a final rule announcing the date. We received no comments objecting to this practice during the 1996 rulemaking, nor have we received comments objecting to this practice since we published a uniform compliance date final rule on December 20, 2018. Therefore, we find good cause to dispense with issuance of a proposed rule inviting comment on the practice of establishing the uniform compliance date because such prior notice and comment are unnecessary. Interested parties will have an opportunity to comment on the compliance date for each individual food labeling regulation as part of the rulemaking process for that regulation. Consequently, FDA finds any further advance notice and opportunity for comment unnecessary for establishment of the uniform compliance date. Nonetheless, under 21 CFR 10.40(e)(1), we are providing an opportunity for comment on whether the uniform compliance date established by this final rule should be modified or revoked.

In addition, we find good cause for this final rule to become effective on the date of publication of this action. A delayed effective date is unnecessary in this case because the establishment of a uniform compliance date does not impose any new regulatory requirements on affected parties. Instead, this final rule provides affected parties with notice of our policy to identify January 1, 2024, as the compliance date for final food labeling regulations that require changes in the labeling of food products and that publish on or after January 1, 2021, and on or before December 31, 2022, unless

ILLUSTRATION 9-3. *Continued*

special circumstances justify a different compliance date. Thus, affected parties do not need time to prepare before the rule takes effect. Therefore, we find good cause for this final rule to become effective on the date of publication of this action.

The new uniform compliance date will apply only to final FDA food labeling regulations that require changes in the labeling of food products and that publish on or after January 1, 2021, and on or before December 31, 2022. Those regulations will specifically identify January 1, 2024, as their compliance date. All food products subject to the January 1, 2024, compliance date must comply with the appropriate regulations when initially introduced into interstate commerce on or after January 1, 2024. If any food labeling regulation involves special circumstances that justify a compliance date other than January 1, 2024, we will determine for that regulation an appropriate compliance date, which will be specified when the final regulation is published.

Dated: December 29, 2020.

Stephen M. Hahn,
Commissioner of Food and Drugs.
Dated: December 30, 2020.
Alex M. Azar II,
Secretary, Department of Health and Human Services.
[FR Doc. 2020–29273 Filed 12–31–20; 4:15 pm]
BILLING CODE 4164–01–P

DEPARTMENT OF THE TREASURY

Internal Revenue Service

26 CFR Part 1

[TD 9937]

RIN 1545–BP46

Rollover Rules for Qualified Plan Loan Offset Amounts

AGENCY: Internal Revenue Service (IRS), Treasury.

ACTION: Final regulations.

SUMMARY: This document sets forth final regulations relating to amendments made to section 402(c) of the Internal Revenue Code (Code) by section 13613 of the Tax Cuts and Jobs Act (TCJA). Section 13613 of TCJA provides an extended rollover period for a qualified plan loan offset, which is a type of plan loan offset. These regulations affect participants, beneficiaries, sponsors, and administrators of qualified employer plans.

DATES:

Effective Date: These regulations are effective on January 6, 2021.

Applicability Date: For date of applicability, see § 1.402(c)–3(b)(2).
FOR FURTHER INFORMATION CONTACT: Naomi Lehr at (202) 317–4102, Vernon Carter at (202) 317–6799, or Pamela Kinard at (202) 317–6000 (not toll-free numbers).
SUPPLEMENTARY INFORMATION:

Background

This document amends 26 CFR part 1, by adding § 1.402(c)–3 to the Income Tax Regulations to reflect changes to section 402(c) of the Code, as amended by section 13613 of TCJA (Pub. L. 115–97 (131 Stat. 2054)).

1. Plan Loans, Eligible Rollover Distributions, and Plan Loan Offset Amounts

Section 72(p)(1) of the Code provides that if, during any taxable year, a participant or beneficiary receives (directly or indirectly) any amount as a loan from a qualified employer plan (as defined in section 72(p)(4)(A)),[1] that amount shall be treated as having been received by the individual as a distribution from the plan. For certain plan loans, section 72(p)(2) provides an exception to the general treatment of loans as distributions under section 72(p)(1).

For the exception under section 72(p)(2) to apply so that a plan loan is not treated as a distribution under section 72(p)(1) for the taxable year in which the loan is received, the loan generally must satisfy three requirements:

(1) The loan, by its terms, must satisfy the limits on loan amounts, as described in section 72(p)(2)(A);

(2) The loan, by its terms, generally must be repayable within 5 years, as described in section 72(p)(2)(B); and

(3) The loan must require substantially level amortization over the term of the loan, as described in section 72(p)(2)(C).

Section 401(a)(31) requires that a plan qualified under section 401(a) provide for the direct transfer of eligible rollover distributions. A similar rule applies to section 403(a) annuity plans, section 403(b) tax-sheltered annuities, and section 457 eligible governmental plans. See generally sections 401(a)(31), 403(b)(10), and 457(d)(1)(C).

Sections 402(c)(3) and 408(d)(3) provide that any amount distributed from a qualified plan or individual retirement account or annuity (IRA) will be excluded from income if it is

transferred to an eligible retirement plan no later than the 60th day following the day the distribution is received. A similar rule applies to section 403(a) annuity plans, section 403(b) tax-sheltered annuities, and section 457 eligible governmental plans. See generally sections 403(a)(4)(B), 403(b)(8)(B), and 457(e)(16)(B).

Sections 402(c)(3)(B) and 408(d)(3)(I) provide that the Secretary may waive the 60-day rollover requirement "where the failure to waive such requirement would be against equity or good conscience, including casualty, disaster, or other events beyond the reasonable control of the individual subject to such requirement." See generally Rev. Proc. 2020–46, 2020–45 I.R.B. 995, which sets forth a self-certification procedure that taxpayers may use in certain circumstances to claim a waiver of the 60-day deadline for completing a rollover under section 402(c)(3)(B) or 408(d)(3)(I), and Rev. Proc. 2020–4, 2020–1 I.R.B. 148, which sets forth procedures that taxpayers may use to request a waiver of the 60-day rollover deadline by submitting a request for a private letter ruling.[2]

Section 1.402(c)–2, Q&A–3(a), provides that, unless specifically excluded, an eligible rollover distribution means any distribution to an employee (or to a spousal distributee described in § 1.402(c)–2, Q&A–12(a)) of all or any portion of the balance to the credit of the employee in a qualified plan. Section 1.402(c)–2, Q&A–3(b), provides that certain distributions (for example, required minimum distributions under section 401(a)(9)) are not eligible rollover distributions.

Section 1.402(c)–2, Q&A–9(a), provides that a distribution of a plan loan offset amount (as defined in § 1.402(c)–2, Q&A–9(b)) is an eligible rollover distribution if it satisfies § 1.402(c)–2, Q&A–3. Thus, an amount not exceeding the plan loan offset amount may be rolled over by the employee (or spousal distributee) to an eligible retirement plan within the 60-day period described in section 402(c)(3), unless the plan loan offset amount fails to be an eligible rollover distribution for another reason.

Section 1.402(c)–2, Q&A–9(b), provides that a distribution of a plan loan offset amount is a distribution that occurs when, under the plan terms governing the loan, the employee's

---

[1] Under section 72(p)(4), a qualified employer plan means a qualified plan, a section 403(a) annuity plan, a section 403(b) plan, and any governmental plan.

[2] Note that the 60-day rollover deadline can also be extended to provide temporary relief during a disaster or an emergency response. For example, in response to the COVID–19 pandemic, Notice 2020–23, 2020–18 I.R.B. 742, extended the 60-day rollover deadline to July 15, 2020, for distributions made between April 1, 2020, and July 14, 2020.

Detailed instructions concerning how to use this resource can be found on the website as well as tutorials. You can save *Federal Register* pages and documents.

▼ How Can You Use Lexis and Westlaw to Retrieve the *Federal Register*?

Another simple method to retrieve *Federal Register* information concerning an adopted or proposed regulation is a computer search of either Lexis or Westlaw. You can search these *Federal Register* databases without regard to a publisher's choice of indexing terms. You may use your own terms to determine whether any regulations concerning your research topic are contained within the *Federal Register*.

▼ How Do You Use the *Federal Register* in Print?

To use the *Federal Register*, you could review the table of contents or the index. The table of contents is found at the beginning of each volume of the *Federal Register* and is organized alphabetically by agency name. An index is published monthly and cumulated for 12 months. This table of contents also indicates that notices and proposed rules are printed in an edition for various agencies.

Just like the online version, the table of contents and the index can be difficult to use because they are arranged by agency rather than by subject. Because of this organization, you first must determine what agency is responsible for regulating the conduct or activity you are researching. It summarizes the regulation.

PRACTICE POINTER

The online sites for the *Federal Register* and *Code of Federal Regulations* are simple to use and provide easy-to-read PDF files. With these features and their updating capabilities, it is much easier to research federal regulations online.

---

b. *Code of Federal Regulations*

During the course of the year, the regulations found in the *Federal Register* are incorporated into a codified version called the *Code of Federal Regulations* (C.F.R.). The code is comprised of 50 titles similar to the titles used in the statutory codes. However, not all 50 titles mirror the titles used in the *United States Code* (U.S.C.). Some titles, such as 26, the Internal Revenue Code, do follow the title of the U.S.C. Title 26 of the C.F.R. contains the Treasury regulations that instruct the researcher on how to apply the relevant statutory code section. The C.F.R. titles are organized by agency, not subjects. The C.F.R. is further divided into chapters, subchapters, parts, and sections.

The C.F.R. is prepared and published by the U.S. Government Publishing Office. However, the C.F.R. is available online through the GPO's govinfo.gov website and online services such as Westlaw, Lexis, and other fee-based companies. These fee-based services offer references to secondary sources and other resources that may assist you in understanding and interpreting a C.F.R. title and section. An unofficial version of the C.F.R. is found at https://www.ecfr.gov/cgi-bin/ECFR?page=browse. It is a compilation of C.F.R. material and *Federal Register* amendments provided by the Office of the Federal Register—part of the National Archives and Records Administration Office and the GPO. It indicates how current the material is.

▼ How Often Is the C.F.R. Updated?

The C.F.R. titles are updated quarterly. Titles 1 to 16 are updated January 1 of the cover year. Titles 17 to 27 are updated April 1 of that year, and titles 28 to 41 are updated on July 1 of that year. Titles 42 to 50 are updated on October 1 of the cover year. C.F.R. volumes are added online when the print volumes are released.

▼ How Do You Use the C.F.R.?

The easiest way to use the C.F.R. is to do it online. Online computer searches may allow easier access to regulations than a print index. You can search the full text of the regulations at the government's website or on both the Westlaw and Lexis systems. With these searches you do not need to rely on the terms contained within the index. Current regulations, as well as many superseded regulations, can be searched online. If you go to the government website, you can search for a regulation by entering keywords, entering a C.F.R. citation, or browsing the titles at the govinfo.gov website. When you browse volumes of the C.F.R., you can select the year you want to review, and then the titles will be shown along with hyperlinks that allow you to jump quickly to that particular text. The C.F.R. is available online in XML, text, and PDF formats. For example, if you select the year 2020, you can then see that Title 21 has the regulations that concern food and drugs. You can download or view that title by clicking the hyperlinks. If you click the PDF icon, you will see the C.F.R. as if it were in print. You also can review the C.F.R. Index and Finding Aids that are listed after the titles. It is an index by subject and agency of rules in the C.F.R. See Illustration 9-4. This page mentions the topic "food labeling." Multiple citations are to Title 21. On the first page, the number 2 is next to the citation for 21 C.F.R. 100—the section about administrative rulings and decisions. On the second page of the illustration, the 2 is next to the citation 21 C.F.R. 101—the section concerning food labeling requirements. It is the section shown in Illustration 9-1. Among the finding aids in the index publication is an alphabetical list of agencies that appear in the C.F.R.

ILLUSTRATION 9-4. C.F.R. Index Pages

```
                    1 Topic    2 CFR citation
CFR Index                                              Food labeling
```

Macaroni and noodle products, 21 CFR 139
Margarine, standards, 21 CFR 166
Meat inspection, mandatory, definitions and
    standards of identity or composition for
    meat products, 9 CFR 319
Meats, prepared meats, and meat products,
    grading, certification, and standards, 7
    CFR 54
Milk and cream, 21 CFR 131
Nutritional quality guidelines, 21 CFR 104
Peanuts, domestic and imported, marketed in
    U.S., minimum quality and handling
    standards, 7 CFR 996
Poultry products and rabbit products,
    voluntary grading, 7 CFR 70
Poultry products inspection, 9 CFR 381
Produce for human consumption, growing,
    harvesting, packing, and holding
    standards, 21 CFR 112
Processed fruits and vegetables and certain
    other processed food products,
    inspection, certification, and standards,
    7 CFR 52
Quality Systems Verification Programs, 7
    CFR 62
Seafood
    Fish and fishery products, processing
        requirements, 21 CFR 123
    Fish and shellfish, general provisions and
        requirements for specific standardized
        fish and shellfish, 21 CFR 161
    Grade standards, 50 CFR 261
    Seafood inspection and certification, 50
        CFR 260
Special dietary foods, 21 CFR 105
Specialty crops, import regulations, 7 CFR
    999
Sweeteners and table sirups, 21 CFR 168
Tree nut and peanut products, 21 CFR 164
Vegetables
    Canned, 21 CFR 155
    Frozen, standards, 21 CFR 158
    Import regulations, 7 CFR 980
    Juices, 21 CFR 156
Voluntary official grade standards;
    development, revision, suspension or
    termination procedures, 7 CFR 36

Food ingredients
See Food additives

Food inspection
See Food grades and standards

Food labeling (1)
See also Foods; Labeling
Bioengineered food, national disclosure
    standard, 7 CFR 66
Cheeses and related cheese products, 21 CFR
    133
Common or usual name for nonstandardized
    foods, 21 CFR 102
Country of origin labeling
    Fish and shellfish, 7 CFR 60
    Lamb, chicken and goat meat, perishable
        agricultural commodities, macadamia
        nuts, pecans, peanuts, and ginseng, 7
        CFR 65
Dairy products, grading and inspection,
    general specifications for approved
    plants and grade standards, 7 CFR 58
Eggs and egg products
    Egg products, voluntary inspection, 9 CFR
        592
    Eggs and egg products, Inspection, 9 CFR
        590
    Shell eggs, voluntary grading of, 7 CFR
        56
Enforcement of Federal Food, Drug, and
    Cosmetic Act and Fair Packaging and
    Labeling Act, 21 CFR 1
Food and Drug Administration,
    administrative rulings and decisions, 21
    CFR 100 (2)
Food Safety and Inspection Service
    General requirements, definitions, 9 CFR
        530
    Importation, 9 CFR 557
    Products and containers; marks, marking
        and labeling, 9 CFR 541
Frozen desserts, 21 CFR 135
Infant formula, 21 CFR 107
Irradiation in production, processing and
    handling of food, 21 CFR 179
Margarine, standards, 21 CFR 166
Meat and poultry products inspection
    Label approval, 9 CFR 412
    Specific classes of product, requirements,
        9 CFR 430
Meat inspection
    Definitions and standards of identity or
        composition for meat products, 9
        CFR 319
    Imported products, 9 CFR 327
    Labeling, marking devices, and containers,
        9 CFR 317

ILLUSTRATION 9-4. *Continued*

In addition, the government offers an integrated version of the C.F.R. called ecfr at https://www.ecfr.gov. This version is updated daily, but it is unofficial. It can be searched by browsing a C.F.R. title and indicates when the online C.F.R. was last updated.

To use the C.F.R in print, consult the index that contains listings of subjects, agencies, and references to the regulations codified within the C.F.R. volumes. The index also provides a list of C.F.R. titles, chapters, subchapters, and parts, and an alphabetical list of the agencies in the C.F.R.

Illustration 9-1 is the page of the C.F.R. referred to under the "labeling" topic in the index: title 21, part 101 of the C.F.R. concerning food labeling. You should scan the sections listed to find relevant sections. For example, suppose you are researching whether health claims may be made concerning raw fruit and the labeling required. You can scan the subpart list and see a listing for section 101.14 "Health Claims: general requirements" shown in Illustration 9-1. You would review that section and any other relevant sections. In this case, section 101.42 appears to be relevant. The C.F.R. part also specifies the enabling statutes. In this case, the enabling statutes are the Fair Packaging and Labeling Act and the Federal Food, Drug, and Cosmetic Act. Citations to the U.S.C. for each act are included under the heading authority. In addition, the relevant citations to the *Federal Register* publication are noted. Finally, the text of the regulation begins under the heading "Subpart A—General Provisions."

PRACTICE POINTER

Videos and other information about how to use the *Federal Register* are available at https://www.federalregister.gov/reader-aids/videos-tutorials.

A video about the Code of Federal Regulations is presented at https://www.youtube.com/watch?v=AYIEYSyMWtU.

▼ When and Why Would You Use Old Regulations?

Often a case will turn on a regulation that was in place at the time of the incident involved. For example, suppose you are representing a client involved in a car accident in 2020. The experts say that the accident occurred because the car manufacturer failed to use a safety device—one that was required by federal regulations. The car was manufactured in 2015. You must research the 2015 regulations to determine what safety regulations applied to that manufacturer.

▼ How Do You Update and Validate Regulations?

Updating is one of the most important tasks you must perform when you review agency regulations. This is especially important because the regulations change frequently. Because the C.F.R. is published annually with quarterly updates, you must determine the currentness of the document. The **List of CFR Sections Affected**, or L.S.A., enables you to update a C.F.R. citation. The L.S.A. identifies which sections have been changed, updated, or removed—in essence, which C.F.R. sections have been affected in any way. A monthly L.S.A. is published with the C.F.R. See Illustration 9-5. The online version is identical to the printed version. Illustration 9-5 is a page that details the parts that changed between April 1, 2021 and June 30, 2021. Because the L.S.A. is updated only monthly, you must check the current *Federal Register* to ensure that a title has not been updated. The Reader Aids section of the daily *Federal Register* has a section entitled "CFR Parts Affected." See Illustration 9-6. This is similar to the L.S.A. Illustration 9-5. However, Illustration 9-6 is a page from the July 23, 2021 *Federal Register* that details only changes in that issue. This daily list of changes is found at the front of the *Federal Register.* At the back of the *Federal Register,* another C.F.R. Parts Affected section details the changes that have occurred within the month of its publication. See Illustration 9-7. Therefore, you must check not only the monthly L.S.A. pamphlet, but also portions of a daily *Federal Register.* The L.S.A. is organized by title. See Illustration 9-5.

▼ How Is the Updating Performed in Practice?

Assume that you have found the regulation that defines the standard for labeling of food in the *Federal Register.* It is 21 C.F.R. §101. Assume also that it is July 23, 2021, and you want to determine if this regulation has been changed since it was last published. You want to be certain that you determine whether there have been any changes to the relevant section through the date of your search.

You should now review the current L.S.A. online. For our purposes, consult Illustration 9-5. This publication discloses any changes to the regulations that occurred between April 1, 2021, and June 30, 2021. Find the title you want to update: in this case, title 21. It was last updated on April 1, 2021, based on the C.F.R. update schedule for its titles. Next review Illustration 9-5. Scan the sections column and determine whether section 101 has been changed since April 1, 2021. In this case, it has not been altered. Note that the sections that have been revised, removed, or amended are noted. A five-digit number appears at the end of each column near the revised, amended, or removed sections. The five-digit number is the *Federal Register* page on which the changes appear.

The monthly LSA includes changes through June 30, 2021 only. Therefore, you need to determine whether any changes were made to the section after that up until the date of your research, July 23, 2021. First, check the last *Federal Register* for July. View the "Reader Aids" section entitled "CFR Parts Affected in August." See Illustration 9-7. Check to see if your citation is listed there. In this case, part 101 of title 21 was not listed, so it was not affected. If there had been changes, you would need to review those *Federal Register* pages to determine if any of the modifications are relevant to your research.

ILLUSTRATION 9-5. L.S.A. Detailing Changes April 1, 2021 to June 30, 2021

1 CFR title   2 CFR parts affected   3 *Federal Register* page number
4 Action taken   5 Dates in citation included in LSA

JUNE 2021   33

⑤ CHANGES APRIL 1, 2021 THROUGH JUNE 30, 2021

① **TITLE 21—FOOD AND DRUGS**

Chapter I—Food and Drug Administration, Department of Health and Human Services (Parts 1—1299) ④

1.74 (a)(1) amended 17060
1.75 (a) amended 17060
1.78 (d) amended 17060
130.10 (b) revised 31137
131.200 Revised.................................31137
131.203 Removed...............................31138
131.206 Removed...............................31138 ③
207.1 Amended 17061
207.3 Amended 17061
207.13 (1)(1) amended 17061
207.49   (a)(15)(i),   (ii)(A),   (B), (iii)(A), and (B) amended..........17061
207.53 (d)(1), (2)(i), (ii), (3)(i), and (ii) amended 17061
510.600 (c)(1) and (2) table amended...17063
520.292 (a) and (c) revised................17063
520.522 (b)(3) added 17063
522.2450 Added..................................17064
② 522.2470 (b)(1) and (2) revised...........17064
524.2098 (c) removed; (d) redesignated as new (c); (a), (b), and new (c)(1) revised.....................17064
528.2001 Added..................................17064
558.128 (e)(4)(xv) revised.................17064
558.342 (d)(3) through (6) revised; (d)(7) and (8) removed...............17064
821.2 (b) introductory text and (c) revised..................................17065
862.1350 Heading and (a) revised 20283
862.2100 (a) revised 20283
866.4750 (a) revised 20283
880.6310 (a) revised 20283
884.2730 (a) revised 20283
892.2010 (a) revised 20284
892.2020 (a) revised 20284
892.2050 Heading and (a) revised 20284

Chapter II—Drug Enforcement Administration, Department of Justice (Parts 1300—1399)

1300.01 (b) added...............................33883
1301.13 (e)(1)(vii) revised; (e)(4) added..33883
1301.72 Heading revised; (e) added 33884

1301.74 Heading and (j) through (l) revised; (m) redesignated as (o); (m) and (n) added...........33884
1304.04 (f) introductory text amended 33885
1304.24 Heading, (a), and (b) revised 33885
1308.11 (b)(73) through (76), (66) through (72), (61) through (65), (57) through (60), (56), (46) through (55), (38) through (45), and (19) through (37) redesignated as (b)(83) through (86), new (75) through (81), (69) through (73), new (64) through (67), new (61), new (50) through new (59), new (41) through new (48), and new (21) through new (39); new (b)(19), new (20), new (40), new (49), new (60), new (62), new (63), new (68), new (74), and (82) added..................22117
1308.11 (b)(67) through (86), (62) through (66), (60), (61), and (39) through (59) redesignated as new (b)(71) through (90), new (65) through new (69), new (62), new (63), new (40) through new (60); new (b)(39), new (61), new (64), and new (70) added 23606
1308.11 (d)(81) through (85) added; (h)(31) through (35) removed 30778
1308.11 (d)(86) added; (h)(36) removed..................................31429
1308.11 (d)(87) Added.......................32634
1308.11 (d)(88) added 33510
1308.12 (b)(1) introductory text revised...................................20286
1308.12 (c)(18) revised 30774
1308.14 (f)(11) through (13) redesignated as (f)(12) through (14); new (f)(11) added; interim 24492
1308.14 Regulation at 85 FR 63019 confirmed 29509
1308.15 Regulation at 85 FR 5562 confirmed 27806
1310.02 (a)(34) through (36) added 24707
1310.04 (g)(1)(vii) through (xiii) and (i) through (vi) redesignated as (g)(1)(x) through (xvi) and (ii) through (vii);

ILLUSTRATION 9-6. Reader Aids of the *Federal Register* Page with C.F.R. Parts Affected Shown

①

Federal Register / Vol. 86, No. 139 / Friday, July 23, 2021 / Contents VII

CFR PARTS AFFECTED IN THIS ISSUE ②

A cumulative list of the parts affected this month can be found in the Reader Aids section at the end of this issue.

10 CFR
50.............................38905
12 CFR
204...........................38905
14 CFR
39 (4 documents) 38907,
    38909, 38912, 38914
71 (3 documents) 38916,
    38918, 38919
Proposed Rules:
39 (5 documents) 38941,
    38943, 38946, 38949, 38950
71 (2 documents) 38953,
    38954

| 1 *Federal Register* date |
| 2 Coverage |
| 3 CFR title |
| 4 CFR Part |
| 5 *Federal Register* page |

③ **20 CFR**
404...........................38920
416...........................38920 ⑤
④ **26 CFR**
Proposed Rules:
1.............................39910
53............................39910
54............................39910
301...........................39910
28 CFR
Proposed Rules:
16............................38955
33 CFR
165 (3 documents) 38925,
    38926
38 CFR
Proposed Rules:
1.............................38958
40 CFR
52 (2 documents) 38928,
    38931
41 CFR
Proposed Rules:
51-1..........................38960
51-2..........................38960
51-3..........................38960
51-4..........................38960
51-5..........................38960
51-6..........................38960
51-7..........................38960
51-8..........................38960
51-9..........................38960
51-10.........................38960
42 CFR
Proposed Rules:
403...........................39104
405...........................39104
410...........................39104
411...........................39104
414...........................39104
415...........................39104
423...........................39104
424...........................39104
425...........................39104
47 CFR
73 (5 documents) 38934,
    38935, 38936, 38937
Proposed Rules:
15............................38969
49 CFR
384...........................38937

Next, you would check the daily "CFR Parts Affected" for July 23, 2021, Illustration 9-7. You would follow the same process you did when you reviewed Illustrations 9-5 and 9-6.

On Lexis and Westlaw, the changes to the regulations already are incorporated.

ILLUSTRATION 9-7. C.F.R. Parts Affected for the Month

1 Date	2 Coverage	3 CFR title
4 CFR Part	5 *Federal Register* page	

i

Reader Aids

Federal Register

Vol. 86, No. 139

Friday, July 23, 2021 ①

CUSTOMER SERVICE AND INFORMATION

Federal Register/Code of Federal Regulations

General Information, indexes and other finding aids	202–741–6000
Laws	741–6000

Presidential Documents

| Executive orders and proclamations | 741–6000 |
| **The United States Government Manual** | 741–6000 |

Other Services

| Electronic and on-line services (voice) | 741–6020 |
| Privacy Act Compilation | 741–6050 |

ELECTRONIC RESEARCH

World Wide Web

Full text of the daily Federal Register, CFR and other publications is located at: **www.govinfo.gov**.

Federal Register information and research tools, including Public Inspection List and electronic text are located at: **www.federalregister.gov**.

E-mail

FEDREGTOC (Daily Federal Register Table of Contents Electronic Mailing List) is an open e-mail service that provides subscribers with a digital form of the Federal Register Table of Contents. The digital form of the Federal Register Table of Contents includes HTML and PDF links to the full text of each document. ③

To join or leave, go to **https://public.govdelivery.com/accounts/USGPOOFR/subscriber/new**, enter your email address, then follow the instructions to join, leave, or manage your subscription.

PENS (Public Law Electronic Notification Service) is an e-mail ④ service that notifies subscribers of recently enacted laws.

To subscribe, go to **http://listserv.gsa.gov/archives/publaws-l.html** **and select** *Join or leave the list (or change settings)*; then follow the instructions.

FEDREGTOC and **PENS** are mailing lists only. We cannot respond to specific inquiries.

Reference questions. Send questions and comments about the Federal Register system to: **fedreg.info@nara.gov**

The Federal Register staff cannot interpret specific documents or regulations.

FEDERAL REGISTER PAGES AND DATE, JULY

34905–35216	1
35217–35382	2
35383–35594	6
35595–36060	7
36061–36192	8
36193–36482	9
36483–36632	12
36633–36986	13
36987–37212	14
37213–37668	15
37669–37890	16
37891–38206	19
38207–38406	20
38407–38536	21
38537–38904	22
38905–39938	23

CFR PARTS AFFECTED DURING JULY ②

At the end of each month the Office of the Federal Register publishes separately a List of CFR Sections Affected (LSA), which lists parts and sections affected by documents published since the revision date of each title.

3 CFR

Proclamations:

10231	35385
10232	38207
10233	38535

Administrative Orders:

Memorandums:

Memorandum of June 29, 2021	35383

Notices:

Notice of July 7, 2021	36479, 36481
Notice of July 20, 2021	38901, 38903

Executive Orders:

14036	36987

5 CFR

890	36872

6 CFR

Ch. I	38209

7 CFR ⑤

457	38537
925	37213
1218	37669
1710	36193
1714	36193
1717	36193
1718	36193
1721	36193
1726	36193
1730	36193
1767	36193

Proposed Rules:

986	35409
1218	38590

8 CFR

212	37670
214	37670
245	37670
274a	37670

Proposed Rules:

214	35410
248	35410
274a.12	35410

9 CFR

352	37216

Proposed Rules:

327	37251
351	37251
354	37251
355	37251
381	37251
500	37251
592	37251

10 CFR

50	38905

52	34905
431	37001

Proposed Rules:

52	34999, 35023
429	36018
430	35660, 35668, 37687, 38594
431	36018, 37069, 37708

12 CFR

204	38905
655	37671
702	34924
1022	35595
Ch. XII	36199

Proposed Rules:

43	38607
244	38607
373	38607
1234	38607

13 CFR

121	38537
124	38537

14 CFR

25	37013, 37015
39	34933, 35217, 35387, 35599, 35601, 36061, 36064, 36202, 36205, 36207, 36483, 36485, 36487, 36491, 36633, 36635, 36638, 37017, 37019, 37219, 37221, 37224, 37226, 37229, 37231, 37891, 38209, 38212, 38214, 38218, 38220, 38223, 38225, 38407, 38410, 38538, 38541, 38907, 38909, 38912, 38914
61	38493
71	34937, 35221, 36210, 36212, 37234, 37235, 37238, 37672, 38229, 38916, 39918, 38919
95	37893
97	34938, 34941, 36641, 36642, 37897, 37899
141	36493

Proposed Rules:

39	35027, 35410, 35413, 35416, 35690, 35692, 35695, 35697, 36241, 36243, 36516, 37087, 37255, 27258, 37936, 38239, 38242, 38608, 38613, 38615, 38941, 38943, 38946, 38949, 38950
71	35233, 35235, 35237, 35419, 35420, 37090, 37939, 37941, 38245, 38419, 38617, 38953, 38954
259	38420
260	38420

ILLUSTRATION 9-7. *Continued*

ii   Federal Register / Vol. 86, No. 139 / Friday, July 23, 2021 / Reader Aids

15 CFR
744 ....35389, 36496, 37901

16 CFR
0..........38542
1..........38542
323..........37022
Proposed Rules:
Ch. I..........35239

17 CFR
Proposed Rules:
246..........38607

19 CFR
Ch. I..........38554, 38556
10..........35566
102..........35566
132..........35566
134..........35566
145..........38553
163..........35566
182..........35566
190..........35566
Proposed Rules:
102..........35422
177..........35422

20 CFR
200..........35221
295..........34942
404..........38920
416..........38920

21 CFR
573..........37035, 37037
1141..........36509
1305..........38230
1308..........37672
Proposed Rules:
1308..........37719, 38619

24 CFR
11..........35391
92..........34943
Proposed Rules:
267..........38607

25 CFR
48..........34943

26 CFR
54..........36872
Proposed Rules:
1..........39910
53..........39910
54..........36870, 39910
301..........39910

27 CFR
9..........34952, 34955
70..........34957
Proposed Rules:
9..........37260, 37265

28 CFR
50..........37674
Proposed Rules
16..........38624, 38955

29 CFR
1910..........37038, 38232
2590..........36872
4000..........36598
4262..........36598
Proposed Rules:
10..........38816
23..........38816
1402..........38627
1910..........36073

30 CFR
550..........38557
926..........37039

31 CFR
1..........35396
589..........37904, 37907
Proposed Rules:
33..........35156
520..........35399

32 CFR
169..........37676
169a..........37676
199..........36213
310..........38560

33 CFR
Ch. I..........37238
100 ....35399, 35604, 37045, 37239, 38233
117..........35402
165 ....34958, 34960, 34961, 34963, 34964, 35224, 35225, 35403, 36066, 36067, 36068, 36070, 36646, 37047, 37049, 37051, 37242, 37244, 37677, 37910, 37911, 37914, 37916, 38236, 38238, 38925, 38926
207..........37246
210..........35225
214..........35226
273..........37053
274..........37249
326..........37246
Proposed Rules:
100..........35240, 37270
165..........35242

34 CFR
Ch. II..........36217, 36220, 36222, 36510, 36648, 37679
Ch. III..........36656
686..........36070

36 CFR
Proposed Rules:
7..........37725

37 CFR
1..........35226, 35229
2..........35229
Proposed Rules:
1..........35429

38 CFR
Proposed Rules:
1..........38958

39 CFR
111..........35606
233..........38413
Proposed Rules:
Ch. III..........36246

40 CFR
51..........37918
52 ....35404, 35608, 35610, 36227, 36665, 37053, 37918, 38562, 38928, 38931
62..........35406
80..........37681
81..........37683
180..........36666, 37055
228..........38563
Proposed Rules:
52 ....35030, 35034, 35042, 35244, 35247, 36673, 37942, 38433, 38627, 38630, 38643, 38652
62..........35044
81..........35254
141..........37948

41 CFR
Proposed Rules:
51-1..........38960
51-2..........38960
51-3..........38960
51-4..........38960
51-5..........38960
51-6..........38960
51-7..........38960
51-8..........38960
51-9..........38960
51-10..........38960

42 CFR
414..........38569
510..........36229
600..........35615
Proposed Rules:
403..........39104
405..........39104
409..........35874
410..........39104
411..........39104
413..........36322
414..........39104
415..........39104
423..........39104
424..........35874, 39104
425..........39104
484..........35874
488..........35874
489..........35874
498..........35874
512..........36322

45 CFR
144..........36872
147..........36872
149..........36872
155..........36071
156..........36872
Proposed Rules:
147..........35156
155..........35156

156..........35156

46 CFR
Ch. I..........37238

47 CFR
Ch. I..........37061
54..........37058, 38570
64..........35632
73 ....34965, 35231, 37058, 37935, 38934, 38935, 38936, 38937
74..........37080
Proposed Rules:
1..........37972
2..........35700, 37982
15 ....35046, 35700, 37982, 38969
73..........37972, 37982
74..........35046, 37982
90..........35700, 37982
95..........35700, 37982

48 CFR
204..........36229
212..........36229
252..........36229
501..........34966
552..........34966
570..........34966
Proposed Rules:
615..........35257
652..........35257

49 CFR
381..........35633
382..........35633
383..........35633
384..........35633, 38937
385..........35633
390..........35633
391..........35633
Ch. XII..........38209
Proposed Rules:
385..........35443
393..........35449

50 CFR
17 ....34979, 38570, 38572
20..........37854
300..........35653, 38415
622..........38416
648..........36669
648..........36671, 38586
660..........36237, 37249
665..........36239
679 ....36514, 38418, 38588
Proposed Rules:
17 ....35708, 36678, 37091, 37410, 38246
218..........37790
635..........38262
648..........36519
665..........37982

▼ How Do You Validate, Shepardize, or KeyCite a C.F.R. Citation?

Cases that construe an administrative regulation are compiled in the *Shepard's®* database on Lexis. For a detailed explanation of how to Shepardize, consult Chapter 5. The KeyCite service through Westlaw also allows you to do a search of regulations so that you can find cases that cite the regulation.

Using *Shepard's* or KeyCite, however, indicates whether the regulation continues to be valid. These services do not replace the need to update the regulation in the manner discussed in the prior sections, though. Updating the regulation provides the most current version of the citation. In contrast, *Shepard's* and KeyCite reveal the judicial interpretations of the citation. Use either *Shepard's* or KeyCite and perform online updating, for your research to be thorough and complete.

▼ How Are the C.F.R. and the *Federal Register* Cited?

Citations to the C.F.R. and the *Federal Register* should follow *Bluebook* **Rule 14**. Title 21 of the C.F.R., part 101 from 2021 is cited per the *Bluebook* as

21 C.F.R. pt. 101 (2021)

Title 21 of the C.F.R., §169.140 from 2021 would be written as

21 C.F.R. §169.140 (2021)

It will be the same based on *ALWD* **Rule 18**.

A *Federal Register* entry from volume 70 beginning on page 35030 from June 16, 2017, would be cited based on the *Bluebook* **Rule 14** and *ALWD* **Rule 18** as

70 Fed. Reg. 35030 (June 16, 2017)

D. DECISIONS

▼ What Else Do Administrative Agencies Do?

Agencies function in a quasi-judicial capacity when they conduct **hearings.** Hearings may resemble court proceedings. However, most hearings are informal. An **administrative law judge** (ALJ) hears cases involving the application of a particular regulation. Often these cases involve the violation of a regulation. After the hearing, the ALJ, who may be an agency employee or an independent attorney, issues an opinion that serves as primary authority. However, most agency decisions do not have the same binding effect as court decisions. Some agency decisions can be appealed in the courts if the parties are not satisfied with the results. Often, however, the federal courts follow agency decisions concerning areas in which the agencies have developed expertise. To determine whether a court will follow an agency ruling, you must review court and agency decisions.

ETHICS ALERT

Some federal agencies permit paralegals to appear before them without an attorney present.

The Administrative Procedure Act requires agencies to publish their decisions and to make them available to the public. Researchers can contact a particular agency to obtain a decision. Administrative rulings are found frequently in the areas of labor, environmental, tax, securities, occupational safety and health, energy, and immigration law. For example, the Consumer Product Safety Commission publishes its advisory decisions at https://www.cpsc.gov/Regulations-Laws–Standards/Advisory-Opinions.

▼ What Kind of Authority Are Administrative Decisions?

Administrative decisions, like decisions of various courts, are primary authorities. Some of these decisions can be appealed to the courts after all agency remedies have been satisfied. For example, an ALJ will determine whether an individual is disabled and qualifies for Social Security. This decision is made following a hearing. The ALJ's decision then can be appealed to the U.S. District Court and subsequently to higher federal courts. The enabling statute defines the type of review each agency decision will be accorded. However, the precedential value of the agency's decision varies. Some agencies do not bind themselves to follow previous decisions. The courts may find that an agency's decision is very persuasive, though, particularly in areas in which an agency has developed an expertise.

▼ Can Administrative Agency Decisions Be Shepardized or Checked on KeyCite?

Yes, administrative agency decisions can be Shepardized or checked on KeyCite.

▼ Other Than the Agency Itself, Where Can You Find
Administrative Agency Decisions?

Sometimes a commercially published service prints administrative agency decisions. Many agency decisions are also available on Westlaw and Lexis. Looseleaf services covering a specific legal topic such as food and drug law or environmental law publish many of the decisions.

E. LOOSELEAF SERVICES

▼ What Are Looseleaf Services?

Looseleaf services cover one topic thoroughly. The publishers compile administrative decisions, rules, regulations, and editorial comments within a single source. Looseleaf services are compiled in all areas covered by administrative law: environmental, labor, energy, and government contracts law. Many researchers think of looseleaf services as mini-libraries because they contain a variety of resources relating to a single legal topic.

The looseleafs started as looseleaf notebooks, but the majority of these services are now available online. Once you become familiar with a practice area, particularly a heavily regulated area of the law, you quickly become familiar with the looseleaf services used in that area.

PRACTICE POINTER

Do not rely on the language of a primary authority you find in a looseleaf. Check the official version of the authority if one exists.

▼ What Type of Authority Are Looseleaf Services?

Looseleaf services as a whole are considered secondary authority because they are not published by a government body in its official law-making capacity. However, looseleaf services contain primary resources such as agency decisions, and frequently a looseleaf service is the only hardcopy resource for the decision. When citing to an agency decision obtained in a looseleaf service, that decision is primary authority.

RESEARCHING ADMINISTRATIVE LAW: SUMMARY

1. Find the enabling statute.
2. Find judicial opinions concerning the enabling statute.
3. Find agency regulations.
   a. Review the index for the appropriate title or look up a title paralleling the statutory title and skim the contents.
   b. Or, look up the agency by name in the index. It will direct you to a C.F.R. part.
4. Find case adjudications. Consult looseleaf services, *Shepard's* and other citators, and the U.S.C.A. or U.S.C.S. annotations.
5. Validate and update your research.

PRACTICE POINTER

Video tutorials and handouts concerning the use of the govinfo.gov site and its resources including the *Federal Register*, its index, and the C.F.R., are available at https://www.govinfo.gov/help/tutorials-handouts.

CHAPTER SUMMARY

Administrative agencies and their power and authority are created by the federal and state legislatures when they enact enabling statutes. These agencies operate on a daily basis to enforce these legislative mandates.

As part of their enforcement duties, the agencies adopt rules and regulations and hold quasi-judicial hearings.

Rules and regulations of the federal administrative agencies can be found in the *Code of Federal Regulations*. These regulations also are available online. A daily paper called the *Federal Register* also reports any new or proposed regulations. States also have codes of regulations and generally a daily record of new and proposed administrative rules and regulations.

Updating these authorities is essential. You must use the *List of C.F.R. Sections Affected* (L.S.A.) to update a C.F.R. citation. These lists are organized by title and section and are included in the daily *Federal Register* publications. You must review both the monthly L.S.A. pamphlets and the *Federal Register* to update a C.F.R. section properly.

Decisions of administrative agencies also can be validated in a manner similar to other case decisions.

Looseleaf services focus on one area of the law. They contain both primary authorities such as statutes, administrative rules, and cases, and secondary authorities such as expert commentary. Some looseleaf services also have digests and citators and some can be found online.

The next chapter will explain how and when to use the computerized legal research systems.

KEY TERMS

adjudicatory

administrative agencies

administrative law judge (ALJ)

Code of Federal Regulations (C.F.R.)

enabling statutes

Federal Register

hearings

List of C.F.R. Section Affected (L.S.A.)

looseleaf services

quasi-judicial

regulations

rules

EXERCISES

PRACTICE SKILLS

Federal Regulations

1. Find a federal regulation that concerns the number of parts of lead allowable in drinking water.
   a. List each source that might contain the regulation.
   b. Map out your search strategy.
   c. List at least two sources and how you would find a regulation in each.
   d. List topics you might consult.
   e. List at least one regulation.
   f. Update the regulation. What steps did you take? Attach a copy of a PDF file of the resources you consulted and your findings.
   g. List the citation in proper *Bluebook* and *ALWD* format.
2. Find a federal tax regulation that specifies how the value of estate property will be determined.
   a. List each source that might contain the regulation.
   b. Map out your search strategy.
   c. List at least two sources and how you would find a regulation in each.
   d. List topics you might consult.
   e. List at least one regulation.
   f. Update the regulation. What steps did you take? Attach a copy of a PDF file of the resources you consulted and your findings.
   g. List the regulation in proper *Bluebook* and *ALWD* format.

State Regulations

3. In your state, where would you look to find state regulations?
4. Find a state regulation that deals with the question of physician licensing.
   a. List each source that might contain the regulation.
   b. Map out your search strategy.
   c. List at least two sources and how you would find a regulation in each.
   d. List topics you might consult.
   e. List at least one regulation.
   f. Update the regulation. What steps did you take? Attach a copy of a PDF file of the resources you consulted and your findings.
   g. List the citations in proper *Bluebook* and *ALWD* format.
5. You must find a federal regulation that concerns small toy parts and children.
   a. List each source that might contain the regulation.
   b. Map out your search strategy.
   c. List at least two sources and how you would find a regulation in each.
   d. List topics you might consult.
   e. List at least one regulation.
   f. Update the regulation. What steps did you take? Attach a copy of a PDF file of the resources you consulted and your findings.
   g. List the citation in proper *Bluebook* and *ALWD* formats.
6. Occupational asbestos exposures are the subject of 29 C.F.R. 1910.1001.
   a. Review the regulation. What is PACM? Provide the citation to that section of the regulation.
   b. What is the date and citation of the first *Federal Register* reference in this regulation?
   c. Find that *Federal Register* entry. Attach a PDF file of the entry to your assignment.
   d. Update the regulation. What steps did you take? Attach a copy of a PDF file of the resources you consulted and your findings.

COMMERCIAL DATABASES

CHAPTER OVERVIEW

This chapter explains the basic concepts of the use of Lexis (also called "Lexis+"), Thomson Reuters Westlaw™ ("Westlaw" or the newest version "Westlaw Edge"), and Bloomberg Law and the way information is organized on the systems. The material in this chapter introduces you to the broad features of the systems. The chapter focuses on Lexis and Westlaw.

The commercial databases have many sophisticated features. However, you must master the basic skills before you use the advanced features. Much of your work with the commercial databases will be focused on updating and validating primary authority and retrieving sources.

Even though we now all have experience searching the Internet, and even with new avenues for computer-assisted legal research, vendor training is still necessary. Vendor training is essential because the databases are very costly to use. Lexis, Westlaw, and Bloomberg Law provide valuable editorial enhancements and accurate up-to-date information. All three have citators. Lexis is the only online system with *Shepard's®*. Westlaw has KeyCite. Bloomberg Law has BCite. Lexis and Westlaw tie the online resources to their respective print publications and research systems, and offer coverage that goes back over 100 years. Commercial databases provide currency, reliability, validity, and accuracy, yet for a cost. The most economical searches are conducted in conjunction with reliable academic and government portals.

Lexis, Westlaw, and Bloomberg Law now all use a "Google-type" query bar that allows broad searching without terms and connectors and without the need to select the specific resource format or document type. Your search will yield more on-target hits if you incorporate a terms and connectors search and know the type of resource you are seeking, or at least are aware of the type of document your research requires. Preliminary research with secondary authorities will show you the vocabulary used in relevant documents and the proximity of the terms within the relevant documents. (See Chapter 6.) Instead of filtering the resources—for instance, for statutes or regulations—when you start the search, you can now filter after you obtain your documents. It is still imperative that you know the types of resources you are after.

The fundamental topics explored in this chapter include:

1. query formulation
2. finding content
3. validation of authority

Although this chapter focuses primarily on Lexis and Westlaw, using computer-assisted legal research in specific research situations is discussed throughout this book. Additionally, cost-effective alternatives to Lexis and Westlaw have emerged, such as Fastcase. Free online websites for legal information are available at Cornell's Legal Information Institute (www.law.cornell.edu), the Government Publishing Office site (govinfo.gov), Findlaw, www.supremecourt.gov (which provides opinions and briefs for free), and Google Scholar, where you can obtain cases. Also, every state has its own website with state primary source documents.

The depth of coverage varies greatly in all the cost-effective sites mentioned. The Lexis and Westlaw alternatives are good places to turn when you are looking for a particular case, statute, regulation, or journal article. The government and academic sites are highly reliable sources of authority. In fact, the government sites offer authenticated resources that are interchangeable with print sources now.

However, these sites do not offer publishers' research enhancements, a wide variety of resources, or validating services such as *Shepard's* or KeyCite. Research enhancements, including Key Numbers and headnotes, related resources produced by the publisher, updating, and validation services are essential for efficient legal research. For older material and a vast array of resources under one site, Lexis and Westlaw products are the way to go. The depth of coverage in both Lexis and Westlaw is vast and deep.

A. INTRODUCTION

Lexis is an online research system owned by RLEX, a British information and analytics business. West, owned by Thomson Reuters, a major legal publisher, also decided to create computerized legal databases and named their system Westlaw. Currently, Westlaw is available as Westlaw Edge to promote the site's capabilities in artificial intelligence (AI). Bloomberg Law is produced by Bloomberg, the major online provider of business information. Lexis+ and Westlaw Edge are the newer versions of Lexis and Westlaw, respectively but text will refer to the databases as Lexis and Westlaw..

A revolution in legal research occurred with the advent of computerized legal research. Researchers can now obtain documents, cases, statutes, bills, regulations, attorney general opinions, slip laws, and many other forms of information, legal and factual, from a myriad of jurisdictions and print it out in full text without leaving the office. In addition, researchers do not have to use an index when obtaining material online. Researchers can select terms or words that need to appear in the ideal document on point. The researcher can then combine the relevant terms in a query, which is used to search the appropriate databank for documents with those words or terms. Computerized research systems continually increase the amount of information and the variety of documents they contain.

Although commercial databanks are costly to use, they offer research enhancements that the scattered, free sites on the Internet often lack. Currently, though, govinfo.gov and Congress.gov are excellent updated resources for federal statutory and regulatory information.

Now you can access up-to-date versions of Lexis, Westlaw, and Bloomberg Law at the following URLs:

Lexis.com or Plus.Lexis.com

Westlaw.com

Bloomberglaw.com

▼ What Are the Benefits of Using Online Legal Research Systems?

The greatest benefit of Lexis, Westlaw, and Bloomberg Law is that all sources are reliable, accurate, and up to date. A vast variety of resources are accessible through your desktop or even your phone. You do not have to travel to various libraries to obtain the information that you need. Also, the material online is never off the shelf or checked out. Currentness is essential in legal research, and the commercial online databases keep everything as current as possible. (See Chapter 5, for example, on how to validate cases on Lexis and Westlaw.) Searching on the commercial databases is smooth.

The database screens have many features to facilitate your search. In addition, *Shepard's* on Lexis and KeyCite on Westlaw permit you to validate the authority that you retrieve with a single click. (At the time of this edition, Bloomberg Law's citator, BCite, only permits validation of cases and selected federal tax resources.) It is essential to know that the authority is still good law before you use it. Both Lexis and Westlaw tie you to their other research products, print and online, by showing you related sources, and both offer editorial enhancements in the form of headnotes, annotations, and summaries. Westlaw has the Key Number system and allows you to customize Key Number searches online for efficient research using the West Digest system. When you use one of these commercial databases, you never have to evaluate whether the site is trustworthy.

NET NOTE

For a quick comparison of the commercial databases' content coverage see the chart created by the Drake Law Library at https://libguides.law.drake.edu/c.php?g=150969&p=992817.

▼ What Are the Major Disadvantages of Using Online Legal Research Systems?

The first major disadvantage is cost. Lexis and Westlaw are still quite expensive, and the charges for searching, connect time, and subscribing add up very quickly. A half-hour search can easily cost well over $100. You can avoid some of the high fees by entering into a special contract with Lexis or Westlaw. Now many types of contracts can be negotiated, including contracts for single-state research or flat annual fees. Sometimes local bar associations have subscriptions you may use.

Although the vendors have made online research easier by adding many user-friendly features—like toolbars and menu-driven and point-and-click searching—many skills must be developed to search in an efficient and cost-effective way. You must take the time to select your search terms to retrieve on-point information. What you enter will limit what you retrieve. Also, browsing through sources is difficult and costly. Make your searches more targeted by taking the time to do some preliminary research to learn the vocabulary. You can also call the help number to ask for assistance with your search before going online.

PRACTICE POINTER

Before using Lexis, Westlaw, or Bloomberg Law to perform any research or to cite check, ask the attorney assigning the project if it is permissible. Sometimes budgets are very restricted.

---

1. Uses for Lexis, Westlaw, and Bloomberg Law

Computerized legal research is a very powerful search tool to find cases that discuss unique fact patterns. For example, suppose you want to find cases that deal with a slip-and-fall-on-a shag carpet issue. An encyclopedia or digest index may have entries under "slip and fall" and possibly under "carpet," but it is very unlikely that there would be an index entry under "shag." Lexis and Westlaw permit you to search "shag carpet" to see where those words appear in a document.

With computerized legal research you also can find documents, cases, statutes, and articles when you only have some information from the cite but not the complete cite. Suppose you hear about a promising Florida Supreme Court case on point. You know the case was decided in April 2003 and the judge's name was Murphy, but you do not have a clue as to the case name. Knowing the court, the year, and the judge will lead you to the case on Lexis or Westlaw.

PRACTICE POINTER

Use Justia and Findlaw for current awareness so that you can read cases in the news. However, you cannot validate the cases.

---

2. Additional Features

Lexis and Westlaw are used very effectively for cite checking, updating, and validating authority. (See Chapter 5 for a full discussion of citators, *Shepard's*, and KeyCite.) The online systems enable you to obtain the subsequent history of a case. Retrieving updated statutory and administrative materials on Lexis and Westlaw is another valuable use of the systems' capabilities because you do not have to consult a number of hardcopy sources, pocket parts, and supplements to find the most current version of a statute or a regulation. Also, administrative and statutory materials often have cumbersome and difficult-to-use indexes.

The full text search capabilities of Lexis, Westlaw, and Bloomberg Law permit you to obtain documents by combining the words and terms relevant to your research problem. Case law and code research from other jurisdictions is performed efficiently on the databases because you do not have to find out-of-state primary sources in hardcopy format. An underused feature of computerized legal research is to access looseleaf services online; subscription and filing fees are saved and the material is always current. Bloomberg Law owns BNA publications, and their looseleaf services and portfolios are online. Lexis has a related content feature on the screen display that provides links to related secondary sources and annotated statutes, if relevant. Westlaw links the user to related West publications and the entire West Key Number system, indexing, and annotated statutes. Lexis and Westlaw provide integrated research so that the retrieval is actually expanded and is tied to the print publications so you can read the source in hard copy.

PRACTICE POINTER

Lexis offers free virtual training. The best course to start with is Lexis Basics.

Go to https://www.lexisnexis.com/university/catalogue.aspx?training= product&product=Lexis%C2%AE. Also, Lexis offers training at all levels. You can find the menu of video training options at https://www .lexisnexis.com/en-us/support/lexis/default.page.

Westlaw offers training for Westlaw Classic and Westlaw Edge. You can find out about Westlaw training options at https://legal .thomsonreuters.com/en/support/westlaw#training-resources.

B. SEARCHING WITH ONLINE LEGAL RESEARCH SYSTEMS

1. General Overview

Lexis, Westlaw, and Bloomberg Law work in a similar fashion. The systems require careful query formulation and selection of search terms to obtain the most relevant information available. Both are **literal searching devices**, meaning that the computer searches for the appearance of the words or terms that you select to appear in the text of the document. You will retrieve a group of documents containing your search terms after executing a search.

The Internet is the gateway to the databanks so there is no need to download software and to update it. The systems are intuitive and are menu driven. You no longer have to locate the names of libraries or databases within the systems, but merely have to point and click on the type of resource you want. The mechanics of using Lexis and Westlaw are now similar to using an Internet browser. Searching now does not require the user to know the database or library, for searching is performed with a series of clicks to narrow the retrieval potential with on-screen filters. Of course, you can type a variety of terms into the search box without connectors and without specifying the document type, but you will locate relevant sources more quickly with search enhancements and refinements.

PRACTICE POINTER

Take the time to find and read a statute or regulation on a government site, such as govinfo.gov and then update and validate the source on Lexis or Westlaw.

Each system has electronic tablet and smartphone search capability.

As stated earlier, although you can use a Google-type search, the most efficient searching is performed with some traditional online research techniques. Begin the search by creating a list of words that would appear in the ideal document on point. (You should educate yourself on the topic before you get online so that you have a research vocabulary that includes synonymous terms.) Then you figure out the relationship between the ideal words or terms. How close together would they appear in the document? Would the words and terms appear in the same sentence? In the same paragraph? Within 100 words of one another? This involves thinking about the context of the words within the document's text and how those words should appear without losing their contextual significance.

NET NOTE

The best comparison chart for terms and connectors is from the Drake Law Library, where search techniques and connectors for the three main commercial databases are compared. You can find the chart at https://libgui des.law.drake.edu/LexisWest.

The process of selecting the terms and determining the terms' contextual relationship is simpler now with natural language searching. Natural language lets you search in plain English using sentences and phrases without selecting connectors between the terms. (More on connectors later in the chapter.) You use a form of natural language searching whenever you enter a search query when you use Google. The system then selects the significant terms from your search and looks for documents containing those terms. Whether you search using a group of words separated by connectors or use natural language, computerized legal research scans the databank for the appearance of those words and retrieves the documents for you.

Electronic retrieval systems do not replace traditional research skills. Electronic resources will not tell you if the source is relevant; you still must read the material to see if it applies. You also must validate any resource you rely on to make sure it is still good law. Even if a case is on Lexis or Westlaw, it may have been overruled. You must take the extra step to validate any primary source authority. Also, the databases are literal searching tools that cannot analyze or reach conclusions, legal or factual. The systems search for terms within the parameters that you specify, the connectors.

The systems are excellent for searching terms that are not ordinarily included in traditional indexes. They are also good for searching for specific facts or legal terms. Remember that the most successful searching occurs after some preliminary research has been performed using secondary sources and digests and, if possible, primary authority. Preliminary research makes you aware of the vocabulary used in topic discussions and the wording in on-point opinions. The preliminary research also helps you to determine the context for the terms, the relationship of the terms, or the proximity of the terms to one another.

The service is very costly when you are using it at a law firm or a corporation. Lexis and Westlaw are not suited to researching broad legal concepts like *breach of contract*. Use your judgment to determine if computerized or hardcopy research is the best route. Statutory research, especially if you have the books, is best started with the hardcopy format and then you can refine and narrow your research online. The best and most effective research uses a combination of hardcopy and computerized sources, drawing on the strengths of both. For instance, if you have the popular name of a federal act, use the popular name table in a hardcopy statute set to find and read the statute. You can then update and validate the statute online. Computerized research is yet another tool in your arsenal of sources.

2. The Basics

▼ How Can You Filter the Information?

Information on both Lexis and Westlaw can be filtered as follows:

1. by jurisdiction: individual states and federal cases and statutes;
2. by topic: for example, bankruptcy, tax, or contracts; or
3. by format: for example, cases, statutes, law reviews, encyclopedias, or news articles.

On Lexis and Westlaw, you can view the types of resources and then select where you want to search. You can select material by jurisdiction, topic, and format, but this is not necessary because you can input the terms in the Go Bar.

All three systems—Lexis, Westlaw, and Bloomberg Law—regardless of version, have state and federal primary authority—statutes, cases, and regulations—as well as secondary sources. The three systems allow you to do a survey of state statutory law on a topic. Lexis and Westlaw have many secondary sources that have a print equivalent such as the A.L.R., Am. Jur. 2d, C.J.S., and formbooks. Westlaw has the West Digest system and the topics and Key Numbers. Lexis has *Shepard's* and terrific news sources. Bloomberg Law has an integrated search and retrieval capability to bring up relevant business information and corporate filings.

On Lexis and Westlaw, you can retrieve a document if you have the citation. Simply type the cite in the search bar. You can also type in the name of a specific source in the search bar to bring up the source.

PRACTICE POINTER

Your employer will probably subscribe to one commercial database, and you can then focus your training on that system.

---

3. Search Formulation

Now that the systems use Google-type searching, there is no need to learn the details of query formulation for each vendor. The new versions start with broad searches and then let you use the on-screen entries to filter your search. You can also enter a citation into the search bar to retrieve a specific document if you have the cite. However, a basic understanding of a terms-and-connector type search will help you to construct a more precise search query.

▼ What Is a Search or Query?

Any group of terms or words that you type into the search bar is a query. The databases are literal searching systems. You must determine the words or terms that you want to appear in a document on point. Your **search** or **query** is the group of terms or words that you select and enter into the system to retrieve on-target information. If you use a terms-and-connectors search, the terms are separated by connectors. Suppose you want to find cases discussing Seminole Indians in Florida, particularly near St. Augustine, and their water, land, or property rights. The terms that you would select are:

> Seminole Indian
> St. Augustine
> water right
> land right
> property right

These are the terms that would appear in the ideal opinion. Use a thesaurus to find synonymous terms to expand the number of documents you will retrieve. Next, if you use connectors, you must determine the placement of the terms in the document's text. Do you want the terms to be close together and to all fall in the same sentence? Do you want the terms to be anywhere in the document? In the same paragraph? Will the contextual meaning or significance of the terms be lost if they are too far apart? Will you fail to retrieve many documents if you indicate that they should be close together? Use connectors to indicate the proximity of the terms.

a. Connectors

Connectors are the special words or symbols devised by Westlaw and by Lexis that link your search terms together to indicate your search terms' physical placement in the document's text. Now with the search bar on Lexis, Westlaw, and Bloomberg Law you do not have to use connectors when entering your terms. However, connectors will yield a more accurate search. Connectors tell Lexis and Westlaw the proximity of the search terms in relation to one another. Lexis uses the following connectors:

and—indicates that the terms are anywhere in the document but both terms must appear in the document. You can also use "&" as "and" and "&" are interchangeable. For example, in typing **seminole and indian**, the word *and* indicates that both terms must appear in the document.

or—indicates that one term or the other term or both terms must appear in the document. A blank space on Westlaw indicates "or." For example, on Lexis, typing **seminole or indian** would cause the retrieval system to look for the occurrence of either *Seminole* or *Indian* or both words in the document. To search for these synonymous terms on Westlaw, input **seminole indian.** The *or* connector is most frequently used for synonymous terms, like *car or vehicle or automobile.* This maximizes the possibility of retrieving a greater number of on-point documents.

w/n—means within *n* number of words. You determine how close the words should appear in relation to one another. In our example, you could use **seminole w/5 indian**, which would tell Lexis to search for the word *Seminole* to appear within 5 words of *Indian*.

Pre/n—This connector is unique to Lexis and is identical to *w/n* except that the first word must precede the second. You are able to set the spacing. For example, **seminole pre/5 indian** would search for the word *Seminole* to precede the word *Indian* by 5 words.

w/s—indicates that the two words must appear in the same sentence in any order. You can also use */s* instead of *w/s*. **Seminole w/s indian** would search for the two terms to appear in the same sentence in any order.

w/p—instructs Lexis to search for the terms within the same paragraph in any order. You can also use */p* instead of *w/p*. **Seminole w/p indian** would search for the appearance of those terms in the same paragraph in any order.

and not—excludes terms. Use it as your last connector. For example, **seminole and indian and not tribe** would retrieve documents with the words *Seminole* and *Indian* anywhere in the document but no documents with the word *tribe* would be retrieved.

Westlaw's connectors are very similar to those of Lexis, but as indicated earlier, Westlaw does have a few unique features:

&—identical to the Lexis **and.**

[blank space]—typing a blank space between two or more terms indicates *or*. For example, the search **auto car vehicle** translates into *auto or car or vehicle*. The **or** connector is most frequently used to indicate synonymous terms, but it is also used to link antonyms, or opposites, like *day or night*.

/s—Westlaw pioneered the within-the-same-sentence connector. It is very handy because you do not have to estimate the proximity of the words to one another. If the words fall in the same sentence, you retrieve the document. Sentences can vary in length, and **/s** approximates written English.

+s—indicates that the two words must appear in the same sentence, but the first term must precede the second. For example, **seminole +s indian** would search for *Seminole* and *Indian* to appear in the same sentence, but *Seminole* must precede *Indian*.

/p—indicates that the two terms appear within the same paragraph. The search **seminole/p indian** would search for those two terms' appearance in the same paragraph in any order.

+p—searches for two terms to appear in the same paragraph, but the first term must precede the second. In our example, **seminole +p indian** would retrieve documents with *Seminole* occurring before *Indian* in the same paragraph.

/n—you can customize the proximity of terms on Westlaw just as you can on Lexis. For example, **seminole/5 indian** would search for the word *Seminole* to appear within 5 words of *Indian*.

+n—this connector allows you to establish the number of words between terms, but the first term must appear before the second. For example, **seminole +5 indian** searches for documents with *Seminole* falling 5 words before *Indian*.

%—excludes the term following the connector.

The following table summarizes connectors.

Description	Lexis	Westlaw
terms within the same document	And or &	&
either or both terms within the same document	or	[blank space]
terms appear within specified number of words of each other	w/n	/n
same as w/n but first term precedes second term	pre/n	+n
terms within the same sentence, any order	w/s	/s
terms within same sentence; first term precedes second term	–	+s
terms within same paragraph, any order	w/p	/p
excludes terms following the connector	and not	%

b. Quotations

If you want to search for a specific phrase or a complete name, enclose the terms in quotation marks. This technique is helpful with searching in the new versions of Lexis, Westlaw, and Bloomberg Law. Without enclosing the terms in quotations, the spaces between the words would be interpreted as *or* on Westlaw. Sometimes you want to search for a phrase that includes articles that are not terms located by either system. In these instances, place the phrase or name in quotations and the system will search for all the terms within the quotes as a unit. For example, you would use quotations to search for cases discussing Megan's Law or the Americans with Disabilities Act. If you do not use quotes, Westlaw would interpret *Megan's Law* to be *Megan's* or *Law*. To obtain the exact phrase in a document enter it as follows: "Americans with Disabilities Act."

c. Plurals

Lexis and Westlaw automatically search for regular plurals. For example, if you enter the word *pattern, patterns* is automatically searched. Irregular plurals like *children* are not automatically searched when the singular term is entered. You can maximize the documents you retrieve by using ! after the root of the word. For instance, instead of searching for commuters, search "commut!" and you will pull up documents with *commuter, commuters, commuting,* and *commuted.* However, you might need to review the documents to determine the relevancy because you might get results with cases about commuted sentences.

d. Irregular Plurals

Lexis and Westlaw have two symbols that assist you in searching for irregular plurals and for words that could have various endings stemming from the root word. The symbol * is like a Scrabble blank: You use it to replace a letter in a term. For example, suppose you are searching for articles about women. Documents on point could have the term *woman* or *women*, so your query would be typed as **wom*n** to increase the potential of retrieving on-point information. If you want documents about children, you could use the term **child***** and retrieve documents with *child* or *children*. The word *childhood* would not appear, however, because you only reserved three spaces after the root of *child*. If you want all possible endings of a word following its root, regardless of the amount of letters, use !. In our example, **child!** would retrieve *children, childhood, child,* and *childish*.

e. Hyphenated Words

If you place a space between two search terms on Lexis, the system will automatically search for the hyphenated version of the word. For example, if you are searching for documents containing the term *full-text*, and you enter **full text** as your query, you will retrieve documents with *full-text* as well as *full text*. On Westlaw, if you use **full-text** as your query, the system will search for the appearance of *full-text* and *full text*. Westlaw interprets a blank space as an *or*, so you must put phrases in quotes so that the system searches for the existence of the phrase or term. For example, you can enter **"full text"** and Westlaw will search for *full-text* and *full text*. The quotes are useful for phrases such as *res ipsa loquitur* so that the entire phrase will be searched for as a whole.

f. Noise Words or Articles

Lexis and Westlaw do not search for the occurrence of articles. Omit *the, a, an,* and *and* from your search queries. The frequent appearance of articles (or "noise words") in text would slow down the computer system if it had to search for them.

g. Capitalizing Proper Nouns and Other Terms

You do not have to worry about capitalization style on any commercial database. Lexis, Westlaw, and Bloomberg Law are not case sensitive, meaning that the databases do not discern between upper- and lowercase letters but search by matching words. Your query can be written as **united w/1 states**, and you will retrieve relevant documents.

4. Other Ways to Restrict Your Search to Retrieve On-Point Information

a. Date and Court Restrictors

Date and court **restrictors** in your query help to narrow your search. On Lexis, Westlaw, and Bloomberg Law, you can filter your retrieved documents by court and by date after you see the search results. You can also start with a date restriction in your search query, or you can filter the search results by date. On both Lexis and Westlaw, you can limit your search to look for documents from a particular time frame. On Lexis, you can restrict your search for information on the Seminole Indians to after 2015, before August 31, 2018, or to a specific date in your search. The searches would look as follows: **seminole w/5 indian and date aft 2015** for documents after 2015; **seminole w/5 indian and date bef 8/31/18** for documents before August 31, 2018; or **seminole w/5 indian and date=10/1/18** for documents pertaining to the date of October 1, 2018. Westlaw has the equivalent method of restricting the date in the search query. On Westlaw, you would search for documents after a certain date as follows: **seminole/5 indian and da(aft 2015)**; before a certain date: **seminole/5 indian and da(bef 8/31/18)**; from a specific date: **seminole/5 indian and da(10/1/18)**. In both Lexis and Westlaw, you can use the display on the screen to narrow a search by date if you did not type the date restriction in the query.

Court restrictors are another method of ensuring that the documents retrieved are pertinent. You can also restrict by court when you enter your search or when you look at the materials retrieved; you can then filter the results by court or by jurisdiction by clicking on the court on the screen or you can include the court in the query.

On Lexis you can limit the courts to only the jurisdictionally relevant ones by using the court segment in the query. An example of this is when you are searching all federal cases and want only those actually decided in a Florida state court or a federal court sitting in the state of Florida. A search using the court segment would look like this: **seminole w/5 indian and court(florida)**. You can also use the courts listed on the screen that are displayed after you run your search and click the court you want.

The systems now have field restrictors on the screen where you can plug in the specific term to look for in a particular part of the document. All the commercial systems have templates for the particular fields that you can search. Cases have set components that can be searched such as the judge's name, the court, the attorney, and the party. For instance, on Westlaw you can click on a field search when looking for cases to restrict the results. You may only want opinions written by Justice Scalia. You would then click: ju. Then you would enter **Scalia** in the box. Lexis and Bloomberg also have templates on the screen for segment searching. Also, you can filter your retrieved sources with on-screen clicks—by court and by jurisdiction—after you obtain your initial search results.

b. Other Restrictors

The following table summarizes the symbols and abbreviations used for search query restriction.

Description	Lexis	Westlaw
replaces a letter in a word or term	*	*
unlimited endings following the root of the word	!	!

c. Fields

Cases and other documents on Lexis contain **segments** and those on Westlaw contain **fields** that can be selected to limit or narrow your search so you retrieve relevant documents. Date and court restrictors are examples of segments or fields. Lexis also has case name, judge, and counsel segments for cases, and Westlaw has counsel, judge, case name, and topic (from the West Digest topics). Every category of information on each database has different segments or fields. Lexis and Westlaw have point-and-click features. Just read the screen, point, and click. Generally, the various ways you can limit your search will be listed on the screen. It is helpful to understand the underlying concepts to achieve more effective searching. Be sure to check with customer assistance because fields might change.

▼ Why Does Integrating Traditional and Computerized Resources Result in the Most Effective Computerized Legal Research?

Beginning your research with traditional sources allows you to become educated in the area of law and to learn the pertinent vocabulary used in decisions and in statutes. (See Chapter 6 for a complete discussion of secondary authorities.) A vocabulary of the words used in on-point opinions lets you construct your search queries most effectively. Online research is very costly, and you cannot afford to use the time online to educate yourself on a topic. It is, in fact, cost-effective to print out the citations and to read sources in hard copy if they are easily obtained.

EXAMPLE

You are asked to find Florida cases discussing abuse of process. Your first reaction to the assignment is that you do not even know what abuse of process is. This is the strategy that you would follow:

1. Consult secondary source materials to educate yourself and to acquire a research vocabulary for search formulation.
2. Begin the education process with a dictionary. For instance, you are asked to find cases from your jurisdiction discussing abuse of process. Your first step would be to look up "abuse of process" in a law dictionary. This will help you construct your query and to sift through the sources you find.

   For our example, abuse of process is a tort and occurs when the process of the courts is used for an improper purpose. Here's an example of abuse of process: An individual enters into a contract with another to purchase rare coins. The two parties draw up an installment contract specifying monthly payments for ten years. After possessing the coins for two years and after making the agreed-on monthly payments, the buyer decides that the market value of the coins has fallen and does not want to continue to make the monthly payments. The buyer sues the seller for fraud, claiming that he was deceived as to the true value of the coins. The buyer sues for fraud not because a fraud actually occurred but because he wants to get out of the contract. This is an abuse of process.
3. Decide the jurisdiction that the materials should be from. You can do a broad search and then filter the results after you retrieve the documents, or you can search for resources from a particular jurisdiction when you enter your query. You will need to know the relevant jurisdiction for your research. In our example, the supervising attorney requested Florida cases, so Florida is the appropriate jurisdiction. Determining the appropriate jurisdiction enables you to narrow your search results.
4. Determine the terms that would appear in the ideal opinion. *Abuse* and *process* would be the terms in this example.
5. Decide the relationship that the terms would have to one another in the text—the proximity of the terms. A little background reading in the law dictionary or a print encyclopedia will give you insight into how the terms relate to each other. How close must the terms appear to maintain the meaning? It is important to ensure that contextual meaning is not lost. This is where you decide what connectors you will use. We are looking for cases defining abuse of process. *Of* is a noise word, so we ignore it for purposes of listing terms for our query, but we know that it falls between two important words. The terms must be close together to retain their contextual meaning in the document. You select *w/3*. The query would be **abuse w/3 process**. If you do not know the proximity of the terms when you initially search, enter a natural language query and then read a

few of the cases. Some cases will be on point. Examine the language in those opinions to draft a new, more precise query.

6. Your goal is to maximize the retrieval of on-point documents. A court can discuss the definition as abusing the process of the courts. To get this decision as well, use a root with a *!*. Your query would be **abus! w/3 process**.

7. You can view the most recent opinions by filtering the retrieval results by date after your search or by adding a date restrictor to your initial query. Use the drop-down menu to plug dates into the date field or segment.

8. If you are frustrated in your attempts to search or your searches result in irrelevant sources, call Westlaw customer service at 1-800-Westlaw, Lexis customer service at 1-800-543-6862, or Bloomberg Law at 1-888-560-BLAW.

5. Retrieving the Results of Your Research

On Lexis, Westlaw, and Bloomberg Law, you can view the citations of documents found. The cite list, the list of documents retrieved from your search, has some text from the actual document with your terms. This allows you to quickly scan your cites to see what is most relevant. You can then select full text by merely pointing and clicking on a citation.

Viewing documents online in full text is time consuming and costly. It is best to obtain citations online and download the documents to a research folder. You can also read the full-text sources on free platforms such as govinfo.gov for federal statutes and regulations and on www.supremecourt.gov for United States Supreme Court decisions. You can also use uniformlaws.org to look at Uniform Laws. Consider reading a free legal encyclopedia at law.cornell.edu to obtain a basic understanding of the issue or terms.

▼ Are There Any Other Ways to Retrieve Documents?

On Lexis and Westlaw, you can retrieve a specific statute or a case if you know the citation. You can merely type the citation into the search bar. If you want to see the text of 121 So. 2d 319, you would type **121 so2d 319** and press **[Enter]**. To view the text of a statute, you would type **28 usc 1485** and press **[Enter]**.

6. Point-and-Click Enhancements

Not only do Lexis, Westlaw, and Bloomberg Law ensure that the information and search capabilities are current, they make searching easier with on-screen buttons to filter your research results. Additionally, all three vendors have made the research services much easier to use by allowing you to use the commands of your Internet browser combined with point-and-click capability instead of learning the searching nuances of each system. The vendors have greatly simplified searching on the systems.

Lexis is at Lexis.com or at plus.lexis.com. On Lexis, the source directory has replaced the libraries. Instead of constructing a query at the top of the page, you click on the terms box. Everything is completely menu driven. Also, just as on any other website, you can link to other resources. You can easily Shepardize on Lexis by merely clicking the "*Shepard's*" icon when a primary source document is on the screen. While reading a document you may see a cite to another document in the text. If the cite is highlighted in blue, you can click on the cite and you then go to the text of the cited document. To go back to the original source, just click your Web browser back.

Lexis has graphics at the beginning of each case to indicate the analysis that case has received. A red stop sign indicates that the case is no longer good law and that there is strong negative analysis. A blue circle means that the available analysis is neutral.

Westlaw is just as simple to use as Lexis.com. Westlaw also has point-and-click capabilities and hypertext links to cited authorities. Westlaw developed KeyCite, a case law validating service with graphics to indicate the strength of the authority. Westlaw relies on flags to indicate how a case has been treated by subsequent courts.

7. Additional Features on Lexis and Westlaw

Shepard's is available on Lexis, and online fees are incurred based on use. The beauty of online cite checking is that you do not have to worry about all of the books being on the shelf or about updating the material. The online services do it. In fact, Shepardizing on Lexis is now the main way that researchers use *Shepard's* citations. Additionally, Lexis permits customized *Shepard's* retrieval by court, jurisdiction, or analysis. *Shepard's* is part of Lexis, so *Shepard's* data are updated nightly online. Additionally, Lexis provides the treatment that the citing case offers regarding the decision you are validating. *Shepard's* on Lexis has color-coded symbols to alert you to the treatment that the case received. Also, you can customize your *Shepard's* retrieval to select only negative or positive treatment.

You do not need a document on the screen to Shepardize online with Lexis. You can click on *Shepard's* when signing on. You can then type in the next citation and press **[Enter]** while the *Shepard's* analysis is on the screen, and the information will reflect the analytical treatment of the succeeding document. You can go through entire lists of citations this way without entering a Lexis library.

Case validation on Westlaw is called **KeyCite**. KeyCite is as current as Westlaw. As soon as a case is placed on Westlaw, it receives KeyCite analysis and is included in that database. KeyCite includes thousands of unpublished opinions and references to law reviews. You can also customize your KeyCite search to focus on a particular jurisdiction, date ranges, and court level. Cases receive boxes to indicate the level of treatment in the cited case. Four boxes indicate that there is more than a page of treatment in the cited case, three boxes equal one page of discussion, two boxes have up to a paragraph, and one box indicates that your case is included in a string cite. The boxes immediately alert you to the depth of treatment in the citing case, which can be a big time saver during research.

A red flag pops up in KeyCite when a case has negative history. This visual clue indicates when a case is no longer good law for one of its points. A yellow flag means that the case has not been overruled but has received some criticism. A blue "H" means that the case has been discussed. You can KeyCite a case by pointing and clicking the KeyCite icon. You can KeyCite a wide range of primary and secondary sources in addition to cases and statutes. Additionally, KeyCite provides subsequent legislative activity for statutes. This is very handy when updating statutory authority. On Lexis, you can Shepardize a document on the screen by merely clicking the *Shepard's* tab. (For a full discussion of cite checking, see Chapter 5.)

Westlaw permits you to view a case as a PDF file so that the case looks identical to its West Reporter version.

Lexis has NEWS resources, which were previously located in the NEXIS library. It is an excellent source for full-text news and periodical articles. It is updated daily and is invaluable when performing factual research on an individual, a corporation, or an event. Lexis also has an extensive Public Records database.

Dow Jones is also available on Westlaw. Westlaw also has a news database with hundreds of newspapers, journals, wire services, and blogs.

Both Lexis and Westlaw, in all versions, have many secondary sources online including legal encyclopedias, law journals, treatises, and formbooks.

Bloomberg Law links all searches to business information and news sources. Many legal matters are based on economic factors. This is one of Bloomberg Law's strengths. Bloomberg Law also has a citator, called BCite, which is currently limited to cases and Internal Revenue Service sources.

All the commercial databases develop new features and add new resources constantly. The best approach is to master the basics of searching. Then, stay current by signing up for e-mail alerts and newsletters from the vendors to learn about new developments on their sites.

8. Comparing Lexis and Westlaw

a. Differences between Lexis and Westlaw

Lexis has news resources, which permit access to full-text articles from hundreds of periodicals. It is an excellent way to perform factual research.

Shepard's, owned by Lexis, is updated nightly and covers all cases and statutes from the 50 states and federal government, as well as many regulations and other resources.

Westlaw permits you to search the West Digest topics and Key Numbers online. This is very convenient because you can customize digest searching by adding date and court restrictors and significant fact terms. Just as Lexis links you to related sources, with Related Content, Westlaw links you to all West legal publishing resources.

News information on Westlaw can be searched as a whole by clicking on the News link on the screen. Dow Jones is part of this database. Westlaw contains hundreds of newspapers, newsletters, journals, and wire services. Westlaw has a validation and citing service called KeyCite. KeyCite tells you the status of the case, its analytical treatment by subsequent courts, and the depth of the treatment.

Thomson Reuters West also publishes U.S.C.C.A.N., as discussed in Chapter 8, which provides the legislative history of selected Public Laws. Consequently, U.S.C.C.A.N. is available on Westlaw.

b. Similarities between Lexis and Westlaw

Both Lexis and Westlaw permit you to research myriad cases, statutes, administrative regulations, articles, factual information, and other documents online using natural language searches that eliminate the cumbersome restrictions imposed by indexes. Westlaw's natural language searching capability is entered through a database. When it is time to construct your query, natural language will be an entry on the screen. You will have a choice of a terms-and-connectors search or a natural language search when entering your query. You can then construct your query as a phrase or sentence without connectors.

Both Lexis and Westlaw have menu-driven searching systems with point-and-click capability so you can search effectively without becoming very familiar with the system. Both are kept up to date and permit you to find documents without having to travel from your keyboard. The accuracy of Lexis and Westlaw is reliable. Both databanks are tied to the respective publisher's hardcopy materials, complete with headnotes, research aids, and practitioners' resources. The databases now use sophisticated artificial intelligence to provide analytics to maximize finding the best authority, in particular, cases. In summary, Lexis and Westlaw are quite similar but competing products that are very powerful when effectively put to use.

NET NOTE

Cleveland Marshall College of Law Library created a research guide "Lexis and Westlaw Compared: Overview" at http://guides.law.csuohio.edu/legal-research. This guide features the up-to-date features and differences in each database's capability and content.

▼ How Do You Use the Computer Most Efficiently?

As discussed earlier in the chapter, the most effective and efficient research is performed after you educate yourself on the topic using hardcopy resources. Doing traditional research gives you a vocabulary that you can use to construct your search queries. It is most efficient and cost-effective to obtain citations to relevant documents online and to read the documents in hardcopy format if they are readily available.

▼ How Do You Cite to Cases Retrieved on Lexis and Westlaw?

Bluebook **Rule 18.3.1** and *ALWD* **Rule 12.14(b)** explain how an unpublished decision found only on either Westlaw or Lexis should be cited. For Westlaw, first provide the name of the case and underline it. The next part of the citation is the docket number. In the example that follows, that number is No. 82-C4585. The next part of the citation is the year that the decision was issued. Next, indicate "WL" for Westlaw and finally the Westlaw number assigned to the case. Place the date in the parentheses.

Westlaw example: *Clark Equip. Co. v. Lift Parts Mfg. Co.,* No. 82-C4585, 1985 WL 2917, at *1 (N.D. Ill. Oct. 1, 1985) — *Bluebook* and *ALWD* format

▼ How Do You Cite a Decision Reported on Lexis?

For Lexis citations, first state the name of the case, the docket number, the year of the decision, the name of the Lexis file that contains the case, and the name LEXIS (in all capital letters) to indicate that the case is found on Lexis. Next place the date in parentheses.

Lexis example: *Barrett Indus. Trucks v. Old Republic Ins. Co.,* No. 87-C9429, 1990 U.S. Dist. LEXIS 142, at *2 (N.D. Ill. Jan. 9, 1990) — *Bluebook* and *ALWD* format

Generally, use the Westlaw or Lexis citation if a decision does not have a reporter citation but is available on a reliable commercial database. This is explained in *Bluebook* **Rule 10.8.1** and *ALWD* **Rule 12.14(b)**.

▼ How Do You Indicate a Page or Screen Number for the Case?

In a pinpoint citation, an asterisk should precede any screen or page numbers. See *Bluebook* **Rule 10.8.1** and *ALWD* **Rule 12.14(b)**.

Westlaw screen no.:   *Clark Equip. Co. v. Lift Parts Mfg. Co.,* No. 82-C4585, 1985 WL 2917, at *1 (N.D. Ill. Oct. 1, 1985) — *Bluebook* and *ALWD* format

▼ What Are the Other Sites for Computerized Legal Research?

There are many sites for cost-effective legal research, such as Justia .com, Cornell's Legal Information Institute at www.law.cornell.edu (one of the best and most reliable free sites), Google Scholar (excellent for finding law review articles and some cases), Findlaw (good for state statutes and specific areas of state law), the Government Publishing Office site at govinfo.gov (excellent for the *Federal Register, Code of Federal Regulations,* the United States Code, and congressional materials), and Congress.gov for federal legislative resources.

All of these sites offer cost-effective alternatives to Bloomberg Law, Lexis, and Westlaw. However, the sites lack editorial enhancements such as headnotes and Key Numbers, links to related legal publications, validation, and citing services. You might find the searching to be a little less user-friendly, and the sites lack many of the on-screen buttons where you can point and click to filter the documents you retrieve. Additionally, many of these sites have materials only from the past 25 years, so they may lack the depth of coverage. If you do not need enhancements or validation and are looking for a specific case, statute, or rule, this may be the avenue to pursue. Always be sure to update and validate any primary source that you will use.

CHAPTER SUMMARY

Computerized legal research opens up a vast realm of research possibilities for the paralegal. You are no longer limited to the resources available at your firm or school library. This chapter introduced you to the basic skills and concepts required to use Lexis and Westlaw, the two major online legal research systems. Bloomberg Law is mentioned, as it is an emerging player in the commercial legal database field. Lexis and Westlaw were also compared to highlight each system's distinguishing features.

Search query formulation is now very easy with natural language integrated into the search bar. This is a Google-type search capability that we are all familiar with. You can filter the material you receive with on-screen buttons or you can refine your search query.

Effective research online comes with careful planning before accessing a commercial database. Take the time to do the training and to watch the videos provided by the services. Learn the vocabulary for your topic. Evaluate whether the expense of online services is justified and within the budget. All the services allow you to manage your work product, and they permit you to save your information in folders to read offline.

Commercial databases are an expensive but powerful research tool.

KEY TERMS

BCite

Bloomberg Law

Congress.gov

connectors

field

Government Publishing
   Office: govinfo.gov

KeyCite

Lexis

Lexis Plus

literal searching devices

natural language searching

query

restrictors

search

segment

Shepard's

www.supremecourt.gov

Westlaw

Westlaw Edge

EXERCISES

SELF-ASSESSMENT

1. What are connectors? Please provide examples of connectors used on Lexis and Westlaw.
2. What is a search query?
3. What is KeyCite on Westlaw?

PRACTICE SKILLS

Application Exercises

4. Is the Torrens system of registering title to real property adopted in your state? If so, locate the pertinent statute section from your state code and find a case from your state's supreme court discussing the Torrens system.

   a. How would you compose the query when searching for the statute section on Westlaw?

   b. How would you compose the query when searching for the statute section on Lexis?

   c. What is the search term or keyword that would appear in a document on point?

   d. How would you compose the query when searching for a state supreme court case discussing the Torrens system on Lexis? Print out the citation to the most recent case that you found.

   e. How would you compose the query when searching for a state supreme court case discussing the Torrens system on Westlaw? Print out the citation to the most recent case that you found.

   f. If you have Lexis available, Shepardize the citation that you used in part d. Print out this information.

   g. If you have Westlaw available, KeyCite the citation that you used in part e. Print out this information.

5. One fine autumn day, Jim and Jean decide to drive to the country in search of the perfect pumpkin. After driving an hour and a half, they pull into Pete's Pumpkin Patch, whose sign states "10,000 pumpkins—state's largest pumpkin patch!" Pete's Pumpkin Patch is packed with shoppers. Jim and Jean eye the perfect pumpkin. As Jim is reaching for the pumpkin, Bob reaches for the very same pumpkin. Bob is a little low on patience that day. Instead of offering to look for another pumpkin, Bob punches Jim right in the jaw. Jim wants to sue Bob for battery.

   The problem raises the issue of whether Bob has committed a battery by punching Jim. The attorney who you work for wants you to sign on to Lexis or Westlaw and find the statute for battery for your jurisdiction. If your jurisdiction does not have a battery statute, find a case discussing battery.
   a. How would you construct the query?
   b. What sources would you consult before going online to become aware of the terms or words that you would use in your query?
   c. How would you filter your search results to find the most relevant source?
   d. How would you validate the case?

6. Imagine that you are employed as a paralegal at a law firm in Detroit. A partner in the firm has just finished interviewing a client who lives in Munster, Indiana. The partner requests that you find out for him whether the courts of Indiana recognize the "Totten" trust as a valid legal instrument in that state.
   a. How would you educate yourself before going online?
   b. Formulate a search query based on the given information.
   c. How would you filter your search results to limit the results to an Indiana statute?
   d. How would you update and validate the authority?

7. Mrs. Donahue comes to your firm because she wants to sue her dentist for malpractice. On April 27, 2021, Mrs. Donahue went to her dentist to have a chipped bridge removed and replaced. In removing her bridge, the dentist broke her tooth. Mrs. Donahue had considerable pain due to the broken tooth. In addition, Mrs. Donahue incurred substantial expenses to repair the broken tooth and to replace the bridge with dental implants. Now that you have done some research and have read some cases, you are familiar with the vocabulary used in relevant court decisions. You are now best equipped to perform online research economically and efficiently.
   a. Use Lexis or Westlaw to find two cases after 1990 that are relevant to Mrs. Donahue's problem.
   b. Download the cases to a folder to read later.
   c. Shepardize or KeyCite the cases and save these results.

8. Use either Lexis, Westlaw, or Bloomberg Law to find any cases from the U.S. Court of Appeals discussing Megan's Law.
   a. What is your query?
   b. Print out the list of citations.
   c. Shepardize the cites on Lexis, KeyCite the cites on Westlaw, or use BCite on Bloomberg Law to validate the cases.
9. Use Westlaw to search *American Jurisprudence 2d* for references to easements in gross. Try to find one reference that defines an "easement in gross."

PRACTICE RULES

CHAPTER OVERVIEW

This chapter provides an overview of practice rules, the sources that contain these rules, and how to find primary and secondary authorities that explain and interpret these rules. You also learn how to ensure that the rule you are relying on is valid. For our purposes, this chapter primarily focuses on the many rules that surround litigation because these rules are the most comprehensive ones you will review and research as paralegals. Most techniques useful for researching these litigation rules also are useful for investigating other rules, such as rules regarding patent and trademark proceedings, workers' compensation, and other administrative law areas as well as ethics rules.

A. OVERVIEW OF RULES OF PRACTICE

▼ What Are Rules of Practice?

Rules govern the practice of law, especially litigation. Some of these rules also govern the conduct of the lawyers, the litigants, and the judges.

▼ What Rules Govern Procedures in the Federal Courts?

The most extensive set of procedural rules for litigation is the **Federal Rules of Civil Procedure.** These rules direct an attorney on how to conduct himself or herself when involved in a court proceeding. The rules cover matters such as the filing of a complaint to begin an action, service of the complaint on the defendant, the answer to the complaint and subsequent motions, and the discovery of information. Postjudgment motions and appeals also are addressed in these rules.

▼ Do the Federal Rules Control Proceedings in State Courts?

No. The federal rules control the course of a civil case pending in federal court only. They do not govern proceedings in any of the state courts. Within the confines of the federal courts, these rules are **primary binding authorities.** Many state courts have patterned their procedural rules after the federal rules. Therefore, the decisions interpreting the federal rules that are similar in nature to the state court rules sometimes are very **persuasive authorities** in the state courts.

▼ What Federal Courts Follow the Federal Rules of Civil Procedure?

All U.S. trial courts follow the federal rules. These rules are not applicable to the U.S. appellate courts or the U.S. Supreme Court. Nor do these rules generally apply in administrative proceedings. See Illustration 11-1.

▼ Are the Federal Trial Courts Governed by Any Other Rules?

The federal district courts also follow the **Federal Rules of Evidence** for motion practice and trial proceedings, and, in criminal cases, the courts are governed by the **Federal Rules of Criminal Procedure.** In addition, many federal courts have adopted a set of rules called **local rules of court** that dictate the small details of practice before each court. For example, the local rules of one district specify the details concerning the electronic filing of documents and motions, including the amount of margin required on a page. You should carefully review the local rules any time you have an action pending in a federal court. In addition to a set of local rules, some courts have general orders that have the effect of local rules. Be sure to note whether the court has such rules. Local rules also can vary among judges within the same court.

ILLUSTRATION 11-1.   Courts and the Applicable Rules

U.S. District Courts
Federal Rules of Civil Procedure
Federal Rules of Criminal Procedure
Federal Rules of Evidence
Local Rules of Orders

U.S. Appellate Courts
Federal Rules of Appellate Procedure
Federal Rules of Evidence
Local Rules of Orders

U.S. Supreme Court
Rules of the Supreme Court
Federal Rules of Evidence

U.S. Bankruptcy Courts
Federal Rules of Bankruptcy Procedure
Federal Rules of Evidence
Local Rules of Orders

▼ What Rules of Procedure Do Federal Appellate Courts Follow?

The U.S. Courts of Appeals follow the **Federal Rules of Appellate Procedure.** These rules are similar in nature to the Federal Rules of Civil Procedure because they are primary binding authority and can be researched in the federal codes and online. Pending changes to the rules can also be found online.

▼ What Rules Govern Practice Before the U.S. Supreme Court?

The **Rules of the Supreme Court** control practice before that Court. Again, these rules are primary binding authority.

ETHICS ALERT

Courts such as the U.S. Supreme Court may sanction attorneys for failing to follow court rules. Be certain to check not only federal or state rules for the court, but local rules as well.

PRACTICE POINTER

If you are assisting with litigation, be sure that you know what general and local rules govern your work. Read those rules carefully.

B. RESEARCHING RULES OF PRACTICE

1. Sources

▼ Where Do You Find These Rules? Are the Federal Rules
Available Online?

The U.S. Courts website, https://www.uscourts.gov/rules-policies, provides links to the Federal Rules of Civil Procedure as well as amendments and proposed amendments to the rules. In addition, it offers full PDF texts of the Federal Rules of Criminal Procedure, the Federal Rules of Appellate Procedure, and the Federal Rules of Bankruptcy Procedure. This court website also provides links to local federal court rules. Lexis and Westlaw offer the Federal Rules of Civil Procedure, the Federal Rules of Appellate Procedure, the Federal Rules of Criminal Procedure, the Federal Rules of Evidence, and the Rules of the United States Supreme Court, as well as some state and local federal court rules. Links to district and appellate federal courts are found at www .uscourts.gov. In addition, information concerning the rulemaking process, proposed rule changes, and commentary are available at the U.S. Courts website. Most individual court websites provide their local rules.

All federal rules of civil and criminal procedure, the evidentiary rules, the appellate procedure rules, and the Supreme Court rules, as well as the bankruptcy rules and official forms, are found in the *United States Code* (U.S.C.), the official federal code published online and printed by the government, as well as annotated statutory codes, *United States Code Annotated* (U.S.C.A.), published by Thomson Reuters and available on Westlaw, and the *United States Code Service* (U.S.C.S.), a LexisNexis product accessible on Lexis. Fastcase also provides federal court and state court rules online. The U.S.C. is available at www.govinfo.gov. Also, PDF versions of the rules are provided at the uscourts.gov website. These PDF files also include historical notes, a table of contents, and a full copy of the rule and the last date it was amended.

When you need an interpretation of a rule, annotated code versions are the best sources to consult. The drafters' commentary is found in the official U.S.C. These codes are discussed in detail in Chapter 7. Several publishers produce the local federal court rules, but the best sources of these rules are the courts' websites. Phone and tablet applications also provide annotated and non-annotated compilations of the federal, state, and local rules. Attorneys and paralegals also still use attorney deskbooks. These are usually paperback books that contain a set of federal, local, and sometimes state rules. These are updated annually.

> ## PRACTICE POINTER
>
> Be certain that the rules found on the Internet are from official rule sources before you rely on them.

2. Steps in Researching Rules and Court Decisions

▼ How Do You Research a Federal Rule?

First, review the rule using one of the online sources listed above or in print in the U.S.C., U.S.C.A., or U.S.C.S. Each of these print publications has an index that allows users to find rules by topic. Next, you will want to locate court decisions and possibly secondary authorities that explain and interpret the rule.

▼ How Do You Find Cases or Secondary Authorities That Interpret and Explain the Federal Rules?

The annotated codes contain excerpts of cases that explain and interpret the federal rules, as well as references to secondary sources such as encyclopedias and law review articles. The research strategy is similar to that involved in researching other statutory materials, explained in Chapter 7, where there is also a complete discussion of the use of annotated codes.

Although some cases that deal with the federal rules are found in the Thomson Reuters *Federal Supplement* or the *Federal Reporter,* many are published in a separate reporter called the **Federal Rules Decisions.** This reporter contains federal civil and criminal cases that focus on the federal rules. These cases have not been designated for publication in the *Federal Supplement.*

In addition to the annotated codes, selected secondary sources such as looseleaf services and treatises focus on the federal rules. The *Federal Rules Service,* 3d published by Thomson Reuters, contains the text of the federal civil rules, local district and appellate rules, and annotations concerning cases, law review articles, and other secondary sources that interpret and explain the rules. This service includes headnotes. The service has a topical digest system with headnotes and an index to its digest similar to the digests discussed in Chapter 4. The *Federal Rules Digest,* 3d, also published by Thomson Reuters, helps you locate cases interpreting the federal rules.

The *Federal Rules of Evidence Service* can assist you in researching the evidence rules. Also published by West, this service includes a digest that includes civil and criminal cases that interpret the Federal Rules of Evidence. Headnotes are used as well as an index system. The *Federal*

Rules of Evidence Digest, also published by Thomson Reuters, is a valuable resource. For more information about how to use this digest, review Chapter 4.

▼ What Sources Are Available to Help Interpret These Rules?

Two multivolume treatises, *Federal Practice and Procedure,* known as Wright and Miller, its original authors, and published by Thomson West is a widely regarded and very persuasive secondary authority that explains the federal rules and provides references to primary and secondary authorities. It continues to be updated. *Moore's Federal Practice* is another well-respected treatise about the Federal Rules of Civil Procedure. It contains the text of each of the Federal Rules of Civil Procedure as well as analysis and secondary information to help researchers understand the rules.

Many circuits have handbooks that are prepared by local bar federal courts committees or the courts. These guides provide you with background and practical information about the courts as well as the time frame and procedure for filing appellate documents. If you are dealing with the Seventh Circuit Court of Appeals, a good reference book is the *Practitioner's Handbook for Appeals to the United States Court of Appeals for the Seventh Circuit,* found online at the court's website, http://www.ca7.uscourts.gov/rules-procedures/Handbook.pdf. Other circuits have similar handbooks or instructions on their respective websites.

When you Shepardize a federal rule online or use KeyCite to validate a rule, secondary resources often are provided. Another useful resource for interpreting federal rules are the federal rules committee comments concerning any changes in the rules or the committee's commentary regarding the purpose and origin of the rule.

Do not forget to consider resources such as encyclopedias, legal periodicals, and the A.L.R. series. For more information about these sources, see Chapter 6.

Consider a review of the federal digests under the topic Federal Civil Procedure for the federal civil rules and other related topics for other sets of federal rules. These digests provide citations to primary and secondary authorities. For a more detailed explanation of how to use the digests, consult Chapter 4.

▼ How Would You Cite the Various Federal Rules?

The federal rules should be cited in accordance with *Bluebook* **Rule 12.9.3** and *ALWD* **Rule 16.1(b)** as follows:

Fed. R. Civ. P. 56
Fed. R. Crim. P. 1
Fed. R. App. P. 26
Fed. R. Evid. 803

Only include the year when the rule is no longer in force by providing the most recent year that it appeared and the year repealed. For example:

Fed. R. Civ. P. 9 (2006) (repealed 2008)

▼ How Would You Cite a Decision Contained in the *Federal Rules Decisions?*

The abbreviation for the *Federal Rules Decisions* is F.R.D. in both the *ALWD* and the *Bluebook* citation guides. A case would be cited according to *Bluebook* and *ALWD* as follows:

Barrett Indus. Trucks v. Old Republic Ins. Co., 129 F.R.D. 515 (N.D. Ill. 1989).

C. STATE RULES OF PRACTICE

▼ What Rules Control the Conduct of State Proceedings?

Most states have adopted rules of civil and criminal procedure. Many of these rules are patterned after the Federal Rules of Civil Procedure or the Federal Rules of Criminal Procedure. Some states have adopted evidence codes, while others rely on the common law and have not approved any evidentiary codes. Note that some of the states that have not adopted evidence codes rely on the Federal Rules of Evidence for guidance. The rules of the state courts control conduct similar to that dealt with in the federal rules. For example, the federal rules describe the procedure and the requirements for the dismissal of a case. Similarly, under some state codes, the rules explain the circumstances that would allow a court to dismiss a case and the procedure to follow to obtain such an order. In addition to state codes, many state courts have local rules or orders similar to local rules issued by the federal courts. Again, check with these courts to determine whether such rules exist for each court.

▼ Where Would You Find State Rules and Local Rules for State Courts?

Many state court websites have links to the state and local rules. The states often include the rules of criminal and civil procedure and the evidentiary rules in their statutory codes. Many bar association websites also offer links to the rules, and several commercially published attorney directories, in print and online, provide the state and local orders of courts in the area covered by the directory. In addition, these rules are available on Westlaw and Lexis. Several tablet and phone applications provide full versions of state rules.

▼ Are Annotations for State Rules Available?

Yes, many annotated statutory codes contain references to cases and secondary authorities that explain or interpret the state procedural rules. These codes can be used in a manner similar to that of the federal annotated codes. For more information about how to use these annotated codes, see Chapter 7.

▼ Are There Any Significant State Rule Treatises or Secondary Authorities?

Each state's set of rules varies, as does the type and number of secondary authorities available to you as researchers. Check with your librarian for relevant materials. Consider reviewing the materials discussed above, such as federal treatises, and those discussed below, such as continuing legal education materials. These may be helpful because the states' rules often are patterned after the federal rules.

D. ENSURING CURRENCY

▼ How Do You Ensure That You Are Reviewing the Most Current Version of the Rule?

You must use online resources to ensure that the rule is valid and current. First, you should both Shepardize the rule online and perform a KeyCite search. Validating a rule also helps you to find cases and other authorities that cite the rule. Validate both federal and state rules by following the same procedures used for the process for cases and statutes. For a more detailed explanation, consult Chapters 5 and 7.

In addition, many court websites will provide information about pending rule changes and recent amendments. It is essential that you review these websites. However, not all court websites may be up to date.

▼ Can State Rules Be Shepardized?

Yes. State rules can be validated using *Shepard's*® or KeyCite.

CHAPTER SUMMARY

The rules that govern the conduct of cases brought before courts vary depending on the court in which an action is pending. Federal rules govern proceedings in the federal courts, and state rules control actions in the state courts.

These rules are primary authorities and generally can be found in statutory compilations online and in print. They also are contained in reference books called deskbooks. The statutory compilations can direct you to cases that interpret and explain these rules. Secondary authorities such as treatises and legal periodicals often explain these rules and provide you with citations to other primary authorities, including cases that focus on the rules. Many rules are available online.

These rules are validated in a manner similar to statutes. When you validate a rule, you also find additional citing authorities.

The next chapter explains ethical rules and how to locate them, as well as how to find cases that interpret these rules. You also learn how to validate the rules.

KEY TERMS

attorney deskbooks
Federal Rules of Appellate
   Procedure
Federal Rules of Civil Procedure
Federal Rules of Criminal
   Procedure

Federal Rules Decisions
Federal Rules of Evidence
local rules of court
persuasive authorities
primary binding authorities
Rules of the Supreme Court

EXERCISES

SELF-ASSESSMENT

1. Find Federal Rule of Civil Procedure 12 in an online source.
   a. What does this rule address?
   b. Where did you find this rule?
   c. Now find the rule online from an official source. Where did you find it?
2. What set or sets of rules or orders apply to cases pending in the U.S. District Court in your state or area?
3. Where can you find the U.S. District Court rules for your state or area online?
4. What set or sets of rules or orders apply to motions and briefs in a case before the U.S. Circuit Court of Appeals in your state or area?
5. Where can you find the rules for the U.S. Circuit Court of Appeals that covers your state online?
6. What set or sets of rules or orders apply to a trial in a federal court?
7. What set or sets of rules or orders apply to a trial in your state court?
8. What set or sets of rules apply to attorneys practicing in the bankruptcy courts generally?
9. List four online sources that contain the U.S. bankruptcy rules.
10. What federal rule concerns a motion to dismiss for lack of jurisdiction?
11. What rules govern practice before the U.S. Supreme Court and where would you find these rules online?
12. What sources contain citations to cases and other authorities that interpret or explain the federal rules?
13. Where would you find rules for the Indiana Supreme Court on the Internet?
14. List a phone or tablet application that provides the full text of practice rules.

PRACTICE SKILLS

15. Find rules on the Internet that concern juvenile procedure in Ohio.
16. Find a local rule concerning pro se parties in the family division of Florida's 11th Judicial Circuit Court. Explain the steps you took to find it and list where you found it. What is the rule number? What does number 1 in the rule specify?

ETHICAL RULES

CHAPTER OVERVIEW

In Chapter 11, you learned about procedural rules. In this chapter, the discussion concerns ethical rules. You learn where to find these rules in print and online and how to retrieve primary and secondary authorities that explain or interpret these rules. You also are shown how to locate ethics opinions, both in print and online. Finally, you are taught about ensuring the currency of these rules.

A. RULES OF PROFESSIONAL RESPONSIBILITY

For the practice of law, individual states determine the rules that regulate the conduct of lawyers. Some of those rules dictate an attorney's

ethical behavior, while others control an attorney's **ability to practice**, such as state licensing rules.

Each court has rules that govern the conduct of lawyers and litigants. Many state courts also have rules that regulate the activities of lawyers who never appear in court. For example, the high courts in many states have rules concerning licensing and registration of attorneys. You always should consider whether any rules exist that govern your conduct or the litigation process in which you are involved. Some rules specify how attorneys must supervise paralegals.

Paralegals must be able to research ethical rules that control the conduct of attorneys and their staffs.

ETHICS ALERT

Attorneys are responsible for ensuring that paralegals follow the rules that govern attorneys. However, you must know what rules to follow so that you do not jeopardize your supervising attorney or your job.

▼ Is There a National Code of Ethics for Attorneys or Paralegals?

No. Each state has its own set of rules that control the conduct of attorneys. Lawyers must follow these rules of conduct. Attorneys also must supervise paralegals and ensure that they also follow these rules. Most, but not all, state ethics rules are patterned after the American Bar Association's (ABA's) *Model Rules of Professional Conduct*, available free on its website. These rules govern issues such as conflicts of interest; client confidentiality; communications; fairness; responsibilities of supervisory lawyers, law firms, and associations regarding nonlawyer assistants; unauthorized practice of law; disqualification from a case; and the reporting of professional misconduct. In most cases, the rules require that attorneys ensure that paralegals follow the same rules designed for attorneys. Paralegals cannot be sanctioned for failing to follow the rules directed at attorney conduct. However, they offer paralegals some direction in how to conduct themselves. In addition to the rules of professional responsibility, cases that interpret the rules also govern the conduct of lawyers.

Also, both major paralegal organizations—the National Federation of Paralegal Associations (NFPA) and the National Association of Legal Assistants (NALA) — have addressed the conduct of paralegals, as have the Standing Committee on Paralegals of the American Bar Association and the ABA House of Delegates. The standing committee drafted the ABA Model Guidelines for the Utilization of Legal Assistant Services, and the ABA House of Delegates first adopted these guidelines in 1991. These were last revised in 2018 and arc found on the ABA website, https://www.americanbar.org/content/dam/aba/administrative/paralegals/ls_prlgs_modelguidelines.pdf. Most states have since adopted state recommendations or guidelines for the use of paralegals. NFPA first adopted a Model Code of Ethics and Professional Responsibility and Guidelines for Enforcement in 1993. In 1997, it adopted the Model Disciplinary Rules. The current version of the NFPA model rules and code is published online at https://www.paralegals.org/files/Model_Code_of_Ethics_09_06.pdf. These rules and the code are advisory only. NFPA also issues and in some cases publishes advisory ethics opinions under the Ethics tab on its website.

NALA adopted its NALA Code of Ethics and Professional Responsibility in 1975 and has revised it multiple times. The current version is available on its website. NALA also has adopted the Model Standards and Guidelines for the Utilization of Paralegals. This publication summarizes case law, guidelines, and state ethics opinions.

▼ What Type of Authority Are These State Rules of Attorney Conduct and Cases That Interpret These Rules?

Rules adopted by a jurisdiction and the subsequent court decisions are primary binding authorities. The *ABA Model Rules of Professional Conduct* is a secondary authority, as are any of the drafters' comments about the origin and purpose of these rules. However, these ethics rules and comments are very persuasive secondary authorities because most state ethics codes or rules are patterned after the ABA models.

▼ When Would You Review the Rules for Ethical Conduct and the Applicable Cases?

You will be asked to review the ethical rules whenever issues involving ethics are presented. Self-interest also demands that you be familiar with the rules. You must follow the rules that govern attorneys. As clients, attorneys, and paralegals become more mobile, conflicts of interest have become a frequent topic for research.

B. RESEARCHING ETHICAL QUESTIONS

1. Primary Sources and Annotated Sources

Many rules of professional responsibility are contained within the codifications of the state's statutes. To find cases, you would use the annotated sources. Most states' ethics rules and opinions are available online at the state court website.

▼ What Is the Value of an Annotated Source for the Rules and Codes?

The annotated rule sources are valuable in a manner similar to the annotated codes. These sources provide citations to primary authorities, such as court decisions, that interpret the rules and citations to secondary authorities such as treatises, and law review articles. See Chapter 7 for additional discussion of annotated codes. Some looseleaf publishers also publish ethics cases.

▼ Where Can You Find the *ABA Model Rules of Professional Conduct?*

An excellent secondary source for your research is the ABA Model Rules found at the ABA's website. This organization publishes the *Annotated Model Rules of Professional Conduct,* a comprehensive guide to the application of these ethics rules for lawyers. The annotated rules book contains the full text of the rules coupled with citations to any interpretations of the rules in court decisions or informal and formal ABA opinions. This source also includes the drafters' commentary about the purpose and design of each rule. It is available for purchase on its website as both a printed publication and e-book.

▼ What Other Secondary Sources Are Useful for Ethics Researchers?

In addition to the ABA annotated sources, many states have annotated guides for their rules of professional conduct. The ABA Center for Professional Responsibility provides online and print resources concerning attorneys' and paralegals' ethical obligations. One valuable publication is called the *Paralegal's Guide to Professional Responsibility* 5th ed., published in 2019. It is available for purchase on the ABA website.

▼ How Do You Use the Annotated Sources?

The best methods for using each of these sources generally involve a review of the table of contents online. The ABA annotated model rules, for example, lists each rule in the table of contents and the subparts. This method is useful if you already know what rule you wish to review. Under the rule is a list of the topics covered by the rule. You could read through each heading to see if the rule applies to your situation. Then click the hyperlink to access the rule. Comments to the rules also are provided.

2. Other Useful Authorities

The ABA and many state and local bar associations render **advisory ethics opinions** for attorneys. These opinions are secondary authorities. Although an **ABA opinion** is a secondary authority that has no force of law, in the ethics area, it is often a very persuasive authority because many ethics rules or codes that govern lawyers are based on the ABA models. The opinions generally are issued after a party requests that the ABA provide such an opinion.

NET NOTE

The ABA Center for Professional Responsibility provides summaries of some of the most recent ABA ethics opinions online at the ABA website. In some cases, the entire opinion is available. The indexes and full opinions can be obtained from the ABA. However, nonmembers will pay a fee for some opinions.

PRACTICE POINTER

Advisory ethics opinions often are excellent sources of rules and cases.

▼ Do State Bar Associations Publish Ethics Opinions Similar to Those Prepared by the ABA?

Yes. Some organizations publish pamphlets or books that contain their opinions while others can be found by reviewing continuing legal education materials, which are discussed in Chapter 13. Some are accessible through the Internet, and others are available from online services.

3. Research Process

▼ How Would You Research an Ethical Question?

First, you would review the rule. Second, you should review any annotations, especially those found in the annotated codes or the annotated rules online or comments. Thomson Reuters Westlaw ("Westlaw") and Lexis provide the rules of professional conduct online. Bloomberg Law also offers ABA ethics opinions, the model rules, practice guides, and state ethics opinions. Next, read any cases or informal and formal opinions. Shepardize or do a KeyCite search of any court ethics cases. Sometimes it is necessary to study a secondary authority to better understand an ethical dilemma. If necessary, perform a search of the rule on the computer to see if any additional cases can be found.

▼ Can You Find State Ethical Rules and Opinions on Westlaw and Lexis?

You can review the ethical rules and perform searches for authorities that discuss these rules on both Lexis and Westlaw. You can access many state ethics rules and opinions on both services. These databases contain secondary authority that has not been adopted in total by any jurisdiction. However, this secondary authority is very persuasive because most states have patterned their ethics rules according to the ABA Model Rules or the ABA Model Code of Professional Responsibility.

To find ethics information of particular interest for paralegals, see the NALA and NFPA websites and the ABA Standing Committee on Paralegals website at https://www.americanbar.org/groups/paralegals/.

▼ Can Ethics Rules Be Validated?

Yes. *Shepard's* lists authorities that cite the ABA Model Code sections, the ABA Model Rules, the Code of Judicial Conduct, opinions of the ABA Standing Committee on Ethics and Professional Responsibility, and state ethics rules and opinions. See Chapter 5 for more information concerning validating authorities.

4. Sample Research Problem

You have been asked to research a conflict of interest question. You work for an attorney who represented K. K. Industries in a matter against R. J. Enterprises in a contract dispute in 2020. R. J. Enterprises has now asked your boss to represent its company against Reynolds Wide Haulers in an unrelated contract dispute. Reynolds Wide Haulers, however, is the parent company of K. K. Industries. Your boss wants to know what rules govern such representation. Your firm is located in Ohio, which has adopted the *ABA Model Rules of Professional Conduct*.

First, brainstorm for possible search topics. Next, look in the index to the Ohio statutes. If you don't find any references concerning conflicts of interest, try the *ABA Model Rules*. One source would be the *ABA Annotated Model Rules of Professional Conduct*. You could look in the index under conflict of interest. You might find topics such as "existing client," "interest adverse to client," or "former client." You would then be directed to rules to review.

The text of each rule is contained in the annotated resource. After each rule is a comment section that explains the rule. There is a list of authorities, including primary authorities.

Next, you should review the authorities. Finally, you should validate the rule and authorities.

▼ How Would You Cite an Ethics Rule Found in the *ABA Model Rules of Professional Conduct*?

The rules for citation of ethics codes are found in *Bluebook* **Rule 12.9.4.** Rule 1.10 of the *ABA Model Rules of Professional Conduct* would be cited as follows:

Model Rules of Prof'l Conduct R.1.10 (2021)

The *ALWD* citation rules for the *ABA Model Rules of Professional Conduct* are found in **Rule 23** and would be cited as follows:

Model R. Pro. Conduct 1.10 (Am. Bar Ass'n 2021)

▼ How Would You Cite an ABA Ethics Opinion?

The rules for citation of ethics opinions are contained in *Bluebook* **Rule 12.9.5** and *ALWD* **Rule 16**. A *Bluebook* and *ALWD* citation of an ABA opinion would be as follows:

ABA Comm. on Prof'l Ethics & Grievances, Informal Op. 1526 (1988) — *Bluebook*

ABA Comm. on Pro. Ethics & Grievances, Informal Op. 1526 (1988) — *ALWD*

CHAPTER SUMMARY

Each state has ethical rules that govern the conduct of lawyers and litigants. Many of these rules are patterned after the *ABA Model Rules of Professional Conduct.*

Often these rules are found in state statutory compilations or attorney deskbooks. The statutory codes provide references to other primary authorities, such as cases and related rules, and to secondary sources. A variety of secondary sources, such as treatises, legal periodicals, and A.L.R. annotations, explain and interpret these rules and include citations to primary authorities.

Many ethical rules are available online, as are some secondary sources that explain and interpret these rules.

In addition to state ethics opinions, the ABA and other bar associations issue advisory ethics opinions. These opinions are secondary authorities. However, they may be very persuasive authorities. These can be found online.

Both the ethics rules and opinions can be validated. The method for validating these authorities is similar to that used for cases, statutes, and rules governing court proceedings.

The next chapter will focus on practical resources that assist you in your research, such as continuing legal education materials, formbooks, and legal directories.

KEY TERMS

ABA Center for Professional
  Responsibility
ABA opinion
ability to practice

advisory ethics opinion
ethical behavior
*Model Code of Professional
  Responsibility*

Model Rules of Professional Conduct
National Association of Legal
  Assistants (NALA)

National Federation of Paralegal
  Associations (NFPA)

EXERCISES

SELF-ASSESSMENT

Find a formal American Bar Association opinion that considers confidentiality issues when counsel seeks to withdraw from a case for nonpayment of fees.

1. How did you find this case?
2. What is the number of this case?
3. What is the date of this case?
4. What Model Rule is at the center of this case?

PRACTICE SKILLS

You are working as a paralegal for a firm that is defending a personal injury action against a manufacturer of recreational bikes. The plaintiff, a resident of Findlay, Ohio, was injured while riding one of the bikes in an event known as the Hancock Horizontal Hundred. While working for the defendant's law firm, Cryer, Wolf and Nonnemaker, you attend depositions and strategy conferences between counsel representing the defendant and counsel representing the codefendant. You had many conferences with witnesses, transcribed statements, and prepared letters to clients after reviewing the files. Although you are working hard on this case, billable hours throughout the firm are down, and you are laid off. You are given two weeks to find a job.

A sole practitioner in Findlay, a town of 25,000, tentatively offers you a job, but you first must do some research. This attorney represents the plaintiff in the above-mentioned action. Before the practitioner will allow you to begin work, you must research whether his firm can hire you and whether the firm can continue to represent the plaintiff in this action.

5. Map out your research plan. What sources will you consult?
6. For each source, note whether you will find secondary or primary authority or both.
7. As you list each print source, note your next step and why you would go to the next source.

PRACTITIONER'S MATERIALS

CHAPTER OVERVIEW

In the preceding chapters, you have learned how to find primary and secondary authorities and how to use the resources that contain these authorities. This chapter focuses on some practical sources, such as formbooks and continuing legal education materials, for you to consider. In addition, you learn about jury instruction sources and how and when to use them.

A. FORMS

Some courts, such as bankruptcy courts, require specific forms. Also, some types of legal documents must be drafted in the statutory form established by the state's legislature. For example, in many states that have living will statutes, living wills must be drafted using the statute's "magic language" to be valid. To assist you in drafting such documents with the appropriate language, some publishers have compiled forms. These often include many federal and state court forms as well as examples of forms that contain the language appropriate for a particular statute. Other forms such as wills provide suggested draft documents for users. These forms can save you time and help in your drafting. However, you must be careful when using these standardized forms for drafting documents that are not standardized, such as wills. Ideally, these forms properly incorporate the language that would make the document legally valid in your state. That, however, is not always the case. Be careful to see whether the form is up to date.

PRACTICE POINTER

You must know what language the current law requires or double-check with the court if you are using a court form. Do not substitute your independent judgment when you use these forms.

Some forms, such as those offered by Thomson Reuters, include references to authorities and library sources such as Key Numbers and encyclopedia materials. However, these books are generally used only for forms.

▼ Where Can Forms Be Found?

Many publishers offer court formbooks. In the probate, real estate, and transaction areas, a variety of publishers issue forms. Forms are available online through Westlaw and Lexis as well as at federal and state court and agency websites. Many can be downloaded in a format that allows the user to customize the form. Westlaw, for example, has a Form Finder. Depending on your subscription, you can limit your content search to the Form Finder and select a particular state. The United States Courts' website, https://www.uscourts.gov/forms/bankruptcy-forms, offers forms for bankruptcy cases. Other forms also are available from the www.uscourts.gov website.

ETHICS ALERT

If you use a form and change it substantially, be certain that an attorney reviews it. Otherwise, this could be considered the unauthorized practice of law.

PRACTICE POINTER

Always check if a specific form is required by statute or rule.

B. OTHER PRACTITIONER'S MATERIALS

1. Checklists

▼ Do Any Publications or Websites Contain Lists of What Steps You Should Follow to Complete a Project?

Many commercial publishers produce **checklists.** These checklists are for a variety of topics, such as estate planning, routine corporate matters, or matrimonial matters. Some checklists provide citations to authorities. Most are updated regularly.

In addition to the commercial checklists, many bar associations, such as the Georgia Bar Association, also offer free checklists on their websites. Here is a link to a Georgia Divorce Action Checklist found on the Georgia Bar Association website: https://www.gabar.org/committeesprogramssections/programs/lpm/upload/dac.pdf. Continuing legal education materials often contain checklists and practical information that may be as valuable for paralegals as it is for lawyers.

Some courts now provide checklists. For example, the Utah Court of Appeals provides appellate court checklists in PDF format at www.utcourts.gov.

NET NOTE

You can search the Internet for checklists. If you enter the term "legal checklists" into various search engines, you will find many such lists. Be careful to consider whether the source is reputable or not.

---

2. Continuing Legal Education Materials

Continuing legal education (CLE) materials generally explain an area of the law. They tend to be written by individual attorneys who are respected practitioners in a particular area. Within each state, a variety of CLE materials are available. These are secondary authorities and have little or no persuasive value. Therefore, do not cite these materials to a court. However, they can be invaluable tools in helping you learn about any area of the law. Many of the materials lack adequate indexes. You generally must use the table of contents, which may not be comprehensive enough for your needs. However, for new areas of the law, these materials might be your only secondary source of information. Often bar associations present seminars with accompanying CLE materials whenever a major change in the law is made. Many law firms and nonprofits offer free CLE materials.

▼ Are CLE Materials Available Online?

Some national and state CLE publications can be found online on Westlaw and Lexis. Some bar associations also provide these materials at their websites. Many law firms and nonprofits offer materials online.

3. Handbooks

▼ What Other Valuable Practitioner's Materials Are Available?

Several publishers produce **handbooks** that provide you with special information about a specialized type of practice such as estate planning, real estate, or trial practice. Sometimes they contain research references and case citations as well as trial aids.

4. Jury Instructions

Jury instructions are provided to juries after they are sworn in and before they deliberate in a case. These instructions explain to the jury members their duties and the applicable law in the case they are considering. In general, attorneys representing all litigants have an opportunity to draft jury instructions and work with a judge to develop a fair and accurate statement of the law that the jurors should be told to apply. Paralegals often assist in finding the appropriate instruction or in the drafting of the instructions. Improperly drafted jury instructions can affect the outcome of a case. Some jury instructions reference books are similar to formbooks because they provide you with sample instructions. Others, however, are pattern or approved instructions.

▼ What Are Pattern Jury Instructions, and How Do They Differ from Other Jury Instructions?

Pattern or **approved jury instructions** must be used in many states. In several states, practitioners must use their state's pattern instruction if one exists concerning a specific point. If an instruction does not exist or if it inaccurately states the current law, then an attorney can submit a proposed jury instruction that varies from the pattern instruction. Be certain that the jury instructions, especially criminal instructions, are up to date. Check the regular supplementary pamphlets. In all cases, review the law and the jury instructions in tandem. Some states have "model" or sample jury instructions that they treat similar to pattern or approved instructions. Often verdict forms on which juries enter their findings are included in both the pattern and model jury instructions.

PRACTICE POINTER

Always determine whether pattern or approved instructions are required.

ETHICS ALERT

Failure to use pattern or approved jury instructions may result in sanctions for an attorney.

Jury instructions generally contain the text of the instruction and case or statutory authorities from which the instruction was derived.

▼ Do the Federal Courts Have Pattern Jury Instructions and Where Can They Be Found?

Federal courts have pattern or model jury instructions. These instructions can be found at the court's website. Here is an example found on the United States Court of Appeals for the Third Circuit website, https://www.ca3.uscourts.gov/model-jury-instructions. Westlaw, Lexis, and Fastcase also have a selection of jury instructions online.

▼ What Type of Research Should Be Done Before You Draft Jury Instructions?

First, you should be somewhat familiar with the case and the underlying law of the case. However, if you are just asked to retrieve a jury instruction this may not be necessary. Jury instructions are read to the juries deliberating a variety of cases. Some jury instructions include references to primary authorities that often are the basis for the instruction. Sometimes these sources can be useful in finding primary binding authority. However, you should carefully read the source to ensure that it in fact states the law as described in the jury instruction.

5. Briefs, Docket Information, Oral Argument Transcripts, or Recordings

The U.S. Supreme Court offers some printed briefs at various depository libraries around the country such as the University of Louisville Law Library and the University of Texas Tarlton Law Library. Electronic versions are available through Westlaw, Lexis, and Docket Alarm, a Fastcase company. Courts often supply docket information online even if they do not provide copies of court documents online. Oral arguments or transcripts also may be available from various appellate courts and the U.S. Supreme Court. The U.S. Supreme Court provides argument transcripts from October 2017 to the present at https://www .supremecourt.gov/oral_arguments/argument_transcript/2020. You can access the transcript for the Mahanoy Area School District case shown in Illustration 3-1 at https://www.supremecourt.gov/oral_ arguments/argument_transcripts/2020/20-255_869d.pdf.

6. Other Tools

▼ What Other Tools Might a Paralegal Use in
Researching a Problem?

Use your ingenuity when researching any problem. Often you are asked to research factual questions as well as legal questions. For example, your firm might want some information about a corporation one of your clients hopes to acquire, and you have been asked to find as much information as possible. One source would be *Dun & Bradstreet*—the producers of *D&B Hoovers™*, which provides information about the corporate officers, the date of incorporation, and capitalization. Additional information often can be obtained from the state's Secretary of State or similar state agency that handles incorporations, registrations, and other state-required corporate documents. Federal agencies also provide factual information about companies.

Lexis is an excellent resource for full-text searches of company profiles, SEC filings, and articles from business and trade publications. It is updated daily and is invaluable when performing factual research on an individual, a corporation, or an event.

Bloomberg Law links to business information and news sources. This is one of Bloomberg Law's strengths.

CCH Intelliconnect contains information to track corporate actions, name changes, mergers, and stock splits.

The S&P NetAdvantage database provides stock reports, corporation reports, and mutual fund and bond reports.

PRACTICE POINTER

Public libraries often have many free databases that contain news articles and business information. Libraries often offer these databases online for remote use by patrons.

▼ How Do You Locate Lawyers and Law Firms in Other States or
Within a State?

A well-known source is the online *Martindale-Hubbell Law Directory*, which lists most attorneys nationwide. This is a voluntary directory, however, so some attorneys have chosen to be excluded. In addition to the free individual listings that include the person's name, address, degrees, and the name of the institute from which the person obtained his or her law degree, some firms pay to publish larger firm directories that list the firm, its areas of expertise, if any, the names of the individual attorneys, and a biography about each attorney. In addition, Martindale has a rating system for lawyers and features reviews. Martindale is available free at www.martindale.com. You can use the Lawyer Locator service in a variety of ways. You can search by lawyer, location and area of practice, by firm, by corporate law department, by U.S. Government Office, or by U.S. law faculty.

Other online lawyers' directories can be found on the Web.

Online services such as Westlaw also allow you to research opposing counsel. If opposing counsel practices in a specific area of the law, you may find relevant cases by researching her or his name in the database. You also will learn about the types of arguments counsel has made in such cases.

CHAPTER SUMMARY

Paralegals find that forms can be invaluable tools. Commercially published formbooks provide guidance in drafting real estate contracts, court motions, estate plans, and the like. However, these are only guides, and the paralegal should always double-check the accuracy and timeliness of the forms they contain.

Practitioner's materials such as checklists and continuing legal education books can be of great assistance to paralegal researchers. Checklists offer step-by-step guidance for handling a variety of legal matters ranging from a real estate closing to the preparation of a will. CLE materials generally concentrate on individual areas of the law and are particularly good at explaining new or developing legal topics. The type and variety of continuing legal education materials available vary by state.

Jury instructions are drafted when a case is presented to a jury. Various books and online sources provide sample jury instructions concerning various legal issues. When a state or court has adopted pattern jury instructions, these instructions must be used.

Legal directories provide information about lawyers, their law firms, and their practices. Some directories also include information about local court phone numbers, rules, and court reporters. There are national and local legal directories.

KEY TERMS

checklists

CLE materials

forms

handbooks

jury instructions

Martindale-Hubbell Law Directory

pattern jury instructions

EXERCISES

PRACTICE SKILLS

Forms
1. Find a sample power of attorney for your state. What source did you review and why? Specify whether it was an online or print source.

Checklists
2. Find a real estate closing checklist for a residential real estate closing. Where did you look and why?

CLE Materials
3. Find a continuing legal education book or materials other than those found at an attorney's website that covers estate planning in your state. Where did you look and why?

Jury Instructions
4. Locate a civil jury instruction for nominal damages in your state.
5. Find a criminal jury instruction for reasonable doubt.
6. Find a criminal jury instruction for the definition of *recklessly* in your state.

Jury Instructions Online
7. Access a state's pattern instructions and find the instruction that defines *exemplary or punitive damages*. List the location of the jury instruction and how you found it.
8. Access a federal pattern instruction that defines circumstantial evidence. List the location of the jury instruction and how you found it.
9. Find a federal jury instruction that explains *retaliatory discharge*. List the location of the jury instruction and how you found it.

Using the *Martindale-Hubbell Law Directory*
10. Search for an attorney in your community. Provide the name and some details from her or his biography.

RESEARCH STRATEGY

CHAPTER OVERVIEW

Research involves planning. The more planning, the more effective the research. This chapter gives you step-by-step techniques to use when researching. This chapter also provides an overview of research strategy to use as a reference when learning about the methods of using each source. Think of this chapter as a road map to legal research strategy. Read this chapter to get the big picture for the process of legal research. Go back to this chapter when you learn about the methods of using sources to see where the sources fit into the overall process of legal research.

Use this chapter as:

• A road map to legal research strategy.
• A preview of the steps you will take when performing legal research.
• A review after you explore the methods of using each type of resource.

Begin by educating yourself on a legal topic that pertains to the issue you are researching. You are then advised to note all of the pertinent information that you find during the research process so that you have a complete record of your findings and complete citations to those findings. Finally, you are reminded to update and to validate all of your findings.

Focusing on your issue and knowing when to stop researching are two skills that you must master. As a paralegal, you must always evaluate how much time it takes to research and to weigh costs and deadlines with accuracy and thoroughness. This chapter provides an overall strategy to help you effectively research a legal topic.

The main research tasks are to:

• Question
• Learn
• Find
• Evaluate
• Update
• Validate
• Record and cite

NET NOTE

At www.law.cornell.edu/wex/legal_research, Cornell's Legal Information Institute provides an overview of the main resource categories for legal research. Review this website's offerings to look at the "big picture" and to check on your thoroughness.

A. QUESTION: DEFINE THE ISSUES AND DETERMINE AREA OF LAW

▼ Where Do You Begin Your Research?

1. Question

We begin the research process with the question. The question is the issue you are asked to answer or to explore. What are you required to find? When you receive the assignment, you will be asked to find something, provide some information, or answer a question. You now have the opportunity to ask questions, too.

When you receive an assignment, determine:

- What law governs? Federal or state or municipal? Which jurisdiction?
- What is the area of law? Torts? Contracts? Real estate? Tax?
- What is the budget?
- What is the deadline?
- What is the format for the result? Memo? Brief? Text? Short e-mail? Letter?

2. Learn

Gather all facts that are relevant to your problem and define the legal issues. The **facts** and the law guide your research. Ask a lot of questions of the client and of the attorney who assigns the problem. Do a quick search on Google to get a few vocabulary terms and to get a very basic overview of the topic. The results from Google are not to be relied on as legal authority and are not validated legal authority but they will give you a glimpse at the big picture—such as whether a statute controls. The Google search will also provide the vocabulary for the topic or issue and the context for the words or terms (how the words or terms appear in proximity to each other). Check the firm's files to see if this issue was researched before. Clarify anything that is unclear. Frame the issue or review the issue framed by the attorney assigning the project.

Use secondary sources with broad coverage, like legal encyclopedias, to learn about an area of law. The legal encyclopedias, *American Jurisprudence and Corpus Jouris Secundum,* discussed in detail in Chapter 6, provide a general overview that is national in scope akin to *Encyclopedia Britannica's* coverage of a topic. The legal encyclopedia will provide the general rule on point. You will get citations to the significant cases and statutes. You will learn whether the topic is controlled by common law (cases) or by statutes. As paralegals, legal encyclopedias will likely provide the information you are looking for so you can locate cases and statutes on point.

Legal encyclopedias are particularly helpful when the issue involves state law and you do not know whether a statute or a case governs the situation. You can access Am. Jur. 2d on Lexis and on Westlaw. The appropriate statute citation would be included, too. When you know if a particular state's law is applicable, state legal encyclopedias are helpful in areas of state law research and enable you to find the general legal rule and citations to important cases for the particular jurisdiction quickly. If a case controls, a citation to the case would be included. For an overview of the law, in a format that is not too scholarly or detailed, use a legal encyclopedia. Also, legal encyclopedias are very efficient to search.

Legal encyclopedias provide you with citations to primary authority, cases, statutes, and regulations, but you must read the source and check if it is still good law. Before you rely on a cited case, statute, or regulation, always read the primary source yourself and always validate, with *Shepard's* or KeyCite, any source cited in a legal encyclopedia.

You will acquire a working vocabulary concerning the topic or issue when you read a legal encyclopedia on the topic. The working vocabulary is essential for successful online searching. You will learn the buzzwords and key phrasing. Additionally, you will come away with the knowledge of how the keywords are used in relation to other words—the context. This also is very helpful when constructing an online search on Lexis, Westlaw, or Bloomberg Law.

At times your knowledge of an area of law is incomplete, even after consulting a legal encyclopedia. You may need to consult additional secondary sources. The *American Law Reports,* the A.L.R., is a great source to consult when you have a narrow, well-defined legal issue. The A.L.R. provides a survey of the law on point concerning the issue. The A.L.R. is available on Lexis and on Westlaw. (See Chapter 6 for a detailed discussion on the A.L.R.)

Before exploring additional resources, consult the assigning attorney. Time and budget limitations may not permit you to perform more detailed research. If time and budget allow, hornbooks about a particular subject are also helpful because they explain the law in everyday language and indicate the legal rules and important cases. Generally, treatises are too detailed for the time constraints that you will be under; however, sometimes they may be valuable. (See Chapter 6 for a complete discussion of secondary sources.) Treatises may be valuable when you are searching for legal authority relating to an obscure issue.

Always be mindful of the time budgeted for the project when researching. Generally, you will be able to find the information you need to locate cases, statutes, and regulations by searching your topic in a legal encyclopedia. If you know the specific state's law that is at issue, then you can use a state legal encyclopedia. Here are the steps to take:

- Make a list of important terms or words that describe the facts and the legal problem.
- Jot down the research vocabulary you acquire from the secondary sources.

- List the cases and statutes that are mentioned that are on point.
- Create an online folder, through the commercial database, to hold the encyclopedia sections and the sources you read. These materials will help later when you perform targeted online research.
- Use a legal dictionary to look up any word or term that sounds unfamiliar. (See Chapter 6 for a discussion on secondary sources.)
- Note unusual facts. An unusual fact may help you narrow your research later on.

B. FIND THE AUTHORITY

▼ How Do You Find Authority?

At this point, you have refined the question and know what you are looking for. You know the jurisdiction, the budget, and the format of the work product you will create. You have educated yourself on the topic. You learned about the rules on the topic or issue by reading a legal encyclopedia. You looked up definitions of unfamiliar words in a law dictionary. You copied the citations to the cases and statutes on point. You learned if the issue is controlled by the common law—cases—or by enacted law—statutes.

If you find that a statute is involved, then use an annotated statute for the relevant jurisdiction to look up the statute section and to find cases that apply to the statute at issue. If the issue is controlled by statute, start your primary source research with an annotated code because statutes control in many issues. Annotated codes will include citations to cases that apply the code section so you can understand how the statute is used. You will look at cases that cite the statute on point because cases will help you determine how to apply and interpret the statute. Additionally, annotated statutes provide many references to other resources from the same publisher. For instance, on Westlaw, annotated codes also provide legislative history information. All annotated codes provide citations to cases that construe and apply the statute section and law review articles. The U.S.C.S., available on Lexis, provides administrative code references.

Administrative code references are essential when figuring out how to implement a code section. After you find the pertinent statute, read and update the corresponding regulations. Regulations provide insight into how the statute should be applied. Always update and validate administrative regulations. See Chapter 9 for a complete discussion of administrative materials.

When you use an annotated code on Lexis or Westlaw, the statute's updates are integrated into the material you retrieve. Updating is essential when using statutes because legislatures are continually revising, amending, and superceding legislation. See Chapter 7 for a detailed discussion on the method of researching with statutes.

If the statute is unclear or there seems to be more than one interpretation, you might have to perform a legislative history, which is very time consuming. Please be mindful of the time constraints and the budget before performing a legislative history. See Chapter 8 for a discussion of legislative history.

If the issue is controlled by the common law cases, read the cases mentioned in the encyclopedia. Even if the case is not from the appropriate jurisdiction, it will still help you learn about the topic. Once you find an excellent case or cases, even from another jurisdiction, go to the digests and use the one good case method to find cases from the appropriate jurisdiction. (See Chapter 4 for a detailed discussion on digest use.)

1. Evaluate

At this point, reexamine the issue that you formulated when you received the assignment. Review the vocabulary words that you listed to describe the legal issue and the factual scenario. Revise the issue to reflect your enhanced knowledge of the subject. Create an outline of the subissues. Remember the terms—review and refine—when you are performing research to find relevant information. Research involves educating yourself; as you learn more about an issue, your research becomes more focused and more precise. You will constantly refine your search.

Evaluate what you find. Ask yourself:

- Do the sources provide an answer to the question?
- Are the sources relevant?
- Are the sources recent?
- How similar are the sources in law and fact to your question or problem?
- Does the source provide a rule or test or standard that can be used to analyze the problem?

Stay focused on your issue or issues. While gathering relevant information, it is easy to stray into related but inapplicable areas. Staying focused on your issues also is cost effective because you do not waste valuable time on irrelevant information.

2. Update and Validate

Most important, once you find pertinent authority to address the issue that you are researching, you must update and validate the authority. Updating and validating authority is performed by using *Shepard's*® on Lexis or KeyCite on Westlaw. *Shepard's* and KeyCite provide citations showing how subsequent courts viewed the decision to indicate whether the case or the statute that you are relying on is still good law. The cited cases in *Shepard's* or KeyCite are also newer cases that interpret the legal rule you are researching. Remember to update your *Shepard's* information by consulting the hardcopy supplements. If you are using Lexis, validate the authority with *Shepard's*. If you are using Westlaw, use KeyCite. If time and money allow, use all of the updating and citing sources available online.

3. Record and Cite

Record keeping and **note taking** are essential to effective legal research because they leave a written audit trail of all the sources consulted and the information derived from those sources. Records should also include sources consulted that did not contain pertinent information so that you do not reexamine those sources if you must expand your research at a later time.

Make a list of each source that you consult. List sources, citations, and any information obtained from the consulted source. For example, you might find a useful A.L.R. annotation. Put the A.L.R. annotation at the top of the page in the correct *Bluebook* format. List all pertinent information relating to your research issue and the pages on which you found that information. Add to the sheet any pertinent cites to cases and to statutes listed in the source. The objective is to create a sheet of information that includes all of the relevant data obtained from the source consulted so that you do not have to go back and review the source again. This includes the precise pages, from within the text, where you obtained the information. Also, include information indicating whether you validated the source and the date Shepardized or KeyCited so that you may redo it if too much time lapses. Note any significant information obtained from *Shepard's* or KeyCite about the document, for instance, if the case was criticized.

When you find terrific sources that are on point, take the time to write out the complete citations in *Bluebook* or *ALWD* format for every source you use. Include the pinpoint citations to the precise page or paragraph where you located the information. Note as you read and indicate in parentheses the page on which you found the information from within the text of the source. This is the pinpoint citation. For instance, if the case begins on page 1382, but the holding is on page 1389, write out the holding and then indicate parenthetically (1389) so that you know exactly where the information was found within the document. Noting the pinpoint citation, as you research, will save you time later.

You will want to note the URL or the database (Lexis, Westlaw, Bloomberg Law, or Cornell's Legal Information Institute, for example) so that you can go back to the source. If you access the information on a site that you found via Google, include the complete URL and the date you visited the site. Establishing the complete citation at the time you are researching means you do not need to retrace your research steps to obtain citation information later on, particularly when you are writing.

4. Complete Your Research

After you complete the research strategy steps, go back to your secondary sources. You will understand the relationship between the sources more completely. Secondary sources do an excellent job of synthesizing primary sources, tying the sources together.

Your research is complete when:

- You used secondary authorities to learn about the issue.
- You located the general rules on point, regardless of jurisdiction.
- You determined if the common law or statutes control.
- You identified the general rules from the appropriate jurisdiction and read the sources.
- You read the primary sources you think you will use.
- You find the same authorities repeatedly when you look for more information.
- You updated and validated the sources you rely on.
- You include pinpoint citations for your sources so you can locate information later.
- You noted the URL and date visited for information retrieved on databases other than Lexis, Westlaw, or Bloomberg Law.
- You run out of time or exceed the project budget.

C. EXAMPLE OF RESEARCH STRATEGY

PROBLEM

The supervising attorney in your department wants to know if there are any rules concerning the labeling of wool products, including clothing and blankets. The attorney wants you to use federal law.

1. Question

You have an idea about the issue. Here, you will want to ask these questions:

- Are there any specific facts?
- Any particular sources you want me to consult?
- How much time should I spend? The deadline? The budget?
- What is the format for the result or answer?

How do you phrase the issue if you are researching the wool labeling problem?

ISSUE

Whether wool products must be labeled.

2. Learn

First, do a quick Google search to see a general discussion of wool labeling, what areas of law are concerned, and the types of resources you may find. The Google search was, "wool products" labeling. "Wool products" is in quotes, as we want the precise terms to appear very close together. When you run a Google search, the results are not necessarily updated or validated but do provide the most general overview so you can build a working vocabulary and know the types of resources to look for. A Google search doesn't always show the language from the most recent version of the statute but does indicate that the topic is controlled by statute, 15 U.S.C. §68. This is a huge head start.

Next, use secondary sources to educate yourself about the area of law. This helps you become familiar with the legal authority controlling the issue. The background research provides specific information indicating the precise statutes, cases, and possibly regulations that apply. If you did not know that the question is controlled by federal law, you would figure out whether state or federal law applies. You should develop a research vocabulary from your readings that helps you construct search queries more effectively. You will discover quickly that this issue is controlled by federal law and is regulated, even if you did not use Google at the start.

Start with a query to search Am. Jur. 2d on Lexis or Westlaw. Your query may be: ""Wool Products" and Label!" From your brief research on Google, you will know that "wool" should be close to "products" in the search. You will also know that you should use the word or term "products" and not "clothing" because "products" is broader. Your results will yield a limited amount of hits. An Am. Jur. Section labeled "Overview" provides the most general discussion, then the following sections go into more detail. You will learn that 15 U.S.C. § 68 is the relevant statute. In our issue, the section "Misbranding Under Wool Products Labeling Act" covers instances when the labeling was inaccurate. Last, the section called "Enforcement of the Wool Products Labeling Act" details compliance and penalties for failing to comply with the Act. You will see that statute sections are cited in the Am. Jur. 2d entries.

You can also search: ""Wool Product" w/s label!" This search is a terms-and-connectors search that uses the context of the terms, that they would appear in the same sentence. Also, the search maximizes how "label" may appear in a document, such as *labeling* or *labeled*.

All of the encyclopedia entries on the topic provide citations to statutes and cases. You can click on the citation to read the source. You will learn that there are statutes on point. You will also learn that there are cases that interpret and apply the statutes.

3. Find

After you learn that there are statutes on point, you can locate the statutes cited in Am. Jur. 2d on govinfo.gov. This would save the client money, as the government website is free. However, you will not get the publisher's references and annotations to cases. You also will not be able to validate the statute on the government's site. However, you can read the current statute, 15 U.S.C. § 68, on govinfo.gov.

After retrieving the relevant code section(s) regardless if you access the statute to read the text on govinfo.gov or Lexis or Westlaw, check the annotated statutes (U.S.C.A. is available on Westlaw and U.S.C.S. is available on Lexis) to see if any relevant cases are cited in the annotations discussing or analyzing the issue. See Illustration 7-6 for an example of 15 U.S.C.S. § 68. Read the statute sections and the cases quickly to see if they are relevant before proceeding. You should then validate any relevant case or statute with *Shepard's* or KeyCite. Note the dates you validate your sources so you can update this information later if necessary.

Shepard's and *KeyCite* are citators, too. Citators tell you where the source is cited in subsequent sources. (See Chapter 5.) When you find a statute or a case on point, you can use a citator to see where it is cited. This step will guide you to additional authorities on point. You might find additional cases that are not included in the annotated statutes. Generally, any source that cites your case or statute will generally have related facts and law.

You may also check if there are any federal regulations in the *Code of Federal Regulations* (C.F.R.) concerning wool labeling. (See Chapter 9 for discussion of administrative materials.) The U.S.C.S. will note if there are any regulations corresponding to the statute section. If you find a relevant regulation, you will have to make sure it is up to date and you will have to validate the cite. Validation also leads you to any newer cases discussing the issue.

4. Evaluate

After finding authorities, a thorough reading of the statutes and decisions is necessary. Do the sources provide an answer to the question? Are the sources relevant? You should make a list of all of the cites checked at this point. Does one source provide the general rule? Does a source provide commentary? Does a source use or apply the general rule in a factual scenario, a case? Which sources are most current? Always reexamine, review, and refine as you perform research. Try to stay focused on the issue.

5. Update and Validate

Use either *Shepard's* or KeyCite to check the validity of the primary source, the United States Code cite, 15 U.S.C. § 68. You will want to see if a statute or regulation is unconstitutional or invalid before relying on it. You will want to see if a case is criticized or overruled before relying on it. Place a check next to the cites that are valid. Add a check next to the cite after you have read the full text of the opinion or statute. This will save you time later if you expand your research. You can merely review your list of cites to see if it is valid and to see if you read the full text of the authority.

6. Record Keeping and Note Taking

Jot down all the sources you consulted. List the relevant authorities you found. Summarize the information you pulled from the authorities with the pinpoint citation indicating precisely where from within the source the information was found. This will help you later when you use the sources to write about the issue. Shepardize or KeyCite any primary source you will rely on and note the date that you validated the source.

At this point, you may want to outline the problem and insert your research findings in the relevant places. Include your citations.

7. Complete Your Research

Your research is complete when you:

- keep on finding references to the same statute, for instance, 15 U.S.C. § 68, and cases applying the statute.
- use a citator and do not find any additional cases.
- use an annotated statute, such as U.S.C.A. or U.S.C.S., and do not find any new links.
- validate primary authorities with *Shepard's* or KeyCite close to the time you will submit your work.
- allow time to write up your research findings in the format that the attorney requested.
- stay within the budget and try to be economical with your time.

▼ What to Do After Completing Your Research

Create a body of information for your discussion or answer to the question. At this point, you must create an outline of the issues and subissues to be addressed. Insert the appropriate legal authority under each outline category. Only expand your research if you do not have sufficient authority to answer the question.

Your detailed note taking and careful citation to references for each source are helpful when you begin to write. Also, keep your complete list of all sources consulted, whether a statute, case, regulation, encyclopedia section, or other source. Your list of sources consulted helps later on if you have a need for more information when you are writing. You can then check the list to see if you already reviewed a source and to see if it was pertinent.

Remember to validate. Shepardize or KeyCite any primary authority that you use in your memo, as this ensures that the authority, whether it is a case, statute, or regulation, is still good or valid law.

Outline the issues that you discuss in your memo or letter. Insert the applicable legal authority under the outline entry.

Review your outline and evaluate whether you have sufficient legal authority to support and to resolve the issues raised by the problem. If you have sufficient authority, begin to write. If you do not have sufficient authority, go back to your list of sources and expand your research. Check your notes and the list of materials found to help you avoid duplicating your efforts and wasting time.

SUMMARY CHECKLIST

1. When you receive the problem: Question
   a. Clarify legal issues being researched.
   b. Determine relevant jurisdiction.
   c. Determine area of the law.
   d. Determine the time required to complete the assignment: How much time should you spend? When is the assignment due?
   e. Determine the format for the answer or the work product: Will you draft a memo, a brief, a text, a short e-mail, a detailed letter?
   f. Gather all of the facts.
   g. Draft a statement of the issue or question that you are researching.
2. Introductory research: Learn
   a. Educate yourself in the area of law to learn the vocabulary and to see if statutes or cases apply.
   b. Do a quick Google search to see the language used, the vocabulary, on the topic.
   c. Learn the relevant vocabulary and use a law dictionary to define unfamiliar terms.
   d. Note the controlling statute and the major cases.
   e. Jot down the general rules on the topic: the tests, standards, and principles used.
   f. Make an outline of the issues and subissues of your problem.
3. Search for authority on point: Find
   a. Use a legal encyclopedia or if the issue is controlled by statute, an annotated statute to find discussion of the legal issue and relevant case and statute citations. Locate the sources that provide

the general rules on point. Acquire a working vocabulary on the issue so you can search effectively.

  b. If you find the general rule from a case cited in the encyclopedia, but from another jurisdiction, go to the digest for the relevant jurisdiction, and use the one good case method to find other cases.

  c. Consult the A.L.R. if you are researching a narrow, well-defined legal issue. Consult the A.L.R. if you did not obtain the needed information from an encyclopedia. The A.L.R. may not always have an annotation on your issue.

  d. Most efficient searching is performed after you obtain a general overview of the topic and you know the vocabulary used.

  e. Look for unique facts and narrow legal issues (for instance, whether malpractice occurred during the insertion of a chin implant), not broad (for instance, whether a breach of contract occurred).

  f. Be thorough and use reliable free government resources to read through statutes and regulations.

4. Evaluate

  a. Review the outline of the issues and subissues that you drafted.

  b. Refine the outline to reflect your increased knowledge of the subject.

  c. Always read any authority that you will rely on. Determine if the authority you found provides enough information.

  d. Summarize statutes and regulations. Brief cases (see Chapter 18) and relate them to one another (see Chapter 23).

  e. Determine if you have enough legal authority to answer the question or if you need more information.

5. Update and validate

  a. Update any statute or regulation to see if the legislature or the agency changed the language or the rule.

  b. Shepardize or KeyCite any case to find what subsequent courts say when the courts mentioned the case.

  c. Shepardize or KeyCite any statute or regulation to determine the validity of the source, whether the source is constitutional, unconstitutional, too broad, or too narrow.

  d. Shepardize or KeyCite to find other cites, as citators are terrific ways to find authority.

  e. Validate any primary source before relying on it as authority.

6. Create an audit trail of your research

  a. Take notes of sources and location, including page number, and write cites in *Bluebook* format to create pinpoint citations.

  b. Note if you found the source in a book, on Lexis, Westlaw, or Bloomberg Law. If you found the sources on an Internet site, note the URL and the date the site was visited.

  c. Note whether validation, Shepardizing or KeyCiting, has been completed and date completed.

7. Organizing your research findings
   a. Review the outline of the issues and the subissues that you created and revise it to reflect any new knowledge. (See Chapter 24.)
   b. Insert the applicable authority discussing the relevant subissue under the appropriate outline heading.
   c. Review the filled-in outline to make sure that you have found adequate authority to address each subissue listed.
   d. If you have sufficient legal authority, begin to write. If you do not have sufficient legal authority to answer the question, expand your research. Always check your list of sources consulted when you are expanding your research to make sure that you do not waste precious time with sources that you have already consulted.
   e. Stay within your time constraints and budget.

PRACTICE POINTER

Take advantage of any training offered at your firm or through legal publishers. Publishers and online database vendors offer training, very often for free, that will enhance your research skills and help you become familiar with new products. Sometimes existing products are very complex, and training will help you use the resources efficiently.

CHAPTER SUMMARY

This chapter led you through the entire research process from initially receiving the project to completing research. Refining the issue at the beginning and focusing on your important sources are as essential as knowing when to stop researching. This chapter and your own experience will guide you through this process. Keep records of all sources consulted and make sure that your citations are accurate; these help when you are ready to write. Also, do not forget to validate all necessary documents and to update all resources. Now you are equipped to write.

KEY TERMS

background research	record keeping
facts	research vocabulary
note taking	

EXERCISES

RESEARCHING IN GENERAL

1. Before you begin a research project, what general questions should you resolve with the assigning attorney?
2. What is the benefit of record keeping when researching?

RESEARCH STRATEGY

3. You have just received a research project. Outline your research plan.
4. Read the following fact pattern and answer the questions.

   John Clark comes to your firm with a question regarding the tax status of his residence. John Clark was just ordained as a Methodist minister. He will be receiving a housing allowance from First Methodist Church, where he will be an assistant pastor. He wants to know if this housing allowance can be excluded from income on his tax return even though the residence is his own.
   a. How would you phrase this issue if you were researching this problem using hardcopy resources?
   b. What would be your research strategy using hardcopy resources?
   c. List three sources that you would consult. Why would you consult them?
   d. Draw a flowchart of your research strategy using a combination of hardcopy and computerized resources.

SKILLS ASSESSMENT

Defining the Issues and Determining the Area of Law

5. Partner Harry Harold asked you to research the following fact pattern based on the law of your jurisdiction.

   Robert and Jan Moore live in Evingston, Anywhere, and are building an addition and repairing the gutters on their house on Ashville Street. There are eight feet between their house and the house belonging to Mrs. Jones, their neighbor. There is no alley in the back and no driveway that goes to their house. The properties are adjoining. The Moores' contractors and construction workers must enter Mrs. Jones's property to the north to perform their work. Mrs. Jones is not very pleased that the workers are entering her property. Mrs. Jones may be induced to permit the work if the Moores obtain a license from her. The Moores came to us to find out what is entailed in obtaining a license.
   a. What is the legal issue?
   b. What is the area of law that you would explore?
   c. What sources did you consult to ascertain the legal issue and the area of law, and why did you consult them? Name three.
   d. What is the query that you would use when searching on either Lexis or Westlaw?
   e. Diagram the research process.

6. What is the Torrens system? Is the Torrens system of registering title to real property adopted in your state? Provide your strategy to arrive at the answer.

7. Diagram the entire research process that you would follow to resolve the following question.

   What is your state's law regarding companies sending unsolicited goods to a consumer? This sometimes occurs with book clubs and subscriptions; when you join initially, you receive a book that you did not order. Be sure that your answer includes validating, Shepardizing, or KeyCiting, and updating your resources. Answers will vary according to jurisdiction.

PRACTICE SKILLS

8. Read the following fact pattern and answer the questions.

   On November 29, 2021, Michael Jones purchased a used truck from Grimy's Auto and Truck Service. At the time of purchase, Grimy's stated that the engine was completely overhauled and consisted of rebuilt and reconditioned parts, all parts were guaranteed, and invoices for all new parts would be provided. On November 14, 2022, after using the truck for almost one year, Jones discovered that several engine parts were not rebuilt or reconditioned and other engine parts were defective, which caused the truck to break down. This resulted in lost wages and lost profits for Jones. Jones made repairs to the truck on November 14, 2022, December 19, 2022, and December 21, 2022. Jones did not attempt to return the truck and did not notify Grimy's that the truck was defective. The truck is currently disabled in Columbus, Ohio. Jones came to your firm because he wants to sue Grimy's for damages for breach of contract.

   Is Jones entitled to receive damages for breach of contract because the truck does not conform to the terms of the agreement? Remember that Grimy's will assert that Jones continued to use the truck for more than a reasonable time and failed to return the truck or to notify Grimy's of its defects in a timely manner.

   a. What would be your overall research strategy?
   b. How would you educate yourself on the relevant topic so that you could find primary sources?
   c. List one secondary source and two primary sources that you would consult. How did you find the primary sources? Why would you consult these sources?
   d. Use either Lexis or Westlaw and formulate a search query that you could use to find primary authority.

9. You are a paralegal with the Law Office of Warren T. Sales. You have been asked to research the following questions and provide answers. These are the facts that Mr. Sales presented to you.

   Your client is Sue A. Seller. She lives at 3225 Wilmette Avenue, Glenview, Yourstate. The defendants are Lee R. Merchant, owner of Mowers-R-Us, in Glenview, Yourstate, and Manny U. Facture, the owner of a manufacturing concern, which is not incorporated, called Mowers, of Rosemont, Yourstate. Ms. Seller went to the defendant's store, Mowers-R-Us, to purchase a lawnmower for her new home. She was a first-time homeowner. She was unfamiliar with lawnmowers. She had never operated a lawnmower because her brothers always had mowed the lawn when she was a child.

When she went to Mowers-R-Us, she asked to speak with the owner. "I want to speak only to the owner," she told Mr. Merchant. "I don't know anything about mowers, and I need to talk with an expert." Mr. Merchant said, "I'm the owner and you couldn't find a better expert anywhere in the state. I have been in the business of selling mowers for more than 40 years. I only sell mowers and the equipment to clean and repair them. Are you familiar with the type of lawnmower you would like?" Mr. Merchant added.

"No, I don't know anything about lawnmowers. I just know that I have to have a lawnmower that will mulch my grass clippings because I cannot bag the clippings. The village of Glenview does not permit me to bag the clippings. So the clippings must remain on my lawn," Ms. Seller told Mr. Merchant.

"You're absolutely correct. You must have a mulching mower," Mr. Merchant said. "That type of mower will grind the grass clippings and you will not notice them on your grass."

"I have the perfect mower for you," Mr. Merchant continued. "It is a used model that will fit into your price range. It is only $200. It is a good brand, a Roro. It will mulch the grass as well as any of the new mowers. This one is true blue. You can purchase a separate mulching blade that will easily attach to it for an additional $50," he added.

"Do you think that I need the mulching blade?" Ms. Seller asked. "I've never used a lawnmower so I don't know what to expect, and you appear to be the expert."

"I think you could do without the mulching blade unless you want the grass ground up very fine," Mr. Merchant said.

"I think that I would like it ground up fine. I'll defer to your judgment. If you think a mulching blade is necessary, then I'll buy that with the mower. Do you think this is the best mower for mulching?" asked Ms. Seller.

"Absolutely. I told you it is a true value. It will mulch with the best of them," Mr. Merchant said.

"If you think it can do the job, I'll trust your judgment," said Ms. Seller. "I'll take the mower and the mulching blade. Can you install the mulching blade? I don't know anything about the installation."

"Sure, we can install any blade for another $30," Mr. Merchant said.

"OK. Do you clean up the machine, too?" Ms. Seller asked.

"We can do it for an additional $40, or you can do it yourself with the special industrial-strength, nontoxic, nonirritant mower cleaner," Mr. Merchant told Ms. Seller.

"Well, I have sensitive skin. Do you really think that the mower cleaner is safe for me to use? I have never used any type of industrial-strength cleaner," Ms. Seller said.

"Absolutely. I've used the cleaner many times. It is very safe and won't hurt your sensitive skin at all."

Ms. Seller purchased the mower, the blade, and the cleaner. She used the mower after Mr. Merchant installed the new mulching blade. It barely cut the grass and certainly didn't mulch the clippings into fine pieces as Mr. Merchant had claimed.

She brought the mower back to Mr. Merchant. He said that he had made no warranties about the mower. He showed her the language on the receipt that said that he did not expressly warrant anything.

Ms. Seller brought the mower to a Roro dealer. The owners of the Roro dealership, Abe Saul and Lou T. Wright, said that the mower Ms. Seller had purchased from Mowers-R-Us was not a mulching mower. It was a mower built before mulching was popular. Therefore, it would not perform the mulching task. It was designed merely to cut the grass. "Any merchant who has been in business for one year or more should have known that mowers built before 1970 were not designed for mulching," Mr. Wright said. He showed Ms. Seller where the manufacturing date appeared on the mower. "Manufactured in August 1969," it said on the plate with the serial number. "Also, mulching blades cannot be placed on these old mowers. Any mower dealer should know that, too," Mr. Wright added. "However, this mower isn't defective. It can cut the grass without mulching it."

The mower wasn't Ms. Seller's only problem. She also had used the cleaner while wearing protective gloves. She broke out in a rash all over her hands. Ms. Seller's dermatologist stated that the cleaner was caustic and permeated the gloves, causing the rash on Ms. Seller's hands.

Ms. Seller is bringing an action against Mr. Merchant and Mr. Facture in the Circuit Court of Cook County, Law Division, in Yourstate. Your research is limited to actions Ms. Seller has against Mr. Merchant for breach of an implied warranty of fitness for a particular purpose.

Answer each of the following questions fully and provide authority—cases, secondary sources, if necessary, or laws—to support your position. Indicate whether the authority is primary or secondary authority and whether it is mandatory or persuasive authority. Remember that your goal is to find the best primary binding authorities.

a. What law of what jurisdiction governs this problem? What is the highest court in the jurisdiction?

b. Where should you begin your research? List any sources you plan to consult. Indicate whether the sources contain primary or secondary sources. Did you use a citator, such as *Shepard's* or KeyCite, to find additional references? List any finding tools you plan to use. Explain why you plan to use each source.

c. Compose a search query after you obtain a working vocabulary on the topic. Run your search. List any secondary and primary sources you consulted. List the sources in order of your consultation. List any finding tools you used. Indicate where you located information in these references.

d. Based on your research in this jurisdiction, can Ms. Seller sue Mr. Merchant for breach of an implied warranty of fitness for a particular purpose with regard to the lawnmower purchase? Provide any authority that supports your position. Use *Bluebook* format for the citations. If necessary, attach additional pages. Write the holding for each authority or a basic summary of the value of that authority. Indicate whether the authority is primary or secondary and whether it is binding. Validate and update any primary authority you will rely on.

e. Based upon the law of this jurisdiction, is Mr. Merchant a merchant? Provide any authority that supports your position. Use *Bluebook* format. If necessary, attach additional pages. Write the holding for each authority or a basic summary of the value of that authority. Indicate whether the authority is primary or secondary and whether it is binding.

f. If Ms. Seller is entitled to recovery of damages for breach of an implied warranty of fitness for a particular purpose in this jurisdiction, does the fact that the mower was a "used product" prohibit Ms. Seller's recovery? Provide any authority that supports your position. Use *Bluebook* format. If necessary, attach additional pages. Write the holding for each authority or a basic summary of the value of that authority. Indicate whether the authority is primary or secondary and whether it is binding.

g. If Ms. Seller is entitled to recovery of damages for breach of an implied warranty of fitness for a particular purpose, does the fact that the mower was not defective prohibit her recovery? Provide any authority that supports your position. Use *Bluebook* format. If necessary, attach additional pages. Write the holding for each authority or a basic summary of the value of that authority. Indicate whether the authority is primary or secondary and whether it is binding.

h. Does Ms. Seller have a cause of action for breach of an implied warranty of fitness for a particular purpose with regard to the cleaner? Provide any authority that supports your position. Use *Bluebook* format. If necessary, attach additional pages. Write the holding for each authority or a basic summary of the value of that authority. Indicate whether the authority is primary or secondary and whether it is binding.

i. Validate your research results on either Lexis or Westlaw before submitting your work. Attach the cite-checking results.

10. The supervising attorney wants you to find the law on the rights of adjoining landowners concerning trees and hedges on the boundary lines of the property.

   a. What is your research strategy? List the steps you would take.

   b. What terms would you use in a search on Lexis or on Westlaw?

   c. Because this is a narrow, well-defined legal issue and you do not know which jurisdiction's law applies, you may consider searching the A.L.R. Take a look at the annotation in the A.L.R., "Rights and Liabilities of Adjoining Landowners as to Trees, Shrubbery, or Similar Plants Growing on Boundary Line" at 26 A.L.R. 3d 1372 (1969). What information would this A.L.R. annotation provide that may help you in your research process?

LEGAL WRITING

GETTING READY TO WRITE

CHAPTER OVERVIEW

Writing involves planning—the more planning, the more effective the written document. Legal writing has three components: prewriting (which includes researching and planning your written document), drafting, and revising. This chapter explains how to plan before drafting documents and how to revise your work so that it is written clearly and concisely. This chapter provides step-by-step techniques to use when preparing to write. To systematically prepare to write, first determine the purpose, audience, and organization of the document. Then, you must carefully revise your work product to tailor it precisely to the assignment, the client, and the facts. This chapter focuses on the fundamentals of good writing. Specific tips are provided to improve your drafts.

A. WRITING GOALS AND HOW TO ACHIEVE THEM

The keys to writing well are **clarity** and **organization**. Your readers must understand what you are trying to convey to them. Whether you are writing a letter or a memorandum, your communication must be clear so that it can be understood. Often several proper formats, used at different times, will make your writing easier to read and understand.

▼ How Do You Plan Your Communication and Revise It?

You must think about what you want to say. Why are you writing? This will highlight the purpose so that you can decide on the format. Who will read your work? This determines the audience. Decide how you want the material you create to sound — this will determine the tone. Outline the communication. Next, write it using correct grammar and spelling, and most important, rewrite it several times. As you rewrite your e-mails, letters, and memos, you will always find that you can eliminate unnecessary words and legalese. Use simple words even though you know more elaborate ones. Doing so makes your writing inviting rather than pompous.

B. THE WRITING PROCESS

Follow a method or format when preparing to write to make the actual drafting process easier. Focus on the mechanics and components of the writing process rather than the finished product. The method that follows is a checklist to ensure thoroughness and to give you confidence in your newly acquired skills. The fundamental components of process writing are assessing the document's purpose and intended audience, drafting a detailed outline before writing, revising your findings to closely reflect the purpose and audience, and outlining and revising your work.

1. Preparing to Write: Purpose and Audience

▼ How Do You Complete the Research Process and Make the Transition to Writing?

Remember that what we plan as we prepare to write is as important as the final product. The more time you can put into the process, the better the product will be. Spend at least 50 percent of the time budgeted for writing in the **prewriting stage**. However, time management is crucial with any assignment because time is money, but allow adequate time to write. Therefore, when the project is assigned, ask how much time you should spend on the project. What is the budget? A good clue as to when you have completed your research is when you do not retrieve any new information; the same sources keep appearing. Ask your law librarian or another paralegal to briefly review your research strategy and ask if there are any other avenues that he or she would have taken.

Take detailed notes and make careful citations to references for each source. Create an outline and put the relevant information under each section. Also, keep a complete list of all sources consulted, whether a statute, case, regulation, periodical article, or other source. Your list of sources consulted helps later on, when you may have to expand your research. You can then check the list to see if you already reviewed a source and to see if it was pertinent.

Shepardize or KeyCite any primary authority that you use in your memo to ensure that the authority, whether it is a case, statute, or regulation, is still good or valid law. Never start to write using a source of authority without Shepardizing or KeyCiting it first.

NET NOTE

For help on word selection, visit thesaurus.com to find synonyms. For definitions, visit dictionary.law.com.

---

a. Purpose

▼ What Is the Purpose of the Document?

When you sit down to write, begin by asking yourself this: What is the **purpose** of the document that I am preparing? Because a legal document has a variety of goals (to inform, persuade, or advise), you must determine the document's intent before writing. Your purpose may also be as simple as to request a document or to transmit a document. The purpose determines the posture and the format of your work product. This is the immediate purpose. All of your work also has an underlying purpose — to convey your professionalism.

If the document is to inform the attorney as to all available law on a particular issue, it is neutral in tone and takes the form of an objective memo. If your goal is to convince another party that your position is correct, then the document may be in the form of a memo for the assigning attorney, a memo for the court, or a trial or an appellate brief, and the tone will be persuasive. Sometimes a persuasive document takes the form of a letter that requests an individual or entity to act in a certain way. Examples of persuasive letters are demand letters requesting payment owed, or eviction letters demanding that a tenant vacate the premises. Sometimes you must convey an attorney's advice to a client. The document may then be in the form of a letter giving counsel, written as simply as possible, to be signed by the supervising attorney. Simplicity is best for a client who may not have a legal education. The purpose of the document determines its format and the rhetorical stance: objective, persuasive, or instructive.

NET NOTE

Cornell's Legal Information Institute provides a brief overview of the types of legal writing at www.law.cornell.edu/wex/legal_writing.

---

b. Audience

▼ To Whom Are You Speaking?

As you prepare to write, determine carefully who the **audience**, or reader, is. Is the reader the assigning attorney? This is often the case when the project is the preparation of an office memo. The memo should be easy for the intended reader to understand; you should insert headings, if necessary, to guide the reader. If the document is intended for a court, then the reader will be a judge and opposing counsel, and your tone will be formal yet persuasive. The assertions or points that you want to prove should be clear and straightforward. Regardless of the audience, it is best to write in plain language so your reader can understand your points after reading the material once.

The document should always be prepared using language that the reader can comprehend; this is also required when drafting texts, e-mails, client letters, and demand letters. Whenever and whatever you write, consider how you can make your work usable and understandable for the reader. The material will likely be read by others later on so you want the material to be clear for the unfamiliar reader, too.

Also, consider how your reader will view the document or written work. You may consider skipping lines between paragraphs to set out information so the reader is not overwhelmed with dense text. Will the reader view the material on a phone screen? On a tablet? On a desktop? In hard copy? The medium will affect how you present the information and also may have an impact on the length and level of detail. It is very hard to read a long document on a phone, for example. Reader-focused writing has the greatest clarity.

PRACTICE POINTER

After you receive the assignment and understand what you are asked to do, inquire as to the number of hours that is budgeted for the project. Also, ask the assigning attorney questions after you have reviewed the assignment, but before you begin to write, to make sure that the purpose and audience are agreed upon so that you stay focused on the attorney's objectives. Remember that there may be other readers who will be copied.

NET NOTE

Check https://www.plainlanguage.gov/guidelines/ for tips on using plain language in your writing.

2. Drafting a Detailed Outline

▼ How Do You Organize Your Ideas?

The next stage is to prepare an **outline** of whatever document you are writing. When you were researching, you likely created an outline and inserted the authorities under each section. You can use this outline to start your writing process. Organize your research findings according to where they are pertinent in your outline. It is best to let your issues or assertions determine where the research should be placed rather than letting the sources determine the placement in the document. Never use your sources as your outline; rely on the issues.

If you are writing an office memo, outline the issues and subissues of points that you want to articulate. Make sure that the outline flows logically. See if there are any gaps by reviewing your outline carefully.

Organization is crucial to effective legal writing to ensure completeness. A complete outline also helps when you have to put your project down for a considerable period of time, or when you must work on more than one matter at a time and want to easily pick up where you left off.

3. Revise for Readability

Your writing should be understandable after a single reading. Consider using the plain language goals set out at plainlanguage.gov. Consider how your reader will view the work. Adjust the content to make your writing more suitable to the medium, whether it is a phone, tablet, desktop, or in hard copy. Also, consider your reader's background. Not every reader will have a legal education.

PRACTICE POINTER

When revising, consult a dictionary to ensure that all of the words are properly spelled and used.

Revision is a continuous part of the writing process and a vital final step. Reread the material after you have reviewed your word choices and eliminated unnecessary words. Revision may seem like a tedious waste of time, but it is one of the most important steps in preparing a well-written document.

Review all the steps you have taken in the prewriting stage. Ask yourself: Is the purpose of the document being prepared according to the assignment, and is it meeting the client's needs? Does the document clearly fulfill its goal of either informing, persuading, or advising? Do the language and format reflect the purpose?

Examine your intended audience. What language is appropriate for the intended reader? What level of sophistication is required? Ask yourself about voice (how it will sound), diction (word choice), and rhetoric (the way you use speech).

Review your outline. Check to see if the outline is well organized, logical, and flows smoothly. At this point, reexamine the issues or assertions that you want to include and make sure that the points are clearly discernible. Insert the appropriate research findings in the relevant place in the outline, as well as the necessary facts and the conclusions that you want to draw. Now you are ready to write. After you write the first draft, revise and pay attention to these details.

PRACTICE POINTER

Review documents in files to see the firm's writing style.

---

4. Example of Process Writing Techniques

Ms. Partner calls you into her office and asks you to prepare a client letter to Mrs. Jones advising her as to a course of action that she can take to rectify the problem of her mislabeled fur coat. The facts of the problem are as follows: Mrs. Jones bought a fur coat from John J. Furriers. The coat was labeled 100 percent raccoon. One day Mrs. Jones was smoking a cigarette and a hot ash fell on the coat while she was wearing it. The ash melted a hole in the coat. Mrs. Jones knew that fur burns, but acrylic melts.

First, what is the purpose of the document? The document's goal is to advise Mrs. Jones as to a course of action against the seller, John J. Furriers. The partner specified the document's form, a letter.

Next, you must examine your audience. Who is your reader? Is Mrs. Jones an attorney? Probably not. You can ask the attorney making the assignment for some background information about the client. This will help you tailor a document to the reader's precise needs. Mrs. Jones is a stock analyst. She is a sophisticated individual but she does not possess a legal education. The language used in the letter must be understandable to Mrs. Jones. The voice — how the letter sounds — should be instructive and advisory without being condescending. The diction, or word choice, should be simple; avoid legalese.

Now outline the points that you want to address in the letter. Begin by restating the facts as you know them. List the points.

1. The fur coat was mislabeled.
2. The seller misrepresented his product.
3. If the misrepresentation was intentional, there is the possibility of fraud.
4. Mrs. Jones would like to obtain a full refund for the coat that she purchased.
5. If a refund is not given in seven days, court action will proceed.

Insert your research findings, in plain language, in the appropriate spot in the outline. Note the pinpoint citations for the authority you use so you have this later if you need it. In a client letter of this nature there is no need to cite to authority. Use the facts to draft a letter for the attorney to advise Mrs. Jones as to how she should proceed with the matter. Remember that an attorney must always review and sign any letter that you prepare that gives legal advice. Only an attorney may sign such a letter.

Check the readability of your work. Can the intended reader understand your document after a single reading? Review all your prewriting steps by checking your purpose, audience, and outline once again.

PRACTICE POINTER

Prewriting preparation is time well spent. Thoroughness and accuracy are so important, and attorneys have little patience for anything besides perfection. Careful note taking, outlining, and citing will provide not only an excellent start to a writing project but ample material if you are called on to discuss a project prior to its completion. Knowing the key points will also help you to draft an e-mail concerning the matter.

Reflect on making the material easy for your reader to understand and to view. Now you are ready to write.

CHECKLIST TO GET READY TO WRITE

1. When you receive the problem
   a. Ask about the intended audience and the subsequent readers.
   b. Ask about the time frame and deadline.
   c. Ask about the budget.
   d. Ask about the format for the work product: e-mail, memo, text?
   e. What is the purpose?
   f. Clarify the legal issues being researched.
   g. Determine the relevant jurisdiction.
   h. Determine the area of the law.
   i. Gather all the facts.
   j. Draft a statement of the issue or question that you are researching.
2. Introductory research
   a. Educate yourself in the area of the law: Review Chapter 14 for research strategy.
   b. Make an outline of the issues and subissues in your problem.
3. Process writing
   a. Purpose: Determine the purpose of the document. The document's goal is either to inform, to persuade, or to advise. Select the appropriate rhetorical stance and determine the format (office memo, court memo, brief, or letter).
   b. Audience: Find out who the reader or readers will be. Determine the language that is most comprehensible to the particular reader. Select an appropriate voice for the purpose, format, and reader. Note your diction.
   c. Outline: Outline the issues, assertions, or points that you want to include. Organize research findings according to the outline. Place facts in the appropriate spot and state the conclusion.
   d. Revise for readability and clarity: Review the purpose and the audience of the intended document and check your outline for appropriateness.

CHECKPOINTS

Check your work as you write. To maintain your focus, ask yourself as you write:

- What is the purpose?
- Who is the audience?
- What is the format expected? Letter, e-mail, memo, brief, text? Is this the suitable format?

- Do you need to revise your outline to reflect any new knowledge, legal or factual? Did you reread the outline to ensure that it is complete and flows logically?
- Is the written work appropriate for the intended audience?
- Can the material or document be written for and readily understood by a variety of audiences?
- How can you ensure the written material best meets the reader's needs?
- How will you, the writer, convey tone?
- Is the writing professional and grammatically correct?
- Did you perform sufficient research? Do you have adequate authority and support for your points and conclusions?
- Will you use the present tense or simple past tense? Will you remove instances of passive voice and avoid the use of the past perfect tense?
- Will you use the active voice?

CHAPTER SUMMARY

This chapter led you through the writing process. This will ensure thoroughness when planning and starting a writing project. Before writing, determine the purpose of your assignment. This will guide your writing. Also, determine the audience for your work. This will determine the style of your writing. Carefully outline the document before writing and then revise the document by preparing an outline of the material that you prepared, an after-the-fact outline. Review the after-the-fact outline to make sure that it is logically organized and includes all points that the issues require to be addressed.

The time that you spend in the prewriting stage ensures a better work product that is produced more efficiently than one created by lunging into the writing process. Think about what you want to say, outline it, and write it using good grammar and correct spelling. Then rewrite and edit your work using the checkpoints. Use these tips even when drafting a short memo or e-mail to an attorney. Prewriting takes planning, but with the methodology outlined in this chapter you will be equipped to write in any format.

KEY TERMS

audience
clarity
organization
    rewriting

outline
prewriting stage
purpose

EXERCISES

BASIC WRITING PRACTICE

1. For this exercise, use a paper that you have written.
   a. Examine the paper. What is the purpose and the audience?
   b. Outline the ideas explained in the paper.
   c. Revise your outline to clarify your ideas.
2. Write a letter to a neighbor discussing the highlights of the past season in your life.
   a. What is the audience and, consequently, the tone?
   b. Rewrite the letter to a government official. In the rewritten letter, express dissatisfaction with a service that is supposed to be provided by the local government and was not provided adequately during the past season. For example, in the letter to your neighbor, you write about the great snowfall during the winter. In the rewritten letter to a government official, you write about the great snowfall, but also include how the locality failed to plow sufficiently. What is the purpose and audience of the letter to the government official?

INTERNET-BASED WRITING PRACTICE

3. Use a document that you need to draft for this exercise. Access the Purdue University Online Writing Lab site at http://owl.english.purdue.edu. Search for materials concerning "prewriting," which will provide ideas on how to plan and outline your draft. This site will help you get started writing and give you points to consider.
   a. What is the purpose of the document you are writing?
   b. How do you plan on achieving this purpose?
   c. List all of your relevant ideas.
   d. Summarize your overall idea.
   e. Make an outline.
   f. Write a first draft.

BRAINSTORMING

4. Start with an assignment that you need to begin. Review the topic in a legal encyclopedia or find a journal article relevant to your assignment. Fill a page with all of your ideas regarding the assignment. Review your notes and make an organized outline, deleting repetitious topics.

PREPARING TO WRITE

5. Why would you use a process method for legal writing?
6. Why would you outline before you write as well as create an outline of your finished document?
7. Why is it important to determine the audience and purpose before writing?

PROCESS WRITING

8. Read the following fact pattern and answer the questions.

John Clark comes to your firm with a question regarding the tax status of his residence. He has just been ordained as a United Methodist minister and will be receiving a housing allowance from First United Methodist Church, where he will be an assistant pastor. He wants to know if this housing allowance can be excluded from income on his tax return even though the residence is his own.

    a. How would you phrase this issue if you were researching this problem?

    b. What would be your research strategy?

    c. Construct an outline of this problem.

9. The assignment partner requests that you draft a letter of your findings to Rev. Clark. List, in detail, the purpose, audience, and resulting outline of the letter.

10. How would the purpose, audience, and outline change if the assignment partner requests a memo concerning your research findings? Once again, how would the purpose, audience, and outline change if you are requested to prepare a court brief?

REVIEWING AND REVISING

11. Use a memo that you drafted. Please look at the discussion section of the memo to answer the following questions to refine and revise your work.

Reviewing the Discussion

12. Did you start with an outline?

13. Is the outline logically organized?

14. Is there enough authority to support the points?

15. Is the intended tone neutral?

Reviewing the Thesis Paragraph

16. Does the discussion start with a thesis paragraph, or paragraph block, written in IRAC format?

17. Does the thesis paragraph start with a broad issue statement?

18. Does the thesis paragraph contain a synthesis of the legal rules starting with the broadest rule so that the reader understands the legal context for the discussion? Does the synthesis provide a legal road map for the discussion to follow?

19. Do you include a general application of the law to the client's facts in about three sentences?

20 Do you include a broad conclusion that mirrors the brief answer but with less detail?

Reviewing the Remaining Discussion Paragraphs

21. Does each paragraph, after the thesis, address a single element?

22. Is each rule, which is the test, standard, or principle the court relied on, stated clearly?

23. Do you include the essential facts from each case so the reader will understand how the issue played out?

24. Is there a clear statement of the court's holding with the signpost, "The court held"?

25. Do you summarize the relevant portions of the court's reasoning in three sentences or fewer, why the court held as it did?
26. The application: Do you clearly draw the parallels and distinctions between the cases and our facts?
27. Are you careful to only conclude on each element and not state the overall conclusion at the end of each IRAC sequence?
28. Are you objective and do you apply the law neutrally?
29. Would a reader who is unfamiliar with the problem be able to understand the memo?

CLEAR WRITING AND EDITING

CHAPTER OVERVIEW

The key to effective writing is clarity. Preparing a first draft of a document can be quite an undertaking, but that is only a start. Until you have carefully edited and revised your drafts at least once, you have not completed your project. This chapter provides you with guidance in editing and revising your documents and preparing them for clients, courts, and attorneys.

A. PURPOSE OF EDITING

Editing and revising are essential if you want to have well-drafted and organized documents. A well-drafted document is one in which your readers understand what you are trying to convey. Be clear and make it easy to read. Few documents are written well after one draft. Good writing entails rewriting. Each time you review your document and revise it, you improve its content and make it more understandable. **Editing** allows you to review your word choices, your grammar, your spelling, and your outline and organization of each sentence and paragraph, as well as the outline and organization of the entire document. It enables you to determine whether the document you wrote is clear and will be understood by your audience. Editing also provides you with the opportunity to enhance your work with additional thoughts and clarify your document by eliminating unnecessary words, ideas, and legalese.

B. PROCESS OF EDITING

The process of editing starts with a first draft and often ends after many more drafts. After you complete your first draft, you must proofread and edit your work. Consider each word you select. Review your overall outline and organization. Then review the outline and organization of each sentence and paragraph.

When you review your draft, you should read it as if you were reading it for the first time. Pretend that you are a stranger to the project and that you don't know anything about it. Ensure that it is understandable. If you have time, put the first draft aside for a day or two and then review it again. It will give you a fresh perspective.

Next, consider whether each part follows the next. The work should flow in a logical order. Consider whether the organization of the document or of any paragraphs or sentences should be revised. Question the structure and organization of each sentence and paragraph. Change passive voice sentences to active voice. For more discussion of passive and active voice, review this chapter's Section C-2, Voice.

Do you notice anything is missing? Sometimes when you read your work aloud, you find that it is missing something needed to get you from point A to point B in the discussion. Add any such missing elements.

Note whether your writing contains transitions and flows easily from one section to the next. If it doesn't, revise it. Add transitional words, phrases, or sentences where necessary. **Transitions** help move readers from one sentence to the next and from one paragraph to the next.

Next, think about whether you can eliminate unnecessary words, a process called tightening or editing. Focus on your words. Change elaborate or unfamiliar words to simpler words—often those you used in grade school. Doing so makes your writing inviting rather than pompous. Make certain that your words provide the reader with a visual image of what you mean. Ensure that your words accurately convey your ideas. Be concise. For additional information about word choice, see this chapter's Section C-1, Diction, below.

Review your grammar and spelling. Ensure that your punctuation is correct and that the elements of each sentence and paragraph are correct. Do not rely on the spell-checker. It does not pick up all of the misspelled words. However, use the spell-checker. Then, review the spelling within the document yourself. Check your citations for errors as well.

C. SPECIFIC ITEMS TO REVIEW WHILE EDITING

1. Diction

▼ What Is Diction?

Diction means choice of words when writing. Selecting the appropriate words to express your idea precisely is a skill that is developed over time. When you are revising a document, consider whether your words convey your ideas precisely. Sometimes you must use a dictionary or thesaurus to assist you in selecting the best word.

Select concrete words that allow the readers to visualize what you are saying. Read the following example:

> He harmed one of his body parts in the device at issue in the case.

It is better to say:

> His arm was severed when the threshing machine stalled and he fell forward in front of the machine.

The second example is clearer because the reader knows what happened and to which body part it happened: The arm was severed. The second sentence also conveys that the device was a threshing machine and that it stalled, throwing the man forward.

▼ What Are Concrete Verbs?

Use **concrete verbs** to exactly describe the action taken. Read the following examples:

> The parties entered into an agreement on July 8, 2021.
> There was an agreement entered into on July 8, 2021.
> The parties agreed to the terms on July 8, 2021.

The last example is the best because it is the simplest and uses the word *agreed* as a verb rather than as a noun. It is the easiest sentence of the three to understand and to visualize.

The first two examples turn the verb *agree* into a noun, a process called **nominalization**. Nominalizations make sentences difficult to understand. The following illustrates a second example:

> The parties entered into an agreement on November 15, 2020, to make a change in the purchase price of the original contract from $1,500 to $2,000.

It is better to say:

> The parties agreed to increase the original contract purchase price from $1,500 to $2,000.

In the second sentence, *entered into an agreement* becomes *agreed* and *to make a change* becomes *increase*. These changes eliminate the use of verbs as nouns.

Here is another example:

> The plaintiff made a statement to police that the defendant ran a red light before the crash.

It is better to say:

> The plaintiff told police that the defendant ran the red light before the crash.

> or

> The plaintiff stated to police that the defendant ran the red light before the crash.

Select simpler words and make sentences short. Review the following example.

> Prior to 9/11, airport security was incomplete.
> It is better to say:
> Before 9/11, airport security was lax.

Before is a simpler word than *prior to* and *lax* is more descriptive than *incomplete*.

Review these statements and determine which is clearer:

> The state driver's license bureau now requires a Social Security card as verification of a person's identity.

> or

> The state driver's license bureau now requires a Social Security card as proof of a person's identity.

The second sentence is clearer. The use of the simple word *proof* rather than the pompous word *verification* makes the sentence easier to understand. Do not make readers use a dictionary.

Keep your writing simple. Use the same word to describe an essential object in the case. For example, if a gun is at the center of the case, use the word *gun* for each reference. Do not alternate and call the object a gun in one reference and a pistol in another. Otherwise, the reader may become confused.

Avoid weak subjects and verbs. The words "it is" are often unnecessary and weaken a sentence. Review the following example:

It is clear that the defendant entered the house at 8:30 p.m.

It is better to say:

The defendant entered the house at 8:30 p.m.

Another phrase to avoid is "it is important to note." If it isn't important, you shouldn't mention it. Instead, start with the part of the sentence that is "important to note." Avoid similar phrases such as "it is evident that" or "it is clear that." Many Web sources will help you avoid such phrases that are often called "throat-clearing" phrases.

▼ How Do You Avoid Legalese or Legal Speak?

Avoid **legalese** or **legal speak**. What does this mean? Use plain English that your nonattorney clients would use. Consider your audience. Your writing should be understandable. Clear writing avoids using unnecessary legal words. For example, do not use the word *scienter* for *intent*. Say *fired* rather than *unilaterally terminated*. At the end of an affidavit, you often see the phrase *Further affiant sayeth not*, which means that the person signing the affidavit has nothing further to say. Because that should be clear without the legalistic phrase, skip it (and others like it that add nothing to your writing). Also avoid words such as *hereinafter, herein, aforesaid, hereafter, henceforth,* and *thereby*.

2. Voice

Voice is the tone of your document. In professional writing, the document's tone is formal. Selecting language that is not colloquial and avoiding slang are ways to ensure that the tone of the document is correct for the law firm or corporate legal department environment. Avoid anything that personalizes the contents. Never use the first person. Conjunctions like *can't* are more casual than *cannot*. When revising, be sensitive to the tone of your document; it should have the requisite formal voice.

▼ What Is the Difference Between Active Voice and Passive Voice?

Active voice is when the subject of the sentence is doing the action of the verb. Active voice emphasizes the actor. Active voice is the preferred voice because it is clearer, more concise, and more lively. Active voice tells the reader clearly who did what.

Active voice: Ben hit a home run.
Sarah danced the tango.
The judge denied the motion.

Passive voice is when the subject of the sentence is being acted on. Although passive voice has its uses, it is generally wordier and not as strong as active voice.

Passive voice: The home run was hit by Ben.
Sarah danced the tango.
The motion was denied by the judge.

Often the word *by* is used in a passive voice sentence. When you see the word *by*, consider rewriting the sentence.

Passive example: Their initial quote for heat stamping equipment was rejected by Abbey.

Rewritten example: Abbey rejected their initial quote for heat stamping equipment.

The second example is clearer and more concise.

Passive voice, however, is sometimes acceptable. In some cases, the person or thing performing the action is unknown. For example:

Taxes were not deducted from her paychecks.

Jenna received health and life insurance benefits.

In other cases, the actor does not need to be mentioned because he or she is less important than the action. If you believe it advantageous to change the emphasis of the sentence from the person doing the action to the action, use passive voice. For example, if your client is the defendant in a proceeding and you do not want to emphasize her action, you would write a sentence in passive voice, as follows:

The action stems from a contract dispute in which goods were rejected by the defendant.

This sentence in active voice would emphasize the defendant, as follows:

The defendant rejected the goods, resulting in a contract dispute.

3. Paragraphs

A **paragraph** is a collection of statements that focus on the same general subject. Effective paragraphs have a unified purpose, a thesis or topic sentence, and transitions between sentences.

The **topic sentence** is generally the first sentence of a paragraph; it tells the reader the subject of the paragraph. This sentence also indicates that a new topic will be discussed. In legal writing, this sentence often introduces the issue or subissues that will be discussed within the paragraph.

You should use transitions to guide your reader from one paragraph to the next. Transitions tell the reader that the ideas follow from each other and are related. A transitional sentence ties two paragraphs together. Think of this sentence as a bridge. Whenever you start your new paragraph, think about how you will relate it to the previous paragraph. Try to vary your transitions.

4. Sentences

A **sentence** is a statement that conveys a single idea. It generally should be written in active voice and must include a subject and predicate. To avoid confusing your reader, do not place the subject too far from the verb. The focus of your sentence should be the idea you wish to convey. Do not make your readers work too hard to understand your sentence. Be direct and to the point. Keep your sentences short, generally not more than 25 words. Shorter sentences are easier to understand. As with any rule, you may break this rule about sentence length, but be careful not to make your sentences too complex.

One common mistake in writing sentences is to use a sentence fragment or incomplete sentence.

Incomplete sentence: The extent of the employer's control and supervision over the worker.

Complete sentence: The court will consider the extent of the employer's control and supervision over the worker.

The first example is a sentence fragment. It is incomplete and is missing a verb. The second sentence is a complete thought. It contains both a subject and a verb.

5. Other Key Rules

Do not start your paragraph or sentence with a citation. Instead, start with the rule summarizing the cited authority.

Use quotations sparingly. Most often, you can paraphrase what a court decision or other authority states. Your words convey the concept more clearly to the reader. Direct quotations that are used to convey an idea often are cluttered with unnecessary words or do not effectively explain a concept in the context of your use of the quotation. An added bonus for you when you paraphrase a court decision or other authority is that you are forced to analyze carefully the language of the authority. This ensures that you understand the concepts presented.

Review the following paragraph. Note that unnecessary words are located in parentheses.

> The plaintiff (made a statement) that in his (own) opinion, during (the course of) (a period of) a year, the defendant (completely) destroyed the furniture the plaintiff hired the defendant to restore. The defendant failed to warn the plaintiff (in advance) that he couldn't restore the piece (properly) and that the price of the work originally estimated (roughly) at $600 would now cost her $2,200.

None of the words in parentheses add anything to the reader's understanding of the sentences or paragraph. The phrase *made a statement* should be shortened to *stated.* Eliminate unnecessary clauses or phrases. Review the following sentence. Note that the unnecessary words are located in parentheses.

The hearing will take place (on or before) January 31, 2022.

The words *on or before* are unnecessary.

When you read your paragraphs, review each word and determine whether it adds to the sentence. If not, delete it.

REVISION CHECKLIST

1. Does the material make sense?
2. Do the words accurately convey what happened?
3. Would another word convey your intended meaning more accurately?
4. Can the reader visualize what occurred?
5. Is it logical?
6. Should the organization of the piece be changed?
7. Does one paragraph flow into the other?
8. Should the paragraphs be rearranged?
9. Does one sentence follow from the next?
10. Should the organization of any sentence be changed?
11. Are there any gaps in the sentence?
12. Review your voice.
13. Is the voice consistent?
14. Is the voice used the intended voice?
15. Can you eliminate passive voice?
16. Be certain the verbs are concrete.
17. Check for nominalizations.
18. Are there any punctuation errors?

19. Are any words misspelled?
20. Are there any typographical errors?
21. Are there any citation errors?
22. Eliminate any legalese.

CHAPTER SUMMARY

This chapter led you through the editing process generally and then more specifically. It outlined essential items to check during your editing process.

Choose your words carefully. Select concrete verbs and avoid legalese. Most often, use active voice in which the subject of the sentence is doing the action of the verb.

Make sure your paragraphs focus on a single subject or aspect of a subject and use topic and transition sentences. Use full sentences that are direct and convey the idea you intend.

Use quotations sparingly to effectively convey your messages.

KEY TERMS

active voice   paragraph
concrete verbs   passive voice
diction   sentence
editing   topic sentence
legal speak   transitions
legalese   voice
nominalization

EXERCISES

PRACTICE SKILLS

1. Eliminate the unnecessary words from the following statements: At the time when the parties entered into the agreement of purchase and sale it is important to note that neither of them had knowledge of contents of the dresser drawer. Because of the fact that previous to the contract the seller did not own the dresser and the seller's mother had not had many valuable pieces of jewelry despite having a large income, the seller had made the assumption that the dresser did not contain anything. Due to the fact that the seller had made a statement to the buyer of the fact that his mother did not own any jewelry in the buyer's thinking, he had no purpose to make any further investigation or inspection of the drawers as he might otherwise have considered making. For these reasons, there was no provision in the contract for an upward modification in the payment to be made by the buyer to the seller in the event that the dresser drawer later proved to be filled with jewels.

2. The police report said that Mr. Harris had a blood alcohol level of 1.7 based on an on-site blood alcohol test and states further that there were swerve marks on the street. The report also stated that there were no brake marks and that the driver was cited by the officer for drunk driving.

3. The personnel manager did all of the hiring and firing of the restaurant and golf course and the part-time accountant manages all bookkeeping and tax work for the restaurant and golf course.

4. Candy Graham who did not have an employment contract was, despite her freedom to set her own hours and work from her own home, also an employee.

5. Which is the best sentence? Why?
   a. A modification to the contract occurred on January 28, 2021.
   b. There was a modification of the contract January 28, 2021.
   c. Harry and Morgan modified their contract on January 28, 2021.

6. Which is the best sentence? Why?
   a. The judge issued a decision on Thursday.
   b. The court issued an opinion on Thursday.
   c. The judge decided the case on Thursday.

TIGHTENING

7. At approximately 7:30 p.m. on May 4, 2021, the plaintiff, Lidia Gregory, was weeding the front garden at her home at 2088 Vista Drive in Phoenix. She was about five feet from the street. The children also were playing in the front yard which was near the street.

8. Based on a blood alcohol test done at the scene of the accident, it was determined that Ronnie Walden was intoxicated.

9. The day the accident occurred it was very clear and had not rained to make the road slick.

10. The issue is whether or not it is a nuisance.

SCREENING FOR LEGALESE: SAY IT IN ENGLISH, PLEASE

11. In the aforementioned case, the funeral home was not found to be a nuisance because the court held that the funeral home in question was "reasonably located on the outskirts of the city."

12. Now comes the plaintiff, by and through her attorney, causes this complaint to be filed with the court.

13. Further affiant sayest not.

14. The party of the first part claims that the party of the second part said that he wanted to cause her to go out of business.

ACTIVE AND PASSIVE VOICE

If the sentence below is written in active voice, note it. If the sentence is written in passive voice, rewrite it in active voice.

15. Two businesses are owned by Max and Sam Maine, and they are being sued in federal court by two former workers for sex discrimination.

16. Ricki Ashton's office supplies and office were provided by Whole In One.

17. The funeral home was controlled by William Halsey and owned jointly by Halsey and Ivy Courier.

18. The subpoena was served by the sheriff.
19. The complaint was filed by the plaintiff in the U.S. District Court for the Northern District of Illinois.
20. Terri Rubin was hit by Debbie Brill's oar as the boats were being rowed by both women.
21. Janice was told she was suffering from shock after an examination at the time of the accident by her son's physician.
22. You represent the defendant. You are describing the plaintiff's claim. Which of the following sentences should you use to describe the plaintiff's claim and why?
    a. $50 was taken from the plaintiff's desk by the defendant.
    b. The defendant took $50 from the plaintiff's desk.

Correct the grammar in the following sentences if necessary, and make the sentences more concise.

23. If our clients' interest in their land is substantially invaded by stables or kennels as a result of odors or sounds created by the proper conduct of those businesses and not taking into account any special sensitivities on the part of our clients, is the harm to our clients significantly more important than the benefit of the stables or kennel to the community?
24. The issue is whether or not it is a malpractice.
25. At 3 a.m. in the morning, the defendant was driving at a rate of 75 miles per hour in a foreign imported car and struck the plaintiff's shed. The end result was that the shed was completely destroyed. The plaintiff had no advance warning. Because of the fact that the shed was destroyed, the plaintiff could not store his bicycle and other bike racing equipment.

WRITING BASICS

CHAPTER OVERVIEW

This chapter reinforces grammar concepts and focuses on problem areas. It provides concrete examples of grammatically correct and incorrect sentences and explains the difference. Because it cannot address all points of grammar that students need to know, you should consult other grammar resources.

A. PUNCTUATION

The punctuation of a sentence, especially the placement of a comma, can change the meaning of that sentence. Therefore, you must carefully place each punctuation mark. The following provides you with some basic rules for checking your punctuation placement.

1. Commas

Commas tell a reader to pause. Use commas to separate a series of items. For example:

Wally ran to the school, the store, the baseball field, and then home.

Be careful not to use commas to divide run-on sentences. The first example below should be two separate sentences.

Incorrect: Tildy's role is merely advisory, although she might be asked to supply facts about the spill, her opinion probably would not form the basis of any final decision.

Correct: Tildy's role is merely advisory. Although she might be asked to supply facts about the spill, her opinion probably would not form the basis of any final decision.

In the second example, the two sentences are correctly separated with a period. Best to avoid using a semicolon and to use two short sentences instead. Shorter sentences enhance clarity. For some run-on sentences, you could divide the sentences with a comma and a conjunction. In the above example, that solution would not cure the problem completely because the second sentence is too long.

Commas also are used to set apart parenthetical phrases where the sentence would be complete without the information between the commas. The information contained between the commas adds more description or information to an already complete sentence. In such a situation, commas should be used in pairs.

The defendant, George K. Dwyer, filed an answer to the complaint.

The name *George K. Dwyer* is parenthetical because the meaning of the sentence would not be changed if the name were omitted. In contrast, read the following examples:

Judges who take bribes should be indicted.

Judges, who take bribes, should be indicted.

In these examples, the phrase *who take bribes* is not parenthetical. If it was omitted, the sentence would say, "Judges should be indicted." The phrase *who take bribes* must be part of the sentence to convey the correct meaning. Therefore, it is not parenthetical, and the commas should be omitted.

Place commas around unnecessary words or phrases. For example, a client has one child, William, and wants to name him as the executor of her estate. In a document to name him as executor, you could use either of the following sentences and the meaning would not be altered.

I name my son, William, as the executor of my estate.

I name my son as the executor of my estate.

Do not place commas around words or phrases that are necessary in order to understand a sentence.

In the next example, your client has two sons, William and Randall. She wants William to be the executor of the estate. The document should read as follows:

I name my son William as the executor of my estate.

The following sentence would be incorrect:

I name my son, William, as the executor of my estate.

2. Special Comma Rules

Commas separate a year from the date.

The plaintiff and the defendant agreed to the settlement on November 18, 2019.

Commas also set off the date from a specific reference to a day of the week.

The judge decided the summary judgment motion on Tuesday, November 12, 2019.

Commas separate a proper name from a title that follows it.

The plaintiff sued RAM Enterprises and Samuel Harris, company president.

Commas and periods should always appear inside quotation marks. This rule is often mistakenly broken.

"But I wasn't in Toledo on the night of the murder," the defendant protested, "I was in Scottsdale with my elderly mother."

3. Semicolons

Semicolons are similar to commas because they tell a reader to pause and they break apart thoughts. Semicolons are used to separate two independent sentences.

Two sentences: The paralegal's responsibilities are broad. They include summarization of depositions.

 One sentence: The paralegal's responsibilities are broad; they include summarization of depositions.

Semicolons separate clauses of a compound sentence when an adverbial conjunction joins the two.

The defendants presented a good case; however, they lost.

Semicolons are used to separate phrases in a list.

The committee members were Robert Harris, vice president of Harris Enterprises; Edna Williams, owner of Walworth Products; Barbara Halley, an attorney; and Benjamin Marcus, an accountant.

Generally, avoid using semicolons to join phrases when you can write two short, complete sentences. Short sentences are clearer for the reader and easier to follow.

NET NOTE

The University of North Carolina's Writing Center has a detailed explanation on semicolon use at https://writingcenter.unc.edu/tips-and-tools/semi-colons-colons-and-dashes/.

---

4. Colons

Colons are marks of introduction: What follow are explanations, conclusions, amplifications, lists or series, or quotations. A colon is always preceded by a main clause, one that can stand alone as a sentence. A main clause may or may not follow a colon.

Help was on the way: Someone had called the police.

Sandra had two assignments: a five-page paper and a book report.

The mayor stepped to the podium: "I regretfully must submit my resignation."

Colons should appear only at the end of a main clause. They should never directly follow a verb or a preposition.

Incorrect: The hours of the museum are: 10:00 A.M. to 6:00 P.M.
Correct: The hours of the museum are 10:00 A.M. to 6:00 P.M.
Incorrect: Marc loved many sports, such as: soccer, tennis, and softball.
Correct: Marc loved many sports, such as soccer, tennis, and softball.

As with any punctuation mark, use colons only when they best serve your writing purpose. Do not overuse them.

5. Parentheses

Parentheses tell the reader that the idea is an afterthought or is outside the main idea of a sentence.

The tort involved a banana peel (the classic culprit) and a crowded grocery store.

Use parentheses infrequently because they tend to break the flow of the sentence. Generally, include the information in the sentence and avoid parentheticals.

6. Double Quotation Marks

These marks enclose direct quotations.

The judge said, "The trial date will not be continued."

Note that the first word of the quotation should be capitalized if it is a complete sentence.

7. Single Quotation Marks

These marks are used to define a quotation within a quotation.

The client told the lawyer, "My boss said, 'You cannot be a good accountant and be a good mother,' and then he fired me."

If you end a quotation with quoted words, you place a single quotation mark and follow it with a double quotation mark.

The witness testified, "The robber said, 'Give me all your money.' "

8. Apostrophes

An apostrophe replaces letters that are omitted in contractions.

> He's the defendant.

He's replaces *he is*. An apostrophe also is used with an *s* to indicate the possessive case.

> The defendant's car struck the plaintiff.

When a noun ends in an *s*, the possessive case is indicated with only an apostrophe.

> The attorneys' clerks researched the applicable law.

To indicate a possessive for one item that two people share, use the apostrophe next to the name of the last person mentioned.

> Ben and Sarah's motion is sound.

However, use an apostrophe after each name if the item is not shared. If Ben has a motion and Sarah also has a motion, the sentence should read as follows:

> Ben's and Sarah's motions are sound.

A common mistake is for a writer to use *it's* when writing about possession. *It's*, however, is a contraction for *it is*.

Finally, **apostrophes** are used to indicate plurals for numbers or letters.

> The attorney told the defendant to watch his p's and q's in the courtroom.

B. MODIFIERS

Modifiers provide a description about a subject, a verb, or an object in your sentence. If you misplace a modifier, you might confuse your reader or convey an incorrect message. A modifier should be placed as close as possible to the subject, verb, or object it modifies. Always ask yourself, who is doing what and how? This will remind you to keep the modifier close to the term it is modifying.

Incorrect: Deadlocked the judge asked the jury to continue to deliberate.

Correct: The jury was deadlocked. However, the judge asked the jury to continue to deliberate.

In the first example, the phrase *deadlocked the judge* incorrectly modifies the judge rather than the jury. This is a dangling modifier. The reader may not know whether the judge or the jury is deadlocked.

C. PARALLEL CONSTRUCTION

Parallel construction is when you make each of the phrases within your sentence follow the same grammatical pattern. Parallel construction is used when the verbs are in the same format in a series. A plural subject must have a plural verb. A singular subject must have a singular verb. You also must use parallel tenses when you are listing a series of activities. Parallel construction also uses nouns in the same format when providing a list. For instance:

> The children are required to bring to school pencils, pens, and notebooks.

A parallel grammatical pattern makes your writing balanced.

Incorrect: The paralegal association set the following goals: recruitment of new members, engaging the community, and improvement of paralegal work conditions.

Correct: The paralegal association set the following goals: recruitment of new members, engagement of the community, and improvement of paralegal work conditions.

In the correct example, the words *recruitment, engagement,* and *improvement* are parallel.

NET NOTE

The Online Writing Lab at Purdue University has a helpful handout on parallel construction at https://owl.purdue.edu/owl/general_writing/mechanics/parallel_structure.html.

D. SUBJECT AND VERB AGREEMENT

Subject and verb agreement, so essential to proper sentence construction, causes great confusion for many writers. The following are sample situations in which errors are most often made. You must use plural pronouns and verbs when the subjects are plural.

Incorrect: Software Developments Inc. sent Cheryl Faith, a company sales representative, and Nicholas Tallis, their plant manager, to Bailey's plant.

Correct: Software Developments Inc. sent Cheryl Faith, a company sales representative, and Nicholas Tallis, its plant manager, to Bailey's plant.

The second example is correct because *Software Developments Inc.* is a singular subject; therefore, the pronoun before *plant manager* should be the singular possessive *its* rather than *their.*

Incorrect: To assert the attorney-client privilege, the claimant must show that the statements were made in confidence and was made to an attorney for the purpose of obtaining legal advice.

Correct: To assert the attorney-client privilege, the claimant must show that the statements were made in confidence and were made to an attorney for the purpose of obtaining legal advice.

The second example is correct because the verbs must be plural when they have a plural noun. In this example, the word *statements* should have a plural verb.

If you have a singular subject, then each of the pronouns in the sentence that describes that subject should be singular.

Incorrect: To receive this protection in the corporate setting, an individual must show that they were a decision-making employee.

Correct: To receive this protection in the corporate setting, an individual must show that he or she was a decision-making employee.

Collective nouns such as *jury, court, committee,* and *group* often pose a problem for writers, especially when the writer's first language is not English. Collective nouns take a singular verb because they are considered one unit. For example, *jury* is considered one unit; it refers to the group, not to individual jurors.

Incorrect: The jury were to eat lunch at noon.
Correct: The jury was to eat lunch at noon.

Compound subjects also cause confusion. Subjects joined by the word *and* usually use a plural verb, regardless of whether any or all of the individual subjects are singular.

Incorrect: The attorney and the paralegal was available for the client.
Correct: The attorney and the paralegal were available for the client.

When a compound subject is preceded by *each* or *every,* the verb is usually singular.

Incorrect: Each attorney and paralegal in the room have access to the library.
Correct: Each attorney and paralegal in the room has access to the library.

When a compound subject is joined by *or* or *nor,* it takes a singular verb if each subject is singular. It takes a plural verb if each subject is plural. If one subject is singular and the other is plural, the verb follows the closest subject.

> **Subjects singular:**   An apple or an orange is my favorite snack.
> **Subjects plural:**   Apples or oranges are my favorite snacks.
> **Subjects singular and plural:**   Neither the mother nor the children were happy.

To avoid awkwardness, place the plural noun closest to the verb so that the verb is plural.

Awkward: Neither the dogs nor the cat was anywhere in sight.
Revised: Neither the cat nor the dogs were anywhere in sight.

Indefinite pronouns may also throw up roadblocks for writers. Indefinite pronouns are those that do not refer to a specific person or thing. Some common indefinite pronouns are

all	nobody
any	none
anyone	nothing
each	one
either	some
everyone	something

Most indefinite pronouns refer to singular subjects and therefore take a singular verb.

Incorrect: Everyone are free to go. Each of the stores were open on Sunday.
Correct: Everyone is free to go. Each of the stores was open on Sunday.

Some indefinite pronouns (all, any, none, some) may take either a singular or plural verb depending on the meaning of the word they refer to.

Singular: All of the library was quiet. (The library was quiet.)
Plural: All of the paralegals were researching the case. (The paralegals were researching the case.)

E. RUN-ON SENTENCES

A run-on sentence is one in which two separate sentences are connected by using a comma, and, or are sentences without punctuation. Be careful not to use commas to divide run-on sentences. The first example below should be two separate sentences.

Incorrect: Tildy's role is merely advisory, although she might be asked to supply facts about the spill, her opinion probably would not form the basis of any final decision.
Correct: Tildy's role is merely advisory. Although she might be asked to supply facts about the spill, her opinion probably would not form the basis of any final decision.

In the second example, the two sentences are correctly separated with a period. For some run-on sentences, you could divide the sentences with a comma and a conjunction if the clauses are related. In the above example, that solution would not cure the problem because the second sentence is too long. Best to limit sentence length when possible.

PRACTICE POINTER

Revise your sentence into two sentences if it has more than two commas but does not contain a list or a modifying phrase. Whenever you use "and" to join two clauses, determine if you can write two short sentences instead.

F. SENTENCE FRAGMENTS

A sentence fragment is a piece of a sentence. It is an incomplete statement as it lacks either a subject or a verb.

Incorrect: The judge presiding over the case.
Correct: The judge was presiding over the case.

Check to see if a sentence has a verb and a subject. If one is missing, add it.

Incorrect: A case on point.
Correct: The attorney cited a case on point.

NET NOTE

City University of New York's Law School has a guide on sentence fragments in legal writing at www.law.cuny.edu/legal-writing/students/grammar/sentence-fragments.html.

G. THAT AND WHICH

Whether to use **that** or **which** depends on whether the clause that follows is essential to convey the meaning of the sentences. If the clause cannot be omitted, use **that**. If the clause can be omitted and the sentence meaning will not change, use **which**. As stated earlier, a clause that can be omitted or that contains superfluous information is set off with commas. A clause that is essential should not be surrounded by commas.

H. PRONOUNS

A pronoun replaces a noun in a sentence. Most often we use pronouns to take the place of a specific noun called the antecedent. Frequently we use personal pronouns. Examples of personal pronouns are "he," "she," "they," "their," and "you." Personal pronouns pose many challenges for legal writers. In many forums, gender-neutral pronouns are common in the third person ("their" or "they" or "them") when not writing about a specific, known person. Often a writer will use a plural pronoun, such as "their" or "they," in a situation requiring a singular pronoun to make the statement gender neutral.

Legal writing requires great precision, so it is considered incorrect to use a plural pronoun when a singular pronoun is required as it creates ambiguity. Our goals as legal writers are to increase clarity and precision. When a word, term, or phrase may have more than one meaning, we try to avoid that wording and opt for the most precise terms.

Legal writers often select one gender when they are writing about a singular subject and use the respective pronoun consistently throughout the document. Legal writers aim for ultra-clarity so they avoid referring to an individual as "they" or using the possessive "their."

It is best to select one gender when you know the gender of the subject. However, there are times when a legal writer is referring to a subject without knowing the subject's gender. You can alternate between "he" and "she." Also, legal writers can avoid using pronouns by using a verb close to a noun without a pronoun. For example, use "Prosecutors work hard" instead of "She works hard as a prosecutor." Additionally, legal writers can use the plural noun so that "they," "their," or "them" work grammatically. For instance, instead of "A paralegal should update her sources," consider, "Paralegals should update their sources."

Please note that you should be sensitive to your client's needs and requests. Often, a client will indicate the pronoun to use when communicating. Sometimes a client will state that the only pronouns he or she uses are "they," "their," and "them."

PRACTICE POINTER

If your firm has a client who requests a specific pronoun reference, please consult with the attorney so that you may respect the client's wishes.

Incorrect:	A teacher may require their student to comply with an Individual Education Plan (IEP).
Correct, but wordy:	A teacher may require his or her student to comply with an Individual Education Plan (IEP).

Legal writers generally will select either "his" or "her." For example:

A teacher may require her student to comply with an Individual Education Plan (IEP).

If you know the gender of the teacher, use the appropriate pronoun.

Avoiding pronoun references:	Teachers may require students to comply with an Individual Education Plan (IEP).

As long as you do not create ambiguity, you can also revise a sentence so that you use a plural subject and a plural pronoun. A plural noun and a plural pronoun will avoid selecting a gender. For example:

Teachers may require their students to comply with an Individual Education Plan (IEP).

CHAPTER SUMMARY

This chapter reviewed basic grammar rules concerning punctuation, modifiers, parallel construction, subject-verb agreement, and pronoun use. It emphasized the importance of correct grammar in legal writing by demonstrating how errors like incorrect punctuation, misplaced modifiers, faulty subject-verb agreement, and ambiguous pronouns can affect meaning. The chapter also discussed the need for sensitivity and awareness when using pronouns.

KEY TERMS

apostrophes	parallel construction
collective nouns	parentheses
colons	pronouns
commas	run-on sentences
compound subjects	semicolons
indefinite pronouns	sentence fragments
modifiers	

EXERCISES

DISCUSSION QUESTION

Before replying to the questions, please read the article, "A Judge, a Lawsuit and One Very Important Comma," printed in *The New York Times* on March 17, 2017. Online at nytimes.com, the article is titled, "Lack of Oxford Comma Could Cost Maine Company Millions in Overtime Dispute," posted on March 16, 2017 at https://www.nytimes.com/2017/03/16/us/oxford-comma-lawsuit.html.

1. What does the article tell the reader about legal writing?
2. Why is precision important in writing?
3. Why is clarity imperative in writing?

SELF-ASSESSMENT

Edit the following sentences. Name the grammar mistake in each sentence (e.g., misplaced modifier, faulty parallelism, and so forth). Then correct the error by rewriting the sentence.

1. At a time when many law firms and corporations are eliminating jobs for the purpose of elimination from the budget excess expenditures, paralegals may become more of an asset.
2. Because of the fact that paralegals' time is charged at lower rates, paralegals may be employed by law firms and corporations to perform tasks previously performed by lawyers.
3. With specificity, paralegals may be asked to perform legal research of case and statutory materials in the event that a client requests an answer to a problem of a legal nature and is concerned about saving money.
4. In the situation where a paralegal is well trained, that paralegal can be asked by an attorney to perform legal research for the purpose of determining a response to the client's question.
5. With regard to ethical considerations, paralegals can perform legal research under the supervision of an attorney.

6. Subsequent to the research, however, the attorney must be the person who renders the legal opinions that need to be made, the reason being that a paralegal cannot provide legal advice.
7. It is important to note that some states are considering allowing paralegals to practice independently.
8. Try this schedule; shower, eat breakfast, drive to the train, go to work, and come home.
9. There are only one hour and thirty-five minutes left to voir dire, the judge stated.
10. Among the defendants was Max Craig, Sam Harris, and Ricki Anya.
11. The prosecutor will attempt to within the course of the trial persuade you that the defendant committed the crime.
12. The foreman, as well as half of the jury, were late for the afternoon court session.
13. Every one of the councilmen we have named to the commission want to serve.
14. The heart of a trial are the witnesses.
15. None of the players were willing to sign contracts.
16. The substance of Walter Mondale's speeches is more similar to Jimmy Carter.
17. The house was vacated by the tenants.
18. The judge said to the jurors, "please refrain from discussing the case."
19. Four of the five jurors were men. (These were Steer, Halsey, Grodsky, and Molitor.)
20. In her testimony, the witness said she remembered that the defendant asked her "Do you have an aspirin"?
21. These modems are shared with the other subscribers, so the more people on the connection the slower.
22. Working at a law firm from 8:30 A.M. to 5 P.M. handling high-level paralegal work may seem ideal, especially if you rarely work weekends.
23. The National Association of Paralegals said 12 percent of the law firms responded to their survey.
24. Mrs. Newman, at first thought her son, Patrick, was dead because of the amount of blood and broken bones that surrounded the car.
25. The extent of the employer's control and supervision over the worker, including directions on scheduling and performance of work.
26. In the lineup the man which was wearing a red shirt committed the crime.
27. The judge based her decision on the case which had a similar set of facts.
28. The juror in green.
29. The 'judge's clerks draft opinions.
30. Law clerks Robert and Karen each wrote a motion. Robert and Karen's motions were excellent.
31. The Whole In One want to show that they are a company who hired these women as independent contractors not employees.

32. Whether the only funeral home in the area, operating since the 1940s, is a nuisance under common law?
33. Ashton worked without supervision from the company offices.
34. The trial court rejected the confession finding that the defendant had not been given a Miranda warning.
35. The plaintiff said "I never consented to sex."

CASE BRIEFING AND ANALYSIS

CHAPTER OVERVIEW

This chapter teaches you how to brief a case and how to apply a case to a specific fact pattern. Applying a case to a specific fact pattern is case analysis and is used to predict how a court may resolve an issue. The chapter discusses the components of a case brief: the issue, the holding, the facts, the rationale or reasoning, and the disposition. You will learn what to include in each section of the brief and how to skillfully draft the brief.

This chapter also teaches you how to use cases to perform legal analysis.

CASE BRIEFING, IN GENERAL

Case briefing is a skill that you must master to effectively record your research results and analyze a case. Often attorneys will ask you to summarize a case in the form of a case brief. The key to a good brief is that it must be usable. You must be able to return to the brief months after you have prepared it and still be able to quickly understand the facts, the issues, the holdings, and the reasoning of the court.

A good case brief can be done in a variety of ways. Always ask an attorney if he or she has a preference. If not, you should consider the method discussed in this chapter.

A. PURPOSE OF A CASE BRIEF

The goal in writing a **case brief** is to summarize a court decision. A well-drafted brief saves you time because you do not have to reread the original decision to understand its significance. You are able to review the brief to obtain any necessary information. The next goal in briefing a case is to put the components of a decision in a uniform format. This is why we have specified eight set categories for a brief: citation, procedural facts, issues, holding, facts, rationale, dicta, and disposition. The rationale contains the basis for the judge's opinion. The judge relies on the relevant legal rule to support her holding. The legal rule is the test, principle, or standard set down in prior opinions. However, many attorneys use their own uniform format, and sometimes that format will depend on why you are briefing a case.

Sometimes you must brief cases in response to a particular legal issue that you are researching. Sometimes you must brief cases just to summarize decisions.

Remember that a brief is a case summary in a uniform format with established categories of information. The set categories make it easier to compare and contrast decisions. Also, this enables you to see how a case supports a client's problem.

B. DIAGRAM OF A DECISION

Before you begin to write your brief, read the case thoroughly several times. See Illustration 18-1. Consider the questions the court was asked to decide. Determine the parties in the action and what each party is seeking. Sometimes this is complicated, and it helps to draw a diagram of the parties. For example, when the parties are involved in a three-way dispute such as a cross-claim, it might take some time to determine what each party is seeking. Make a column for each party in which you list an issue raised and a remedy sought. After you have read the case, you are ready to write the case brief.

ILLUSTRATION 18-1.   Sample Case, *Seymour v. Armstrong*

612   64 PACIFIC REPORTER.   (Kan.

ance with the requirements of the statute, the precise offense of which the appellant was convicted, and the judgment of the court below will be affirmed. All the justices concurring.

(1) (62 Kan. 720) (2)

SEYMOUR v. ARMSTRONG et al. (3)

(Supreme Court of Kansas. April 6, 1901.)

CONTRACT—VALIDITY—CONSTRUCTION—EVIDENCE.

(4) 1. A contract may originate in an advertisement or offer addressed to the public generally, and, if the offer be accepted by any one in good faith, without qualifications or conditions, it will be sufficient to convert the offer into a binding obligation.

2. If the acceptor affixes conditions to his acceptance not comprehended in the proposal, there can be no agreement without the assent of the proposer to such conditions.

3. If persons carrying on a trade or business give to words and phrases a technical or peculiar meaning, they will be presumed to have contracted with reference to such meaning or usage, unless the contrary appears.

4. Where a term employed in a written contract has a meaning different from the ordinary meaning when used in connection with a trade or business, evidence is admissible to show such meaning, and the sense in which it was used by the parties.

(Syllabus by the Court.)

Error from court of appeals, Northern department, Eastern division.

Action by T. F. Seymour against Armstrong & Kassebaum. Judgment for defendants was affirmed by the court of appeals (61 Pac. 675), and plaintiff brings error. Affirmed.

J. A. Rosen and David Martin, for plaintiff in error. Isenhart & Alexander, for defendants in error.

(5) JOHNSTON, J. This was an action to recover damages for the breach of an alleged contract. On February 15, 1896, Armstrong (6) & Kassebaum, commission merchants of Topeka, inserted an advertisement in a weekly (7) newspaper, which, among other things, contained the following proposition: "We will pay 10½c., net Topeka, for all fresh eggs shipped us to arrive here by February 22. Acceptance of our bid with number of cases stated to be sent by February 20th." On February 20, 1896, T. F. Seymour, a rival commission merchant of Topeka, sent the following note to Armstrong & Kassebaum in response to their proposition: "I accept your offer in Merchants' Journal, 10½ cents, Topeka, for fresh eggs, and will ship you on C., R. I. & P. R. R. 450 cases fresh eggs, to arrive on or before February 22d. The eggs are all packed in new No. 2 white wood cases, and I will accept 15 cents each for them, or you can return them, or new ones in place of them." On receipt of this note, Armstrong & Kassebaum at once notified Seymour that they would not accept the eggs on the terms proposed by him. Notwithstanding the refusal, Seymour pro-

cured a car, and loaded it with eggs. Not having a sufficient number of eggs to fill the car, Seymour found two other commission merchants who were willing to co-operate with him, and who furnished 190 of the 450 cases, which were loaded in Topeka, only a few hundred feet away from the place of business of Armstrong & Kassebaum, sealed up, and then pushed a short distance over to their business house. They refused to receive the eggs, and Seymour shipped them to Philadelphia, where they were sold for $391.83 less than they would have brought at the price named in Seymour's note of acceptance. For this amount the present action was brought, and the plaintiff is entitled to recover if the defendants' offer on eggs was unconditionally accepted. At the trial a verdict was returned (8) in favor of the defendants, and the result of the general finding is that the pretended acceptance of Seymour was not unconditional, and that no contract was, in fact, made (10A) between him and the defendants.

Did the negotiations between the parties result in a contract? A contract may originate in an advertisement addressed to the public generally, and, if the proposal be accepted by any one in good faith, without qualifications or conditions, the contract is complete. The fact that there was no limit as to number or quantity of eggs in the (9) offer did not prevent an acceptance. The number or quantity was left to the determination of the acceptor, and an unconditional acceptance naming any reasonable number or quantity is sufficient to convert the offer into a binding obligation. It is e- (11A) sential, however, that the minds of the contracting parties should come to the point of agreement,—that the offer and acceptance should coincide; and, if they do not correspond in every material respect, there is no acceptance or completed contract. In our view, the so-called "acceptance" of the plaintiff is not absolute and unconditional. It affixed conditions not comprehended in the proposal, and there could be no agreement (9) without the assent of the proposer to such conditions. It is true, the plaintiff agreed to furnish eggs at 10½ cents per dozen, but his acceptance required the defendant to pay 15 cents each for the cases in which the eggs were packed, or to return the cases, or new ones in place of them. It appears from the record that according to the usages of the business the cases go with the eggs, as was done in this case.

One of the grounds of complaint is that (10B) the court erred in admitting testimony as to the sense in which the word "net" was used in the negotiations between the parties, and in submitting to the jury the question of whether the offer of the defendants was accepted. The plaintiff is hardly in a position to question the propriety of receiving evidence as to the meaning of the word "net," used in the offer and acceptance.

ILLUSTRATION 18-1. *Continued*

Kan.)   CITY OF KANSAS CITY v. SMILEY.   613

He was the first to open an inquiry, and to bring out testimony as to what was meant by the term when used in connection with a sale of eggs. Aside from that consideration, **(11B)** the term appears to have a meaning in connection with the business different from the ordinary meaning, and in such case evidence of the meaning given by usage of the trade or business is admissible. If persons carrying on a particular trade or business give to words or phrases a technical or peculiar meaning, they will be presumed to contract with reference to the usage, unless the contrary appears. There was abundant evidence to show that the use of the word "net," according to the usage of the business, includes the cases of eggs like the one question. The witnesses stated that it **(11A+B)** was a price clear to the purchaser without commissions, cartage, or any charge for cases. The finding of the jury, in effect, that it was understood and agreed that the cases went with and were included in the price quoted for the eggs, and the acceptance, therefore, did not correspond with the offer, nor complete the contract. We think that under the circumstances parol testimony of the sense in which the terms were used, and as to what the parties intended by them, was properly received, and that the court properly charged the jury as to the elements entering into a contract. Cosper v. Nesbit, 45 Kan. 457, 25 Pac. 866. Others of the instructions are criticised, but we find nothing substantial in any of the objections made nor in any of the grounds assigned for reversal. The judgment of the court of appeals and the district court will be affirmed. All the justices concurring. **(12)**

1	Citation
2	Case name
3	Date of decision
4	Syllabus by court
5	Judge's name authoring the opinion
6	Opinion
7	Facts
8	Procedure
9	Rationale or reasoning
10A	Issue 1
10B	Issue 2
11A	Holding 1
11B	Holding 2
12	Disposition

Reprinted with permission of Thomson Reuters.

Write the brief in your own words and paraphrase rather than quote a court's statements unless the statements are well-phrased, concise, and understandable. Paraphrasing the information from the cases helps you analyze a case and allows you to understand the brief quickly when you return to it later. Also, paraphrasing cases helps when you are writing about an opinion in a memo. The memo will read more smoothly if you use your own voice when you import the information from case brief rather than using quoted language from the opinion.

IN-CLASS EXERCISE

Compare the writing styles in the *Seymour* and the *Lefkowitz* decisions in this chapter. You will notice that the writing styles differ. When you brief cases and use the cases in an assignment, if you paraphrase the points from the cases, your writing will be smoother. Use your own language but always provide citations to authority.

C. ANATOMY OF A CASE BRIEF

Because a brief is a summary of a decision in a uniform format, there are set categories. You should label the sections of the brief: citation, procedural history or procedure, issue, holding, rationale (which includes the legal rule or standard), dicta (if they exist in the case), and disposition.

1. Citation

The case brief starts with a **case citation**, which allows you to find the case at a later date. First, note the name of the case, which is generally found at the top of the page. Then add the case citation or docket number of the case. See Illustration 18-2. Be sure to include the date of the decision and the name of the deciding court. Next, you might want to make a note concerning whether the decision is primary binding or primary persuasive authority. (For more information about binding and persuasive authority, see Chapter 2.) Follow either *Bluebook* or *ALWD* rules for case citation format.

ILLUSTRATION 18-2. Sample Case, *King v. Miller*

KING v. MILLER
1000 E.R. 108 (Karen Ct. App. 2019)

Evelyn King, an insurance agent who worked for the defendant, Miller Company, filed a lawsuit claiming that the defendant discriminated against her on the basis of her sex in violation of Title VII, 42 U.S.C. § 2000e et seq. Upon a motion for summary judgment, the district court granted the motion in favor of Miller. The district court found that King was not an employee of the defendant. She did not work in a manner consistent with an employee. The court said that King was an independent contractor. As an independent contractor, her discrimination claim was outside the protection of the federal law. King appealed the trial court's decision.

In 2014, King was hired by Miller to work as an "employee agent." As such, she was paid a salary. Income taxes and Social Security were withheld by Miller. She was promoted to "independent contract agent." King could not remain an employee agent for more than one year. When she was promoted she had to sign an agreement that stated that she was an independent contractor.

ILLUSTRATION 18-2. *Continued*

As an independent contract agent, King earned a commission on her sales and some bonuses. She did not receive any paid holidays, sick days, or vacation days. She paid for her own health, life, and disability insurance.

Miller, however, provided office space, furniture, file cabinets, rate books, forms, shared secretarial services, stamps, computers, and Miller's stationery. King purchased her own personalized stationery, pens, and business cards. Miller paid King's tuition for required special insurance seminars, provided lunch at such programs, and rented the space for the sessions.

King had wanted to work for Miller because Miller had a good reputation. Before coming to Miller's office, King worked for three other insurance companies. King was a single, 30-year-old mother of two children. Before her experience in the insurance industry, she worked as a sales clerk at a local boutique.

While working as an independent contract agent for Miller, King could not sell insurance for any other company. She also could only sell insurance in the county designated by the company manager. She had to work at the Miller office three and one-half days a week and every third Saturday, attend two hour-long meetings each week, and retrieve mail every day.

King was responsible for finding her own customers and deciding which products to offer. She could set the hours she worked and she worked without direct supervision. Miller did not regularly review her work. King was fired in 2015, and a man was hired to take her place.

The district court found that based upon these facts, King was an independent contractor, not an employee. The court focused on the economic realities test. One of the factors it considered as part of its test for determining whether King was an employee or an independent contractor was Miller's right to control King. *Spirides v. Reinhardt*, 613 F.2d 826, 831 (D.C. Cir. 1979), is the leading case regarding the question of whether an individual is an employee, or an independent contractor, under the federal discrimination laws. The *Spirides* court adopted an 11-part test. These factors are:

> 1) the kind of occupation, whether the work is usually done under the direction of a supervisor or without a supervisor; 2) the skill required; 3) whether the "employer" provides the equipment used and the workplace; 4) how long the individual has worked; 5) how the individual is paid, whether by assignment, piece, or time; 6) how the work relationship is to be terminated, i.e., was notice required; 7) whether vacation is provided; 8) whether retirement benefits are provided; 9) whether the employer deducts social security and income tax payments; 10) whether the work is an integral part of the employer's business; and 11) the intention of the parties.

Id.

The Karen district court focused on five of those factors: 1) the extent of Miller's control and supervision of King concerning scheduling and

ILLUSTRATION 18-2. *Continued*

performance of work; 2) the kind of occupation and the nature of the skill required; 3) the division of the costs of the operation, equipment, supplies, and fees; 4) the method and form of payment and benefits; 5) length of job commitment. Central to its decision was the lack of control Miller exercised over King. The court found that King had a great deal of freedom to select her hours, her clients, and the insurance products she sold.

King must prove that an employment relationship existed between herself and Miller in order to maintain a Title VII action against Miller. Independent contractors are not protected by Title VII. *Spirides*, 613 F.2d at 831. Title VII defines employee "as an individual employed by an employer." 42 U.S.C § 2000E(f). "In determining whether the relationship is one of employee-employer, courts look to the 'economic realities' of the relationship and the degree of control the employer exercises over the alleged employee." See *Unger v. Consolidated Foods Corp.*, 657 F.2d 909, 915-916 n.8 (7th Cir. 1981).

On appeal, King contends that the district court placed too much weight on the "control factor" and the fact the Miller did not supervise King's work and did not dictate King's hours, products, or customers. Based upon this emphasis, King argues that the district court's decision was erroneous.

However, this court finds that the district court correctly considered other facts such as that King was paid on commission, did not receive benefits, and provided many of her own supplies, including stationery and business cards.

Although this court was not asked to determine whether the district court should have considered all of the facts that were relevant to each of the 11 factors stated in the *Spirides* economic realities test, this court finds that the district court should have done so.

Although we think that the district court should have focused its analysis on all 11 factors, we do not think that its decision is clearly erroneous; therefore, we affirm the decision of the district court in granting summary judgment for the defendant, Miller.

2. Procedural History

This section of the case brief should be labeled **procedural history** or simply procedure. These facts explain the status of the case. You will summarize how this case traveled through the court system to reach this point. See Illustration 18-3. In this section, you note the action of the prior courts. For example, if the decision concerns an appeal to a federal appellate court, note that. Also, state whether the court reversed or affirmed the lower court's decision and whether the case was remanded.

> ### *PRACTICE POINTER*
>
> Always validate any case that you brief by using *Shepard's*® or KeyCite. Note the date validated at the top of the brief so that you know to update if necessary.

ILLUSTRATION 18-3.   Sample Case Brief, *King v. Miller*

KING v. MILLER
1000 E.R. 108 (Karen Ct. App. 2019)

PROCEDURAL HISTORY

The case was on appeal from the District Court's grant of summary judgment for the defendant Miller.

ISSUE

Is King, a worker subject to only minimal company control and who was paid commissions rather than a salary and benefits, an employee protected by Title VII or an independent contractor who is outside the protection of the federal law?

HOLDING

King, a worker subject to only minimal company control and who was paid commissions rather than a salary and benefits, was an independent contractor rather than an employee protected by Title VII.

FACTS

King first worked for Miller as an employee agent. During that time, she received a salary and the company withheld income tax and Social Security payments. King later was promoted to independent contract agent.

As an independent contract agent, King earned a commission and bonuses but did not receive a salary. She signed an agreement that stated that she was an independent contractor. As a contract agent, she did not receive paid holidays, sick days, or vacation days, and she paid for her own health, life, and disability insurance. King supplied her own personalized stationery, business cards, and pens. She found her own customers, decided which products to sell, and set her own hours.

For its contract agents, Miller supplied office space, furniture, file cabinets, forms, shared secretarial services, stamps, computers, and stationery. Miller also paid for required insurance seminars. Miller required that contract agents, such as King, attend weekly meetings, work in the office three and one-half days per week and every third Saturday, check their mail and retrieve messages daily, and sell only Miller insurance. Miller also restricted King's sales area. Miller did not regularly review King's work.

ILLUSTRATION 18-3. *Continued*

REASONING

In order to determine whether an individual is an employee or an independent contractor, the employment relationship between the parties needs to be evaluated based upon the economic realities and circumstances of the relationship. The court considered the control exercised by the "employer" over the worker; the method of payment; who paid for the individual's benefits, such as life and health insurance; and who paid for the operation. In this case, the court found that King was an independent contractor because she was paid on commission, she paid for her own benefits, she supplied her own supplies, and she controlled her work. The court found that she set her own hours, selected the product she sold, and generated her own clients. Based upon these facts, the appellate court found that King should be considered an independent contractor rather than an employee.

DICTA

The 11-part test set by the *Spirides* court should be applied to determine whether an individual is an employee or an independent contractor.

DISPOSITION

The Court of Appeals affirmed the district court's judgment in granting summary judgment for the defendant.

PRACTICE POINTER

Obtain all of the citation information when you are using the reporter or accessing the case online. Record all of the citation information in the brief, including the precise pages where you obtained the information, the pin cites. Write the cites in *Bluebook* or *ALWD* format. Later, when writing, you will not have to revisit the decision to get the cite information.

3. Issues

Next, list the **issue** or issues presented in the case. See Illustration 18-3. Although determining the issues in a case is a difficult process at first, it does get easier with practice.

The issues are the questions the parties asked the court to decide. In most cases, multiple issues are presented. To determine the issues, you must understand the legal rules that govern a particular case. If you are briefing a case and you have not been assigned an issue to research, list all the issues presented in the case. If you have been given a research assignment, you need only brief the issues that are relevant to your research, listing each one separately.

▼ How Do You Determine the Legal Issue or Issues Presented When Examining a Client's Problem?

To understand this process, assume you have been asked to research whether your firm's client, Whole In One, will be subject to the federal antidiscrimination laws. Whole In One is a seasonal restaurant and golf course in Glenview, Illinois. Two women, Victoria Radiant and Karen Walker, brought suit against Whole In One for sex discrimination. Their claims are based on a federal antidiscrimination statute commonly known as Title VII. You have been asked to research whether Whole In One is an employer and whether the women are employees under the definitions included in the federal law. During your research, you find the case of *King v. Miller.* Review Illustration 18-2.

To determine the issue, read the case. Ask yourself, "What did the parties ask the court to determine?" Sometimes the court will note the issue directly in its opinion. Other times, you must search through the opinion to determine the issue. After you have read the *King* case, you should note that it involves a question of sex discrimination. However, your research is limited to the issues that concern the definitions of *employer* and *employee.* Therefore, the case brief should focus on issues that relate to your research problem.

Once you have read the *King* case, you will find that it addresses the question of whether an individual is an employee protected by Title VII. Now you are ready to draft the issue.

▼ How Do You Draft a Statement of the Issue or Issues?

For the *King* case, you might start with this brief issue:

> Is King an employee protected by Title VII or an independent contractor who is outside the protection of the federal law?

Now that the issue is presented in question format, you could leave the issue section here. However, the issue would be more meaningful for your research if you included more information about the legal issue the court focused on in making its determination. In its discussion, the *King* court focused on the amount of control that an employer must exercise before an individual is viewed as an employee rather than an independent contractor. You could incorporate the court's focus on control into the issue as follows:

> Is King, a worker subject to only minimal company control, an employee protected by Title VII, or an independent contractor who is outside the protection of the federal law?

You also should include relevant facts in your issue statement. Again, this will make the issue more meaningful for your research. In this case, for example, you might add some facts about the company's method of payment and its lack of provisions for benefits:

> Is King, a worker subject to only minimal company control who was paid commissions rather than salary and benefits, an employee protected by Title VII, or an independent contractor who is outside the protection of the federal law?

The final issue statement is the best because it incorporates the relevant facts that affect a court's decision concerning this issue and the **rule of law** that will be applied.

You might wonder why the issue did not focus on the appellate court's consideration of the district court's action in granting the motion for summary judgment in favor of the defendant. Students often phrase such an issue as follows:

> Did the district court err in granting summary judgment in favor of the defendant?

However, this issue focuses too heavily on the procedural question posed in the *King* case and does not include the applicable law or any of the legally significant facts. Your issue should concern the legal, not the procedural, questions a court was asked to decide. As you learned above, the *King* case involved a motion for summary judgment.

To find the substantive legal issue, determine the legal question the parties asked the court to answer in the motion for summary judgment. In the *King* case, the parties asked the court to determine whether, as a matter of law, King was an independent contractor rather than an employee. This is the central legal issue. By focusing on this substantive issue rather than the procedural issue, your brief will be more useful to you in your research of the Whole In One case.

Some of you might wonder why you do not focus on the question of discrimination in your issue section. Remember the issue you were asked to answer with your research. You were asked to deal with the issues of the definitions of *employee* and *employer.* You should tailor your brief to address only these issues.

4. Holding

The next section should be your **holding**. Essentially a holding is the court's answer to the issue or question presented. However, it is not a yes, no, or maybe answer to the issue. The holding should be a full sentence that responds directly to the issue posed and that incorporates both the legal standards and the most significant legal facts on which the answer is based. A holding differs from a legal rule in that a legal rule is the standard, test, or principle that the court uses in its rationale, or reasoning, to explain its holding or to arrive at its holding. The holding addresses the specific question before the court.

▼ How Do You Draft a Holding?

The process for drafting the holding is similar to the process for writing your issue statement. First, your holding should be a statement that answers the issue. Assume you selected the first issue statement considered in this discussion:

> Is King an employee protected by Title VII or an independent contractor who is outside the protection of the federal law?

You might consider answering it as follows:

> King is an independent contractor rather than an employee and therefore is outside the protection of Title VII.

While this statement is simple and direct, similar to the first issue statement, it does not contain any relevant facts or incorporate any legal standards. This holding should be rewritten, incorporating the elements or legal standards that would be considered. Such a change would make the holding more meaningful in the context of this research.

The rewritten issue, for which we will draft a holding, could read:

> Is King, a worker subject to only minimal company control, an independent contractor, or is she an employee protected by Title VII?

Again, you might want to include additional facts the court considered in determining that King was an independent contractor. For the holding, rewrite the final issue statement drafted above in the form of a statement.

> King, a worker subject to only minimal company control who was paid commissions rather than salary and benefits, was an independent contractor rather than an employee protected by Title VII.

The key to drafting a clear issue statement, holding, or any other component of the brief, is rewriting and editing. You must make your holding broad enough so that it could be useful for various research projects involving different fact patterns. However, a clear holding incorporates facts from the case at hand that make it unique and that limit the holding so that you can understand the facts that form the basis for the court's decision. These facts are the **legally significant facts**. Also, try to make the statement of the holding narrow enough so that it reflects the unique legal issue in the case. Refine your statements and assess whether they are helpful in your research summary.

Also, be careful to incorporate the facts and the underlying law into your holding statement, as you did in your issue statement. A holding such as:

The district court did not err in granting summary judgment in favor of the defendant.

is not valuable for your research. It does not explain why the court found that the district court's decision was correct.

5. Facts

The next section of the brief should be the **facts**. Be certain to include the names of the parties, a notation concerning whether the party is a plaintiff, a defendant, an appellant, or appellee, and some details about the party, such as whether it is a corporation or an individual. State the relevant rather than procedural facts in this section. Also, explain why a party sought legal assistance.

▼ What Are the Relevant Facts?

Relevant facts are those facts that may have an effect on the legal issues decided in a particular action. To write this section, you must clearly understand the issues decided by the court. Decide which facts the court relied on to make its decision. Those are the facts that you should include in this section. The facts should be presented in a paragraph form rather than in a list or in bullet points. Also, mention any facts that will assist you in understanding the relationship between the parties and the nature of the dispute.

In the *King* case, the court relied on facts that explained the relationship between King and the Miller Co. For example, the court considered that King earned commissions and bonuses rather than a salary. That fact should be listed. Before you write your facts statement in paragraph format, make a rough outline of all the facts that the court considered in making its decision. Sometimes a chronological timeline helps when organizing the facts. For the *King* case, your outline might look like this:

King first worked as an "employee" agent
    As an employee agent, King was paid salary, and the company withheld taxes

King later was designated an "independent contract" agent, earned commission and bonuses but no salary
    King signed an agreement that she was an independent contractor
    Did not receive paid holidays, sick days, or vacation
    Paid for her own health, life, and disability insurance

Miller supplied office space, furniture, file cabinets, forms, shared secretarial services, stamps, computers, and Miller stationery

Miller paid for insurance seminars and lunches at the seminars

Miller required that King attend weekly meetings, work in the office three and one-half days per week and every third Saturday, check her mail and retrieve messages daily, and sell only Miller insurance

Miller restricted King's sales area

Miller did not regularly review King's work

King supplied her own personalized stationery, business cards, pens

King found her own customers, decided which products to sell, and set her own hours

The court listed additional facts, such as:

King had wanted to work for Miller because Miller had a good reputation

Before coming to Miller's office, King worked for three other insurance companies

King was a single, 30-year-old mother of two children

Before her experience in the insurance industry, she worked as a sales clerk at a local boutique

Note that for its decision the court did not consider any of the facts contained in the outline under additional facts. Therefore, they are not relevant, or legally significant, facts and should not be included in your brief. After you have made your outline and determined which facts are relevant, you should draft your facts statement in paragraph format. A list is not as helpful as a paragraph when you want to review the brief at a later date.

▼ How Do You Organize Your Facts Statement?

Your facts statement could be written in chronological order, in topical order, or using a combination of the two methods. Chronological order often works best when the case involves facts that need to be placed in order according to when they occurred. For example, in a personal injury action that results from a car accident, a chronological set of facts is best. Start with the first fact that occurred and work forward.

A chronological organization for the facts in the *King* case would read as follows:

In 2014, King started to work for Miller. King first worked for Miller as an employee agent. During that time, she received a salary and the company withheld income tax and Social Security payments. King later was promoted to contract agent. King was fired in 2015, and a man was hired to take her place.

A topical organization is the best choice for facts that have no temporal relationship. Instead, these facts are grouped by topic or legal claim. In this case, the topic is the legal question of whether King was an independent contractor. Therefore, you would group together all the facts that relate to this question.

> As an independent contract agent, King earned a commission and bonuses but did not receive a salary. She signed an agreement that stated that she was an independent contractor. As a contract agent, she did not receive paid holidays, sick days, or vacation days, and she paid for her own health, life, and disability insurance. King supplied her own personalized stationery, business cards, and pens. She found her own customers, decided which products to sell, and set her own hours.
>
> For its independent contract agents, Miller supplied office space, furniture, file cabinets, forms, shared secretarial services, stamps, computers, and Miller stationery. Miller also paid for required insurance seminars. Miller required that contract agents, such as King, attend weekly meetings, work in the office three and one-half days per week and every third Saturday, check their mail and retrieve messages daily, and sell only Miller insurance. Miller also restricted King's sales area. Miller did not regularly review King's work.

In the *King* case, a combination of a chronological and topical organization works best. The *King* brief facts statement might read as follows:

> King first worked for Miller as an employee agent. During that time, she received a salary and the company withheld income tax and Social Security payments. King later was promoted to independent contract agent.
>
> As an independent contract agent, King earned a commission and bonuses but did not receive a salary. She signed an agreement that stated that she was an independent contractor. As a contract agent, she did not receive paid holidays, sick days, or vacation days, and she paid for her own health, life, and disability insurance. King supplied her own personalized stationery, business cards, and pens. She found her own customers, decided which products to sell, and set her own hours.
>
> For its contract agents, Miller supplied office space, furniture, file cabinets, forms, shared secretarial services, stamps, computers, and Miller stationery. Miller also paid for required insurance seminars. Miller required that contract agents, such as King, attend weekly meetings, work in the office three and one-half days per week and every third Saturday, check their mail and retrieve messages daily, and sell only Miller insurance. Miller also restricted King's sales area. Miller did not regularly review King's work.

The above facts statement begins with a chronological organization. It explains the beginning of the relationship between King and Miller. Next, it states all the facts that pertain to King's benefits and her control of her work. The next paragraph explains what Miller provided for the independent contract agents and what Miller required of them. Following this facts section, you should include a reasoning or rationale section in a brief.

6. Reasoning

In the **reasoning** or **rationale** section, you should explain the court's thought process and relevant cases or statutes, then apply the law to the facts of the case you are briefing. Essentially, you will explain the law the court relied on in making a decision and why the court reached its decision. The court will base its opinion on the relevant legal rule. The legal rule is the principle, test, or standard. Sometimes the court uses more than one rule. For example, the *King* court reviewed the definition of *employee* contained in Title VII and past case precedent, such as *Spirides v. Reinhardt*, 613 F.2d 826, 831 (D.C. Cir. 1979), and *Unger v. Consolidated Foods Corp.*, 657 F.2d 909, 915-916 n.8 (7th Cir. 1981), to determine that independent contractors are not protected by Title VII. Both of these cases are from different jurisdictions. The *Spirides* case is primary binding authority only in the District of Columbia Circuit and *Unger* is primary binding authority only within the Seventh Circuit. However, both are persuasive authorities in other circuits. Explain in this section whether the court relied on binding or persuasive authority.

You also must review a decision for any tests a court considered in making its decision. In *King*, the court considered the economic realities test. Finally, note how the court applied the law to the facts of the particular case.

For the *King* case, you might include the following reasoning section in your brief:

> To determine whether an individual is an employee or an independent contractor, the employment relationship between the parties needs to be evaluated based on the economic realities and circumstances of the relationship. The court reviewed several of the factors set forth by the District of Columbia Circuit Court in *Spirides v. Reinhardt*, 613 F.2d 826, 831 (D.C. Cir. 1979), a persuasive authority, and the economic realities of the situation as defined by the Seventh Circuit court in *Unger v. Consolidated Foods Corp.*, 657 F.2d 909, 915-916 n.8 (7th Cir. 1981), another persuasive decision. Based upon these factors, the *King* court considered the control exercised by the "employer" over the worker; the method of payment; who paid for the individual's benefits, such as life and health insurance; and who paid for the operation. In this case, the court found that King was an independent

contractor because she was paid on commission, she paid for her own benefits, she provided her own supplies, and she controlled her work. The court found that she set her own hours, selected the products she sold, and generated her own clients. Based on these facts, the appellate court found that King should be considered an independent contractor rather than an employee.

Or you could prepare the reasoning section without any reference to the underlying, or embedded, case law.

To determine whether an individual is an employee or an independent contractor, the employment relationship between the parties needs to be evaluated based on the economic realities and circumstances of the relationship. The *King* court considered the control exercised by the "employer" over the worker; the method of payment; who paid for the individual's benefits, such as life and health insurance; and who paid for the operation. In this case, the court found that King was an independent contractor because she was paid on commission, she paid for her own benefits, she provided her own supplies, and she controlled her work. The court found that she set her own hours, selected the products she sold, and generated her own clients. Based on these facts, the appellate court found that King should be considered an independent contractor rather than an employee.

In the reasoning section, you should include an application of the law to the facts of the case and a mini-conclusion that summarizes the court's decision. In the above example, the following section is the application of the court's reasoning to the facts of the case.

In this case, the court found that King was an independent contractor because she was paid on commission, she paid for her own benefits, she provided her own supplies, and she controlled her work. The court found that she set her own hours, selected the products she sold, and generated her own clients.

This also provides insight into the legally significant facts, so that when you examine your problem, you will look at parallel facts to determine if the client was an employee.

In the above example, the following statement is the mini-conclusion:

Based on these facts, the appellate court found that King should be considered an independent contractor rather than an employee.

In some cases, you will find that a court bases its decision on reasons other than statutes or past cases. For example, a court might consider whether its decision would be fair under the circumstances. This type of analysis is called the court's consideration of policy, which sometimes is a question of what would benefit society, such as equal rights in an educational setting. Incorporate this policy into your reasoning section whenever it is useful for your research. After the reasoning or rationale, discuss any dicta contained in the court's decision.

7. Dicta

If a court makes a statement concerning a question that it was not asked to answer, this statement is called **dicta**. Although dicta does not have any binding effect, it is often useful to predict how a court might decide a particular issue in the future. Therefore, you want to include any dicta that might affect your case.

In the *King* case, the court stated that it was not asked to decide whether the district court should have considered all 11 factors before it rendered its decision. However, the court stated that the district court should have based its decision on all 11 factors. This statement by the court was dicta. It is helpful for your research problem because it states the factors that this circuit court might consider in determining whether an individual is an independent contractor rather than an employee.

The dicta section for the *King* case might read as follows:

The 11-part test set by the *Spirides* court should be applied to determine whether an individual is an employee or an independent contractor.

8. Disposition

The final section of your brief is the **disposition**. The disposition of a case is essentially the procedural result of the court's decision. For example, in the *King* case, the court found that the district court's decision to grant summary judgment for the defendant was correct. Therefore, the disposition section would state:

The court of appeals affirmed the district court's judgment in granting summary judgment for the defendant.

Finally, remember to rewrite your brief, but do not spend too much time rewriting it. Use your own words rather than many quotes from the court opinions. Paraphrasing in your own words helps you analyze the case and better understand it when you review your brief in the future. Also, paraphrasing allows you to import the information from the brief into a document that you draft later. You may even cut and paste portions of a well-drafted brief into a memo. Try to limit the length of the brief to one page typed. The single page makes it easier to use the case when writing. The short format also enables us to compare and contrast opinions easily.

ILLUSTRATION 18-4. *Lefkowitz v. Great Minneapolis Surplus Store, Inc.*

Lefkowitz v. Great Minneapolis Surplus Store, Inc.

Supreme Court of Minnesota

December 20, 1957

No. 37,220

Reporter
251 Minn. 188 *; 86 N.W.2d 689 **; 1957 Minn. LEXIS 684 ***

Morris Lefkowitz v. Great Minneapolis Surplus Store, Inc.

Prior History: [***1] Action in the conciliation court of Minneapolis, Hennepin County, for damages for defendant's alleged failure to sell to plaintiff certain items as advertised in the newspaper. After removal to the municipal court of Minneapolis, the court, Lindsay G. Arthur, Judge, found for plaintiff, and defendant appealed from an order denying his motion for a new trial.

Disposition: Affirmed.

Core Terms

advertisement, newspaper, unilateral, terms

Counsel: *Louis F. Davis*, for appellant.

Morris Lefkowitz, pro se, for respondent.

Judges: Murphy, Justice.

Opinion by: MURPHY

Opinion

[*189] [**690] This is an appeal from [***2] an order of the Municipal Court of Minneapolis denying the motion of the defendant for amended findings of fact, or, in the alternative, for a new trial. The order for judgment awarded the plaintiff the sum of $ 138.50 as damages for breach of contract.

This case grows out of the alleged refusal of the defendant to sell to the plaintiff a certain fur piece which it had offered for sale in a newspaper advertisement. It appears from the record that on April 6, 1956, the defendant published the following advertisement in a Minneapolis newspaper:

"Saturday 9 a.m. sharp

3 Brand New

Fur Coats

Worth to $ 100.00

First Come

First Served

$ 1

Each"

On April 13, the defendant again published an advertisement in the same newspaper as follows:

"Saturday 9 a.m.

2 Brand New Pastel

Mink 3-Skin Scarfs

Selling for $ 89.50

Out they go

Saturday. Each $ 1.00

1 Black Lapin Stole

Beautiful,

worth $ 139.50 $ 1.00

First Come

First Served"

[*190] The record supports the findings of the court that on each of the Saturdays following the publication of the above-described ads the plaintiff was the first to present himself at the appropriate counter [***3] in the defendant's store and on

ILLUSTRATION 18-4.   *Continued*

Lefkowitz v. Great Minneapolis Surplus Store, Inc.

each occasion demanded the coat and the stole so advertised and indicated his readiness to pay the sale price of $ 1. On both occasions, the defendant refused to sell the merchandise to the plaintiff, stating on the first occasion that by a "house rule" the offer was intended for women only and sales would not be made to men, and on the second visit that plaintiff knew defendant's house rules.

The trial court properly disallowed plaintiff's claim for the value of the fur coats since the value of these articles was speculative and uncertain. The only evidence of value was the advertisement itself to the effect that the coats were "Worth to $ 100.00," how much less being speculative especially in view of the price for which they were offered for sale. With reference to the offer of the defendant on April 13, 1956, to sell the "1 Black Lapin Stole * * * worth $ 139.50 * * *" the trial court held that the value of this article was established and granted judgment in favor of the plaintiff for that amount less the $ 1 quoted purchase price.

1. The defendant contends that a newspaper advertisement offering items of merchandise for sale at a named price [***4] is a "unilateral offer" which may be withdrawn without notice. He relies upon authorities which hold that, where an advertiser publishes in a newspaper that he has a certain quantity or quality of goods which he wants to dispose of at certain prices and on certain terms, such advertisements are not offers which become contracts as soon as any person to whose notice they may come signifies his acceptance by notifying the other that he will take a certain quantity of them. Such advertisements have been construed as an invitation for an offer of sale on the terms stated, which offer, when received, may be accepted or rejected and which therefore does not become a contract of sale until accepted by the seller; and until a contract has been so made, the seller [**691] may modify or revoke such prices or terms. *Montgomery Ward & Co. v. Johnson, 209 Mass. 89, 95 N.E. 290*; *Nickel v. Theresa Farmers Co-op. Assn. 247 Wis. 412, 20 N.W. (2d) 117*; *Lovett v. Frederick Loeser & Co. Inc. 124 Misc. 81, 207 N.Y.S. 753*; *Schenectady Stove Co. v. Holbrook, [*191] 101 N.Y. 45, 4 N.E. 4*; *Georgian Co. v. Bloom, 27 Ga. App. 468, 108 S.E. 813*; Craft v. Elder & Johnston Co. 34 Ohio L.A. 603, 38 N.E. [***5] (2d) 416; Annotation, 157 A.L.R. 746.

The defendant relies principally on Craft v. Elder & Johnston Co. *supra*. In that case, the court discussed the legal effect of an advertisement offering for sale, as a one-day special, an electric sewing machine at a named price. The view was expressed that the advertisement was (34 Ohio L.A. 605, 38 N.E. [2d] 417) "not an offer made to any specific person but was made to the public generally. Thereby it would be properly designated as a unilateral offer and not being

supported by any consideration could be withdrawn at will and without notice." It is true that such an offer may be withdrawn before acceptance. Since all offers are by their nature unilateral because they are necessarily made by one party or on one side in the negotiation of a contract, the distinction made in that decision between a unilateral offer and a unilateral contract is not clear. On the facts before us we are concerned with whether the advertisement constituted an offer, and, if so, whether the plaintiff's conduct constituted an acceptance.

There are numerous authorities which hold that a particular advertisement in a newspaper or circular letter relating to [***6] a sale of articles may be construed by the court as constituting an offer, acceptance of which would complete a contract. *J.E. Pinkham Lbr. Co. v. C.W. Griffin & Co. 212 Ala. 341, 102 So. 689*; *Seymour v. Armstrong & Kassebaum, 62 Kan. 720, 64 P. 612*; *Payne v. Lautz Bros. & Co. 166 N.Y.S. 844*, affirmed, *168 N.Y.S. 369*, affirmed, *185 App. Div. 904, 171 N.Y.S. 1094*; Arnold v. Phillips, 1 Ohio Dec. (Reprint) 195, 3 Western L.J. 448; *Oliver v. Henley (Tex. Civ. App.) 21 S.W. (2d) 576*; Annotation, 157 A.L.R. 744, 746.

The test of whether a binding obligation may originate in advertisements addressed to the general public is "whether the facts show that some performance was promised in positive terms in return for something requested." 1 Williston, Contracts (Rev. ed.) § 27.

The authorities above cited emphasize that, where the offer is clear, definite, and explicit, and leaves nothing open for negotiation, it constitutes an offer, acceptance of which will complete the contract. The most recent case on the subject is Johnson v. Capital City Ford Co. [*192] (La. App.) 85 So. (2d) 75, in which the court pointed out that a newspaper advertisement relating to the purchase and sale [***7] of automobiles may constitute an offer, acceptance of which will consummate a contract and create an obligation in the offeror to perform according to the terms of the published offer.

Whether in any individual instance a newspaper advertisement is an offer rather than an invitation to make an offer depends on the legal intention of the parties and the surrounding circumstances. Annotation, 157 A.L.R. 744, 751; 77 C.J.S., Sales, § 25b; 17 C.J.S., Contracts, § 389. We are of the view on the facts before us that the offer by the defendant of the sale of the Lapin fur was clear, definite, and explicit, and left nothing open for negotiation. The plaintiff having successfully managed to be the first one to appear at the seller's place of business to be served, as requested by the advertisement, and having offered the stated purchase price of the article, he was entitled to performance on the part of the defendant. We think the trial court was correct in holding that there was in the conduct of the parties a sufficient mutuality

ILLUSTRATION 18-4. *Continued*

Lefkowitz v. Great Minneapolis Surplus Store, Inc.

of obligation to constitute a contract of sale.

[**692] 2. The defendant contends that the offer was modified by a "house rule" to the effect that [***8] only women were qualified to receive the bargains advertised. The advertisement contained no such restriction. This objection may be disposed of briefly by stating that, while an advertiser has the right at any time before acceptance to modify his offer, he does not have the right, after acceptance, to impose new or arbitrary conditions not contained in the published offer. *Payne v. Lautz Bros. & Co. 166 N.Y.S. 844, 848*; *Mooney v. Daily News Co. 116 Minn. 212, 133 N.W. 573, 37 L.R.A. (N.S.) 183*.

Affirmed.

End of Document

Reprinted from LexisNexis with permission. Copyright 2021 LexisNexis. All rights reserved.

PRACTICE POINTER

Reread your brief as if you were unfamiliar with the case. If you cannot understand what happened, rewrite your brief.

NET NOTE

A basic overview of how to brief a case is found at www.lib.jjay.cuny.edu/research/brief.html.

IN-CLASS EXERCISE

Sometimes learning to brief can seem like an abstract exercise. The following exercise is designed to hone your brief drafting skills. It is best for students to read the illustrations for this exercise before class. Read the *Lefkowitz* case in Illustration 18-4 and the brief in Illustration 18-5, then go back to the case and try to find where the issue, facts, holding, and reasoning were obtained. This will give you insight into the information that must be pulled from a case to write a brief.

ILLUSTRATION 18-5.   *Lefkowitz* Brief

CITATION

LEFKOWITZ v. GREAT MINN. SURPLUS STORE, INC.
86 N.W.2d 689 (Minn. 1957).

PROCEDURE

The defendant appealed the decision of the Municipal Court of Minneapolis after the court awarded the plaintiff $138.50 as damages for breach of contract.

ISSUE

Whether a newspaper advertisement is considered a valid offer that when accepted forms a contract or merely an invitation to make an offer of sale.

HOLDING

A newspaper advertisement constitutes an offer when the terms in the advertisement are definite, certain, and clear leaving nothing open for negotiation. A merchant cannot arbitrarily alter the terms of the sale after the merchant publishes the advertisement and the terms of the sale were met.

FACTS

The defendant, the Great Minneapolis Surplus Store, published two advertisements in the local newspaper. The first stated that the store would sell three fur coats, for $1.00 each, "worth up to $100" the following Saturday at 9 a.m. first come, first served. The plaintiff, Mr. Lefkowitz, appeared at the store at the stated time, on the stated day. The store refused to sell the coats to Mr. Lefkowitz, stating that there was a house rule that the sale was for women only. The next week, the defendant published an advertisement stating that the store would sell a black lapin stole, valued at $139.50 for $1.00 on the Saturday after the ad appeared. The advertisement also stated: "first come, first served." The plaintiff was again the first person at the store as the stated time and day. The defendant refused to sell the plaintiff the stole for $1. The defendant again claimed that there was a house rule that the sale was for women only. The plaintiff filed suit for the value of the articles.

RATIONALE

Newspaper advertisements that are clear, definite, and explicit where the terms leave nothing open for negotiation constitute offers where the offer's acceptance will result in the formation of a valid contract. The court stated that the value of the three fur pieces in the first ad was speculative and uncertain. However, the court stated that the terms in the advertisement, for the sale of the black lapin stole, were clear and precise. The store named the value of the item, and described the conditions under which the stole would be sold. The plaintiff satisfied the terms of the sale as stated in the ad. The court stated that when terms of an advertised sale are definite, clear, and leave nothing open for negotiation, the terms cannot be arbitrarily altered once the ad is published and once the party has met the terms of the offer. The ad constituted an offer and once the terms of the offer were accepted, a valid contract was formed.

DISPOSITION
  Affirmed.

CHECK YOUR WORK

Here are some questions to ask yourself after you brief a case:

1. Is the issue before the court clearly and accurately stated?
2. Does the brief include a factual and legal basis for the holding and not just a terse answer to the question raised in the issue?
3. Are the facts succinct? Are there adequate facts so that you can understand and remember the context without having to go back to the decision? Are the facts organized logically?
4. Does the brief include the legally significant facts in the facts section of the brief?
5. In the reasoning section, is the court's reason, or basis, for its holding clearly stated?
6. Is the brief a single page typed?

D. CASE ANALYSIS

Case analysis requires you to compare and contrast decisions to assess the outcome of an issue posed by a client's factual scenario. Case analysis is particularly important when you want to evaluate a client's situation and get an idea of how the law will determine the outcome. We look to prior cases to anticipate how a court will rule on the issue we are researching. You determine if the question before the court, the issue, is the same as or different than the question the client's problem raises. You must examine the facts of the case and the facts of the client's problem to ascertain the similarities and differences. Sometimes only one component of the decision addresses one part of a client's problem. Last, you must use the relevant cases from the appropriate jurisdiction.

NET NOTE

An example of the process of performing a legal analysis can be found at http://userwww.sfsu.edu/dlegates/URBS513/howtodoa.htm.

1. Sample Single Case Analysis

Read the following abridged case and then read the fact pattern from the client's situation.

ILLUSTRATION 18-6. *Shila Morganroth, Plaintiff-Appellant v. Susan Whitall and The Evening News Association, Inc.*

SHILA MORGANROTH, PLAINTIFF-APPELLANT v. SUSAN WHITALL AND THE EVENING NEWS ASSOCIATION, INC., A CORPORATION, DEFENDANTS-APPELLEES

Docket No. 91215

COURT OF APPEALS OF MICHIGAN

161 Mich. App. 785; 411 N.W.2d 859; 1987 Mich. App.

LEXIS 2608; 14 Media L. Rep. 1411

April 14, 1987, Submitted

July 21, 1987, Decided

Abridged decision

"Truth is a torch that gleams through the fog without dispelling it."
—Claude Helvetius, *De l'Esprit.*

In this heated dispute, the trial court granted summary disposition in favor of defendants on plaintiff's claims of libel and invasion of privacy by false light. Plaintiff now appeals and we affirm.

Plaintiff alleges that she was libeled and cast in a false light by an article written by defendant Whitall which appeared in the Sunday supplement of the *Detroit News* on November 11, 1984. The article was entitled "Hot Locks: Let Shila burn you a new 'do.'" The article was accompanied by two photographs, one depicting plaintiff performing her craft on a customer identified as "Barbara X" and the second showing Barbara X and her dog, identified as "Harry X," following completion of the hairdressing. Central to the article was the fact that plaintiff used a blowtorch in her hairdressing endeavors. According to the article, plaintiff's blowtorch technique was dubbed "Shi-lit" and was copyrighted. The article also described two dogs, Harry and Snowball, the latter belonging to plaintiff, noting that the canines have had their respective coats colored at least in part. The article also indicated that the blowtorch technique had been applied to both dogs. Additionally, the article described plaintiff's somewhat unusual style of dress, including a silver holster for her blowtorch and a barrette in her hair fashioned out of a $100 bill. Much of the article devoted itself to plaintiff's comments concerning her hairdressing and the trend of what, at least in the past, had been deemed unusual in the area of hair styles.... [Editor's note: Text removed from original opinion.]

ILLUSTRATION 18-6. *Continued*

Plaintiff's rather brief complaint alleges that the article, when read as a whole, is false, misleading, and constitutes libel. More specifically, the complaint alleges that the article used the terms "blowtorch lady," "blowtorch technique," and the statement that plaintiff "is dressed for blowtorching duty in a slashed-to-there white jumpsuit" without any factual basis and as the result of defendants' intentional conduct to distort and sensationalize the facts obtained in the interview. The complaint further alleges that the article falsely portrayed plaintiff as an animal hairdresser, again as part of a deliberate action by defendants to distort and sensationalize the facts. In her brief on appeal, plaintiff also takes exception to her being cast as an animal hairdresser and claims as inaccurate the portrayal in the article that she does "mutt Mohawks for dogs" and the reference to "two canines who have been blowtorched.".... [Editor's note: Text removed from original opinion.]

... [Editor's note: Text removed from original opinion.] The elements of defamation were stated by this Court in *Sawabini v. Desenberg*, 143 Mich App 373, 379; 372 NW2d 559 (1985):

> The elements of a cause of action for defamation are: "(a) a false and defamatory statement concerning plaintiff; (b) an unprivileged publication to a third party; (c) fault amounting at least to negligence on the part of the publisher; and (d) either actionability of the statement irrespective of special harm (defamation per se) or the existence of special harm caused by the publication (defamation *per quod*)." *Postill v. Booth Newspapers, Inc.*, 118 Mich App 608, 618; 315 NW2d 511 (1982), *lv den* 417 Mich 1050 (1983), citing Restatement Torts, 2d, § 558; *Curtis v. Evening News Association*, 135 Mich App 101, 103; 352 NW2d 355 (1984); *Ledl v. Quik Pik Food Stores, Inc.*, 133 Mich App 583; 349 NW2d 529 (1984).

See also *Rouch v. Enquirer & News of Battle Creek*, 427 Mich 157, 173-174; 398 NW2d 245 (1986).

The *Sawabini* Court further commented on the appropriateness of dismissing a defamation claim by summary disposition:

> The court may determine, as a matter of law, whether the words in question, alleged by plaintiff to be defamatory, are capable of defamatory meaning. See, *e.g., Ledsinger v. Burmeister*, 114 Mich App 12, 21; 318 NW2d 558 (1982). Where the words are, as a matter of law, not capable of carrying a defamatory meaning, summary judgment under GCR 1963, 117.2(1) is appropriate. See *Lins v. Evening News Association*, 129 Mich App 419, 422; 342 NW2d 573 (1983).
>
> "A communication is defamatory if it tends so to harm the reputation of another as to lower him in the estimation of the community

ILLUSTRATION 18-6. *Continued*

or to deter third persons from associating or dealing with him. *Nuyen v. Slater*, 372 Mich 654, 662, fn; 127 NW2d 369 (1964); *Ledsinger v. Burmeister*, 114 Mich App 12, 21; 318 NW2d 558 (1982)." *Swenson-Davis v. Martel*, 135 Mich App 632, 635-636; 354 NWd 288 (1984), *lv den* 419 Mich 946 (1984). In assessing whether language is defamatory, the circumstances should be considered. *Ledsinger v. Burmeister, supra.* [143 Mich App 379-380.]

In determining whether an article is libelous, it is necessary to read the article as a whole and fairly and reasonably construe it in determining whether a portion of the article is libelous in character. *Sanders v. Evening News Ass'n*, 313 Mich 334, 340; 21 NW2d 152 (1946); *Croton v. Gillis*, 104 Mich App 104, 108; 304 NW2d 820 (1981).

Reading the article as a whole, we believe that it is substantially true; therefore plaintiff's complaint lacks an essential element of her defamation claim, namely falsity. In looking at plaintiff's specific allegations of falsity, for the most part we find no falsehood. Considering as a group the various references to plaintiff's using a "blowtorch" in hairstyling, we note that *The Random House College Dictionary, Revised Edition* (1984), defines "blowtorch" as follows:

[A] small portable apparatus that gives an extremely hot gasoline flame intensified by air under pressure, used esp. in metalworking.

In looking at the photographic exhibits filed by defendants, we believe that the instrument used by plaintiff in her profession can accurately be described as a blowtorch.[2] Accordingly, while the use of the term "blowtorch" as an adjective in connection with references to plaintiff or her hairdressing technique may have been colorful, it was not necessarily inaccurate and certainly not libelous. As for the reference that plaintiff was "dressed for blowtorching duty in a slashed-to-there white jumpsuit," we have examined the photographic exhibits submitted by defendant at the motion hearing and we conclude that reasonable minds could not differ in reaching the conclusion that plaintiff did, in fact, wear a jumpsuit "slashed-to-there."

Finally, while having disposed of the allegedly libelous claims contained in the complaint, we briefly turn to the additional allegations of false statement listed in plaintiff's brief on appeal. In her brief, plaintiff claims that defendants inaccurately described her as being a hairdresser for dogs, giving dogs a Mohawk cut, and using a blowtorch on the dogs. While it appears that plaintiff did do hairdressing on dogs, it

---

[2]We acknowledge that *The Random House Dictionary's* definition did not list hairdressing as an example. However, we are not persuaded that the dictionary's editors intended their examples to be exclusive. See also "blowtorch," *Webster's New World Dictionary, 2d College Edition* (1976).

ILLUSTRATION 18-6. *Continued*

is not necessarily certain at this point that she did, in fact, use the blow-torch on the dogs. However, as noted above, plaintiff filed no response to the motion for summary disposition in the trial court and, thus, presented no affidavits or other evidentiary showings that the statements in the article were false. Thus, there has been no showing by plaintiff that the statements relating to the dogs were false.

Moreover, inasmuch as it appears undisputed that plaintiff at least dyed the fur of the dogs, which would constitute hairdressing of dogs, we are not persuaded that the article, when read as a whole, becomes libelous because of an inaccurate reference to using the blowtorch on the dogs. This is particularly true since, by plaintiff's conduct, she asserts that blowtorching is a safe practice when performed on humans. Therefore, it would appear that, from plaintiff's perspective, blowtorching would also be safe on dogs, even if she did not engage in such a practice. Furthermore, her claim that she was libeled by labeling her as both a dog hairdresser and a human hairdresser is unsupported in light of the tinting of the dogs' hair. Since the undisputed factual showing indicates that plaintiff did blowtorch her human clientele and style her pooch's fur, we will not split hairs at this point to conclude that the statement that she used her blowtorch on dogs, even if inaccurate, is libelous.

For the above-stated reasons, we conclude that, when reviewing the article and accompanying photographs as a whole, the article was not libelous.

On appeal, plaintiff also argues that the article invaded her privacy by casting her in a false light.... [Editor's note: Text removed from original opinion.]

See Restatement Torts, 2d, § 652 E, comment a. Furthermore, comment b to § 652 E, p 395, explains that:

> "The interest protected by this section is the interest of the individual in not being made to appear before the public in an objectionable false light or false position, or in other words, otherwise than as he is. In many cases to which the rule stated here applies, the publicity given to the plaintiff is defamatory, so that he would have an action for libel or slander.... In such a case the action for invasion of privacy will afford an alternative or additional remedy, and the plaintiff can proceed upon either theory, or both, although he can have but one recovery for a single instance of publicity.
>
> "It is not, however, necessary to the action for invasion of privacy that the plaintiff be defamed. It is enough that he is given unreasonable and highly objectionable publicity that attributes to him characteristics, conduct, or beliefs that are false, and so is placed before the public in a false position. When this is the case and the matter attributed to the plaintiff is not defamatory, the rule here stated affords a different remedy, not available in an action for defamation."

ILLUSTRATION 18-6. *Continued*

As indicated in the above discussion under the theory of defamation, with the exception of certain references to hairdressing dogs, none of the conduct attributed to plaintiff in the article was false. Therefore, it could not place plaintiff in a false light. With reference to the assertions concerning her hairdressing of dogs, we do not believe that a rational trier of fact could conclude that, even if inaccurate, those references are unreasonable or put plaintiff in a position of receiving highly objectionable publicity. The article did not indicate that plaintiff harmed, injured, or inflicted pain upon the dogs. Rather, at most, the article inaccurately stated that plaintiff used techniques on the dogs, such as blowtorching, which she also used on humans. While the article may have overstated the techniques that she uses on dogs, inasmuch as she advocates those techniques for use on humans, we cannot conclude that plaintiff would believe it highly objectionable that those techniques also be performed on dogs. Similarly, she cannot have been placed in false light as being both the hairdresser of dogs and humans inasmuch as the tinting of the canines' fur would constitute hairdressing. Thus, it would not be placing plaintiff in a false light to indicate that she served both dog and man. Accordingly, we believe that summary disposition was also properly granted on the false light claim.

In summary, although the manner in which the present article was written may have singed plaintiff's desire for obtaining favorable coverage of her unique hairdressing methods, we cannot subscribe to the view that it was libelous. We believe that the trial court aptly summarized this case when it stated that "this Court is of the Opinion that the Plaintiff sought publicity and got it." Indeed, it would appear that the root of plaintiff's dissatisfaction with defendants' article is that the publicity plaintiff received was not exactly the publicity she had in mind. While the publicity may have been inflammatory from plaintiff's vantage point, we do not believe it was libelous. At most, defendants treated the article more lightheartedly than plaintiff either anticipated or hoped. While this may give plaintiff cause to cancel her subscription to the *Detroit News*, it does not give her cause to complain in court.

Affirmed. Costs to defendants.

CLIENT'S FACTUAL SCENARIO

The partner asked you to apply the *Morganroth* case to the client's facts. Mrs. Smith came to your firm because she was concerned that an article published in the local newspaper, *The Star News*, was defamatory. *The Star News* reported that Mrs. Smith is a professional pancake flipper and cheerleader for she dresses in a cheerleader's outfit and performs cheers when she delivers the platters of pancakes. Mrs. Smith claims that the article's depiction is untrue. Mrs. Smith asserted that she is a business owner and a professional chef. Mrs. Smith hoped that the article would provide a restaurant review highlighting the culinary integrity of her cuisine. Additionally, the article had a picture of Mrs. Smith in a cheerleader's skirt and a letter sweater. Also, there was a picture of Mrs. Smith jumping in the air after she delivered a platter of pancakes to a table. Mrs. Smith claims that she is merely energetic and enthusiastic. Mrs. Smith also claims that the outfit fits in with the restaurant's theme as it is called "Collegiate Cakes." Mrs. Smith claims that the article is libelous because portraying her as a cheerleader is inaccurate. Additionally, Mrs. Smith claims that her customer volume declined, after the article's publication, from 125 customers per day to 100 customers per day, on average.

The first task is to brief the case focusing solely on the issue that Mrs. Smith raised. Mrs. Smith's sole issue is whether the newspaper article portraying her as a cheerleader was libelous. The case also analyzes the issue of false light but since this is not relevant for our analysis it will not be included in the brief.

ILLUSTRATION 18-7.   Brief of *Morganroth v. Whitall*

MORGANROTH v. WHITALL
411 N.W.2d 859 (Mich. Ct. App. 1987)

PROCEDURE

Plaintiff, Shila Morganroth appeals the trial court's decision granting summary disposition to the defendants on the libel claim.

ISSUE

Whether the plaintiff was libeled in an article, written by Whitall, a reporter for *The Evening News*, entitled: "Hot Locks: Let Shila burn you a new do" indicated that the plaintiff used a blowtorch to style hair, that she also styled dogs' hair, and that she wore a jumpsuit "slashed-to-there" that when read as a whole, can be fairly and reasonably construed as true.

ILLUSTRATION 18-7. *Continued*

HOLDING

The article was not libelous because as a whole it was true as the instrument the plaintiff used to style hair could be considered similar to a blowtorch, she did color dogs' hair, and her jumpsuit, as shown in photos, was revealing.

FACTS

The plaintiff, Ms. Morganroth, was a hairdresser. The article about Ms. Morganroth and her hair styling techniques was in the Sunday supplement of the *Detroit News* on November 11, 1984. The article stated that Ms. Morganroth used a blowtorch to style hair and that she styled the hair of both humans and dogs. Additionally, the article stated that Ms. Morganroth dressed in an unusual manner and wore a holster to hold her blowtorch. The article also had pictures of Ms. Morganroth in a jumpsuit with a deep slash in the front. The plaintiff alleged that the defendant's article was libelous as it did not contain any factual basis when it used the terms "blowtorch lady," "blowtorch technique," and "is dressed for blowtorching duty in a slashed-to-there white jumpsuit."

REASONING

The court examined the rule of defamation. The court noted that the first element, of defamation, requires that for a statement to be defamatory, it must be false. The court also noted that the words may be examined to determine if they alone have defamatory meaning. The article must be read as a whole to evaluate its meaning to see whether it is libelous completely or whether a part of it is. An article read as a whole will not be capable of defamatory meaning when it is substantially true. The words alone must be false. The court stated that the article, when read in totality, was substantially true. The court interpreted the dictionary definition of "blowtorch" and determined that the photographs of the plaintiff showed that the instrument she used matched the dictionary definition of "blowtorch." Also the photographs showed the plaintiff wearing a revealing jumpsuit. Consequently, because the article as a whole was true, it was not libelous.

DISPOSITION

Affirmed.

PROCESS FOR CASE ANALYSIS

The second task is to look at the parallels between the case and the client's situation.

Both the case and the client's facts concern an allegedly libelous (libel is a defamatory statement that is written or printed) newspaper article. In both instances the articles were substantially true. In our facts, Mrs. Smith does dress in a cheerleading skirt and letter sweater when waiting on tables. Mrs. Smith also jumps in the air at the restaurant. Although jumping in the air may not be a "cheer," it is pretty similar to cheerleading.

The court, in *Morganroth*, stated that if the article read as a whole is false and misleading then it constitutes libel. However, the court noted that if the article is substantially true then it is not libelous, and consequently not defamatory. Here, Mrs. Smith actually dresses in a cheerleading skirt and letter sweater when she waits on tables. The article in *The Star News* depicted Mrs. Smith, both in text and in photos, as she actually dressed at work and therefore the article is substantially true. Because the article in *The Star News* is substantially true, the article did not convey any false information, it lacked an essential element of the claim for defamation. Defamation requires the statement concerning the plaintiff to be false. Therefore, based on *Morganroth*, the article in *The Star News* is most probably not libelous.

2. Sample Analysis Using Two Cases

Review *Seymour v. Armstrong* at the beginning of this chapter, and *Lefkowitz v. Great Minn. Dept. Store*. How are the cases similar? How are they different? Best to compare the briefs you created for each case. How would you apply the cases to the following fact pattern?

> An attorney asked you to apply the holdings of *Seymour* and *Lefkowitz* to the following fact pattern. Mrs. Johnson, the owner of Frocks, Etc., ordered 50 dresses at the price of $35 per dress to be delivered in one week. Mrs. Johnson ordered the dresses from ABC Dress Company and sent a contract stating that she requests 50 dresses at $35 per dress, totaling $1750 payable upon receipt of the dresses. Mrs. Johnson assumes that when ABC ships the dresses this indicates that they are assenting to the contract by their action. However, ABC sends an invoice for the dresses for $1750 plus shipping fees of $106. The attorney wants to know, in light of the holdings in *Seymour*, and *Lefkowitz*, if ABC imposing a new condition in the contract, results in no agreement between ABC and Frocks, Etc.?

Notice how the facts are examined in our client's situation and applied to the holdings from the cases. We also try to parallel the courts' reasoning when we insert our facts into the tests that the courts used. These are essential parts of legal analysis. Also, compare and contrast the decisions. View each of the briefed cases on a single page, in the uniform categories, to compare and contrast decisions easily. Look carefully at the facts that the judge used to apply the law to the issue raised in the case — this provides crucial insight into legally significant facts. Examine the reasons why the court ruled; this provides the court's rationale or the basis for its holding.

Legal analysis is different than rules synthesis. Rules synthesis requires us to combine more than one legal rule to create a mini body of law on point. Legal analysis, especially when you use two or more cases, requires us to examine the facts in the cases and our client's facts to determine the factual parallels and distinctions between the cases and our client's facts. We perform legal analysis to support our prediction as to how a court would apply the law to our client's situation or to support an argument that the law should apply in a certain way. When we write a legal memo or a persuasive document, we often have to synthesize legal authority and perform legal analysis. In an objective memo's discussion section, you can find the detailed legal analysis in the application portion of the IRAC sequences.

The basis of our analysis: The cases and our client's facts concern whether a contract was formed. In our case the terms of the offer and the acceptance did not match. In *Seymour v. Armstrong,* the acceptance included the additional cost of the crates. In *Lefkowitz,* there was an offer and an acceptance, but the offeror added the new term when Lefkowitz accepted the original offer, that only ladies can accept the offer. The relevant portion of *Seymour v. Armstrong* states: "It is essential, however, that the minds of the contracting parties should come to the point of agreement,—that the offer and acceptance should coincide; and, if they do not correspond in every material respect, there is no acceptance or completed contract." Additionally, *Lefkowitz* states, regarding the formation of a contract, that "…where the offer is clear, definite, and explicit, and leaves nothing open for negotiation, it constitutes an offer, acceptance of which will complete the contract." *Lefkowitz,* 86 N.W.2d at 691.

The analysis: In Johnson's case, since the offer and the acceptance did not coincide, the parties did not form a binding contract. Just as the facts in *Seymour v. Armstrong,* ABC added an additional term in the acceptance with the inclusion of shipping costs of $106. Johnson's offer was clear, definite, and explicit. Since ABC added a new term in the acceptance, the parties did not have a meeting of the minds and a contract could not be formed. However, unlike the facts in *Lefkowitz,* ABC did not add an additional term after the offer was accepted. In Johnson's case, as in *Seymour* and *Lefkowitz,* the parties did not have a meeting of the minds as the offer was not accepted without additional terms or conditions. Consequently, a contract between Johnson and ABC was not formed.

PRACTICE POINTER

Evaluating cases: When you evaluate which case or cases to use, remember that cases from the appropriate jurisdiction are essential for binding precedent. Also, newer cases are stronger than older cases. Cases from higher courts are stronger than those from lower courts.

CHAPTER SUMMARY

A case brief has several components, including a citation, the procedural history, an issue, a holding, the relevant facts, the reasoning, and the case disposition. These briefs are designed to assist you and sometimes an attorney in understanding a case. The components of a case brief are:

- *The Citation:* The location of the source so you attribute credit.
- *The Procedural History:* How the case progressed through the court system to arrive at this court.
- *The Facts:* Contextual facts and legally significant facts. Legally significant facts are the facts the court relies on to resolve the controversy.
- *The Issue:* Specific question that the court is asked to determine.
- *The Holding:* The answer to the question that the court is asked; always more than a simple reply, for it includes at least one fact.
- *The Reasoning, or Rationale:* This is the basis for the court's holding. In the reasoning you need to include the rule, which is the test, standard, or principle the court relied on to arrive at its holding. You will glean the rule from reading the opinion. Be very careful to not cite to the cases cited in the opinion. The court relies on prior holdings to resolve the controversy before it, precedent, however, we are concerned with what this court is saying and how this court is interpreting the law. We try not to cite the embedded cases.
- *The Disposition:* How the court ruled.
- *Dicta, if included in the opinion:* Dicta is not in every opinion. Dicta is a statement by the court about something that is unrelated to the specific issue before it. It could be a comment about politics or a social program.

We rely on case briefing to summarize decisions in a uniform format so we can compare the decisions easily and apply the decisions to our issue.

This chapter also provided you with your first exposure to legal analysis. You learned the step-by-step process of drafting a case brief as well as how to compare briefed cases with one another and with a legal problem. Comparing the case's facts and issue with our problem's facts and issue is the process of legal analysis. The process of legal analysis will enable you to use legal authorities to answer a legal question.

KEY TERMS

case analysis	issue
case brief	legally significant fact
case citation	procedural history
dicta	rationale
disposition	reasoning
facts	relevant facts
holding	rule of law

EXERCISES

IN-CLASS

Issues

1. Review the following issues prepared for a case brief of the *King* case. List any problems you find. Which issue of the following five is best, and why?

Issue 1. Was the district court's decision that King was an independent contractor rather than an employee of the Miller Co. erroneous?

Issue 2. Whether King was an employee of Miller or an independent contractor for these reasons:

a. The control factor, in which agents are restricted in the selling of insurance as to whom or where. Agents also have mandatory requirements for working at designated times and dates. In addition, they are expected to attend weekly meetings and engage in daily office tasks.
b. The economic factor, in which agents are not allowed to sell products for anyone but Miller and that agents are "integral" to Miller's business.
c. As with employees, services, supplies, and education expenses are provided. Compensation is made in the form of commissions.
d. Work hours are based on flexibility for prime selling.
e. Performance evaluations and documents of rules of conduct are customary requirements of an employer-employee relationship.

Issue 3. Whether, in finding the plaintiff was not an employee under the Title VII definition, the trial court erred by:

f. failing to properly evaluate the nature of insurance sales;
g. failing to evaluate and weigh the integral economic relationship between the defendant and the plaintiff; and
h. failing to discuss other evidence regarding the "control" criterion used to judge eligibility.

Issue 4. Whether the district court was clearly erroneous in determining that an insurance agent is an independent contractor rather than an employee when the individual is paid commissions and bonuses rather than a salary and her work is not supervised by the company.

Issue 5. Does an employer have to exercise control over a worker before that individual is considered an employee under Title VII?

Holdings

2. Review the holdings below that were drafted for a brief in the *King* case, list any problems you see with each, and note which is the best.

Holding 1. The court of appeals affirmed the lower court's decision that King is an independent contractor rather than an employee of the Miller Co.

Holding 2. Because the trial court did understand the law and its factual findings are not clearly erroneous, its decision is affirmed.

Holding 3. The district court's underlying factual findings are not clearly erroneous; therefore, the decision of the district court was affirmed.

Holding 4. Yes. An employer must exercise control over a worker before that individual is considered an employee under Title VII.

SELF-ASSESSMENT

3. List two reasons to brief a case.
4. List two essential items that should be noted in the case brief.
5. What is the procedural history?
6. What are the issues?
7. What is the holding?
8. What are relevant facts?
9. What are dicta and why would you include them in a brief?
10. What is the case's disposition?
11. What is the case's rationale?
12. Whom is the brief generally designed to assist?

APPLICATION OF BRIEFING CONCEPTS EXERCISES

For the following exercises, review *Hornick v. Borough of Duryea*, 507 F. Supp. 1091 (1980).

13. Which is the best issue statement regarding the part-time employees' concerns in the *Hornick* case?
    a. Whether part-time workers who are hired, controlled, and paid by a company are counted as one of a company's 15 employees under Title VII, even though they work only a few hours a day.
    b. Whether the defendant had at least 15 employees so as to be considered an employer for Title VII purposes.
       Subissue: Whether part-time workers were to be counted as employees in determining if a person is an employer under Title VII.
    c. Whether the plaintiff was discriminated against solely because of her sex, based on a height and weight requirement, according to the theory of disparate treatment and disparate impact.
    d. Whether part-time workers who work only a few hours a day are considered employees for Title VII purposes.
14. Read the following statements. Which is the best holding and why?
    a. Yes. Even though they work only a few hours a day, part-time workers are counted as one of the 15 employees required for Title VII application, when they are hired, controlled, and paid by a company.
    b. Yes. The defendant had at least 15 employees and therefore was subject to Title VII coverage.
       Subissue: Yes. Part-time workers are to be counted as employees to determine if a person is an employer for Title VII purposes.

    c. According to disparate impact theory and disparate treatment theory, plaintiff was discriminated against solely based on a discriminatory height and weight requirement.

    d. The court found that it was not significant that the worker worked only a few hours a day with minimal pay. These workers were hired, controlled, and paid by the employer and were therefore considered "employees" for Title VII purposes.

    e. The court held that the non-CETA full- and part-time employees exceeded the jurisdictional requirement of Title VII.

PRACTICE SKILLS

15. Brief *Kalal v. Goldblatt Bros.*, 368 N.E.2d 671 (Ill. App. Ct. 1977).

16. Brief the following abridged case:

KREIGER v. KREIGER

No. 371

SUPREME COURT OF THE UNITED STATES

334 U.S. 555

February 2-3, 1948, Argued

June 7, 1948, Decided

...The parties were married in New York in 1933 and lived there together until their separation in 1935. In 1940 respondent obtained a decree of separation in New York on grounds of abandonment. Petitioner appeared in the action; and respondent was awarded $60 a week alimony for the support of herself and their only child, whose custody she was given.

Petitioner thereafter went to Nevada where he continues to reside. He instituted divorce proceedings in that state in the fall of 1944. Constructive service was made on respondent who made no appearance in the Nevada proceedings. While they were pending, respondent obtained an order in New York purporting to enjoin petitioner from seeking a divorce and from remarrying. Petitioner was neither served with process in New York nor entered an appearance in the latter proceeding. The Nevada court, with knowledge of the injunction and the New York judgment for alimony, awarded petitioner an absolute divorce on grounds of three consecutive years of separation without cohabitation. The judgment made no provision for alimony. It did provide that petitioner was to support, maintain, and educate the child, whose custody it purported to grant him, and as to which jurisdiction was reserved. Petitioner thereafter tendered $50 a month for the support of the child but ceased making payments under the New York decree.

Respondent thereupon brought suit on the New York judgment in a federal district court in Nevada. Without waiting the outcome of that litigation she obtained a judgment in New York for the amount of the arrears, petitioner appearing and unsuccessfully pleading his Nevada divorce as a defense. The judgment was affirmed by the Appellate Division, two judges dissenting. 271 N.Y. App. Div. 872, 66 N.Y.S.2d

798. The Court of Appeals affirmed without opinion, 297 N.Y. 530, 74 N.E.2d 468,... Respondent does not attack the bona fides of petitioner's Nevada domicile.

... [W]e hold that Nevada had no power to adjudicate respondent's rights in the New York judgment and thus New York was not required to bow to that provision of the Nevada decree. It is therefore unnecessary to pass upon New York's attempt to enjoin petitioner from securing a divorce or to reach the question whether the New York judgment was entitled to full faith and credit in the Nevada proceedings. No issue as to the custody of the child was raised either in the court below or in this Court. The judgment is

Affirmed.

MR. JUSTICE FRANKFURTER dissents....
MR. JUSTICE JACKSON dissents....

17. Brief *Talford v. Columbia Med. Ctr. at Lancaster Sub., L.P.*, 198 S.W.3d 462 (Tex. App. 2006).
18. Brief *DeMercado v. McClung*, 55 Cal. Rptr. 3d 889 (Ct. App. 2007).

ANALYSIS

19. When we use a case to analyze a problem, the problem focuses our reading so that we examine the case for particular issues that our problem also raises. We also analyze the case to look for facts that are either parallel to the facts in our problem or that are different, that are distinguishable. This exercise uses a case to resolve a client's issue. We will use *Seymour v. Armstrong* in Illustration 18-1 to determine if a company is imposing a new condition in a contract.

    Review *Seymour v. Armstrong* in Illustration 18-1. An attorney asked you to apply the holding in *Seymour* to the following fact pattern.

    Facts: Mrs. Johnson, the owner of Frocks, Etc., ordered 50 dresses at the price of $35 per dress to be delivered in one week. Mrs. Johnson ordered the dresses from ABC Dress Company and sent a contract stating that she requests 50 dresses at $35 per dress, totaling $1,750 payable upon receipt of the dresses. Mrs. Johnson assumes that when ABC ships the dresses this indicates that they are assenting to the contract by their action. However, ABC sent an invoice for $1,750 plus $106 for the cost of shipping, with the dresses.

    Question: The supervising attorney wants to know, in light of the holding in *Seymour*, if ABC is imposing a new term, with no agreement existing between ABC and Frocks, Etc.

20. One of the purposes of briefing cases is to be able to easily compare and contrast cases as they are in the same format. You probably noticed that both *Seymour v. Armstrong*, Illustration 18-1, and *Lefkowitz*,

Illustration 18-4, dealt with contracts and advertisements. Answer the following questions to compare the decisions.

1. Was there a meeting of the minds in the contract in *Lefkowitz?* A meeting of the minds occurs when both parties have the same intentions concerning the agreement and both parties agree to the substance of the agreement and its terms.
2. Was there a meeting of the minds in the contract in *Seymour?*
3. How is *Lefkowitz* similar to *Seymour?*
4. How does *Lefkowitz* differ factually from *Seymour?*
5. Do the cases rely on precedent? We do not include the cited cases in our briefs though.

21. Please read the following paragraph and describe the legal analysis in the paragraph.
    a. Does the example provide the reader with insight into how the law will determine the outcome?
    b. Are there any similarities between the cases and the Murrays' facts?
    c. Does the example provide enough information from the cases so that you can see the factual similarities and differences?

    The following example uses two cases. One case defines an easement in gross and then another case explains how an easement in gross is retained. Both cases discuss easements in gross, yet one expands on the other. The facts on which the example is based are as follows:

    > Robert and Jan Murray live in Evanston and are building an addition to their house on Ashland Avenue. There is eight feet between their house and their neighbor Mrs. Brown's house. The properties are adjoining. A driveway does not separate the houses. Also, there is no alley that would provide access to either property. The Murrays' contractors and construction workers must enter Mrs. Brown's property to work on the addition. Mrs. Brown is not very pleased that workers are entering her property. The Murrays came to our office wondering whether they should purchase an easement from Mrs. Brown, their neighbor.

EXAMPLE

The Murrays should purchase an easement in gross from Mrs. Brown so that the workers can enter the Brown's property, for the limited purpose, to perform construction on the Murray home. An easement in gross, sometimes called a personal easement, is a right in the land of another that is not permanently part of the title of the property. An easement in gross allows for use of the land of another for a limited purpose. *Willoughby v. Lawrence,* 4 N.E. 356 (Ill. 1886). The easement in gross belongs to the easement holder independent of his ownership or possession of any tract of land and does not benefit the possessor of any tract of land in his use of it. *Schnabel v. County of DuPage,* 428 N.E.2d 671 (Ill. App. Ct. 1981). The Murrays are building an addition to their house. They want to have a right to use the adjoining land only to perform the construction of their addition. They do not need an easement that would be a permanent part of the property's title. The interest that the Murrays have in Mrs. Brown's land is personal and would not benefit either tract of land. Therefore, the Murrays can purchase an easement in gross from Mrs. Brown that would permit the workers to enter the Brown property for the limited purpose to complete the construction project.

THE LEGAL MEMORANDUM

CHAPTER OVERVIEW

This chapter introduces you to the legal memorandum. You learn about your audience and how to write objectively. You are introduced to the components of the memorandum, such as the issues, conclusion or brief answer, facts, and discussion sections. The chapter concludes with a brief overview of the process of writing a memorandum and some key tips.

A. THE LEGAL MEMORANDUM

▼ What Is an Objective Legal Memorandum and Why Is It Written?

An **office memorandum**, often called a memo, explains in an objective rather than a persuasive or argumentative manner the current state of the law regarding an issue. It clarifies how that law applies to a client's transaction or legal problem. A memo should explain the current law—both favorable and unfavorable—and any legal theories related to the issues.

The balanced approach of a legal memo helps an attorney see the strengths and weaknesses of a transaction or dispute. Only when an attorney can see all sides of an issue can he or she determine how best to represent a client. Sometimes your research will determine whether the client has a case or not. If in writing a memo you advocate a single position or attempt to persuade an attorney, the attorney cannot make an informed decision about a dispute or transaction. This can be a very costly error in terms of money, time, client loyalty, court favor, and legal ethics.

A memo also assists an attorney in predicting how a court might decide a particular issue. A memo could be drafted to address an issue raised as a case progresses in court. As a paralegal, you might research whether the law provides for the dismissal of an action; your research and memorandum might form the basis for such a motion to dismiss or for subsequent court documents. You might also write a memo to assist an attorney in drafting an appellate brief, a document used to appeal a trial court's decision.

ETHICS ALERT

You must provide an attorney with an accurate representation of the law. It is an ethical violation if an attorney presents a knowingly false representation of the law. For example, if the case is a well-known and often cited case, but one you omit from a memo and that the attorney later omits from the court brief, the attorney may be sanctioned. See Rule 3.3 Candor Toward the Tribunal of the ABA Model Rules of Professional Conduct.

B. AUDIENCE

▼ Who Reads a Memorandum?

You will usually research a legal question to determine whether a client has a claim or should proceed with a case. Following your research, you generally prepare a memo for an attorney. Your memo also might be sent to the client. Your primary audience, then, is the assigning attorney, and the secondary audience is the client. When drafting your memo, think about how to best explain the problem so that each audience understands it.

Often memoranda are saved in **memo banks** accessible to all firm or corporation attorneys and paralegals, so other attorneys and paralegals might review your memo.

ETHICS ALERT

Do not send a research memo you drafted to a client unless an attorney has reviewed and approved the document.

C. COMPONENTS OF A MEMORANDUM

▼ What Is Included in a Memorandum?

A memorandum can have a variety of components arranged in different orders. The components and their order often vary from attorney to attorney. Ask the assigning attorney if your firm or corporation has a particular style. Review a sample memo so that you can study the style he or she prefers, or go to the memo bank to review a sample. The format discussed in this chapter is one commonly accepted style. See the sample memo in Illustration 19-1.

ILLUSTRATION 19-1.   Sample Memorandum

**ATTORNEY WORK PRODUCT PREPARED
FOR LITIGATION**

MEMORANDUM

To: Benjamin Joyce
From: William Randall
Date: November 7, 2021
Re: *Harris v. Sack and Shop*

QUESTION PRESENTED
Is Sack and Shop, a grocery store, liable for injuries sustained by Harris, a store patron who slipped on a banana peel that had been left on the grocery store floor for two days after the store employee and manager had been told it was there?

BRIEF ANSWER
Probably yes. Sack and Shop, a grocery store, likely breached its duty of care to a store patron, Rebecca Harris, who was injured when she slipped on a banana peel that the grocery store had allowed to

ILLUSTRATION 19-1. *Continued*

remain on the grocery store floor for two days after both the store employee and manager knew about the peel.

FACTS

Rebecca Harris is suing our client, Sack and Shop Grocery Store, for negligence.

Harris went to the store to purchase groceries on July 8, 2021. While she was in the produce section, she slipped on a banana peel that a grocery store employee dropped on the floor. The employee had dropped the peel on the floor two days earlier. The employee had failed to clean it up, even after a patron, who saw him drop it, asked him to clean it up. The patron also told the store manager about the banana peel and the manager asked an employee to clean it up. The employee still failed to clean up the peel and the manager failed to ensure that the employee removed the peel.

Harris sustained a broken arm and head injuries as a result of the slip and fall.

DISCUSSION

The issue presented in this case is whether Sack and Shop Grocery Store was negligent when Rebecca Harris slipped in the store's produce section. A defendant is negligent if the defendant owed the plaintiff a duty, the defendant breached that duty, and the defendant's breach of that duty was the proximate cause of the plaintiff's injury. *Hills v. Bridgeview Little League Ass'n*, 745 N.E.2d 1166 (Ill. 2000). A grocer owes a duty of reasonable care to its patrons, and the grocer will be found negligent if a store employee or manager breached the store's duty of reasonable care to its patrons, and, as a result of that breach, the patron was injured. *Ward v. K Mart Corp.*, 554 N.E.2d. 223 (Ill. 1990); *Thompson v. Economy Super Marts, Inc.*, 581 N.E.2d 885 (Ill. App. 1st). A store owner may be liable when a patron, who is a business invitee, is injured by slipping on a foreign substance, if a store owner knew of the presence of the foreign substance or should have discovered it. *Olinger v. Great Atl. & Pac. Tea Co.*, 173 N.E.2d 443 (Ill. 1961). In our case, Sack and Shop owed a duty of reasonable care to Harris because she was a store patron—a business invite. Based on that duty of reasonable care, Sack and Shop must keep its store floor free of foreign substances that it knew of or should have discovered. In this case, Sack and Shop knew about the foreign substance—the banana peel. However, Sack and Shop failed to remove the banana peel that the store employee dropped. The store failed to clean it up for two days, even after both the employee and the store manager had been told to clean up the peel from the floor. Therefore, Sack and Shop is likely to be found liable for the injuries Harris sustained.

The first element to consider is whether Sack and Shop owed a duty of reasonable care to Harris. A business owes a duty to its invitees or patrons to exercise reasonable care to maintain its premises in a "reasonably safe condition for use by the invitees." *Ward*, 554 N.E.2d at 226. Harris was a customer in the store. Sack and Shop, a grocery store, is a

ILLUSTRATION 19-1. *Continued*

business. Therefore, Sack and Shop owed Harris a duty of reasonable care to maintain the premises.

The next question to consider is whether Sack and Shop breached its duty of reasonable care to Harris. A store will be found to have breached its duty of reasonable care to a patron if a store employee fails to properly and regularly clean the floor of the store. *Olinger v. Great Atl.& Pac. Tea Co.*, 173 N.E.2d 443 (Ill. 1961), or if the business had knowledge of the dangerous condition. *Id.* Also, if a business created the hazard, the business can be found to have breached its duty of reasonable care to a patron. *Pabst v. Hillman's*, 13 N.E.2d 77 (Ill. App. 1st 1938). In *Pabst*, the grocery store had overfilled a display of green beans, and the green beans spilled onto the floor. A patron slipped on one of the green beans. The court found that it could infer that the grocer had created the dangerous situation because the beans were on the floor next to the overfilled basket. *Id.* In our case, Sack and Shop's employee had two days to clean the floor before Harris fell. That could be considered a failure of the store's duty of reasonable care to properly maintain the premises and to regularly clean the store floor. Also, as in the *Pabst* case, Sack and Shop through its agent—an employee—had created the dangerous situation because the employee dropped the banana peel on the floor. In addition, a customer had placed the store employee and the manager on notice of the banana and neither one cleaned up the banana peel. Therefore, Sack and Shop breached its duty of reasonable care to Harris.

The plaintiff, however, still must establish proximate cause, that is, that the injury resulted as a natural consequence of Sack and Shop's breach of its duty of reasonable care. In *Pabst*, a store owner's failure to clear green beans from a store floor, resulting in injury to a patron who slipped on the floor, was found to be the proximate cause of the patron's injuries. *Id.* at 80. In this case, Sack and Shop's failure to clean the peel from the floor was a breach of its duty of care to Harris. This breach resulted in injury to Harris when she slipped on the neglected banana peel. Sack and Shop's breach of its duty will be found to be the proximate cause of Harris's injuries.

The final element that must be established for Sack and Shop to be liable to Harris for negligence is that the plaintiff, Harris, suffered injuries. In this case, Harris sustained a broken arm and head injuries as a result of the slip and fall on the banana peel. Therefore, Harris will be able to show that she was injured.

CONCLUSION

Sack and Shop owed Harris a duty of reasonable care. The store is likely to be found to have breached that duty of reasonable care because an employee and the store manager failed to remove a banana peel—a foreign substance—from the grocery store floor during the preceding two days. The injuries Harris sustained were directly caused by a slip on the banana peel. Therefore, Sack and Shop is likely to be found liable to Harris for negligence.

> ## PRACTICE POINTER
>
> Place the words "Attorney Work Product" or "Attorney Work Product Prepared for Litigation" on any legal memo you prepare. The attorney *work product doctrine* is to protect legal materials prepared for legal representation against disclosure to third parties. The doctrine, however, is not a complete protection. Federal Rule of Civil Procedure 26 (b)(3) provides that disclosure of such materials may be compelled for "substantial need" and "undue hardship." To help preserve this protection if challenged in court, label your memos.

ILLUSTRATION 19-2.   Sample Memorandum: Dwyer Battery Action

ATTORNEY WORK PRODUCT PREPARED IN ANTICIPATION OF LITIGATION

MEMORANDUM

To: William Houck
From: Ivy Courier
Date: November 7, 2021
Re: Dwyer Battery Action

QUESTION PRESENTED

Did an actionable battery occur when Mann intentionally struck Dwyer with a bucket, without Dwyer's consent, causing Dwyer to suffer physical and monetary injuries?

CONCLUSION

Mann's intentional striking of Dwyer with a bucket and sand was an actionable battery.

FACTS

Our client, Mary Dwyer, a 36-year-old bank teller, wants to bring an action for battery against Carol Mann, a 36-year-old mother, who threw a metal bucket filled with sand at Dwyer at a local park. While Dwyer sat on a park bench, she teased Mann's seven-year-old son. Mann did not like this teasing and threw a bucket filled with sand at Dwyer. Sand landed in Dwyer's eyes while she was wearing soft contact lenses. As a result, Dwyer's contacts had to be replaced. The bucket also cut Dwyer's eye and cheek. She had stitches in both places. Dwyer asked Mann to pay for her doctor bills and for the new contacts. Mann refused and added, "I'm not sorry. I meant to hurt you."

ILLUSTRATION 19-2. *Continued*

DISCUSSION

The issue presented is whether Mann's intentional touching of Dwyer with a bucket rather than her person is an actionable battery. A battery is the intentional touching of another without consent or privilege, which causes injury or offensive contact. *Anderson v. St. Francis-St. George Hosp., Inc.*, 77 Ohio St. 3d 82, 671 N.E.2d 225 (1996); *Love v. Port Clinton*, 37 Ohio St. 3d 98, 524 N.E.2d 166 (1988), quoting the Restatement of Law 2d, Torts (1965). A touching can occur directly or indirectly such as when an object or a substance rather than an individual's body contacts the other party. *Leichtman v. WLW Jacoc Communications, Inc.*, 92 Ohio App. 3d 232, 634 N.E.2d 697 (1994). In this case, Mann intentionally struck Dwyer with a bucket without Dwyer's consent and that touching resulted in injuries. Therefore, a battery occurred.

The threshold issue is whether a touching occurred when the bucket struck Dwyer. An indirect contact between a defendant and a nonconsenting party can be a battery. *Leichtman v. WLW Jacoc Communications, Inc.*, 92 Ohio App. 3d 232, 634 N.E.2d 697 (1994). In *Leichtman*, one person blew cigar smoke at another person, resulting in injuries. The court found that the contact from cigar smoke, although not a direct touching by a person, was still battery. In essence, the court found that the smoke was an extension of the person and that contact between the smoke and the nonconsenting person met the requirement of a touching for civil battery. In this case, Mann threw the bucket at Dwyer, and the bucket contacted her face. That was an indirect touching. Following the reasoning in the *Leichtman* case, the bucket contact, although indirect, would be an extension of Mann's body, and the contact between Dwyer and the bucket would be considered a touching under the theory of civil battery.

Next, the question to consider is whether Mann intended to touch Dwyer when she struck her with the bucket. The "essential character" of the conduct will be considered in determining whether a person intends his or her conduct. *Love v. Port Clinton*, 37 Ohio St. 3d 98, 524 N.E.2d 166 (1988). In *Love*, a police officer handcuffed the plaintiff. The court found that the officer must have intended his actions because you could not accidentally handcuff a person. *Love*, 524 N.E.2d at 168. In Dwyer's case, Mann aimed the bucket at Dwyer and purposefully tried to strike her. Mann later told Dwyer that she deliberately threw the bucket at her. The essential character of these acts and Mann's own statements indicated that Dwyer probably will be able to establish that Mann had the intent.

The next factor to consider is whether Dwyer caused injury. A battery occurs only if a plaintiff sustains physical injuries as a result of the touching. *Anderson v. St. Francis-St. George Hosp., Inc.*, 77 Ohio St. 3d 82, 671 N.E.2d 225 (1996). Dwyer sustained cuts on her face, and the sand flew out of the bucket into her eyes. Dwyer should be able to show that she sustained physical injuries as a result of the contact with the bucket.

1. Heading

In Illustrations 19-1 and 19-2, the first part of the memo is the **heading.** A sample heading also is shown in Illustration 19-3. The first notation in the heading of these illustrations is the word "MEMORANDUM," placed in all capital letters at the top of the page. The next notations in Illustrations 19-1, 19-2, and 19-3 tell the reader who the memorandum is written to and from, the date, and the subject. The regarding line, indicated by "Re:," varies depending on the firm's style. For example, some insurance clients ask that you include claim numbers in the regarding line. Some attorneys prefer court case numbers, and still others prefer clients' billing numbers and file numbers.

ILLUSTRATION 19-3.   Sample Memorandum Heading

MEMORANDUM

To: Sarah E. Lillian
From: Kelsey Barrington
Date: July 8, 2021
Re: Negligence Action between Sack and Shop Grocery Store and Rebecca Harris

---

2. Questions Presented or Issues

The next portion of the memo seen in Illustrations 19-1 and 19-2 is the questions presented section, which is sometimes called the issues section.

The terms **issues** or **questions presented** are synonymous. For our purposes, we will use the terms *question presented* or *questions presented.* The questions presented are the specific legal questions an attorney has asked you to research. The question presented is phrased in the form of a question concerning the legal issue posed, and it includes a reference to the applicable law and some **legally significant facts.** The legal issue shown in Illustration 19-4 is whether the grocery store owner was negligent and whether he owed a duty to the patron. The legally significant facts are that the patron slipped on a banana peel that had been on the grocery store floor for two days. (A detailed explanation of how to draft the questions presented is provided in Chapter 20.) Note the facts included in the questions presented section of Illustration 19-2. These facts are the legally significant facts. They are interwoven with the standard of law applicable to this case.

ILLUSTRATION 19-4.   Sample Question Presented

Is a grocery store owner liable for injuries sustained by a store patron who slipped on a banana peel that had been left by a grocery store employee on the grocery store floor for two days, even after the employee and the store manager had been told to remove it by a patron?

3. Conclusion or Brief Answer

You should follow the questions presented section with a **brief answer** or a **conclusion.** Brief answers and conclusions differ in format, although their purposes are similar. A brief answer is a short statement that directly answers the question or questions presented. See Illustration 19-5. A conclusion is similar, but it is usually longer. In Illustration 19-1, you will find an example of a conclusion. If there were two issues presented, you would include two conclusions, placed in the same order as the issues that they answer.

ILLUSTRATION 19-5.   Sample Brief Answer

Probably yes. Sack and Shop, a grocery store, likely breached its duty of care to a store patron, Rebecca Harris, who was injured when she slipped on a banana peel that the grocery store had allowed to remain on the grocery store floor for two days after both the store employee and manager knew about the peel.

▼ What Is the Difference Between a Conclusion and a Brief Answer?

Some attorneys prefer a brief answer immediately following the question or questions presented and a formal conclusion at the end of the memo. The brief answers should be presented in the same order as the questions they answer.

For other attorneys, a conclusion without a brief answer is sufficient. A conclusion is an in-depth answer to the question presented. There is no set length for a conclusion; it should be a succinct statement that summarizes the substance of the memo. See Illustration 19-6. As you can see in Illustration 19-6, the conclusion is more in-depth than the brief answer. However, note that both the conclusion and the brief answer include references to the legally significant facts: the failure to remove the banana peel from the grocery store floor. In the conclusion, you provide your opinion concerning the case. However, a paralegal should refrain from telling an attorney how to proceed. For example, do not say "I think that we will lose this case, so we should settle it." Instead, say "This case is not likely to be won." Allow the attorney to determine whether the case should be settled. (Drafting conclusions and brief answers is explained in detail in Chapter 20.)

ILLUSTRATION 19-6. Sample Conclusion

A grocery store owner owes a patron a duty of reasonable care. The store owner is likely to be found to have breached that duty of reasonable care because he failed to remove a banana peel from the grocery store floor two days after an employee had dropped the banana peel and after a patron had told the employee and the store manager to remove the peel. The injuries the patron sustained were directly caused by a slip on a banana peel. Therefore, the grocery store owner is likely to be found liable to the patron.

4. Facts

Following the conclusion or brief answer, you should include a **facts statement** that explains the status of the case and all the facts that might have a bearing on the outcome of a client's case. These facts are called legally significant facts. You should include facts that cast your client's dispute or transaction in a good light and those that shade it in a negative light. See Illustration 19-7. The presentation of facts should be balanced rather than slanted.

ILLUSTRATION 19-7. Sample Facts Statement

Rebecca Harris is suing our client, Sack and Shop Grocery Store, for negligence.

Harris went to the store to purchase groceries on July 8, 2021. While she was in the produce section, she slipped on a banana peel that a grocery store employee dropped on the floor. The employee had dropped the peel on the floor two days earlier. The employee had failed to clean it up, even after a patron, who saw him drop it, asked him to clean it up. The patron also told the store manager about the banana peel and the manager asked an employee to clean it up. The employee still failed to clean up the peel and the manager failed to ensure that the employee removed the peel.

Harris sustained a broken arm and head injuries as a result of the slip and fall.

5. Discussion

Following the facts, you will include your **discussion,** in which you will explain the current state of the applicable law, analyze the law, and apply the law to the legally significant facts noted in the facts statement. Any problems posed in the client's case and counterarguments should be presented here. This should not be an exhaustive review of the history of the law but should be focused analysis of the current state of the law. The law should be applied to each of the legally significant facts. Note if the law is primary binding or merely persuasive authority. Use only highly persuasive secondary authorities if primary authorities are not available.

Finally, following the discussion, you should include a conclusion if a brief answer rather than a conclusion has been used earlier. Review the discussion sections in Illustrations 19-1 and 19-2. Note that Illustration 19-2 contains multiple issues, and they are discussed separately within the memo.

PRACTICE POINTER

Review memos prepared previously for the attorney who assigned the memorandum. Follow that format or ask the assigning attorney what format he or she prefers.

D. STEPS IN DRAFTING A MEMORANDUM

▼ What Steps Should You Take in Drafting a Memo?

1. An attorney will assign a research problem to you. Discuss the problem thoroughly with the attorney. Be certain to ask the attorney questions to clarify the legal issues and the facts of a dispute or transaction. Ask for guidance concerning possible topics to research and resources to consult.
2. Immediately following your meeting, draft a preliminary statement of the legal issues and the relevant facts.
3. Begin your research. To develop an understanding of the issues and the general legal rules applicable to your problem, and to provide you with some search terms, read secondary authorities such as encyclopedias and *American Law Reports.* During your research, you often will discover other issues that may be relevant, and you will find additional facts that are important. If you are uncertain whether to pursue these additional issues, ask the attorney who assigned the case whether the issues are relevant.
4. If you have additional questions about the facts of a case, ask the attorney or the client for additional facts to assist you in determining what authorities are relevant to your research.

5. Find primary binding authorities. If you are unable to find those, locate persuasive primary or secondary authorities.
6. After you find relevant authorities, validate the authorities and review the citators for more current, valuable authorities. If necessary, review these additional authorities.
7. Prepare case briefs of the relevant cases. (See Chapter 18 for a detailed discussion of case briefing.)
8. After you have completed your research, rewrite the questions presented.
9. Rewrite the facts and then draft the brief answers or conclusions (or both).
10. Next, outline the discussion section. (See Chapter 24 for a discussion of outlining and organizing the memorandum.) While you are preparing your outline, you should synthesize the legal authorities. (This process is explained in Chapter 23.) You should formulate your discussion and paragraphs in a special format called IRAC, which is an abbreviation for the formula Issue, Rule, Application, and Conclusion. (This format is discussed thoroughly in Chapter 22.) You can now begin to write your memorandum.

E. MEMO DRAFTING TIPS

You should be careful to guide your reader through each section of your memo and from issue to issue. To do this, introduce the legal issues in the facts section and again in the discussion section. Also, use headings and transitions to guide your reader into the new sections. Your memo should be clearly written, accurate, concise, and thorough. Use everyday language rather than legalese. Write the memo as if the reader is unfamiliar with the law, but do not be condescending.

CHECKLIST FOR DRAFTING A MEMORANDUM

1. Discuss the case with the attorney.
   a. Discuss the legal issues presented.
   b. Discuss the known facts.
   c. Determine whether additional facts should be investigated.
   d. Determine what law governs.
   e. Check the memo bank to determine the firm's style and to learn whether the issue has been researched previously.
2. Draft a preliminary statement of the facts.
3. Draft a preliminary statement of the legal issues or questions presented.

4. Research the legal issue or issues.
    a. If you find additional relevant issues, discuss them with the attorney.
    b. Determine whether additional facts should be considered in light of the new issues; ask the attorney or client about additional facts.
    c. Research the new issues, if necessary.
5. Rewrite the issues or questions presented after your research has allowed you to focus them better.
6. Draft a brief answer or a conclusion (or both).
7. Rewrite the facts statement of the memo.
8. Draft an outline of the discussion section of the memo; organize the discussion.
9. Draft the discussion section.
10. Reevaluate the facts and rewrite the facts statement to include only legally significant facts.
11. Rewrite the conclusion.

Your memo should not trace the legal history of the law. Instead, it should be a statement of the current state of the law.

When you approach a legal rule, start with the rule rather than the citation for the authority. Doing so makes your discussion stronger.

Be certain that your discussion supports your conclusions. Incorporate the relevant facts into your discussion.

CHAPTER SUMMARY

The legal memorandum is composed of issues, conclusions and brief answers, facts, and a discussion section. These are written for attorneys and clients. Memoranda are designed to assist them in determining the current state of the law regarding a legal issue and how that law applies to the facts presented in a particular case.

In the next few chapters, you will learn about each one of the components of a memorandum: the questions presented, the facts, the conclusions, the brief answers, and the discussion.

KEY TERMS

brief answer
conclusion
discussion
facts statement
heading
issues

legally significant facts
memo banks
office memorandum
questions presented
work product doctrine

EXERCISES

SELF-ASSESSMENT
TRUE OR FALSE

1. A memorandum should be persuasive in its style.
2. A memorandum should present only facts that are favorable to your client's position.
3. A memorandum should inform the attorney and the client about the favorable authorities and known facts as well as the authorities and facts that pose problems for a client's case.
4. Your memorandum will never be read by a client.
5. You should include descriptive words in the facts section that slant the facts in favor of your client's position.

CHAPTER 20

QUESTIONS PRESENTED AND CONCLUSIONS OR BRIEF ANSWERS

CHAPTER OVERVIEW

Chapter 19 introduced you to the legal memorandum and its components. This chapter explains the reasons for drafting questions presented, issues, brief answers, and conclusions and teaches you how to draft these items.

A. QUESTIONS PRESENTED OR ISSUES

The **questions presented** or **issues** are the problems you must research to answer the attorney's or client's questions. These questions provide a preview to the reader about the applicable legal standards and the relevant facts. They are always posed in the form of a question.

▼ Who Reads the Questions Presented Statement?

The questions presented statement often is the first portion of a memorandum an attorney reviews. Many attorneys focus on these questions and the **conclusions** or **brief answers**. Some attorneys read these questions and answers without reading the entire memorandum. Therefore, your questions presented statement must be easy to understand and allow the reader to quickly grasp the legal questions that the memo will address.

1. First Draft

The first draft of the questions presented should be done following the receipt of the initial research assignment from the attorney. Draft a simple statement that explains the questions you were asked to research. For example, suppose an attorney provides you with the following facts:

> While driving a car Ronnie Randall struck Janice Kahn's son at 5:00 p.m. on August 29, 2021. It was bright and clear. No skid marks appeared on the dry street following the accident.
>
> Janice Kahn was working in her garden about five feet from the accident scene at the time of the accident. Her son was playing a game in the street before Randall's car struck him. Kahn saw Randall turn his car steering wheel to turn the car to strike her son. At first, she thought her 11-year-old son was dead. He was covered with blood and had several broken bones. However, Kahn's son was conscious after the accident.
>
> Immediately after the accident, police tested Randall's blood alcohol level and found that it was 0.11. Police cited Randall for drunk driving and driving with a suspended driver's license. Police had charged him with drunk driving and had suspended his license two weeks earlier after the car he was driving struck another child at the same spot. Randall had a drinking history.
>
> Following the accident, several witnesses said Randall was upset and wobbled as he walked. One witness said that Randall intentionally turned the steering wheel to hit Kahn's son. Kahn stated that Randall often swerved down her street to get her attention.
>
> Rhonda Albert, Kahn's neighbor, said she heard Randall say he would get even with Kahn after Kahn broke off a ten-year relationship with him. During Kahn and Randall's ten-year relationship, Randall was close to Kahn's son. He took him to ball games, including one in April, and attended the son's baseball games. Randall knew that Kahn's son was the most important person in her life.
>
> Since the accident, Janice Kahn vomits daily and suffers from anxiety and headaches. Dr. Susan Faigen, Kahn's internist, states that the vomiting, anxiety, and headaches are the result of the accident.

The attorney wants you to research whether Janice Kahn has a claim against Ronnie Randall for intentional infliction of emotional distress. Your first draft of the question presented might be:

> Does Janice Kahn have a valid claim for intentional infliction of emotional distress against Ronnie Randall?

This statement is devoid of legally significant facts.

▼ What Are Legally Significant Facts?

These are facts that will have an impact on a jury's or judge's decisions concerning Kahn's claim. This question as presented is too vague. To make your question more understandable in the context of Kahn's case, you must incorporate **legally significant facts**.

Legally Significant Facts

Kahn saw Randall turn the steering wheel and car to strike her 11-year-old son.
Randall struck the boy with his car.
Kahn now suffers from anxiety, headaches, and vomiting.

You might rewrite the question presented with the fact that Kahn saw Randall turn the steering wheel and the car and she saw Randall's car strike her 11-year-old son. Those facts are legally significant. The rewrite might read as follows:

> Does Janice Kahn have a valid claim for intentional infliction of emotional distress against Ronnie Randall when Kahn **saw** Randall turn the car and strike her 11-year-old child with the car?

By incorporating some legally significant facts, you have drafted a question presented that places the issue in perspective for the reader and that clearly identifies the parties in the action. This question presented allows the reader to understand the legal issue in the context of the factual circumstances surrounding the claim.

2. Research the Issue and Revise It

Now you are ready to research the issue. After you complete your research, you determine what law applies to a claim for intentional infliction of emotional distress. Once you determine the legal standard, you rewrite the question presented to incorporate that standard and only the legally significant facts. Your rewrite should frame the questions presented around the applicable legal standard and should present the applicable legal standard in the context of the facts that will affect the determination of a claim.

In the case of Janice Kahn, you learn from a decision of the highest court in your state that intentional infliction of emotional distress is "an act done by a person which is extreme and outrageous, done with intent to cause another to suffer severe emotional distress, and which results in distress and emotional injury to another. The emotional injury must manifest itself with a physical problem." If you rewrite the question presented above to incorporate the legal standard and legally significant facts, it might read as follows:

> Does Janice Kahn have a valid claim for intentional infliction of emotional distress against Ronnie Randall after Kahn saw Randall turn his car to strike Kahn's 11-year-old child in front of her, causing her to suffer from anxiety, headaches, and vomiting?

This question presented incorporates legally significant facts and provides these facts in the context of the legal standard. Randall's intention is one of the legal factors or elements in determining whether Kahn has a claim for intentional infliction of emotional distress. The question presented notes the legally significant fact that Randall turned his car to strike the child. The fact that Kahn now suffers from anxiety, headaches, and vomiting also is legally significant and relates to the legal standard because it may show that Kahn suffers from severe emotional distress. Although you should mention legally significant facts and the legal standard, keep the issue short enough for the reader to understand.

When you have multiple questions presented, the conclusion section should answer the questions in the same order in which they were presented.

Review the question presented in Illustration 20-1. Determine what legal issue is presented. Then find the legally significant facts that are included in the question presented. Before you review Illustration 20-1, please review the facts presented in Illustration 19-1 in Chapter 19.

ILLUSTRATION 20-1.   Question Presented

Is the grocery store owner liable for injuries sustained by a store patron who slipped on a banana peel that had been on the grocery store floor for two days?

3. Specificity and Precision

The facts should be **specific** and your characterization of the parties and the issues should be **precise**. For example, consider a case that concerns whether an individual, Walker, is an independent contractor or an employee of the Whole In One company. Walker did not work for any other companies. She paid her own taxes quarterly rather than through payroll deductions. She worked with limited company supervision. You could pose the question presented as follows:

> Was Walker an employee when she worked exclusively for Whole In One, paid her own taxes quarterly rather than through deductions, and worked with limited company supervision?

The facts in this case are specific: Walker paid her taxes quarterly rather than through payroll deductions. However, the question presented is not precise because it does not characterize the legal issue presented completely. The legal issue is whether Walker is an independent contractor rather than an employee. Therefore, the question presented could be refined as follows:

> Was Walker an independent contractor rather than an employee when she worked exclusively for Whole In One, paid her own taxes quarterly rather than through deductions, and worked with limited company supervision?

You must only ask a question in the questions presented statement, not provide an answer. You will answer the question presented in the brief answer or conclusion section. See Illustration 19-1 in Chapter 19.

If you have more than one issue or question presented, place them in a logical order and make that order consistent throughout the memo. The first question presented, then, should be answered first in the conclusion or brief answer statement and should be the first issue addressed in the discussion.

B. BRIEF ANSWERS AND CONCLUSIONS

1. Brief Answers

Brief answers are the quick answers to the question or questions presented. A brief answer is a short statement. Some attorneys prefer a brief answer that is later accompanied by a formal conclusion at the end of the memorandum. The brief answer allows an attorney to read a memo in a hurry and determine the legal issues. See Illustration 20-2.

ILLUSTRATION 20-2. Question Presented and Brief Answer

Question Presented: Does Janice Kahn have a valid claim for intentional infliction of emotional distress against Ronnie Randall after Kahn saw Randall turn his car to strike Kahn's 11-year-old child in front of her, causing her to suffer from anxiety, headaches, and vomiting?

Brief Answer: Yes. Kahn can bring a successful action for intentional infliction of emotional distress against Ronnie Randall because she saw Randall turn his car to strike her 11-year-old son, causing her to suffer severe anxiety, headaches, and vomiting.

The brief answer should include a brief statement of the applicable law and some relevant facts. A brief answer for the question presented above in Illustration 20-1 could be presented as follows in Illustration 20-3.

ILLUSTRATION 20-3. Brief Answer

Probably yes. A grocery store owner probably will be liable based upon negligence for injuries sustained by a store patron who slipped on a banana peel that had been on the grocery store floor for two days.

In the memorandum, it would appear as follows:

Question Presented: Is the grocery store owner liable for injuries sustained by a store patron who slipped on a banana peel that had been on the grocery store floor for two days?
Brief Answer: Probably yes. A grocery store owner probably will be liable based upon negligence for injuries sustained by a store patron who slipped on a banana peel that had been on the grocery store floor for two days.

The legal standard of conduct applicable to this case, negligence, is mentioned in the brief answer along with legally significant facts.

2. Conclusions

A conclusion also is an answer to the question presented and a summary of the discussion section. For some attorneys, a conclusion without a brief answer is sufficient. However, other attorneys prefer both a brief answer and a conclusion.

▼ How Is a Conclusion Different from a Brief Answer?

A conclusion does not have a set length, but it is generally longer than a brief answer. It is not a detailed or in-depth discussion of the legal issue presented in the case. It is a succinct summary of the substance of the memo. The conclusion should include legally significant facts and the applicable legal standard. In the conclusion, you must answer the question presented and provide your best prediction concerning the outcome of the case. It is acceptable to use terms such as *likely* or *probably* when you think that the outcome of an action is uncertain.

3. Drafting Conclusions

Before you draft your conclusion, review the questions presented and your preliminary facts statement. (A detailed explanation of the facts statement is presented in Chapter 21.)

Next, write the conclusion as an answer to the question presented and incorporate some of the relevant facts contained in the facts section of the memo. Refine the conclusion so that the reader understands the legal standard and the applicable facts. Conclusions often work well when drafted in an IRAC formula: Issue, Rule, Application, and Conclusion. (For a thorough discussion of the IRAC formula, see Chapter 22.)

For the facts and the question presented in the *Kahn* case, the following conclusion might be prepared:

> The central question is whether Janice Kahn has a valid claim for intentional infliction of emotional distress against Ronnie Randall. To successfully prove a claim for intentional infliction of emotional distress, Kahn must show that the act that caused the distress was extreme and outrageous and done with intent. In the case, Kahn saw Randall turn his car to strike her 11-year-old child, Bill. Seeing this accident caused Kahn to suffer from anxiety, headaches, and vomiting daily. Several witnesses can testify that Randall said he intended to harm Kahn, and Kahn states that Randall turned the car to strike her son. Two factors, however, might show that Randall lacked intent: the statement that he made to the police that he did not intend to hit the child and the fact that his blood alcohol level was 0.11, possibly preventing him from formulating the needed intent. Kahn probably has a claim for intentional emotional distress.

This conclusion provides a summary of the writer's prediction of the outcome of the case after the legal standards are applied to the legally significant facts:

> Janice Kahn probably has a valid claim for intentional infliction of emotional distress against Ronnie Randall.

Facts such as that Kahn saw Randall turn the car to strike her son and that witnesses can testify concerning what Randall said he intended to do are relevant to the question of whether the act was extreme and outrageous. The legal standard provides that the act must be extreme and outrageous before an individual can be liable for intentional infliction of emotional distress. In addition, the extreme and outrageous act must be done with intent. Randall's intent also is discussed in the conclusion.

Many students include an authority, such as a statute or case, in the conclusion. Most often, however, your analysis of a claim requires that you synthesize a number of authorities to determine the applicable law. It would be misleading, therefore, to include only one authority in your conclusion. You might include an authority if it is the sole authority governing a claim.

When two or more questions presented are noted in the memorandum, a conclusion or a brief answer should be stated for each question. The conclusions or brief answers should be noted in the same order as the questions presented. See Illustration 20-4.

ILLUSTRATION 20-4. Questions Presented and Conclusion

QUESTIONS PRESENTED

1. Does Janice Kahn have a valid claim for intentional infliction of emotional distress against Ronnie Randall after Kahn saw Randall turn the steering wheel of his car to strike Kahn's 11-year-old child in front of her, causing her to suffer from anxiety, headaches, and vomiting?

2. Does Janice Kahn's 11-year-old child, Bill, have a claim against Randall for battery after Randall turned his car to strike Bill, and did strike him, breaking Bill's bones?

CONCLUSIONS

1. The central question is whether Janice Kahn has a valid claim for intentional infliction of emotional distress against Ronnie Randall. To successfully prove a claim for intentional infliction of emotional distress, Kahn must show that the act that caused the distress was extreme and outrageous and done with intent. In the case, Kahn saw Randall turn the steering wheel of his car to strike her 11-year-old child. Seeing this accident caused Kahn to suffer from anxiety, headaches, and vomiting daily. Several witnesses can testify that Randall said that he intended to harm Kahn, and Kahn states that Randall turned the car to strike her son. Two factors, however, might show that Randall lacked intent: the statement that he made to the police that he did not intend to hit the child and the fact that his blood alcohol level was 0.11, possibly preventing him from formulating the needed intent. Kahn probably has a claim for intentional emotional distress.

2. Bill Kahn is likely to make a successful claim for battery against Randall. A battery is the intentional touching of another without consent, which causes injury. A touching can occur when an object rather than an individual's body contacts the other party. In this case, Randall struck Bill Kahn with his car without Bill Kahn's consent and that touching resulted in injuries. Intent may be an issue because Randall said he did not intend to hit the child and his blood alcohol level was 0.11, possibly preventing him from formulating the needed intent. However, the fact that he turned the wheel to strike Bill Kahn is likely to show intent.

> ## PRACTICE POINTER
>
> When you have multiple questions presented, the conclusion section should answer the questions in the same order in which they were presented.

CHAPTER SUMMARY

In this chapter, you learned how to draft questions presented, issues, brief answers, and conclusions. Questions presented or issues should incorporate legally significant facts and the rule of law. Legally significant facts are facts that will affect a decision concerning an issue of law.

Legally significant facts and the current rule of law also should be included in the conclusions or brief answers that answer the questions presented or issues.

Some attorneys prefer both a brief answer and a conclusion, while others require only a conclusion.

The process of writing the questions presented, issues, brief answers, and conclusions requires that you rewrite these components of a memorandum several times. The questions presented or issues should be drafted before you perform your research. The conclusions or brief answers also should be rewritten in light of the facts presented in a case.

In the next chapter, you learn how to draft facts statements for your memoranda.

KEY TERMS

brief answers
conclusion
issues
legally significant facts

precise
questions presented
specific

EXERCISES

SELF-ASSESSMENT

1. What is a brief answer?
2. How does a brief answer differ from a conclusion?
3. Is an issue or question presented written as a statement or a question?
4. If you have four questions presented, how many conclusions or brief answers should you have?
5. What is the purpose of a question presented?
6. What is the purpose of a conclusion?

PRACTICE SKILLS
Questions Presented
Draft questions presented for memos in the following cases.

7. You work as a paralegal for the county prosecutor's office in Houcktown County. One of the assistant prosecutors asks you to research whether Bonnie Bill has committed aggravated burglary under the Houcktown Rev. Code § 2911. The attorney has provided you with the following facts:

> Merriweather Halsey and Bonnie Bill were at the Masonic Temple for a fundraiser to fight AIDS. During the fundraiser Bill told a drunken Halsey that she intended to steal the $8,000 fundraiser proceeds from the Masonic Temple after the fundraiser and that she intended to steal a pearl necklace from Alice McKinley.
>
> Bill, who had helped organize the fundraiser, watched as the chairperson of the fundraiser opened the safe and placed the money in it. She memorized the combination and decided that she would use it later to steal the money.
>
> After the fundraiser, Bill walked home to get a credit card and a crowbar to open the door if she needed it. Bill went to the Masonic Temple after the fundraiser, wearing a disguise, showed the guard her invitation, and told him that she lost her mother's diamond brooch inside. Although the guard did not remember her, he allowed her to go into the temple. She wandered around the building for about an hour with the brooch inside her purse.
>
> When the guard decided to eat his supper and call home, Bill went to the safe. She opened it and pulled out all the money, except for $1,000. Bill told the guard she found the brooch and then left. She went to Alice McKinley's home, entered the house through an open ground-floor window, took the pearl necklace she had seen McKinley wearing earlier, and then left.
>
> The relevant statute is as follows:

§ 2911 Aggravated Burglary

> (A) A person is guilty of aggravated burglary when the person, by force or deception, trespasses in any house, building, outbuilding, watercraft, aircraft, railroad car, truck, trailer, tent vehicle or shelter with the purpose of committing a theft; and

>> (1) inflicts or attempts or threatens to inflict physical harm to another; or
>> (2) the person has a deadly weapon, which is any instrument, device, or thing capable of inflicting death or designed or specially adapted for use as a weapon; or
>> (3) the person has a dangerous ordnance such as any automatic or sawed off firearm, zip gun or ballistic knife, explosive or incendiary device; or
>> (4) the structure is the permanent or temporary dwelling of a person.

8. An assistant county prosecutor wants you to research whether Merriweather Halsey committed aggravated burglary based on the following facts. Draft a question presented for this problem based on the aggravated burglary statute noted in Exercise 7 above.

> Merriweather Halsey considered borrowing money from a friend who worked at the local bulb factory. She wandered into the factory around 4:00 a.m., after an AIDS fundraiser. The guard had stepped away from the door for a break. She headed toward her friend's workstation, but she stumbled into an open office where the petty cash was kept. She fell over a secretary's desk. Her leg caught the desk and pulled open a drawer that contained $500. She thought about taking the money, but she passed out before she took it. She woke up at about 6:00 a.m., when a secretary found her and summoned the security guard.
>
> Halsey then fell onto the security guard, causing him to crash his head into a planter. The guard cut his head and later required six stitches. Halsey thought the security guard was a robber, so she grabbed a letter opener from a nearby desk and told the security guard to back off. The security guard took the letter opener. Halsey's mind was still fuzzy from the alcohol, but she decided to pull a squirt gun out of her pocket to scare the robber.

Conclusions

9. Draft a conclusion for the problem discussed in Exercise 7.
10. Draft a conclusion for the problem discussed in Exercise 8.
11. Review the following facts. Make a list of the legally significant facts. Then prepare an issue statement and a conclusion for this problem.

> Your client, Hospitality Resorts International, Inc., which does business in your state, is defending an action against James Panhandle, a 70-year-old doctor from Akron, Ohio, who slipped and fell at a London hotel bearing the name Hospitality Resorts of London on January 28, 2021. Panhandle, a semi-retired general practice physician, smashed his head on some wet marble flooring next to the pool. A sign saying "slippery when wet" was set up next to the pool, but Panhandle didn't see the sign. He sustained severe and permanent injuries and was unable to practice medicine for two years.
>
> Panhandle often stayed at the Hospitality Resorts. The resorts were known for cleanliness and hospitality. The staff was friendly and always helpful. The advertising for the resorts claimed that it was the "cleanest in the world. We stay on top of our hotels." Most advertisements stated that the hotels were independently owned and operated. Some ads, such as the one that appeared in *Doctor's Weekly,* which Panhandle read, did not state that independent owners owned the London hotel. That ad boasted about the resort, "We care about you. We take care of you. We take care of your home — our resort."
>
> Hospitality Resorts was a trade name. The company that licensed the name Hospitality Resorts to other hotels was called Hospitality Resorts

International, Inc. (HRII), your client. Hospitality Resorts licensed its trade name to Fred and Ethel Carrigan of London, England, for use in a hotel there. The Carrigans called the hotel Hospitality Resorts of London. As part of the license agreement, Hospitality Resorts provided training to the staff. The Carrigans hired and fired the staff. HRII had no authority to hire and fire staff.

Panhandle did not know anything about the training or the connection between the London hotel and HRII.

HRII provided operations manuals and suggested procedures and menus. Personnel from HRII regularly traveled to London to advise the hotel employees about their jobs. HRII had no ownership interest in the London hotel. HRII was not authorized to act on behalf of the hotel nor was the hotel authorized to act on behalf of HRII.

The license agreement between HRII and Hospitality Resort of London only provided for HRII to provide its name Hospitality Resort to the London hotel as well as some manuals and technical assistance. It did not authorize the London hotel to act as its agent and HRII was not an agent of the London hotel. HRII did include the Hospitality Resort of London in its list of Hospitality Resorts. That list appeared in many ads as well as in a brochure.

Plaintiff filed suit against the Hospitality Resort in London and Hospitality Resorts International, Inc., alleging that HRII is in an agency relationship or apparent or ostensible agency relationship with the London Hospitality Resort. Thus, plaintiff claims that HRII and the London hotel are both responsible for his injuries. This suit was filed in the United States District Court for your area. All the rules of that court and the Federal Rules of Civil Procedures apply.

Does our client have a good defense to the plaintiff's claim that it was in an agency relationship with the London hotel?

Assume that the highest court in your state has held that a hotel owner can be liable based upon the theory of apparent agency. Under that theory, if a business allows another to hold itself out as its representative or the individual or entity holds itself as acting on behalf of the business, the business may be liable for the acts of the individual or entity. Also assume that a decision of the federal appellate court in your area follows your high court's decision.

12. Review this question presented and this conclusion. What legally significant facts are included in the question presented? What legally significant facts are included in the conclusion?

Question Presented
    Did an actionable battery occur when Mann intentionally struck Dwyer with a bucket, without Dwyer's consent, causing Dwyer to suffer physical and monetary injuries?

Conclusion
    Mann's intentional striking of Dwyer with a bucket and sand was an actionable battery.

13. Prepare an issue statement for this problem:

> You are a paralegal with the firm of Probing and Will. You must research whether Sarah Wakefield can renounce Adam Antwernt's will and collect a portion of the estate in your state.
>
> Your firm's client is Sarah Wakefield. She was married to Adam Antwernt. Antwernt died in your state following a long illness. Wakefield was Antwernt's second wife. She had been married to him for more than 20 years and lived in their home in your state before Antwernt died. Antwernt purchased the home with his first wife, Carry MacOver. MacOver died while she was still married to Antwernt. Wakefield subsequently married Antwernt. When Antwernt married Wakefield he never changed the deed for the home to include Wakefield. Wakefield kept her maiden name. Antwernt adopted a son with MacOver. The son, who is now 30 years old, is Grayson Antwernt.
>
> Antwernt drafted his will before he married Wakefield. He and Wakefield were getting along fine when he died. However, she was not included in his will. He did not leave her any property. Instead, he left all of his property to Grayson. Antwernt's will was admitted to probate.
>
> Wakefield wants to know whether Antwernt's will is valid and whether he can divest her of the marital property or whether she can renounce the will and collect a portion of the estate. Grayson is out of town and his attorney told Wakefield that she will get her share of the estate once Grayson returns. He is scheduled to return later this month.

14. Draft an issue statement for the Late case below. You work for a firm that has been retained by Mrs. Late. She would like to know if McCool can prove that Mr. Late gave him all Mr. Late's interest in the company:

> Nate Late, a business owner, has two partners in the operation of Loose Cannon Manufacturing in Anytown in your state. He owns one-third of a $3 million company. Late is ill but is not dying. He is grooming a 26-year-old boy, Ivan T. McCool, to run the business. He tells his family that he likes the boy and wants to teach him the business. The business owner, Nate Late, dies. The most current will leaves the estate of Late to his wife, Shirley Late, and his only son, Lou Sier. McCool tells Mrs. Late that Late intended to give McCool Late's one-third interest in the company, and that Late told this to McCool in front of a banker on the day of his death. The conversation took place during a meeting and the agreement was never put into writing. Before this meeting, on the day of Late's death, other employees of Loose Cannon heard Late say that he intended for McCool "to get" the business. Family members knew that Late intended for McCool to run the business and for McCool to get something if the business was sold. None of the family believed that Late intended to give the business to this newcomer. Late's shares of stock were never given to McCool. The shares were in the safe deposit box shared by Late and his wife of 24 years.
>
> Rob R. Baron also claims that Late promised to give him the shares in the future. Baron admits that Late did not physically give him the shares

before he died, but Baron insists that Late said, "I shall give you my shares in two years."

Mrs. Late said that Mr. Late planned to give her the shares. He told her this when he opened the joint safety deposit box and gave her the key.

Conclusion: Drafting Exercises

15. Assume that the statute in your state provides that Wakefield, the spouse, can renounce the will within six months of its admission to probate and that she would be entitled by statute to one-third of the estate and Grayson would be entitled to the remainder of the estate. Prepare a conclusion for the Wakefield problem in Exercise 13.

16. Assume that the statements below are the law in your state concerning a gift. Draft a conclusion for the problem outlined in Exercise 14.

A gift is a voluntary transfer of property from one person to another without any compensation or consideration. To be a valid gift, it must actually be made or executed. A gratuitous promise to make a gift in the future is not binding.

A living gift is called a *gift inter vivos.*

There are three requirements for such a gift: donative intent, acceptance of the gifts, and delivery.

Clark v. Davis: Clark told Davis, a friend, that after he got his life together, he would give Davis his coin collection. Until that time, Clark planned to use the collection, show it, and maybe sell some of it. Court said that a donor must have a present mental capacity and intent to give away his property. Court held that there was no present intention to make a gift of the collection to Davis. Therefore, a gift was not made.

Wally v. Allan: Wally gave Allan a guitar for use in his rock band. The court found that Allan accepted the gift. When a gift, such as the guitar, is beneficial to the donee, acceptance is presumed.

Lois v. Kate: Lois told Kate that she planned to give her a CD. Kate asked when she would give it to her. Lois said that she would leave the CD at the front desk of her record company. Lois left the CD at the desk and did not mention that Kate needed to leave any money to pay for the CD. Therefore, the court said that delivery of a gift occurred when Lois left the CD at the front desk, although delivery generally occurs when a party hands over the gift to the other party. The above situation also amounts to delivery.

17. Prepare a question or questions presented in this case and then prepare a conclusion or conclusions for this case.

Your firm has a client, an individual, Kris Rizzo, who claims he was injured when he was driving a car rented from Bear Cubs Car Rental and the brakes failed. The case was brought in state court in Arizona. Bear Cubs wants to move the lawsuit to federal court based on diversity jurisdiction.

Bear Cubs Car Rental had its car service area inspect the brakes four months before the accident. The service told management the brakes must be inspected in four months and likely replaced then.

The case is brought in state court in Arizona.

Bear Cubs Car Rental is owned by Hope Motors, a national rental car company.

Hope Motors is based on Western Avenue in Chicago, Illinois.

All of the company decisions concerning the operations of Hope Motors and its rental companies in various states are made at its Chicago headquarters. All officers work in Chicago.

Bear Cubs Car Rental operates in Phoenix, Arizona.

Federal diversity jurisdiction requirements are specified in a federal law 28 U.S.C. § 1332.

Where can this case be brought?

FACTS

CHAPTER OVERVIEW

This chapter explains the purpose of a facts statement and how to draft one. To do this, you need to learn how to determine which facts are legally significant. The chapter discusses the difference between a fact and a legal conclusion and demonstrates the different organizational structures for the facts section.

A. FACTS STATEMENT

The **facts statement** is a summary of the information that is relevant to determine whether a legal claim exists or whether a defense to such a claim can be made. It is also a summary of the status of a pending case.

A fact statement is an integral part of the office memorandum. Often, an attorney reads this statement to refresh his or her memory about the facts of the case before meeting with a client or a judge. The facts detailed in a memorandum also provide a reference point for your research and the framework for the application of the law.

1. Defining *Fact*

A **fact** may be something that is known with certainty. It can be an event. It can be an observation. The answer is not clear-cut. Some facts are pure facts, which means there is no dispute about them. For example, an individual's birth is a **pure fact**.

Facts in a court document, such as a complaint or an answer, are **asserted facts**, which means the individual is claiming they occurred. Some information can be objectively tested. That is a fact. For the purpose of the facts statement, note all of this information as facts.

2. Legally Significant Facts

▼ What Facts Should Be Included in the Facts Statement?

All facts that might have an impact on the issues presented in a particular case must be included in the memo. These facts are called **legally significant facts**. A good rule is that if you plan to include a fact in your discussion of the law, it should be mentioned in the facts statement.

Legally significant facts are those facts that may affect how a court would decide a particular legal issue. To determine which facts are legally significant, you must understand the legal issue or issues presented in your case. A **legal claim** is comprised of components called **elements** that must be proven before a claim is successful. Legally significant facts are those facts that might prove or disprove any of those elements.

For example, you are asked to research the factors a court will consider when it decides whether Sack and Shop Grocery Store was liable to Rebecca Harris, a patron, for a slip-and-fall accident that occurred in the store. Ms. Harris was injured when she slipped on a banana peel that a store employee failed to remove from the store floor for two days. Ms. Harris's shopping list included bananas, cherries, and strawberries.

You determine that the action or legal claim is based on negligence. You learn that negligence is the breach of a duty of reasonable care that results in an injury to another person. The legal elements of negligence are as follows:

* Existence of a duty
* Breach of that duty
* Injury caused by the breach of the duty

Legally significant facts are those facts that might prove or disprove any of those elements. In this case, the legally significant facts and the legal element that they might prove or disprove would include:

* The slip and fall occurred in the store. (injury, breach)
* Rebecca Harris slipped on a banana peel that a store employee left on the store floor for two days. (injury, caused by breach)
* Rebecca Harris suffered injuries as a result of the fall. (injury)
* Rebecca Harris shopped daily at the store. (duty)
* Rebecca Harris went to the store to make a purchase. (duty)

A fact that is not necessarily legally significant is:

* Rebecca Harris's shopping list included bananas, cherries, and strawberries.

This fact does not prove or disprove any of the elements.

Do not omit any legally significant facts even if you think that an attorney should remember them from client meetings. Attorneys are responsible for multiple cases, and these statements often are used to refresh their recollection. If a fact is not legally significant, you generally would exclude it. However, if the fact explains how a dispute or transaction arose or explains the relationship between the parties, then that fact should be noted. Such a **procedural fact** would assist the reader in understanding the status of a case.

Facts statements provide facts that are advantageous for your clients and those facts that are unfavorable to them. Remember that this is an objective memo. The facts should be presented in a neutral manner, devoid of emotion. Compare the following two examples.

EXAMPLE ONE

Our client, Janice Kahn, seeks to sue Ronnie Randall for intentional infliction of emotional distress following a car accident in which Randall brutally struck Kahn's only child while the precious child was playing T-ball in the street with his friends. This brutal act was done in the presence of Ms. Kahn, a caring mother, who was gardening while watching her child play. As a result of the incident, Kahn was devastated and emotionally distraught.

EXAMPLE TWO

Our client, Janice Kahn, seeks to sue Ronnie Randall for intentional infliction of emotional distress following a car accident in which Randall struck Kahn's child while the child was playing T-ball in the street with his friends. After Randall struck the child, he backed up and struck the boy again, running over his head with the rear tire. Ms. Kahn was gardening nearby while watching her child play.

The first example contains several words that slant the statement in favor of Kahn. The statement "Randall brutally struck Kahn's only child" characterizes the action as brutal. This is not a statement of fact. The word *brutal* should not be included in a facts statement. The second example is devoid of these **emotional adjectives**. Instead of using the word *brutal,* the second example details the underlying acts that constitute a brutal strike:

> After Randall struck the child, he backed up and struck the boy again, running over his head with the rear tire.

Example Two allows readers to draw their own conclusions. The facts statement should not be slanted. Facts such as that Kahn was "a caring mother" or that the child was "precious" should not be incorporated into a facts statement. You should mention only facts, not legal conclusions or definitions of the law.

PRACTICE POINTER

When drafting a facts statement, include favorable and unfavorable facts. It should be balanced so that the attorney knows the problems with a case.

PRACTICE POINTER

Omit any emotional words in the facts statement.

---

3. Fact Versus a Legal Conclusion

A fact is a piece of information that might explain to the reader what occurred in a particular case. In contrast, a **legal conclusion** is an opinion about the legal significance of a fact. Read the following facts statement:

> Our client, Janice Kahn, seeks to sue Ronnie Randall for intentional infliction of emotional distress following a car accident in which Randall maliciously struck Kahn's only child while the child was playing T-ball in the street with his friends. This malicious and intentional act was done in the presence of Ms. Kahn, a caring mother, who was gardening while watching her child play.

The statements that the act was *malicious* and *intentional* are legal conclusions because the writer makes assumptions about the state of mind of the actor. The term *malicious* is a legal element of many claims; it describes a wicked state of mind. *Intentional* also describes a legal element. You should exclude such characterizations from your facts statements. Instead, describe the acts a person committed that could be considered malicious, or statements that could indicate that an act was intentional. For example:

> Randall struck Kahn's only child after he told a neighbor that he intended to hit the child with his car while the child was playing T-ball. Randall struck the child with his car while the car was traveling at 25 miles an hour.

The information about Randall's comments to the neighbor, coupled with the speed at which he struck the child, could indicate that Randall struck the child maliciously and intentionally. The proper place to discuss whether an act is either malicious or intentional is in the discussion section of the memo. A definition of the law also is not a statement of fact and should be noted only in the memo discussion.

PRACTICE POINTER

Do not use legal conclusions in a facts statement. Use such conclusions in the memo discussion section instead.

---

4. Source of Information for a Facts Statement

Most often, information from a client interview is the basis for your facts statement. See the example in Illustration 21-7 later in this chapter. During a court dispute, information for the facts statement also can be found in witness statements, complaints, answers, or discovery materials, such as depositions and interrogatories. For these facts, note the source of the information. For transactions, information might be contained in various business records or contracts.

B. ORGANIZING THE FACTS STATEMENT

A facts statement can be organized in several ways: chronologically, by claim or defense, by party, or a combination of these three methods.

▼ What Are the Different Methods of Organizing
a Facts Statement?

1. Chronological Organization

A **chronological organization** is based on the order of events. You start with the event that occurred first and end with the event that occurred last. You also can write the statement in **reverse chronological order**, beginning with the last event and ending with the first. For some claims, such as those stemming from an accident, a contract dispute, or a criminal case, chronological organization works well because these concerns often are ordered by time. See Illustration 21-1.

The statement in Illustration 21-1 first introduces the claim. In the succeeding paragraphs, the events are detailed in chronological order from start to finish. Illustration 21-2 starts with the last event and ends with the information about the beginning of the day.

ILLUSTRATION 21-1. Chronological Organization

Dr. James Panhandle is suing our client, Hospitality Resorts International, Inc., for negligence stemming from injuries he sustained when he slipped and fell on January 28, 2021, at the Hospitality Resort of London. The doctor seeks $16 million in damages.

On the day of the accident, children were playing in the pool at 8:00 a.m. The children splashed water out of the pool and onto the marble floor near the pool. The floor had not been mopped at any time during the day.

At 8:00 p.m., Dr. Panhandle was walking slowly out of the hotel coffee shop that was adjacent to the pool. He slipped on the wet marble floor next to the pool.

The doctor hit his head on the marble floor, causing him to crack his skull and to bleed.

ILLUSTRATION 21-2. Reverse Chronological Order

Dr. James Panhandle is suing our client, Hospitality Resorts International, Inc., for negligence stemming from injuries he sustained when he slipped and fell on January 28, 2021, at the Hospitality Resort of London. The doctor seeks $16 million in damages.

The doctor hit his head on the marble floor, causing him to crack his skull and to bleed.

ILLUSTRATION 21-2. *Continued*

At 8:00 p.m., Dr. Panhandle was walking slowly out of the hotel coffee shop that was adjacent to the pool. He slipped on the wet marble floor next to the pool.

On the day of the accident, children were playing in the pool at 8:00 a.m. The children splashed water out of the pool and onto the marble floor near the pool. The floor had not been mopped at any time during the day.

2. Organization by Claim or Defense

Facts statements also can be **organized by claim or defense**. In statements of this kind, legally significant facts that relate to a claim or a defense are grouped together. See Illustration 21-3. This method is useful when the issue does not concern events that can be organized by time sequence and the information involves individuals who are not parties to the action.

ILLUSTRATION 21-3. Organization by Claim or Defense

Our clients, the Black Hawks, want to know whether the attorney-client privilege can be asserted by a former company president, Debbie Irl, and a current employee, Meredith Tildy, head of the cleaning staff. These questions arose while the plaintiff's attorney was deposing these individuals on July 8, 2021, as part of the discovery in a personal injury lawsuit stemming from a slip and fall at the stadium.

Irl, president of the Hawks at the time of the accident, left the organization in June 2018. During her tenure with the organization, she was a decision maker and she drafted the cleaning policy for the stadium. Irl had spoken with the Hawks' attorney, Ace Rudd, about the accident on July 10, 2020. Irl is not named as a party in the lawsuit and is merely a witness. During the deposition, the plaintiff's attorney asked Irl about her conversation with Rudd. Irl asserted the attorney-client privilege.

Meredith Tildy, the current head of the Hawks' cleaning staff, knew about the accident. Beer had been spilled the night before the accident. A patron told the staff to mop up the beer when it happened. Tildy knew that the cleaning staff had failed to clean up the beer. In her position, Tildy schedules the staff and decides whether the stadium should be cleaned completely each night. On July 10, 2020, Tildy spoke with Rudd, the company attorney, about the accident. The plaintiff's attorney asked Tildy about her conversation with Rudd. Based upon Rudd's advice, Tildy asserted the attorney-client privilege.

In Illustration 21-3's sample facts statement, the details are organized by claim. The first paragraph introduces the claims — the assertion of attorney-client privilege by Irl and Tildy. The next paragraph includes the facts that are legally significant to Irl's claim of attorney-client privilege. The final paragraph focuses on the facts that are legally significant to Tildy and Tildy's assertion of the attorney-client privilege. Because neither Irl nor Tildy is a party, this organization works well.

3. Organization by Party

Another way to organize the facts is to **organize by party**, grouping the facts according to the party the facts describe. This method is useful when multiple parties are involved in a dispute. See Illustration 21-4, which involves a dispute between three parties: a company and two individuals. The memo focuses on whether Whole In One is an employer and whether two individuals are employees or independent contractors.

The first paragraph in Illustration 21-4 introduces the claim. The next paragraph describes one of the parties, Whole In One. The next paragraph describes another party, Walker. The final paragraph tells the reader about Radiant, the third party in the action.

ILLUSTRATION 21-4.   Organization by Party

Victoria Radiant and Karen Walker, two former Whole In One Enterprises workers, brought a federal sex discrimination lawsuit, based upon Title VII, against our client, Whole In One Enterprises, owned by Nancy and Craig Black. The lawsuit, filed in the U.S. District Court for the Northern District of Illinois, stems from the dismissal of the two women by the Blacks during 2021.

The Blacks own Whole In One Enterprises, which operates a miniature golf course and restaurant in Glenview, Illinois. During the 24-week 2021 restaurant season, 10 people worked full-time and 14 people worked part-time for Whole In One. However, no more than 14 people worked on any one day. Of those 14 people, only 3 were full-time employees. The other full-time employees regularly took days off during the summer restaurant and golf season.

Among the full-time workers was Karen Walker, who worked as a public relations director for Whole In One. Walker responded to an ad that said that "an employer" sought an individual to perform public relations work. Whole In One hired Walker without a contract and told her she was prohibited from working for other firms. However, Walker worked from home and set her own hours. Whole In One required Walker to attend weekly staff meetings at the company offices, where Whole In One would review and revise Walker's work. The company supplied Walker with paper, pencils, stamps, and telephone service and paid for her life and health insurance. Whole In One did not withhold taxes from Walker's commissions.

Victoria Radiant, who had a two-year employment contract with the company, provided marketing services to Whole In One from October of 2019 until she was fired in 2020. Although Radiant worked in the company office, Whole In One management rarely supervised her work. The company paid for her continued education, provided her with bonuses, and deducted taxes from her weekly salary.

4. Combination of Chronological and Claim or Party Organization

Some facts statements do not lend themselves to one type of organization. Some facts should be arranged by the order of the events, and others do not fit neatly into this arrangement. Therefore, you might group facts in chronological order and by party or claim.

The facts statement in Illustration 21-5 concerns the question of whether Janice Kahn can successfully pursue a claim against Ronnie Randall for intentional infliction of emotional distress after Randall struck Kahn's 11-year-old son with Randall's car. The accident itself is best described in a chronological manner because the events can be explained in a sequential order. However, the witness statements and other "facts" that relate to whether Randall intentionally struck the child and whether Randall intended to cause emotional distress when he struck the child should be organized by issue or claim.

In some instances, your organization should be structured by the sequence of the events and by the parties. See Illustration 21-6.

ILLUSTRATION 21-5. Chronological and Claim Organization

While driving a car, Ronnie Randall struck Janice Kahn's son at 5:00 p.m. on August 29, 2021. The sun was bright and the weather was clear. No skid marks appeared on the dry street following the accident. Janice Kahn was working in her garden about five feet from the accident scene at the time of the accident. Her son was playing a game in the street before Randall's car struck him. Kahn saw Randall turn the steering wheel of the car and strike her 11-year-old son with the car. At first, Kahn thought her son was dead. He was covered with blood and had several broken bones. However, Kahn's son was conscious after the accident.

Immediately after the accident, Randall, who had a blood alcohol level of .11, was cited for drunk driving and driving with a suspended driver's license. Police had charged him with drunk driving and suspended his license two weeks earlier after the car he was driving struck another child at the same spot. Randall has a history of alcohol abuse.

Following the accident, several witnesses said Randall was upset and wobbled as he walked. One witness said that Randall intentionally turned the steering wheel to hit Kahn's son. Kahn stated that Randall often swerved down her street to get her attention.

Rhonda Albert, Kahn's neighbor, said she heard Randall say he would get even with Kahn after Kahn broke off a ten-year relationship with him.

During Kahn and Randall's ten-year relationship, Randall was close to Kahn's son. He took him to ball games, including one in April, and attended the son's baseball games. Randall knew that Kahn's son was the most important person in her life.

Since the accident, Kahn vomits daily and suffers from anxiety and headaches. Dr. Susan Faigen, Kahn's internist, states that the vomiting, anxiety, and headaches are the result of the accident.

ILLUSTRATION 21-6.   Chronological and Party Organization

Merriweather Halsey and Bonnie Bill were at the Masonic Temple for a fundraiser to fight AIDS. During the fundraiser Bill told a drunken Halsey that she intended to steal the $8,000 proceeds from the Masonic Temple and a pearl necklace from Alice McKinley after the fundraiser. Bill, who had helped organize the fundraiser, watched as the chairperson of the fundraiser opened the safe and placed the money in it. She memorized the combination and decided that she would use it later to steal the money.

After the fundraiser, Bill walked home to get a credit card and a crowbar to open the door if she needed it. Bill went to the Masonic Temple after the fundraiser, wearing a disguise, showed the guard her invitation, and told him that she had lost her mother's diamond brooch inside. Although the guard did not remember her, he allowed her to go into the temple. She wandered around the building for about an hour with the brooch inside her purse.

When the guard decided to eat his supper, Bill went to the safe. She opened it and pulled out all the money, except for $1,000.

Bill told the guard she had found the brooch and then left. She went to Alice McKinley's home, entered the house through an open ground-floor window, and took the pearl necklace she had seen McKinley wearing earlier, and then left.

Merriweather Halsey considered borrowing money from a friend who worked at a local bulb factory. She wandered into the factory around 4:00 a.m., after the fundraiser. The guard had stepped away from the door for a break. She headed toward her friend's workstation, but she stumbled into an open office where the petty cash was kept. She fell over a secretary's desk. Her leg caught the desk and pulled open a drawer that contained $500. She thought about taking the money, but she passed out before she took it. She woke up about 6:00 a.m., when a secretary found her and summoned the security guard.

Halsey then fell into the security guard, causing him to crash his head into a planter. The guard cut his head and later required six stitches. Halsey thought the security guard was a robber, so she grabbed a letter opener from a nearby desk and told the security guard to back off. The security guard took the letter opener. Halsey's mind was still fuzzy from the alcohol, but she decided to pull a squirt gun out of her pocket to scare the guard she thought was a robber.

The question is whether Bill or Halsey can be convicted of aggravated burglary under Houcktown County law.

In Illustration 21-6, the first paragraph introduces both parties, Bonnie Bill and Merriweather Halsey. The facts statement details most of the night's events in chronological order. However, the parties, Bill and Halsey, leave the fundraiser separately. At this point, the organization changes from chronological to one focusing on each party. First, facts that are legally significant to Bill's escapades are explained. These are noted in chronological order from start to finish. After the facts concerning Bill's adventure, the facts related to Halsey's acts at the bulb factory are detailed. These facts also are explained in chronological order. The final paragraph tells the reader the issues that will be considered in the memo.

C. WRITING THE FACTS STATEMENT

1. Prepare a List of Facts and Preliminary Statement

After you meet with an attorney to discuss your research assignment, make a list of the facts and draft a preliminary facts statement. Illustration 21-7 shows an excerpt from a client interview. Following the interview is a list of the facts and a preliminary facts statement, shown in Illustration 21-8, that includes all the facts provided in the interview.

ILLUSTRATION 21-7. Excerpt from a Client Interview

Attorney: What can I do for you today, Mr. Grocer of Sack and Shop?

Grocer: Rebecca Harris, one of my regular customers, is suing me for $1 million.

Attorney: What happened?

Grocer: Ms. Harris came to the store to purchase cherries, strawberries, and bananas. When she was turning the corner in the produce section, she slipped on a banana peel.

Attorney: How long had the banana peel been on the floor?

Grocer: Two days.

Attorney: Did you or any of your employees know about the banana peel on the floor?

Grocer: Yes. One of the patrons told the head of the produce department to clean up the banana peel two days before Ms. Harris fell.

Attorney: Why wasn't it picked up?

Grocer: The produce department head was in a hurry to leave and forgot to do it. The next day, he was very busy and he kicked the banana peel into a corner. Apparently it somehow was knocked out of the corner and to the middle of the floor where Ms. Harris slipped on it.

Attorney: Were there any witnesses?

Grocer: I saw her slip.

Attorney: What was Ms. Harris doing when she slipped?

Grocer: She was walking toward the green peppers.

ILLUSTRATION 21-7.   *Continued*

Attorney: What day did the incident occur?

Grocer: July 8, 2021. The same day another accident occurred in the produce section that involved a piece of cut cantaloupe.

Attorney: Was Ms. Harris injured?

Grocer: She hurt her head and broke her arm. At least I think she broke her arm because the bones didn't seem to be connected properly. It looked like part of the bone was dangling.

Attorney: Was anyone injured in the second accident?

Grocer: Yes. A man slipped on the cantaloupe and broke his finger.

ILLUSTRATION 21-8.   Sample Preliminary Facts Statement Based on the Client Interview

BRIEF LIST OF FACTS:
Client: Sack and Shop Grocery Store
Plaintiff: Rebecca Harris

Slip and fall at grocery store on July 8, 2021.

Plaintiff slipped on a banana peel, which had been left on the store floor for two days.

Harris was walking to the green peppers.

Another accident happened in the same section when a man slipped on a cantaloupe and broke his finger.

A patron told the store employee to clean up the banana peel two days earlier.

The employee kicked it into a corner.

Somehow the peel got to the middle of the floor again.

Harris came to the store to purchase cherries, strawberries, and bananas.

Preliminary Facts Statement

Our client, Sack and Shop Grocery Store, is being sued for negligence by Rebecca Harris.

Harris went to the store to purchase cherries, strawberries, and bananas on July 8, 2021.

While Harris was in the produce section, she slipped on a banana peel that had been left on the floor by a grocery store employee. The employee dropped it on the floor two days earlier and had failed to clean it up after a patron asked him to do so. The employee had kicked the peel into the corner two days before the accident. Somehow the peel found its way to the middle of the floor on the date of the accident.

ILLUSTRATION 21-8. *Continued*

Harris sustained a broken arm and head injuries as a result of the slip and fall. Another man was injured in the produce department that same day when he slipped and fell on some cantaloupe.

2. Research the Issue

After you prepare your list and preliminary facts statement, the next step is to research the legal issue or issues and to determine the applicable law.

3. Revise to Include Only Legally Significant Facts

Revise your list so that it includes only the legally significant facts, the facts that will have a bearing on the applicable law. See Illustration 21-9. To draft this list, you must determine the legal elements necessary to establish a claim. In the case of negligence, you would learn that negligence is the breach of a duty of reasonable care that results in injuries to another person. The elements then would be:

- duty of reasonable care
- breach of the duty
- a link between the breach of the duty and the resulting injuries
- injuries

You should review the facts and determine which facts may affect whether the plaintiff can establish one of these elements or whether the defendant would be able to disprove one of the elements — in other words, the legally significant facts. In this case, you should include all of the facts listed in Illustration 21-9. In that illustration, the element of the legal theory is noted in parentheses next to the legally significant fact. The fact that Harris was purchasing cherries, strawberries, and bananas is not legally significant. Similarly, the fact that another patron was injured in the produce section that day did not affect whether Harris was injured and therefore is not legally significant.

ILLUSTRATION 21-9.   List of Legally Significant Facts

- The slip and fall occurred in the store on July 8, 2021. (breach and duty)
- Rebecca Harris slipped on a banana peel that had been left on the store floor for two days. (breach and duty)
- The store employee dropped the banana peel on the floor two days earlier. (breach and duty)

ILLUSTRATION 21-9. *Continued*

- A store employee knew about the banana peel on the floor two days before the accident. (breach and duty)
- The employee kicked the peel into the corner after a patron told him to clean it up. (breach and duty)
- Rebecca Harris suffered injuries as a result of the fall. (link and injuries)

4. Organize the Facts

After you have made your list of facts, decide how to organize them. After you select your organizational method, group the legally significant facts together in the organizational style you have selected.

PRACTICE POINTER

Sometimes you will use multiple organization methods.

---

5. Rewrite the Facts Statement

The facts contained in Illustration 21-9 lend themselves to a chronological organization because they can be ordered by time. Illustration 21-10 is a rewritten facts statement that includes only the legally significant facts. Finally, remember to introduce the legal issue or issues presented in the facts statement, as shown in the first paragraph of Illustration 21-10.

ILLUSTRATION 21-10.   Sample Facts Statement for Slip-and-Fall Case

Rebecca Harris, a store patron, is suing our client, Sack and Shop Grocery Store, for negligence.

While Harris was in the produce department, on July 8, 2021, she slipped on a banana peel that had been left on the floor by a grocery store employee. The employee dropped it on the floor two days earlier and had failed to clean it up after a patron asked him to do so. When he was told to pick up the peel, the employee kicked the peel into the corner.

Harris sustained a broken arm and head injuries as a result of the slip and fall.

CHAPTER SUMMARY

A facts statement is designed to refresh an attorney's memory about a case or to educate a new attorney about the case. It is a statement of all facts that are legally significant (facts that might affect the outcome of a legal issue). Facts that are not legally significant should be omitted from a facts statement.

Facts statements can be organized in chronological or reverse chronological order, by claim or defense, by party, or any combination of these three.

To draft your statement, make a list of the facts, plan your organization, then write the statement. Next, research the legal issue, then rewrite your facts statement because the legally significant facts may have changed based on your research.

In the next chapter, you will learn how to organize using the IRAC methodology.

KEY TERMS

asserted facts
chronological organization
elements
emotional adjectives
fact
facts statement
legal claim

legal conclusion
organization by claim or defense
organization by party
procedural fact
pure fact
reverse chronological order

EXERCISES

SELF-ASSESSMENT

1. What is a facts statement?
2. What are legally significant facts?
3. What are pure facts?
4. What are asserted facts?
5. What are procedural facts?
6. What facts should be included in the facts statement?
7. What is the difference between a fact and a legal conclusion?
8. Where do you find the information to include in the facts statement?
9. List several methods for organizing a facts statement.
10. Explain two methods of organization.

PRACTICE SKILLS
Drafting a List of Relevant Facts

11. Review the following Uniform Commercial Code section and read the list of facts that follows. Make a list of the legally significant facts based on the statute. Next to each fact, list the relevant portion of the statute.

§ 2-315 Implied Warranty of Fitness for a Particular Purpose

Where the seller at the time of contracting has reason to know any particular purpose for which the goods are required and that buyer is relying on the seller's skill or judgment to select or furnish suitable goods, there is unless excluded or modified under the next section an implied warranty that the goods be fit for such purpose.

Facts

Your client is Sue A. Buyer. She lives at 3225 Wilmette Avenue, Sylvania, Ohio. The defendants are Lee R. Merchant, owner of Mowers R Us, in Toledo, Ohio, and Manny U. Facture, the owner of a manufacturing concern that is not incorporated called Mowers, of Rossford, Ohio. Ms. Buyer went to the defendant's store, Mowers R Us, to purchase a lawn mower for her new home. She was a first-time homeowner and was unfamiliar with lawn mowers. She had never operated a lawn mower because her brothers had always mowed the lawn when she was a child.

When she went to Mowers R Us, she asked to speak with the owner. She told Mr. Merchant: "I don't know anything about these mowers, and I need to talk with an expert." Mr. Merchant said, "I'm the owner, and you couldn't find a better expert anywhere in the Northwest Ohio. I have been in the business of selling mowers for more than 40 years. I only sell mowers and the equipment to clean and repair them. Are you familiar with the type of lawn mower you would like?"

"No, I don't know anything about lawn mowers. I just know that I have to have a lawn mower that will mulch my grass clippings, because I cannot bag the clippings. The city of Sylvania does not permit me to bag the clippings, so the clippings must remain on my lawn."

"You're absolutely correct. You must have a mulching mower," Mr. Merchant said. "That type of mower will grind the grass clippings, and you will not notice them on your grass. I have the perfect mower for you. It is a used model that will fit into your price range, only $200. It's a good brand, a Roro, and will mulch the grass as well as any of the new mowers. This one is true blue. You can purchase a separate mulching blade, which will easily attach to it for an additional $50," he added.

"Do you think that I need the mulching blade?" Ms. Buyer asked, "I've never used a lawn mower, so I don't know what to expect, and you appear to be the expert."

"I think that you could do without the mulching blade unless you want the grass ground up very fine."

"I think that I would like it ground up fine. I'll defer to your judgment. If you think a mulching blade is necessary, then I'll buy that with the mower. Do you think that this is the best mower for mulching, or should I go with a new one?"

"Absolutely the used one is best; I told you: it's a true value. It will mulch with the best of them."

"If you think it can do the job, I'll trust your judgment," said Ms. Buyer, "I'll take the mower and the mulching blade. Can you install the mulching blade? I don't know anything about the installation."

"Sure, we can install any blade for another $30."

Ms. Buyer purchased the mower and the blade. She used the mower after Mr. Merchant installed the new mulching blade. It barely cut the grass and certainly didn't mulch the clippings into fine pieces as Mr. Merchant had claimed.

She brought the mower back to Mr. Merchant. He said that he had made no warranties about the mower. He showed her the language on the receipt that said that he did not expressly warrant anything.

Ms. Buyer brought the mower to a Roro dealer. The owners of the Roro dealership, Abe Saul and Lou T. Wright, said that the mower Ms. Buyer had purchased from Mowers R Us was not a mulching mower. It was a mower built before mulching was popular. Therefore, it would not perform the mulching task. It was designed merely to cut the grass. "Any merchant who has been in business even for one year should have known that mowers built before 2000 were not designed for mulching," Mr. Wright said. He showed Ms. Buyer where the manufacturing date appeared on the mower. "Manufactured in August 1999," it said on the plate with the serial number. "Also, mulching blades cannot be placed on these old mowers. Any mower dealer should know that, too," Mr. Wright added. "However, this mower isn't bad. It can cut the grass without mulching it."

Ms. Buyer brought an action against Mr. Merchant and Mr. Facture in the Lucas County Common Pleas Court in Toledo, Ohio.

OBJECTIVE WRITING

12. Write three different discussions about your high school career. One discussion should present the experience in a negative manner. The second should attempt to persuade the reader that the experience was positive. Finally, write about your experience in a neutral manner, without any emotion. Compare the three discussions.

DRAFTING A FACTS STATEMENT

13. Draft a facts statement for our client, Ronnie Randall. Janice Kahn, the plaintiff, brought an action against Randall for intentional infliction of emotional distress. You should prepare your facts statement based on this excerpt from a deposition transcript, witness statements, and a police report. The facts statement will be included in a memo that discusses the issue of intentional infliction of emotional distress. For the purpose of this memo, intentional infliction of emotional distress is defined as follows:

An act by a person that is extreme and outrageous conduct, done with intent to cause another to suffer severe emotional distress, and which results in distress and emotional injury to another. The emotional injury must manifest itself with a physical problem.

Below is a portion of Janice Kahn's deposition transcript.

Q. What were you doing when the accident occurred?

A. Working in my garden. I planted tomatoes, green peppers, carrots, and broccoli.

Q. Where is your garden located on your property?

A. In the front, near the street. It is next to a brick wall. I can't see the garden from my house.

Q. What direction were you facing in your garden?

A. North.

Q. Does that direction face the street?

A. No.

Q. What do you usually do in your garden when you work?

A. Weed it.

Q. What were you doing in your garden when the accident occurred?

A. Weeding it.

Q. Where is the street in relation to your garden?

A. About five feet.

Q. Where do the children generally play?

A. In the backyard.

Q. Where were the children playing on the day of the accident?

A. They were playing T-ball in the front yard.

Q. Were you watching the children at the time of the accident?

A. Yes, I could see them.

Q. Did you see the accident occur?

A. Sort of.

Q. Did you or did you not see the accident?

A. I saw my son, who is 11 years old, on the ground covered with blood, and blood all over the front of the Cadillac.

Q. Did you actually see the driver strike your son?

A. No. But I know Ronnie hit him. I saw my son next to Ronnie's car. I heard him swerve.

Q. Did you know the driver?

A. Yes.

Q. How did you know him?

A. We met at a state fair. We dated for ten years. I broke up with him two weeks before the accident.

Q. Did he know your son?

A. He knew my son was the most important person to me, and he tried to kill him to pay me back for dumping him.

Q. Are you accusing the driver of intentionally striking your son?

A. Yes. He wanted to get back at me, so he hit my boy.

Q. What happened to your son on the day of the accident?

A. He sustained head injuries and several broken bones. He can't play T-ball for the rest of the season, and we had to cancel our vacation to the Dells because he's been hurting so much.

Q. Was he conscious when you first saw him after the accident?

A. He was awake, but I thought he was dead at first. He had blood everywhere. I knew the driver, Ronnie, was drunk when he hit him. He wasn't even looking where he was going. He always swerves down our street to get my attention.

Q. Did your son speak to you right after the accident?

A. Barely. I told him that Ronnie was speeding and trying to run him down on purpose. I was horrified to see the blood and the broken bones. I couldn't move and I was so angry at Ronnie because I knew he did this on purpose.

Q. Did you go to the doctor after this accident?

A. I went by ambulance with my son to the doctor. His doctor looked me over and said I was suffering from shock. Since then, I suffered from anxiety and headaches. I throw up every day.

Q. Have you seen a doctor for your complaints?

A. Yes. She said that they are related to the accident. I just keep thinking back to that day when the neighbor told me that Ronnie intentionally turned the wheel to hit my boy.

Q. Was your son able to move after the accident?

A. Slightly. He looked just like our neighbor's son did after Ronnie hit him with his car two weeks before at the same curve.

Police Report, State of Illinois

Ronnie Randall, the driver of a 2018 Cadillac, was cited for driving while under the influence of alcohol and/or drugs, reckless driving, and driving with a suspended license. I will ask the prosecutor to consider either reckless assault charges or vehicular homicide, depending upon the condition of the boy. I tested Randall for alcohol intoxication. His blood alcohol level was .11. Randall struck another boy, Tommy Albert, at the same site two weeks earlier. He was cited for reckless driving for that accident and drunk driving. As I arrested Randall, he said that he was daydreaming during the accident and that he did not mean to hit the child. There were no skid marks. The street was dry.

The boy's mother, Janice Kahn, was working in her garden about five feet from the accident scene at the time of the accident. Her son, Billy Kahn, was playing a game in the street.

Witness Statement

Two days before the accident, Rhonda Albert, a neighbor of Janice Kahn, heard Randall say that he planned to get even with Kahn after Kahn broke off her ten-year relationship with Randall. Albert saw the car strike Kahn's son. According to Albert, after the car struck the boy, Randall got out of his car and said, "Oh, my God. I didn't mean to hit him. Is he okay?" Albert could smell alcohol on Randall's breath.

Witness Statement

Rebecca Mark saw the driver, Ronnie Randall, turn the car toward Kahn's son.

REVIEW OF FACTS STATEMENTS

14. Now that you have reviewed the facts for the Janice Kahn case and have drafted a statement of your own, read the following statements of facts. Determine which facts statement is best. List any errors you find in any of the statements.

A. The plaintiff, a single mother, and the defendant, her ex-boyfriend, are involved in a lawsuit. The plaintiff alleges in her deposition that the defendant was driving recklessly and intentionally struck her son with his car. The defendant's motive was to pay her back for ending their relationship. He tried to kill her son for this reason. As a result of the accident, the plaintiff went into shock and suffers from anxiety, headaches, and vomiting.

B. The plaintiff was working in her tomato garden located in the front of the property about five feet from the street. She could see the children playing in the front yard. She did not see the driver, Ronnie Randall, hit her son with his Cadillac but did see blood on the front of the Cadillac and on her son, who was on the ground.

    The plaintiff dated Randall for ten years and had just ended their relationship. She states that Ronnie hit her son to pay her back for ending their relationship. Two weeks before, Ronnie had hit a neighbor's son at the same curve.

    The plaintiff states that her son was covered with blood, able to move slightly. He suffered head trauma and broken bones.

    The plaintiff is suffering from shock after seeing her son. She remembers a neighbor telling her that Ronnie intentionally turned the wheel to hit her son.

    The plaintiff suffers from anxiety and headaches and vomits daily.

C. Janice Kahn is bringing an action against Ronnie Randall for the intentional infliction of emotional distress. Ronnie Randall struck her son with his car on the street in front of the Kahn home. At the time of the injury, Kahn was working in the front yard near her son. Her son went into the street and Randall hit him. At the time of the accident, Randall was legally drunk and driving with a suspended license.

    Randall had previously told Kahn's neighbor, a Ms. Albert, that he was going to get even with Ms. Kahn over the breakup of their ten-year relationship. He also told Ms. Albert that he knew that Ms. Kahn's son was very important to her.

    Since the accident, Kahn vomits daily and suffers from anxiety and headaches. She has stated that Mr. Randall often drives by her home in an erratic fashion and on another occasion hit a neighbor's child. Kahn feels that Randall hit her son intentionally. Kahn did not see the injury take place but was at her son's side immediately after the injury. Kahn also says that Randall never slowed down until after he hit her son.

D. On August 12, 2019, Janice Kahn filed a lawsuit against Ronnie Randall for intentional infliction of emotional distress stemming from an accident involving Kahn's 11-year-old son.

On July 8, 2019, Janice Kahn was weeding her tomato garden while her children played T-ball a few feet away from her in the street. As she worked, Kahn heard a car swerve. She looked up to see her son, covered in blood, lying on the ground in front of a Cadillac. Ronnie Randall drove the Cadillac.

Two neighbors witnessed the accident. Rebecca Mark saw the driver, Ronnie Randall, turn the car toward Kahn's son. Rhonda Albert also saw the car strike Kahn's son. According to Albert, after the car struck the boy, Randall got out of his car and said, "Oh, my God. I didn't mean to hit him. Is he okay?"

Albert could smell alcohol on Randall's breath. Police tested his blood alcohol level and found that it was .11. Police cited Randall for drunk driving, speeding, and reckless driving.

After police arrived, an ambulance took Kahn and her son to the hospital, where he was treated for head injuries and broken bones. The doctor who treated Kahn's son told Kahn that she should be treated for shock. Since the accident, Kahn has suffered from anxiety and headaches and vomits daily. Her doctor said that the anxiety, headaches, and vomiting are the result of the accident.

The driver of the car involved in the accident was Kahn's former boyfriend. They had dated for ten years; however, Kahn broke off the relationship about two weeks before the accident. Kahn stated in her deposition that she believes Randall intentionally struck her son to pay her back for ending the relationship.

Also, two days before the accident Albert heard Randall say that he planned to get even with Kahn after Kahn broke off their ten-year relationship. However, the police report stated that Randall said that he was daydreaming during the accident and that he did not mean to hit the child. Since the breakup, Kahn has seen Randall often swerve down the street in front of her home. Two weeks before the accident, Randall hit Rhonda Albert's son with his Cadillac at the same curve.

15. Read the following statement. Make a list of the legally significant facts. Then prepare a facts statement for a memo that would explain the possible interests of all of the parties. What type of organization did you use and why?

Nate Late, a business owner, has two partners in the operation of Loose Cannon Manufacturing in Gurnee, Your State. He owns one-third of a $3 million company. Late is ill but is not dying. He is grooming a 26-year-old man, Ivan T. McCool, to run the business. He tells his family that he likes McCool and wants to teach him the business. The business owner, Nate Late, dies. The most current will leaves the estate of Late to his wife, Shirley Late, and his only son, Lou Sier. McCool tells Mrs. Late that Late intended to give McCool Late's one-third interest in the company and that Late told this to McCool in front of a banker on the day of his death. The conversation took place during a meeting and the agreement was never put into writing. Before this meeting, on the day of Late's death, other employees of Loose Cannon heard Late say that he intended for McCool "to get" the business. Family members knew that Late intended for McCool to run the business and for McCool to get something if the business was sold. None of the family believed that Late intended to give the business to this newcomer. Late's shares of stock were never given to McCool. The shares were in the safe deposit box shared by Late and his wife of 24 years.

Rob R. Baron also claims that Late promised to give him the shares in the future. Baron admits that Late did not physically give him the shares before he died, but Baron insists that Late said, "I shall give you my shares in two years." Mrs. Late said that Mr. Late planned to give her the shares. He told her this when he opened the joint safety deposit box and gave her the key.

You work for a firm that has been retained by Mrs. Late. She would like to know if McCool can prove that Mr. Late gave McCool all of Mr. Late's interest in the company.

16. Rewrite this statement using a different type of organization. Does this organization make sense? If not, why not? If so, why?

FACTS DRAFTING

17. Make a list of the legally significant facts for the following problem. Then draft a facts statement.

You are a paralegal with the firm of Probing and Will. You must research whether Sarah Wakefield can renounce Adam Antwernt's will and collect a portion of the estate in your state.

Your firm's client is Sarah Wakefield. She was married to Adam Antwernt. Antwernt died in your state following a long illness. Wakefield was Antwernt's second wife. She had been married to him for more than 20 years and lived in their home in your state before Antwernt died. Antwernt purchased the home with his first wife, Carry MacOver. MacOver died while she was still married to Antwernt. Wakefield subsequently married Antwernt. When Antwernt married Wakefield he never changed the deed for the home to include Wakefield. Wakefield kept her maiden name. Antwernt adopted a son with MacOver. The son, who is now 30 years old, is Grayson Antwernt.

Antwernt drafted his will before he married Wakefield. He and Wakefield were getting along fine when he died. However, she was not included in his will. He did not leave her any property. Instead, he left all of his property to Grayson. Antwernt's will was admitted to probate.

Wakefield wants to know whether Antwernt's will is valid and whether he can divest her of the marital property or whether she can renounce the will and collect a portion of the estate. Grayson is out of town and his attorney told Wakefield that she will get her share of the estate once Grayson returns. He is scheduled to return later this month.

18. Make a list of legally significant facts and then draft a facts statement for this problem.

> Your firm has a client, an individual, Kris Rizzo, who claims he was injured when he was driving a car rented by Bear Cubs Car Rental and the brakes failed. The case was brought in state court in Arizona. Bear Cubs wants to move the lawsuit to federal court based on diversity jurisdiction.
>
> Bear Cubs Car Rental had its car service area inspect the brakes four months before the accident. The service told management the brakes must be inspected in four months and likely replaced then.
>
> The case is brought in state court in Arizona.
>
> Bear Cubs Car Rental is owned by Hope Motors, a national rental car company.
>
> Hope Motors is based on Western Avenue in Chicago, Illinois.
>
> All of the company decisions concerning the operations of Hope Motors and its rental companies in various states are made at its Chicago headquarters. All officers work in Chicago.
>
> Bear Cubs Car Rental operates in Phoenix, Arizona.
>
> Federal diversity jurisdiction requirements are specified in a federal law 28 U.S.C. § 1332.

THE IRAC
METHOD

CHAPTER OVERVIEW

This chapter focuses on the IRAC writing method used for the discussion portion of the memo. IRAC is an acronym for Issue, Rule, Application, Conclusion. These are the building blocks of a memo's discussion. IRAC is used most frequently in objective writing. You will learn to identify issues and applicable legal authority. You will also learn how to extract the legally significant facts and apply them to the relevant law to draw substantiated conclusions. You will learn to identify effective IRAC use by dissecting discussions and labeling the IRAC components, and you will learn to draft IRAC sequences as well.

A. PURPOSES OF IRAC

▼ What Is IRAC?

IRAC stands for Issue, Rule, Application, Conclusion. IRAC is the architectural blueprint for the discussion portion of a legal memo. It gives legal writing continuity and clarity and organizes the contents of the discussion. The IRAC format provides an organizational structure for your document. IRAC provides legal support and analysis for the issues posed by the problem and guides the writer toward a well-supported conclusion.

IRAC benefits both the writer and the reader because the components are essentially a checklist designed to ensure that the discussion is analytically well thought out and that it contains the necessary legal authority. IRAC is used in objective writing to allow the reader to see:

- the particular legal point being addressed
- the relevant legal rule
- the application of the law to the facts
- the conclusion

IRAC is formula writing in the same way that formula movie romances, Westerns, and thrillers are. The predictability of the IRAC format enables the reader to obtain information quickly.

NET NOTE

The CUNY Law School Writing Center website has information on using the IRAC format at www.law.cuny.edu/legal-writing/students/irac-crracc/irac-crracc-1.html.

B. IRAC COMPONENTS

Each IRAC sequence is composed of an issue, which is really a legal element or component; the **legal rule** or holding from a case or statutory authority; the application, which is a demonstration of how the legal authority applies to the problem that you are writing about; and the conclusion, the final assessment of how the rule applies to the facts of your problem.

▼ What Does an IRAC Paragraph Look Like?

This fact pattern forms the basis of the IRAC paragraph example.

> On August 9, 2021, Ms. Howard went to Rough & Tough Pawn Shop in Chicago to obtain a loan using a diamond ring as collateral. Rough & Tough loaned Ms. Howard $800, and she agreed to pay $75 per month for

a total of 13½ months. Ms. Howard knew that she would have to pay off the balance of $1,025 in 12 months because at that time Rough & Tough would have the right to sell the ring. On September 13, 2021, Ms. Howard received a postcard from Rough & Tough stating that it was selling the shop and all of its assets to Able Pawn. Mr. Sam Able would assume the business of Rough & Tough, including all pawned items and outstanding loans. On the bottom of the postcard was a notice stating; "If you want your item, please pick it up by September 29, 2021, and pay off your note by September 29, 2021." Because Ms. Howard did not have the money to pay off the note, she decided to pay Able Pawn the $75 per month once the loan was transferred in the sale. In October 2021, Able Pawn was robbed and all the jewelry, including Ms. Howard's ring, was stolen. Able Pawn had a security alarm system and a guard dog to protect the property, but the robbers were able to circumvent these obstacles.

We will work through the following sample IRAC paragraph, based on the Howard fact pattern, and its components to illustrate how to draft an IRAC paragraph.

(**I**) Whether a bailment for the mutual benefit of Rough & Tough and Howard existed. (**R**) A pawn is a form of bailment, made for the mutual benefit of bailee and bailor, arising when goods are delivered to another as a pawn for security to him on money borrowed by the bailor. *Jacobs v. Grossman*, 141 N.E. 714, 715 (Ill. App. Ct. 1923). In *Jacobs*, the court found that a bailment for mutual benefit arose because the plaintiff pawned a ring as collateral for a $70 loan given to him by the defendant. *Id.* (**A**) Similarly in our problem, Howard pawned her ring as collateral to secure an $800 loan given to her by Rough & Tough, the pawnbroker. (**C**) Therefore, Howard and Rough & Tough probably created a bailment for mutual benefit.

Note that the first sentence of the IRAC paragraph is a statement of the issue that will be examined in the paragraph. The issue is narrowly defined and focused on one of the analytical elements of the problem. The rule of law, the next component of the paragraph, provides the legal basis for the analysis of the issue. Then, it is appropriate to discuss some of the facts of the cited case if these facts help explain how the legal rule can be applied to your facts. Notice that everything that comes from an opinion is given citation credit.

The most important component of the IRAC paragraph is the application portion. The application is where you use the facts of your problem to demonstrate, but not to conclude, why the legal rule should apply to the issue posed. You draw the parallels and distinctions here between your facts and the case's facts. This is the legal analysis. (See Chapter 18 for more discussion.) The facts speak for themselves when you demonstrate how the legal rule applies to the scenario at hand by contrasting or paralleling the facts of the case and the problem. After laying out this relationship, you will then draw a conclusion. The conclusion answers the issue posed. The issue is the question being examined in the discussion, and the conclusion is the answer.

This example illustrates how the conclusion responds directly to the issue:

Issue: Whether a bailment for the mutual benefit of Rough & Tough and Howard existed.

Conclusion: Therefore, Howard and Rough & Tough probably created a bailment, for it was for their mutual benefit because a loan was given upon the receipt of valuable collateral.

1. Issues

The question presented is the overall legal **issue** that will be resolved in the memo. A **subissue** in the IRAC paragraph is a point or query that must be addressed to substantiate one legal element of the problem. When analyzing and writing about a legal problem objectively, it is often important to address subissues in the order in which they must be resolved to support legal analysis. For example, the general rule for arson in Illinois is the malicious burning of the dwelling house of another. The question presented for a memo on arson would be:

Whether Mr. Smith committed arson by intentionally burning down his brother's factory.

The subissues addressed in the IRAC paragraphs would be:

Whether there was a malicious burning

Whether the factory is a dwelling house

Whether the factory of Mr. Smith's brother constitutes the property of another person

The subissues form the **topic sentences** of the IRAC paragraphs. They provide the analytical steps that you must take in your thought process and your legal reasoning to resolve the overall issue the problem poses; the overall question is the question presented for the entire memo. The topic sentences in the IRAC paragraph introduce the legal element in question that needs to be resolved to complete the steps necessary to thoroughly examine the problem and to determine a response to the question presented.

▼ What Is the Difference Between the Question Presented and the Issues in IRAC Paragraphs?

The question presented is the overall problem that must be resolved in the objective memo. The question presented for the Howard fact pattern is:

Whether Ms. Howard has a claim against Rough & Tough or against Able Pawn Shop for the value of her ring.

The subissues are determined by the legal elements or tests involved in the problem. The elements are discussed individually along with the relevant legal rule. There is a certain logical order when presenting the elements. Let the legal rules guide you in establishing the order of the subissues. Notice that each issue centers on a single step or element of the legal analysis necessary to examine fully the question presented.

The subissues that form the topic sentences of the IRAC paragraphs in a memo addressing Ms. Howard's problem would be as follows:

The first issue is what type of relationship do a pawner and a pawnee have?

What property rights do Ms. Howard and Rough & Tough Pawn have when they enter into a mutual bailment?

Can Rough & Tough Pawn transfer its interest in Ms. Howard's property to Able Pawn?

Did Rough & Tough Pawn receive the proper consent for the transfer of the ring from Ms. Howard?

Is Rough & Tough liable for the loss of Ms. Howard's property after transferring its interest to Able Pawn?

Is Able Pawn liable for the theft of Ms. Howard's property while it was in its possession?

All of these queries are really elements that must be addressed, step by step, to resolve the question presented.

Each of the subissues will be a topic sentence of the IRAC paragraph highlighting the analytical focus of the legal discussion in that paragraph. Each issue is a step in the thought process required to thoroughly prove all of the underlying elements necessary to address the question presented.

Notice how one issue statement logically leads into the next. A good test to see if your discussion is well organized is to write down all your issue statements from your IRAC paragraphs. If the issue statements flow logically, one to the next, then the organization of your discussion will be logical.

To analyze the problem thoroughly, a number of issues must be examined in the discussion. To make the analysis logical, the issues must be examined in a certain order.

2. Rules of Law

The **legal rule**, or synthesized compilation of the pertinent legal rules, follows the issue at the beginning of the IRAC paragraph. (For an in-depth discussion of the process of synthesizing authority, see Chapter 23.)

A rule of law is the court's test, standard, or principle on the point. A rule also can be a statute and the legal elements stated in the statute provision. A synthesis of a statute and a case applying or interpreting the statute also constitutes a rule.

In our IRAC example, note that the first sentence is the issue, and the second sentence is the legal rule.

Issue:	Whether a bailment for the mutual benefit of Rough & Tough and Howard existed.
Rule, followed by pinpoint citation:	A pawn is a form of bailment, made for the mutual benefit of the bailee and the bailor, arising when goods are delivered to another as a pawn for security to him on money borrowed by the bailor. *Jacobs v. Grossman*, 141 N.E. 714, 715 (Ill. App. Ct. 1923).

When organizing the discussion, first discern what issues are to be addressed, then find the pertinent mandatory authority that addresses the issues raised. Do not write the discussion around the authority but make the authority address the issues. To demonstrate clearly how the authority supports or addresses the issues raised, discuss the pertinent facts of the cited case after you state the case's legal rule. This is particularly helpful when the rule is very broad. You must demonstrate that the cited case truly supports the premise discussed in the IRAC paragraph. Your reader will want to see why the case is relevant and will want to understand what happened in the case factually.

▼ Why Is Citation Important?

Citation is an essential component of the rule portion of the IRAC paragraph. (See Citation Appendix.) You must always give proper credit in *Bluebook* or *ALWD* format to any statement made that is not wholly your own. Any legal principle or authority must be attributed to its source. Proper attribution of authority tells the reader where you obtained the legal principle that supports the discussion. The cite allows the reader to find the source, too. Most important, the cite tells the reader whether the authority is primary mandatory authority, primary persuasive, or secondary authority. A cite also provides information without including the information in the discussion's text. For example, you could write a rule as follows:

> The state of Kimberly Supreme Court held in 1983 that individuals have a right to privacy. *Jones v. City of Moose*, 121 Kim. 12, 13 (1983).

A more effective version of the same rule, to include in the rule portion of the IRAC paragraph, is:

> Individuals have a right to privacy. *Jones v. City of Moose*, 121 Kim. 12, 13 (1983).

The citation itself provides the information about the court, its jurisdiction and level, and the year. The text need not repeat this information. Your reader wants to know the point of the case, its test, standard, or principle. Citations are valuable sources of information about the legal authority presented in the rule component of the IRAC paragraph.

3. Application of the Law to the Problem's Facts

▼ How Do You Use the Legally Significant Facts?

Think of the legal rule as a test or a series of elements requiring certain facts to be used to support the outcome of the test. The facts used are **legally significant facts** because they bear legal significance as to the outcome of an issue. Our arson example mentioned earlier in the chapter illustrates this point.

THE ARSON HYPOTHETICAL

John Smith lived in Arkville. John Smith's brother, Richard Smith, lived in Barkville Estates. Richard Smith owned a factory in downtown Barkville. John Smith was consumed by a jealous rage over his brother Richard's success and intentionally and maliciously burned down the factory in Barkville. The question to be examined is whether John Smith committed arson by intentionally and maliciously burning down his brother's factory.

The general rule for arson is the malicious burning of a dwelling house of another. This general rule would be the legal authority used in the rule portion of the IRAC paragraph.

An IRAC paragraph on this topic would be as follows:

Issue:	Whether John Smith committed arson when he burned down his brother's factory.
Rule:	Arson is the malicious burning of a dwelling house of another. 9 Stat. §§ 21, 23 (2021).
Application:	John Smith's actions were intentional and malicious when he burned down the factory of his brother, Richard. Richard resides in Barkville Estates.
Conclusion:	Although John's actions were intentional and malicious, John did not commit arson because he burned down his brother's factory, not his brother's residence or dwelling house.

The **application** lays a factual foundation on which the conclusion can be based. The facts are selected because each fact illustrates a legal point related to your rule of law: the malicious act, the intentional burning down of a building, the use of the building—whether it serves as a residence or dwelling house or whether it serves another purpose. The rule indicates which facts you should examine. In our example, the rule requires us to focus on the type of building. Here, the building was a factory and not a dwelling house. After you lay the factual foundation by using the problem's facts to illustrate how the law should apply, you can draw a conclusion.

4. Conclusion

The **conclusion** resolves the issue posed at the beginning of the IRAC sequence. The conclusion should reflect directly the issue posed. If you remove the rule and the application portions of the IRAC paragraph, the issue and the conclusion should read as if they are a question and an answer. The conclusion generally restates the issue and includes the basis for the answer. The arson example with John Smith illustrates the role of the conclusion.

> **Issues:** Whether John Smith committed arson when he burned down his brother's factory.
>
> **Conclusion:** John Smith did not commit arson because he burned down his brother's factory, not his residence or dwelling house.

Notice how the conclusion responds directly to the issue posed. The conclusion focuses directly on the question raised at the beginning of the IRAC sequence. Each element of the discussion is resolved before addressing the next element or issue.

PRACTICE POINTER

To test if your conclusion is focused on the issue raised, read the issue at the beginning of the IRAC sequence, then read the conclusion. If the issue and the conclusion read like a question and a reasoned answer that responds directly to the question raised, then you have stayed focused and adequately addressed the issue.

CHECKPOINTS FOR FOLLOWING THE IRAC FORMAT

1. Does each paragraph, after the thesis, address a single element?
2. Is each rule, which is the test, standard, or principle the court relied on, stated clearly?
3. Did you include the essential facts from each case so the reader will understand how the issue played out?
4. Are the case facts limited to three sentences or less?
5. Is there a clear statement of the court's holding with the signpost "The court held"? The holding is the answer to the specific question before the court.

6. Do you introduce the summary of the reasoning with "The court reasoned"?
7. Did you summarize the relevant portions of the court's reasoning in three sentences or fewer—why the court held as it did?
8. For the application, do you clearly draw the parallels and distinctions between the cases and our facts?
9. Do you state the conclusion for each element, and not state the overall conclusion for the memo, at the end of each IRAC sequence?
10. Is the memo objective and does it apply the law neutrally?

CHAPTER SUMMARY

IRAC—standing for Issue, Rule, Application, Conclusion—provides the structure for the legal discussion. The IRAC structure provides a checklist for you to make sure that you have included all the necessary components in the discussion and supported every premise with legal authority. Because it follows a predictable pattern, IRAC permits the reader to obtain information quickly. Mastering the IRAC format requires practice, which involves rereading and revising your work. Once you feel comfortable with the IRAC format, you should be confident that the discussion portions of your memos are logically ordered and analytically complete.

KEY TERMS

application	legal holding
citation	legal rule
conclusion	legally significant facts
IRAC	subissue
issue	topic sentence

EXERCISES

SELF-ASSESSMENT
1. What does IRAC stand for? Define each component.
2. Why do we use the IRAC format?
3. What is a legally significant fact?

DIAGRAMMING IRAC COMPONENTS
4. Diagram the IRAC components of each paragraph in the discussion section below. Note where the writing digresses from the IRAC format.

Discussion
To be successful in a claim against Rough & Tough or Able Pawn, Ms. Howard would have to prove that Rough & Tough was liable for the loss of her ring. First, for an action against Rough & Tough, she would have

to show that the company had no right to transfer her pawned property without her written consent. Illinois Pawnbrokers Act, 205 Ill. Comp. Stat. 510/10 (2020). If pledged property was transferred without written consent of the property owner, the pawnbroker can be held responsible for loss or theft of pawned property because the property was in his safekeeping and was transferred illegally. *Jacobs v. Grossman*, 141 N.E. 714, 716 (Ill. App. Ct. 1923). Rough & Tough did not get a written consent for the transfer of Ms. Howard's property. In its defense the company could claim that written correspondence without the written consent would be enough to inform the pawner of the transfer of her property. Second, for an action against Able Pawn, Ms. Howard would have to show negligence in its care of her pawned ring. Illinois courts have ruled that in bailment for mutual benefit, the ordinary care or diligence that one would give to one's own property would be adequate to avoid negligence. *Id.* at 715; *Bielunski v. Tousignant*, 149 N.E.2d 801, 803 (Ill. App. Ct. 1958). Ms. Howard would have to prove that a security system and a guard dog would not be ordinary care and diligence. In his defense Mr. Able could argue that these were sufficient to be considered ordinary care and diligence. For a claim against Village Jewelers to be successful, Ms. Howard would have to establish that she held good title to her property because a thief cannot convey good title to stolen property. *Hobson's Truck Sales v. Carroll Trucking*, 276 N.E. 89, 92 (Ill. App. Ct. 1971). Village Jewelers, which purchased the ring from the robbers, could not have good title to Ms. Howard's ring. Ms. Howard probably could have a successful claim against Rough & Tough and Village Jewelers. She probably would not be able to prove Able Pawn negligent in the care of her ring.

Does a pawnbroker have the right to transfer pawned property or interest in that property without written consent of the pawner? Pawned property cannot be transferred within a year from the pawner's default without written consent of the pawner. Illinois Pawnbrokers Act, 205 Ill. Comp. Stat. 510/10. One Illinois court ruled that a pawnbroker had no right to transfer the plaintiff's pledged diamond ring to another pawnbroker within a year of the plaintiff's default of her loan, without written consent of the pawner. *Jacobs*, 141 N.E. at 716. In our situation, Rough & Tough sold its shop and assets to Sam Able within two months of Ms. Howard's pawning her grandmother's engagement ring. Because the sale occurred within a year of Ms. Howard's transaction with Rough & Tough, the company had a legal obligation under the Illinois statute to require a written consent for the transfer of her property. Also, the statute states that the time period for requirement of written consent for transfer of pledged property is established from the time of the pawner's default. 205 Ill. Comp. Stat. 510/10. Our client has not defaulted, and she deserves at least all the rights offered by the statute to a pawner who is in default. Rough & Tough did send Ms. Howard a postcard notifying her that it had sold all the pawned items and outstanding loans, including her ring, but it did not get her written consent for the sale of her property. Rough & Tough did not have the right to transfer Ms. Howard's ring without her written consent, and the sale of her property was probably not a legal sale.

Is a postcard sent to a pawner by a pawnbroker sufficient notice for the transfer of pawned property? Personal pawned property cannot be sold by a pawnee within one year from the time the pawner has defaulted in the interest payment unless the pawner has given written consent. Illinois Pawnbrokers Act, 205 Ill. Comp. Stat. 510/10. The statute uses a definite and clear term: "written consent." Ms. Howard did not default, and she would have at least all the rights of a pawner that did default. Therefore, the pawnbroker was required to receive her written consent before transferring her property. A postcard with written notice of a sale of pawned property is not a written consent by the pawner and would probably not be sufficient notice to constitute a legal sale.

5. Diagram the IRAC components of each paragraph in the discussion section. The facts and the issues are provided to help you understand the context for the discussion. Note where the writing digresses from the IRAC format.

Facts
The Blacks came to us with the following problem and want to know what type of damages they are entitled to.

Mr. and Mrs. Black wanted to have a chair and a loveseat made to match the living room in their new home. The Blacks searched for weeks at various local furniture retailers for a furniture style and fabric that they liked but were unsuccessful. Finally, the Blacks went to a fabric sale at Fabric Retailers and found the upholstery fabric of their dreams. The Blacks purchased 50 yards of the fabric to make sure that they would have enough for any project. Mr. Black called all the furniture retailers in the area to inquire whether customers can have furniture covered in their own material. Finally, Comfy Furniture said that they permit customers to bring in their own material to cover upholstered furniture ordered from Comfy. The Blacks hurried over to Comfy with the 50 yards of fabric and placed an order for a chair and a loveseat using their own fabric. The price agreed on was the base price of $500 for the chair and $800 for the loveseat. Mr. Blaine, of Comfy Furniture, was their salesperson. Mr. Blaine said that the fabric was ideal for the styles selected because it required no matching. He added that there was plenty of yardage because 30 yards is adequate for jobs of this nature. The fabric was a small paisley print, with the right side having a lovely sheen and vibrant coloration. The Blacks placed the order on July 8, 2019, because they were planning a family reunion for Thanksgiving and felt that that date would give them plenty of time to completely decorate their living room. The new pieces would provide plenty of seating for the family reunion. The Blacks indicated to Mr. Blaine that they needed the furniture for the reunion. Mr. Blaine asserted that the furniture would be ready by September 16. The Blacks gave Comfy Furniture a deposit of $1,000. The loveseat and the chair were delivered to the Black home on September 10, but the furniture was upholstered with the fabric's reverse side showing. The Blacks were devastated.

Issues

Whether the Blacks are entitled to damages from Comfy Furniture for incorrectly upholstering their furniture.

Whether the Blacks are entitled to damages from Comfy Furniture for the expense of decorating their living room to match the furniture they did not receive in the agreed-on condition.

Discussion

Are the Blacks entitled to special damages from Comfy Furniture for the cost of the redecoration of their living room? An Illinois Appellate Court decided that the nonbreaching party should be put back in the position that it was in when the contract was formed. *Kalal v. Goldblatt Bros.*, 368 N.E.2d 671, 673 (Ill. App. Ct. 1977). The Blacks stated their intention at the beginning concerning the fabric, the redecoration of the living room, and the family reunion. This fact was a part of their original position. The living room was redecorated. The furniture was delivered; however, the fabric was incorrect. Therefore, the Blacks have a right to recover consequential damages for the cost of the redecoration of their living room because the end result was not achieved: correctly upholstered furniture, newly redecorated living room to match, and sufficient seating for the reunion. The conditions of the original contract were not met, and there was a breach of contract as embodied by the incorrectly upholstered furniture.

Under contract law, what damages are the Blacks entitled to pursue? Damages for breach of contract should place the plaintiff in a position he would have been in had the contract been performed. *Kalal*, 368 N.E.2d at 671. The plaintiffs in *Kalal* received a sofa that had been reupholstered in the wrong fabric after numerous delays, during which they had chosen three different fabrics in succession. *Id.* The court held that the defect could be remedied by the cost of reupholstering the sofa in the proper fabric. *Id.* at 674. The Blacks' sofa and loveseat were improperly upholstered. Comfy Furniture upholstered their furniture with the reverse side of the fabric showing. Therefore, they were entitled to damages equal to the cost of upholstering their furniture correctly. However, the Blacks' situation is distinguished from *Kalal* in that their furniture was delivered before the date set in the contract, and it can be argued by Comfy that there was time to remedy the defect before their target date of Thanksgiving.

Are the Blacks entitled to compensation for the loss of use of their furniture? The question of compensation for loss of use of the furniture was considered by both parties in *Kalal* to be appropriate since the plaintiffs in the case were without their furniture for several months while waiting for it to be reupholstered. *Id.* The Blacks have been similarly inconvenienced in that they, too, have been without the use of their new furniture. Thus, they are entitled to compensation for the loss of use of the furniture. However, it can be argued by Comfy Furniture that the furniture in the *Kalal* case was used and had been removed from the home for the purpose of reupholstering it. *Id.* In the present case, the furniture was new and had never been in the Blacks' home, and Comfy may argue that the Blacks did not actually suffer loss of use of the new furniture.

Are the Blacks entitled to damages for the expense of decorating their living room to match the furniture they did not receive in the agreed-on condition? The redecorating of the living room in *Kalal* was not in the contemplation of either party at the time the contract was executed. *Kalal*, 368 N.E.2d at 671. Subsequently, the court held that the only damages that were recoverable for breach of contract are limited to those that were reasonably foreseeable and were within the contemplation of the parties at the time the contract was executed. *Id.* at 674. By the express terms of the Uniform Commercial Code, the court cannot follow tort theories to award damages. The legislative history of the U.C.C. indicates that contractual disputes should apply to the findings of the court. *Moorman Mfg. Co. v. National Tank Co.*, 435 N.E.2d 443, 453 (Ill. 1982). The Blacks only told Mr. Blaine that they needed the furniture to be completed in time for a family reunion. Comfy knew that the Blacks were under a time constraint for the delivery, but apparently there was no communication regarding the redecorating of the living room. With regard to Comfy Furniture, the redecorating of the Blacks' living room was an unforeseeable event, and consequently they would not be held responsible for the expense. Because the fact that the redecorating of the living room was unforeseeable, it was not included within the terms of the contract. Therefore, Comfy only breached the express terms of the contract. The Blacks probably will not be awarded compensatory damages.

PRACTICE SKILLS

6. Write an IRAC paragraph using the following information. You need not include all the information. The issue is whether the plaintiff can show that his attorney's failure to attend hearings was excusable neglect. A number of the text blocks below contain statements of rules. Other text blocks include legally significant facts. In some paragraphs, conclusions have been drawn for you. Combine the rules where necessary and form an IRAC paragraph for the issue.

Fed. R. Civ. P. 60(b) provides for relief from judgment if plaintiffs can show that a mistake was made or that there was excusable neglect on the part of their attorney.

Rule 60(b) is an extraordinary remedy, granted in only exceptional cases. *Harold Washington Party v. Cook City. Illinois Democratic Party*, 984 F.2d 875 (7th Cir. 1993).

In this case, the plaintiff's attorney, Mark Adly, missed four court-set status hearings. He failed to appear. He failed to answer motions. Court status hearings are routinely held every three months.

Adly claims he did not have any notice of the hearings. Adly knew status proceedings normally were held. He attended depositions in this matter. Court records show that he was sent notices of the hearings to the address Adly says is correct.

"Excusable neglect may warrant relief under Rule 60(b)." *Zuelzke Tool & Eng'g v. Anderson Die Casting*, 925 F.2d 226 (7th Cir. 1991). In this case, the defendant relied on a third party who told them to refrain from further action because efforts were being made to have the defendant removed as defendant. *Id.* at 228. Anderson did not answer any complaints or file any pleadings. *Id.* The lack of response led the court to enter a default judgment against the company. *Id.* at 229. The district court refused the motion to vacate, saying that the defendant had voluntarily chosen not to control its fate in the litigation. *Id.*

7. Review the following paragraph. Note the issue, the rule, the application of law to facts, and the conclusion.

An important factor in determining whether a funeral home is a nuisance is the suitability of its location. "Funeral homes are generally located on the edge of purely residential but not predominantly residential areas." *Bauman v. Piser Undertakers Co.*, 180 N.E.2d 705, 708 (Ill. App. Ct. 1962). A carefully run funeral home may be located on a property zoned for business at the edge of a residential neighborhood. *Id.* The funeral home in this case is located in a predominantly rural area. It is outside the boundary lines of the Up and Coming Acres subdivision. It is a lawful business located on a parcel zoned for business. The funeral home is in a suitable location.

8. Read the following facts carefully.

Mr. and Mrs. Mortimer reserved the party room at Harvey's Restaurant and gave Harvey's a $500 deposit. Their party was scheduled for November 6, 2021. Mrs. Mortimer sent the invitations out on October 4, 2021. The Mortimers agreed to the quoted price of $62.50 per person. The purpose of the event was for Mr. Mortimer to establish relationships with current and prospective legal clients.

On October 18, 2021, Mrs. Mortimer called Harvey's to confirm party details. She was informed that the party room was under demolition and could not be used for the party. Mrs. Harvey offered to lower the price to $57.50 per person and reserve a portion of the dining room. Although she believed these arrangements were not suitable, Mrs. Mortimer agreed to use the dining room since the invitations were sent and many people accepted.

Mrs. Mortimer ordered lump crabmeat as an appetizer for the party. A waitress told Mrs. Mortimer that imitation crabmeat was used when Mrs. Mortimer inquired about the crab's unusual crunchiness.

The Mortimers want to sue Harvey's for breach of contract and believe that they relied to their detriment on this contract. They assert that Harvey's failed to notify them of the changes in a timely manner, consequently preventing them from making other arrangements. Additionally, the Mortimers want to know if they have a cause of action for the substitution of imitation crabmeat for genuine.

The following is a portion of a memo relating to one of the issues raised by the Mortimers. Read the paragraphs carefully and revise in IRAC format. Remember that each IRAC sequence can span more than one paragraph (for example, paragraph 1—issue and rule; paragraph 2—application and conclusion).

Did the Mortimers suffer a loss of business because of Harvey's Restaurant's promise of the entire party room? The Mortimers can argue that a false representation surrenders the restaurant's interest. "When parties enter into a contract for the performance of the same act in the future they impliedly promise that in the meantime neither will do anything to harm or prejudice the other inconsistent with the contractual relationship they have assumed. . . . If one party to the contract renounces it, the other may treat the renunciation as a breach and sue for damages at once." The restaurant can argue that the contract did not cover the entire performance but was modified; therefore, no harm was done to the contractual relationship. *Pappas v. Crist*, 25 S.E.2d 850, 852 (N.C. 1943). The Mortimers can argue that "damages are not speculative merely because they cannot be computed with mathematical exactness, if, under evidence they are capable of reasonable approximation." *Hawkinson v. Johnston*, 122 F.2d 724, 727 (8th Cir. 1941). The "rainmaking" potential was minimized because of the restaurant's failure to supply the room contracted for.

The restaurant would argue that the "period for which the damages can be reasonably forecast or soundly predicted in such a situation must depend on the circumstances and evidence of the particular case." *Id.* at 727. Therefore, the Mortimers can only quantify the number of RSVPs, not the number of rejects due to the smaller room.

9. This exercise highlights organizational problems in the discussion and will help you to write more logically. Review the discussion section of a previously drafted memo. Label, in the margin, the issues, the rules, the application portions, and the conclusions. Examine each component to see where you diverge from the IRAC format in the discussion. Revise the discussion to conform more closely to the IRAC format.

10. Label the components of the following discussion to indicate Issue, Rule, Application, and Conclusion, and where each component begins. The discussion is based on these facts:

Drake Industries has been leasing warehouse space at 2700 North Bosworth Avenue in Chicago, Illinois, from the owner of the building, Michael Martin. Drake began leasing space from Martin beginning January 1, 1993, at $700 per month until the lease expired on December 31, 2004.

Martin offered a new lease to Drake on November 25, 2004, to be signed and returned by December 31, 2004. The new lease began January 1, 2005, and expired on December 31, 2022, and the rent increased to $850 per month, payable on the first of each month. Drake never signed and never returned the new lease, but did pay the increased rent amount during the term of the unsigned lease ending December 31, 2022. Since then, Drake has continued paying $850 on the first day of each month. On August 15, 2022, Martin requested that Drake surrender the premises. Drake came to our firm to find out what type of tenancy the lease has and whether Martin gave Drake proper notice to quit the premises.

Discussion

Is Drake Industries a holdover tenant? A holdover tenancy is created when a landlord elects to treat a tenant, after the expiration of his lease, as a tenant for another term upon the same provisions contained in the original lease. *Bismarck Hotel Co. v. Sutherland*, 415 N.E.2d 517, 520 (Ill. App. Ct. 1980). In *Bismarck*, defendant Sutherland's written lease expired. Bismarck presented her with a new lease, which included a rent increase. Sutherland began to pay the increase but did not sign the new lease. Sutherland could not be a holdover since the terms of the old lease were not extended to the terms of the new, unsigned lease. Drake Industries was offered a new lease in 2004, which included a rent increase. Since the terms were different from the original lease, Drake could not be considered a holdover tenant.

It is the intention of the landlord, not the tenant, that determines whether the tenant is to be treated as a holdover. *Sheraton-Chicago Corp. v. Lewis*, 290 N.E.2d 685, 686 (Ill. App. Ct. 1972). When a landlord creates a new lease and presents it to the tenant, it is clear that it is his intention that a new tenancy is created. *Holt v. Chicago Hair Goods Co.*, 66 N.E.2d 727, 728 (Ill. App. Ct. 1946). Martin presented Drake with a new lease to sign in November 2004 with new terms beginning January 1, 2005. It was never his intention to hold over the same lease from 1993. Therefore, Drake was not to be a holdover tenant and has never been one. 735 Ill. Comp. Stat. 5/9-202 (West 2020) could not apply to Drake, and Martin could not demand double rental fees from Drake when it remained in possession of 2700 N. Bosworth after the written lease expired on December 31, 2004.

Is Drake Industries a year-to-year tenant? When the payment of rent is annual, there arises a year-to-year tenancy, even if the agreement provides for a payment of one-twelfth of the annual rental each month. *Seaver Amusement Co. v. Saxe et al.*, 210 Ill. App. 289, 297 (1918). The terms of the 1993-written lease would have to have said "$8,400 a year rent, payable in monthly installments of $700" for it to be considered a year-to-year lease. Since the terms of the 1993 lease provided for monthly payments only and not a yearly rental rate, Drake was not a year-to-year tenant. 735 Ill. Comp. Stat. 5/9-205 (2020) does not apply at all to Drake, and Martin would not be required to tender 60 days' written notice to terminate the tenancy.

Is Drake Industries a month-to-month tenant? A month-to-month tenancy is created when a tenant remains in possession of the premises after a lease expires under different terms of tenancy. *Bismarck*, 415 N.E.2d at 517. By paying Bismarck's increased rental amount, different terms of the tenancy were established, so Sutherland's tenancy was considered month-to-month by the court. Drake remained at 2700 N. Bosworth after its lease expired in 2004, but began paying the increased rent to Martin under the new terms of the unsigned lease. This established different terms of tenancy, so Drake has been a month-to-month tenant since January 1, 2005.

What type of tenancy is created under an oral lease? When a tenant goes into possession of real estate under a verbal leasing agreement for a term over one year at monthly rental, the agreement is voidable under the Statute of Frauds. The most that the tenant in possession can claim is that the leasing is from month-to-month and that the landlord can terminate the tenancy by providing 30 days' notice in writing to the tenant. *Creighton v. Sanders*, 89 Ill. 543, 545 (1878). Charles Creighton had a verbal agreement to lease a house from Patrick Sanders for a five-year term. When Creighton ceased paying rent, Sanders gave him a written notice to quit the premises. Creighton maintained that he had a five-year lease, but the most the court allowed was that he was a month-to-month tenant, based on the oral lease. When Drake never signed and never returned the new lease, he entered into an oral lease agreement with Martin. Martin cannot hold Drake to any terms of that lease because the tenancy was for a duration of over 18 years, well over the one-year limit under the Statute of Frauds. The most Martin can claim is that Drake is a month-to-month tenant.

What type of notice is necessary to vacate the premises? Under 735 Ill. Comp. Stat. 5/9-207 (2020), notice to terminate a month-to-month tenancy must be made with 30 days' notice, in writing, before any action for forcible entry and detainer can be maintained. Drake said that on August 15, 2022, Martin "requested" that Drake surrender the premises. An oral request may not be sufficient, and Drake may maintain that proper notice has not been made and that he need not surrender the premises by September 15, 2022. A forcible entry and detainer action could not be entered and maintained, and Drake need not surrender the premises until proper notice has been given.

DRAFTING PRACTICE

11. Write an IRAC paragraph based on the following facts, issue, and cases.

Facts
Ms. Jones was waiting to get off the commuter train in the train's vestibule. The commuter train pulled into the station and Ms. Jones descended the stairs to disembark from the train. The conductor exited the train first to watch the passengers exit the train and then signal to close the doors for the train to start rolling. Ms. Jones was carrying her briefcase, which had a long strap. As Ms. Jones exited the train the briefcase strap was behind her. The train doors shut with Ms. Jones on the platform but with the briefcase strap still inside the door. The train dragged Ms. Jones about ten feet and she suffered a broken shoulder. The issue you have to consider is whether the conductor's negligence by signaling for the train to start was the proximate cause of Ms. Jones's broken shoulder.

Issue
The issue on which you should focus is whether the conductor's failure to see that Ms. Jones's briefcase strap was inside the door as he signaled for the train to start moving is the proximate cause of her broken shoulder.

Cases
Smithers v. Atlantic City Railroad, 12 Nowhere 2d 5 (2021)

Mr. John Smith was injured on the Atlantic City Railroad when the train lurched with great violence as it rounded a curve on the track. The train was overcrowded. Smith was injured without fault on his part. The motorman drove the overcrowded car too fast around the curve, so as to cause it to give a severe lurch. Where a passenger train is overcrowded and the employees operating the train know of such condition, it is their duty to exercise additional care commensurate with the dangers. The motorman knew of the overcrowded conditions and failed to exercise additional care when rounding the curve. Mr. Smith was injured when the train lurched as it rounded the curve because he fell onto another passenger. The motorman's failure to exercise the requisite care was the proximate cause of Mr. Smith's injuries.

Blue v. Boardwalk Railroad, 15 Nowhere 2d 9 (2020)

Mr. Robert Blue was blinded by a sudden gust of steam and fell underneath the train he was in the process of boarding at the station. Mr. Blue's arm was severed by the train as it started to leave the station. Regular inspection of couplings is a required duty of conductors. Failure to inspect the couplings for leaks is a negligent act on the part of the defendant. Railroad's allowing steam to escape was the proximate cause of Mr. Blue's injury, since a man of ordinary prudence could have foreseen that escaping steam would result from leaks in the uninspected couplings. The consequence of the escaping steam, due to the railroad's failure to inspect the couplings, resulted in a foreseeable injury to a passenger or person waiting on the platform.

12. Write an IRAC paragraph based on the following facts, issue, and statutes.

Facts
Ms. Jones was waiting to get off the commuter train in the train's vestibule. The commuter train pulled into the station and Ms. Jones descended the stairs to disembark from the train. The conductor exited the train first to watch the passengers exit the train and then signal to close the doors for the train to start rolling. Ms. Jones was carrying her briefcase, which had a long strap. As Ms. Jones exited the train the briefcase strap was behind her. The train doors shut with Ms. Jones on the platform but with the briefcase strap still inside the door. The train dragged Ms. Jones about ten feet and she suffered a broken shoulder. The issue you have to consider is whether the conductor's negligence by signaling for the train to start was the proximate cause of Ms. Jones's broken shoulder.

Issue
The issue that you should focus on is whether the conductor's failure to see that Ms. Jones's briefcase strap was inside the door as he signaled for the train to start moving is the proximate cause of her broken shoulder.

Statutes

Chapter 131 Nowhere Revised Code § 12 (2021)

An operator of a common carrier must perform regular inspections of all components of the common carrier. Failure to do so constitutes negligence. The failure to perform inspections and the resulting negligence will be considered the proximate cause of all injuries occurring aboard a common carrier.

Chapter 131 Nowhere Revised Code § 14 (2021).

It is the duty of an operator of a common carrier to exercise additional care when dangers are foreseeable.

SYNTHESIZING CASES AND AUTHORITIES

CHAPTER OVERVIEW

You will learn about the methods of synthesis used when writing a memo. Synthesizing authority requires finding a common theme from two or more sources that ties together the legal rule. Cases are synthesized because it is hard to find a single decision that articulates the precise rule of law to support a point in a memo or brief. Often one case rule will expand on another, so the two rules can be combined, or synthesized, to reflect an accurate statement of the law.

You will also become adept at synthesizing statutory authority, often called enacted law, as well as combining case law and statutes. Constitutions should be given the highest regard in the hierarchy of authority, then statutes. You will probably not use many constitutional provisions in your writing, but statutes play a very large role in legal research and writing. If you find case law that applies or interprets a statute, synthesize the statute and the rule from the case.

A. SYNTHESIS

Synthesis is the bringing together of various legal authorities into a unified cohesive statement of the law. The process of synthesizing authority requires finding a common theme or thread that relates to the various legal rules and tying the rules to that unified theme. Discussing related decisions and statutes separately in a memo makes your points sound more like a list than an integrated, well-thought-out whole. Synthesis adds analytical insight to your legal documents and makes reading the discussion easier. When you synthesize your legal authorities, you relate the authorities to your points rather than merely present summaries of your sources.

▼ What Is the Process of Synthesizing Legal Rules?

We synthesize cases and enacted law because memos and opinion letters are organized by legal issue and not by cited references. Frequently, more than one source of primary authority addresses a particular legal issue. The synthesis of related legal principles enables you to compare and contrast the legal rules easily as well as to demonstrate how factual applications differ and to show how legal rules expand or contract. Often enacted law and case law are synthesized because the case law applies the statute or interprets the extent to which the statute can be applied. Sometimes the rules that are on point are derived from relevant statutes only. Enacted law that comes from more than one statute section also must be synthesized under a common legal principle to promote cohesiveness and to add your analytical viewpoint to the memo.

▼ Why Do We Synthesize Legal Authority?

The legal issues form the framework for the discussion. The synthesized authority groups the legal rules together to address the issues raised.

The following example demonstrates how one case defines an easement in gross and then another case explains how an easement in gross is retained. Both cases discuss easements in gross, yet one expands on the other. The facts on which the example is based are as follows:

> Robert and Jan Murray live in Evanston and are building an addition to their house on Ashland Avenue. There is eight feet between their house and their neighbor's, Mrs. Brown's, house. The properties are adjoining. A driveway does not separate the houses. Also, there is no alley that would provide access to either property. The Murrays' contractors and construction workers must enter Mrs. Brown's property to work on the addition. Mrs. Brown is not very pleased that workers are entering her property. The Murrays came to our office wondering whether they should purchase an easement from Mrs. Brown, their neighbor.

EXAMPLE

The Murrays should purchase an easement in gross from Mrs. Brown so that the workers can enter the Brown property, for the limited purpose, to perform construction on the Murray home. An easement in gross, sometimes called a personal easement, is a right in the land of another that is not permanently part of the title of the property. An easement in gross allows for use of the land of another for a limited purpose. *Willoughby v. Lawrence*, 4 N.E. 356 (Ill. 1886). The easement in gross belongs to the easement holder independent of his ownership or possession of any tract of land and does not benefit the possessor of any tract of land in his use of it. *Schnabel v. County of DuPage*, 428 N.E.2d 671 (Ill. App. Ct. 1981). The Murrays are building an addition to their house. They want to have a right to use the adjoining land only to perform the construction of their addition. They do not need an easement that would be a permanent part of the property's title. The interest that the Murrays have in Mrs. Brown's land is personal and would not benefit either tract of land. Therefore, the Murrays can purchase an easement in gross from Mrs. Brown that would permit the workers to enter the Brown property for the limited purpose to complete the construction project.

B. TYPES OF SYNTHESIS

▼ What Are the Four Methods of Synthesizing Authority?

As we discussed previously, synthesizing primary authority requires finding a common theme that is used to unify all of the various rules related to the issue. The common legal theme can be developed by grouping the applicable precedent into categories. There are four basic ways to combine and to analyze legal rules to create a coherent distillation of the law:

1. **Primary authority** can be grouped by related rules of law found in the text of the decision or in the statute or constitution.
2. Synthesis can be focused around the **reasoning** that the judges use as the basis for the holdings.
3. The various **facts** from different cases can form the foundation of the synthesis.
4. The **causes of action** can be the focus of case synthesis.

To synthesize primary authority in our examples, you will group related legal rules. All the examples focus on this method of synthesis. Detailed instruction follows as to how to synthesize various sources of case law, case law combined with statutory authority, as well as two sources of statutory authority.

C. STEP-BY-STEP PROCESS TO SYNTHESIZING LEGAL RULES

The most effective synthesis of legal rules follows conscientious case briefing and careful reading of enacted law (statutes and constitutions). Case briefing requires summarizing a decision in set categories: citation, procedure, issue, facts, holding, legal rule (the test or standard the court used to arrive at its decision), rationale (the court's reason for its holding), and disposition. (See Chapter 18.) The following steps take you through the synthesizing process.

1. *Summarize enacted law. Brief relevant decisions.* Once you have summarized enacted law, constitutional provisions, and statutes, after reading for their plain meaning, and carefully and meticulously briefed all the decisions that you plan to use in your memo, you can establish categories of legal rules to make comparing and contrasting authorities easier. It is far simpler to compare and to contrast seven rules from summarized statutes and briefed decisions than to flip through printouts of the authority.
2. *Outline the problem.* The next step is to formulate the analytical outline of your letter or memo and to pinpoint the issues and subissues that must be addressed to fully explore the memo topic. Here, you focus on the elements of the problem or the issue.
3. *Relate research to legal issues raised.* To organize the primary authority, relate the research findings to the issues the problem raises. Remember, legal writing is never organized around your sources of authority but around the issues the problem poses. After identifying the legal issues that will be explored, decide on the general rule relating to that point of law.
4. *Under each issue, organize your primary sources by hierarchy of authority.* Enacted law comes before common law, constitutions come before statutes, newer case decisions interpreting statutes come before common law cases, higher court holdings come before lower court holdings, and newer case holdings are more relevant than older holdings on the same point of law from the same court.
5. *Compare and contrast legal rules and statutes.* Using the case briefs that you prepared and the notes you made from the plain reading of the enacted law, compare and contrast the legal rules from the cases and statutory texts.
6. *Formulate a statement of the law.* Your statement should incorporate all the primary sources that will be used under the subissue heading. Start with the broadest statement of the rule. Ask yourself: What are the similarities and differences between the various cases and statutes? In the cases, how do the legal rules or tests the court used differ from or expand on one another? How do the facts differ? What do the documents have in common? Does one rule expand or

narrow another? Draft the synthesized legal support for each point in your outline.

7. *Correct citation.* Remember that you must attribute the authority for any legal statement, even if it is a clause, using the proper *Bluebook* or *ALWD* citation.

NET NOTE

The CUNY Law School Writing Center has information on rule synthesis at www.law.cuny.edu/legal-writing/students/irac-crracc/irac-crracc-3.html.

D. EXAMPLES OF CASE SYNTHESIS

This example demonstrates synthesizing the rules from two legal decisions. A problem and two fictitious legal decisions are provided below on which case synthesis is performed.

PROBLEM

Mr. and Mrs. Black wanted to have a chair and a loveseat made to match the living room in their new home. The Blacks searched for weeks at various local furniture retailers for a furniture style and fabric that they liked but were unsuccessful. Finally, the Blacks went to a fabric sale at Fabric Retailers and found the upholstery fabric of their dreams. The Blacks purchased 50 yards of the fabric of their dreams to make sure that they would have enough for any project. Mr. Black called all the furniture retailers in the area to inquire whether customers can have furniture covered in their own material. Finally, Comfy Furniture said that they permit customers to bring in their own material to cover upholstered furniture ordered from Comfy. The Blacks hurried over to Comfy with the 50 yards of fabric and placed an order for a chair and a loveseat using their own fabric. The price agreed on was the base price of $500 for the chair and $800 for the loveseat. Mr. Blaine, of Comfy Furniture, was their salesperson.

Mr. Blaine said that the fabric was ideal for the styles selected because it required no matching. He also offered that there was plenty of material, that 30 yards was adequate for a job of this nature. The fabric was a small paisley print, with the right side having a lovely sheen and vibrant coloration. The Blacks placed the order on July 7, 2022. They were planning a family reunion for Thanksgiving and felt that ordering in July would give them plenty of time to completely decorate their living room. The new pieces would provide plenty of seating for the family reunion. The Blacks indicated to Mr. Blaine that they needed the furniture for the reunion. Mr. Blaine asserted that the furniture would be ready by September 16. The Blacks gave Comfy Furniture a deposit of $1,000. The loveseat and the chair were delivered to the Black home on September 9, but the furniture was upholstered with the fabric's reverse side showing. The Blacks were devastated.

The legal issue is whether the Blacks are entitled to damages for the breach of the contract to upholster the furniture.

The legal principle surrounding this problem is the expectation interest in a contract. The expectation interest is the expectation of gain from the performance of the contract. The damages are assessed to give the nonbreaching party the measure of gain that he or she would have received if the contract was performed as agreed. Sometimes special or consequential damages are awarded in addition to the expectancy interest.

CASE A

The Cahill family ordered a sofa to be upholstered in red tapestry from the Acme Furniture Company on June 5, 2019. It was due to be delivered in six weeks, on July 19, 2019. The Cahills paid $600 for the sofa at the time of the order. In the meantime, the Cahills decorated their living room to match the red sofa. After ten weeks, Acme delivered a sofa upholstered in gold fabric to the Cahill home. The Cahills called Acme to complain, and Acme picked up the sofa with the promise that it would be reupholstered in red fabric. The sofa was delivered six weeks later upholstered in green fabric, not in red as requested. After the sofa was delivered upholstered in green fabric 16 weeks after the initial order, the Cahills sued Acme for breach of contract and for damages resulting from the breach, which included the cost of redecorating their living room to match the red sofa. The legal rule is that the nonbreaching party can only collect damages to recoup the expected gain from the contract if performed as agreed. The nonbreaching party cannot receive damages for expenses incurred that were not in contemplation at the time the contract was formed. The court held that the Cahills are entitled to damages for the upholstering of the sofa in the incorrect color and are entitled to compensation for the loss of the use of their sofa for 16 weeks as well as the cost of a new red sofa.

CASE B

Jane Smith ordered a new car from Lunar Motors on June 3, 2019. The Lunar coupe in black was ordered, but the salesperson suggested that the gray floor model, which was used only for demo drives, would represent a $300 savings off the sticker price of the Lunar coupe. Ms. Smith agreed to purchase the floor model for $15,700 rather than pay $16,000 for the special-order car. The salesperson once again asserted that the floor model was new, was used only for demo drives, and had only 5 miles on the odometer. Ms. Smith returned to Lunar Motors on June 4, 2019, paid the $15,700 for the gray floor model Lunar coupe, and drove home. While driving home, Ms. Smith noticed that the car veered dramatically to the left. Ms. Smith took the car to her mechanic, who reported that the car was in an accident previously and had been repaired, but the frame was bent in such a manner as to distort the alignment. Ms. Smith contracted for and expected to receive a new, undamaged car with mileage and wear and tear due to demo drives. Ms. Smith did not contract to receive a damaged car. The salesperson asserted the car was like new. The rule is that the nonbreaching party is entitled to the gain expected from the performance of the contract as agreed, and if the contract is not performed as agreed, the nonbreaching party is entitled to receive the benefit that she would have received if the contract had been performed as agreed. The court held that Ms. Smith is entitled to a complete refund of the $15,700 she paid for the car plus the daily cost of the loss of the use of the automobile to be tabulated by the fair market rental value per day of a Lunar coupe.

▼ What Is the Process to Synthesize the Rules?

To synthesize the rule, or tests, from the fictitious cases, you would find a common theme that ties together the rules of law from both decisions. You would start with the most general statement of the rule. Basically, both cases state the rule as the nonbreaching party in a contract is entitled to receive the benefit of the deal that would have been received if the contract had been performed as agreed. First, write a general statement of the rule. Then, mention the legal rules from Case A and Case B as they pertain to the general statement of the law.

EXAMPLE OF EFFECTIVE SYNTHESIS for The Black Factual Scenario

Are the Blacks entitled to damages compensating them for the breach of the contract to reupholster the loveseat and the chair? Damages are assessed in a breach of contract action in a very specific manner. Damages are assessed to give the nonbreaching party the measure of gain that he would have received if the contract had been performed as agreed. Case A; Case B. The nonbreaching party can collect damages to recoup the gain expected from the contract if the contract had been performed as agreed. Case A; Case B. If the contract is not performed as agreed, the nonbreaching party is entitled to the benefit he would have received if the contract had been performed as agreed. Case B. The nonbreaching party cannot be compensated for expenses incurred that were not in contemplation at the time the contract was formed. Case A. In the alternative, the nonbreaching party can be compensated for expenses incurred that were in contemplation at the time the contract was formed. Case A. In our problem, the Blacks contracted to have the chair and loveseat upholstered in paisley fabric with the correct side showing. The furniture was upholstered with the wrong side of the fabric showing. When ordering the furniture, the Blacks stipulated that they needed the pieces for a family reunion and that the pieces would provide the necessary seating. The Blacks were without their furniture because of Comfy Furniture's error. The Blacks communicated the need for the seating at the time of the contract formation. The Blacks should receive the benefit they expected from the performance of the contract as agreed as well as compensation for the expense of providing alternative seating for the family reunion based on the rental cost of chairs.

An ineffective case synthesis based on our hypothetical problem would be as follows:

> Are the Blacks entitled to damages from Comfy Furniture for breach of contract? "The nonbreaching party is entitled to the gain expected from the performance of the contract as agreed and if the contract is not performed as agreed, the nonbreaching party is entitled to receive the benefit that she would have received if the contract had been performed as agreed." (Rule from) *Case B.* The Blacks were the nonbreaching party and anticipated a loveseat and a chair to be upholstered in paisley with the correct side showing. Therefore, the Blacks are entitled to be compensated by a damage award to put them in a position as if the contract had been performed as agreed. Are the Blacks entitled to be compensated for not having adequate seating for the family reunion? Case A states that the nonbreaching party cannot receive damages for expenses incurred that were not in contemplation at the time the contract was formed. (Rule from) *Case A.* The Blacks alerted Mr. Blaine, the salesperson, that the chair and loveseat were needed for a family reunion at Thanksgiving. The Blacks indicated that the additional seating provided by the chair and the loveseat would be necessary at the reunion when ordering the furniture. Since the need for the seating that the furniture would provide was in contemplation at the time the order was placed, the Blacks should be compensated for not having adequate seating at the time of the reunion. The damages should be measured by the cost of providing alternative seating.

This example, although clear and coherent, is ineffective because it does not synthesize the decisions and unify the concepts articulated in the cases. Each rule is addressed separately, although one rule relates to the other. Also, the rules are presented in the form of holdings because they read as answers to the question before the court rather than as a rule. The authority is presented more as a list than as a cohesive unit. Also, try never to start a sentence with a case name. The case name does not provide helpful information. The reader wants to know the rule from the case and then its citation.

▼ What Is the Difference Between a Rule and a Holding?

The rule is the test, standard, or principle the court uses to resolve the question before it. The holding is the answer to the specific question that the court is asked to resolve. For instance, the court may be asked whether a suspect is guilty of arson. The court may hold that the suspect is not guilty of committing arson. The rule that the court would apply to determine the holding may be, "arson is the malicious burning of the dwelling house of another."

▼ How Do You Synthesize Statutes and Cases?

When you have found a relevant statute for a problem, give it the highest regard, because statutes are on a higher rung than cases in the hierarchy of legal authority. (See Chapters 1 and 2.) Generally, synthesize statutes separately from case law holdings. However, if you find cases that interpret and apply the relevant statutes, synthesize the statute text with the application found in case law. Always apply the plain meaning rule to statutes. The plain meaning of the statute text is derived from a reading of each word at its face value.

The problem below illustrates the synthesis of a statute and a case.

PROBLEM

FACT PATTERN

On August 4, 2021, our client, Jane Howard, obtained an $800 loan from Rough & Tough Pawn Shop, using her grandmother's engagement ring as collateral. Howard agreed to make monthly payments on the loan for a minimum of 13 months. After 12 months, Rough & Tough had the right to sell the ring and to refund Howard the difference between her outstanding debt and the price received for the ring.

On September 9, 2021, Howard received a postcard from Rough & Tough stating that its shop and its assets would be sold to Able Pawn. The postcard also stated that Able would assume the business of Rough & Tough, including the items pawned and the loans outstanding. The postcard alerted Howard to pick up the ring and to pay off her note by October 2, 2021, if Howard wanted to reclaim her property. Howard decided to continue to make her monthly payments to Able Pawn, where her loan would be transferred.

On October 3, 2021, Able Pawn was robbed and all the jewelry was stolen, including Howard's ring. The premises were protected by a security alarm system and a guard dog.

ISSUE

The issue to be examined is whether Rough & Tough had authority to sell its interest in Howard's ring.

STATUTORY AUTHORITY

The applicable statute is from the Pawnbrokers Regulation Act, 205 Ill. Comp. Stat. 510/10 (2021).

Sale of property. No personal property pledged or received on deposit by any pawnbroker shall be permitted to be redeemed from such pawnbroker for a period of 48 hours after the delivery of the copy and statement required by Section 7 of this Act required to be delivered to the officer or officers named therein. No personal property purchased by any pawnbroker shall be sold or removed from the place of business or transferred to another pawnshop location of such pawnbroker for a period of 10 days after the delivery of the copy and statement required by Section 7 of this Act required to be delivered to the officer or officers named therein. If the pawner or pledger fails to repay the loan during the period specified on the pawn ticket, the pawnbroker shall automatically extend a grace period of 30 days from the default date on the loan during which the pawnbroker shall not dispose of or sell the personal property pledged. The parties may agree to extend or renew a loan upon terms agreed upon by the parties, provided the terms comply with the requirements of this Act.

RELEVANT CASE LAW

This decision interprets and applies the relevant statute, so the statute and the decision should be synthesized.

JACOBS v. GROSSMAN
141 N.E.2d 714 (Ill. 1923)

DUNCAN, J.

This case is brought to this court on a certificate of importance and appeal from a judgment of the Appellate Court for the First District, affirming a judgment of the municipal court of Chicago in favor of the appellee and against appellant in the sum of $330. Appellee, Minnie Jacobs, on April 8, 1921, began an action of replevin (replevin is an action where the owner of property attempts to recover the property from someone who wrongfully took or held the property) in the municipal court of Chicago against appellant, Harry Grossman, a licensed pawnbroker, to recover possession of a diamond ring delivered by herself to appellant to secure the payment of $70 borrowed from him. . . . The case was heard before the court without a jury.

On June 3, 1919, appellee placed in pawn with appellant, a licensed pawnbroker doing business at 426 South Halsted Street, Chicago, the ring, and received thereon the sum of $70. Interest on the loan was paid to June 7, 1920. The pawn ticket issued to appellee contained this statement, "This office protected by the Chicago Electric Protective Company," and described the location and name of the pawnbroker as "Metropolitan Loan Bank, 426 South Halsted St." The ticket further described the goods pawned, the amount loaned, and the time of redemption. Between October 7 and 10, 1920, appellant sold all his interest in whatever pledges he had to Jacob Klein, another duly licensed pawnbroker at 502 South Halsted Street, for the sum of

$16,000 or $17,000, which represented the principal sums loaned on said pledges with interest thereon. The pledges were sold by appellant to Klein upon the express understanding that the pledgors might redeem from Klein in the same manner as they could from appellant, had he not sold his interest in the pawns. It was admitted that Klein is a reputable business man, and it was also conceded by appellant that no notice was given by him, either expressly or impliedly, to the appellee of the transfer of her property. On January 8, 1921, the pawnshop of Klein was entered by four armed robbers. The robbers ordered the clerks employed there to hold up their hands, and they forcibly took from a safe a large number of articles, including the diamond ring in question of appellee, which has never been recovered....

Counsel for appellant relies for a reversal of the judgment on two propositions: First, that a pawnbroker is bound only to use ordinary care for the safety of the pawner's property, and, if the property is lost or destroyed without the negligence of the pawnee, then he is not liable; second, that a pawnbroker has the right to assign or sell to another his interest in an article pledged to him.

A pawn is a species of bailment which arises when goods or chattels are delivered to another as a pawn for security to him on money borrowed of him by the bailor.... It is a class of bailment which is made for the mutual benefit of the bailor and bailee. All that is required by the common law on the part of a pawnee in the protection of the property thus entrusted to him is ordinary care and diligence. Consequently, unless a failure to exercise such care and diligence is shown, a pawnee is not answerable for the loss of the article pledged. 30 Cyc. 1169; *Standard Brewery v. Malting Co.*, 171 Ill. 602, 49 N.E. 507. This is an elementary principle, and there can be no question as to the accuracy and correctness of appellant's first proposition.

But the question arises as to whether or not appellant was guilty of negligence in transferring the interest of the pawner without giving her any notice of such transfer. Appellant's duty to her was to safely keep and protect the property pledged. It was a legal obligation on his part to appellee, from which he could not relieve himself by transferring the pledge to another without her consent. Appellee relied upon him to keep and protect her property where it would be reasonably safe, and he had in substance assured her by the language on the ticket that her property was insured or safeguarded. He violated this duty or obligation to her by transferring the possession of her property to another, to be kept at another place, which the evidence does not show to be protected by a protective company, and without giving her notice of such custody and transfer.

Whatever may be the right of the parties in a bailment for the mutual benefit of the bailor and the bailee, it is unquestionably the law that the parties may increase or diminish these rights by stipulations contained in the contract of bailment. 30 Cyc. 1167; *St. Losky v. Davidson*, 6 Cal. 643. The sum and substance of appellant's contract was that he would keep appellee's property at his office or shop described as aforesaid, and which was protected as aforesaid. The pawning of the ring by appellee under the circumstances imposed a personal trust upon appellant to personally keep the property at his shop and under the assurance of protection as aforesaid, and he could not at his will, without the consent of appellee, transfer the possession and custody thereof to another without such consent. The rule is stated in 3 R.C.L. 112, that any attempt on the part of the bailee in an ordinary simple bailment of a pawn to sell, lease, pledge, or otherwise part with the title or possession of the bailment, constitutes a conversion in every case where the bailment can be properly regarded as a personal trust in the bailee.

There is another controlling reason for holding that appellant is liable for the loss of the ring, and for holding that he could not transfer the possession of the article pawned to him to another and escape liability for a conversion. Section 10 of the Pawnbroker's Act (Smith-Hurd Rev. St. 1923, c. 107 1/2) provides, in part, as follows:

> No personal property pawned or pledged shall be sold or disposed by any such pawnbroker within one year from the time when the pawner or pledger shall make default in the payment of interest on the money so advanced by such pawnbroker, unless by the written consent of such pawner or pledger.

Appellant claims that the proper interpretation of this statute is that it prohibits the sale of an article, including the interest of the pledger or pawner as well as his own, and does not refer to a sale of only the interest of the pawnbroker or pledgee. The statute is not subject to such construction. It should be construed to mean what it says: That the property must not be sold or disposed of by the pawnbroker without the written consent of the pledgor. The statute does not confine itself to a sale, but also forbids any disposition of the same without consent as aforesaid. It cannot be seriously disputed that appellant did dispose of the property without the consent of appellee, within the meaning of the foregoing section of the statute.

The judgment of the Appellate Court is affirmed.

Judgment affirmed.

SAMPLE SYNTHESIS

Whether Rough & Tough has the authority to sell its interest in Howard's ring. Unless the pawner and pawnbroker agree, pawned property may be sold or disposed of by any pawnbroker only after 30 days from the time the pawner defaults in the payment of interest on the money advanced by the pawnbroker. 205 Ill. Comp. Stat. 510/10 (2021). Where a pawnbroker neglected to give notice of the intent to sell his interest in a particular property and neglected to receive written consent for such sale, the pawnbroker lacked authority to transfer his interest in the property, the ring, to another. *Jacobs v. Grossman*, 141 N.E. 714, 715 (Ill. App. Ct. 1923). Although Rough & Tough gave Howard notice of its intent to sell the shop and its assets, R&T failed to obtain Howard's written consent to sell her ring. Additionally Jane Howard continued to make the payments on the loan so default is not an issue. Rough & Tough's transfer of the ring, the property, occurred during the term of the loan. Therefore, a court will probably find that Rough & Tough lacked the authority to sell its interest in Howard's ring to another pawnbroker.

The above example synthesizes the statute and the *Jacobs* case as they relate to the issue of whether a pawnbroker has authority to sell its interest in a pawned item without the consent of the pawner. Notice how the statute is mentioned first because its authority ranks higher than the case. The *Jacobs* case rule follows the statute because the rule is more detailed on the issue of a pawnbroker's duty to give notice before selling his interest in the pawner's property, a ring, and the facts are similar to Jane Howard's situation. Two sources of primary authority, a statute and a case, are used together in this sample synthesis because both sources relate to a single legal issue. Also, cases provide information on how a statute is applied to a specific set of facts.

▼ How Do You Synthesize Two Sources of Statutory Authority?

Often you must use two or more sections of a statute in conjunction to explain the legal rule completely. Sometimes definitional provisions are located in one section and the applicable code section is located in another.

Facts: Mr. Thomas was arrested on charges of domestic battery. He punched his wife in the face three times and broke her nose. Mr. and Mrs. Thomas live in Illinois, but they are living apart.

Issue: Whether the Illinois domestic battery statute applies to an estranged husband and whether punching is considered battery.

This problem requires you to use two statutory provisions. One section defines the relevant terms, and the other section details actions that constitute domestic battery. The statutory definition of family and household members as pertaining to domestic battery follows.

725 Ill. Comp. Stat. 5/112A-3(b)(3) (2021)

"Family or household members" include spouses, former spouses, parents, children, stepchildren, and other persons related by blood or by present or prior marriage, persons who share or formerly shared a common dwelling, persons who have or allegedly have a child in common, persons who share or allegedly share a blood relationship through a child, persons who have or have had a dating or engagement relationship, persons with disabilities and their personal assistants, and caregivers . . . For purposes of this paragraph (3), neither a casual acquaintanceship nor ordinary fraternization between 2 individuals in business or social contexts shall be deemed to constitute a dating relationship.

The Domestic Battery Statute at 720 Ill. Comp. Stat. 5/12-3.2 (2021):

(a) A person commits domestic battery if he or she knowingly without legal justification by any means:

(1) causes bodily harm to any family or household member;

(2) makes physical contact of an insulting or provoking nature with any family or household member.

Here is a sample synthesis using two statutory provisions:

We must determine whether the domestic battery statute, 720 Ill. Comp. Stat. 5/12-3.2 (2021), applies to married couples living apart, and if so, whether Mr. Thomas, an estranged husband, committed domestic battery when he punched his wife. The domestic battery statute applies to family members. "Family members" is defined to include "spouses formerly sharing a common dwelling." 725 Ill. Comp. Stat. 5/112A-3(b)(3) (2021). "A person commits domestic battery if he intentionally or knowingly without legal justification by any means: (1) Causes bodily harm to any family or household member 720 Ill. Comp. Stat. 5/12-3.2 (2021).

Since Mr. Thomas is a spouse who formerly shared a common residence with his wife, he is a family or household member, and the domestic battery statute is applicable. Mr. Thomas punched his wife in the face three times, which caused her nose to break. The facts do not state that his mental capacity was altered by inebriation or severe mental illness, so his actions can be deduced to be intentional. The facts also do not indicate if Mr. Thomas was provoked to commit battery by extreme jealousy. It appears that there was no legal justification for the bodily harm inflicted on Mrs. Thomas by Mr. Thomas. Although Mr. Thomas is a spouse formerly sharing a common dwelling with Mrs. Thomas, he is a family member and is governed by the domestic battery statute. By punching his wife, breaking her nose, and causing her bodily harm, Mr. Thomas committed domestic battery.

CHECKLIST TO SYNTHESIZE AUTHORITIES

1. Summarize the relevant statutes and brief the relevant cases.
2. Outline the problem.
3. Organize the primary authority.
4. Arrange your primary sources by hierarchy of authority under each issue.
5. Compare and contrast the case holdings and statutory text.
6. Formulate a statement of the law that incorporates all the primary sources that will be used under each subissue or element.
7. Check to see if the source is valid and still good law on *Shepard's* or KeyCite.
8. Attribute the authority for any legal statement by using the proper *Bluebook* or *ALWD* citation.

PRACTICE POINTER

When synthesizing authorities, always cite to every source you use. When you use a case, often the information gathered from the authority is not from the first page of the decision. You must use pinpoint cites to indicate from exactly where within the decision the information is obtained. Also, often you will use authorities, cases, and statutes more than once. This calls for subsequent citation format for cases and statutes. Use the Bluebook or the ALWD Guide to Legal Citation for guidance on short citation when citing cases and statutes subsequently.

CHAPTER SUMMARY

Learning to synthesize authority is a mechanical process at first. Brief the cases and summarize the statutory authority. Insert the applicable authority in your outline by grouping together related statements of the law. Draft cohesive statements of the legal authority that you grouped together. Use your own language to summarize the authorities but be certain that you stay true to the points in the sources. Cite all authority accurately even if string citations are needed or if two separate clauses in a single sentence are each supported by a different authority.

As you become more adept at synthesis, you will see that your writing is smoother and less redundant. Synthesizing authority lets you write in one voice rather than awkwardly switching back and forth between your words and the words of the court.

KEY TERMS

causes of action   reasoning
facts   synthesis
primary authority

EXERCISES

SELF-ASSESSMENT

1. Why do we synthesize authority?
2. What are the four basic types of synthesis?
3. What are the steps required to synthesize legal rules?

PRACTICE SKILLS

4. Read the following fact pattern and cases carefully. Draft a paragraph in which you synthesize the holdings of the cases. The issue that you will address is provided as well. Remember that proper synthesis requires you to relate the authority to a common legal theme. The problem's issue will guide you in synthesizing the authority.

Facts

On November 29, 2021, Michael Jones purchased a used truck from Grimy's Auto and Truck Service. At the time of purchase, Grimy's stated that the engine was completely overhauled and consisted of rebuilt and reconditioned parts, all parts were guaranteed, and invoices for all new parts would be provided. On November 14, 2022, after using the truck for almost one year, Jones discovered that several engine parts were not rebuilt or reconditioned and other engine parts were defective, which caused the truck to break down. This resulted in lost wages and lost profits for Jones. Jones made repairs to the truck on November 14, 2022, December 19, 2022, and December 21, 2022. Jones did not attempt to return the truck and did not notify Grimy's that the truck was defective. The truck is currently disabled in Columbus, Ohio. Jones came to your firm because he wants to sue Grimy's for damages for breach of contract.

Issue

Whether Jones continued to use the truck for more than a reasonable time after noticing the defects and failed to properly reject the truck and to notify Grimy's as to the defects.

Case A

A buyer of goods must alert the seller as soon as he discovers that the goods are not as agreed on. A buyer must rescind a sales contract as soon as he discovers the breach or after he has had a reasonable time for examination. The buyer waives the right to rescind a contract for the sale of goods by continuing to use allegedly defective goods for more than a reasonable time.

Case B

To meet the requirements of an effective rejection, the buyer must reject the goods within a reasonable time and reasonably notify the seller.

5. Read the following fact pattern and cases carefully. Draft a paragraph in which you synthesize the holdings of the cases. The issue that you will address is provided as well.

Facts

Robert and Jane Moore live in Evanston and have to repair the gutters on their house. There is eight feet between their house and their neighbor's. The properties are adjoining; the neighboring Kandler house is north of the Moore house. The Moores' contractors and carpenters must enter the Kandler property to work on the gutters on the north side of the house. Mrs. Kandler is not very pleased that workers are entering her property. The Moores came to our office to find out what they should do. The Moores specifically asked if they should obtain an easement to grant them a right of way on Mrs. Kandler's property to make the repairs.

Issue
What legal access would allow the contractors and carpenters, repairing the gutters on the Moore house, to enter the adjoining property belonging to Mrs. Kandler?

Statutory Authority
Ch. 12 § 99: If the repair and maintenance of an existing single-family residence cannot reasonably be accomplished without entering onto the adjoining land, and if the owner of the adjoining land refuses to permit entry onto that adjoining land for the purpose of repair and maintenance of the single-family residence, then the owner of the single-family residence may bring an action in court to compel the owner of the adjoining land to permit entry for the purpose of repair and maintenance where entry will be granted solely for the purposes of repair and maintenance.

Case Y
The need to enter the land of an adjoining property for the purpose of making repairs to one's own property should not mandate that an easement be acquired. An easement grants a right of way, but only the landowner can create an easement. The adjoining landowner may view the repairs as a nuisance and not grant the easement. Sometimes repairs must be performed on a single-family residence that require entering the adjoining land. Statute Ch. 12 § 99 was created to avoid the need to obtain an easement to enter adjoining land when the sole reason for the right of way is to make repairs on a single-family residence.

REINFORCEMENT EXERCISES

Case Synthesis Concepts
6. Review a memo that you have recently completed. Examine the body of the discussion carefully. Highlight a paragraph that states the rule, its application, and conclusion. Examine a subsequent paragraph that expands on the initial rule by citing a separate opinion. Reformulate the rules statement to incorporate the initial rule and the subsequent rule to create a comprehensive statement of the law, in a single paragraph, on that particular point. Check your citation format.

7. Read the facts and the two cases and answer the questions that follow.

Facts
Ms. Jones was waiting to get off the commuter train in the train's vestibule. The commuter train pulled into the station and Ms. Jones descended the stairs to disembark from the train. The conductor exited the train first to watch the passengers exit the train and then

signal to close the doors for the train to start rolling. Ms. Jones was carrying her briefcase, which had a long strap. As Ms. Jones exited the train, the briefcase strap was behind her. The train doors shut with Ms. Jones on the platform but with the briefcase strap still inside the door. The train dragged Ms. Jones about ten feet and she suffered a broken shoulder. The issue you have to consider is whether the conductor's negligence by signaling for the train to start was the proximate cause of Ms. Jones's broken shoulder. The issue that you should focus your case synthesis on is whether the conductor's failure to see that Ms. Jones's briefcase strap was inside the door as he signaled for the train to start moving is the proximate cause of her broken shoulder.

Smith v. Atlantic City Railroad, 12 Nowhere 2d 5 (2014)

Mr. John Smith was injured on the Atlantic City Railroad when the train lurched with great violence as it rounded a curve on the track. The train was overcrowded. Smith was injured without fault on his part. The motorman drove the overcrowded car too fast around the curve, so as to cause it to give a severe lurch. Where a passenger train is overcrowded and the employees operating the train know of such condition, it is their duty to exercise additional care commensurate with the dangers. The motorman knew of the overcrowded conditions and failed to exercise additional care when rounding the curve. Mr. Smith was injured when the train lurched as it rounded the curve because he fell onto another passenger. The motorman's failure to exercise the requisite care was the proximate cause of Mr. Smith's injuries.

Blue v. Boardwalk Railroad, 15 Nowhere 2d 9 (2010)

Mr. Robert Blue was blinded by a sudden gust of steam and fell underneath the train he was in the process of boarding at the station. Mr. Blue's arm was severed by the train as it started to leave the station. Regular inspection of couplings is a required duty of conductors. Failure to inspect the couplings for leaks is a negligent act on the part of the defendant. The railroad's allowing steam to escape was the proximate cause of Mr. Blue's injury, since a man of ordinary prudence could have foreseen that escaping steam would result from leaks in the uninspected couplings. The consequence of the escaping steam, due to the railroad's failure to inspect the couplings, resulted in a foreseeable injury to a passenger or person waiting on the platform.

a. Brief the cases to extract the holdings.
b. What are the similarities and differences between the *Blue* case and the *Smith* case?
c. How do the facts differ?
d. How do the holdings differ?
e. What do the cases have in common?
f. Formulate a statement of law that incorporates the holdings from the *Smith* case and the *Blue* case.

8. Read *Seymour v. Armstrong*, 64 P. 612 (Kan. 1901), and *Lefkowitz v. Great Minneapolis Surplus Store, Inc.*, 86 N.W.2d 689 (Minn. 1957), reprinted in Chapter 18. The two cases involve similar issues.
   a. What are the similar issues?
   b. What is the subject matter of each case?
   c. Draft a statement of the law combining the holdings or rules from both cases.

OUTLINING AND ORGANIZING A MEMORANDUM

CHAPTER OVERVIEW

In Chapters 19 to 23, you learned about the components of a legal memorandum as well as some drafting pointers. This chapter teaches you how to organize the discussion section of your memorandum. The outlining techniques presented here are suggested techniques only. You may have a technique of your own that works well. Feel free to use it. In this chapter, you also learn how to draft thesis paragraphs for your discussion.

A. PURPOSE OF OUTLINING

The key to a well-organized memo is a well-drafted outline. **Outlining** allows you to organize your discussion easily so that it is smooth and cogent. An outline ensures that you cover all the legal rules and apply all the legally significant facts to those rules. An outline also simplifies your discussion drafting.

B. STEPS TO OUTLINING

The outline should be done in two stages, each of which consists of a number of steps. In the first stage, you compile a **list of legal authorities**, which includes the names of and the citations to authorities, a note about the legally significant facts presented in any case, and a statement that summarizes each authority's significance to the issues presented in your research problem. See Illustration 24-1. In the second stage, you arrange the discussion sections concerning each issue and, in some cases, arrange each paragraph. See Illustration 24-3.

1. Steps in Compiling a List of Legal Authorities

1. Draft the statement of the facts, the questions presented, and the conclusions.
2. Research your issues.
3. Read the cases.
4. Brief the authorities as discussed in Chapter 18. Once you have briefed the authorities, you will write a holding for each case. These holdings should be used in your list of authorities. These holdings will summarize the significance of the authorities. If the holdings are well written, they will incorporate important facts derived from the authorities.
5. Write a summary statement for each statute or other noncase authority you plan to cite.
6. Prepare a list of each of the relevant authorities. Note that not all authorities will be relevant. Include only those that help you to determine the law involved in your case. For your list, include the name of the authority. If the authority is a case, list the holding or summary statement of the significance of the authority. Note the complete citation. It is also helpful to list whether the authority is a primary binding, primary persuasive, or secondary authority.

Now review Illustrations 24-1, 24-2, and 24-4. Illustration 24-1 is a list of legally significant facts. Illustration 24-2 is a list of the significant authorities for the memo in Illustration 24-4.

ILLUSTRATION 24-1.   List of Legally Significant Facts

Mary Dwyer is a 36-year-old bank teller.

Dwyer wants to sue Carol Mann.

Mann is a 36-year-old mother.

Mann threw a metal bucket filled with sand at Dwyer at a local park.

Dwyer sat on a park bench and teased Mann's seven-year-old son.

Mann did not like this teasing.

Mann threw a bucket filled with sand at Dwyer.

Sand landed in Dwyer's eyes while she was wearing soft contact lenses.

Dwyer's contacts had to be replaced.

The bucket also cut Dwyer's eye and cheek. She required stitches in both places.

Dwyer asked Mann to pay for her doctor bills and for the new contacts.

Mann refused and added, "I'm not sorry. I meant to hurt you."

ILLUSTRATION 24-2.   List of Authorities

1. *Anderson v. St. Francis-St. George Hosp., Inc.*, 77 Ohio St. 3d 82, 671 N.E.2d 225 (1996): A battery is the intentional touching of another without consent or privilege, which causes physical injury or offensive contact. (primary binding)

2. *Leichtman v. WLW Jacor Communications, Inc.*, 92 Ohio App. 3d 232, 634 N.E.2d 697 (1994): A direct or indirect contact between a nonconsenting individual and a substance or an object such as cigar smoke is sufficient to be a touching within the context of the tort of civil battery. (primary binding)

3. *Love v. Port Clinton*, 37 Ohio St. 3d 98, 524 N.E.2d 166 (1988): A person intends his or her conduct when the essential character of the conduct is considered and when he or she undertakes an action with a knowing mind. (primary persuasive)

PRACTICE POINTER

When you cite to a dissent, concurring, or other opinion rather than the majority opinion, you must indicate that within the citation with the name of the opinion author.

ILLUSTRATION 24-3. Outline of Battery Discussion

Element or Subissue 1

Issue: Did a touching occur?

Rule: Substances or objects are extensions of body parts. Contact with a substance or an object can be touching (*Leichtman*)

Application of law to facts: Bucket contacted Dwyer.

Conclusion: A touching occurred.

Element or Subissue 2

Issue: Did Mann intend to hit Dwyer?

Rule: A person intends an act when it is done purposefully and when the character of the act is assessed. (*Love*)

Application of law to facts: Mann purposefully threw the bucket at Dwyer and said she intended to strike her.

Conclusion: Mann had intent.

Element or Subissue 3

Issue: Did Dwyer suffer the requisite physical injuries as a result of the contact?

Rule: Physical injuries must result from contact for battery. (*Anderson*)

Application of law to facts: Dwyer sustained cuts and eye irritation from bucket and sand contact.

Conclusion: Dwyer had requisite physical injuries.

ILLUSTRATION 24-4. Sample Memorandum: Dwyer Battery Action

ATTORNEY WORK PRODUCT PREPARED IN ANTICIPATION OF LITIGATION

MEMORANDUM

To: William Mark
From: Ivy Courier
Date: November 7, 2020
Re: Dwyer Battery Action

QUESTION PRESENTED

Did an actionable battery occur when Mann intentionally struck Dwyer with a bucket, without Dwyer's consent, causing Dwyer to suffer physical and monetary injuries?

CONCLUSION

Mann's intentional striking of Dwyer with a bucket and sand resulting in physical injuries to Dwyer was a battery.

ILLUSTRATION 24-4. *Continued*

FACTS

Our client, Mary Dwyer, a 36-year-old bank teller, wants to bring an action for battery against Carol Mann, a 36-year-old mother, who threw a metal bucket filled with sand at Dwyer at a local park. While Dwyer sat on a park bench, she teased Mann's seven-year-old son. Mann did not like this teasing and threw a bucket filled with sand at Dwyer. Sand landed in Dwyer's eyes while she was wearing soft contact lenses. As a result, Dwyer's contacts had to be replaced. The bucket also cut Dwyer's eye and cheek. She required stitches in both places. Dwyer asked Mann to pay for her doctor bills and for the new contacts. Mann refused and added, "I'm not sorry. I meant to hurt you."

DISCUSSION

The issue presented is whether Mann's intentional touching of Dwyer with a bucket rather than her person is an actionable battery. A battery is the intentional touching of another without consent or privilege, which causes injury or offensive contact. *Anderson v. St. Francis-St. George Hosp., Inc.*, 77 Ohio St. 3d 82, 671 N.E.2d 225 (1996). *Love v. Port Clinton*, 37 Ohio St. 3d 98, 524 N.E.2d 166 (1988), quoting the Restatement of Law 2d, Torts (1965). A touching can occur directly or indirectly such as when an object or a substance rather than an individual's body contacts the other party. *Leichtman v. WLW Jacor Communications, Inc.*, 92 Ohio App. 3d 232, 634 N.E.2d 697 (1994). In this case, Mann intentionally struck Dwyer with a bucket without Dwyer's consent and that touching resulted in injuries. Therefore, a battery occurred.

The threshold issue is whether a touching occurred when the bucket struck Dwyer. An indirect contact between a defendant and a nonconsenting party can be a battery. *Leichtman v. WLW Jacor Communications, Inc.*, 92 Ohio App. 3d 232, 634 N.E.2d 697 (1994). In *Leichtman*, one person blew cigar smoke at another person, resulting in injuries. The court found that the contact from cigar smoke although not a direct touching by a person was still battery. In essence, the court found that the smoke was an extension of the person and that contact between the smoke and the nonconsenting person met the requirement of a touching for civil battery. In this case, Mann threw the bucket at Dwyer, and the bucket contacted her face. That was an indirect touching. Following the reasoning in the *Leichtman* case, the bucket contact, although indirect, would be an extension of Mann's body, and the contact between Dwyer and the bucket would be considered a touching under the theory of civil battery.

The next question to consider is whether Mann intended to touch Dwyer when she struck her with the bucket. The "essential character" of the conduct will be considered in determining whether a person intends his or her conduct. *Love v. Port Clinton*, 37 Ohio St. 3d 98, 524 N.E.2d 166 (1988). In *Love*, a police officer handcuffed the plaintiff. The court found that the officer must have intended his actions because you could not accidentally handcuff a person. *Love*, 524 N.E.2d at 168. In Dwyer's

ILLUSTRATION 24-4. *Continued*

case, Mann aimed the bucket at Dwyer purposefully trying to strike her, Mann later told Dwyer that she deliberately threw the bucket at her. The essential character of these acts and Mann's own statements indicate that Dwyer will probably be able to establish that Mann had intent.

The next factor to consider is whether Dwyer caused injury. A battery occurs only if a plaintiff sustains physical injuries as a result of the touching. *Anderson v. St. Francis-St. George Hosp., Inc.*, 77 Ohio St. 3d 82, 671 N.E.2d 225 (1996). Dwyer sustained cuts on her face and the sand flying out of the bucket got into her eyes. Dwyer should be able to show that she sustained physical injuries as a result of the contact with the bucket.

2. Organize Issues

After you have prepared a detailed list of authorities, you are ready to organize your issues and to determine each of the legal elements that your memo should address. Each legal theory is defined as several factors called **elements.** You can think of the elements as pieces of a puzzle. You must consider each element before you complete your discussion. You can think of your discussion of these elements as a discussion of the subissues of the questions presented. Your discussion of some of these subissues will be cursory; some elements can be discussed in a single sentence. Most subissues, however, will be discussed in one or more paragraphs, generally organized in the IRAC (Issues, Rules, Application, Conclusion) format discussed in Chapter 22.

▼ **What Steps Should You Follow in Preparing Your Outline of Each of the Issues?**

The first step in organizing your outline is to write a **thesis paragraph.** This is the first paragraph of your discussion. It usually is a summary of the legal issue you plan to discuss. In the thesis paragraph you introduce the issue, define the applicable rule of law, introduce each legal element, apply the legally significant facts to the rule of law, and provide a short conclusion, usually one sentence long. When you have multiple issues, the thesis paragraph will introduce all the issues presented and give readers a road map of what will be discussed. Then, each issue will begin with a separate thesis paragraph.

3. Draft a Thesis Paragraph

The best and most typical format for the thesis paragraph is the IRAC format. (For a full discussion of this format, see Chapter 22.) The first sentence of a thesis paragraph introduces the overall issue presented in the memo. The second sentence explains the rule of law. The next sentence applies the rule of law to the facts of your case, and the final sentence states a conclusion. A general outline for a thesis paragraph, then, is:

1. Introduce the legal issue or question presented.
2. Summarize the legal rule for the question presented and each legal element to be discussed.
3. Apply the legally significant facts to the legal rule.
4. Conclude.

Review the thesis paragraph in Illustration 24-5. It is the first paragraph of the discussion section of the memo in Illustration 24-4. The first sentence introduces the issue: whether a battery occurred when Mann struck Dwyer with the bucket. This sentence mirrors the question presented. The second sentence is the rule of law. In this sentence you introduce each of the legal elements or factors that will be discussed. In the *Dwyer* case, the elements are touching, intent, and resulting physical injury. Each of these elements is discussed separately in the succeeding memo paragraphs. A thesis paragraph should introduce the reader to as many legal elements as possible in the thesis paragraph. The fourth sentence of this thesis paragraph is the application of the law to the facts. In this sentence, you explain to the reader the relationship between the relevant law and the facts of your case. In Illustration 24-5, the fact that Mann struck Dwyer with the bucket resulting in physical injury applied to the rule of law stated in the two prior sentences. The final sentence is a conclusion. This sentence explains to your readers your view of how the law and facts relate to each other. In the *Dwyer* case, the writer concluded that a battery occurred.

ILLUSTRATION 24-5. Thesis Paragraph

The issue presented is whether Mann's intentional touching of Dwyer with a bucket rather than her person is an actionable battery. A battery is the intentional touching of another without consent or privilege, which causes injury or offensive contact. *Anderson v. St. Francis-St. George Hosp., Inc.*, 77 Ohio St. 3d 82, 671 N.E.2d 225 (1996). *Love v. Port Clinton*, 37 Ohio St. 3d 98, 524 N.E.2d 166 (1988), quoting the Restatement of Law 2d, Torts (1965). A touching can occur directly or indirectly such as when an object or a substance rather than an individual's body contacts the other party. *Leichtman v. WLW Jacor Communications, Inc.*, 92 Ohio App. 3d 232, 634 N.E.2d 697 (1994). In this case, Mann intentionally struck Dwyer with a bucket without Dwyer's consent and that touching resulted in injuries. Therefore, a battery occurred.

ILLUSTRATION 24-5. *Continued*

OUTLINE OF THESIS PARAGRAPH FOR DWYER CASE

1. Introduce the battery issue or question presented.
2. Summarize the legal rule: Battery is the intentional touching of another that results in physical injury; touching can be done with an object.
3. Apply the legally significant facts to the legal rule: Touching occurred when bucket struck Dwyer.
4. Conclusion: Battery occurred.

---

4. Determine Which Element to Discuss First

The next step is to determine which element to discuss first. If a legal claim has a threshold issue or element, it should be discussed first. A threshold issue is an issue that, if decided one way, would eliminate any further consideration of the legal claim. For example, in a breach of contract case, you must decide first whether a contract was formed before determining whether a breach occurred. Because courts sometimes change current law or approach legal claims differently than expected or than the law provides, you should fully discuss all subissues or elements, even if your threshold issue would dispose of the legal claim. For the memo in Illustration 24-4, the touching is the threshold issue. If Mann did not touch Dwyer, then Dwyer could not bring an action for battery. Therefore, this issue must be considered first.

5. List Elements or Subissues

Next, make a list of the elements or subissues to discuss. In the *Dwyer* case, the elements list might be as follows:

touching

intent

physical injury

6. Add Authority

Now add the authority or authorities that relate to each element:

touching (*Leichtman, Love*)

intent (*Love*)

physical injury (*Anderson*)

7. Refine Issues

You might refine the issues so that they include facts from your case or incorporate further questions that are raised by the issues. For example, the issue of touching involves a secondary question of whether contact with an object rather than a person is a touching sufficient to constitute a battery. Your new list might be as follows:

touching (*Leichtman, Love*) →

indirect rather than direct touching by an object rather than person (*Leichtman*) →

intent (*Love*) →

physical injury (*Anderson*)

8. Arrange the Order of Elements

Now arrange the order of the elements. Touching is the threshold element or subissue, so you should discuss it first. The order of the other issues is a value judgment. If one or more elements can be easily discussed in a single sentence, often it is best to consider them after the threshold issue. If none of the elements is a threshold issue, then consider those elements that can be discussed easily first.

9. Organize into IRAC Paragraph

After you have determined the order of the elements, organize each element or subissue into an IRAC paragraph. Introduce the issue, present the rule, apply the law to the facts of your case, and conclude. For the *Dwyer* memo, the discussion outline for each element might be as shown in Illustration 24-3. Review Illustration 24-3 and compare it to the text of the memo in Illustration 24-4. The discussion is derived entirely from the outline and follows it closely in IRAC format.

> ### PRACTICE POINTER
>
> If your outline is well drafted, your writing of the discussion will flow easily from it.

C. MULTI-ISSUE MEMORANDUM

If you have a multi-issue memorandum, you will use many of the same techniques discussed above.

▼ How Do You Organize a Multi-Issue Memorandum?

1. Determine how many issues you will discuss. Often an attorney will help you make this determination. Decide which issue should be discussed first. Again, consider whether there is a threshold issue. In the memo above, the first issue is whether Mann committed a battery. If a touching did not occur when the bucket struck Dwyer, then the later issues do not need to be addressed. Therefore, this issue is the threshold issue and should be placed first. However, you should still discuss the later issues even if you determine that the first issue would be decided in a manner that would dispose of a case. Courts are unpredictable and might decide the issue differently than you did.
2. Determine the legal elements you will discuss and a logical order for this discussion.
3. Prepare a detailed outline of the discussion. For each issue, note each legal element you will address, the authority related to that element, and the legally significant facts applicable to that element.
4. Write a thesis paragraph. For a multi-issue memo, such as the one in Illustration 24-4, introduce the issues and explain the rules of law in the thesis paragraphs that introduce each issue. Your organization for a multi-issue memo might be as follows:

Thesis Paragraph
  Introduce all legal issues or questions presented
  Conclusions

Thesis Paragraph for Issue or Question Presented #1
  Introduce the legal issue or question presented
  Summarize the legal rule for the question presented #1 and
    each legal element to be discussed
  Apply the legally significant facts to the legal rule
  Conclusion

First Legal Element or Subissue
  Introduce the legal element
  Summarize the legal rule
  Apply the legally significant facts to the legal rule
  Conclusion

Second Legal Element or Subissue
  Introduce the legal element
  Summarize the legal rule
  Apply the legally significant facts to the legal rule
  Conclusion

Thesis Paragraph for Issue or Question Presented #2
    Introduce the legal issue or question presented
    Summarize the legal rule for the question presented #2 and
        each legal element to be discussed
    Apply the legally significant facts to the legal rule
    Conclusion

First Legal Element or Subissue
    Introduce the legal element
    Summarize the legal rule
    Apply the legally significant facts to the legal rule
    Conclusion

Second Legal Element or Subissue
    Introduce the legal element
    Summarize the legal rule
    Apply the legally significant facts to the legal rule
    Conclusion

5. Use headings to introduce new issues. Use transitions to guide the reader from one issue to another and one paragraph to another.

Illustration 24-7 is an outline of the memo shown in Illustration 24-6.

Once you complete your outline, you are ready to begin writing your discussion. Follow your outline and use the applicable law and the facts from cases when they are useful. Once you have completed your draft, compare the draft to the outline to ensure that you have incorporated all the components in your outline and that your text matches your outline organization.

Review Illustration 24-7 and compare the outline provided to the discussion section that follows. Now compare this to the discussion sections that concern this point of law found in Illustrations 24-4 and 24-6.

ILLUSTRATION 24-6.   Multi-Issue Memorandum: Dwyer Battery Action

---

ATTORNEY WORK PRODUCT PREPARED FOR LITIGATION MEMORANDUM

To: William Mark
From: Ivy Courier
Date: November 7, 2020
Re: Dwyer Battery Action

QUESTIONS PRESENTED

1. Did an actionable battery occur when Mann intentionally struck Dwyer with a bucket, causing Dwyer to suffer physical and monetary injuries?

ILLUSTRATION 24-6.   *Continued*

2. Does eight-year-old Rachel Dwyer have a valid claim for intentional infliction of emotional distress against Carol Mann after the child saw Mann throw a rusty metal bucket of sand at her mother's face and head, causing physical injuries to the elder Dwyer and resulting in the child suffering from anxiety, headaches, and vomiting?

3. Was Camp Cougar vicariously liable for the intentional torts of Mann, a volunteer whom camp officials asked to supervise children in the sandbox?

CONCLUSIONS

1. When Mann intentionally struck Dwyer on the head and in the face with a rusty, metal bucket and sand and Dwyer was injured, a battery occurred.

2. Eight-year-old Rachel Dwyer has a claim for intentional infliction of emotional distress against Carol Mann because the child can show that she suffered emotional distress as a result of Mann's extreme and outrageous act of intentionally throwing a rusty, metal bucket at the child's mother, causing the older Dwyer to suffer physical injuries and the child to suffer from anxiety and post-traumatic stress syndrome — mental anguish no child should be expected to endure.

3. Camp Cougar will not be found vicariously liable for an intentional act of its agent, Mann, because it did not benefit from that act nor did the camp control Mann's actions.

FACTS

Our client, Mary Dwyer, a 36-year-old bank teller, seeks to bring an action for battery against Carol Mann, a 36-year-old mother, who threw a rusty, metal bucket filled with sand at her at a local camp. She also wants to bring an action against Camp Cougar for vicarious liability for the intentional torts of camp volunteer Carol Mann. Camp Cougar enlisted Carol Mann, a camper's parent, to act as volunteer supervisor of the sandbox during Parent Visitor Day at Camp Cougar. Camp Cougar officials told Mann to ensure that no one was injured while playing in the sandbox. Mann had handled this responsibility during Parent Visitor Day in the past. Mary Dwyer came to see her eight-year-old daughter, Rachel, during Camp Cougar Parent Visitor Day. While Dwyer sat on a camp bench, she teased Mann's seven-year-old son. Mann did not like this teasing and threw a rusty, metal bucket filled with sand at Dwyer's head and face. Sand landed in Dwyer's eyes while she was wearing soft contact lenses. As a result, Dwyer's contacts had to be replaced. The bucket also cut Dwyer's head, eye, and cheek. She lost a lot of blood from her head, requiring a transfusion of one pint of blood. She had stitches on her eyelid and cheek. After the bucket struck Dwyer, Mann told Dwyer in front of three witnesses, "I'm not sorry. I meant to hurt you."

ILLUSTRATION 24-6. *Continued*

Immediately after Rachel Dwyer saw her mother bleeding, she began to cry and vomit. She told the camp counselors that her head hurt and she would not go with the camp director to the hospital. She said she was afraid the director would throw a bucket of sand at her if she didn't like what she said. The child missed the remainder of camp because she suffered from daily headaches and vomiting and she was afraid of the adults at the camp. A child psychologist examined the child and said she was suffering headaches, vomiting, and anxiety as a result of seeing a bucket thrown by an adult at her mother. He said she was experiencing post-traumatic stress syndrome.

DISCUSSION

This memo first will address whether Carol Mann can be held liable for battery when she intentionally struck Dwyer with a rusty, metal bucket, without Dwyer's consent, causing Dwyer to suffer physical and monetary injuries. Next, the discussion will consider whether eight-year-old Rachel Dwyer has a claim for intentional infliction of emotional distress against Mann after the child saw Mann throw a rusty, metal bucket of sand at her mother's head and face, resulting in injury to her mother and causing the young girl to suffer from anxiety, headaches, and vomiting. Finally, the memo will explore whether Dwyer can establish that Camp Cougar was vicariously liable for the intentional actions of one of its volunteers, Carol Mann, that resulted in injury to Dwyer.

1. WAS MANN'S INTENTIONAL TOUCHING OF DWYER WITH A BUCKET BATTERY?

Did an actionable battery occur when Mann intentionally struck Dwyer with a bucket, causing Dwyer to suffer physical and monetary injuries? A battery is the intentional touching of another without consent or privilege, which causes injury or offensive contact. *Anderson v. St. Francis-St. George Hosp., Inc.*, 77 Ohio St. 3d 82, 671 N.E.2d 225 (1996); *Love v. Port Clinton*, 37 Ohio St. 3d 98, 524 N.E.2d 166 (1988), quoting the Restatement of Law 2d, Torts (1965). A touching can occur directly or indirectly such as when an object or a substance rather than an individual's body contacts the other party. *Leichtman v. WLW Jacor Communications, Inc.*, 92 Ohio App. 3d 232, 634 N.E.2d 697 (1994). In this case, Mann intentionally struck Dwyer with a bucket without Dwyer's consent and that touching resulted in injuries. Therefore, a battery occurred.

The threshold issue is whether a touching occurred when the bucket struck Dwyer. An indirect contact between a defendant and a nonconsenting party can be a battery. *Leichtman v. WLW Jacor Communications, Inc.*, 92 Ohio App. 3d 232, 634 N.E.2d 697 (1994). In *Leichtman*, one person blew cigar smoke at another person, resulting in injuries. The

ILLUSTRATION 24-6. *Continued*

court found that the contact from cigar smoke, although not a direct touching by a person, was still battery. In essence, the court found that the smoke was an extension of the person and that contact between the smoke and the nonconsenting person met the requirement of a touching for civil battery. In this case, Mann threw the bucket at Dwyer, and the bucket contacted her face. That was an indirect touching. Following the reasoning in the *Leichtman* case, the contact with the bucket, although indirect would be an extension of Mann's body, and the contact between Dwyer and the bucket would be considered a touching under the theory of civil battery.

The next question to consider is whether Mann intended to touch Dwyer when she struck her with the bucket. The "essential character" of the conduct will be considered in determining whether a person intends his or her conduct. *Love v. Port Clinton*, 37 Ohio St. 3d 98, 524 N.E.2d 166 (1988). In *Love*, a police officer handcuffed the plaintiff. The court found that the officer must have intended his actions because when the essential character of his action was considered, the court found that the officer could not accidentally handcuff a person. *Love*, 524 N.E.2d at 168. In Dwyer's case, Mann aimed the bucket at Dwyer, purposefully trying to strike her, Mann later told Dwyer that she deliberately threw the bucket at her. The essential character of these acts and Mann's own statements indicates that Dwyer probably will be able to establish that Mann had the intent.

The next factor to consider is whether Dwyer caused injury. A battery occurs only if a plaintiff sustains physical injuries as a result of the touching. *Anderson v. St. Francis-St. George Hosp., Inc.*, 77 Ohio St. 3d 82, 671 N.E.2d 225 (1996). Dwyer sustained cuts on her face and the sand flying out of the bucket got into her eyes. Dwyer should be able to show that she sustained physical injuries as a result of the contact with the bucket.

2. IS MANN LIABLE FOR INTENTIONAL INFLICTION OF EMOTIONAL DISTRESS?

The next issue to consider is whether eight-year-old Rachel Dwyer has a claim for intentional infliction of emotional distress against Carol Mann. To successfully prove intentional infliction of emotional distress, Dwyer must show that Mann intentionally committed an extreme and outrageous act that proximately caused emotional distress that no reasonable person could be expected to endure. *Yeager v. Local Union 20*, 6 Ohio St. 3d 369, 453 N.E.2d 666 (1983); *Pyle v. Pyle*, 11 Ohio App. 3d 31, 34, 463 N.E.2d 98, 101 (1983). In the case, Rachel Dwyer, a child, saw Mann, an adult, throw the rusty, metal bucket filled with sand at her mother's head and face, causing her mother to bleed. Seeing this act caused the child to suffer from anxiety, headaches, and vomiting daily. Several witnesses can testify that Mann said that she intended to harm Dwyer. A child should not be expected to endure the pain of

ILLUSTRATION 24-6. *Continued*

seeing her mother injured. Therefore, Rachel Dwyer has a claim for intentional emotional distress.

The threshold issue is whether Mann's act of throwing a rusty, metal bucket at the head and face of another adult in front of children was an extreme and outrageous act. An act is extreme and outrageous if it goes "beyond all possible bounds of decency," *Yeager* 6 Ohio. St. 3d at 375, 453 N.E.2d at 672, and is regarded as "atrocious, and utterly intolerable in a civilized community." *Id.* In this case, Mann, an adult who was asked to supervise the sandbox and ensure the safety of others, threw a rusty, metal bucket filled with sand at another adult in front of young children, including her child and Rachel Dwyer. The bucket struck the older Dwyer, causing her to bleed. That act went beyond all possible bounds of decency and was atrocious and utterly intolerable in a civilized community. This is especially true since Mann was charged with ensuring the safety of people in the sandbox area. Therefore, Mann's act would be found to be an extreme and outrageous act.

Next, the young Dwyer must show that the act was done with intent. A person intends his or her conduct when he or she undertakes an action with a knowing mind. *Smith v. John Deere Co.*, 83 Ohio App. 3d 398, 614 N.E.2d 1148 (1993). If an actor knew or should have known that his or her actions would cause serious emotional distress, intent is established. *Hale v. City of Dayton*, 2002 Ohio App. Lexis 474 (2002). In this case, Mann not only knew or should have known that throwing a rusty, metal bucket filled with sand at the head and face of another adult in front of the other adult's child resulting in the adult bleeding would cause an eight-year-old child to suffer serious emotional distress. For those reasons, the young Dwyer should be able to show intent.

The third element Dwyer must establish is that the extreme and outrageous act was the proximate cause of her emotional and physical distress. Proximate cause exists when an act precedes and produces an injury that is likely to have occurred as a result of the act or which might have been anticipated. *Jeffers v. Olexo*, 43 Ohio St. 3d 140, 143, 539 N.E.2d 614, 617 (1989). In this case, the young Dwyer can show that a child likely would experience emotional distress when she saw her mother injured and bleeding. Therefore, the child will be able to establish that the extreme and outrageous act was the proximate cause of her emotional distress.

Finally, the child must show that she suffered from serious emotional distress. To establish serious emotional distress, the mental anguish she suffered must be serious and of a nature that "no reasonable man could be expected to endure it." *Id.* Serious emotional distress goes "beyond trifling mental disturbance, mere upset or hurt feelings" and "may be found where a reasonable person, normally constituted, would be unable to cope adequately with the mental distress engendered by the circumstances of the case." *Paugh v. Hanks*, 6 Ohio St. 3d 72, 78, 451 N.E.2d 759, 765 (1983). It is not necessary to prove any physical harm.

ILLUSTRATION 24-6. *Continued*

Pyle v. Pyle, 11 Ohio App. 3d 31, 34, 463 N.E.2d 98, 101 (1983). Various neurosis, psychosis, and phobias are examples of serious emotional distress. *Paugh v. Hanks,* 6 Ohio St. 3d 72, 78, 451 N.E.2d 759, 765 (1983). In this case, a psychologist examined the child and found that she suffered from post-traumatic stress syndrome and physical symptoms such as headaches and vomiting after she saw an adult throw a bucket at her mother. Post-traumatic stress and anxiety coupled with these physical manifestations should be sufficient for young Dwyer to establish serious emotional distress that is beyond mere upset or hurt feelings and that a reasonable person would be unable to cope.

3. WAS CAMP COUGAR VICARIOUSLY LIABLE FOR MANN'S INTENTIONAL TORTS?

The final claim to consider is whether Camp Cougar will be vicariously liable to both Dwyers for Mann's intentional torts. An entity can be held vicariously liable for the actions of its agent. *Byrd v. Faber,* 57 Ohio St. 3d 56, 58-59, 565 N.E.2d 584-586 (1991). A principal-agent relationship is established when one party exercises control over the actions of another and those actions are done for the benefit of the party exercising control. See *Hanson v. Kynast,* 24 Ohio St. 3d 171, 173, 494 N.E.2d 1091 (1986). However, a master can be vicariously liable for its agent's intentional tort only if the entity controlled the agent's conduct and the agent's acts benefited the entity. *Id.* In this case, Camp Cougar directed Mann to supervise a camp activity. Therefore, Mann may be found to be Camp Cougar's agent. However, Mann's actions did not benefit the camp, nor did the camp exercise control over her actions. In fact, these actions may have harmed the camp. Therefore, it is unlikely that Camp Cougar would be found liable for Mann's torts.

The threshold issue is whether Mann is Camp Cougar's agent. A principal-agent relationship is established when one party exercises control over the actions of another and those actions are for the benefit of the party exercising control. See *Hanson v. Kynast,* 24 Ohio St. 3d 171, 173, 494 N.E.2d 1091 (1986). In this case, Camp Cougar directed Mann to act as the sandbox supervisor and specifically directed her to keep people safe. Therefore, Mann is likely to be found to be an agent of Camp Cougar.

The next issue to consider is whether a master can be vicariously liable for its agent's intentional torts. A master can be vicariously liable for its agent's intentional tort only if the master controlled the agent's conduct and the agent's acts benefited the master. See *Hanson v. Kynast,* 24 Ohio St. 3d 171, 173, 494 N.E.2d 1091 (1986). The camp did not direct Mann to injure Dwyer, nor did the camp benefit from Mann's actions. Therefore, Camp Cougar would not be vicariously liable for Mann's act of throwing the bucket of sand at Dwyer or causing young Dwyer's serious emotional distress because it did not control Mann's actions, nor did the camp benefit from Mann's actions.

ILLUSTRATION 24-7. Multi-Issue Outline

Thesis Paragraph
    Introduce issues
        Whether Carol Mann's touching of Dwyer was battery
        Whether Carol Mann committed the tort of intentional inflic-
        tion of emotional distress
        Whether Camp Cougar can be vicariously liable for Carol
        Mann's acts

Heading: Issue #1 or Question Presented #1
    Introductory issue: Did Carol Mann commit the tort of battery?
    Rules: (1A) A battery is the intentional touching of another
      without the consent of the person touched that results
      in injury. (*Anderson*) (primary binding) (first element or
      subissue) (1B) A contact between a nonconsenting party
      and object rather than the actor's body can be a battery.
      (*Leichtman*) (primary binding) (first element or subissue)

    Rule (2) A person intends his or her conduct when he or she
      undertakes an action with a knowing mind. (*Smith*) (pri-
      mary binding) (second element or subissue)

    Rule (3) A battery occurs only if a plaintiff sustains physical
      injuries as a result of the touching. (*Anderson*) (primary
      binding) (fourth element or subissue)

    Application of law to facts: In Dwyer's case, Mann not only
      aimed the bucket at Dwyer purposefully to strike her, she
      struck Dwyer with it and the sand. The bucket and the sand
      striking Dwyer would be sufficient to establish that a "touch-
      ing" occurred. Mann later told Dwyer that she deliberately
      threw the bucket at her. Dwyer did not consent to being hit
      by the bucket and that touching resulted in injuries.
    Conclusion: The touching was a battery.

First Legal Element or Subissue #1
    Issue: Did a touching occur?
    Rule: Objects are extensions of body parts. Contact with a sub-
      stance or an object can be touching. (*Leichtman*)

    Application of law to facts: Bucket contacted Dwyer.
    Conclusion: A touching occurred.

Second Legal Element or Subissue #2
    Issue: Did Mann intend to hit Dwyer?
    Rule: A person intends an act when it is done purposefully.
      (*Smith*)

    Application of law to facts: Mann purposefully threw the bucket
      at Dwyer and said she intended to strike her.
    Conclusion: Mann had intent.

ILLUSTRATION 24-7. *Continued*

Third Legal Element or Subissue #3

> Issue: Did Dwyer suffer the requisite physical injuries as a result of the contact?
>
> Rule: Physical injuries must result from contact for battery. (*Anderson*)
>
> Application of law to facts: Dwyer sustained cuts and eye irritation from bucket and sand contact.
>
> Conclusion: Dwyer had requisite physical injuries.

Thesis Paragraph to Introduce Issue #2

> Issue: Does eight-year-old Rachel Dwyer have a claim for intentional infliction of emotional distress against Carol Mann?
>
> Rule: Intentional infliction of emotional distress occurs when an individual intentionally commits an extreme and outrageous act that causes emotional distress that no reasonable person can be expected to endure. (*Yeager*) (primary binding)
>
> Application of law to facts: Rachel Dwyer, a child, saw Mann, an adult who was asked to supervise the sandbox and ensure the safety of others, throw the rusty, metal bucket filled with sand at her mother's head and face, causing her mother to bleed. Seeing this act that was "beyond all possible bounds of decency" and therefore extreme and outrageous caused the child to suffer from anxiety, headaches, and vomiting daily—symptoms no reasonable child should be expected to endure. Several witnesses can testify that Mann said that she intended to harm Dwyer.
>
> Conclusion: Rachel Dwyer has a claim for intentional emotional distress.

Issue #2 First Element or Subissue #1

> Issue: Did Mann commit an extreme and outrageous act?
>
> Rule 1: An extreme and outrageous act is one that no reasonable person can be expected to endure. (*Yeager*) (primary binding) (*Pyle*) (primary persuasive)
>
> Rule 2: An act is extreme and outrageous if it goes beyond all possible bounds of decency and is intolerable in a civilized community. (*Yeager*) (primary binding)
>
> Application of law to facts: Mann, an adult who was asked to ensure safety in the sandbox, threw a rusty, metal bucket filled with sand at another adult in front of young children, including her child and Rachel Dwyer, the injured party's daughter. That act goes beyond all possible bounds of decency and would be intolerable in a civilized community.
>
> Conclusion: Mann's act would be found to be an extreme and outrageous act.

ILLUSTRATION 24-7. *Continued*

Issue #2 Second Element or Subissue #2

Issue: Was the extreme and outrageous act done with intent?

Rule 1: A person intends his or her conduct when he or she undertakes an action with a knowing mind. (*Smith*) (primary binding)

Rule 2: If an actor knew or should have known that his or her actions would cause serious emotional distress, intent is established. (*Hale*) (primary binding)

Application of law to facts: Mann said she intended to harm Dwyer. In addition, Mann not only knew or should have known that throwing a rusty, metal bucket filled with sand at the head and face of another adult in front of the other adult's child resulting in the adult bleeding would cause an eight-year-old child to suffer serious emotional distress.

Conclusion: The young Dwyer should be able to show intent.

Issue #2 Third Element or Subissue #3

Issue: Was the extreme and outrageous act the proximate cause of Dwyer's emotional and physical distress?

Rule: Proximate cause exists when an act precedes and produces an injury that is likely to have occurred as a result of the act or which might have been anticipated. (*Jeffers*) (primary binding)

Application of law to facts: A child would be expected or likely to experience emotional distress when she witnesses her mother injured and bleeding.

Conclusion: The young Dwyer will be able to show that the act was the proximate cause of her emotional and physical distress.

Issue #2 Fourth Element or Subissue #4

Issue: Did the child suffer from serious emotional distress?

Rule 1: To establish serious emotional distress, the mental anguish must be serious and of a nature that "no reasonable man could be expected to endure it." (*Paugh*) (primary binding) Serious emotional distress goes beyond mere upset or hurt feelings, but exists when a reasonable person is unable to cope. *Id.*

Rule 2: Physical harm need not be shown. (*Pyle*)

Rule 3: Neurosis, psychosis, and phobias can establish serious emotional distress. (*Paugh*) (primary binding)

Application of law to facts: A psychologist found that the child suffered from post-traumatic stress syndrome and suffered anxiety and physical symptoms such as headaches and vomiting. That should be sufficient to establish serious emotional distress that is beyond mere upset or hurt feelings and that a reasonable person would be unable to cope.

Conclusion: Young Dwyer can show she suffered from serious emotional distress.

ILLUSTRATION 24-7. *Continued*

Introduce Issue #3

Issue: Was Camp Cougar vicariously liable for Mann's intentional torts?

Rule 1: An entity can be held vicariously liable for the intentional actions of its agent if the entity controlled the agent's conduct and benefited from it. (*Byrd*)

Application of law to facts: Mann may be found to be an agent for Camp Cougar. However, Mann's actions did not benefit the camp, nor did the camp exercise control over her actions.

Conclusion: Even though Mann is likely to be found liable for these intentional torts and a master can be found liable for the intentional torts of its agent, it is unlikely in this case that Camp Cougar would be found liable for Mann's torts.

Issue #3 First Element or Subissue #1

Issue: Is Mann Camp Cougar's agent?

Rule: A principal-agent relationship is established when one party exercises the right of control over the actions of another and those actions are for the benefit of the party exercising control. (*Hanson*) (primary binding)

Application of law to facts: Camp Cougar directed Mann to act as the sandbox supervisor and specifically directed her to keep people safe, exercising control over her actions and deriving benefit from her actions.

Conclusion: Mann is likely to be found to be an agent of Camp Cougar.

Issue #3 Second Element or Subissue #2

Issue: Is Camp Cougar, a master, vicariously liable for its agent's intentional torts?

Rule: A master can be vicariously liable for its agent's intentional tort only if the master controlled the agent's conduct and the agent's acts benefited the master. (*Hanson*) (primary binding)

Application of law to fact: Camp Cougar did not direct Mann to throw the bucket nor did the camp benefit from Mann's conduct.

Conclusion: Camp Cougar would not be held liable for Mann's intentional acts.

ILLUSTRATION 24-8. Writing from an Outline

Outline
First Legal Element or Subissue #1

> Issue: Did a touching occur?
>
> Rule: Objects are extensions of body parts. Contact with a substance, even cigar smoke or an object, can be a touching. (*Leichtman*)
>
> Application of law to facts: Bucket touched Dwyer when Mann threw it.
>
> Conclusion: A touching occurred.

Paragraph Drafted from Outline

I. Did a battery occur when Mann struck Dwyer with a bucket and sand?

Whether Mann committed the tort of battery turns on whether an intentional touching occurred when a bucket Mann threw struck Dwyer. A touching can occur directly or indirectly, such as when an object or a substance rather than an individual's body contacts the other party. *Leichtman v. WLW Jacor Communications, Inc.*, 92 Ohio App. 3d 232, 634 N.E.2d 697 (1994).

In *Leichtman*, one person blew cigar smoke at another person, resulting in injuries. The court found that the contact from cigar smoke, although not a direct touching by a person, was still battery. In essence, the court found that the smoke was an extension of the person and that contact between the smoke and the nonconsenting person met the requirement of a touching for civil battery. In this case, Mann threw the bucket at Dwyer, and the bucket contacted her face. That was an indirect touching. Following the reasoning in the *Leichtman* case, the bucket contact, although indirect, would be an extension of Mann's body, and the contact between Dwyer and the bucket would be considered a touching under the theory of civil battery.

IN-CLASS EXERCISE

Review the memo in Illustration 24-9. Prepare an outline of authorities and an outline based on this memo. (This is the reverse of the process you would normally use.) Then discuss your outline. Make a list of legally significant facts and note the legal standard.

ILLUSTRATION 24-9. Sample Memorandum: Slip-and-Fall Case

ATTORNEY WORK PRODUCT PREPARED FOR LITIGATION

MEMORANDUM

To: Benjamin Joyce
From: William Randall
Date: November 7, 2020
Re: *Harris v. Sack and Shop*

QUESTION PRESENTED

Is Sack and Shop, a grocery store, liable for injuries sustained by Harris, a store patron who slipped on a banana peel that had been left on the grocery store floor for two days after the store employee and manager had been told it was there?

BRIEF ANSWER

Probably yes. Sack and Shop, a grocery store, likely breached its duty of care to a store patron, Rebecca Harris, who was injured when she slipped on a banana peel that the grocery store had allowed to remain on the grocery store floor for two days after both the store employee and manager knew about the peel.

FACTS

Rebecca Harris is suing our client, Sack and Shop Grocery Store, for negligence.

Harris went to the store to purchase groceries on July 8, 2020. While she was in the produce section, she slipped on a banana peel that a grocery store employee dropped on the floor. The employee had dropped the peel on the floor two days earlier. The employee had failed to clean it up, even after a patron, who saw him drop it, asked him to clean it up. The patron also told the store manager about the banana peel, and the manager asked an employee to clean it up. The employee still failed to clean up the peel, and the manager failed to ensure that the employee removed the peel.

Harris sustained a broken arm and head injuries as a result of the slip and fall.

DISCUSSION

The issue presented in this case is whether Sack and Shop Grocery Store was negligent when Rebecca Harris slipped in the store's produce section. A defendant is negligent if the defendant owed the plaintiff a duty, the defendant breached that duty, and the defendant's breach of that duty was the proximate cause of the plaintiff's injury. *Hills v. Bridgeview Little League Ass'n*, 745 N.E.2d 1166 (Ill. 2000). A grocer owes a duty of reasonable care to its patrons, and the grocer will be found negligent if a store employee or manager breached the store's

ILLUSTRATION 24-9. *Continued*

duty of reasonable care to its patrons, and as a result of that breach, the patron was injured. *Ward v. K Mart Corp.*, 554 N.E.2d. 223 (Ill. 1990); *Thompson v. Economy Super Marts, Inc.*, 581 N.E.2d 885 (Ill. App. 1st). A store owner may be liable when a patron, who is a business invitee, is injured by slipping on a foreign substance, if a store owner knew of the presence of the foreign substance or should have discovered it. *Olinger v. Great Atl. & Pac. Tea Co.*, 173 N.E.2d 443 (Ill. 1961). In our case, Sack and Shop owed a duty of reasonable care to Harris because she was a store patron — a business invite. Based on that duty of reasonable care, Sack and Shop must keep its store floor free of foreign substances that it knew about or should have discovered. In this case, Sack and Shop knew about the foreign substance — the banana peel. However, Sack and Shop failed to remove the banana peel that the store employee dropped. The store failed to clean it up for two days, even after both the employee and the store manager had been told to clean up the peel from the floor. Therefore, Sack and Shop is likely to be found liable for the injuries Harris sustained.

The first element to consider is whether Sack and Shop owed a duty of reasonable care to Harris. A business owes a duty to its invitees or patrons to exercise reasonable care to maintain its premises in a "reasonably safe condition for use by the invitees." *Ward*, 554 N.E.2d at 226. Harris was a customer in the store. Sack and Shop, a grocery store, is a business. Therefore, Sack and Shop owed Harris a duty of reasonable care to maintain the premises.

The next question to consider is whether Sack and Shop breached its duty of reasonable care to Harris. A store will be found to have breached its duty of reasonable care to a patron if a store employee fails to properly and regularly clean the floor of the store, *Olinger v. Great Atl. & Pac. Tea Co.*, 173 N.E.2d 443 (Ill. 1961), or if the business had knowledge of the dangerous condition. *Id.* Also, if a business created the hazard, the business can be found to have breached its duty of reasonable care to a patron. *Pabst v. Hillman's*, 13 N.E.2d 77 (Ill. App. 1st 1938). In *Pabst*, the grocery store had overfilled a display of green beans, and the green beans spilled onto the floor. A patron slipped on one of the green beans. The court found that it could infer that the grocer had created the dangerous situation because the beans were on the floor next to the overfilled basket. *Id.* In our case, Sack and Shop's employee had two days to clean the floor before Harris fell. That could be considered a failure of the store's duty of reasonable care to properly maintain the premises and to regularly clean the store floor. Also, as in the *Pabst* case, Sack and Shop through its agent — an employee — had created the dangerous situation because the employee dropped the banana peel on the floor. In addition, a customer had placed the store employee and the manager on notice of the banana peel, and neither one cleaned up the banana peel. Therefore, Sack and Shop breached its duty of reasonable care to Harris.

ILLUSTRATION 24-9. *Continued*

The plaintiff, however, still must establish proximate cause—that is, that the injury resulted as a natural consequence of Sack and Shop's breach of its duty of reasonable care. In *Pabst*, a store owner's failure to clear green beans from a store floor, resulting in injury to a patron who slipped on the floor, was found to be the proximate cause of the patron's injuries. *Id.* at 80. In this case, Sack and Shop's failure to clean the peel from the floor was a breach of its duty of care to Harris. This breach resulted in injury to Harris when she slipped on the neglected banana peel. Sack and Shop's breach of its duty will be found to be the proximate cause of Harris's injuries.

The final element that must be established for Sack and Shop to be liable to Harris for negligence is that the plaintiff, Harris, suffered injuries. In this case, Harris sustained a broken arm and head injuries as a result of the slip and fall on the banana peel. Therefore, Harris will be able to show that she was injured.

CONCLUSION

Sack and Shop owed Harris a duty of reasonable care. The store is likely to be found to have breached that duty of reasonable care because an employee and the store manager failed to remove a banana peel—a foreign substance—from the grocery store floor during the preceding two days. The injuries Harris sustained were directly caused by a slip on the banana peel. Therefore, Sack and Shop is likely to be found liable to Harris for negligence.

CHAPTER SUMMARY

Outlining is an important component of legal writing. It helps you organize the discussion section of your legal memorandum. To outline a legal memorandum, first draft a list of legal authorities. Second, arrange the discussion sections concerning each issue and, if necessary, arrange each paragraph of the memorandum.

The list of legal authorities should include the names and citations to the authorities, a note about the legally significant facts contained in the authority, if any, and a statement that summarizes the significance of the authority.

The legal issues of the discussion should be organized in the IRAC format discussed in Chapter 22. Each element of a legal issue should be addressed in this format.

Before you can begin writing your memorandum, you must organize your thesis paragraph. The thesis paragraph is the first paragraph of your discussion. It summarizes the legal issues you will discuss in the memorandum. This paragraph also should be organized in IRAC format, if possible.

You have been shown how to draft questions presented, issues, conclusions, brief answers, facts statements, and discussion sections. In addition, you have been taught how to synthesize authorities and how to use a legal writing convention called IRAC.

KEY TERMS

elements
list of legal authorities
outlining

thesis paragraph
threshold issue

EXERCISES

SELF-ASSESSMENT

1. How do you organize a thesis paragraph?
2. How do you compile a list of legal authorities?
3. How do you determine which element to discuss first?
4. What format should each paragraph take?

PRACTICE SKILLS

5. Review the memo in Illustration 24-9. Prepare an outline of authorities and an outline based on this memo. (This is the reverse of the process you would normally use.) Then discuss your outline. Make a list of legally significant facts and note the legal standard.
6. Write the discussion section only for the memo below.

MEMORANDUM

To: Ruth Abbey
From: Gail Michael
Date: January 20, 2021
Re: *Kahn v. Randall,* Civ. 95 No. 988, File No. 8988977

QUESTION PRESENTED

Does Janice Kahn have a valid claim for intentional infliction of emotional distress against Ronnie Randall after Kahn saw Randall turn his car to strike Kahn's 11-year-old child in front of her, causing her to suffer from anxiety, headaches, and vomiting?

CONCLUSION

Janice Kahn probably has a valid claim for intentional infliction of emotional distress against Ronnie Randall. Kahn saw Randall turn his car to strike her 11-year-old child. Seeing this accident caused Kahn to suffer from anxiety, headaches, and vomiting daily. This act could be considered extreme and outrageous conduct if it was done with intent. Several witnesses can testify that Randall said that he intended to harm Kahn, and Kahn states that Randall turned the car to strike her son. Two factors, however, might show that Randall lacked intent: the statement that he made to the police that he did not intend to hit the child and the fact that his blood alcohol level was 0.11, possibly preventing him from formulating the needed intent.

FACTS

While driving a car Ronnie Randall struck Janice Kahn's son at 5 p.m. on August 29, 2021. The sky was bright and clear. No skid marks appeared on the dry street following the accident.

Janice Kahn was working in her garden about five feet from the accident scene at the time of the accident. Her son was playing a game in the street before Randall's car struck him. Kahn did not see the car strike her 11-year-old son. When she first looked up from her garden, she thought her son was dead. He was covered with blood and had several broken bones. However, Kahn's son was conscious after the accident.

Immediately after the accident, Randall, who had a blood alcohol level of 0.11, was cited for drunk driving and driving with a suspended driver's license. Police charged him with drunk driving and suspended his license two weeks earlier after the car he was driving struck another child at the same spot. Randall has a drinking history.

Following the accident, several witnesses said Randall was upset and wobbled as he walked. One witness said that Randall intentionally turned the steering wheel to hit Kahn's son. Kahn stated that Randall often swerved down her street to get her attention.

Rhonda Albert, Kahn's neighbor, said she heard Randall say he would get even with Kahn after Kahn broke off a ten-year relationship with him.

During Kahn and Randall's ten-year relationship, Randall was close to Kahn's son. He took him to ball games, including one in April, and attended the son's baseball games. Randall knew that Kahn's son was the most important person in her life.

Since the accident, Kahn vomits daily and suffers from anxiety and headaches. Dr. Susan Faigen, Kahn's internist, states that the anxiety, headaches, and vomiting are the result of the accident. The prevailing case is *George v. Jordan Marsh Co.*, 359 Mass. 244, 268 N.E.2d 915 (1971). In that case, the court held that one who without a privilege to do so by extreme and outrageous conduct intentionally causes severe emotional distress to another, with bodily harm resulting from such distress, is subject to liability for such emotional distress and bodily harm.

7. Review the discussion section in the multi-issue Dwyer memo above and draft a list of authorities. Then draft an outline of the discussion section.
8. You are a paralegal with the firm of Probing and Will. You must research whether Sarah Wakefield can renounce Adam Antwernt's will and collect a portion of the estate in your state.

Your firm's client is Sarah Wakefield. She was married to Adam Antwernt. Antwernt died in your state following a long illness. Wakefield was Antwernt's second wife. She had been married to him for more than 20 years and lived in their home in your state before Antwernt died. Antwernt purchased the home with his first wife, Carry MacOver. MacOver died while she was still married to Antwernt. Wakefield subsequently married Antwernt. When Antwernt married Wakefield he never changed the deed for the home to include Wakefield. Wakefield kept her maiden name. Antwernt adopted a son with MacOver. The son, who is now 30 years old, is Grayson Antwernt.

Antwernt drafted his will before he married Wakefield. He and Wakefield were getting along fine when he died. However, she was not included in his will. He did not leave her any property. Instead, he left all of his property to Grayson. Antwernt's will was admitted to probate.

Wakefield wants to know whether Antwernt's will is valid and whether he can divest her of the marital property or whether she can renounce the will and collect a portion of the estate. Grayson is out of town and his attorney told Wakefield that she will get her share of the estate once Grayson returns. He is scheduled to return later this month.

What rights does Ms. Wakefield have to the estate? How must she exercise those rights in your state?

9. You are a paralegal with the Securities and Exchange Commission.

A hedge fund and its founder, Theodore Stalling, have been operating as an investment advisor, registered with the Securities and Exchange Commission, for ten years. Within the first year, eight qualified investors invested more than $100,000,000 in the fund — the Stalling Growth Fund, run by Stalling Group, an RIA.

Stalling directed the Fund's day-to-day activities and the Fund's acquisitions of securities. Stalling also met and communicated with investors. He prepared and distributed the Fund's newsletters, monthly reports, and portfolio statements to investors. He also provided information to the Fund's auditors.

Stalling solicited new investors and frequently met with existing investors. Stalling managed the Fund in exchange for fees. The fees were calculated on the basis of the Fund's asset value. Each quarter, the Fund received a 1 percent annualized advisory fee based on the reported assets. The Fund also received an annual incentive fee equal to 20 percent of the net profits of the Fund calculated as of the last business day of the year. Stalling, who owned 80 percent of the Fund, collected most of the fees.

During this time, Stalling and the hedge fund told investors in the private placement memoranda (PPMs) that the Fund's NAV "at any date shall be determined on an accrual basis of accounting in accordance with GAAP in the United States and certain other provisions."

The auditor, United Auditor Services, said that the Fund's audited statements were not prepared in accordance with GAAP and that the financial statements were the responsibility of the Fund's management.

The PPM also stated that the investments would be traded on "listed exchanges." In addition, the securities listed on the national securities exchanges were to be valued at their last sales price, or at the mean between the "bid" and "ask" prices if no sales occurred. Not all of the investments were made on listed exchanges, nor were they valued in the manner stated in the PPM, according to the Fund's former portfolio manager, Brett Flanagan.

Each month, Stalling sent a newsletter to its investors and prospective investors. The newsletter showed the return for the month. Each month, it showed a return that was at least 10 percent higher than the actual return. The newsletter also provided a value for the securities the Fund held. The value was not calculated in accordance with the statement made in the PPM. The value was at least 40 percent higher each month than the actual value of the securities. In addition, Stalling provided investors with a fake monthly portfolio statement of its holdings. It did not hold the equities and other holdings listed in the monthly portfolio report.

When one major investor, Rapid Fire, sought to redeem its $100 million investment, it did not receive any of the money it invested.

What, if any, sections of the federal securities law did the hedge fund and its founder violate? Prepare a detailed outline of authorities. Then, prepare both a memo outline and a memo for your supervising attorney stating whether the SEC could bring an action against Stalling.

CORRESPONDENCE

CHAPTER OVERVIEW

This chapter explains letter-writing basics, such as formats and types of letters. It provides examples of a variety of letters you might use in practice. Paralegals draft letters more frequently than any other type of written work.

Letter writing is one of the basic tasks you will perform as paralegals. Most letter-writing conventions apply to legal correspondence in much the same way as they do to other business communications. Regardless of the medium, professionalism is important, even if you send a letter via e-mail or a text via Slack. Paralegals should be aware of the components of basic letters as well as some special rules for legal communications.

A. BASICS OF LETTER WRITING

The mechanics of letter writing are similar to those of any other legal writing project. You plan it, draft it, and revise it. In planning your communication, you must determine your audience and outline what you plan to say to your reader. Always consider the tone of any written communication that you send. Tone is basically how your writing sounds to your reader. When revising the letter, use proper grammar and consider any revisions that would make the letter clearer. Proofread your letter.

▼ What Formats Are Used?

Letters may be drafted using a variety of formats. Letters may be sent via post, facsimile, e-mail, or text message. Today, most correspondence is sent via e-mail or text. Regardless of the mode of transmission, professional formatting is still required. Often the firm letterhead is set in the template for any e-mail correspondence. When in doubt as to style, always ask the supervising attorney, but it is best to always err on the side of formality. Look through the firm's correspondence file to get an idea of the format you should use. Firm style or your supervising attorney's guidelines generally determine the format of your letters. The formats are **full block, block, modified block**, and **personal style.** Full block style is the most frequently used in professional correspondence sent via e-mail.

In a full block letter, you do not indent the paragraphs. You will use the full block format for correspondence sent via e-mail. The paragraphs, the complimentary close, and the dateline are flush left. See Illustration 25-1. For block format, all paragraphs and notations are flush left, except for the date, the reference line, the complimentary close, and the signature lines, which are just right of the center of the page. See Illustration 25-3. In a modified block style letter, the first line of each paragraph is indented about five characters. See Illustration 25-6. In a personal style letter, often written to friends, the inside address is placed below the signature at the left margin.

B. COMPONENTS OF A LETTER

1. Letterhead and Headers

A letter is divided into several sections: the date, the name and the address of the addressee (called the inside address), a reference line, a greeting to the addressee, the body of the letter, and the complimentary closing.

You should draft the first page of a letter on firm letterhead. The **letterhead** is the portion of the firm's stationery that identifies the firm, generally the attorneys, and sometimes the firm's paralegals. It usually includes the firm's address and its telephone and facsimile numbers. Additional pages should not carry the firm letterhead but should be placed on matching paper with a **header** on each page. The header identifies the letter and is generally placed on the top left side of the page. A header includes the name of the addressee, the date, and the number of the page:

Margo Smith
November 15, 2022
Page Two

ILLUSTRATION 25-1.   Full Block Letter

[1]Vail McCann & Graham
888 Toledo Road
Ottawa Hills, Ohio 43606
(419) 535-7738
[2]November 8, 2022

[3]<u>Via Federal Express</u>
Mr. Stuart Shulman
Navarre Industries
708 Anthony Wayne Trail
Maumee, Ohio 45860

[4]Re: Settlement of <u>Kramer v. Shulman</u>

[5]Dear Mr. Shulman:

[6]I have enclosed a copy of the settlement agreement that we drafted and that has been signed by Mr. Kramer. Please sign the agreement and forward it to me at the above address by November 29, 2022.
If you have any questions, please feel free to call me at (419) 535-7738.

[7]Sincerely,

Mara Cubbon
Legal Assistant

[8]cc: Randall Fuzzwell

[9]Enc.

[10]MAC/wlk

1. Letterhead: Often the letterhead is built into the firm's letter template. It can be accessed as a macro or with a few keystrokes.
2. Date
3. Recipient's address and method of service
4. Reference line
5. Greeting
6. Body of the letter
7. Closing
8. Carbon copy notation
9. Enclosure of notation
10. Initials of drafter/typist

ETHICS ALERT

Check your state law as to whether your name may appear on the letterhead.

2. Date

The **date** should be placed at the top of the letter just below the firm's letterhead. The date is one of the key components of a letter concerning any legal matters. Date the letter with the same date as the date of mailing. This date can be crucial in determining a time line in a legal proceeding. Timing in sending documents and correspondence is often important in legal transactions and litigation matters. Therefore, be careful to include the date of mailing rather than the date of writing the letter. For example, if you prepare a letter on July 7 after the last mail pickup, you should date the letter July 8 because that is the date it would actually be mailed. This may seem like a purely technical distinction if you put the letter in the mail on July 7. However, some court cases and negotiations turn on the date of mailing. With e-mail, the date is easily discerned, but the recipient will consider the date of receipt the next business day.

3. Method of Transmission

If the letter is being sent by a method other than U.S. mail, it should be indicated above the address and then underlined as follows:

<u>Via E-mail and U.S. Mail</u>
Cheryl Victor
Vice President
Arizona Currency Traders
1000 Tempe Road
Phoenix, Arizona 85038

This notation should start at least two lines below the date. See Illustration 25-1.

4. Inside Address

The next part of the letter, the **inside address**, should contain the name of the person to whom the letter is addressed, the individual's title if he or she has one, the name of the business if the letter is for a business, and the address.

5. Reference Line

The **reference line** is a brief statement regarding the topic of the letter. For example, if the letter concerns a contract for the sale of a particular property, your reference line would say:

Re: Sale of commercial property—2714 Barrington Road, Toledo, Ohio

Some firms and corporations ask that the reference line contain a client number, claim number, or case number, so investigate your firm's style. Reference lines are also used on e-mail correspondence. You can use the reference line for the subject for the e-mail that will appear in the recipient's inbox. Aim for a maximum of eight words in the subject line or reference line. Try to place the most important words at the beginning of the subject line or reference line. You will catch the reader's attention.

PRACTICE POINTER

If possible, review letters written by the assigning attorney. You will find the letters in the attorney's correspondence file or on the firm's intranet. Note the attorney's style for the reference line and follow it. You may also see examples of correspondence for a particular client.

---

6. Greeting

In general, your **greeting** depends on how familiar you are with an individual. An individual whom you do not know should be addressed as "Dear Ms. White." If you know an individual well, you may address that person by first name. If you are uncertain whether to address the individual by first name, use a title and the individual's last name. If you are addressing a letter to a particular person, such as the custodian of records, but you do not know the person's name, try to determine the person's name. If necessary, call a company or agency to determine the appropriate recipient for the letter. Your letter is more likely to be answered quickly if it is addressed to the appropriate person rather than "To whom it may concern." In addition, it may provide you with an opportunity to establish a rapport with the individual to whom the letter is addressed.

PRACTICE POINTER

E-mails are now the predominate vehicle for communication, yet you should take the same care and use the same professionalism that you would use in hardcopy letters. You should always start the letter, even in e-mail format, with a professional, cordial greeting. Additionally, you should end the letter with a cordial closure just as you would in a letter that is mailed.

---

7. Body of Letter

The **body** of the letter follows the greeting and should begin with an opening sentence and paragraph that summarizes the purpose of the letter. Draft the body of the letter carefully. Outline the letter before writing it to be sure that you address all the necessary points. List each point you want to cover. For Illustration 25-1, your outline might read as follows:

1. enclose settlement agreement
2. ask for signature and specify return date
3. ask addressee to call if he has questions

Consider your audience. If you are writing to a layperson unfamiliar with the law, explain any legal terms you use often using definitions provided in a dictionary, or use simple language. However, do not provide any legal opinions. If you are addressing your letter to an individual who is familiar with the law, such as a judge, a paralegal, an in-house counsel, or an attorney, you do not need to explain such terms. To do so might be considered condescending.

ETHICS ALERT

Do not offer any legal advice or opinions in the letter. If an attorney is not signing the letter, do not request the recipient to take any action that would change her legal position or require her to make a legal decision.

---

8. Closing

End your letter with a **closing** in which you invite a response, such as "Please do not hesitate to call if you have any questions," or thank the addressee for assistance, such as "Thank you in advance for your cooperation." Finally, end the letter with a complimentary closing such as "Sincerely," "Very truly yours," or "Best regards" placed two lines below the final line of the body of the letter. Use a cordial closing even if you are writing a demand letter. You should always be professional. Place your name four lines below the closing to allow for a signature. Include your title, that is, paralegal or legal assistant. The guidelines to close a letter also apply to e-mail correspondence.

ETHICS ALERT

Be sure that your reader knows that you are a paralegal rather than an attorney. The easiest way to do this is to add your title after your name in the closing. If the letter is to be written for the attorney's signature, present the letter to the attorney for review and for her signature prior to sending.

Do not provide legal advice in your letter or represent yourself as an attorney. Ethical codes and state laws prohibit paralegals, who are not licensed to practice law, from providing legal opinions or from representing themselves as attorneys. To avoid any confusion or possible misrepresentation, include your title after your name when you write a letter.

---

9. Copies to Others and Enclosures

If you are copying a third party on the letter, you might want the original addressee to know this. In a letter sent via post, note it with a "cc" at the bottom left margin of the letter following the closing. The cc indicates **carbon copy** sent to the person listed. (Although photocopies have replaced carbon copies, cc is still used.) Indicate to whom a copy of the letter was sent as "cc: Mike Sterner." See Illustration 25-2. If you do not want the original addressee to know that you copied a letter to another person, note on the draft or file copy "bcc," which means **blind carbon copy.** That notation should only appear on the draft or file copy of the letter and not on the recipient's letter. If the letter is sent via e-mail, the recipient will know that you sent a copy via "cc" because when the recipient's name is posted, the party "cc'd" will be included below. The recipient will not see the party that received the e-mail via "bcc."

ILLUSTRATION 25-2.   Letter Confirming Deposition

Law Offices of Sam Farrell
2714 Barrington Road
Findlay, Ohio 45840
(419) 267-0000

January 28, 2022

Ms. Karen Dolgin
2903 W. Main Cross Street
Findlay, Ohio 45840

Re: Deposition of Robert Harrold
     Harrold v. Sofer

Dear Ms. Dolgin:

This letter is to confirm our conversation today in which you stated that you will present the plaintiff, Robert Harrold, for a deposition at the law office of Sam Farrell, 2714 Barrington Road, in Findlay, on March 18, 2022, at 2 P.M. This deposition is being rescheduled at your request because the plaintiff had a family commitment on February 11, 2022, the date originally set for the deposition.

If you have any questions or additional problems, please feel free to call me at (419) 267-0000, extension 608.

Best regards,

Craig Black
Paralegal
cc: Sam Farrell
     Wally Sofer
CMB/klm

The next notation is for **enclosures**, such as court orders, contracts, or releases. Place the abbreviation **Enc.** or **Encs.** at the bottom left margin of the letter. See Illustration 25-1. If you are sending attachments via e-mail, note in the body of the e-mail that the documents are attached. The attachments will also appear as links at the top of the letter.

Finally, the letter should note your initials in all capital letters as the author of the letter and then the initials in lowercase letters of the person who typed the letter. If your initials are RAS and the typist's are HVS, then the notation under the enclosure or cc notation would read RAS/hvs.

C. TYPES OF LETTERS

Paralegals write letters to clients to confirm deposition dates, meeting dates, hearing dates, or agreements. These letters are called confirming letters. Other letters provide a status report of a case or summarize a transaction. Some letters accompany documents, such as those for document productions, contracts, or settlement releases. These are called transmittal letters. Other letters may request information. Some letters explain the litigation process to clients. See Illustration 25-3. Some letters, written by a paralegal but signed by an attorney, make a demand.

1. Confirming Letters

Confirming letters reaffirm information already agreed to by you and the recipient. It is a good practice to follow up any conversation with a client or an opposing attorney or paralegal with a confirming letter that summarizes the conversation, any agreements made, or any future acts to be accomplished. See Illustration 25-2. For example, after you discuss a document production with a client and set a meeting date to review the records, send a letter summarizing the conversation. Confirming letters provide a reminder of the conversation and allow anyone who reviews the file later to know what you and the client discussed should you be unavailable. Pay close attention to the tone as you want to sound informative, yet professional. You do not want to convey that you are inconvenienced or irritated. Often to expedite this process, confirming letters are sent via e-mail and the billing partner and supervising attorney are copied on the correspondence.

If opposing counsel has agreed to produce documents or provide a witness for a deposition at a particular time, write a confirming letter to the opposing counsel summarizing these facts and asking to be contacted if there are discrepancies. This can be sent via e-mail with the supervising attorney's permission. Whenever a deposition is rescheduled or continued, it is imperative that a confirming letter be sent via e-mail and post to avoid future discovery disputes. Whenever your client is deposed, send him or her a copy of the deposition for review. A sample of such a letter is found in Illustration 25-4.

2. Status Letters and Transaction Summary Letters

Often you will be asked to provide a **status report** of a case, especially to insurance companies and other clients. See Illustration 25-5. These letters provide clients with an overview of the current activities in a court case, transaction, or other legal matter.

ILLUSTRATION 25-3.   Letter Concerning Deposition Schedule

Law Offices of Sam Farrell
2714 Barrington Road
Findlay, Ohio 45840
(419) 267-0000

January 21, 2022

Wally Sofer
Chief Executive Officer
1000 Hollywood Way
Houcktown, Ohio 44060

Re: Deposition of Wally Sofer
Harrold v. Sofer

Dear Mr. Sofer:

This letter is to advise you that you are required to submit to a deposition by the plaintiff's attorney at 10 A.M. on March 2, 2022, at the law office of Karen Dolgin, 2903 W. Main Cross Street in downtown Findlay. During this deposition, the plaintiff's attorney will ask you questions related to the above-referenced court case, and you will provide answers while under oath and in the presence of a court reporter. Mr. Farrell also will be present to represent you during the deposition. Mr. Farrell and I would like to meet with you at least once before the deposition to discuss your case and this important part of your case.

I will call you Friday, January 28, 2022, to schedule an appointment next week to prepare for your deposition.

Please bring any accident reports, citations, or other documents that relate to the accident if you have not already provided them to our office.

I look forward to speaking with you this week.
Sincerely,

Craig Black
Paralegal
cc: Sam Farrell
CMB/klm

Transaction summary letters often follow a business transaction such as a real estate closing. In these letters, you summarize a transaction.

ILLUSTRATION 25-4. **Letter Enclosing Deposition Transcript**

Law Offices of Sam Farrell
2714 Barrington Road
Findlay, Ohio 45840
(419) 267-0000

July 15, 2022

Mr. William Gary
709 Franklin Street
Findlay, Ohio 45840

Re: Deposition on July 8, 2022

Dear Mr. Gary:

Enclosed is a copy of the transcript of your July 8, 2022, deposition. Please review the transcript carefully and note any statements that were incorrectly transcribed. You may not rewrite your testimony, but you should note any inaccurate transcriptions. You may correct the spelling of names and places. If you find any serious mistakes, please call me to discuss these problems.

When you review the deposition, please do not mark the original transcript. Instead, note any discrepancies on a separate sheet of paper. Please note the page and line of any discrepancies. I will have my secretary type a list of the discrepancies, and we will discuss these changes before we send them to the court reporter. These changes must be received by the court reporter within 30 days; therefore, I would appreciate your prompt review of the transcript and would like to review your changes by July 29, 2022. If we fail to provide the changes to the court reporter within 30 days, we will forfeit your right to correct the transcript and any inaccuracies will be part of the record.

If you have any questions, please do not hesitate to call me.

Thank you in advance for your cooperation.

Best regards,

Benjamin Farrell
Paralegal

Enc.
BSF/jas

ILLUSTRATION 25-5.   Status Report Letter

Martin Marshall & Smith
960 Wyus Boulevard
Madison, Wisconsin 53606

June 13, 2022

Mr. Cal L. Grist
Pockets Insurance Company
10 Wausau Way
Wausau, Wisconsin 54401

Re: <u>Kelsey v. Cocoa</u>
Your claim number: C100090888

Dear Mr. Grist:

This letter is to provide you with a status report concerning the progress of the above-referenced matter. To date, we have requested that the plaintiff answer interrogatories and requests for admissions. I sent a copy of these requests to you about a week ago. The plaintiff is required to answer these requests within 30 days. We will send you a copy of the plaintiff's answers as soon as we receive them. We are scheduled to depose the plaintiff on September 6, 2022.

The plaintiff's attorney is scheduled to depose a representative of Oleo Company on October 13, 2022.

At this time, the court has not scheduled a settlement conference, but is likely to do so before the end of the year.

Please feel free to call if you have any questions.

Sincerely,

Alicia R. Samuel
Legal Assistant

ARS/yml

In other letters, you will **request information**, often from the custodian of records. See Illustration 25-6.

Often you will be responsible for coordinating document productions. Illustration 25-7 shows a sample **transmittal letter** to a client concerning a request to produce documents.

Many letters will be written to accompany documents, releases, and checks. See Illustrations 25-8 and 25-9.

ILLUSTRATION 25-6.   Request for Information

Vail McCann & Morris
960 Wyus Boulevard
Madison, Wisconsin 53606

August 12, 2022

Sarah Ray
Custodian of Records
Federal Deposit Insurance Corp.
9100 Bryn Mawr Road
Rosemont, Illinois 60018

Re: Freedom of Information Act Request

Dear Ms. Ray:

Based on the Freedom of Information Act, 5 U.S.C. § 552 et seq., I am requesting that your agency provide copies of the following:

Each and every document that relates to or refers to the sale of the property located at 2714 Barrington Road, Glenview, Illinois, 60025.

The documents should be located in your Rosemont, Illinois office.

Under the act, these documents should be available to us within ten days. If any portion of this request is denied, please provide a detailed statement of the reasons for the denial and an index or similar statement concerning the nature of the documents withheld. As required by the act, Smith, Langdon and Oleo agrees to pay reasonable charges for copying of the documents upon the presentation of a bill and the finished copies.

Thank you in advance for your cooperation in this matter.

Sincerely,

Lillian Eve Farrell
Paralegal

LEF/dag

ILLUSTRATION 25-7. Request to Produce Documents

Carthage Katz & Kramer
1001 B Line Highway
Darlington, Wisconsin 53840

February 28, 2022

Ms. Karen Taylor
Carolton Corp.
1864 Merrimac Road
Sylvania, Ohio 43560

Re: <u>Carolton v. Franklin</u>

Dear Ms. Taylor:

Enclosed please find a request from the defendants asking you to produce documents. The date scheduled for the production of these documents is April 4, 2022. Some documents may be protected from disclosure because they may contain confidential trade secret information, and others may be protected because they are communications between you and your attorney or the result of your attorney's work. We must respond in writing by March 25, 2022 in order to raise any of these claims.

As we must review the documents to determine whether any documents are protected, we should compile the documents no later than March 18, 2022. This will allow us time to review, to index, and to number each document.

I will be available to assist you in gathering documents to respond to this request. I will call you this week to schedule an appointment.

If you have any questions, please feel free to call.

Sincerely,

Eileen Waters
Paralegal

Encs.
EDW/jnn

ILLUSTRATION 25-8.   Letter Accompanying Document

Janis Max & Jordan
1600 Bradley Street
Wilmette, Illinois 60091

March 4, 2022

Eve Lilly
Lake County Recorder of Deeds
18 N. County Street
Waukegan, Illinois 60085

Re: 1785 Central Street
    Deerfield, Illinois 60015

Dear Mrs. Lilly:

Enclosed please find two original quit claim deeds, one dated December 30, 2021, and one dated January 3, 2022, relating to the above-referenced property. Both deeds have been marked "exempt" from state and county transfer tax. A check for $50.00 to cover the recording fees ($25 each) is enclosed. Please record these deeds at once and return the originals to Jacki Farrell at the 1785 Central Street address.

Thank you for your assistance.

Sincerely,

Jennifer Laurence
Legal Assistant

Encs.
cc: Jacki Farrell
JML/jch

ILLUSTRATION 25-9.   Letter Accompanying Check

Howard & Farrell
Central and Carriage Way
Evanston, Illinois 60202

April 21, 2022

William Green
Chicago Bar Association
124 Plymouth Court
Chicago, Illinois 60611

Re: Commercial Real Estate Contract Prepared by the Real Property
Law Committee

Dear Mr. Green:

Enclosed please find a check for $30.00 to cover the mailing fees and
the cost of a copy of the Real Estate Contract referenced above. Please
send me a copy of the contract at your earliest convenience.

Thank you for your cooperation.

Sincerely,

M. Seth Jordan
Paralegal

Enc.
cc: Rachel Jones
MSJ/ear

3. Demand Letters

A **demand letter** is a letter that states your client's demands to another
party. The demand can request a party to act in a particular way, to pay
a debt, or to stop acting in a particular way, such as to cease contact with
the client. Paralegals are often assigned to write demand letters. Often
the demand letter seeks to collect debts. Demand letters may need
to comply with the requirements of your state's fair-debt-collection
laws. Always check with the supervising attorney to make sure that
the demand letter complies with state and local law. As a paralegal,
you will draft the demand letter, but an attorney may be required to
sign it because it asserts that a party change his legal position. See
Illustration 25-10.

A demand letter has several goals and guidelines. In the demand letter, you will:

- Tell the reader who you are and why you are writing. This also provides credibility.
- Include the relevant facts without adding emotional adjectives. Use precise dates, quantities, dollar amounts, and times. The supervising attorney will provide guidance as to the level of detail required here. Be careful not to be too detailed and just include the essential facts. We aim for a professional yet assertive tone.
- State your client's precise demand. Follow the demand with the general legal support, without citations, for your demand, if suitable. Your supervising attorney will instruct you as to the nature of the demand, the request, and relevant legal authority. Always follow the supervising attorney's instruction as to whether to include the legal support. Sometimes an attorney uses the demand letter to state the client's legal rights.
- Indicate clearly the date compliance is expected and the consequences of failing to comply with your client's demand. Indicate the date or time frame for the demand to be met.
- Always end a demand letter with: "Please contact me if you have any questions or concerns."
- Close the demand letter with a professional closure, even if you or the client is angry. An example of a professional closing is: "Very truly yours." Always use professionalism and close cordially. This is an opportunity to demonstrate your professional ethos when writing the letter.
- Ask the assigning attorney if she would be more comfortable if she signed the demand letter. An attorney must sign the letter if the demand letter will change the recipient's, or your client's, legal position, or advocates that the reader should change her legal position.
- Write short paragraphs in demand letters because each paragraph is used to state a separate point or component so that they stand out for the busy reader. The topic sentence for each paragraph should state the paragraph's point. You should be able to discern the outline of the letter from just the topic sentences.
- Use plain language to make the letter understandable for the immediate audience as well as for subsequent readers. The letter should be readily understandable for the busy, unfamiliar reader. The reader should not need a legal education to understand the letter. You can invite the reader to contact you if she has any questions. Your letter may be placed in a file and the subsequent reader may be unfamiliar with the matter. The reader should be able to understand the letter after a single reading. Short paragraphs and terse sentences enhance the letter's persuasive, assertive tone.

In a demand letter, if the issue involves a debt, you should state that your firm represents the creditor or other client, as well as the client's desire for full payment of the claim. Specify the amount demanded or state the action sought, and ask the debtor either to make payment or to contact your office within a certain number of days. Then state the action that the firm will take if the demand is not met within the specified time period. It is best to send a demand letter via post. Even if the attorney chooses to e-mail a copy of the demand letter, also ask the attorney to send a hard copy.

ILLUSTRATION 25-10.   **Demand Letter**

Law Office of Randall William
145 Franklin Street
Madison, Wisconsin 53606

April 4, 2022

Michelle Hunt
889 Barrington Road
Middleton, Wisconsin 53608

Re: Furniture Crafters Account 4155

Dear Ms. Hunt:

Our office represents Furniture Crafters in the collection of the $468.00 debt due on the above-referenced account. Furniture Crafters requests that you pay the full amount of the debt, $468.00, immediately.

You must pay this amount in full or contact our firm at the above telephone number or address within seven days. If we do not hear from you within seven days, we will proceed to court in this matter.

Sincerely,

Randall William
Paralegal

RAW/bgh

---

4. Opinion Letters

Opinion and advice letters advise clients about the legal rules that apply to their situation. Often a client will request that the firm issue a legal opinion about the legal consequences of an intended transaction. The opinion is then documented in an opinion letter. The client may then make a legal decision. Most law firms will not have paralegals draft even a preliminary opinion letter. If your firm asks you to draft a preliminary letter, be sure not to sign the letter with your name. Always have the supervising attorney review the opinion letter carefully before it is sent to another attorney for signing. An **opinion letter** must be signed by an attorney because, as its name suggests, the letter states a legal opinion. Many firms require that opinion letters are signed only by partners, as the letter makes the firm responsible for the opinion offered.

ETHICS ALERT

If you sign an opinion letter, this could be construed as the unauthorized practice of law. If you sign the attorney's name, without her consent, that is tantamount to practicing law.

If you must draft a preliminary version of an opinion letter, the process is similar to writing an IRAC paragraph. Start with a statement of the legal issue. Your next sentence, however, should answer the issue. The reader will want to see the bottom line up front, or the actual conclusion on the matter. In the paragraph following the answer to the issue, state the law and apply the legally significant facts to the law. Provide information about any legal issues that present problems and incorporate the legally significant facts into that discussion.

The final paragraph should state your opinion as to the conclusion or answer to the issue presented and provide your prediction of the outcome for the legal situation. Clients often request opinion letters prior to entering a business transaction or to request the tax consequences of a proposed business transaction.

Discuss this letter with the attorney who will be signing it and be sure that it is the attorney's opinion rather than your own that is conveyed to the client. Be sure that the attorney reviews the letter before signing it. If the attorney does not initiate a discussion with you about the letter, you should do so to ensure that the attorney reviewed it. Although you may draft the letter for the attorney to review, be sure that the attorney signs the letter before it is sent to the recipient. Even under direction by an attorney, a paralegal can never give legal advice, suggest a change in a legal position, or reach a legal conclusion. Opinion letters provide legal advice, suggest that a client change his legal position, and also reach a legal conclusion; this is why it is imperative for the supervising attorney to sign the letter.

5. E-mail

Most professional correspondence is now sent via e-mail. Often, for important letters, an additional copy of the correspondence is sent via mail. Many of the same drafting rules that we use for professional letters apply in the same way to an e-mail note. Professionalism is just as important in e-mail as it is in letters sent via post. Maintain a professional tone in e-mails even though the format is considered casual.

Please avoid sarcasm and jokes in professional e-mails, as they may be misunderstood. Consider your purpose and audience and then outline what you plan to say.

When writing an e-mail, use proper grammar. Proofread your e-mail. If you would address a letter using a title such as Mr. or Mrs., do so in the e-mail. Do not use all capital letters in an e-mail. That is considered screaming. Also, be careful with bold font, as it is distracting.

Include your mailing address and your telephone number so that the party can contact you using methods other than e-mail. Use a cordial closing in an e-mail, too. If you are sending an **attachment,** such as a document to be reviewed, be sure you mention the attachment in the letter so that the person doesn't mistakenly delete the attachment, believing it may contain a virus.

Often short notes sent via e-mail are designed to fill a single screen on a smartphone. Use the full block style when formatting your e-mail letter. Additionally, watch your sentence length in e-mail communication. Sentences in e-mails should be no longer than 16 to 18 words. In e-mail correspondence, paragraphs should be limited to four or five sentences with a line skipped between paragraphs. This prevents the reader from experiencing a visual block of text. Spacing on the screen is very important in e-mail communication.

PRACTICE POINTER

Check with your firm concerning policies regarding any e-mails that include client confidences. E-mails can be intercepted and may not be secure. Some firms, however, have security measures in place to safeguard such communications. Most firms have a confidentiality warning as part of the firm's e-mail template. However, e-mails can still be forwarded and intercepted. If a matter is very sensitive, consider alternative ways to communicate such as printed letters sent via post or even a telephone conversation.

When sending e-mails, remember that they can be forwarded to other recipients. Also, any e-mail that you create while at work is now a permanent part of the firm or company's document files. Even if you delete the e-mail, the encryption can often be retrieved. Be very careful with what you write and how you write it when you are at work. Ask the supervising attorney if e-mail is the best format for the correspondence.

Most firms now include confidentiality information in the e-mail template stating that the e-mail should be viewed only by the intended recipient. Whenever writing an e-mail in any context, always make sure that it is professional, truthful, and accurate before sending it.

Although emojis are used to convey tone, it is best to use emojis sparingly in professional correspondence. Emojis should be used only between close colleagues working on ongoing matters. Limit emojis to smiley faces if you opt to include them at all.

It is best to avoid using e-mail to discuss human resource issues, to share personal information, and to express condolences.

E-mail Etiquette Guidelines

- Reply promptly
- Be succinct, professional, and clear
- Be careful when replying and forwarding
- Evaluate whether information is necessary to share
- Use a meaningful subject line
- Select legible fonts and colors
- Include your contact information
- Remember that this is professional correspondence

Never:

- Use sarcasm
- Convey condolences
- Discuss human resources issues
- Share confidential information
- Use "Reply All" if unnecessary

Remember to:

- Avoid inappropriate jokes
- Only say what you may feel comfortable if a message is forwarded
- Close your e-mail cordially
- Forward with care
- Edit and proofread
- Make a phone call if needed

PRACTICE POINTER

Some e-mail programs allow you to request a return receipt that lets you know that the reader opened the e-mail. For critical e-mails, it is a good idea to request such a receipt. If something is time critical and you must ensure that the party received the document, consider sending the letter by messenger.

▼ How Do You Draft Subject Lines for E-mail?

When you draft a subject line, ask yourself "What is my e-mail's point?" To create an attractive and accurate subject line, place the most important words to the left. The subject line is a chapter heading or a title for your e-mail and accurately summarizes its content.

An accurate, attractive subject line increases the likelihood that your e-mail will be read. Limit the subject line's length to three to eight words and provide adequate detail. A subject line may also be called a reference line. You can use the subject line in the reference line in the e-mail letter.

Instead of a vague subject line, such as "Need Answer," consider: "Answer Required by Friday—Lease Renewal Trent Properties." Note that the subject line "Answer Required by Friday—Lease Renewal Trent Properties" provides specific information as well as a request for action.

Always update your subject line for the matter that you are corresponding about. Do not use an old e-mail thread for a new topic even if the same parties are involved.

6. Social Media

Social media, such as Facebook, LinkedIn, blogs, and Twitter, are now frequently used by many legal professionals. Law firms and corporations rely on social media for marketing and networking. Client and professional correspondence have not yet adopted social media as a form of communication in the law firm environment. Most firms have adopted social media policies. Before using social media at work to communicate to clients and other parties, ask your supervising attorney if it is appropriate. Although Twitter would seem like the ideal method to quickly communicate concise information with a large group, it is still considered too informal for professional correspondence. A user must have a Twitter account, too. Many senior legal professionals have not adopted social media, although younger workers are comfortable with it. Twitter has a unique characteristic in that each "tweet" is limited to 280 characters. Also, with Twitter, the sender cannot control where the "tweet" goes and who reads it, so many client confidentiality issues are raised. The Twitter message can easily be broadcast to a large audience.

Facebook and LinkedIn require the user to subscribe, and not everyone subscribes to such services. Facebook and LinkedIn may be viewed as marketing tools rather than vehicles for professional correspondence. Always ask the supervising attorney if social media is an appropriate format for communication prior to corresponding. Always be professional in all of your communication, regardless of format. Any electronic communication has the ability to live on past the transaction or representation and be viewed by unintended recipients.

PRACTICE POINTER

Before using any form of social media in the work environment, check if the firm or company has a social media policy in place. Remember that social media has not been adopted by everyone and may be considered very informal for professional correspondence. Consider the age and background of the recipient, too, when deciding on the format for the correspondence. Additionally, be aware of client confidentiality when using social media for professional communication. If the topic is very sensitive, ask the supervising attorney if a telephone call may be the best way to communicate at the outset.

CLASS DISCUSSION

Read over the following letter and find the flaws.

Law Office
Attorneys at Law
1818 Main Street
Ossining, New Jersey 07555

Mr. Ronald Tolbert
1501 South Street
Morris City, New Jersey 07345
Dear Mr. Tolbert:

Thank you for your correspondence recently. We will see where we can get this week and then write again next week. I do think we should try to get this done in the next few weeks and then put this matter to bed. As previously indicated, I do have a substantial problem with time this week but lets see where we can get.

I don't have time now to respond to all your points and I don't know that we necessarily agree or for that matter disagree with any of the various issues, legal or other that you raise. I can respond more fully as to our position on thise various items as we go forward. I don't know that we need to get into those issues now anyway. I would like to comment on our need to receive a copy of the settlement letter.

I know that the settlement letter is important for our client. Please send the settlement letter as soon as you are able. In any event, if I am missing something, please let me know.

Sincerely,
Diane Russell
Paralegal

7. Texting

Texting is a very popular form of communication now. Many firms use Slack for internal messaging or have their own messaging service.

Although texting is very informal, professionalism is still necessary. Avoid using the firm's messaging service to share details about your weekend with your co-workers. You can omit greetings and closures on subsequent texts, sent within a short time frame, regarding the same matter. Always edit and proofread your messages. The notes in a text are not as structured or as formal as letters, but still require clarity. Examine the use of abbreviations and acronyms, as they are not always immediately understood. Your professional image is conveyed even in a simple text.

PRACTICE POINTER

Before sending a message, consider the purpose and the audience. Check your tone for professionalism.

CLASS DISCUSSION

Please read over the following texts to find the flaws. Focus on ways to make the series of messages more professional.

<u>From Mitch</u>

Hi Ron, Do you know if the lender plans on issuing the borrowers 1099s in connection with the deed in lieu of foreclosure? Thanks, Mitch

<u>From Ron:</u>

Checking

<u>From Mitch:</u>

Hi Ron,

Any chance you can get an answer on this today? My client has a call with their investors tomorrow morning and that question will likely be discussed.

Thanks,

Mitch

<u>From Ron:</u>

Trying.

<u>From Mitch:</u>

We would greatly appreciate an answer about the 1099.

Thanks.

<u>From Ron:</u>

Pressing the lender. What document?

<u>From Mitch:</u>

We are concerned with the 1099s. Will each TIC's 1099 be for its respective pro rata share of the outstanding mortgage debt?

From Ron:

Not sure. We can write with you.

From Mitch:

Does "write with you" mean "work with you" or did you intend something else?

From Ron:

Yes! Ugh. Airport texting always challenging. Thanks!

CHECKLIST

1. "Never give legal advice" is the first rule of letter writing for paralegals.
2. If you sign a letter or any correspondence, identify yourself as a paralegal.
3. Be informative.
4. Determine the purpose of the correspondence. The purpose will help you develop the format and the content.
5. Consider your audience. If you are addressing a client, do so courteously and write at a level that the client will understand. This applies to e-mail correspondence, too. If you were asked to answer a client's questions, be sure that you do. You should always be respectful to the addressee. Think about the client's and the reader's level of sophistication when deciding if you should send a letter or an e-mail.
6. Choose your words carefully. You want to make certain that your words express what you intend.
7. Establish your tone. Aim for a professional yet cordial tone in most correspondence. A greeting and a closure establish tone.
8. Avoid acronyms and abbreviations. If you must use an acronym or an abbreviation, define it in parentheses the first time you use it.
9. Write succinctly and directly. Your reader is busy so you want to communicate clearly and in as few words as possible. Avoid unnecessary details.
10. Use updated, accurate, and enticing subject lines in e-mail.
11. Always be professional even if e-mail or texting is the selected transmission format.
12. Proofread all correspondence. Check for spelling, word choice, clarity, and tone.

CHAPTER SUMMARY

Letter writing is an essential part of your daily routine as a paralegal. Most letter-writing conventions that apply to business communication apply to legal correspondence. However, paralegals should be careful about dating letters concerning legal matters. Letters should be dated with the date of mailing, which may or may not be the date of drafting.

A letter should contain a date, the name and address of the addressee, a reference line, a greeting to the addressee, the body of the letter, and the complimentary closing.

Confirming letters reaffirm information already agreed to between you and the recipient. Status letters provide an up-to-date review of the process of a pending matter. Transaction summary letters explain particular transactions. Letters also are written to accompany documents, such as releases and checks, or to state your client's demands to a third party, such as for payment.

As with any written document, letters should be outlined, written, and then rewritten if necessary. Careful writing is also important in the e-mail and text formats. Even if the mode of transmission is e-mail or text, always opt for professionalism.

It is important to avoid the unauthorized practice of law when writing letters, regardless of the transmission method. Do not give any legal advice in a letter that you sign. A letter must be signed by an attorney when it contains legal advice, suggests that a client change her legal position, or states a legal conclusion. Last, in any professional communication, regardless of the format or the medium, professionalism and client confidentiality are of paramount importance.

KEY TERMS

attachment
blind carbon copy (bcc)
block letter
body
carbon copy (cc)
closing
confirming letter
date
demand letter
e-mail
enclosure line
full block letter
greeting

header
inside address
letterhead
modified block letter
opinion letter
personal style letter
reference line
request information
social media
status report
transaction summary letter
transmittal letter

EXERCISES

DISCUSSION QUESTION: CHECK YOUR TONE

1. This exercise requires you to write three very short e-mails. Each e-mail has a different purpose and a different audience. You will consider your tone carefully when writing the e-mails.
   - E-mail 1: Write a short introductory e-mail to your classmates so that they can get to know you.
   - E-mail 2: Write a thank you note after a job interview for a paralegal position to thank the interviewer.

- E-mail 3: Write an out-of-office message that will post as an automatic reply for when you are on vacation. You are an entry-level paralegal at a company.

Each e-mail should be a maximum of 125 words.

Answer the following questions about the e-mails:

a. What is the purpose in each of the e-mails?

b. Who is the audience for each of the e-mails?

c. Is each e-mail appropriate for the intended audience?

d. Can each e-mail be written for a variety of audiences?

e. How did you, the writer, make each e-mail conform to the reader's needs?

f. What are the main differences between the e-mails you drafted?

g. How did you convey "tone" in your e-mails?

h. How did the tone differ in each e-mail?

i. Is the writing professional and grammatically correct?

SELF-ASSESSMENT

2. What are the basic components of a letter?

3. What is a reference line?

4. How do you indicate that you are sending a copy of a letter to another person?

5. How do you indicate that you want someone to receive a copy, but you don't want the addressee to know that the other person received a copy of the letter?

6. What are confirming letters?

7. What is a status report letter?

8. What are transmittal letters?

9. What are demand letters?

10. Should you provide a legal opinion in a letter?

PRACTICE SKILLS

Prepare the following letters as if you were a paralegal with the law firm of O'Connor Hackett & Black, 1000 Madison Way, Madison, Wisconsin 53606. Addressee names are identified for you, but you may supply each one's address yourself.

11. Write a letter to Madison Insurance Corporation explaining that your law firm will be representing Carol White for a lawsuit against its insured, Harold Watson, stemming from an automobile accident that occurred on September 1. The Madison claims adjuster is Howie Mark. Harold Watson's insurance policy number is 1280. You once had a difficult time dealing with Mr. Mark and Madison Insurance in the past, so send your letter by certified mail. Enclose a copy of the police report. Send a blind copy to your client. You write it at 5 p.m. on December 24. You realize that December 25 is a holiday and that mail will not go out until the next business day.

12. Your firm represents a client, Karen Taylor, who sustained a neck injury during an automobile accident between Carter McLaughlin and Robert Carroll. Write a letter to Dr. Nancy Martin asking for a detailed report concerning the present and future medical problems of that client. Dr. Martin

is an orthopedic surgeon. Indicate that you have a signed release from the client to enclose.

13. Your firm represents Margaret Weston in a divorce case. Write a short letter to her informing her of the final hearing date in her divorce case. The date is June 16, in Lucas County Domestic Relations Court, 900 W. Adams Street, Toledo, Ohio 43602.

14. Your client needs to give testimony at a deposition on November 15, at 10 a.m. at your offices. Draft a letter asking William Hesse to be at the deposition. Explain to him that you will meet with him in advance to discuss his testimony.

15. Your firm has just settled a case involving Karen Douglas and your client, the Wentworth Industries, in Morristown, New Jersey. The case was settled for $88,000. The Wentworth Corporation paid Douglas for injuries she sustained when she fell at a Mexican hotel. You do not want to admit any liability in your letter or admit any ownership interest in the Mexican hotel, the CanCan. You merely want to tender the check to Douglas in full satisfaction of any claims she or her husband have against Wentworth. You also have the signed settlement agreement and the court dismissal of the action to send her.

16. You are assigned the preparation of a letter that explains the status of a pending insurance defense litigation matter. The matter is set for trial on November 15 of this year. Two depositions have been taken—the plaintiff's and the defendant's. Interrogatories have been answered by both sides, and a settlement conference is scheduled with the judge in the case on October 31. The judge is Eve G. Halsey of Ohio Common Pleas Court in Columbus, Ohio. You expect that a representative of the restaurant where the incident took place will attend the settlement conference and that an insurance company representative also will attend as required by the local court rules. Your firm will be calling several witnesses from the restaurant to testify at the trial and you and the partner on the case, Wally Taylor, will be preparing these witnesses to testify beginning in October. Send this letter to your client, Schroeder Insurance Enterprise, 250 W. Wilson Street, Hinsdale, IL 60521. The person you deal with at the insurance company is Thomas Kennedy, a claims manager. You are sending this letter via Express Mail. The letter is being typed by Taylor's secretary Jan Marie Maggio. She will send a blind copy of the letter to an associate on the case, Janis Farrell. She also will send a carbon copy of the letter to Mr. Taylor.

17. The following letter was written and signed by a paralegal. List three problems that could arise from this letter.

January 1, 20_____

Sent by Mail and Fax to:

Re: Contract to purchase real estate dated December 15, 20_____

Dear Mr. Smith:

Per your request the Seller hereby agrees to extend the attorney approval contingency until 5:00 p.m., January 15, 20_____.

I specifically note to you that I am in receipt of your first amendment and its Exhibits A, B, and C.

As to paragraph 3 of your first amendment, I note to you that I am posting in the mail to you a proposed limited warranty and a Waiver and Disclaimer of Implied Warranty of Habitability. I request that you review the same after I have advised you that my client has reviewed the same. I am also posting it in the mail to them. It is specifically noted that what will be provided will be a limited warranty and that we will expect the parties to sign a waiver and disclaimer and I further note that I want to end this thing and accordingly, I provide for a date of January 15, 20_____.

I expressed to you that I was unhappy with the contingencies in paragraph 5 of the contract. In fairness, I request that if it does not appear that your client will be able to meet the contingencies, namely, either sell her home or secure financing, that she will notify us at the earliest date and to then voluntarily agree to a termination of the contract.

Looking forward to a closing with you soon.

> Very truly yours,
> Mary Walton
> Paralegal

APPLICATION OF CONCEPTS

For the following exercises, assume that you are a paralegal with the law firm of Coffield, Kurth and Taylor, 30 N. Wacker Drive, Chicago, Illinois 60606. The phone number is 312-792-3161.

18. Prepare a letter to Attorney Gene Williams of the Law Office of Gene Williams, 20 E. Washington Street, Chicago, Illinois 60611. You want to tell Mr. Williams that you are sending him a copy of a real estate contract

between your clients, Laura and James Hirsh, and his clients, Michelle and Jordan Bream, for the purchase of 2629 Canterbury Lane, Northbrook, Illinois 60062. You also are including a $41,000 certified check for the escrow for the property. This represents 10 percent of the purchase price. The closing is tentatively set for April 1 of this year. The letter is being hand-delivered by a messenger from your law firm. The letter is being typed by your secretary, Carly Alice Connelly. A blind copy is being sent to the partner on the case, Wally Taylor.

19. You are responsible for mailing interrogatories to the plaintiff's lawyer, Joanna Mark, at the Law Office of Joanna Mark, 25 E. Randolph Street, Chicago, Illinois 60611. You complete the interrogatories on October 30 of this year at 11 p.m. What date should you put on the letter, and what date will the letter be mailed? Draft this letter. Your secretary, Carly Alice Connelly, will be typing the letter, and a carbon copy should be sent to the partner, Alicia Coffield.

20. You are sending a letter via facsimile and U.S. mail to Beth Baker, 30 S. Taylor Street, Milwaukee, Wisconsin. Baker works at Baker, Corvino and German. This letter is to confirm negotiations for the purchase of a business, Hocking Enterprises, in Brown Deer, Wisconsin. The negotiations are set for 10 a.m. at your offices on June 12 of this year. You expect that your clients, Eric and Debbie Hocking, will be at your office and that Ms. Baker will be bringing her clients. The partner on the case is Wally Taylor. His secretary, Jan Marie Maggio, is typing your letter and will make certain that Mr. Taylor receives a copy of the letter. Draft the letter.

21. Draft a letter to Barry and Debbie Williams telling them that you are sending them a copy of their wills and a living trust. These are their signed copies for their files. Tell them to place these documents in a safe place and that you will keep copies at your office. Thank them for allowing your firm to handle this matter and tell them that you are looking forward to working with them on setting up a new business enterprise during the next year. Send a copy of the letter to the partner Wally Taylor and to the associate Edna Steer. The letter is being typed by your secretary, Carly Alice Connelly. The date of the letter should be today's date. This letter is being sent by Federal Express.

22. Write an e-mail to your client Naomi Polisky. Explain that you have researched her claim and will file a complaint in the Common Pleas Court of Hancock County, Ohio. Tell her your contact information.

23. Draft an e-mail to tell your client Seth Jacob that you are sending the final contract for the Rachel Sarah Evening Theater to him for his review. Ask him to return the signed contract to you at your law firm within a week. Provide contact information.

CITATION

The *Bluebook* is the guide to citation form for all legal documents, whether office memos or Supreme Court briefs. The *Bluebook*, formally known as the *Uniform System of Citation*, 21st edition, governs because of convention and tradition rather than by the mandate of the state legislature. In law, and legal writing, any point, idea, or rule must be cited. We generally cite after every statement that is not our own idea. Because none of us create legal authority, this means that we cite often.

We now have new citation formats due to the advent of electronic resources, including podcasts, and nonproprietary cases, called public domain citations, in which the case is not attributed to a publisher. The *Bluebook* and *The ALWD Guide to Legal Citation*, 7th edition, guide you on how to cite traditional resources such as cases, statutes, and regulations and on how to cite to nonprint and Internet resources. *ALWD* references the *Bluebook*, 21st edition. Both guides offer easily comprehended citations. *ALWD* contains "Fast Formats" for every category of citation. These provide terrific examples of formats for all legal resources. *ALWD* provides exceptional examples and diagrams of citations that make the format and the spacing clear.

Generally, the *Bluebook* is the universal resource for citation format for all legal personnel. Attorneys and paralegals use the *Uniform System of Citation*, commonly called the *Bluebook*.

The content in the *Bluebook* and *ALWD* are very similar. However, the *Bluebook* is still the standard resource for citation format if there is a discrepancy between the sources. This appendix is designed to give you a start in your citation process. If ever in doubt as to citation format, rely on the *Bluebook*.

▼ What Is a Citation?

A citation is really an address indicating where the cited material can be found so that anyone reading your document can find the material if he or she wants to. Also, **the citation** provides the location of the source so you attribute credit. The abbreviations must be consistent so that everyone knows what they mean. We rely on a similar convention with street addresses and postal abbreviations. The abbreviation for avenue is Ave.; the postal abbreviation for New York is NY. See the diagram of a case citation at the beginning of *Bluebook* **Rule 10** for an overview of case citation's components. To get started, there are helpful charts with Basic Citation Forms at the beginning of *Bluebook* **Rules 10, 12,** and **14.** Check the Fast Formats and Snapshots for cases, statutes, and Regulations in *ALWD*.

NET NOTE

Georgetown University Law School Library has a terrific research guide covering *Bluebook* citation that includes videos. You can find the guide at https:guides.ll.georgetown.edu/bluebook.

▼ What Documents Are Cited?

Any source of authority that you discuss in any legal document is cited. Any concept or idea that is not your own must be cited; this is called attributing authority to your ideas. Citing credits the source from which the idea or legal rule came. You will also have to indicate the specific page or paragraph that you used from within the document. When we include or reference a part of the decision, we cite to the specific part of the case. This is the pinpoint citation. When we cite to a part of a case that has a public domain citation, we cite to the paragraph within the decision.

The citation also tells the reader where to find the original source. Citations are used for all authority, whether it is primary authority such as a case or a statute or secondary authority such as a treatise or a law review article. Also cited are practitioners' materials and newspaper articles.

The *Bluebook* has two citation formats, one for court documents and memos and the other for law review articles. *ALWD* includes formats for court documents and for academic footnotes. Paralegals rely on the court documents and memo format for citation. See the "Quick Reference: Court Documents and Legal Memoranda" inside the back cover of the *Bluebook*. Although the print in the *Bluebook* may lead you to think otherwise, please underline or use italics for case names. Most practitioners italicize case names now. *ALWD* makes the type-face very clear with the Fast Formats and the Snapshots. See *ALWD* **Chart 1.1** for detailed information about underlining and italicizing parts of the citation.

ETHICS ALERT

Always provide complete citations to anything that is not your own idea or a client's fact.

▼ What Are the Components of a Citation?

Generally, the components of a cite are the name of the particular document, the volume or title where the document is located, the name of the publication that contains the document, and the specific page, section, or paragraph where the document is found. The number after the initial page number is the pinpoint citation — the specific page from within the document where you obtained the information. Also included is the year that a case was decided or the publication date of a book or volume of statutes. For example:

Jacobs v. Grossman, 310 Ill. 247, 248, 141 N.E. 714, 715 (1923)

The name of the document is the case name, *Jacobs v. Grossman*. Parallel citations are given just for the purposes of this example so that you can see the citation for the case in both reporters; the official reporter is always mentioned first and the unofficial reporter mentioned second. Each state has its own rules regarding the necessity of including parallel citation information for documents submitted to its court. For instance, Illinois no longer requires parallel citations and only requires citation to the regional reporter. In fact, most states no longer require citation to state reporters, only citations to regional reporters, and many states now use public domain citations for recent decisions. However, local court rules may require parallel citations. Even if parallel cites are not required by the local court rules, it may be a courtesy to provide parallel citations. Always ask the supervising attorney about his or her preference for citation format when writing internal memos and research for clients. In all other circumstances, the court rules and the *Bluebook* control.

PRACTICE POINTER

Do not rely on the cite format that the publisher provides in their reporters at the beginning of a case. Always consult the *Bluebook* for citation format.

Some states do not have state reporters and rely on the regional reporters so parallel citation is not an issue. Now, if a case is included in an office memo, you will use only the regional reporter. The *Bluebook* will indicate, in **Table 1**, which reporter to cite to when submitting a document to the court. You can also check the local court rules. The first number preceding the reporter abbreviation is the volume number of the reporter. Next is the reporter abbreviation and then the page number where the case begins in the reporter. The year that the case was decided is included in parentheses. *Bluebook* **Table T.1** lists reporter abbreviations, as does *ALWD* **Appendix 1**. *ALWD* **Chart 12.2** details the abbreviations for frequently used reporters.

Using the *Bluebook* takes practice. The *Bluebook* is organized by rules. Each rule details the citation format for each type of document. The index is very helpful in finding specific references to the citation format for an individual document such as a statute, an administrative regulation, or a law review article. For additional examples, use the Fast Formats in *ALWD*. The Fast Formats are easily located in the *ALWD* index, under the relevant topic heading.

The following portion of this appendix provides examples of the materials and sample cite formats. These examples will help you navigate your way. If the illustration here does not provide adequate information, you can turn to the *Bluebook* or *ALWD* rule mentioned to obtain more detailed treatment.

▼ How Are Pending and Unreported Decisions Cited?

You should provide the docket number, the court, and the full date of the most recent disposition of the case, as well as the full case name. The *Bluebook* states in **Rule 10.8.1** that when an unreported case "is widely available on a widely used electronic database, it may be cited to that database." The citation for the pending or unreported decision, when using a database, should include the case name and complete docket number yet without the judge's initials, the database identifier (LEXIS, Westlaw, or Bloomberg), court name, and date of case.

unreported case available on Lexis:	*Wood v. Mut. Redevelopment Houses, Inc.,* No. 14 Civ. 07535, 2017 U.S. Dist. LEXIS 233583, at *2 (S.D.N.Y. Mar. 1, 2017) — *Bluebook* **Rule 10.8.1(a)**; *ALWD* **Rule 12.15(b)**
slip opinion cite:	*Gillespie v. Willard City Bd. of Educ.,* No. C87-7043 (N.D. Ohio Sept. 28, 1987) — *Bluebook* format, **Rule 10.8.1**; *ALWD* format, **Rule 12.15**
with page cite:	*Gillespie v. Willard City Bd. of Educ.,* No. C87-7043, slip op. at 3 (N.D. Ohio Sept. 28, 1987)

Some jurisdictions prohibit the citation of unpublished opinions in court documents as these jurisdictions consider unpublished opinions to lack precedential authority. According to *ALWD*, always check the local court rules to see if unpublished cases can be cited. See *ALWD* **Appendix 2**.

▼ How Do You Cite a State Case?

Bluebook **Rule 10**, *ALWD* **Rule 12.6(c)(4)** and **Rule 12.6(c)(5)** discuss citation formats for state cases. Also check the *Bluebook* for the jurisdiction-specific rules and Style Guides at **BT2** for local court citation rules. If using *ALWD*, consult **Appendix 4(B)** for state court abbreviations. The first example below shows the citation for an Illinois case with parallel authority included. You may use parallel cites for an office memo if your supervisor requests it. The second example shows the same case cited in a brief to an Illinois court or to the United States District Court for the Northern District of Illinois.

With parallel cites: *Thompson v. Economy Super Marts,* 221 Ill. App. 3d 263, 581 N.E.2d 885, 163 Ill. Dec. 731 (App. Ct. 1991) — *Bluebook* format but only if an attorney requests parallel cites for the Illinois case

Thompson v. Economy Super Marts, 221 Ill. App. 3d 263, 163 Ill. Dec. 731, 581 N.E.2d 885 (1991) — *ALWD* format

In a brief: *Thompson v. Economy Super Marts,* 581 N.E.2d 885 (Ill. App. Ct. 1991) — *Bluebook* and *ALWD* formats. Note that parallel cites are not included in citations for documents submitted to an Illinois or federal court.

Check the jurisdiction's citation rules and the firm's requirements when you use a state decision in a memorandum or a brief. See *Bluebook* **Table T.1** and *ALWD* **Appendix 2**. If you are citing a state case to a state court in which the case was decided follow the court rules or the assigning partner's requests. If you need to use parallel citations, always list the official citation first. When you cite a state case in a memorandum addressed to a federal court or to a court of a state different from the state that decided the case, include only the regional citation as the example for citing in a brief, above, shows. If you are using only the regional citation, remember to place the abbreviation for the deciding court in parentheses. When citing a case from a state's highest court, though, do not include the court's name. See *Bluebook* **Rule 10.4** and *ALWD* **Rule 12.6(a)**. Additionally, follow the local court rules references in *Bluebook* blue pages **BT2** and for state courts in **BT2.2**, *ALWD* **Appendix 2**, and *ALWD* **Rule 12.4**. However, if parallel citations are required, see *ALWD* **Rule 12.4(c)** and *Bluebook* **Rule B10.1.3**, "Parallel Citation in State Court Documents."

Every state has its own rules regarding the reporter designated as "official" and whether the state has adopted public domain citations. Always check with the supervising attorney and the court rules. *Bluebook* **Table T.1** lists websites for each state, and *ALWD* **Appendix 2** provides websites for the courts to access the court's local citation rules. You must look up the rules for each state. Some states do not have state reporters but use the regional reporters. For instance,

Wyoming did away with the Wyoming Reports in 1959 and used the Pacific Reporter as the official reporter after 1959.

States that have adopted public domain citations as their official cites should be cited in accordance with *Bluebook* **Rule 10.3.3** and *ALWD* **Rule 12.11** (also called neutral citations). For example, Oklahoma requires the public domain citation format for all cases decided after May 1, 1997. Many states adopted public domain citation formats but you must check the *Bluebook*, **Table 1** for the specific dates when each state requires citation to the public domain format for cases. Also, *ALWD* **Appendices 1**(B) in hard copy and **2(B)** online note under each jurisdiction whether the jurisdiction uses the public domain format. These cites are designed to allow readers to find the case in a computerized system that does not rely on commercial publishers.

The public domain format is as follows: case name, followed by the year of the decision, the deciding court, and the sequential number of the decision. In some jurisdictions, the sequential number of the decision is the docket number. To cite to a specific portion of the decision, you may add a reference to the paragraph. If available, and if the jurisdiction requires, a parallel cite must be listed.

Sometimes a jurisdiction requires a specific public domain citation format. It is best to always check **Bluebook Table T.1** for each jurisdiction's requirements for public domain citation format. *ALWD* **Appendix 2** is available online and provides the updated local court citation rules. Although many states have adopted public domain formats for recent decisions, the federal courts have not yet adopted public domain citation formats for opinions from the federal courts although many decisions are available electronically.

Public domain citation: *State v. Kienast,* 1996 S.D. 111, ¶2, 553 N.W.2d 254, 256—*Bluebook* and *ALWD* formats

Use neutral, or public domain, citations when local court rules permit according to *ALWD* **Rule 12.11**. See *ALWD* **Sidebar 12.6** that lists states that use the public domain citation format.

▼ How Do You Cite Decisions Found in the *Federal Reporter* or the *Federal Supplement*?

Bluebook **Rules 10.1-10.6** along with **Table T.1** cover most requirements for citing cases. *ALWD* **Rule 12.6(c)(1)** and *ALWD* **Appendices 1 and 4(A)** provide detailed coverage of the citation format for cases from the *Federal Reporter* and the *Federal Supplement*. The case name is placed first and italicized. Next, place the volume number. The reporter abbreviation is next. For the *Federal Reporter*, the abbreviation is "F." The number of the series, second or third, should be placed next to the "F." For the *Federal Supplement*, the reporter is abbreviated "F. Supp." The page number follows the abbreviation for the reporter. Next, place an abbreviation denoting the appropriate court and the date of the decision. Be certain to include a geographic designation for the district courts.

Federal Reporter case: *Zimmerman v. North Am. Signal Co.*, 704 F.2d 347 (7th Cir. 1983) — *Bluebook* and *ALWD* formats

Federal Supplement case: *Musser v. Mountain View Broad.*, 578 F. Supp. 229 (E.D. Tenn. 1984) — *Bluebook* and *ALWD* formats

▼ How Do You Cite a Decision Contained in the *Federal Rules Decisions* Reporter?

The abbreviation for the *Federal Rules Decisions* is F.R.D. A case would be cited according to *Bluebook* **Table T.1** and *ALWD* **Appendix 1**, as follows:

Barrett Indus. Trucks v. Old Republic Ins. Co., 129 F.R.D. 515 (N.D. Ill. 1989)

PRACTICE POINTER

When starting an in-house memo assignment, ask the attorney about his citation preferences and look at examples in the firm's memo and brief bank. For in-house documents, sometimes the attorney's preferences will differ from the court rules.

▼ How Do You Cite a U.S. Supreme Court Case?

According to the *Bluebook*, once a U.S. Supreme Court case is published in an advance sheet of the *U.S. Reports*, the *U.S. Reports* citation, and only the *U.S. Reports* citation, is the proper citation, without any parallel citations. See **Rule 10** and **T1.1**, and *ALWD* **Rule 12.6(b)** generally. The cite format is diagrammed on page 95 of the *Bluebook*.

> *Erie R.R. v. Tompkins*, 304 U.S. 64 (1938) — *Bluebook* and *ALWD* formats. *ALWD* **Rule 12.4(b)(3)** provides guidance as to which reporter to select to cite a Supreme Court decision and states that one reporter should be selected. *ALWD* **Rule 12.4**.

Generally, if a Supreme Court opinion has been published in the *West Supreme Court Reporter* but not yet in the *U.S. Reports*, the *Supreme Court Reporter* citation should be used. If a Supreme Court opinion has not yet been published in *U.S. Reports*, or the *Supreme Court Reporter*, the *U.S. Reports, Lawyers' Edition* citation should be used. See *Bluebook* **Table T1.1**.

If a Supreme Court opinion has not yet been published in *U.S. Reports*, *Supreme Court Reporter*, or *U.S. Reports, Lawyers' Edition*, then you should cite to *United States Law Week*. See *Bluebook* **T1.1**. The court designation, "U.S.," should be placed in parentheses with the full date. See *Bluebook* **Rule 10.4(a)**. The citation would read as follows:

UAW v. Johnson Controls, 59 U.S.L.W. 4209 (U.S. Mar. 20, 1991)

▼ How Do You Use Short Citation Forms?

Short citation forms and subsequent cite formats are explained in *Bluebook* **B4**, and **Rule 10.9**. Also see *ALWD* **Rule 12.16(b)-(c)**.
Full citation:

Seymour v. Armstrong, 64 P. 612, 613 (Kan. 1901)

Subsequent citation when there is an intervening cite:

Seymour v. Armstrong, 64 P. at 613 — *Bluebook* **Rule 10.9**

Seymour, 64 P. at 613 — *Bluebook* and *ALWD* **Rule 12.16(b)** if using only the first party will not cause confusion

A subsequent citation without an intervening cite requires the use of *Id.* Use *Id.* only when the preceding citation is a single source.

Example of *Id.*:

Id. at 613 — *Bluebook* B10.2 and *ALWD* **Rule 12.16(a)**

Parallel short citations
Use of *Id.* with parallel citations. Note: Follow local court rules to determine requirements for parallel citation:
Full cite for parallel citation:

Thompson v. Economy Super Marts, 221 Ill. App. 3d 263, 581 N.E.2d 885, 163 Ill. Dec. 731 (App. Ct. 1991)

Short cite for parallel citation without intervening citations:

Id. at 263, 581 N.E.2d at 887, 163 Ill. Dec. at 733 — *Bluebook* **Rule 10.9(b) (ii)**

Id. at 263, 63 Ill. Dec. at 733, 581 N.E.2d at 887 — *ALWD* **Rule 12.16(d)**

Short cite for parallel citation with intervening citations:

Thompson, 221 Ill. App. 3d at 263, 581 N.E.2d at 887, 63 Ill. Dec. at 733 — *Bluebook* **Rule 10.2**

Thompson, 221 Ill. App. 3d at 263, 63 Ill. Dec. at 733, 581 N.E.2d at 887 — *ALWD* **Rule 12.16(d)**

▼ How Do You Cite a Decision Reported on a Commercial Database?

Generally, use the Westlaw or Lexis citation if a decision does not have a reporter citation but is available on a reliable commercial database.

Bluebook **Rule 10.8.1** and *ALWD* **Rule 12.14(b)** explain how an unpublished decision found only on Westlaw or Lexis, and other reliable electronic databases, should be cited.

▼ For Decisions Reported on Westlaw

For Westlaw, first provide the name of the case. The next part of the citation is the docket number. In the example that follows, that number is No. 82-C4585. The next part of the citation is the year that the decision was issued. Next, indicate "WL" for Westlaw and finally the Westlaw number assigned to the case. Place the date in the parentheses. However, *ALWD* requires that if a reporter citation is available for the case, cite to the reporter.

Westlaw example: *Clark Equip. Co. v. Lift Parts Mfg. Co.*, No. 82-C4585, 1985 WL 2917, (N.D. Ill. Oct. 1, 1985) — *Bluebook* and *ALWD* format

Bluebook **Rule 10.8.1** and *ALWD* **Rule 12.14(b)**

▼ For Decisions Reported on Lexis

For Lexis citations, first state the name of the case, the docket number, the year of the decision, the name of the Lexis file that contains the case, and the name LEXIS (using all capital letters) to indicate that the case is found on Lexis. Next place the date in parentheses.

Lexis example: *Barrett Indus. Trucks v. Old Republic Ins. Co.*, No. 87-C9429, 1990 U.S. Dist. LEXIS 142, at *2 (N.D. Ill. Jan. 9, 1990) — *Bluebook* and *ALWD* format

▼ How Do You Indicate a Page or Screen Number for a Case Retrieved on a Commercial Database?

An asterisk should precede any screen or page numbers. See *Bluebook* **Rule 10.8.1** and *ALWD* **12.14(b)**. See the example of the Lexis cite, above.

Westlaw screen no.:   *Clark Equip. Co. v. Lift Parts Mfg. Co.*, No. 82-C4585, 1985 WL 2917, at *1 (N.D. Ill. Oct. 1, 1985) — *Bluebook* and *ALWD* format

If a decision is published in a hardcopy reporter, you should use the reporter citation, even if you access the decision on Westlaw or Lexis. If a public domain citation is available, you should include it but follow the requirements for the jurisdiction as explained in *Bluebook* **T.1**. You can still access the case electronically but provide the reporter information so the reader can access the decision. For example, Westlaw always includes the reporter citation for their reporters if it is available. See *Bluebook* **Rule 10.3** and **T.1** and *ALWD* **Rule 12.14(b)**.

▼ How Do You Cite Internet Resources?

Bluebook **Rule 18** covers Internet materials and electronic media. The newest edition of the *Bluebook* also covers citation format for blogs, podcasts, nonprint media, images, and recordings. *ALWD* **Rule 21.5** covers periodicals online. In *Bluebook* **Rule 18.1**, General Citation Forms are provided for electronic media and digital sources. *Bluebook* **Rule 18.2** provides general guidance for citing sources retrieved on the Internet. You can use sources on the Internet in lieu of the hardcopy source when the online format is the official resource for the publication or the document, or if the online source is identical to the hard copy, such as the *Federal Register*. In this situation, you do not need to include a URL. This is occurring more frequently with federal, state, and municipal legislative and administrative resources. The *Bluebook* states that printed resources should be used and cited, when available, "unless there is a digital copy of the source available that is authenticated, official, or an exact copy of the printed source. . ." *Bluebook* **Rule 18.2**. *ALWD* states that if a periodical is available in print and electronic formats and it is exactly the same, cite to the print source and then you may add the URL, after the comma if it helps to access the source.

> Karin Mitra, *Information v. Commercialization: The Internet and Unsolicited Electronic Mail*, 4 Rich. J.L. & Tech. 6 (Spring 1998), *www.richmond.edu/jolt/ v4i3/mitra.html* — *Bluebook* **Rule 18.2.1(b)(ii)**

> Karin Mitra, *Information v. Commercialization: The Internet and Unsolicited Electronic Mail*, 4 Rich. J.L. & Tech. 6 (Spring 1998), http://*www.richmond. edu/jolt/v4i3/mitra.html* — *ALWD* **Rule 21.5**

PRACTICE POINTER

It is both cost- and time-efficient to attach PDF versions of cases and statutes to e-mailed memos rather than printing or photocopying the resources. govinfo.gov has the United States Code, the *Code of Federal Regulations*, and the *Federal Register* in PDF.

▼ How Do You Cite Documents Retrieved in PDF Files?

Documents are widely available for retrieval in Portable Document Format (PDF). Lexis and Westlaw now permit most resources to be saved and printed in PDF. Documents in PDF maintain the pagination from the hardcopy source and do not permit end-user manipulation.

Bluebook **Rule 18.1** provides an example for citing to PDF documents. *ALWD* **Rule 30.2** details citing to online materials that are official or authenticated sources.

▼ How Do You Cite Federal Statutes?

Always cite to the official statutory compilation. The first entry in the citation is the title number, then the abbreviation for the statutory compilation, and then the section or paragraph number. *Bluebook* **Rule 12** and *ALWD* **Rule 14** detail all the various rules pertaining to citing statutes and codes, state or federal. The Fast Formats at the beginning of *ALWD* **Rule 14** are particularly helpful.

Here is an example of a code section currently in force:

12 U.S.C. § 211 *Bluebook* and *ALWD* formats

It is now optional to include the date of publication of the code volume if the statute is currently in force. If you can obtain the statute in the official code, the United States Code, then cite to the official code.

If a code section is well known by a popular name, then include the name in the citation. For example:

Strikebreaker Act, 18 U.S.C. §1231 (2012) *Bluebook* and *ALWD* formats

You may rely on an unofficial version for updating purposes. All the following are citations to the identical statute.

26 U.S.C. § 61 *Bluebook* and *ALWD* formats.

Use the dates when the statute is divided between the main volume and the updates in the supplement. — *Bluebook* **Rule 12.2.2** and *ALWD* formats.

26 U.S.C.A. § 61 (West 2011 & Supp. 2021)

26 U.S.C.S. § 61 (LexisNexis 2014 & Supp. 2021) — *Bluebook* and *ALWD* formats

As with the U.S.C., the year included in the citation is the year that the code volume was published, not the year that the statute was enacted. In the U.S.C.A. example above, the first year mentioned, 2011, is the year that the particular volume of the code was published; the second date, 2021, is the year of the pocket part supplement that updates the code volume. For the unofficial codes, the publication date is printed either on the title page of the bound volume or on the back of the title page. Note that the title and section do not change in the codes published by different companies.

The precise, current version of the United States Code is now available at govinfo.gov in PDF format. You can cite the United States Code, even when you obtain it at govinfo.gov, in the exact same way as the print code. For instance, this a cite to the print version of the U.S.C.:

26 U.S.C. § 61

If you were to obtain the code section on govinfo.gov, the cite would be:

26 U.S.C. § 61 — You do not include a URL.

See the *Bluebook*, **Rule 12.10** for short citation format for statutes. When you are citing to the exact same statute subsequently, without an intervening cite, you can now use *Id. ALWD* details, in **Rule 14.5(a)**, the use of *id.* when short-citing statutes when there are no intervening citations.

PRACTICE POINTER

Ask your supervising attorney if she prefers the use of *Id.* for subsequent citations to the same statute or the short cite format.

▼ How Do You Cite a Section of a Constitution, Federal or State?

Bluebook **Rule 11** and *ALWD* **Rule 13** outline the citation format. The United States Constitution citation refers to the particular article, section, and clause being used. For example:

U.S. Const. art II, § 2, cl. 1 — *Bluebook* and *ALWD* formats

Note that a year is not included in the cite when the constitutional provision is currently in force. Also, in *Bluebook* format you may use upper- and lowercase lettering when typing the citation for a section of a constitution. In *ALWD* format you will also use upper- and lowercase type.

The above cite is used when you are referring to the body of the Constitution. A special citation format is required when you are referring to an amendment currently in force. For example:

U.S. Const. amend. II

State constitutions are indicated by the name of the state in the *Bluebook* abbreviated format. *Bluebook* **Table T.1** and *ALWD* **Appendix 1** indicate the accepted state name abbreviation; this is not necessarily the postal abbreviation. For example, the state of Washington's postal abbreviation is WA, but the *Bluebook* and *ALWD* abbreviation is Wash. A section of the Washington state constitution would be cited as follows:

Wash. Const. art I, § 2 — *Bluebook* and *ALWD* formats

Years or dates are not included in citations to constitutions, state or federal, that are currently in force. Parenthetical notations after the citation indicate the year a constitutional provision was repealed or amended. An example is the Eighteenth Amendment to the U.S. Constitution prohibiting the sale of liquor. The Twenty-First Amendment later repealed this. *Bluebook* **Rule 11** and *ALWD* **Rule 13.3(b)** cover this:

U.S. Const. amend. XVIII (repealed 1933) — *Bluebook* format

U.S. Const. amend. XVIII, *repealed by* U.S. Const. amend. XXI — *ALWD* format

▼ How Do You Cite to the Components of the Legislative Process and the Legislative History of a Statute?

Bluebook **Rule 13** and *ALWD* **Rule 15** detail the citation format for all the components of the legislative process: the bill, the committee report, the debates, and transcripts of the hearings.

▼ How Are the *Code of Federal Regulations* and the *Federal Register* Cited?

Rule 14 of the *Bluebook* and *ALWD* **Rule 18** provide the citation format for administrative and executive materials, which include the *Code of Federal Regulations* and the *Federal Register*. See also *Bluebook* **T.1** for each jurisdiction's administrative material. Note that the date is the date the volume of the C.F.R. was published. Generally, the entire C.F.R. is published annually with 25 percent of the titles published every three months. See Chapter 9.

Title 21 of the C.F.R. § 169.140 from 2021 is cited as:

21 C.F.R. § 169.140 (2021) — *Bluebook* format and *ALWD* format

According to the *Bluebook*, **Rule 18.2.1(a)** and *ALWD* **Rule 18.1(e)**, if the C.F.R. or the *Federal Register* is accessed online at govinfo.gov, and it is the official or precise copy of the print source, cite as if to the original printed source and do not include a URL. You can cite to the original printed C.F.R. or *Federal Register* when the online version is the exact copy, online authenticated copy, of the print source. This also applies when citing to state administrative materials, as many states no longer print administrative codes and rules.

A *Federal Register* entry from volume 82 where the entry is on page 23,241, from May 3, 2021, would be cited as:

86 Fed. Reg. 23,241 (May. 3, 2021) — *Bluebook* and *ALWD* formats

▼ How Do You Cite to a Legal Dictionary?

The information for the correct citation format for dictionaries is found in **Rule 15.8** of the *Bluebook* with an excellent example at **B15.1** and in **Rule 22.1** of *ALWD*.

> *Easement,* Black's Law Dictionary (11th ed. 2019) *Bluebook* format; note that the title is either underlined or italicized in *Bluebook* format.
>
> *Easement, Black's Law Dictionary* (11th ed. 2019) — *ALWD* format

ALWD states that the pinpoint page is not included because the term is the reference. No editor is included in a citation to *Black's Law Dictionary.*

▼ How Are Legal Encyclopedias Cited?

Bluebook **Rule 15.8** and *ALWD* **Rule 22.3** discuss print legal encyclopedias. Note the section is the pinpoint cite, so no need for page numbers. A citation to the discussion of easements would be as follows:

> 1 Am. Jur. 2d *Adjoining Landowners* § 20 (2004 & Supp. 2021) — *Bluebook* and *ALWD* formats

If the encyclopedia is available in print and on a commercial database, you may cite to the database. For example:

> 1 Am. Jur. 2d *Adjoining Landowners* § 20, Westlaw (database updated May 2021) — *Bluebook* **Rule 15.9** and *ALWD* **Rule 22.3(f)**

▼ How Do You Cite to *American Law Reports?*

This is found in **Rule 16.7.6** of the *Bluebook* and **Rule 22.5** of *ALWD*.

> William B. Johnson, Annotation, *Locating Easement of Way Created by Necessity,* 36 A.L.R.4th 769, 773 (1985 & Supp. 2021) — *Bluebook* and *ALWD* formats

Note that you can include a pinpoint cite for the specific part of the annotation you relied on. You can indicate the pinpoint citation with page numbers or section numbers. Here, the example used the precise page of the reference, "773." In newer series of the A.L.R. you would use the section number.

You can cite to a commercial database if you retrieved the A.L.R. annotation on LEXIS or Westlaw. According to *Bluebook* **Rule 15.9**, if a source is available in both print and on a commercial database, you may cite to the database. You must include the complete citation described in **Rule 16.7.6** as well as a cite to the database. *Bluebook* **Rule 16.8**. The underlying goal here is for the reader to be able to access the source with the citation you provide.

William B. Johnson, Annotation, *Locating Easement of Way Created by Necessity*, 36 A.L.R.4th 769, Westlaw (1985 & database updated April 19. 2021) — *Bluebook* format

William B. Johnson, Annotation, *Locating Easement of Way Created by Necessity*, 36 A.L.R.4th 769 (Westlaw through April 19, 2021) — *ALWD* format

▼ How Do You Cite to a Law Review or Law Journal?

Bluebook **Rule 16** and *ALWD* **Rule 21** indicate the citation form for a law review article, as follows:

Mitchell N. Berman, *Justification and Excuse, Law and Morality*, 53 Duke L.J. 1, 3 (2003) — *Bluebook* and *ALWD* formats

Abbreviations for most journal names are found in **Table 13** of the *Bluebook* and *ALWD* **Appendix 5**. Now, **Appendix 5** is only available online so that it is current. A newspaper is cited according to *Bluebook* **Rule 16.6**.

Wayne Smith, *Remote Access: Striking a Balance*, Law Tech. News, Jan. 2005, at 11 — *Bluebook* and *ALWD* formats

ALWD details citation format for newspapers in **Rule 21.3(f)**.

▼ How Do You Cite the Restatements?

Bluebook **Rule 12.9.4** indicates that the Restatements are cited as follows:

RESTATEMENT (SECOND) OF CONTRACTS §235 (AM. L. INST. 1981) — *Bluebook*— note the use of large and small capitals may be used for stylistic purposes in court documents but is not required. The use of large and small capitals is shown as an example of how the citation would look, but is not required. See *Bluebook* **Rule B2**.

Restatement (Second) of Contracts § 235 (Am. L. Inst. 1981) — *ALWD* **Rule 23.1**

Note that for both the *Bluebook* and *ALWD* format, the year is the date that the Restatement section was published. You can find the year of publication on the title page or on the verso of the Restatement volume.

When you are citing to a comment that follows the Restatement section, **Rule 3.4** of the *Bluebook* applies. For example:

RESTATEMENT (SECOND) OF CONTRACTS § 235 cmt. a (AM. L. INST. 1981) — *Bluebook* format

Restatement (Second) of Contracts § 235 cmt. a (Am. L. Inst. 1981) — *ALWD* format

ALWD considers a comment a form of a pinpoint reference like a page number or an illustration.

Note that in Restatement cites, *ALWD* only requires the use of small and large capitals in the citation when used in academic footnotes.

▼ How Do You Cite to a Uniform Law?

Unif. Certificate of Title Act § 2 (Unif. Law Comm'n 2005) — *Bluebook* Rule 12.9.4

Unif. Certificate of Title Act § 2 (2005) — *ALWD* Rule 23.6

▼ How Do You Cite an Ethics Rule Found in the *ABA Model Code of Professional Responsibility*?

The rules for citation of ethics codes are found in *Bluebook* **Rule 12.9.5** and *ALWD* **Rule 23.5. Rule 1.10** of the *ABA Model Code* would be cited as follows:

Model Code of Pro. Resp. DR 2-103 (Am. Bar Ass'n 1980) — *Bluebook* and *ALWD*

▼ How Do You Cite an ABA Ethics Opinion?

The rules for citation of ethics opinions are contained in *Bluebook* **Rule 12.9.5** and *ALWD* **Rule 16.2.** For example:

ABA Comm. on Pro. Ethics and Grievances, Informal Op. 88-1526 (1988) — *Bluebook* and *ALWD* formats

▼ How Do You Cite the Various Federal Rules?

Cite the federal rules in accordance with *Bluebook* **Rule 12.9.3** and *ALWD* **Rule 16.1** as follows:

Fed. R. Civ. P. 56

Fed. R. Crim. P. 1

Fed. R. App. P. 26

Fed. R. Evid. 803

Only include the year when the rule is no longer in force by providing the most recent year that it appeared in an official source and the year repealed. For example:

Fed. R. Civ. P. 9 (2006) (repealed 2008) — *Bluebook* **Rule 12.9.3** and *ALWD* **Rule16.1(d)**

CITATION EXERCISES

APPLICATION OF CONCEPTS

1. For the following citation, *Sloan v. Walker*, 671 F. Supp. 325 (D.N.J. 1987), provide the following:
   a. The plaintiff's name
   b. The defendant's name
   c. The volume number
   d. The reporter
   e. The page number where the case can be found
   f. The court and what its abbreviation means
   g. The year of decision

CITATION CORRECTION EXERCISES

Correct the following citations. Consult *Bluebook* **Rule 10** or *ALWD* **Rule 12**.

2. Smith v. PPG Industries, 100 F.3d 229 7th Circuit Court of Appeals (2000).
3. Taylor v. Canteen Corporation, 69 F.3d 773 7th Circuit Court of Appeals Fair Employment Practice Case (Decided November 30, 1995).
4. Larry Steele and Max Steele, d/b/a Steele Farms, Appellants v. Paul E. Harrison, D.D.S.
   552 P.2d 957. Decided in the Supreme Court of Kansas on July 23, 1976.
5. Lefkowitz v. Great Minneapolis Surplus Store, Incorporated. 86 N.W. Second 689 (Supreme Court of Minnesota 1957).

PROVIDING CITATIONS EXERCISES

Please provide the correct citations for these problems.

6. Plaintiffs have elected to resist the motion for summary judgment by trying to create issues involving immaterial facts rather than the "material" facts emphasized by Rule 56, F.R.C.P.
7. A complaint must be dismissed if a claim is lacking.
   Federal Rule of Civil Procedure 12 b 6.
8. How would you cite rule 803 of the Federal Rules of Evidence?
9. How would you cite rule 22 of the U.S. Supreme Court Rules?
10. How would you cite Federal Rule of Appellate Procedure 10?
11. *United States v. Upjohn*, 449 U.S. 383
12. What, if anything, is missing from the following citation?
   Consolidation Coal Co. v. Bucyrus-Erie Co., 89 Ill. App. 2d 103 (1982).

CASE CITATION PRACTICE

For the following citations, assume that these cases are being used in a brief for the U.S. District Court for the Northern District of Ohio. Correct the citation, if possible. If not, specify what is wrong. If an item is missing, note it and tell where it belongs.

13. How would you cite the following slip opinion?

Michele Greear et al., plaintiffs, vs. C.E. Electronics, Inc. et al., defendants, decided in the United States District Court for the Northern District of

Ohio Western Division, docket number C 87-7749, decided by Judge Richard B. McQuade, Jr. on September 12, 1989.

14. When responding to a motion for summary judgment, the plaintiff must submit proof of each and every element of his claims so that a reasonable jury would find in his favor. Anderson v. Liberty Lobby, Inc., 477 U.S. 242, 105 S.Ct. 989, 10 L.Ed. 2d 1111 (1986).

15. When the relationship of the parties is so clear as to be undisputed, it can be decided as a matter of law that no apparent or actual relationship existed. Mateyka v. Schroeder, 504 N.E.2d 1289 (1987).

16. In a diversity action, a court must apply the conflict of law principles of the forum state. Dr. Franklin Perkins School v. Freeman, 741 F.2d 1503, 1515, n.19 (1984); Pittway Corp. v. Lockheed Aircraft Corp., 641 F.2d 524, 526 (7th Cir.); Klaxon Co. v. Stentor Electric Mfg. Co., 313 US 487, 496 (1941).

17. Gizzi v. Texaco, 437 F.2d 308 (3rd).

18. Zimmerman v. North American, 704 F.2d 347 (1983).

19. E.E.O.C. v. Dowd, 736 F.2d 1177.

20. Musser v. Mountain View Broadcasting, 578 F. Supp. 229 (1984)

21. United States v. Upjohn, 449 U.S. 383.

22. Indicate what, if anything, is missing from this citation: Consolidation Coal Co. v. Buryus-Erie Co., 89 Ill. App. 2d 103 (1982).

CITATION PRACTICE

Provide the correct citation form for the following; use case name abbreviations found in either the *Bluebook* or the *ALWD Guide to Legal Citation.*

23. Trzcinski v. American Casualty Company 901 Federal Reporter Second Series 1429 Seventh Circuit Court of Appeals 1990

24. Wade v. Singer Company 130 Federal Rules Decisions 89 Northern District Court of Illinois 1990

25. Pryor v. Cajda 662 Federal Supplement 1114 Northern District Court of Illinois 1987

26. Longman v. Jasiek 91 Illinois Appellate Court Reports Third Series 83 46 Illinois Decisions 636 414 North Eastern Second Series 520 Third District Court of Appeals 1986

27. Gulf Oil Corporation v. Gilbert 91 Lawyers Edition 1055 330 United States Reports 501 67 Supreme Court Reporter 839 1947

28. Wyness v. Armstrong World Industries Incorporated 131 Illinois Reports Second Series 403 546 North Eastern Reporter Second Series 568 Supreme Court of Illinois 1989

29. Title 28 of the United States Code, section 1404(a) from the year 2018

30. Title 42 of the Code of Federal Regulations, part 400.200 from the year 2021

SHORT CITATION

31. Write the following information in short citation format.
    Smith v. Jones, 96 N.E.2d 17 (Ill. App. Ct. 1965). You are using text from p.18 of the N.E.2d. 31.
    How would you cite this the first time?

How would you short-cite it to page 18 if it is cited in full in the immediately preceding citation?

32. Cranshaw v. Marge, 321 F.2d 97 (5th Cir. 1935). You need to short-cite this case to reflect attributing authority to page 99 of the decision.

CITATION FOR RESOURCES OTHER THAN CASES

33. How would you cite to a federal statute that appeared in the 2021 pocket part of Title 42 of the United States Code Annotated at section 1201 that was in a volume published in 2011?

34. How would you cite a law review article that appeared in volume 78 of the Columbia University Law Review in 1985? The article is entitled Tax Aspects of Marital Dissolution, and begins on page 1587. The author is John Reese.

35. How would you cite Megan's Law found in Title 42 of the United States Code at section 14071(e) in the 2018 Code?

36. How would you cite volume 63 of the Federal Register at page 59,231 from October 1, 1991?

CITATIONS FOR ONLINE RESOURCES

37. How would you cite an unreported opinion available on Lexis where you are relying on a statement from page 3 of that opinion? The opinion is from 2005 and was found in the US Dist Ct file. The Lexis case number is 15976. The date of the decision is April 13, 2005. The case name is *Panera Bread Store v. Baguette Company*. The docket number is No. 05-1721.

38. You have found a new C.F.R. provision on Westlaw and you know it was printed in hard copy in the 2021 C.F.R. The provision is in Title 5 at section 12.

39. You retrieved a recent final regulation in the *Federal Register*, volume 82 at page 32135. It will be codified in the C.F.R. at 33 C.F.R. part 100. The material was accessed at govinfo.gov. Assume that the *Federal Register* is from July 19, 2021 and the CFR is from the current year. Please provide the citation according to the *Bluebook* or *ALWD*.

40. You have found an article in the Yale Law Journal. You know that the journal is available in hard copy at the law school library in another city and the identical article is available in full text on the Web. You want to cite to both sources to improve access. What rule do you follow in the *Bluebook*?

    The article is from volume 114, number 7, May 2005. The article is titled: "The Sarbanes-Oxley Act and the Making of Quack Corporate Governance" by Roberta Romana. The article begins on page 1521. The Yale Law Journal site is https://www.yalelawjournal.org/.

INDEX